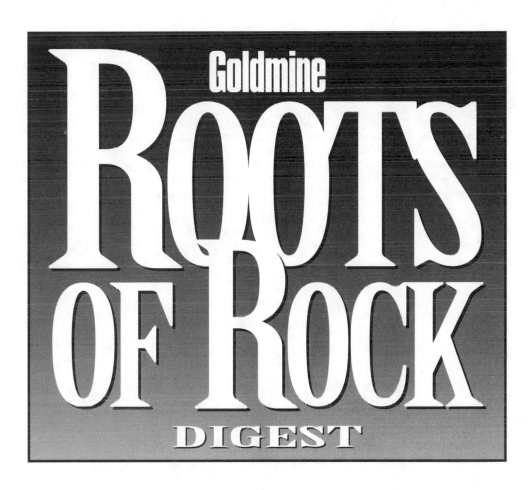

COMPILED BY THE EDITORS OF
GOLDMINE MAGAZINE

Published by

**krause
publications**

700 E. State Street • Iola, WI 54990-0001
Telephone: 715/445-2214

Please call or write for our free catalog.
Our toll-free number to place an order or obtain a free catalog is 800-258-0929
or please use our regular business telephone 715-445-2214
for editorial comment and further information.

Library of Congress Catalog Number: 99-86936
ISBN: 0-87341-775-5

Printed in the United States of America

Table of Contents

Introduction...4
Photo Credits...6

Part I: The Pioneers

Johnny Ace 9
Bo Diddley...11
Fats Domino..17
Bill Haley...25
Les Paul..29

Part II: The '50s Rockers

Chuck Berry...51
Eddie Cochran..61
Buddy Holly...67
Jerry Lee Lewis...79
Little Richard...87
Carl Perkins...95
Elvis Presley..113
Gene Vincent...127
Link Wray...141

Part III: The Teen Idols

Fabian...153
Rick Nelson..157
Bobby Rydell..163

Part IV: The Early '60s Rockers

Chubby Checker..173
Lesley Gore..179
Wanda Jackson...191
Brenda Lee...195
Roy Orbison...211
Gene Pitney..217
Del Shannon..225

Part V: Behind The Scenes

Dick Clark...237
Alan Freed...247
Leiber and Stoller..253
Sam Phillips...261
Phil Spector...273

Part VI: To The Present

25 Great Rock 'n' Roll Movies..285
The 45 — In The Beginning...289
2000 Fan Club Directory..293
Foundations, Societes, et al..309

Introduction

This is the second in a planned series of *Goldmine* "digests." The idea continues to evolve, but the primary goal is to reprint articles that first appeared in the pages of *Goldmine*, the world's foremost record and compact disc collectors' magazine.

Over the years, many top recording artists have sat down for at least a few minutes and discussed their careers and plans with a *Goldmine* writer. In many cases, these were the first lengthy interviews the subject had given in years. A couple years ago, the editorial staff of the magazine discussed ideas for new book projects, and the idea of reprinting some of these pieces arose. We all liked it. After all, it's a minority of *Goldmine* readers who saw every one of these when it was first printed.

The first of these projects, the *Goldmine Classic Rock Digest*, was released in 1998 and is still available. That also contains a bonus compact disc as part of the book that reflects the diversity of artists you might find in *Goldmine* over a period of time. Some of the featured artists are Frank Zappa, Curtis Mayfield, Bill Wyman, Todd Rundgren and The Knack, among others.

This book is called the *Goldmine Roots Of Rock Digest*. It covers those people who, in the years leading up to the British Invasion of 1964, influenced what came after. All of these were performers when the music was still called "rock 'n' roll" and was considered a threat to the moral foundations of America. (Don't laugh. Some people really felt that way. Sadly, some still do.)

Obviously, this covers a wide area. So we chose to narrow our focus.

Every performer we chose for the book either is best known as a solo artist or was the leader of a band that bore his or her name. That, of course, discounts the role of vocal groups. But we plan to cover that area in a future *Goldmine* digest.

Given that restriction, it was still not easy to decide what to include. Some were obvious – of course Elvis Presley has to be in here, as do Buddy Holly and Chuck Berry. But who else?

We decided to divide the book into several parts. Within all but the last section, the subjects are arranged alphabetically.

First we have "The Pioneers." These are people who had hits before rock 'n' roll broke out. In many cases, they still had hits once the music became big. All of them were highly influential on what came afterwards. We've even included one non-rock performer among this group, without whom rock 'n' roll as we came to know it could not possibly exist, and that's Les Paul.

Next we have "The '50s Rockers." I hope this category is self-explanatory.

Then, "The Teen Idols." Actually, many of the people in the other categories were "teen idols," too. But these handful seem to fit best in their own category.

Next, "The Early '60s Rockers." Most of them didn't rock as hard as their 1950s forbears. But denying any of these artists, whose peak of popularity were the years 1960-1963, the title of "rocker" would be wrong. It would play into the hands of those who felt that these years were the dark ages of rock 'n' roll. They were not! A lot of memorable music was made during this time, some of it by the performers we feature in this section.

Then, "Behind the Scenes." Many non-performers played a significant role in the popularity of rock 'n' roll – composers, producers, disc jockeys – and *Goldmine* has done articles on many of those as well.

Finally, a section we call "To The Present." Most of this material is exclusive to the *Goldmine Roots Of Rock Digest*. These pieces take some of the ancillary things that rose out of rock 'n' roll – for example, the rock 'n' roll movie and the fan club – and bring them to now.

We admit that some of the placement of articles was arbitrary. Some of the people we put in one category could easily fit in another. But that's life.

In our process of deciding what to use, we came up with 29 articles. In so doing, we tried to keep in mind the concept of the book – to present both the biggest and most influential people from the years 1955-1963 who were related to the rockin' side of the "new music" and had been profiled in the magazine.

The oldest of these was in a 1979 issue; the newest, in 1999. So even the long-time reader of the magazine probably missed at least a few of these over the years.

We used all different kinds of work in here. Some are strictly in a question-and-answer format. Others are articles with an interview woven throughout. Sometimes, the subject of the article was not available to be interviewed, either because of premature death or unwillingness. Some of these articles either are historical pieces, often with appropriate quotes from other sources placed throughout. Others use the words of close associates to tell the tale (Buddy Holly, Phil Spector). In one case, we reprinted an artist's obituary, which contained past quotes from the performer.

During the final editing process, I can't help but think about who we left out, not because the articles weren't up to par, but because in our brainstorming sessions, the name never came up. Fortunately, most of them can be used in later "digests."

We've basically decided to leave the articles as they were printed at the time, except to correct grammatical and stylistic errors that may have crept through. (*Goldmine* has used many styles in its Q&A articles over the years; we've standardized them in here.) A couple of the articles were shortened a bit, but we feel that the integrity of the original remains in those rare cases where we did so.

Each piece has a newly written introduction. This helps to explain why this artist belongs in the book, and in some cases, it catches up with the article's subject since the article first appeared. (In some cases, too, the note explains my own fascination with the performer in question.) Also, the introductions always tell you when the article first appeared in the pages of *Goldmine*, so if some things seem to be out of date (as they will), you can check the date and see how current the information is.

We considered running complete vinyl discographies with each piece. However, that could have doubled the length of the book, especially when you start factoring in the seemingly countless reissues and label variations. Instead, we've done two things.

So you can gauge the collectibility of the artists, in the first four sections we list a "Most Valuable 45" and a "Most Valuable LP," as listed in the *Goldmine Price Guide To 45 RPM Records, 2nd Edition* (Krause, 1999) and the *Goldmine Record Album Price Guide* (Krause, 1999). In case of ties, we list the earliest release. The values attached to these are for near mint copies – in other words, they must look as if you just bought them new in a store! Lesser condition records go for considerably less. For more information like that, *Goldmine* has, in addition to the two books listed above, another source available – the *Standard Catalog Of American Records 1950-1975*. If you want to see what was released on vinyl by any of these artists, and what the records are fetching on the collector's market, we recommend any of these three.

Following those, we offer a "Recommended Introduction" and "If you want to hear more…" series of selections. These are geared toward the reader whose collection consists primarily of compact discs, or to one who may finally be starting a CD collection after all these years. We hope that you will be interested enough in the subject of the article to actually want to hear their music!

For the "Recommended Introduction," I asked myself, "If I wanted to give someone who maybe has heard one or two songs by this artist a better idea of what they were like at their peak, which disc would I buy for them?" Thus the "Recommended Introduction." If you own only one CD by the artist, this should be the one. With rare exceptions, I was able to choose a U.S. release for this selection, for which we can be thankful. Usually, these are easier to find and less expensive than imports.

Sometimes I had to fudge. In a couple instances, I recommended two CDs, because I frankly couldn't decide which one was best; I leave it to you to choose which one you want to try. You can't really go wrong with either one. Also, my goal was to recommend something that was currently in print. On a couple of occasions, the best introduction is a CD that is officially no longer available, though they may still crop up in retail stores, used shops or the record clubs such as Play/ Columbia House or BMG Music Service. Finally, with artists whose original material was on the Cameo-Parkway family of labels, I had to recommend hard-to-find imports that may or may not be legitimate issues, but are all we have right now. The Abkco label, which owns the rights to those two key Philadelphia labels, has not yet seen fit to issue any of that material on compact disc in the United States.

For the "If you want to hear more…" section, I went through the (sometimes lengthy) lists of currently available CDs and important out-of-print ones to give the listener some other places to explore. In this category, I did not hesitate to recommend imports if necessary; the Bear Family box sets from Germany, especially, are an incredible resource for people who can't get enough of a given artist, and they aren't that difficult to find in America.

I didn't list every CD available by an artist. In a case such as Elvis Presley, the list would have been ridiculous, because – unless you're a fanatic – only a relative handful need to be in your collection. I did, however, split the Elvis recommendations into a third category, which I called "If you want to hear a LOT more…." For that, I listed the six compilations of music that were released from 1991-94 that cover nearly every important master that was released during his lifetime. Most of the other boxes and collections are for the die-hard or collector only; those you can discover on your own.

I also avoided re-recordings unless there was no alternative (say, with Chubby Checker). While some are OK, they usually lack the same spirit and feel as the originals. However, I didn't hesitate to recommend newer or recent releases by the artists in the book if they stood with their earlier work. Sometimes, these do have new versions of old songs, but more often, they don't. Again, I tried to list only those CDs that were still in print as of the summer of 1999; some box sets, compilations and later works are, alas, no longer officially available.

Certainly, the listed CDs are not the only worthwhile ones by the artists. But I do offer a word of warning: The bargain bins are littered with re-recordings and live versions, often made years after the performer's peak. Many of them sound that way, too. If you can, listen before you buy so you don't get taken in.

Finally, before I leave you to the often fascinating articles contained in the next 300 pages or so, I want to tell you that, even though my imprint is found throughout, compiling this book was a true collaborative effort.

Greg Loescher, the editor of *Goldmine* magazine, helped a lot in choosing the artists and keeping the project focused. Cathy Bernardy, associate editor of *Goldmine*, was the "point person" for the fine photographs you'll see within these pages. She is our liaison with photo agencies and photographers for the magazine and does a fine job there, so why mess with success? She also assembled the fan-club directory, our first up-to-date listing in several years.

Because most of these articles appeared in *Goldmine* before the era of computer archiving, they had to be re-typed into the system from the actual magazines; many thanks to Krause Publications' data entry people for doing so in a timely manner, and just as many thanks to our proofreading staff for making sure the material is as perfect as humanly possible. The art and production departments did the design of the cover and interior pages, respectively, and did a fine job.

Finally, I'd like to thank the photographers and writers who have contributed such excellent work over the years. And the performers featured within, who gave *Goldmine* something to write about.

Tim Neely
Goldmine book editor and research director
September 1999

Photo Credits

Johnny Ace, p. 9, Showtime Archives, Toronto.

Bo Diddley, p. 11, Star File/Pictorial Press, London, 1965.

Bo Diddley, p. 13, Star File/Al Pereira.

Fats Domino, p. 17, Glenn A. Baker Archives, Australia.

Bill Haley, p. 25, London Features International.

Bill Haley And The Comets, p. 26, London Features International.

Les Paul, p. 29, Star File/Jeffrey Mayer, 1998.

Chuck Berry, p. 51, Star File/Barrie Wentzell, 1972.

Chuck Berry and Alan Freed, p. 52, Glenn A. Baker Archives, Australia.

Eddie Cochran, p. 61, London Features International.

Eddie Cochran, p. 63, Glenn A. Baker Archives, Australia.

Buddy Holly, p. 67, Larry Matti, Feb. 1, 1959, Green Bay, Wis.

Buddy Holly And The Crickets, p. 71, London Features International.

Jerry Lee Lewis, p. 79, London Features International/John Reggero, 1982.

Jerry Lee Lewis, p. 80, Star File/N. Thomas.

Little Richard, p. 87, Star File/Chuck Pulin.

Carl Perkins, p. 95, London Features/Simon Fowler.

Carl Perkins, p. 102, Star File/Bob Alford.

Elvis Presley, p. 113, Glenn A. Baker Archives, Australia.

Elvis Presley, p. 120, London Features International.

Gene Vincent, p. 127, Star File/Pictorial Press, ca. 1957.

Gene Vincent And His Blue Caps, p. 134, Star File/Pictorial Press.

Link Wray, p. 141, Glenn A. Baker Archives, Australia.

Fabian, p. 153, London Features International/Curt Gunther.

Rick Nelson, p. 157, London Features International/Ron Wolfson.

Bobby Rydell, p. 163, Star File/Pictorial Press.

Chubby Checker, p. 173, Glenn A. Baker Archives, Australia.

Lesley Gore, p. 179, Star File/Pictorial Press.

Wanda Jackson, p. 191, Glenn A. Baker Archives, Australia.

Brenda Lee, p. 195, Glenn A. Baker Archives, Australia.

Roy Orbison, p. 211, Star File/Pictorial Press, London, 1968.

Gene Pitney, p. 217, Star File/Harry Goodwin.

Del Shannon, p. 225, Showtime Archives, Toronto.

Dick Clark, p. 237, London Features International/Ron Wolfson, 1996.

Alan Freed, p. 247, Glenn A. Baker Archives, Australia.

Leiber & Stoller, p. 253, Star File/Jeffrey Mayer, 1996.

Sam Phillips, p. 261, Showtime Archives, Toronto/Colin Escott.

Phil Spector, p. 273, Star File/Chuck Pulin.

Photos of records, sleeves, sheet music and other ephemera are from either the *Goldmine* files or the Tim Neely collection.

Part I
The Pioneers

Johnny Ace

by Peter Grendysa

"The Late Great Johnny Ace." That's how Paul Simon immortalized him in his song, which also drew parallels with the assassination of John Lennon. Today Johnny Ace is known for two things: "Pledging My Love," his posthumous hit, and, as this short piece that was originally published September 25, 1987 points out, the event that made such a hit possible. Johnny Ace, it could be argued, was the first rock 'n' roll casualty. Whether by accident or misadventure, dying sometimes has been the best career move a rock musician can make.

An untimely death in the world of show biz is usually a sure ticket to headlines and fortune (the latter for the stricken survivors, of course). It used to be accidents that took the toll, but it became apparent that a lengthy public demise was the best kind of demise. A lingering illness, preferably self-induced, during which your adoring public could watch you going to hell, was by far the best, and Janis, Jimi, and Elvis all agree on that.

So, Johnny Ace did it all wrong with his suicide. It looked as if he didn't mean to do it, it was an awfully dumb thing to do, and he forgot to leave his kindly old boss, Don Robey, a whole stack of unreleased masters to issue for the next 20 years. We will just have to be content to remember Johnny Ace for what his wax showed him to be – a wonderful singer with the bluest pipes around, the guy with a tear in his voice.

John Marshall Alexander was born June 9, 1929, in Memphis, and took up piano playing after his discharge from the Navy in 1947. He was soon gigging around his hometown with a loosely-knit bunch of musicians and singers called the Beale Streeters, amongst whom were found Bobby Bland, Earl Forrest, Roscoe Gordon and B.B. King. Whoever had the best thing going at the time was the boss, so you had Bobby Bland chauffeuring B.B. around for awhile, and perhaps B.B. backing Gordon on a club date. When B.B. got really big and left the gang, the others pretty much split, too. The band recorded for the Biharis [founders of the labels Modern and RPM – ed.] in 1952, but Ace's track was not issued until much later.

Ace was added to the very slim talent roster at Duke Records by the owner, David James Mattis, a deejay in Memphis. His first for Duke was "My Song," an autobiographical excursion that entered the R&B charts in August 1952, hit #1, and stayed alive for 20 weeks. Original 45 pressings of this tune have an incised area around the center hole, raised "typed style" "P-45 20B" on the A-side vinyl, and a flash line around the outer edge.

The popularity of this record was the reason Don Robey wanted the Duke label, and his arrangement with Mattis soon left the deejay out in the cold. Ace was hot, however, and hit followed hit. For two years, all but one of his records hit the charts, and original pressings are fairly common today. His second release, "Cross My Heart," featured him on Hammond organ, and his delicate touch on that much-abused instrument, countered with lovely vibraphone work, is an R&B masterpiece.

The third hit for Ace, "The Clock," has a melody "borrowed" from "Two Loves Have I," highly original lyrics, beautiful tenor sax work by Bill Fort, and Ace's own laid-back keyboard tinkling. The public liked it, too, forcing it up to #1 the summer of 1953. The flip is an instrumental which may include Ace on piano with the Johnny Otis band, or may not. Throwaway flip sides were not invented by Phil Spector.

Jump sides by Ace generally don't come off as well as the ballads. "Yes Baby" and the hard-punching "You've Been Gone So Long" are credible, but were no threat to Wynonie Harris or Little Richard, then or now. "Saving My Love For You" was written by Sherman "Blues" Johnson, and "Please Forgive Me," another weeper tailor-made for the Ace style, was penned by Joseph "Gorgeous Eyes" August. Beginning with Duke #128, original labels no longer carried the notation "Peacock Records Affiliate" on right center.

After "Never Let Me Go" failed to make the charts in late 1954, Ace shot himself, but the connections are tenuous. He was in a good mood, by most accounts, when he put the gun to his head backstage at the Houston City Auditorium on Christmas Eve and pulled the trigger. This had a dramatic effect on the other people in the dressing room at the time, but those dressing rooms were the pits anyway.

Don Robey was devastated, and tearfully claimed writer's credits for Ace's three posthumous records. Of these, "Pledging My Love" was the biggest hit of Johnny Ace's career, and is heard even today on lily-white "rock oldies" stations. In 1960 it was recoupled with "Anymore" and both sides were overdubbed with a vocal group. The reissue was given #136, so buyer beware. The original version is once again available, and is the one played on the air, while the overdub is never heard. Duke also issued 10- and 12-inch LPs and a couple of EPs after Ace's death.

One can only speculate on what the future would have held for Johnny Ace, had he not suffered from terminal foolishness, but his meager recorded legacy earned him a measure of immortality, and his end certainly beat being found floating face down in somebody's swimming pool.

Most Collectible 45

"Midnight Hours Journey" (Johnny Ace not on B-side), Flair 1015, $150.

Most Collectible LP

Memorial Album For Johnny Ace, Duke DLP-71, red vinyl, $4,000.

Recommended Introduction

Johnny Ace Memorial Album, MCA 31183 (posthumous compilation that has been in and out of print with varying titles since 1955)

Bo Diddley

by Bill DeYoung

Have you ever heard "(Marie's The Name) His Latest Flame" by Elvis Presley? "I Want Candy" by either the Strangeloves or Bow Wow Wow? "Not Fade Away" by either the Crickets (with Buddy Holly) or the Rolling Stones? "Faith" by George Michael? Maybe you've heard George Thorogood and the Destroyers chugga-chugging through "Who Do You Love." Then you've heard the distinctive "Bo Diddley beat." Yet Bo himself had exactly one record make the top 20 of the Billboard pop charts – his proto-rap record "Say Man." His influence reverberates anywhere musicians churn out that familiar rhythm, whether in original songs or, as with Thorogood, a remake of a Diddley original. After decades of obscurity, he re-entered the American consciousness and got a career boost when he appeared with baseball and football player Bo Jackson on one of the most famous TV commercials of all time – the line "Bo, you don't know diddley!" became a national catchphrase much as "Where's the beef?" had been several years earlier. Bo – Diddley, not Jackson – continues to perform today, chugga-chugging the beat on his rectangular-bodied guitar. The following interview appeared in the February 28, 1997 issue of Goldmine, shortly after Diddley had been nominated for his first Grammy Award in 37 years!

Ellas Bates McDaniel, a.k.a. Bo Diddley, has lived the life of a rural squire in North Florida since 1983, when a dentist, making small talk; told him about some acreage deep in the woods – with a two-story log cabin and a bass-fishing lake outside the back door – that an acquaintance had up for sale.

Bo Diddley snapped it up, and except for a two-year stretch in the early '90s when he relocated to New Mexico to "cool out" and resolve some family problems, he's never resided anywhere but Florida.

Currently, Bo and Sylvia – his fourth wife – live on 75-plus acres in Levy County, about halfway between Gainesville and the Gulf of Mexico. They're in a constant state of visitation from his children, her children, his grandkids and great-grandkids. There are a dozen dogs claiming residence on the property, which is mostly piney woods and scrub palmetto. The McDaniel home – a modest, white, one-level affair – sits at the end of a long limerock road through the woods (Bo built the road himself, sitting on top of one of his beloved tractors).

Behind the house is a smaller building full of mixing boards, speaker cabinets and ratty-looking electronic gadgets with wires exposed and guts spilling out. Here, Bo has his workshop, and he spends hours with screwdriver and soldering iron, taking apart drum machines and re-fitting them into guitar bodies. There's also a pretty nice eight-track demo studio in the back, and video equipment.

His latest delight is a vocal harmonizer, which he's combining with a rhythm machine to turn himself into a one-man band for the occasional charity shows he does in the area.

Maybe six times each month, he packs an overnight bag, grabs one of his rectangular guitars and his Bo Diddley ranger's hat, and hops a plane ("If the price is right, boom, I'm out of here") for Elsewhere, U.S.A. That's when the guy from Levy County, Fla. becomes the mighty Bo Diddley and kills 'em with "Who Do You Love," "Mona," "Say Man" and "Bo Diddley." In January, he spent 10 days touring Japan with a band from that country called Bogumbo.

For important gigs in the big stateside cities, he plays with the New York-based Debby Hastings Band; most of the time, the local promoter books him a pickup band, locals who are instructed only to play slow blues and the Bo Diddley beat, and then hang on.

At 68, he's slowed down a bit – more the result of 1995 surgery to repair his back than advancing age – but the one-time boxer is still as punchy as ever on the subject of his lost revenues (he sold his publishing 20 years ago) and what he perceives as lack of recognition from the rock 'n' roll powers that be.

Bo received a Grammy nomination this year for the album *A Man Amongst Men*, a "comeback" he really wasn't party to. The album, which got him on the radio for the first time in decades, featured a passel of friends and admirers including longtime chums Ron Wood and Keith Richards, Jimmy Vaughan and Richie Sambora.

He was nominated once before, in 1960, but didn't win, and hasn't been acknowledged by the Grammy people since.

Goldmine*: You've been nominated for a Grammy Award. How do you feel about it?*

Bo Diddley: I'm glad to get it. It excites me, but not the way most people see it. Because I'm 40 years in the business, and I've been overlooked, shoved aside and all this.

People say 'Aw, Bo Diddley's always crying the blues' and all this, but I don't cry unless I'm hurtin'. And it actually hurt that I see people that's in the business for two or three years, and they got nominations and Grammys, and they ain't did nothin' like what I've done.

It's been 10 years since your induction into the Rock and Roll Hall of Fame.

I was slapped in the face with that, too. It was a great thing being inducted into the Hall of Fame, but I ask myself all the time 'What does it mean?' I was very sick when they were getting ready to open it, and I was sent an invitation but I wasn't asked to perform.

Now, nobody knew I was sick. I didn't get the opportunity to say 'I'm sick; I'm not able.' And they had cats on that stage that shouldn't have been in the parking lot. That hurt.

So are you saying that these awards – the Hall of Fame, the Rhythm & Blues Foundation Lifetime Achievement Award, and the Grammy nomination – are a case of too little, too late?

I don't want to say it's too late. But why did it take 40 years for somebody to look back and say 'Oh! Bo Diddley'? And I'm the sucker that everybody copied. A lot of guys in country music right now are writin' songs with my beat. And I don't get recognized. Somebody writes a song, puts his name to it, says 'I did this,' he's a goddamn liar.

If I played something that sounds like the Rolling Stones, I would recognize them or the Beatles. I'd say 'I got a little bit of Beatles kicking here.'

In America, it looks like you gotta die in order to be really recognized. And to me, that's a crock of crap. Honor me while I'm alive, so that I know you really appreciated me. Don't wait till I'm dead and gone and then stand up and cry over me and all that kind of stuff.

(Looking at his Hall of Fame statue) If I got hungry, I couldn't pawn this. I couldn't get ten dollars for it. Now, if I'm dead, this sucker means a whole lot. You understand what I'm saying?

Do you think about that, about what will happen after you're gone?

Sure, I think about it. I'm at that age where you can't help but think about it. I ain't young and dumb and runnin' all over, everywhere clowning, and not thinking about tomorrow. I think about everything now.

A lot of people don't know that I do a lot of charity work, I go to the schools and talk to the kids, and steer 'em away from drugs and all that kind of stuff.

That little statue doesn't mean a lot to you, does it?

I look at it this way: What's going to happen to it if I'm deceased? Right away, somebody'll tell you 'Oh, it's not yours. It's our property.' What the hell do you mean, it's your property? Somebody'll get ahold of it, and you'll need a truckload of lawyers to get it back.

You did many things before your career as musician began. Do you ever think about what your life might be like today if you'd kept up as a carpenter or a mechanic?

If I'd done something else, I don't think I'd have what I have. I've worked hard to get what you see. I'm not in poverty or anything, but I'm not a rich man. I'd lie if I said I don't need to work.

I don't think I would've stayed in that predicament, because I'm a person that thinks. My studio looks like shit, but it works. And that's what I want. I don't want no elaborate place. A beautiful studio doesn't show

people where the record was cut. You could cut a record in your garage.

You're always out here tinkering with your equipment.

I ain't got time to be out here standin' on the streets bullshitting, 'Whoop here it is.' I try to tell everybody, not only my black brothers but my white brothers, too: Hey man, get up off of it and go try to get something. Because ain't nobody gonna give you nothin.'

I done figured this out. Now I'm out here 40 years, and if I don't know now, I'll never learn.

My mother used to get on me about building stuff in the house when I was a kid. But she didn't understand that I didn't want to be like Uncle Leroy or Uncle So-and-So, I had my own ideas. And that's the reason why I can say I'm not my brother's keeper. My brother's got a different brain structure – he wants to do this, and I want to do that.

People have a habit of judging you by something your brother did. And that's wrong. Your brother is a different person. My brother is a minister, Rev. Kenneth Haynes in Biloxi, Mississippi. Beautiful person. But he wanted to be a minister, I wanted to play music.

You went entirely the other way.

It was just a gas to be able to go and do all these things. Here I was, a youngster 26, 27 years old, quit school at 16 years old – and I thought I was raised in hell, here I was makin' like 700 bucks a week, and I got a band. Couldn't nobody tell me nothin', you understand what I'm saying?

Out of school with no diplomas, no nothin.' I don't even think they got a record of where I went to school. I didn't know that I was gettin' ripped off then.

I'd like to ask you about your back problem. What exactly happened?

I got up out of the bed, went to the washroom, washed my face, came back and put my pants on. And my socks were about two feet away from me. I leaned over sideways to pick 'em up, instead of forward. And when I did that, I screamed. That is the worst pain, worse than a toothache. I just locked up, cracked a disc in three places. And I couldn't walk.

It scared the hell out of me. This whole (left) leg here, it was just like it wasn't there. I was getting ready to go out and ride my tractor, grade my roads, you know? And I never made it.

This is a message, 'cause Bo knows: When your back starts to acting up, you go to the doctor! Because something is definitely wrong.

Did you have an existing back problem already?

No, man, I used to fight, box, rassle, jump fences and do all sorts of stuff. The doctor said it was somethin' I did 30 years ago. And it just caught me.

If anything, it could've happened one time I fell off the stage overseas. And I fell off the stage in

Texas, because I walked through a curtain and they didn't have no rail there. I just stepped off the son of a gun and hit the ground. If I hadn't been as husky as I was, I'd have crushed my shoulder.

It could've been one of those times.

You had corrective surgery in mid-1995. You seem to be walking pretty good – but you can't stand and play the guitar, can you?

No. I get up for a few minutes and then after a while I say 'Uh-oh, here it comes,' and I sit back down. You have to remember one thing – I'm not 21 any more. That's one thing that the doctor told me. And things don't heal as fast with you when you get my age.

To be honest with you, I'm scared. I'm not gonna lie to you. I'm scared to death, because I do not want to deal with no wheelchair! So I don't do nothin' funny.

I feel like I'm doing the right thing – I piddle around, and slowly but surely, I'm gettin' stronger. I'm not weak and broke down where I can't function at all, but I'm not going to run around here pickin' up stuff. My wife catches me pickin' up stuff, she starts hollerin' and screamin'.

I'll pick up something, but maybe later that night I'll pay for it. And that tells me don't do it.

Most of the work you do is with a pick-up band, a different group in each city. I've always wondered what that was like.

I rehearse with the band for a few minutes and see if they, you know ... I rely mostly on the drummer and the backup guitar. I say 'If you can't do the gig, let me know right now, because I don't want to turn around on stage and say something to you.' Because that's very unprofessional.

I've worked with some bands that were really terrible, but I didn't want to destroy 'em by saying something to them. I just suffer through.

In other words, these guys might have been hungry. The dude might need to feed him and his kids, and I'll say, 'Hey man, we'll make it, come on,' you understand what I mean? I can relate to that, being hungry. Hell, yes.

Don't you have to have an understanding with the band? Do you tell them, I play this way...

First of all, I tell them 'Don't get scared because it's Bo Diddley. That's bullshit. Let's work. I'm a cat who's got to pay bills just like you. So let's go ahead and make the money.'

Some guitar players won't play 'cause they're scared to death they're gonna step on me. I say 'Naw, you can't step on me. I can get out of your way real quick.'

If I have a beef with one that's on the stage with me, I don't jump on him on the stage. I wait 'til he gets in the dressing room, and then I chew him out. I say 'I ain't never seen you before, man.' I say 'Now,

if you want to stay in this business, you better cool that act that you got.'

Was it a good experience, making the new album with all those people in New York?

I didn't work with any of them. They asked me what did I think about it, and I said 'Sure, this'll be great.' There was only one guy on there I didn't know, I can't remember his name.

To be honest, I really didn't get involved in anything that went on with the thing. I just went there, recorded, and did it, and I left. And they took it and did whatever you heard later.

Weren't you happy to have a major label record coming out?

Well, this was good, but I have to say this. I've been out here 40 years, and I don't expect people will like everything that I do. That's impossible.

But I can't stand for somebody to inflict their ideas on me, because it's not me. I am the person that came up with something that everybody grabbed, and I feel like if I'm going to stay out here and deal with the public like I've done in the past, it's me that's got to come up with something. I can't be somebody else. I have to still be Bo Diddley.

Now, it's up to me to entice the new kid on the block. I can't do it with somebody else's throw.

Are you saying it was more (producer) Mike Vernon's record than yours?

A lot of stuff went into it I didn't understand. It came out great, Mike did a damn good job, but I think in some tunes, it kind of stepped out from Bo Diddley. See, I'm a rhythm fanatic, beats, rhythm and precision, where everybody's not playing on top of one another.

All this screaming guitars and stuff like that kind of worried me. But it's a good album. I think we reached the generation we were trying to get to.

I guess the idea was to contemporize...

But, see, I don't even understand 'contemporary.' I don't understand DAT, analog and all this, you understand what I mean? Because I've got stuff in (my studio) that I've cut, and you can't tell me what it was cut on. Your ears only hear certain things.

I got the impression that a lot of the parts were overdubs. That the musicians weren't always in the studio at the same time.

No, they weren't. It was great that I went over to England to (work) in Ronnie Wood's studio. He's a great guy. And Keith, too, you know.

You've known the Stones for a long time. Tell me about that relationship.

They're a bunch of great guys. But Mick is kind of standoffish. He's always been that way, kind of a

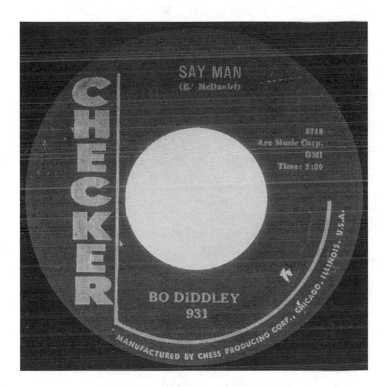

loner. It kind of worried me. He'll talk to you, but Mick, he kind of stands to himself.

What do you remember about that British tour in '63, where the Stones opened for you?

When Tom Jones was tryin' to get somebody to listen to him, he used to follow us in a little ol' raggedy MG, and get on the show where we was at. I didn't know who in the heck he was, but later I found out.

Was it tough getting work in the '60s, after the British music thing was happening?

Yeah, I like to have starved to death. And I bought all the stuff you see me with from Penny-Pincher, a hundred bucks here, 50 dollars here. Bought all this equipment piece by piece, until I got enough.

You own 75 acres out here. Do you still have to work?

Oh yeah. I'm pretty cool on paper, I'm not hungry, but I have to work because I haven't got what's due me. Somehow or another, there's a lot of forks in the road. And the money went to somebody else's house.

I was taught the honest trip. And I like being honest, my word is my bond. I might promise you something, and I might not be able to do it that day, but I won't forget it.

But do you still enjoy it?

It's turned into a job. It's not a fantasy – no, not fantasy, what's that called when you can't wait to get out there? It ain't that no more. It's turned into a job.

I don't like to go as much as I've been going. But I love it, and I still love my fans. God bless rock 'n' roll and God bless America.

And I'd like to say one more thing. I think it's time people my age start squawking – because our offspring is not capable of doing it – about all of the dirty lyrics that are played on the radio and television.

Young kids today need to be governed to a certain age, and *then* turn 'em loose.

Everybody sits around and talks about kids doing drugs, and I write a song that I think is very attractive, saying, 'Kids, Don't Do It.' Saying, don't make your mother and daddy give up on you.

What's wrong with that message? I can't get the son of a bitch played.

These children today need some guiding because if somebody don't stop 'em, the police will stop 'em. You can't win all of 'em, but you can slow some of 'em down. Make 'em stop and think.

Most Collectible 45

"Diddley Daddy"/ "She's Fine, She's Mine," Checker 819, maroon "checkerboard" label, $60.

Most Collectible LP

Bo Diddley, Checker LP-1431, black label, $200.

Recommended Introduction

Bo Diddley: His Best, Chess/MCA 9373 (20 of his greatest hits)

If you want to hear more...

Bo Diddley: The Chess Box, Chess/MCA 19502 (a 2-CD set of 45 tracks he recorded for Checker from 1955-69)

This Should Not Be, Triple X 51130 (a 14-track collection recorded in the late 1980s)

A Man Amongst Men, Atlantic 82896 (his 1996 "comeback" with many guest stars)

Fats Domino

by Rick Coleman

Long before the music was called "rock 'n' roll," Antoine "Fats" Domino was playing rock 'n' roll. One could make an argument that his first record, "The Fat Man," was the first rock 'n' roll record, but to do so would be to ignore the roots of even that seminal recording. Domino lasted long enough to become hugely popular once rock 'n' roll broke nationally. While his own "Ain't It A Shame" was outdone on the charts by Pat Boone's pale cover version in 1955, no one was going to top his reading of the standard "Blueberry Hill." Domino was still charting records into the 1960s, and he influenced countless other artists – The Beatles' 1968 hit "Lady Madonna" was Paul McCartney's attempt to write a Fats Domino song, and Fats himself actually recorded it for his "comeback" album Fats Is Back *later in the year. Today, Fats is in his 70s, yet he continues to perform and occasionally record – he finally did a Christmas album,* Christmas Is A Special Day, *in 1993. The following piece on "The Fat Man" and his peak period both creatively and commercially, the 1949-61 Imperial Records years, appeared in* Goldmine *in the May 17, 1991 issue.*

E 1950. Alan Freed is rolling Beethoven records in Cleveland. Bill Haley is twangin' hillbilly in Philly. Elvis gazes out the window of Humes High in Memphis.

Somewhere in America a crackling sound is heard as a 78 zips into a rumbling 88-key overdrive that will electrify airwaves and burst jukebox speakers for years to come. The bombing piano frenzy is accompanied by popping flak rimshots and air-raid siren horns as our pilot into this brave new musical world, his cherub cheeks bugling his triumph like a judgment day kamikaze, boldly radios through the static his name, weight and street address to a shell-shocked planet.

> They call, they call me the Fat Man
> 'Cause I weigh 200 pounds
> All those girls they love me
> 'Cause I know my way around
> I was standin', I was standin' on the corner
> Down on Rampart and Canal
> I was watchin', watchin'
> Watchin' all those Creole gals.

On December 10, 1949 bandleader Dave Bartholomew brought his latest discovery to record with his band in Cosimo Matassa's tiny J&M studio on Rampart and Dumaine Street. The song they put down, "The Fat Man," would contribute to the birth of a new form of music.

Johnny Otis, who led the hottest R&B band in the country in 1950, was dumbfounded by "The Fat Man." He says, "I consider that a revolutionary record ... I remember we were eating in a restaurant and a jukebox man was changing the records. When he got through he punched a few buttons to play a few and we were hearing a lot of new sides we hadn't heard. And suddenly 'The Fat Man' came on. I remember my guitar player, Pete Lewis, and I ran over to the jukebox to see what that was. We said, 'Shit, that's something we wished we had done!'"

Antoine "Fats" Domino's musical roots were divided between the boogie-woogie and blues pianists he heard on jukeboxes and the traditional New Orleans songs he was taught by his brother-in-law Harrison Verrett, a guitar player for Papa Celestin and other jazz groups. Among local favorites was the ancient blues of the imprisoned addicts, "Junker Blues," which formed the basis for "The Fat Man." Domino had played his stomping version of the song – often as an instrumental – and attracted large crowds to the hole-in-the-wall Hideaway Club in the Ninth Ward section of New Orleans.

Dave Bartholomew, the top bandleader in the city along with the recently-deceased Paul Gayten, had been assigned by Lew Chudd of Imperial Records in Los Angeles to find local talent. Together they checked out the chubby, 21-year-old pianist one night at the Hideaway and were impressed enough to sign him up.

"The Fat Man" defined both Domino and his sound the way "Bo Diddley" would for Ellas McDaniel five years later. Domino's piano work is taken almost note-for-note from New Orleans blues patriarch Champion Jack Dupree's 1941 Okeh recording of "Junker Blues," but is faster, rawer, rougher. The lyrics composed by Bartholomew and Domino are fun-loving and self-mocking – nothing is going to stop Fats from having a good time. He even unabashedly bugles like a kazoo.

"It's part of that transmitting from him to you the good feeling," notes Cosimo Matassa. The riffing horns and pulsing rhythm section keep up the monumental pounding. Simply, it was rhythm 'n' blues with a joyful New Orleans parade feeling and beat that would come to be known as rock 'n' roll.

Domino has said, "I wouldn't say that I started it, but I don't remember anyone else before me playing that kind of thing."

Domino's all-important second hit after three flops was "Every Night About This Time," which featured his affecting vocals and his first extensive use of hammering piano triplets. "I was really singin' the blues then," says Domino. "I used it (the 6/8 triplets ever since. I first heard it on an Amos Milburn record."

After two disastrous road trips with Domino (the latter including Professor Longhair), Bartholomew came home and had a falling out with Lew Chudd over a Christmas bonus. For the next year Domino would record on his own.

Domino's band, consisting of Walter "Papoose" Nelson or Harrison Verrett (guitar), Billy Diamond (bass), Cornelius "Tenoo" Coleman (drums), Wendell Duconge (alto) and Buddy Hagans (tenor), was not nearly as professional as Bartholomew's band, and many of the songs it recorded were searing combo blues, instead of the more uptown variety that had hit for him.

The mid-tempo boogie "Rockin' Chair," with Domino's jolly vocal belying the woeful lyric, reached #9 nationally (according to Joel Whitburn's *Top R&B Singles 1942-1988*) in December 1951, and was often performed by Little Richard.

Despite unbalanced instrument levels and a raw sax solo by Buddy Hagans, "Goin' Home" hit a live nerve with returning Korean War veterans. "When he'd play 'Goin' Home Tomorrow' he'd bring the house down," recalls Billy Diamond. "That was our national anthem song then."

"Goin' Home" 's cannonading triad horn riff would be heard in dozens of songs, notably Guitar Slim's R&B #1 "The Things That I Used To Do." Released in March 1952, "Goin' Home" made #1 in

Billboard's R&B chart in June, the week before Lloyd Price's, "Lawdy Miss Clawdy," featuring Domino's piano and Bartholomew's band, took over the chart. The stage was set for the emergence of the New Orleans sound.

While away from Imperial, Bartholomew had recorded his own original version of "My Ding-A-Ling" for King, "Lawdy Miss Clawdy" for Specialty and Shirley and Lee's first hit "I'm Gone" for Aladdin. Lew Chudd smartly made amends and Domino and Bartholomew were reunited.

Domino's marvelous version of Longhair's "Mardi Gras In New Orleans" was advertised as the A-side of his new single as he played a three-day stint at Los Angeles' 5-4 Ballroom in mid-April 1953. However, "Going To The River," a down-in-the-mouth blues with strong lyrics and a brief sax solo by Herb Hardesty, became a #2 R&B hit.

Hardesty would soon do the majority of Domino's saxophone solos and would join him on the road: "It was hard work because we was doing nothing but one-nighters. And during that period we would sleep one night and travel the other night to skip a night's rest ... We had to strictly stay in black hotels, and a lot of them wasn't hotels. A lot of them was guest houses. And this was not very pleasant..."

"Please Don't Leave Me," a raw stomper with Domino's wild, "woo-woo's," was put together by Domino and the band in the frenzied atmosphere of the Show-boat Club in Philadelphia. It and the second version of "Rose Mary" (a promise by Fats to his wife to come home and stop touring) from June kept Fats burning on the charts in the last part of 1953.

A September 1953 session included "Fats' Frenzy," an instrumental with scintillating fingering by Domino and awesome sax blowing, and two songs which would foreshadow his future styles. "Don't Leave Me This Way" uses pauses in the music for dramatic effect and "Something's Wrong" has a soft, warm vocal and catchy bridge.

In March 1954 Domino was the #1 R&B artist on *Billboard*'s juke box operators' poll. "Something's Wrong" and "You Done Me Wrong," a rousing variation on "Please Don't Leave Me," kept him on the charts through mid-1954. Domino was on the road so much in 1954 that he only recorded eight songs, all of which failed to make the best-seller list.

Nineteen-fifty-five opened with a bang indicative of the surprises to come when Alan Freed presented his "Rock 'n' Roll Ball" in New York City. Both it and a 60-day package tour featured many R&B superstars, among them Big Joe Turner, the Clovers, the Moonglows and Clyde McPhatter and the Drifters.

In February 1955 "Don't You Know," which again featured pauses in the music, was released and created quite a stir. *Life*, doing a story on the rock 'n' roll phenomenon, photographed Domino's fans going wild at one of his record-breaking shows at the 5-4 Ballroom in Los Angeles in April as Herb Hardesty played "Don't You Know" 's sax solo lying on his back.

Then came "Ain't It A Shame."

Billboard wrote on April 30: "First week reports on this new Domino release indicate that it is a powerhouse." All hell was about to break loose.

One June 4 *Billboard* reported on Domino's having a show in Bridgeport, Connecticut banned in a news item titled "Fear of Rock-Roll Nixes Conn. Date."

The next week "Ain't It A Shame" topped the R&B charts for the first of 11 consecutive weeks. A month later the almost unthinkable happened when Domino followed Pat Boone's lachrymose glucose overdose, re-titled "Ain't That A Shame," into the pop charts. Domino's wall-of-sound beat blasted everything else off the radio. It would not be superseded until Little Richard's catacylsmic "Tutti Frutti," recorded in the same studio with Bartholomew's band.

Early the next year Domino would again trail an inferior version up the pop charts when the barnyard novelty "Bo Weevil" was covered by winsome warbler Teresa Brewer. However, a *Billboard* article in October 1955 noted that sentiment among pop disc jockeys was shifting toward the original R&B hits.

Bartholomew and Domino had experimented over the last year or so with great success, using stop-time beats, pop hooks and country tunes. Their songs on the next record, released in March 1956, set the patterns for many of the recordings to come.

In the grooving rocker "I'm In Love Again" the pair had finally hit on the perfect formula for rock 'n' roll: tight, concise songs – faintly country, faintly pop – with a heavy beat and simple lyrics.

Giving a big beat to pop standards had long been a tradition in New Orleans jazz. In December 1955 Domino followed that tradition in his own unique way when he did "My Blue Heaven."

"Harrison Verrett had a little black book," says Billy Diamond. "He taught Fats all of them (standards) ... See, Harrison used to sing all them kinda tunes with Papa Celestin."

"He used to tell me always to play some of those standard old songs because they never die," admits Domino. "You know, like 'My Blue Heaven' or 'When My Dreamboat Comes Home.'"

In later years a long procession of standards would be detrimental to Domino's career, but early on the colorful lyrics added a warm visual imagery to Fats' thick Creole drawl ("Mah Bleuuu Ha-vawwnn"), making his records ooze with personality. Additionally, the song was already known by the parents of the rock 'n' roll generation, so his popularity was immediately broadened. The record was a huge, double-sided hit for Domino, and his first in Britain.

After an R&B package tour that included Little Richard among the opening acts, Domino headed to the West Coast, where in July 1956 his show triggered a massive "rock 'n' roll riot" in San Jose that nearly got rock 'n' roll banned in the state of California. It was one of dozens of riots and brawls in the '50s that got Domino a lot of unwanted publicity and show cancellations.

Bass player Lawrence Guyton toured with Domino in 1956 until he was injured in a riot in which North Carolina police used tear gas. "You see, it was a free-for-all fight, everybody was fightin'," he recalls. "I seen women get cut, people layin' on the floor, all cut up. So at that particular time people thought that when they see us on the bandstand we didn't go through it, but every night a row would start out there. That was every night!"

The standard "When My Dreamboat Comes Home" was coupled with the superbly performed blues ballad, "So Long," for another pop/R&B hit. "Dreamboat" was driven along by the saxes and two thrilling solos by Herb Hardesty, and was performed live in September on the *Steve Allen Show.*

Around this time *Jet* magazine reported with interest on the first black rhythm 'n' blues star to make it huge in the pop world: "In a single evening, Domino sometimes grosses nearly $2,000 ... Money has brought Fats no pain. It has, instead, equipped him with a fire-engine red El Dorado trimmed in gold, a shocking pink Fleetwood Cadillac, a Chrysler station wagon, 50 suits and 200 pairs of shoes. It also has brought a goodly measure of the finer things of life to his wife, Rosemary, and their six children..."

Hot on "Dreamboat"'s heels was a record cut in Los Angeles in July. Domino's inspiration for "Blueberry Hill" was Louis Armstrong's 1949 version: "I liked to hear him sing on account of his voice," says Fats. "He had a gravel voice. I liked the way he did that 'Blueberry Hill.' I told Dave, 'I want to record that number.'"

The song was recorded in Los Angeles and pieced together by Master Recorders engineer Bunny Robyn: "We never got a full good take, but between the varied takes we had I edited in," he says. "And we had no real ending to it, so we did a repeat thing and just faded out on the end."

Ironically, it was "Honey Chile" that got the first airplay, as Imperial promotion man Eddie Ray recounts: "When it first came out in Philadelphia, I believe it was, they jumped on 'Honey Chile,' and it got tremendous response. So I recall talking and goin' out with that record." Because of this initial feedback, Domino lip-synched "Honey Chile" with his band for the movie *Shake, Rattle And Roll*, along with "Ain't It A Shame" and' "I'm In Love Again," instead of "Blueberry Hill."

Imperial followed up at #1 on the R&B charts with a totally different classic, the stomping worker's lament "Blue Monday," which had moldered in the vaults for a year and a half. "Blue Monday," seen in abbreviated form in the movie *The Girl Can't Help It*, was the favorite song of Chudd, Bartholomew and Domino, because, as the writers say, "It's a true story."

In January 1957, Domino recorded his next #1, "I'm Walkin'."

"(Fats) had an idea and we were working together in Philadelphia," says Bartholomew. "He said he always like songs with 'walkin'' in 'em. So we got together and we worked out 'I'm Walkin',' with the tremendous help we had from our guitarist (Papoose Nelson), who was a great guitar player. Earl Palmer thumps his bass drum and we're off on a second line parade at a gallop."

"It all comes from those marching bands," says Palmer. "It was a hit and when I came out here (Los Angeles), Rick Nelson got me to play on his when he did the cover on 'I'm Walkin'.'"

Domino then went on an eastern tour, which was extended by 80 days on February 15, as headliner of the first edition of Irving Feld's "Greatest Show of 1957." "It would be about 12 to 14 artists on the same show," remembers Herbert Hardesty. "Fats would be the headliner of the show. And we would start maybe from New York and go completely through Canada ...

into Oregon and all through California, and working back through every state. We did this Irving Feld tour maybe about four or five times."

After 22 weeks at #1 in the R&B Best Sellers, Domino was finally dethroned by Chuck Berry's "School Day" in May. "When me and Little Richard and Chuck Berry toured together we all had our records on the charts," remarks Domino. "Every week that *Billboard* came out everybody want to look and see how their number stand."

"Valley Of Tears," with an awful choir overdubbed on the 45, was a letdown saleswise. It was Domino's last Top 10 pop hit for a year and a half.

Fats was touring almost non-stop in 1957 and his material consequently suffered. In June, Bartholomew recorded tracks that Domino would later overdub. It seems likely given the huge number of sessions he is credited with in 1957 – many on dates when he was on tour – that he actually overdubbed several times. Moreover, New Orleans session pianists were occasionally used on the tracks laid down, though how much of this actually appeared on Domino records is doubtful "Edward Frank, James Booker and Allen Toussaint could all play Fats like Fats," says Cosimo Matassa. "There were certainly some Domino things that Domino wasn't playing piano on."

On tour Domino was at his peak. Near the end of "The Biggest Show of Stars for '57" in November, he was headlining the most incredible rock 'n' roll tour package of all time: Fats Domino, Chuck Berry, Buddy Holly and the Crickets. the Everly Brothers, Clyde McPhatter, LaVern Baker, Frankie Lymon, Paul Anka, Buddy Knox, Jimmy Bowen, Eddie Cochran, the Diamonds and the Drifters! The "good" seats cost $3.50. He followed it by topping the bill at the end of the year at the legendary Alan Freed Brooklyn Paramount show with Jerry Lee Lewis.

Domino ended the year with two songs from movies ("Wait And See" from *Jamboree* and "The Big Beat" from *The Big Beat*) that barely made the Top 40. At the time doomsayers were predicting Domino's fall because some of his 45s only sold half a million copies. Lew Chudd countered the critics: "You should cool off like he has."

Looking at the charts did not make Domino too happy in 1958. His biggest hit was Chris Kenner's funky rocker "Sick And Tired," which at midyear made #22 pop and #15 R&B among the best sellers. "Young School Girl," a fluffy teen idol ballad which listed teenage activities Fats knew about as well as Martians, was the nadir, just barely cracking the Top 100 at #92 in September and threatening to break Domino's string of consistent chart-making since the beginning of 1955.

Domino's slump was abolished when "Whole Lotta Loving" made the Top 10 in early 1959. Domino is the whole show, from his sparkling piano figures to his smacking kisses into the microphone.

After Domino and his band's magnificent workout on the Dixieland warhorse "When The Saints Go Marching In" stalled halfway up the charts in March, Domino followed with the sledgehammer parade propulsion of "I'm Ready," written by the songwriting team of Sylvester Lewis and Al Bradford (who also wrote the dissimilar "Tears On My Pillow").

Domino seemed to be showing some wear in June 1959 in the tired-sounding, almost monotonous, sentimental ballad "I Want To Walk You Home," redeemed by the punchy bridge. Apparently the song's hypnotic effect made it Domino's first R&B #1 in over two years in September 1959.

The flip side, "I'm Gonna Be A Wheel Someday," was perfect ambition/revenge cruising music. Bartholomew had recorded the song twice before in 1957 with its author, Cajun Roy Hayes, and with local R&B singer Bobby Mitchell. The band streamlined the song like a new Cadillac, with a gliding guitar by Ernest McLean, nifty bass figures by Frank Fields, handclaps and shouts.

Domino and Bartholomew were presented with their next hit, "Be My Guest," by teenager Tommy Boyce (who would later co-write many of the Monkees' hits) and his music publisher John Marascalco (who co-wrote many of Little Richard's hits). Although it mentions *American Bandstand* dances, "Be My Guest" was unusual in that, as author and historian Charlie Gillett explained: "The guitar plays 4/4 time while the drummer bashes on the off-beat, so the song is like the bluebeat or ska sound of Jamaican music five years later." Several other Domino songs have a similar beat, dating back to "She's My Baby" in Domino's first session, and he had a huge influence in Jamaica, where he toured in 1961.

Probably due to a shortage of current recordings (Domino only recorded six songs in 1959), the shrill novelty "Country Boy" was finally released after a year in the can in January 1960. It was the first Domino single in five years not to make any of the R&B charts, though it made #25 in the pop charts.

Domino's chart slide was accompanied by the noticeable shift among black audiences from his sound to the dynamic and sexy soul of artists like Jackie Wilson and Sam Cooke, as was noticeable in an Easter week show at the Apollo in 1961. "We only had two good nights the whole week," Harrison Verrett recalled in 1961. "Jackie Wilson, every night he was there they couldn't get in."

In April 1960 Domino and Bartholomew took a major step. "Bobby Charles came up with 'Walking To New Orleans' and I recorded on Claiborne Avenue in rehearsal," says Bartholomew. "After we cut it I told Cosimo, 'I don't know where to turn – this ain't doin' nothin'.'" Bartholomew added strings with the help of an arranger from the New Orleans Symphony.

The song summed up Fats Domino's unshakable love affair with his hometown. "Right now when I go away," says Domino, "I still got home on my mind, especially New Orleans, anyway." The strings add a whole other atmosphere, like a warm Southern breeze echoing Fats.

Bartholomew's gamble paid off, as "Walking To New Orleans" was a major hit in the summer of 1960. However, the strings were overbearing on most of the ballads recorded over the summer. The exceptions were the next hit, "Three Nights A Week" and the languorous "Rising Sun."

In the midst of this sea of strings, Domino recorded two romping rockers, the parade beat square dance "Shu Rah" and the locomotive rocker "My Girl Josephine," which kept him in the Top 20 at the end of 1960.

Domino's December 1960 session was strong, producing four Top 40 hits – "It Keeps Rainin'," "What A Price," "Ain't That Just Like A Woman," and "Fell In Love On Monday" – all of which should have been bigger.

"What A Price" was Domino's finest blues ballad since "So Long" in 1956, with great presence in the unusually soulful vocal. The song was the first of several written for Domino by south Mississippi songwriters Pee Wee Maddux and the late Jimmy Donley,

and was Domino's fourth consecutive Top 10 R&B hit in early 1961. The B-side was "Ain't That Just Like A Woman," a grinding version of Louis Jordan's boogie with Lee Allen blasting out a tribute to "Chattanooga Choo Choo."

The origin of the next record, "It Keeps Rainin'," gives some insight into Domino's creative and recording process. "The name of the song was 'Little Rascal,'" recalls the song's co-author, Bobby Charles. "When they sent the copy of the tape to Fats in Philadelphia they didn't put the vocal on the tape, all they put was the track. He liked the track, so he wrote some other words. He wrote "It Keeps Rainin'."

In April, Domino began a major package caravan, "The Biggest Show of Stars for 1961." He still headlined, but only Bo Diddley was left out of those he had shared bills with in the '50s.

Domino's version of Bartholomew's "Let The Four Winds Blow," with booming drums by Cornelius Coleman and saxes blowing like the four winds, kept him cookin' in the summer of 1961, though it would be his last Top 20 pop hit (#2 R&B).

The two Hank Williams songs recorded at the second June session – "You Win Again," and "Your Cheatin' Heart" – fit Domino's style perfectly, as did his joyful *fais-do-do* version of Williams' anthem to Louisiana cooking, "Jambalaya (On The Bayou)," recorded in November.

The raucous "What A Party," "Jambalaya" and "You Win Again" kept Fats in the Top 30 from November 1961 to April 1962. On February 28 Walter "Papoose" Nelson died in New York City. Sax player Clarence Ford sums up the opinion of everyone connected with Domino: "He was the greatest blues guitar player I ever heard. He was a natural."

An April 1962 session included Domino's first acknowledgment of the Twist, "Dance With Mr. Domino." Although the beat was closer to "Whole Lotta Shakin' Goin' On," there was no doubt that Domino was copying his "namesake" Chubby Checker. The following month Domino would co-headline his last Biggest Show of Stars, with Brook Benton. "Dance With Mr. Domino" only made #98; people couldn't twist that fast.

The last song recorded was a triplet ballad with blasting horns not far removed from "Goin' Home." Domino sings, "Nothin' new, it's the same old thing/ You got me singin' the blues again." He concludes the session, "Ha! Ha! Ha! What a laugh!" It was Fats Domino's last Imperial session.

Perhaps the most fitting way to remember the Fats Domino Imperial years is the "What A Party" session from September 1961. Clarence Ford recalls: "What A Party" was a party! It must've started around two o'clock in the evening. We'd get there maybe one-thirty, and Fats would always come there a little later. They had whiskey and all that there before the session started. It was a real party. I'll never forget that session. He had everything – whiskey, beer and sandwiches."

The song pretty well summed up the dozen years during which Domino's band had been creating parties everywhere, having started perhaps the biggest party music of all. Domino starts with a laugh: "Ha! Ha! Ha! Let's go!" and dives into a mad melee, with people yelling, clapping and clinking glasses.

"The girl was dancin' with no shoes on
The big tenor man really blew his horn
What a party! Lawdy! Lawdy!
Big fat piano man he sure could play.

It ends with Hardesty blasting a mind-messing solo. Domino starts to repeat the first verse, as the guitar and bass trail off. Someone complains, "Aw, man, he was tellin' me to stop."

In 1963 Lew Chudd sold Imperial Records and disappeared from the record business. The rock 'n' roll founder who had started first and lasted longest was now destined to the fate of the others – which, judging from the fortunes of Chuck Berry, Jerry Lee Lewis, Buddy Holly and Little Richard, at that time, seemed to be unemployment or worse, though we now know better.

Turn out the lights. The party's just beginning.

Most Collectible 45

"The Fat Man"/ "Detroit City Blues," Imperial X5058, blue label, $2,000.

Most Collectible LP

Rock and Rollin' With Fats Domino, Imperial LP-9004, maroon label, $150.

Recommended Introduction

The Fat Man: 25 Classic Performances, EMD/Capitol 52326 (contains almost all his biggest hits on Imperial; supersedes the 1990 *My Blue Heaven* collection, EMD/Capitol 92808, also excellent, and also still in print)

If you want to hear more...

Rock And Rollin' With Fats Domino/This Is Fats Domino, Collectables 2721 (a twofer containing two of Fats' original Imperial albums on one CD)

Rock And Rollin'/Million Sellers By Fats, Collectables 2722 (a twofer containing two of Fats' original Imperial albums on one CD)

Here Stands Fats Domino/This Is Fats, Collectables 2723 (a twofer containing two of Fats' original Imperial albums on one CD)

The Fabulous Mr. D/Fats Domino Swings, Collectables 2724 (a twofer containing two of Fats' original Imperial albums on one CD)

The Early Imperial Singles, 1950-1952, Ace 597 (UK import with the A and B sides of his first 15 Imperial singles)

The Imperial Singles, Volume 2, 1953-1955, Ace 649 (UK import with the A and B sides of the next 15 Imperial singles, including "Ain't It A Shame")

The Imperial Singles, Volume 3, 1956-1958, Ace 689 (UK import with the A and B sides of the nest 15 Imperial singles, including most of his biggest rock 'n' roll hits)

Fats Is Back!, Bullseye Blues 619616 (his 1968 "comeback" album, including his renditions of "Lady Madonna" and "Lovely Rita")

Bill Haley

by Brad Elliott and Denise Gregoire

Rodney Dangerfield always said that he "don't get no respect." Neither, it seems, does Bill Haley. Our in-house index of past feature articles, which we used to compile this book, said that the last piece Goldmine *did on Haley was in 1988, a short item that appeared along with profiles of many other artists who had been named to the Rock and Roll Hall of Fame. (At least that controversial body realized Haley's importance – he was in the first class of inductees.) But I could have sworn I saw him featured in* Goldmine *more recently than that. I recall reading that he had been part of a group called the Sundowners that actually had made a Vogue Picture Record or two during those novelty items' post-World War II heyday. I also recall seeing a photo of a label of another Haley-related record, a 78-only release on the Atlantic label. I thought for sure that I had seen this material in* Goldmine. *It turns out that my memory wasn't playing tricks on me –* Goldmine *featured the rock 'n' roll pioneer on the cover of its April 19, 1991 issue. But somehow, it was missing from the index. Oh well. Instead, we offer the below article that appeared in the April 1981 issue of* Goldmine, *in the wake of Haley's passing. Why is he so important? All he did was make rock 'n' roll a viable commodity with his "(We're Gonna) Rock Around The Clock." Without that hit, which spent two months at No. 1 a full year after its original release, then returned to the Top 40 in 1974 after it was used as the original theme for the TV series* Happy Days, *RCA Victor likely would never have gone searching for a hillbilly cat named Elvis. Haley had several other hits from 1953-56, but he faded fast from the charts after that. The British never stopped liking or respecting him, though. They've always had more room in their hearts for our pioneers.*

Bill Haley, whose recording of "Rock Around The Clock" became virtually synonymous with '50s rock and roll, died February 9 at his home in Arlington, Texas.

Haley, at the time of his death, was a study in the ways of American musical popularity. While everyone who even casually listened to the radio or watched television knew "Rock Around The Clock," few knew anything about the man or would have known who he was if his name was mentioned.

In other countries it was different.

After Haley's popularity in the U.S. waned in the late '50s, he found substantial recording contracts overseas (with Mexico's Orfeon in the early 1960s and Sweden's Sonet since 1968). A 1961 Orfeon LP of his, *Twist*, is the biggest selling album of all time in Mexico. In both that country and Europe, he was still a star when he died.

Haley's place in the history of rock 'n' roll is unique. Unlike Elvis, the Beatles or even Chuck Berry, Haley did not leave a lasting stylistic imprint on the face of rock music. And, despite what many novice fans think, Haley did not create rock and roll. Authorities disagree on what was the first rock 'n' roll record, but there is no doubt there were several before Haley scored with "Rock Around The Clock."

A look at Haley's recording career reveals that even he was performing rock 'n' roll before he recorded his world-famous hit. In 1951, Haley covered "Rocket 88," which in its version by Jackie Brenston is often cited as the first rock and roll record.

Haley's importance rests instead with the fact that he almost single-handedly made rock 'n' roll a national phenomenon.

His cover of Joe Turner's "Shake, Rattle And Roll" went to the No. 7 position of *Billboard*'s charts in the fall of 1954. "Rock Around The Clock" hit the number one spot July 9, 1955 and went on to sell more than 22 1/2 million copies worldwide. (It should be noted that Elvis Presley's "Heartbreak Hotel" would not hit for another eight months.)

When Haley recorded "Rock Around The Clock" April 12, 1954, it was not a likely choice to start a revolution in popular music. Neither "Clock" nor its flip side, "Thirteen Women," were covers of R&B hits (as was "Shake, Rattle And Roll"). When initially released in May 1954, "Clock" did nothing. It was not until the song was included as a teenage anthem in the film "Blackboard Jungle" that it took off up the charts.

Haley's contribution to the popularity of his hits was more than just performance. Although he and other early white rock and roll performers were later criticized for it, they rewrote their covers of R&B songs so they would be less offensive to white audiences.

For example, the unexpurgated version of "Shake, Rattle And Roll" opened:

Get out of that bed,
And wash your face and hands. (twice)
Get into the kitchen,
Make some noise with the pots and pans.
Well you wear low dresses,
The sun comes shinin' through. (twice)
I can't believe my eyes,
That all of this belongs to you.

The Haley version is much less sexually suggestive:
Get out in that kitchen,
And rattle those pots and pans. (twice)
Roll my breakfast,
'Cause I'm a hungry man.
You wear those dresses,
Your hair done up so nice. (twice)
You look so warm,
But your heart is cold as ice.

One verse of the original version is missing completely from Haley's recording.
I said over the hill
And way down underneath. (twice)
You make me roll my eyes,
And then you make me grit my teeth.

While it can be argued that what was done amounted to "tampering," it is probably a fair statement to say "Shake, Rattle And Roll" would not have been the big hit it was if Haley had not deleted the rawness of the R&B version.

Bill Haley (third from left, with his trademark "spit curl" on his forehead) plays with the Comets in the 1950s.

"We steer completely clear of anything suggestive," Haley once told an interviewer. "We take a lot of care with lyrics because we don't want to offend anybody. The music is the main thing and it's just as easy to write acceptable words."

Suggestive lyrics were part and parcel of the very forthright and emotional R&B music Haley's roots were in.

William John Clifton Haley Jr. grew up in a musical family – specifically, a country and western family. His father played banjo and he was introduced to the guitar at an early age.

Haley was born in Highland Park, Michigan. His actual birthday is the subject of debate. For many years, Haley indicated he was born in March 1927, but the evidence points instead to July 6, 1925.

When he was quite young, Haley's family moved to the Philadelphia area. In his early teens, Haley started playing guitar with local country and western groups. At 15 he left home to travel with the Downhomers. Several years later, he formed his own group, first called the Four Aces of the Western Swing, later the Saddlemen and finally the Comets. For the first few years, when he wasn't performing he worked at radio stations. For a brief time, he served as program director for WPWA in Chester, Pa.

Haley's group started out playing western swing – basically upbeat country music with a dance beat. But it wasn't long before Haley began including features

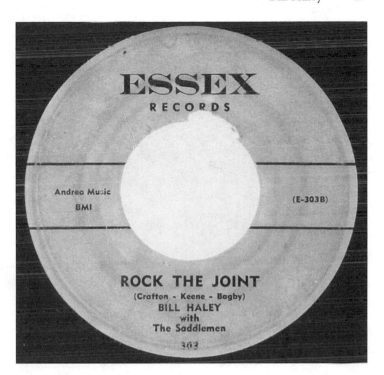

drawn from other styles of music, especially the "back beat" of black dance music.

"The style we played way back in 1947, 1948, and 1949 was a combination of country and western, Dixieland and the old-style rhythm and blues," Haley said in 1962.

"Around the early '50s, the musical world was starved for something new," he recalled four years later. "The days of the solo vocalist and the big bands had gone. About the only thing, in fact, that was making noise was progressive jazz, but this was just above the heads of the average listener. I felt then that if I could take, say, a Dixieland tune and drop the first and third beats, and accentuate the second and fourth, and add a beat the listeners could clap as well as dance, this would be what they were after. From there the rest was easy."

Haley certainly wasn't the image of a rock star, a fact that undoubtedly led to his fall from popularity in the U.S. His only visual trademark was his spit curl tumbling onto his forehead. Once others figured out the music, it wasn't long before he was replaced in the eyes of the public by handsome singers like Elvis and Pat Boone.

Haley's only Top 10 hit after "Rock Around The Clock" was "See You Later, Alligator." His last Top 40 hit was "Skinny Minnie." His last entry on the charts was "Skokiaan, which peaked at No. 70 almost exactly five years after "Rock Around The Clock" hit the top position.

When the Mexican audience discovered him, Haley responded by moving to that country, where he met and married his wife, Martha. Mexico remained home base for Haley up until his death.

Haley regularly toured Europe and South America during the 1960s and 1970s. The lineup of the Comets constantly changed, with the exception of the sax player Rudy Pompilli. In 1976, after a tour of Brazil, Pompilli died and Haley seemed to have lost all interest in performing. He was coaxed into a European tour in 1977, but appeared lifeless on stage. At the tour's completion, he dropped from sight, apparently by choice.

Then, in March 1979, he toured Britain for a month and was very successful. He cut a new album during the summer. In November, he played through Europe, climaxing his tour with a performance before the Queen of England at the Royal Variety Show. In April 1980, he played a set of South African concerts – his last on-stage performances.

At the time of his death, Haley reportedly was set to record a new album. Interestingly, the planned LP was to be a return to his roots – a country and western record.

Haley was in Arlington, Texas on a vacation when he died February 9. The official cause was a heart attack at about 6:30 a.m.

Right to the end, Haley continued to play his own style of rock 'n' roll. Even though he had long ago been passed over by American audiences, he was still a star in many places. It was only right. He may not have been the "Father of Rock and Roll," but he was most certainly the midwife who brought it to the world.

Most Collectible 45

"Rock The Joint"/ "Icy Heart," Essex 303, red vinyl, $1,800.

Most Collectible LP

Shake, Rattle And Roll, Decca DL 5560, 10-inch LP, $800.

Recommended Introduction

The Best Of Bill Haley And His Comets: The Millennium Collection, MCA 11957 (a 1999 release, and the only one of the "Millennium Collection" we can recommend without reservation, it has 12 of his Decca hits on it, which is about the right number for an introduction to Haley)

If you want to hear more...

From The Original Master Tapes, MCA 5539 (the first U.S. Haley retrospective, it has 20 tracks consisting of the A and B sides of his first 10 Decca singles)

Rock The Joint: The Original Essex Recordings 1951-1954, Rollercoaster 3001 (U.K. import, it contains 22 songs he recorded for the Philadelphia label, including the original "Rock The Joint" and his first hit, "Crazy Man Crazy")

American Legends: Bill Haley, Laserlight 12750 (budget-label collection of 12 of his Warner Bros. recordings, the best source for these in the U.S.)

The Decca Years And More, Bear Family 79005-11550-6 (a 5-CD German import with material he recorded from 1954-59; much of this material has not been reissued in the U.S.)

The Warner Bros. Years And More, Bear Family 79005-16157-2 (a 6-CD German import with material he recorded from 1960-69; much of this material has not been reissued in the U.S.)

Les Paul

by Lenny Kaye

    If he had done nothing more than invent the solid-body electric guitar – it's not called a Gibson Les Paul for nothing – and make multi-track recording techniques feasible, Les Paul would be praised as one of the people who made rock 'n' roll possible. Chuck Berry never could have played a guitar like a-ringin' a bell, for example, without Les Paul. (Indeed, he's in the Rock and Roll Hall of Fame for these very reasons.) As a musician, though, he's often seen as one of the performers that rock 'n' roll saved us from – after all, he and ex-wife Mary Ford had a string of hits in the early 1950s, most of which fit right in with the pop pabulum of the era. But there's a notable exception… In retrospect, it's amazing that the rocking, frenetic, barely two-minute long version of "How High The Moon" even got airplay in 1951, much less spent over two months at #1 in Billboard. This was a prototype of rock 'n' roll, complete with a really cool electric guitar solo that even today, roughly 50 years later, still sounds fresh. As of the time this article appeared in Goldmine – Jaunary 29, 1999 – Les Paul was still playing his guitar in public at the age of 83, jamming for patrons in a small nightclub.

If the 20th century will ultimately be known musically as the heyday of the guitar – and despite the myriad of instrumental innovations and relative new-found popularity of everything 1900's, from the saxophone to the synthesizer, I believe it will be – there will be few names written as large as Les Paul.

It is not only that his stage moniker graces the headstock of one of the premier electric guitars ever made, though it's probably true that many who play that very instrument have only a foggy notion of what its originator sounded like; or that, for a time in the early '50s, his hit records – with Mary Ford as songstress – defined the postwar sense of optimal abundance and possibility that coincided with America's ascendance into pop cult superpower.

Neither is it his considerable instrumental skills, his hotshot jazz chops, his chordal knowledge, his digital (as in fingers) speed and nose for a good tune. Nor, truth be told, is it his survivor's drive and instinct that keeps him on stage at the age of 83 every Monday night at Club Iridium, in the shadow of Lincoln Center, a cultural archive of memory, wit, off-color jokes, guest artists, and rippling, fluid solos that flurry from one end of the neck to the other. Two sets. Autographs after the show.

Les Paul will be remembered for his Sound. The New Sound, he called it, shortly after overdubbing himself into synched-up bliss (he would later schematic the first multi-track recorder) with the conceptual leap of 1948's "Lover" and "Brazil"; but really, he had been hard at work conceiving his own noise since barely a teenager.

The story is as simple as any bolt-of-lightning creation myth. Playing in the parking lot of Beekman's barbeque stand in Brookfield, Wis., perched midway between Milwaukee and his home town of Waukesha, Les was performing as a one-man band, blowing harmonica, singing, toe-tapping a bass drum and strumming his guitar. He'd already rigged up a primitive microphone and speaker system from his family radio, but in so doing was drowning out his guitar playing. Even then, Les knew that his singing voice wouldn't take him very far, and there wasn't a lot of call for even the most virtuoso of harp players.

Les went home, dismantled his father's Kolster radio-phonograph, and jabbed the needle into the wood, an inoculation of electricity the reverbs of which are still being felt today.

In a sense, he short-circuited record-collecting. He became his own record. Over the years, as he refined his sense of captured sound, amplified and treated and made musical by the new blue plate special of frequency and wave, he opened the world's ears to a music that sprang from outside the instrument itself – a perspective on sound, and no less effective on the emotions.

This sense of on-the-go technology and music – the reasoned numbers of science mixing with "Here's a number that's an old favorite..." – is really the story of musical growth at any given time, the resources used in order to reconstruct the tune running around in your head, and the rhythm of your life. But in the interstices between those who figure out how things work and those working "by ear" must lie gifted individuals who see these disparate strands and weave them together into a rope, which they then gather and yank the whole oxcart a step forward.

That's Les. He walks into his living room, circa 1929, and sees the differing streams of technology that have blossomed there since the turn of the century. The telephone. The radio and phonograph. The player piano. All devoted to the transmission of sound. Then he looks down at the acoustic hollow-body guitar in his hands, and an electric light flicks on in his head.

It is a sensibility of manipulated sound that would lead to such well-loved 20th century arcana as the feedback solo, "Bohemian Rhapsody," Phil Spector, the Chipmunks, and the basic instrumental blueprint for at least half the world's guitarists (the other half wield Fender Strats, so I've been told).

But Les wasn't just a six-string version of Thomas Edison. What makes him unique – and to my mind, what makes his music also sound otherworldly – is his musicality. Even from his earliest recordings, recently collected on a 2-CD set, *The Complete Trios – Plus* (1936-1947) (Decca/MCA), you can hear his chordal inventiveness, articulated speed, madcap glisses and slides and whoop-de-doos that took him through the heat of after-hours jam sessions in each of the world's jazz capitals at an important juncture: Chicago's post-Dixieland late-20s–early-30s; New York's late-30s pop swing mainstream; L.A. in the Hollywood royal flush of the '40s.

Throughout, he shared experiences and musical relations with the grand poobahs of pop, from Fred Waring and the Andrews Sisters to Bing Crosby and Chet Atkins, traded licks with Art Tatum and George Barnes and, more recently, Jimmy Page – names so interwoven with the fabric of our pop lives, their revolutionary evolutions so absorbed into the mainstream musical vocabulary that you sometimes forget that someone visionary had to dream these innovations up from scratch. Especially Les. If anything, his Sound would prove so futuristic that it would take a generation or three to even catch up, to become aware of how his tinkering with the wave-form paved the way for rockabilly's echo chamber deluxe, The Beatles' use of jazzy harmonies in straightforward teen pop songs, for the effects pedal to be a part of every guitarist's and studio's arsenal, and for the 1959 tiger-flamed Les Paul Gibson to become the vintage guitar mart's Holy Grail.

At one of the first Rock and Roll Hall Of Fame nominating committee meetings, the name of Les Paul came up for inclusion in the Early Influences category. "He's pop music," scorned one Golden Era record company president whose considerable groundbreaking achievements in the new rockin' rhythm & blues helped knock Les off the charts in the early years of the rock 'n' roll wars.

It was a strange generation gap I perceived, the battles still being fought over Then and Then-Then. To me, even if the music Les played was of an older, more complex and sophisticated pop form, his wildcard energy and the very electricity of his approach pointed more toward Jimi Hendrix and Eddie Van Halen than did any of his contemporaries. The wattage had intensified as the chords had gotten simpler. Les' arc bridged the gap between the haves (and have-nots) of the century. Thus he accepted his award (there had been many previously and many since) at the next year's induction ceremony.

Les Paul was originally a Polsfuss, born on January 9, 1915, in Waukesha, Wis., *Goldmine*'s home state, and his mother imbued him with his perfectionist sense of will and application. It is this determined sensibility – his motto, learned when he was given his first harmonica by a black ditchdigger at the age of eight, was "Don't say you can't 'til you've proved you can't" – has helped him survive through obstacles that would cause a less determined individual to shrug and hit the remote. Through trial and error, he built his own equipment; a lot of it didn't work when he first plugged it in. Sometimes he had to drastically rethink the problem, especially when it became personal. On the eve of his first

solo Capitol release in 1948, the aforementioned "Lover" and "Brazil," Les was involved in a terrible car crash. His right arm shattered, he had to virtually relearn the mechanics of guitar playing.

Similarly, when he put his mind to the lutherial science of guitar building, he used it to enhance his own playing to the point where it threatened to overshadow his considerable virtuosic grasp. It is probably true that, at times, Les seemed to want to show off his technical gadgetry at the song's expense, that Mary could open her mouth and out would come Bing's voice, and that one guitar could become four, effects piled on effect. More or Les, that was his continual artistic conundrum.

Always though, his love for the guitar balanced him, and it continues to do so, each Monday night at Iridium in New York. Backed by a bass-and-rhythm guitar duo that makes him a trio, he perches on a bar stool, guitar straddling his left thigh, like a classical musician might hold the instrument, instead of the more familiar folk crouch on the right leg, spinning out "Misty" and "Caravan" and "Over The Rainbow," a touch riding the strings with the old-friends familiarity of the many places his music has witnessed these nigh-seventy years.

Interviewing Les Paul can be a daunting task, if only because each of the scenes he arpeggiated and comp-chorded his way through are so fascinating in themselves. Where do you spend time delving? By the time he was 20, he had already been a veteran of the road, playing with such radio gypsies as the Ozark Apple Knockers, moving to St. Louis before settling in Chicago in the early '30s. He acquired the stage name Rhubarb Red, a hillbilly moniker that he soon dropped in favor of the more euphonious Les Paul, discovering the recordings of Django Reinhardt and the jazz-soaked musicians' hangouts scattered across the Windy City's South Side. He played with everyone and anyone, a brash, ambitious guitarist with an insatiable energy. On May 20, 1936, he cut his first official solo releases (he had been home-recording himself for years previously), four sides that ultimately appeared on the Montgomery Ward label in June 1937: "Just Because"/"Deep Elem Blues" and a sequel, "Answer To Just Because"/"Deep Elm Blues #2."

Released as Rhubarb Red, complete with singing, they ironically became Les' farewell to his hokum alter-ego. He juggled his two musical selves for a while, but left his hick character behind when he moved his trio to New York in 1938. There he secured a job with Fred Waring and became an in-demand session player on the radio broadcasts that blanketed the country with live "remotes." In 1943, he followed his musical opportunities to California and settled in Hollywood.

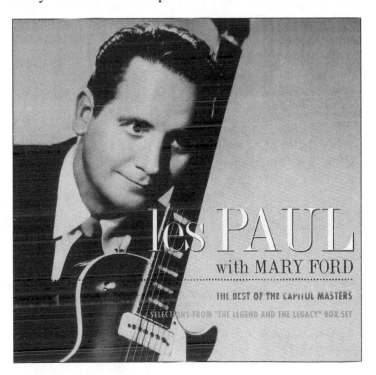

Les PAUL with MARY FORD

THE BEST OF THE CAPITOL MASTERS

SELECTIONS FROM "THE LEGEND AND THE LEGACY" BOX SET

All the while he was refining his idea of the electric guitar. Still regarded as a novelty, the instrument had never progressed beyond the semi-acoustic. Les dreamed of a solid body to increase sustain and dispel unwanted feedback howls. In 1941, he built a prototype called "The Log," literally a chunk of lumber with wings clamped on each side – to make it resemble a traditional guitar – and a pair of pickups. It would be another 10 years before his dream became Gibson's reality.

Les was successful in Hollywood, his brash go-for-it persona placing his flashy runs alongside established stars like Nat King Cole and Bing Crosby. The latter scored a major hit with "It's A Long, Long Time" in 1945, interplaying with Les' obligattos and fulfilling a long-time dream of Les' to play with Der Bingle.

He might have stopped there, a musician's musician, a studio pro, but despite these achievements, his tale had only begun. Setting up a recording studio in the garage behind his house at 1514 North Curson Avenue in Hollywood, Les began experimenting with the possibilities of recording. He would often plug his electric guitar directly into the mixing board, all the better to shape its pure signal. One night, with his friend Lloyd Rich, he happened on the idea of using "a playback pickup behind the recording head" to generate short tape echoes. Later, he would prevail on Ampex to build him a multi-track recorder so he wouldn't have to painstakingly layer his records dub-by-dub, losing sound quality all the while.

And then there was the human element. In 1945, Les met Colleen Summers, one of the country-inflected Sunshine Girls. Two years later, Les had convinced her to change her name to Mary Ford, and on December 29, 1949, the pair were formally married. He had already begun experimenting with overlaying her voice over his guitar instrumentals. Capitol, pleased with Les' success on "Lover," but feeling that perhaps it was a novelty hit, released "Until I Hold You Again," in May 1949, with "three" Marys on lead vocal. It was not a hit, but the '50s had yet to begin.

In the meantime, a version of the old 1922 chestnut, "Nola," became Les' second solo hit in the spring of 1950. Given some commercial room by Capitol, and moving back east to New York, Les continued to create settings for Mary. It was a vocalist's time, and his experience on tour with the Andrews Sisters had given him an understanding of close several-part female harmony. For a few months in early 1951, Capitol positioned Mary as a Patti Page competitor – Les & Mary scored a minor hit with "Tennessee Waltz," and then a much larger one with "Mockin' Bird Hill." Any thoughts that the duo were overdubbed flash-in-the-pan novelties were quickly dispelled by the green-cheese chart success of "How High The Moon," which owned the #1 slot during the spring of 1951, and made Les and Mary one of the most recognizable couples in mid-century pop music.

They were everywhere: on radio, television, constantly traveling. Les would even carry recording equipment in the couple's car, setting it up in motel rooms during days off from their grueling schedule of personal appearances. The hits still sound unlike anything recorded before or since – "Vaya Con Dios," "The World Is Waiting For The Sunrise," "Bye Bye Blues" – and for a good few years, until rock 'n' roll irrevocably changed the musical landscape, Les and Mary's "New Sound" took them to heights unimagined.

There was little separation between church and state, however. Les' round-the-clock work habits gave Mary no respite from the road, even when they moved to a mountainside home in Mahwah, N.J., where Les built another studio. Increasingly, as the rockin' '50s sidelined the couple's recorded output, stress fractures began to show in the Pauls' marriage. Even a shift in record labels to Columbia in 1958, where president "Sing Along With" Mitch Miller promoted "good" music over rock 'n' roll, did nothing to revive their fortunes. Though Les and Mary's partnership lasted until the early '60s, both professionally and matrimonially, the handwriting was on the wall.

Meanwhile, Les had endorsed Gibson guitars in the early '50s, and had designed a special signature Les Paul model for the company. He accompanied his technological innovations with the Les Paulverizer, an electronic device that attempted to recreate live the overdubs he'd engineered in his home studio. And as the years passed, '60s passing into '70s, Les found his legend overtaking many of the ups and downs he had survived over the years. In 1976, when he dropped into Nashville to visit Chet Atkins and record *Chester & Lester* for RCA – ultimately to win a Grammy for the collaboration – he had become part of a pantheon of six-string wizards whose contributions have far outstripped chord shapes and scale patterns.

We spoke over the phone on two consecutive Wednesdays in November, each conversation lasting a gracious hour and a half in length. As we moved through the layers of events, the songs played and roads traveled, you could hear the enthusiasm mounting in Les' voice. He unraveled his memories like an off-the-cuff solo, following tangents, unexpected lyricisms, flip asides, tickling the strings, getting serious, flashing back to the main theme, quickly spinning into the next tune in the medley. Somewhere there's music... A saloon 'neath the moon and how high it will be....

Goldmine: *What was it about the guitar that initially attracted you?*

Les Paul: Well, I started out on the harmonica. It was when I was very young, just after kindergarten, when I'd begun school. Playing the harmonica, I needed something to go with it. I was so small. I tried the saxophone, I tried a banjo, I tried a drum. My mother guided me. She said, "You have to have something that you don't have in your mouth, and you have to have something to go with your foot." So from the banjo, Mother suggested I get a guitar. I sent to Sears, and at about nine years old, I got my first guitar.

The guitar is a very physical, hands-on instrument.

It's complementary to everybody. That was it. From that point on, why, I was playing the harmonica and the guitar. One night at a drive-in halfway between Waukesha and Milwaukee, some young guy in the rumble seat of a car wrote a note and gave it to the carhop, and she gave it to me. I had a PA system rigged up with my mother's radio, and I was singing into a telephone. He said "I can hear your voice and the harmonica fine, but the guitar's not loud enough." So I went home and told my mother. I figured I would go down to my dad, rob another telephone and his radio and play the guitar through that. I found that didn't work. So I jabbed a phonograph needle into the top of the guitar, turned that on, and man, it was loud.

Goldmine is essentially a record collector's magazine. It strikes me that you actually built the rarest of records there – the musical instrument as amplified disc. You turned your guitar into a phonograph record.

That's right. I understood how the sound transfers when I took apart phonographs. I took everything apart and rebuilt it. In the late '20s, I had my own illegal broadcast station in the basement. Oh, I was doing the whole thing, playing through the radio at home and broadcasting in the neighborhood. The whole nine yards. (laughs)

It's amazing, all this new technology coming along in the late '20s. You could suddenly be as intimate and personal with your words and music as need be, and still reach thousands and millions of listeners.

I was always inquisitive to find out. That part over there had nothing to do with this other part, but what was it doing? I would get on my bicycle and pump right out to the transmitter, and knock on the door. Make sure it was raining so the guy would let me in. The guy at the transmitter, he'd say, "What do you want?" He'd see it was raining, and me standing in the rain, and I'd asks, "Can I talk to you, Mister?" and he'd say, "Get in here out of the rain," and the next thing you know I'm getting a lesson every week. I was studying electronics. Right when I got my guitar, I was already into electronics.

There's a certain mathematics with playing music as well as with electronics. Did you bridge the gap?

Sure. They're related. They're such companions that it's just a natural. You want to change the volume, you want to change the tone, you want to do this, that, you're dealing with frequencies. It's related, all the way through.

Radio stations have cycles and so do the wave forms of music.

Absolutely. I can't imagine me ever getting along without both. One is related to the other so much.

It's like the right and left half of the brain, where one is very analytical, and the other maneuvers through intuitive emotion. You seemed determined to unite the two.

That's right. I grew up not knowing what I was into. It was all in my living room. See, my mother had a player piano, and I'd come running home every night after school because I could pump the piano for her. When I got the chance, I would punch extra holes in it with an icepick. If I missed, well, I would put a piece of tape over it and move the hole. The next thing you know I would rig up a way of putting in the particular note that I wanted. So when I had a C, and I'd want to add a B-flat in there to make it a seventh, I'd experiment. I didn't know they were even sixths and sevenths, 'til one day I started counting them out. And the piano and the piano roll were natural things to make multiples. I had wild chords going. Here I am, in the '20s, not knowing that the player piano is leading me right to the phonograph, which was also in the living room. Had a crank on it. It was a Victor Victrola. I had that, I had the radio, I had the telephone. I had everything in the living room, and I didn't have to leave it. I had all the things that I have today. It was all there. The receiving part that you're listening to me on the telephone – that's nothing but the same magnet and a coil that's under the string. That's exactly what it is. And so when I took that part of it, and put it under the string, I damn near went crazy.

You did bring that sense of technology and science to the guitar. Not, remarkably enough, in your playing. To me, you're not really a scientific player. You tap into your emotion, beyond technique.

These are things you crave to hear, and we couldn't hear them – so if you can't buy one, you build one. It was fun, not knowing what I was doing. I looked at the crank phonograph and I said, Jesus, if Edison can record on that thing, I must be able to, too. So I went to my dad, and the next thing you know I'm building a recording machine, and I'm recording my singing and harmonica. I used the telephone for a mike. With the radio there, I needed nothing. I didn't have to leave my living room.

I built my recording machines, my broadcasts. I had my own little circus going. It turned out to be fun. Then I got the guitar and of course, playing in the goddamn barbeque stand, and this guy sitting in the back seat wrote me a note. He says, all I can hear is your singing and the harmonica. I can't hear the guitar. So I says, "Ma, I got a critic. Some guy told me the guitar's not loud enough." I'm thinking of getting Dad's radio, and plugging my guitar into it with another telephone. Then the idea hit me, what would happen if I put a phonograph pickup in the top of the guitar, and turned that on instead of a record. So I did. Here I got a crystal pickup in the top of my guitar, and holy Christ, it was loud. But it fed back. So I filled the guitar full of rags. Then I took plaster of Paris and poured it in there. And I ended up with a solid body guitar.

That weighed 75 pounds!

Then I made one out of a steel railroad track, to prove whether wood was better than steel. And of course, the steel railroad track sustained forever. Then I took the part of the telephone with the coil and magnet in it, and put that under the strings and jeez, I'd found the end of the world. It was humbucked yet. Bell Telephone gave that to me. All I had to do was open the telephone and I had my pickup. Everything was in my living room. My brother would always say, "Mother, he's at it again!" I was the busiest...

You even made some test records then.

That is correct. But it was all in the living room. So if I never went out, I had everything I needed to make the recordings. I'm thinking, when it comes in that antenna, it's gotta get in the radio, and if I find where that is, I can take my telephone and plug it where the antenna goes in. Then I've got the sound. And when I moved around to the other side, I felt the speaker moving, and I said if that's moving, then there must be a way of taking that same thing I'm going in with, and working on the out of it. So there's an in and an out of the whole system. When you go in, you're going to the out of it, and when you go to the output, you're listening to what you put into it.

It was no time at all that I had a recording lathe there, with a crank, and I'm gouging out my very first record. In 1928, I built my first recording machine with which I could actually hear myself. When I sang in Milwaukee, my mother actually dropped the needle on there, and I had my first record, which was in December of '28. The date is on there, my mother wrote the date on the disc. If you get down on your knees and put your ear to the speaker, you can hear me singing and playing the harmonica.

You must have only been 13 or 14 then.

Oh, I left home at thirteen. I was gone. At thirteen, my mom got on a Greyhound bus and took me to St. Louis. I got my first job. I had a job previous to that, with a cowboy band, that went all over Minnesota, Wisconsin, Michigan, Illinois. I was Red Hot Red, and then I went to St. Louis, and that's where they changed my name to Rhubarb Red. I started on the radio on a Saturday night. The first Saturday night was canceled, for some reason. Still, I got more mail, that my mother had sent, from Wisconsin, saying how great I was, and I wasn't even on the radio. Her friends, she'd called them up on the phone. The program director comes in, and says "You got more mail and you weren't even on yet!" That was in 1930.

It was a good year technologically.

Everything was under way. You had the movies making their transition from silents to talkies, electrical recording. I think of it as a beginning of modern mass communication. It sure was. I was listening on all the radio stations that existed, which were few, but there they were. I'd listen to WLS (Chicago), I'd listen to Nashville, Wheeling, W. Va. And then I'd be listening to the broadcasts from the Grand Terrace, Earl Hines and Coleman Hawkins. I'm hearing the Art Tatums. Everything. And it would only be a couple of years until I would be playing with the very people that I was listening to a couple of years earlier. I listened to the broadcasts and that's where I set my goal. I'd bum a ride with my brother into Milwaukee. He had a Model T Ford, and he had to deliver clothes to be cleaned. They cleaned them in Waukesha, and he'd have to drive them 19 miles each day back to Bell Dye Works. He'd throw those clothes in the truck and say "Red, you want to go in?" I'd go to Milwaukee to the only music store, called Orth's, and would buy a record. It would cost 19 cents or something to get a record of Duke Ellington or some country guy. In 1929 I'd come home with records by Gene Autry, Nick Lucas, Eddie Lang, some of the pioneers in their day.

Nick Lucas and Eddie Lang would seem to be a real starting point for the guitar in this century.

It was. I brought them both home, a record of each, and I thought, which one am I going to listen to here? And I quickly decided that Eddie Lang was the guitar player to follow.

Why would you say that? I would agree with you, by the way.

Technically. He was hammering strings, pulling strings, he had the vibrato going. He was playing a Gibson L-5. Everything that he did seemed to be right, while Nick Lucas was accompanying himself with a more Italian style of playing. I call them spaghetti chords. He was doing all the little runs, while Eddie Lang was doing all the big stuff. He was playing harmonics, everything, so I chose to go with Eddie Lang, and got his book, and started studying that, and listening to him, and figured out how he was playing. Copied him and then went on.

Did you ever hear any of the recordings he made with Joe Venuti?

Oh, sure. Probably the second time I went to Orth's Music I had "Kicking That Dog Around" and all the things with Joe. I knew everything about "Four-String Joe," "April Kisses"...everything that Joe or Lang did. I had 'em all.

It's really a sad thing that Eddie died so early in life.

It sure was. Little did I know that I would be sitting in his chair a few years later with Bing Crosby. I knew that's where I would like to go, and that's who I listened to. Bing in 1929: I was glued to the radio to hear his first broadcast, and to hear Eddie Lang behind him. And then Carl Kress, I would hear him with the Boswell Sisters, and Eddie Lang with the Boswells, I'm listening to these guys in the late twenties. That's all I needed.

Were you familiar with the work of Roy Smeck?

Sure, when I came to New York, we were very dear friends, right away.

Though your music doesn't sound alike, some of your stage patter might have something in common.

(Laughs) Yeah, yeah. He played the harmonica, and he walked out on the stage and he did his shtick. He lived in Sunnyside, over on the (Long) Island. When I came in '37 to New York, I lived in Jackson Heights, in Queens, where all the musicians were. I believe every musician that lived in the east found a place in Jackson Heights. The building I was in had the Pied Pipers, had the Merry Macs, had Artie Shaw's band, Fred Waring's band, Blue Barron's band. Just anybody that was any good. Bob Crosby. They were all in that

neighborhood. George Smith was across the hall, Bobby Hackett was in the building. I built an illegal radio station there. We broadcast every Wednesday night, and we had the most wonderful musicians there, in the studios of the basement in Jackson Heights. It was tremendous.

Did you play the vaudeville circuit at that time?
Sure.

Three, four, five shows a day?

You want to go for eight and nine? The most I did was nine. That's when you go on, you go off, and when you go off, you're on again. They're calling a half hour from when you walk off the stage. Before you know, it's time for another one.

Roy Smeck... the ukulele was quite the instrument in the late twenties. Did you ever try your hand at that?

No, I just knew Roy as a friend, seeing that he lived in Sunnyside. In '37-'38 he had to go to Brazil because his wife was on him, and he had to leave the country. When he came back he played the Palace Theatre, and I went down with him. He walked out there and got electrically shocked and he played the harmonica for the whole show, cause he didn't dare play his steel guitar. Just before he died, I asked him if he would play at the Edison Labs in Menlo Park for a commemorative show. I was emceeing with Governor Brendan Byrne. Roy was there, and he was too feeble; he had arthritis real bad. He played very little, and he had a young guy who played with him, that did the playing. That's the last time I saw him, and then he passed on. Eubie Blake was there as well.

A convention of great innovators...

I interviewed Eubie before the show and was able to get some good questions for him. As well as Roy. Yes, I knew Roy very well.

You went on your own in 1934. I believe you went to Chicago around then?

First I went to St. Louis, and that was in 1930. I joined the union in St. Louis. That was where I started. From there I went to Springfield, Mo., and then to Chicago. In 1933 I was in Chicago for the World's Fair, and I was on the Columbia Broadcasting System, doing shows from Chicago. I was making what would be a fortune today. I was making some 1200 dollars a week.

And this in the midst of the Depression.

You better believe it. And I didn't save any of it. I'd just go in a club and buy everyone a drink. I was playing for the Roger Touhys, the Al Capones – in the middle of that whole thing. I was playing on the soap operas. I saw Amos and Andy when they were Sam and Henry. Before they were known. I was at the beginning of all of it. And then when I left Chicago, I came to New York.

It was in May 1936 that you cut your first sides for the Montgomery Ward label as Rhubarb Red. What was it like being in the studio for those early recordings?

It was great. I had made some recordings in 1931 for Decca Records, only it wasn't Decca then, it was World Transcriptions. I made those prior to Rhubarb Red. The studio was in the (*New York*) *Daily News* building. We made 111 of them, and I remember they were on Western Electric cutters. It was what they called vertical recordings – hill and dale – and I cannot find the masters. The music is recorded, and it should be out there somewhere. I don't think it would be thrown away. Then I didn't record anymore until 1935, when I went over to Decca Records and made some sides. Then right after that I cut some of my own recordings, and that's what came out under the name of Rhubarb Red.

That was mostly hillbilly stuff...

Mine was, and I know I went up there that day with just one guitar. They had a song called "Just Because" and wanted me to do my hillbilly stuff. I only had my L-5, and I didn't have my flat-top round-hole guitar, so I didn't play finger-style. I used a pick, and played like Eddie Lang. Behind Georgia White I played Eddie Lang-style, and on the country stuff, I got the wrong guitar, and a pick, and so I did it with that. My mother didn't like it. She said, "You don't sound country, why'd you do that?" Well, I was there with the wrong guitar. I used my jazz guitar for country. She said, "Well, you sound like Gene Autry, or one of those drugstore cowboys." (laughs)

That's interesting, because you're not known for finger-style guitar playing.

No. People don't even know I play bluegrass. Like Earl Scruggs on a banjo, only this is my own little thing. It's country as hell, though. A different ball game. I got a ton of masters where I just used finger picks. Bluegrass. They're just great. The records don't have a scratch on them. I have over 50 Rhubarb Red sides sitting here. They go back into the '30s. They're very well recorded; I did them on my own machine, nothing but a bass and a guitar, and finger-style guitar.

You formed your own trio after that, with Jimmy Atkins, Chet's brother, and Ernie Newton. And then you came to New York and hooked up with Fred Waring.

It was actually my third trio. I joined him in '37. I played for him in the hallway, by the elevator. It was on the eighth floor of the building where David Letterman is now (The Ed Sullivan Theatre). Major Bowes had his offices in there, Paul Whiteman was in there. They were all in there. I said, "Can we play something while you're waiting for the elevator? He said, "Look, I can't feed the 60 Pennsylvanians I've already got."

But when we played for him, he said, "Get in the elevator." Of course, we knew right away that we had the job. When we went in the rehearsal room, he stopped the glee club and the band, and he told them that if they liked us, we were in. We knew we were home with that line. We had the electric guitar, and that was a rare thing, too. He loved it. We played two numbers, "Casey Jones" and "After You've Gone" and (laughs) we got the job.

You were playing the electric guitar all this time. You must've been familiar with Charlie Christian's take on it.

I was prior to Charlie. I was playing in '31 with my own guitar and even goes back into the '20s when I played the barbeque stand. But when I came to Chicago, the problem was people didn't like the electric guitar. To sing and play with it, it wasn't yet very good, coming through a Motorola speaker. It wasn't what you'd call the best speaker. In '31, I kind of figured out that I had to get a decent case for my amplifier. I can't go around with Mother's radio in tow. So I went over to Bell & Howell, who made projectors for people that wanted to play films, 8 or 16 mm film. I explained that I just wanted the carrying case and amplifier. I didn't want a projector. I wanted something with a handle on it that was already made. They got interested in me and gave it to me. They thought it was pretty cute. I still have it. It's an amplifier in a case for the projector. It had a little tone control on it, and a speaker built in with a field supply on it. To this day it sounds good, and that was in 1931. Then I went over to Lyon and Healy, a music store in Chicago; they picked up on the cabinet. If you look at Gibson's first amplifier ever, you're going to look at my amp, and there it is. Gibson copied Lyon and Healy; it's identical.

Did playing the electric guitar change the way you approached the instrument? For a while, the electric guitar was just regarded as an amplified version of an acoustic guitar.

There was so much flap over the electric guitar. In '33, I used them at the Big Yank workshirt company at the World's Fair, and we broadcast over WLS in Chicago. I had the guitar amp, but I don't know if there's any recordings. I'd just go over there as part of the World's Fair Duo and that's it. In '34, I went to the Bismarck Hotel, and on Friday nights, I'd go on NBC. I had a jazz quartet. It had a violin, two guitars, and bass. And we sang. It was the biggest thing in Chicago. Oh, man, was it making noise. My violin player was a klutz, and he would stand on my goddamn cable. And I would walk to go up to the microphone, and he would rip the pickup right out of the guitar. We're off the air. And so NBC would call me after that, and ask what happened. I'd tell them it was an accident, and they suggested that maybe on the broadcast, I shouldn't use the electric, because then we know you're not going to screw the broadcast up. I would use the amplifier for the audience. Come showtime, we'd put the guitar up to the mike, and let the guitar amplifier go to the audience. We wouldn't mike the amplifier. So I don't think – now I haven't gone through all the recordings I have back here – but I do have some from the Bismarck, but I'm not sure if I have any with an electric guitar. That was '34. The mail came in, with people liking it and not liking it. Musicians would call in, write in, saying they didn't like it as well as an acoustic, it doesn't sound as good, or another person would say they like it better. There was a lot of controversy about it.

By the time Charlie started playing the concept of the electric guitar was more accepted.

In 1938, I was visiting my mother back in Waukesha, and mom says, "I wish you'd get off that high-class show with Fred Waring playing every night. It's just too spiffy." Too high class. I said, "What would you want me to do?" and she said, "I'll show you Saturday night." And she tunes in Bob Wills, over KVOO, in Oklahoma. Out in Tulsa. She says, "That's where you should be, Lester." I said, "Geez, I'm coast-to-coast. You're telling me a guy you can hardly get out there, a local program..." She says, "That's the kind of music you should be doing." That was her kind of music. "Listen," she'd say. "It's got a drum in it and everything."

So my bass player Ernie and I decided to go out there. We were on vacation, with nothing to do for another week. We got in the car and drove out to Tulsa. In '38, we're in Tulsa, and I'm jamming with the band, with Bob Wills and the Playboys, in this Quonset hut of a ballroom. During the intermission, after we played – aw, hell, we were having a great time – this black guy comes up to me, this skinny kid, and he says, "Mr. Paul, my name is Charlie, and I was wondering if I could play your guitar."

I asked him if he could play, and he nodded. So I handed it down to him from the stage. He did a few runs, and I asked him if he wanted to get up and play the next set. So he got up and he played, knocked me out, and that's where I met Charlie. The next time I heard from him, he was on his way to New York to join Benny Goodman. I ran into him on 53rd and Broadway, at the music store called New York Band & Instrument Co. It was on Sixth Avenue, near 50th. Eddie Bell was over there, and I ordered a guitar for Charlie and myself. They were in a maple cabinet like the one from Bell and Howell only made of one-inch maple, and we had this thing with 37 tubes in it!

It was an AC-DC amplifier, and one was also made for Roy Smeck. So we picked up our amplifiers over on Sixth Avenue, and we carried them over to 53rd and Broadway. We picked up a pair of them and we carried those sonsabitches over to 53rd and Broadway, and he says, "Let's rest here." And we're right where the subway is, and I asked, "How do you feel?" He says, "I'm tired." I said, "Yeah, I am too. These fuckin' things are too heavy." He said, "I don't think we're going to make it with these." I felt very bad. It was my idea to have one made for him and one made for me. They were godawful heavy. Between the amp and the guitar, boy, we were both dyin'. So we took them back to New York Band & Instrument Co. and said "make us two regular ones." That's what we did. Then when Charlie went with Benny Goodman, he made the electric guitar famous. He just did great.

Were there any elements of his style you particularly appreciated?

He was a stomper. Charlie, he played one note while I was playing 10. I was a technique guy, and he was one that just went for the right note in the right place. I admired him very much.

What about someone like Django Reinhardt?

He fractured me. When I heard him, I said "Oh, my God." Harry Zimmerman was an organist I worked with at WJJD in Chicago – this was in 1934 – and I was musical director there. It was my job to go over to Lyon and Healy and buy the records. In those days, you weren't given the records by the record company. You went out and bought 'em. So I went out to buy the records for WJJD and WIND, and I had an allowance of maybe a hundred dollars that I could spend for records. I used to love to pick out the records, cause I'd get what I liked, whether it was Count Basie, or Andre Konstelantz or Eddie Lang. That's where I picked up all the records – Joe Venuti, Bing Crosby, Russ Columbo, all that. Rudy Vallee. Everything. Louis Armstrong, the Boswell Sisters, Paul Whiteman. It was the same world. It wasn't long before we had Benny Goodman, Lionel Hampton. This particular week I said to Harry Zimmerman, "Can you go pick out the records for me this week." It was something we did once a month. And he brought back Django.

Did you ever think of moving in a more purely jazz direction?

No. I made that decision when I was Rhubarb Red, right before switching over to Les Paul. I said, there's two kinds of jazz. There's a jazz where people walk away from it, and then there's the kind of jazz that entertains. From doing burlesque, and doing the radio shows, and working with the entertainers, I felt I knew where it was at. If I want to impress another guitar player, then I'll go into jazz. When I grew up in Chicago with the Earl Hineses and the Nat Coles, I had that choice. I decided real fast that even though I would sit and play with the Art Tatums and play their kind of music, when it was time to make a recording or do anything... no, no, no. Just like when I play at the club. I play for the people.

That's an admirable thing. Sometimes musicians all too often forget their audience, though I think you have to strike a balance between doing your art and what's predictable and expected. I mean, you didn't purely follow trends. You certainly were an innovator, and it's nice when you can take people along with you.

If you can educate them without hurting anybody, without stepping off the curb, you're OK. If I have a choice of making a jazz thing of, let's say, in those days it would be "Cherokee," I would say, no, no, no. I'm going to leave the other guy to play "Cherokee," or "C Jam Blues." I'm not going to do it that way. I'll go over here, and I'll do "Vaya Con Dios," or "World Is Ready For the Sunrise" or "How High The Moon." I'm going to do it commercial. I was criticized for it by a lot of the jazz people, because they knew I could play jazz. They just couldn't understand why I wouldn't play just for them. It was simple.

Still, I don't think I confined myself stylistically. I liked country; I liked jazz. I liked popular music. I wanted to make records that every station would play. Today, if it's jazz, a country guy would never play it. You could never hear it in Nashville. You would never hear it in New York on a country station.

For a time, musicians worried that getting played on the radio would hurt their live popularity.

When I joined Fred Waring he was anti-recording. He had a whole scene going with Whiteman, the Dorsey Brothers, Benny Goodman, to ban recording. Fred was the leader of it. And he had musicians signing up, pledging not to make a phonograph record. I said, "Me for one disagrees with you. There's nothing in my contract that say I can't make a phonograph record, so I'm going over and make one." We had a big argument about it. Finally Fred had to say, "OK, you're legally right, but I disagree with you." Later on, he would come to me and ask me to talk to Capitol Records for him. Everybody deserted him. Nobody stopped recording, and Fred realized he was wrong.

It's like the people who were against the electric guitar. Sometimes you can't stand in the way of progress. It'll run you over.

It was 1937 when I joined Fred Waring, and he made a remark I'll never forget. "Les," he said, "I don't understand it. Your trio draws more mail than I get. What's the reason for it?" I told him most of it was controversy over the electric guitar. I said, "We'll record both shows tonight. On the first show I'll use the straight guitar, and the second one I'm going to play the electric." And then we'd listen to both of them. We did our broadcast from the Hotel Vanderbilt, and then we went back to the offices on Broadway. Waring asked if he could come with us. We walked over to 53rd, and we sat down and listened to the first show and second. Fred says, "Why don't we take a vote?" We all were there – Scotty, Fred's engineer, and Fred – and we all unanimously chose the electric. I said to Fred, "Why did you pick the electric?" and he said, "Well, everybody can hear you. You make different sounds. You're no longer competing with a loud saxophone or a drummer. You can actually turn that thing up and drown them all out! You've got command."

Did you find that it changed the way you played the instrument?

Absolutely. Before, we'd have to scrub a chord, or beat on it like a banjo. We'd have to do something to even the volume difference. Four strings are louder to your ear than one. Technically it's not; technically, when you're making a recording, the four strings go to zero on the dial, and if you play one note, you bring it up to zero also. But one is much more intimate than four. One note is more powerful than four, the same as one singer is more powerful than four singers; that is, for getting the message across. Not loudness. If Bing Crosby comes out alone, he's more powerful than if he comes out with three guys. The Andrews Sisters, one is more powerful than three. If you're standing on the stage, there's more concentration if the person can look only at you. He can concentrate on one thing. So what I found out was single-string playing is much more definite than chords. If I go out with a straight acoustic guitar, I just don't have the power. So I'd have to hit four strings, and when you hit

four strings, it's just not as concentrated. You got four to listen to; it's busier. I saw that Bing had much more power than the Mills Brothers. You got three Andrews Sisters. Which one are you going to look at? Can you look at all three? You can't.

So this idea got into my head. I realized now that if you're playing with one string, and it's got a big ballsy sound, and then you go hit a chord, it just doesn't ring right. You say, why is that? Well, if you're hearing a line, like Dorsey on the trombone, "Sentimental Over You" (he sings bompbom dada dee dah dah dah)... if he could hit a chord on the trombone, it wouldn't be as good. Now you've changed your style of playin', this is an entirely different ball game. You don't play like Django. When Django went to the electric, that was almost his Waterloo, though Django was quick to adapt to it

It's like when microphones became commonplace. That Al Jolson style of throwing your arms out and singing to the back balcony went out, and a more intimate form of singing could result. They had to rethink how they sang.

It's a good analogy. Bing would go in there and steal your teeth by just moving into the microphone as he sang. He'd wipe the other guy who's back there belting his note out. And strangely enough, his idol was Al Jolson. Bing always admired him. I watched them sing together on the radio, and when you heard them side-by-side, you could see how much alike they were. They whistled, Bing and Jolson did the ba ba ba boos... you just had to look for it. You just had to look for the similarities. I once asked him, "Who is your mentor?" and he says Al Jolson. I was surprised. Probably, if he hadn't told me, I never would have connected the two.

What kind of a guy was Bing? In some ways, he seems like such an enigma.

He was a loner. It took a lot to get to know him. He had very few people that ever got close enough where you could go out and get drunk with him. He'd ask me what I was doing, and I'd say whad'ya have in mind... We'd go out together and we'd sit in some saloon down in the bowels of L.A. and he'd throw his rug in the car. No hat on. It was a different Bing. I never saw Bing rehearse. As many times as I'd visit him at his house, I never saw him playing a record over and over and over to learn a part. That sonofabitch would walk in, and ask what he was doing, and they'd tell him and he'd say OK. And the first take, it's over. That's it. Sinatra would have 29 takes to get one right. Not Bing. If you did two takes or three takes, it's because the band screwed up. I never saw anybody like Bing. He was a rock, the most stable guy. He'd take his shot of whiskey before the show. One before the show, one after, and one in between there somewhere. He had

enough in his little bottle for three shots, and that was it. If I was around him, he'd say, "Hey, you want one?" and I'd say no, and he'd say, "Thank you!" He had 'em all measured out.

You met him in Hollywood when you moved out there in the '40s. It must've been an exciting boom town in those days.

I moved out there in '42. I was in the right place at the right time, like I'd been in Chicago and New York. All of 'em. And when you ask where is the right place, well, it's when it's happening. In '42, in L.A., it was perfect.

You were well on your way to building your first recording studio. It was great that the armed forces helped give you an engineering degree.

(Laughs) That's a wild story. A guy named Bob Summers asked me to fill in a couple of shows for him because his mother died. One was at KNX – that was just five steps from my house. I was living at Gordon, there at Gower, over on the next block. So I went home and got my guitar and had to do "The Whistler," or "Suspense" – it was one of those drama shows for Autolite – and there's nothing for me to play. There's maybe three or four chords I have to play. So I'm jamming with the guys. I had my electric there, and Gordon Jenkins was the leader of the band, and he's sitting at the piano and we're going at it. A guy taps me on the shoulder. It was Meredith Willson. He asked me my name, and said if I ever got my induction papers, if that happens, contact me. He was going to start an outfit called the Armed Forces Radio Service. I said, "Meredith, I got my papers yesterday!" And I'd already contacted Glenn Miller, and Glenn is going to request me. He said, "Would you authorize me to kill it. Maybe I could do something about it?" I said I don't know. He said that the Armed Forces Radio Service would be based in Hollywood, and I wouldn't have to move. I could live at home, and work in the band, and he'd make room for my trio as well. He even said we'd be working with Bing. So I was the third guy to go in – there was Colonel Lewis, Loretta Young's husband; the Captain was Meredith Willson; and then they got Private Paul. We picked out the members of the band, and it was on the same street I lived on. Two blocks down the hill! That was the most convenient war I ever saw. I ended up playing more with Bing than had I been a civilian. My trio would play for all the Armed Forces Networks broadcasts. Kate Smith would come on, she wouldn't want to use the big band. Same with Bing. They'd use the Les Paul Trio. I probably recorded more than anybody in the world.

Hollywood seemed good to you. You made hit records with Bing and the Andrews Sisters. You went on tour with them, didn't you?

I got along with all three of them.

Were they as close in temperament as they were in harmony?

LaVerne was unhappy. She wanted to quit. We were on our way to Boston at the time. We tried our damnedest to convince her not to quit, but she wanted to quit.

She was a true Andrews Sister; you couldn't just replace her with someone outside the family.

Sooner or later, certain things happened. She just wanted to get the hell out. She bought a liquor store for her boyfriend – and he was a trumpet player with Fred Waring. I knew him many years before LaVerne ever met him. The liquor store was at the corner of Sunset and LaBrea, and they just wanted to get off from all that traveling and stuff.

You liked traveling though. There's all these stories about you driving everywhere and anywhere. You're a restless guy.

How do you convince someone to stay on the road when they don't want to be on the road? There was no law about the Andrews Sisters. They didn't have a life contract in any way.

You had started inventing the "New Sound" about this time. When you would overdub your guitars, say in something like "Brazil," how would you get them to hook up harmonically? Vari-speed?

I had it mathematically worked out. Like we were saying very early in the conversation, it's mathematical. Slow or increase the tape speed so much and over-dub your new part. That not only includes the guitar, it goes for everything in electronics, everything in music. You play your instrument, whether it's mechanical – no matter what it is – it doesn't matter. It still comes down to mathematics. Everything I worked out was figured out.

So say you're working on "Brazil" and you're over-dubbing that guitar on top. What would you have to do to get it in sync with the rest of the arrangement?

First, you'd have to think about what you're going to do. You have to put it down and think about what it will sound like. I know Roland has come to me, Korg has come to me, all the major companies – Boss – they all ask what the formula is, and I've told them. They haven't figured it out yet. I actually sat down and gave it to Lexicon, but they haven't got it yet. They should have it by now.

How did you feel when you heard something like "Lover" come back over the speakers?

Knew that I had something that was unique. I didn't tell anyone. W.C. Fields was in the backyard to do his album. I didn't know he was there. When I finished laying down the 12th or so part to "Lover," he snuck in and said, "You sound like an octopus!" He was the first one to hear it. When I finished the recording of "Lover," we decided to visit a friend, Jim Moran. He lived up on Fairfax and Sunset, in a garage in the backyard. He had Laurence Tierney there, Artie Shaw, Mary and myself. They were all smoking pot or whatever they were doing before we arrived, and I brought a dub of "Lover" with me. I sneaked it in to the stack of records on Jim's record player. I just wanted to see what Jim thought of it, what their reaction would be. I didn't say, hey, I have a record of mine. It would just show up, and they wouldn't know it was me. They're all laying on the floor, and then the record came on. Nobody knew what it was. The reaction was stunning.

It was truly a new sound. It was space age.

It was different. It was completely fresh.

The sounds you were creating were so otherworldly, it's almost as if you needed a voice like Mary's to give it a human warmth.

It did. It's normal to have a picture and want to put a frame around the picture. What I did, from the beginning on, was not to change the picture but to change the frame. In that way, you always knew it was Les Paul and Mary Ford. Everything could move, but you always knew it was Les and Mary. Even today, I try to keep that same perspective. If you're outside of the club and you hear what I'm doing, you'll know it's Les Paul. Whether it's sped up, whether it's normal, whether it's got funny boxes on it or anything to change it, it must have an identification. That goes back to the night my mother heard me on the radio with the Andrews Sisters. She said I had to do something about my sound because everybody was starting to sound like me. I said, "Well, that's because of the electric guitar." But she wanted to be able to tell me from the other guys. So I thought the sound I got should be different in tone and texture.

I can hear, even in your standard recordings without the effects, a Les Paul approach, an element of style.

Style is included in this whole approach. When a guy is stuck with a style, no matter who he is.... I've had that privilege. I've had to start over and rethink what it is I do. If I'm in an automobile accident, and I can't use my arm anymore, I have to figure out a way to get around that. This was in 1948.

That's quite a moment in time. Here you have your first records – "Lover" and "Brazil" – coming out that very month... and there's no melody on it.

I've got to play it with a thumb pick and a cast, and I'm saying "Holy Christ, how am I going to do that?" I had to learn a new technique of playing in '48. Completely different, because the elbow moves. You don't realize it, but on the first string your elbow is here, and on the sixth string it's in a different place. Now I have to think of how to tilt the guitar to compensate what would have been your elbow moving. When the hands freeze up with arthritis, things change again. As the bones fuse together, none of my fingers bend. So I had to learn to play one more way. There's no movement in the fingers.

The reason you can hold a pick is with the pinch you can make between your thumb and first finger. Well, there is no pinch anymore. What you do is put sandpaper on the pick, and then find a pick that's large enough, that you will hold in your hand as you squeeze the thumb and first finger. It's not held by pinching the fingers; it's held by stuffing something between there that will remain there. So now, if you don't have any movement of the elbow, and only your wrist – which is under strain because it's taking over all the load of what the fingers used to do, and the elbow used to do – it goes to your shoulder. It's your shoulder and nothing moves but your wrist. That's all you got. And like I say, you beat the wrist up. It's an entirely different way of touching (the strings) then you would normally. Normally, you have all these muscles and joints moving, and when they freeze up they're not there anymore. I only got two guys working, that's my shoulder and my wrist.

A lesser guy would've given up long ago. What do you think gives you your drive?

I was asked that Monday night. I think what it's got to do, is that when you give up on that, you've got nothing. It's almost – you defy it, knowing that it's worsening. It's not getting better. You just have to adjust. If you stepped on a bug and broke his leg, he would run without that leg. He's going to survive. I think I'm no better than that bug.

There's a sense of a very strong will running through you.

I know I have that. That will and that power applies to keeping your head straight, your act straight, otherwise you could end up in Looneytown.

Focus and concentration. To focus and relax at the same time, there's the trick.

Probably most people play their best when they're dying. They really have to get nailed to the wall before they say, "Holy Christ, who am I going to turn to now?" There's no place to turn to. So if you want the power to fight, you've got to say to yourself, "Hey there, Junior, let's get our act together. We gotta do something about this." If you rationalize it, you'd probably be better to chuck the whole thing. Do something else.

But what if nothing else gives you your spark?

I could do a bio on myself for A&E, which they want, and that would be much more advantageous than to go down and play to a couple hundred people. Realistically, you're not going to be getting any better, so why the hell are you doing it? You're doing it for other reasons. Not to get the bio out. Get the bio out

after I'm gone. I don't care about that. It's right now that you care about.

You do it because it's who you are. A musician is a very high calling.

When they did the heart bypass, the doc made me promise that I'd work hard. He said by working hard, you're going to live longer, and have a better life. And it's so true. I think this applies to a lot of people who retire. Some can go and retire and it works out fine. The guy that owned *Guitar Player* magazine, he retired at a very young age, went around the world three times, goofing around, and then he had a stroke and died. He's gone. A young kid. But he did everything he wanted to do and was very successful. Got a boat and went around the world. And that's what he wanted to do, and it worked. In my case, rather than get a boat and go around the world, I'd rather go down to the Iridium and play.

Why do you think you and Mary Ford struck such a chord with popular music in the early 1950s? What was it about your combination? What were you expressing in your songs?

Oh, so many things. The melody was there, and with Mary, the warmth of the lyrics were there. Otherwise everything would be an instrumental. I wanted to break it up.

How come you didn't sing? On your early Rhubarb Red sides, you have quite a nice voice.

I never thought... I sang novelty songs. I used it to kid around with. Mary was a real voice, and that made a big difference. She was very talented.

What kind of things would you be thinking about as you'd watch Mary sing through the recording glass?

She was never over the glass. She was always in the same room. There was no glass between us. We were on the same wavelength. Mary automatically knew what to sing. That was a great advantage because you don't have to sit down and explain anything. I didn't have to say, well, here's the harmony part. She already had got that down. Rarely would I have to direct her. Sometimes I would say, I want you to double this in unison, I want to sing this note. She might tell me she wouldn't be able to hit that note, and I'd have to speed it up so she could hit that note. On that part I would speed it up and then bring it back to normal. Or I would sing that part. She was almost like a robot. She'd sing whatever way you wanted. This is a talent. It's fortunate for me that's the way we worked. She left the arranging up to me. She'd say, "How would you like it?" and she'd sing it that way. Never a question, or an argument in working together. She loved recording more than anything. That was the easiest part. It was the personal appearances she didn't like.

You had quite a sense of humor in your music. Do you think that would sometimes hurt people's acceptance of you as an emotional player?

I don't know. I think the humor wouldn't hurt anything. When I was serious, I was serious. There are musicians that are terribly, terribly serious, and they wouldn't be caught dead kidding – on the stage or in the music. That's not me. There are times when things get serious. Things should get a little lighter. A humorous line makes the serious stuff go down a little easier.

Do you think a player such as Speedy West might have listened to you at one time and imported some of your wilder stylings into his steel playing?

Oh, he did. He told me so. We were friends. I haven't seen him for years. I knew Jimmy Bryant; I was much closer to him than Speedy.

Did you ever play together?

Not really. We'd get together every once in a while and hack over the old times.

What did you think of Alvino Rey?

I thought he was great. He did what he could do well. I loved his band when he had it. A nice person.

I notice on "Nola" you're credited as playing steel guitar. Did you ever play steel regularly?

No. The only time I played it was one time on a Hawaiian album, when Mary became ill, and was in the hospital, and I thought I would fill in with something different because she wasn't there. I don't remember playing it on "Nola."

Was that "Lover's Luau"?

Yeah. She came out of the hospital just long enough to sing it, and then went right back in. You can see in the picture she didn't look very well.

How do you feel about your work together with her now? There was certainly something more than the rapport between a singer and a guitar player.

She was incredible. We loved each other very much. But the work just got too hard. Personal appearances. For a gal, that's rough anyway. The business is rough. It wasn't that we didn't love each other; it was just too hard. She wanted to retire, just like Mary Livingston with Jack Benny, or Gracie Allen with George Burns. The women say that's enough.

Being on the road is a grueling thing at best.

That's rough, especially for a gal, that is. Here I am, 83, and working all the time.

You never say enough!

No. I love it. I love to play in a club and keep going. But they like to have kids, retire, and cook. That's really... that was what Mary wanted to do.

I imagine that the radio shows took an immense amount of time.

Nope, one day. I wrote all the dialogue on my own, and the engineering, the playing. I got it all ready. It took a week, and on Friday we put it all together. We did four numbers in one day. We did all those multis, and they were sound-on-sound then. All done on a quarter-inch tape machine. I mailed them on Friday, and they played them the following Friday. It was a lot of work. I'd never do that again.

"Vaya Con Dios" was probably your biggest record. How did you first come upon the song?

When I heard "Vaya Con Dios," Mary was sitting on the bed in Minnesota, where we were playing. I was listening to Anita O'Day sing it on a record. It was coming over the radio in the room. I asked Mary if she liked it. I didn't even know what it was called "Vagas Contigious" or something. I didn't even have it close. I just knew it was a catchy song. So we called the radio station, picked up the record, and we loved it so much we decided to drive straight through from Minneapolis to New Jersey. Not only that, when we got home, we recorded it, called Capitol up and told them they had a hit. We told them to stop the one that they were getting ready to release, "I'm A Fool To Care," and hold that one back, put it in the corner, and I had a new one for them. I told them it was "Vaya Con Dios." They said, we own that song. It's a dog. I said it's not a dog anymore. We got it, and it's great. They refused to put it out at first, but after I sent it to them, they liked it. They sent it out, but I'll be darned if the song I wrote on the other side, "Johnny Is The Boy For Me," didn't look like the hit. I finally had to go to seven cities and talk to the disc jockeys about flipping the record over. Capitol was glad to do that because they owned the song, but I was more convinced than anybody at Capitol that "Vaya Con Dios." The jockeys felt they were doing a favor to me

by playing "Johnny," since I wrote it. But as soon as they turned the record over, "Vaya Con Dios" was the biggest hit we ever had. It shows you how things can reverse themselves.

One of my favorite albums of yours is called Time To Dream. It's got some beautiful songs and standards.

It's mine, too. We made that all in one night. The whole idea of that was not to rehearse it. To do the first shot and let it go through with that. So I made the complete background and then called Mary in from the kitchen and said, I just want you to sing it once. If we get through it, that's it. One after another, we just sang them all. I love the album. I have the masters here; if I was to remix that again, which I would like to do, I would just add a little more rhythm, a little more bass, just to bring it up a little more, and the balance would've been a little better.

It was around this time that you first endorsed the Les Paul guitar from Gibson. I've heard the story of how they came out to your hilltop in Stroudsburg, Pa. How did they react to your ideas on guitar building?

I worked on them 10 years to get them to make a solid-body guitar. They didn't believe in it. Finally I called them and said Leo Fender is coming out with one. If you don't, you'll be left behind. Ten years they had The Log there. Finally, I got with the chairman of the board, Mr. M.H. Berlin, the key guy at the whole company, and we sat down and designed that guitar. I came in with my thoughts on it, and he asked if I would consider making it look like a violin? He took me to his vault where he had all the violins. We got very excited about the fact that we would arch the top, which would make it different than the plank of wood Leo had. I picked the colors out for the guitar, which is black and gold. I hadn't thought of gold until he first asked me, and black would show off the guitarist's hands better. Four knobs, the electronics... it was all thought out.

I always find it ironic that the sound that players today associate with the Les Paul is so thick and distorted, overdriven and feedbacked, and your sound was completely different.

Ted McCarty of Gibson begged me for the pickups to give him that sound, and I wouldn't do it. I told him, that's my identification. That I will not give you. It was my trademark.

Very few people think of the Les Paul guitar as a delicate instrument. But if you turn it down and put it through a small amplifier, it's got quite a filigree touch. Very bell-like. These are qualities usually associated with Gibson's rival, Fender.

You hit it right with the Les Paul guitar. When you open the back up on the amp, and you have a small amplifier, it gets some of that rumble out of the bottom end. Then the guitar sound can penetrate and get through like mine. Fender is a fine, fine instrument, and I have nothing but good things to say about Leo and the guitar. They do an excellent job for what it is. And I think the same is true for our guitar. The Les Paul guitar. The whole thing was, and this was what I had to convince Gibson on, that when you wake up in the morning and look at that Les Paul guitar, you have a beautiful instrument. You love it more than your wife, and you can love it, because it looks great.

You always want to pick up a beautiful instrument.

The Fender was just a plank of wood. I wanted to make ours with the finest finish and make it a beauty. When I convinced Gibson, which I did – I worked years on them. By the time they got to the late '50s, we were doing our own television and radio shows. *The Listerine Show* started in '53. But where it really got strong was in the later '50s, and oddly enough, the Fender guitars reached their peak at the same time. The momentum of our hit records, and the radio and television, and even commercials, made those guitars reach that unbelievable pitch. So if you have a '57, '58, '59 guitar, you know how valuable they are today. We were constantly appearing. Exposure, exposure, exposure. And Gibson followed it up.

Did you know Leo Fender?

Leo was in my backyard all the time. We'd discuss which sound we liked. He was trying to get the sound I had, too, and I wouldn't let him know what it was. I wanted to keep that sound, like on "Time To Dream," "Sunny Side Of The Street," "Three Little Words," "Whispering," "How High The Moon"... that sound was distinctly different.

Did you ever play any of his Fenders?

Never. He gave me one in 1948 or '49. It has his name on it, but he hadn't yet called it a Broadcaster or Telecaster. That's when I called Gibson and said, "You have to be fools if you don't get with it. This thing is going to come out on the market." Leo wanted me to be partners and go in with him, and we'd combine our knowledge and our efforts. A Les Paul Fender. Imagine that. The whole thing would've been different. In 1961, I was going through a divorce and asked Gibson to hold off on the guitars until the divorce was over. That space of time when there were no Les Paul guitars out, that was because of the divorce. As soon as the divorce was settled, then Fender came immediately to me to do the same thing again. But I called Gibson and told them that I'd go with Fender unless they woke up. And they told me – this was in the early '60s – that they were phasing out the electronic division. It's over. The electric guitar is extinct. I said, you're wrong. I went to have coffee with them – flew to Chicago. We stayed up all night. We sat there and pleaded with them – Mr. M.H Berlin, Mark Carlucci, Zeke Manners, and myself – and finally we decided to go into it and do it. I convinced them that The Beatles, Jimmy Page, Eric Clapton, Jeff Beck – they were not running up and down 48th St. paying $10,000 for a guitar for laughs. These people were the cows with the bell on it. They're telling you to go back and make the guitar again. And Mr. Berlin says, it's yours. Don't let anybody tell you what to do. You do it and I'll back you up. And he did.

It's a strange twist of fate that rock 'n' roll, which seemed to change the playing field so much for you in the '50s, would ultimately provide you with a new lifeline.

Those guys did so much for me. Them and many more. They were the ones that made it possible to convince Gibson to go back and make the guitar. They only had an SG out, that's all they had out, and the reason the SG was out there was because I said, "If you're going to make a guitar that flimsy, take my name off it."

You like a guitar with some weight to it.

I do. The SG is too anemic. You can shoot arrows with it. I said, I want a strong guitar, with balls in it. But Gibson faithfully stuck by me 'til the divorce was over, and in the meantime, Mr. Berlin decided to sell off the electronic division. At that time, whatever had a pickup on it, I got a royalty on it. It could be a banjo, mandolin, balalaika... a kazoo. If it had a pickup on it, I got a royalty.

How did you feel about rock 'n' roll when it came in during the '50s? It certainly changed the way people listened to music.

I didn't quite agree with rock in its infancy. I thought that it was a very simple type of music. I have to put it this way, because this is the way it was in our minds. It was a type of music that some of it wasn't very impressive, and it sure made it rough on Sinatra, on Peggy Lee, on Les Paul & Mary Ford. On Nat Cole, Benny Goodman, Count Basie. It was changing our world from good music to what we considered a very simple, crude type of music, a guy stomping on a board doing these simple changes. But I also saw the fact that they were rebelling against bebop, rebelling against the old way of music and said it's time for a change. We could see, and did see, the rock side, and when they asked us to do rock, we said we'll try it. And we did, and we said, no no no. If you want rock, you go get rock. A lot of it was good. We'd go down to hear Roy Buchanan, we'd go down to hear The Temptations, we'd go down to hear Bill Haley and The Comets, or they would come to hear us. You can listen to Bill Haley and many of those people and hear us in them. There was a mar-

riage, not between Benny Goodman and rock, but between Les Paul & Mary Ford and rock. There was a definite marriage in there, and when I heard people like Carl Perkins, Elvis, the Everly Brothers, I liked what they were doing.

I would imagine the rockabilly players, especially with their use of echo, were not a million miles from your type of sound.

Absolutely. And so while it sort of put us in a bad spot, because we're not about to go into rock, it had an effect. The Beatles – I was talking to Paul McCartney about it – and Paul said, "We were terribly influenced by you, Les. But we didn't want to clone you. We had to be careful not to sound like you. We had to be deliberately influenced by you and not show it." He said the first tune the Beatles learned was "The World Is Waiting For The Sunrise," exactly like our version. "John Lennon and I went for our job...we did one of our songs, and the owner of the club said 'You're going to die with that. Can you play something that's up a little bit?'" And they did "World" and he said "That's what I want." It was the first number they played that night in the club.

The Beatles were very sophisticated tunesmiths. They had major sevenths in their songs, diminished chords. You had a great deal of technique at your command. You understood the ins and outs of the instrument to such a degree that I would imagine you would look on someone as an interloper who gets up and bangs away at three chords. Still, they were playing your guitar.

The same thing that was happening to the guitar here was happening over there, in England, because as far as guitars were concerned, I was terribly pleased that Gibson did what they did, and Fender did what they did. I thought Leo was on the right track; I thought we were on the right track, and here it is 50 years later, and what do we have? We got exactly that. We got a Fender and a Les Paul.

Heads or tails.

Everything else is a copy of (Fender and Les Paul), other than the Martin guitar, and Martin with the electric just never made it.

Do you play much acoustic these days?

None. I just stay with the electric. I love the sound of it. I love what you say with it. Imagine in a club if I was playing an acoustical guitar? I couldn't get arrested. You don't have to sacrifice any sound. No two guitars are alike. You play 'em without turning them on, listen to them acoustically. And if they sustain and don't have wolf tones and it's got a good sound to it, then you plug it in and turn it on. Then you have a good instrument. But you get four of the

same model, and each one has its own pimples, wrinkles, loss of hair, right?

I think you can say the same thing about guitarists, too. You can give the same guitar to a number of guitarists and they'll all make it sound very different. I'm thinking specifically of your Chester And Lester *album. The way you both approach the instrument. How was that album to make?*

It was fun, and simple. One day, and that was rehearsal. Chet says, "Now we take the weekend off, and Monday we'll go for a take." I says, "That is the take, I'm leaving." He says, "Les, you can't leave now." I said, "I'm all done. My hand's killing me, I'm out of here." I left him with the rehearsal tape.

I love your version of "Long Long Time," the Bing Crosby song.

Chet's doing pretty good. I talked to Chet a couple days ago. He's had a rough time. He's been pretty damn sick. We were kidding with each other, and saying we'd both get good and strong and make another album. Chet loves that idea.

He learned a lot of your licks when he was coming up. How would you describe the differences in your respective styles?

His style is part me and part Merle Travis. That's how I'd explain him. As far as I'm concerned, I would be part Django, part Eddie Lang. I'm over there somewhere.

And a part Thomas Edison.

Well, that's something I don't know. I was very lucky. It just happened that it was all in my living room.

Was there anything you tried to invent that you never could quite pull off?

There's some that I worked on my whole life. Different things. There's some that I put on a back burner, and all of a sudden a light lights and I said, "Oh my God almighty"... and usually it's after years and years of going down a wrong road with a great idea but you don't have the solution to it. If I was to give you an analogy, I would be getting out of the car and drop my keys, OK, and a guy comes along and says, "What, did you lose something?" I'm standing over by a streetlight. He says, "Where did you drop them?" I say, "Over there." "What are you looking over here for?" he asks me. "'Cause it's lighter. There's more light over here." That's what you do in inventing. Sometimes you're looking where the light is stronger but not where you dropped your keys. You've got to look in the right place. If you beat your brains out and get nowhere, it means you have to go back and review the case. You back up from it. You say, am I wasting my time here? Then, as you broaden your perspective, you look at it and you say, this is a dead-end street. If I did get it, what is the end result?

Start with the phonograph record. You've got a farmer and he's got a horse and a plow. And he's gouging this record out, and you drop a needle in it and play it back. As you go to the inside of the record, the velocity gets less and less, so there's going to be a loss in the frequency response as you go to the inside of that record. Had you gone the way Edison made it, on a cylinder, there is no loss. It's the same at the beginning on a cylinder as it is on the end. He was right. When you go to a phonograph record, a platter, the needle goes to the center. You are deteriorating the sound to nothing. A flat phonograph record will never make it. We're monkeying with the wrong idea. It's a dead end street.

So the next guy says, "We have tape." With tape, you can only grind the oxide for so long. The tape is limited. Pasting oxide on a piece of tape has an extremely short life. It's going to leave us. You can only grind it smaller, smaller, and the slower the speed, the worse the response. You could always go 200 ips a second, but that's not the way to go. In almost every case, you have to say, where do we go next?

You go to digital. I can't go beyond digital because my head won't go there, but when we get done with digital, we'll have something that far surpasses digital. That's the way it goes. It's amazing, the world we live in now. We've been here a billion years and we can't pour piss out of a boot, and all of a sudden all hell breaks loose. It's frightening how fast we're going.

The advances in the last hundred years are awe-inspiring. The concept of recorded sound was only about 20 years old at this point in the last century.

And you know what? The guitar hasn't changed a bit in 50 years. It's a coil under the string, and a crystal that I jabbed in the top of my guitar. Nothing has changed. Now you put a Piezo (pick-up) in there... that is a crystal. That's all it is. Put it at the bridge, and it ain't going to go nowhere. That's it. You put a magnet under the string, or you can get finer wire. You can chase a pickup for a million years – smaller wire, more turns, less turns, more wire, stronger magnet, weaker magnet – and you're chasing your tail. It's limited.

And unlimited in the sense that there's so many guitar players and they're all approaching it in their own unique way.

It's the guy who picks the guitar up that can say so much. It's unlimited as to how you're going to play that same passage – up, down, across, hammer it, pull it. You've got a million ways to caress that note. They all say – Benny Goodman, Artie Shaw, Art Tatum, whoever – it's like a voice. You can tell Bing Crosby from Ella Fitzgerald.

Or you. I've been listening to the Trio recordings and can hear your voice, even backing up Georgia White in 1936, when you're only 20 years old. Your style is there.

Isn't that amazing? That's your genes, and they show up from the second you play, from the beginning to the end. You say, that's Benny Goodman. That's Les Paul. A guy got out of the car and come down to the Iridium, and he says, "I wondered if that's the Les Paul we used to listen to." And by the time he got to the door, he said, "That's him." He wasn't even in the club. As soon as he heard a note, he knew it was me. That's an identification tag. I remember my mother came to me one time – we were at the Oriental Theatre in Chicago. She said, "I heard you last night, Lester, and you were real good." I said, "Mom, I've been doing seven shows at the Oriental for a month now. I haven't been anywhere else," and she said, "You should do something about it. There's people that sound just like you." Now if your own mother can't tell if it's you...

I quit the show with the Andrews Sisters, and I said, "I'm going to go back home and lock myself in the garage. I'm going to make music that makes me different than anybody else so that my mom will know me." And that's where I come up with that New Sound. The multi-tracks and all the different sounds. Then I distinctly went for the Sound. The style is inbred. That's part of you. I've changed over the years, but you can still tell the same person who played behind Georgia White is still there.

Of all the recordings you've made over the years, is there any one that stands out in your mind as being a very special moment?

Oh, there's so many moments. It just never ends. There isn't any one. Doing the radio shows back there when Mary and I started, and we were broke. That was "The World Is Waiting For The Sunrise" and "How High The Moon" and "Whispering" and those things. Those were probably the most creative and probably the time when things were at a peak.

Do you know why people loved you and Mary so much? What you touched in them?

No. I have no idea. People will come up to me and express a lot of their feelings. From Finland, Japan, Russia... they all have reasons. I don't believe any of them, I don't take any of them seriously. I appreciate the compliments; I'm not a humble guy, but I don't think I did anything that wasn't there to be done. I'm just another guy who wished I could do better. That's the end of it. I never seriously think I'm good. Well, I think I'm good. I just think I'm not nearly as good as I'm rated by someone who comes up to me and says nice things. I appreciate them. But I don't believe them.

You seem to be into the work. That's where you find your reward. The creation of the sound and the playing.

I worked hard and know so little and am glad that I got lucky and some things came out good. I'd hate like hell to have to try and go back and try to do it again. Then I might say, Jesus Christ almighty, that's good. At the time I made them, I'd say, oh, that's OK for now. I thought they were good, we were proud of them that day, and the next day it's old hat and you want to try and do something better. A lot of times you work at it and it gets worse and worse and worse. You don't know when you're doing something good. It's like an artist with a painting. You're too close to the picture.

You're involved with the making of it. That's where your thrill is. When it's done, it belongs to whoever listens to it.

Something else happens too a lot of times. Sometimes your limitations, as you grow older, may make you think more. An example would be, if you play one note or 10 notes, the only reason you might play one note is you're not capable of playing 10, and you find the one note is better than the 10 notes. If you're not wise enough to use the blessings of technique, you spend it. It's like a kid with all that energy. You see a four- or five-year-old, they just burn up energy on their tricycle. They're not using it wisely.

They have to learn to direct it.

You have to learn when to lay back. When not to play so much. You can sing too much. You can be too perfect. You can put too much in. I find out at the Iridium which is the best way to go. Count Basie. He only played one note, but it was the goddamnedest note I ever heard. Isn't that wonderful? He's got that whole band screaming, and he comes in with his thumb and just hits one note and you say, "That's the best note I've heard." Louis Armstrong did that.

Did you ever play with Louis Armstrong?

Oh, yeah... 1929. At the Regal Theatre on the south side of Chicago. When I walked off, I said to the stagehand, who is that fellow playing there now? He says go out and look at the marquee. I didn't even know who he was. I was on the same bill with Eddie South, the "dark angel" of the violin, and I was playing guitar for him. The act that followed us was Louis. The only reason I asked the stagehand was because he kept missing the last note. He'd build up to it, and he'd miss it. He said, "I'll go back and get it." He was tearing that audience up. They were going crazy out there. And when he finally hit the note....

You obviously missed performing during the years you weren't doing it.

I quit 10 years. It was... I didn't miss it. I was busy doing other things, but after I come out of my surgery and everything, the doctor says, "I want you to promise me you'll work hard, because that's going to keep you alive." I took a piece of paper and drew a line down the center, and I thought, "I'm going to figure out what I liked in my lifetime and what I didn't like, and maybe that paper is going to tell me what I should do, if I go back to work again. Do I want to be a manager? Do I want to play again? Where was I happiest?" It pointed down to a little saloon somewhere where you could play for an intimate crowd, no pressure on you, where you could just have fun, meet people. You could keep your old friends and make new friends. You're not nailed down to an 18-minute show or an hour show with 50,000 people going from town to town. You can do what you want to do. It's a little saloon. So I found a nice club, Fat Tuesday's in New York. When they closed I moved up to the Iridium. When I first started, Mary called, and says, "I hear you're going into a club. Can I go in with you?" I says, "I thought you didn't want to work." She says, "That's not work. That's in a little saloon. There's no pressure." I say, "I love it in there." She says, "A lot of people will think that you're broke. I said "That's easy... I'll put my bank account in the window." (laughs)

My manager says, "Les, what are you doing in a joint? You could be in Carnegie Hall." But that's pressure. I don't want any pressure. I want to play in a little saloon. The audience doesn't mind. They like it just as well if I sit there and tell them a story as if I'm playing the guitar. If I miss a note, hey, I'll get it next time!

Most Collectible 45

"How High The Moon"/ "Walkin' Whistlin' Blues," by Les Paul and Mary Ford, Capitol F1451, $25.

Most Collectible LP

Hawaiian Paradise, Decca DL 5018, 10-inch LP, $100.

Recommended Introduction

The Best Of The Capitol Masters, Capitol 99617 (20 hits by Les and Mary from the early 1950s, their glory years; unfortunately, it appears to be out of print in general, but it is still available through the Play/Columbia House CD club)

If you want to hear more...

The Guitar Artistry Of Les Paul, One Way 22085 (reissue of Vocalion LP that consisted of 10 Les Paul Trio recordings for Decca)

The Complete Decca Trios Plus, Decca/MCA 11708 (2-CD set of his 1930s and 1940s work for Decca, including as backing group for Bing Crosby and the Andrews Sisters, among others)

V-Disc, Collectors' Choice 6667 (27 recordings Les made for the U.S. Armed Forces during World War II)

Lovers' Luau, Sony Music Special Products A 8086 (Les and Mary's Hawaiian album)

Chester And Lester, RCA D 113033 (his 1976 duet album with Chet Atkins, still available through the BMG Music Service, though otherwise out of print)

The Legend And The Legacy, Capitol 97654 (now out of print, this is the 4-CD box that has all his Capitol hits plus lots of other stuff, all from Les' original masters)

Part II
The 50's Rockers

Chuck Berry

by John Etheredge

Flash back to 1955. On the Billboard singles charts at the same time that "Rock Around The Clock" was holding down the top spot was an even more revolutionary sound. This was a record by a black man that no white artist could possibly cover (although there were some pretty lame attempts). "Maybellene" by Chuck Berry would get to No. 5 on the best-seller list and pave the way for even more revolutionary sounds by the guy who played a guitar just like ringin' a bell. Since the below article appeared in Goldmine, *in November 1983, a lot has happened. Berry has been the subject of a biopic,* Hail! Hail! Rock 'n' Roll! *He's had a run-in or two with the law once again. He was a charter inductee of the Rock and Roll Hall of Fame. And he still goes out on the road, duckwalking across stages, using whatever local band will back him up, and playing "Johnny B. Goode" and "Sweet Little Sixteen." Berry's in his seventies but has shown no signs of slowing down. Hail, hail, rock 'n' roll indeed.*

What can be said about Chuck Berry that hasn't already been said? Very little indeed. He is the single most influential figure rock 'n' roll music has ever known. To each person who has ever heard him or been moved by one of his songs, he means something else. Every person has his Chuck Berry story. This is mine.

1966: I'm 15 years old. I notice this name that keeps cropping up in the composer credits on albums by my favorite groups: the Beach Boys, the Beatles, the Rolling Stones, Jan and Dean, Johnny Rivers, the Animals, the Hollies, the Kinks. I thought that must be a pretty good job, writing songs for all these great performers. The name is Chuck Berry.

If I had asked one of my older sisters, they probably could've enlightened me. But eventually I stumbled across Chuck Berry myself, in the record bin of the Western Auto store in Mt. Pleasant, Texas, the only place in town to buy records. There was a copy of *Chuck Berry's Greatest Hits* on Chess, the one with the blue cover and the photo of the sly-looking dude with the wavy hair and the pencil-thin mustache. Aha! So this guy makes records, huh? I decide to take a chance and invest my $3.29.

1968: I'm a senior in high school, and on a weeknight at 11:30 p.m. I'm sound asleep in bed where I'm supposed to be. But my mother, knowing what a Chuck Berry fanatic I am, has the good sense to wake me up when she hears Johnny Carson announce that Chuck is going to be a guest on his show that night. Chuck talks at great length about Berry Park, his estate near Wentzville, Missouri, about 30 miles west of St. Louis. And, get this, he invites all his fans to come stay there, for free yet! He said something to the effect of "Everything I have, I got from the public. If any of my public wants to come stay at my place, they're welcome." His picture should've been put in the dictionary under "benevolent."

1970: I'm driving solo from Waco, Texas, to Minneapolis, Minnesota. My route takes me through St. Louis, at about three o'clock in the morning. I pull into an empty parking lot and sleep in my car until dawn. Now I'm thinking, "Should 1, or shouldn't I?" I mean after all, he invited me. I decided to take him up on the offer. After all I could use a place to crash.

But actually, all I really want is a chance to meet The Man, the thrill of shaking his hand. Wentzville is not much more than a wide place in the road, with a feed mill or some such thing and not much else. The zip code is E.I.E.I.O. A phone booth is my first stop, to see if there's anybody named Berry listed. I'm thinking to myself, "Nah, he couldn't be that easily located." The Wentzville phone book is about the thickness of a comic book. And there, right in front of my eyes, are the listings: Berry, Chuck; Berry Music, Inc.; Berry Park.

I feel just like the dumb-ass fan that I am when I dial Chuck's number. And the woman that answers the call insists that I come be their guest. She gives me directions to Berry Park, and when I arrive she shows me to an empty guest room in the lodge. While taking a shower I am interrupted by a young man who tells me that they've made a mistake. This room has been reserved by a party of hunters, and it was the last empty room. So they're gonna have to put me up in "the house." I'm thinking, "The house? Does this mean I'm going to be put up in *Chuck*'s house?"

I couldn't believe my luck. When I finally meet Chuck himself, my excitement must be difficult to hide. But Chuck goes out of his way to make me feel at ease. I offer to pay for my food and lodging, but he is adamant that the treat is on him. He is apologetic that the lodge is full, and I would have to make do with his living room couch.

So that's where I rest up before pressing ahead to Minneapolis. Right there on Chuck-goshdang-Berry's living room couch, under one of those dayglo-on-black-velvet paintings of a black woman with an Afro. My life is complete. I go away a happy man, with a great tale to tell when I get to Minneapolis – I slept at Chuck Berry's house.

1982: I get a phone call from a total stranger, who explains that she is producing a Chuck Berry concert in Eugene, Oregon, where I've been doing my weekly oldies radio program for about 11 years. She wants to know how much I would charge to emcee this event. Somehow I have the presence of mind to not blurt out that I would

Legendary disc jockey Alan Freed looks on as Chuck Berry plays. Because of his role in getting the record played, Freed "earned" co-writer's credit with Berry on "Maybellene."

pay her for such a privilege. A deal is made, and I'm on cloud nine. I'd enjoyed hearing Chuck in concert a half dozen times in the past, but the last time was nearly 10 years ago. This is gonna be a real treat.

A few days later, this would-be concert promoter calls me back to tell me to forget it, the show was off. Her financial backing had fallen through. I ask her exactly how much up-front money might be required for such a venture, and when I find that it might be within my own financial range, I said, "Let's talk." So now I'm in the concert promotion business.

I keep thinking of these scenes in the old "Our Gang" comedies where Darla would suggest, "We could use Daddy's barn to put on a show, and we'll get Spanky's mom to help with the costumes," or something to that effect. Somehow or other we manage to pull this deal off, and it becomes apparent several days before the scheduled concert that we are going to have two packed houses for Chuck's two shows. So here we are, we're gonna make a bunch of money, and we're gonna be rockin' with Chuck Berry. My ecstasy is made complete when, a day before the concert, we get a call from the William Morris Agency asking us to please meet Chuck at the airport and give him a lift into town.

The bubble pops about 10 seconds after Chuck sets foot in the airport. I approach him and introduced myself as an associate of the concert promoter, and explain that I have been asked to provide him with transportation. Chuck fixes me with a stare that more or less says, "Who the ---- are you?" and walks straight for the rent-a-car desk. Well, I'm just naive enough to figure that if you treat a person honestly, fairly, and with respect, he's gonna treat you that way right back. I know that our business dealings have been handled honestly and fairly, and I know that I am treating him with respect at the airport. So I tell myself that perhaps he misunderstood me.

I approach Chuck at the rent-a-car desk and say, "Mr. Berry, you don't need to rent a car if you don't want to. Your agency asked us to provide you with transportation, and I'll be glad to take you anywhere you want to go." Without even looking at me, Chuck says, "O.K., fine," picks up his rent-a-car keys, and heads out of the terminal. So much for trying to do a favor for one of your idols. I find it difficult to imagine that this is the same man who had made me feel so comfortable a dozen years earlier at Berry Park.

But of course, back then I was just a fan. Now I am in the concert promotion business. I get the impression from this encounter, and from our other contact before the beginning of the first of his two shows that night, that he considers me to be The Enemy. The Ofay. Whitey. Like I'm supposed to be guilty of the sins of every promoter who may have given Chuck a raw deal over the years. Like I'm the judge who sent him to prison in the early '60s for what was really only a mild indiscretion. Like I'm the one who put him back in prison in the late '70s for tax evasion while rapists and muggers and crooked politicians walk the streets. I want to tell him I'm just an old fan, and I mean him no harm.

Perhaps in the morally loose '80s it is hard for us to gauge just why rock 'n' roll musicians in the '50s posed such a threat to authority, why Jerry Lee, Elvis and Chuck Berry had to be thwarted by the powers-that-were. Today, the antics they participated in during the '50s would hardly raise an eyebrow. But when they emerged on the scene as legitimate threats to the innocence and order of the era, they had to be stopped.

For Berry, the burst bubble came when he was arrested under the Mann Act for allegedly transporting a minor across state lines. A two-year trial followed, Berry was convicted and spent more than two years in prison. When he emerged he was, according to most who knew him, a changed man. And so was the rock 'n' roll he helped to define; it something different now. By the time Berry was back on his feet again, the English had arrived.

If anything, it can now be seen, the arrival of acts such as the Rolling Stones and Beatles actually helped Berry. Those groups revered him and they put the life back into the music that had been sapped from it by the likes of Avalon, Vinton and Rydell in the wake of Berry's sentencing. By turning young fans on to Berry's music, the English bands helped him keep his ground. But other than scoring a few more hits, the spotlight was no longer Chuck's; he was relegated to the oldies circuit, where he remains today.

It has been nearly 30 years now since Chuck Berry's first hit, "Maybellene." came forth on Chess 1604. His life before that was similar to those of many black musicians. Born Charles Edward Berry in San Jose, California, on October 18, 1926, his family soon moved to St. Louis, Missouri. Berry's life was always troubled. In his teens he spent three years in a reform school for attempted robbery. Although he'd learned to play the guitar, when he got out he supported himself in the immediate post-war era by working for General Motors and as a hairdresser. By 1952, he was accomplished enough on guitar to be asked by pianist Johnny Johnson to join his trio. The two would stay together throughout Berry's career.

In 1955, Berry met a longtime idol, Muddy Waters, who encouraged the young singer/songwriter/guitarist to go see the Chess brothers at their record company. Berry did so, and was immediately signed. The brothers liked his audition number, "Ida Red," which Berry had also written, but suggested that he change the title. It became "Maybellene." Backed with a slow blues, "Wee Wee Hours," "Maybellene" went all the way to number five on the *Billboard* charts.

In rapid succession, he followed that tune up with "Roll Over Beethoven," "School Day," "Rock & Roll Music," "Sweet Little Sixteen," "Johnny B. Goode," and several others, all now bona fide rock classics. He appeared on TV, in concerts, and in films, putting his growing earnings into Berry Park, a piece of real estate in Wentzville, Missouri that includes a fairground, motel and more.

It was in 1959 that the bill came down and Berry's troubles with the law began. While the trial and subsequent jailing took place, Berry became a hero to thousands of English rock 'n' rollers: the Beatles, Stones, Animals, Yardbirds, Kinks and most of the rest knew Berry's repertoire inside out by the time he was released from jail.

Berry regained some of his popularity in the mid-'60s, and scored with such hits as "Nadine," "You Never Can Tell" and "No Particular Place To Go." After that stretch, he switched to Mercury Records, where he had no major hits but recorded an interesting album backed by San Francisco's Steve Miller Band. His remakes of some of his Chess hits were forgettable, and he returned to Chess when the Mercury contract ended. Ironically, it was on Chess in 1972 that Berry scored his biggest hit and only number one record, "My Ding-A-Ling," a silly, childlike song poking fun at the male sex organ.

Perhaps his newfound rebirth of fame was a hindrance in some ways, as it sparked the Internal Revenue Service to investigate Berry's tax situation and discover that he withheld his income tax for a couple of years in the early '70s. By the end of the decade, Berry was doing time again. As a condition of his parole, he was required to serve a number of hours playing benefit concerts, which he was still in the process of doing at the time of this article. According to most observers, the experience left him a bitter man, perhaps with good reason. If such a great cultural icon as Chuck Berry can be imprisoned for the same thing thousands of corrupt business and government officials get away with every day, something is wrong somewhere.

Howard DeWitt, in his book *Chuck Berry: Rock 'n' Roll Music*, notes that after Chuck's first prison stretch in the early '60s his "temperament had changed dramatically since the '50s. He was no longer a friendly, garrulous performer. Now he had a tendency toward guarded behavior and sullen attitudes." From my own experience, I can say that Chuck was literally looking for a fight.

The interview that follows was recorded in Chuck's dressing room after the first of his two shows that night in November 1982. With no sound check and no rehearsal with his pickup backup band (he always plays backed by a local band – he figures every band knows his group), Chuck performed a lackluster 40-minute set that left the audience hollering for more, then booing when he refused to do an encore.

As several reporters gathered in his dressing room between shows, a local photographer had his camera to his eye and his finger on the button when Chuck said, "No photos." The click of that button and the last syllable of "photos" were heard simultaneously. Berry reacted quickly and angrily. He immediately grabbed the camera and tried to wrestle it away from the photographer, but it was strapped around the photographer's neck. So here we were, about to begin a visit with a guy who up to now hasn't exactly been Mr. Warmth, and a fight breaks out in the dressing room between Chuck and this luckless photographer.

All the spectators to this scene were taken completely by surprise, and there was a very uncomfortable feeling in the room. A couple of the people present decided at that point that an interview with Chuck probably wasn't going to be worth the effort, and left the room. Not wanting to suffer the same fate as the photographer, I was very careful to politely ask him if it was OK if I turned on my tape recorder for the interview. Berry nodded that that would be OK, while he occupied himself with trying to figure out how to get the film out of the camera he had confiscated.

As the interview progressed, Chuck loosened up considerably. The tension that marked the beginning of the session gradually disappeared, Chuck seemed to relax, and he seemed to actually be enjoying himself. Later, when he hit the stage for his second show of the night, he was a different performer than had taken the stage earlier that night. His second set was much more "up," much tighter, much more exciting, and considerably longer than his first show. He still left them hollering for more, and he still refused to do an encore, but there were no "boo's" after that show, and the audience was clearly satisfied and happy. As a fan, I felt better that he left on an up note. That's the Chuck Berry I want to remember.

Goldmine: When you were playing the clubs in St. Louis, before your recording career began, what kind of music were you playing?

Chuck Berry: More blues than rock. You see, rock wasn't named rock. It got named rock during

the time I was there. Little Richard had "Tutti Frutti" out before I had "Maybellene." And Bill Haley had "Rock Around The Clock" before I left. But I had recorded, and my record "Maybellene" was doing things up around WENY in New York.

You shared composer credits on that with Alan Freed and Russ Frato.

You know who Russ Frato was? Russ Frato had the stationery shop next door to Leonard Chess' shop that did all of Leonard's stationery. And he got in on that song. Of course, you know how Freed got in on it. A piece of the action. Do you know when I got the rights to that song back? Last year. At the time, I didn't even know you got money for writing songs and they had me sign them away. That's ignorance. Can't blame them.

Who do you consider to be the chief influences on your music, and on the rock 'n' roll of the '50s?

The music was here long before Louis Jordan, but to my recollection, Louis Jordan was the first one that I heard play rock 'n' roll. Louis Jordan's music was popular, but the white population didn't hear it until I came along. Not until *I* came along, but until the *period* when I came along, when the radio stations started lifting the ban on black music. There were radio stations in St. Louis that didn't play any black music. If they didn't play it, you didn't hear it. When Alan Freed started his exploitations, and he saw 'em dancin' and rockin' on the floor, doin' the barrelhouse roll, you know, so it was rock 'n' roll music. That's where the "brand" came from. But Louis Jordan was playin' it long before me, Fats, any of us.

What kind of music do you like?

Oh, that's unfair. I came up with Tommy Dorsey and Nat Cole and Glenn Miller. Swing, man. Swing was my thing. And that's really what I'm playin' now. I'm only playin' it with three pieces, which makes it rock 'n' roll. Most of the stuff I do could've been wrapped up in Tommy Dorsey's "Boogie Woogie," Count Basie, "Tuxedo Junction," "Flying Home," Lionel Hampton, Carl Hogan. (Note: Carl Hogan played electric guitar with Louis Jordan's Tympany Five. Check out his solo on Jordan's "Blue Light Boogie.")

Don't you think that stuff is coming back?

Comin' back? It never left, baby, if you wanna know something. People don't want to see 17 pieces up there in neckties. That's what they don't want. They wanna see some jeans out there, and some gettin' down, and some wigglin'. They don't want it just straight. Charlie Christian was the best guitar player, and he never looked up from his guitar. The greatest guitar player that ever was, Charlie Christian. (Note: Charlie Christian played amplified guitar with the Benny Goodman Sextet and in the Benny Goodman Orchestra.) And Carl Hogan, he never looked up from his guitar. Most of my licks came from Carl Hogan and Charlie Christian. But because I've put a little dance with it, I guess they appreciate hearin' somethin' along with seein' somethin'.

Music seems to be getting back to the basics, with groups like the Stray Cats and the Blasters. Have you heard any of that, and do you think it's a good direction?

I don't agree entirely with what you're sayin', that it's going back. Some groups come out, just as you say. But it's a segment. And they may get hot as fire, for a while. But most of the people are searching for something new to hit the market, to make the money. This is America. Everybody wants to make a living. So they'll do something new. Now don't try to persecute these punk rockers or whatever you call them. They're trying to search for something new. And it's hard to find. Chuck even finds it hard to find. I think I have a great imagination for lyrics. But every time I turn around, some guy's got somethin' that I only dreamed about, and was gettin' ready to come up with. And you can't barge in on it. If you want to be original, it has to be brand new.

If people are always looking for something new, then how come you've lasted so long in the music business?

That's a very good question, and somehow or another I'll explain it in my book. Right now "Ole Blue Eyes" ain't doin' as much as Barry Manilow. But if Barry Manilow don't stay in there, he'll never be remembered like "Blue Eyes." Because of the status, I mean those years and years. That's what does it.

What do you think of some of the newer music?

Rock is rock. When you add punk to it, then that's takin' on rock. They may play some rock, and call it punk. But it's not a change in music. I don't hear too much difference in punk and rock 'n' roll music-wise. But their attitudes are altogether different. You know, we're out there in tuxedos goin' "Oo-wah doo-wah doo-wah doo-wah," and they come out with fire and bustin' up their guitars. Well, that's exciting, yeah. But it has nothing to do with the sound of music. You can't see a guitar on fire on the record.

You have earned only one RIAA certified gold record in your career, and that was for "My Ding-a-Ling." It's remarkable that so many of those classics that you introduced in the '50s didn't earn gold records. Is there any explanation for that?

Well, I don't know how many anybody else earned. To earn a gold record, I don't know if any one person would know, because too many people have their hands in the pie. BMI and ASCAP are the only ones that really know how many gold records. They don't even really know. They know what's reported, how many records sold. But if they report a million, then you know you got a million. So far as BMI is concerned, there's more than one. And as long as they pay me the bread, it can stay one, the way I have problems with my taxes. (At this point, Chuck leaned closer to the microphone, as if to make sure he would be heard.) So yes, there's been one, I.R.S., there's been one. (Chuck laughs.) I'm payin' my taxes now, so it doesn't make any difference. There's been more than one, let's put it that way.

Out of all the people that have recorded your songs, is there any one performer or group that you could point to and say "Hey, I really like the way they did that!?

Every one of them. Excepting the very first one I heard. I'll tell you who it was. The Beach Boys did "Sweet Little 16" and it was called "Beach ... uh ... something".

"Surfin' U.S.A."

That's it, yes. Well, that's no compliment. They named it different. But BMI noticed it, and here come the royalties. So it doesn't really matter. Most of them, it wouldn't matter whether I liked it or not, as long as the public liked it. If the public likes it, that's where the royalties come in. It all boils down to when you're makin' a livin', when you create a product, and somebody else uses it, that's gratification. If I hated it, it didn't matter to me. How could you hate something that brings in 40 thousand dollars? It could sound like "Purple People Eater." If it brought in 40 thousand dollars, it's a beautiful purple.

Your music must be more to you than just a business.

Well, I'll tell you. With about one-eighth of my wealth now, I could live to be 100 and have it pretty good. But I darn sure wouldn't be out there for the next 20 years doin' benefits. I don't know how many times I've been asked, "Doesn't it hurt you to see another artist doing your number, and making more than you made out of it?" In the first place, he never gets it for nothing, because anything that you create, you get a royalty from it. But people think that should hurt me, because someone else made two million off something, and I only made two or three hundred thousand. You'd have to be black to know what I'm gettin' ready to say now. That's happened to me so many times that it's just a passin' thing now. You become immune to hurt. It's an everyday thing, to be turned back so many times. The next turnback, you say "Well, OK, it's one of those things." But if you've never been turned back, you can see where if I get my fifteenth turnback, and you happen to see it, and you've never been turned back, you should think it would kill me dead. But it's nothin' to be turned back, or turned down, or whatever.

What does hurt you?

It's not hurt that you're talkin' about. It's fear. There's no such thing as hurt. You're either in fear, or you're in happiness. Fear is the father of all negative emotions. If you feared nothing, it couldn't hurt you. I haven't conquered it, but I've mastered it. I feel a little, but when I think of why I fear something, you can diminish it and squash it right out. You just have to analyze your hurt as you go along. And you can prevent it, or you can cure what comes that you didn't prevent.

What are you doing these days?

Livin' like a champ. Payin' my taxes. Boy, this tax thing that I was in was no bum rap. It was straight, true. It was a bum rap in the sense that it was a little more, it was about fifteen percent that they added on, but that's nothing to kick about. In other words, they were 85 percent right and 15 percent wrong. But what made it so bad is, if I had known that there was more than just payin' it back, if I'd have known that there was a penalty to it ... No, I went that route. I've had some penalties. And every penny I still had in my safe. I didn't want nobody to find *the* dollar with *the* number on it. I just thought, "Well, whenever they catch up with ya..." Six years I had it. Six years I held that bread. And I told them that I still had it. I was just lettin' 'em know, "If y'all want it back, y'all know where it is". (Chuck laughs). And they said "Mmm, you mean you got $400,000 somewhere?"

Nobody ought, to have that around the house, because you can't get interest in it. Yeah, but this, I didn't want it to go through the bank. And they said, "That's unusual. OK, we'll put that down." But I had all the bread. But not only was there a penalty on time, there was a penalty on interest. You learn this after you pay. So that's the way that was. So they analyzed seven more years, all the seven years after that, straight as a block. I always did pay my taxes, except for those two years. I was with some crooked guys that encouraged me. Big New York guys. And so I took the cash. They said, "Nobody'll ever find this, baby." But Sam and them computers come in '72 and '73 and '74. And by '75, when those computers began to work, they came all the way down to Missouri, and went all out in Wentzville. That was out in the country, man. (Chuck laughs.) I'm not tellin' a lie, baby. We had some rock roads out there. Now we don't figure no computer's goin' down a rock road.

How's Bo Diddley? Have you seen him lately?

Yeah, but Bo's not makin' the money. Bo's really been clipped. His manager was even clippin' him. And that ain't all. He clipped him financially and socially. Even had his wife move all the way to Florida. You see, Bo doesn't have too much education, and Bo's satisfied with a few little mature toys, like color cameras where he can take pictures and see 'em right back and things like that that excite him. I love him. Here's a guy that's down and don't even know he's down. And he's good. He's good because he's down, I guess. You gotta love an ignorant person that's not belligerent. You gotta love him. He plays what he knows. So was Presley, playin' what he knows. But he got some backin' up and some guidance. Bo didn't have no guidance. It's a shame, too. Domino had schoolin'. Domino knew what he was doin'. He had a nice manager. And McPhatter, he ruined his stomach. Lloyd Price is a smart guy, but Lawd, he didn't get the breaks that Domino got, or that Bo Diddley or I got. Larry Williams was very belligerent. Larry had a chance to do *American Hot Wax* and blew it. He wanted seven hundred dollars instead of five. And at that time, when he was down, it would have raised his exploitation, you know, among the public. I hate to talk about my colleagues like that. I just thought it was belligerent. Little Richard's so wishy-washy. That's a good artist, man. Boy, I liked his songs. Man, he sang. He had a beautiful voice for rock 'n' roll. Beautiful voice. I think Richard oughta get back in there.

People say I don't like to do interviews, man. We've been in here an hour and a half. I'm havin' fun. If I can get out after a show, I'm gone, baby. Especially in Spokane, and all them. Missoula, Montana. I was gettin' my ticket in Newark, New Jersey. I told her I wanted to go to Missoula from St. Louis. I was pickin' up the tickets so when I got back home I would pick up my wardrobe and go on to Missoula. It was an Oriental clerk. She said, "You cannot go from St. Louis to Missoula. St. Louis is *in* Missoula." (Chuck laughs.)

How often do you play these days?

I play about six to eight gigs a month. If I did more, I'd fall short on my administration. I have 26 pieces of property that I'm takin' care of. And nine of them are out here on the coast. It takes some time to keep up with what comes up and get the answers back. It's just not all telephone work. You gotta look at some of these things.

What kind of properties?

Commercial properties and apartments. One's in Canada. It cost 28 grand in '71, and now it's worth 76 grand. Now this is an accomplishment to me as much as having written the song "Johnny B. Goode." I got a piece of property right in L.A. I paid 90 for, and I was offered 250 for it.

Tell us about Berry Park.

It's 98 acres, with 45 acres improved. Three lakes, a tennis court, motel, dance hall, and a baseball diamond. A guitar swimmin' pool, adminstration building, and it's my office for music and everything.

When you perform, you use local bands as backup bands. Has that worked out OK, or have you ever had an instance where it's been a terrible backup band?

I've done a thousand dates in the last five years. Two have been ridiculous, but still wound up with the audience hollering for "more, more, more." Because there's something behind that. People kind of like mistakes. When mistakes happen, you can

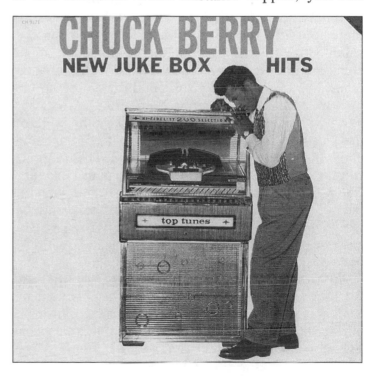

make a joke out of them that's almost better than the music that they came expecting to hear. Because it's brand new. There's no two mistakes alike. And I doubt if there's ever any two handled alike.

You played some blues tonight that was really good.

I know. But that's not makin' money. That's entertainin' the people. You put it on record, it'd sell 17 copies. But tonight I may have thrilled a thousand people with that one blues. But on record, it'd sell 17 copies. But it's a status, you know. People think, "I know he's playin' the real thing because he knows what's happening, and if he don't, he should." (Chuck laughs.)

After nearly 30 years, what does it feel like every time you hit the stage?

B.B. King has wrote the song "The Thrill Is Gone." I enjoy it if I satisfy the people, which is accomplishing the mission, it's good. But as far as the thrill ... I'd have never gone out there tonight if they had been just one thousand dollars short. Because I don't think I deserve to have any less than what I'm accepting, which is less than the average act of my status.

You say the thrill is gone, but you appear to be having a good time on stage.

Don't you think I'm not. I wouldn't be out there if I didn't. I don't need to be out there. I turned down a $22,000 job, because I should've made $30,000 on this particular job. Now you know the thrill ain't gone. If the thrill was really gone, I'd have took the 22, because. that would be money sure enough. When you know you're bein' hit, forget it. Especially if you don't have to do it. Forget it. But I enjoy it. When I was playin' the blues up there tonight I felt like I was in Chicago, on the south side. I seen 'em on the south side. Them chicks come in there and say "I'm takin' you home." "I'm married." "You comin' home with me or I'm cuttin' you." I seen it. Sometimes I wonder if any of these guys know what's on the other side of the world. (Here Chuck is referring to his backing band that night, Johnny Limbo and The Lugnuts from Portland, Oregon, and their piano player.) There's places where he would play that kind of music, and before he got up from the piano he would be married. He'd have three wives, yessir, and they'd all have knives. (Chucks laughs.) The blues are so true. It's just like country music. There's a song that I like so well, "Third Rate Romance." Man, there's some lyrics: "Third rate romance, and low rent rendezvous". That's hittin' it on the head, man. Truck driver checkin' into these jive motels fallin' in love, got a wife at home.

Are you writing any new songs?

Yes. I'm doing a double album, four sides. My daughter Ingrid is doing five numbers and I'm doing the other 31. And it really is a mix. As a matter of fact, there's even two spirituals. One in Spanish. Doing a blues. I have seven country, 10 rock, four swing. Swing in the sense of Tommy Dorsey. Horns and the whole bit, 14 pieces.

Who are you recording it for?

I don't know. I'm just gonna shop. I came out here to CBS, man, and didn't get no further than the lobby. I didn't know you had to have an appointment. But I'm gonna shop it around, and I'll get some action out of it, I suppose.

What made you decide to go back to the studio?

I never left the studio. I own a studio. I just haven't had the time to go in it. I do it on my own time because I'm on my own and I'm not with any record company. I can go in there at four o'clock in the evening and leave at six, or stay 'til 12. And do all my dubbing. It's got a $115,000 mixing board.

Any plans to retire?

People don't retire. My father, and all these people, they cut grass. They fix their porches. Is that retirin'? You might as well do something beneficial. I come out here and do my type of cuttin' grass. I can go back and have six cats to cut grass. Twenty cats to cut grass. So I'll do what they want me for, and get somebody else to cut grass.

What's down the road for you?

Same thing. I'm satisfied.

Most Collectible 45

"Oh Marie" by Joe Alexander and the Cubans, Ballad 1008 (his first appearance on record as the uncredited guitarist), $1,500.

Most Collectible LP

After School Session, Chess LP-1426, $200.

Recommended Introduction

Chuck Berry: His Best, Volume 1, Chess/MCA 9371 (the original hit versions of 20 of his most renowned classics from 1955-58)

If you want to hear more...

Chuck Berry: His Best, Volume 2, Chess/MCA 9381 (20 more Berry hits covering the years 1959-72)

Chuck Berry: The Chess Box, Chess/MCA 80001 (a 3-CD set with 71 Chess recordings)

Rock 'N Roll Rarities, Chess/MCA 92521 (20 rare, previously unissued takes and stereo mixes that works as an alternate overview of his career as well)

The London Chuck Berry Sessions, Chess/MCA 9295 (his 1972 "comeback" album recorded in England, containing, for better or worse, the full-length version of "My Ding-a-Ling")

Eddie Cochran

by Bruce Eder

Take a look back at the history books, most notably Joel Whitburn's hefty compilations of chart singles and albums, and you'll notice something strange when you look up Eddie Cochran. Most of the time, there's a blip, a sudden recognition of loss, when an artist dies young (or even old). Records that had been ignored or were in the pipeline at the time of the artist's death suddenly become big, probably much bigger than if the artist had survived. It happened with Johnny Ace in 1955; Chuck Willis in 1958; Buddy Holly and Ritchie Valens in 1959; Sam Cooke in 1964-65; Otis Redding in 1968; Jim Croce in 1973-74; Elvis Presley and Lynyrd Skynyrd in 1977-78; and John Lennon in 1980-81. But with Eddie Cochran, who was killed in a car crash while on tour in England in 1960, nothing. None of his albums, even his posthumous ones, charted. There was no sudden burst of interest in any single he had out at the time. It's almost as if his home country had forgotten about him, even when he died. To most, he remains a one-hit wonder, the guy who gave us the classic teenage lament "Summertime Blues," a song that transcends the generations so powerfully that it's been a hit several times since, most recently by Alan Jackson, who took it to the top of the country charts in the summer of 1994. But the British recognized him for much more than that and have helped keep his memory alive. It's said that when John Lennon met Paul McCartney in 1957, the first song Paul played for John was Eddie Cochran's "Twenty Flight Rock." Goldmine ran this story on the forgotten American rocker in the September 8, 1989 issue.

I t's been nearly 30 years since Eddie Cochran died, in a car crash outside of Chippenham, England in April 1960, but his reputation looms even larger today than it did then. Indeed, thanks largely to Cochran's British fandom, there is more of his material available now than at any time when he was alive. After years of neglect, during which Cochran was often overlooked by the rock press in favor of his friend and fellow musician Gene Vincent, his induction into the Rock and Roll Hall of Fame in 1987 marked a breakthrough in the United States, and Cochran's fame as a guitarist arranger and producer has at last begun catching up with his renown for recording and co-writing "Summertime Blues."

In a way, this neglect was understandable. Cochran was more of a musician and less a "natural" rock 'n' roll idol like Elvis Presley or Buddy Holly – his devotion to his guitar and his early work as a session musician seemed to fit him more easily into the role of a Scotty Moore, Chet Atkins or James Burton than a "star" of the magnitude and charisma of Elvis, while his country music roots remained prominent for far longer than those of many other early rockers, and put him more easily into the role of a latter-day Hank Williams than a rock 'n' roll rebel.

Edward Ray Cochran was born on October 3, 1938 in Albert Lea, Minn. near the Iowa border about 100 miles south of Minneapolis, the fifth child of Frank Cochran and the former Alice Whitely, originally of Oklahoma City. Neither of his parents was musical, but Eddie's oldest brother, Bill, who was already serving in the army while Eddie was growing up, owned a Kay guitar and later a Martin. Their mother doesn't recall either being played very much, however, according to William J. Bush in *Guitar Player* (December 1983). The first important manifestation of Eddie's musical longings came at age 12 when he tried to join the school orchestra, first as a drummer and later a trombonist. The director didn't think he had the right "lip" for the trombone, however, and suggested the clarinet as an alternative, but Eddie refused.

"He didn't like hearing that," Alice Cochran recalled, in *Guitar Player,* of her son's rejection from the band, "so [his second oldest brother] Bob showed him a few chords on Bill's guitar." Soon after, he got his first chord book, Nick Manoloff's *Complete Chord And Harmony Manual*, and his relationship with the instrument grew from there. By the time he was 12, he was referring to the guitar as his "best friend."

In 1951, the family moved to Bell Gardens, Calif, a suburb of Los Angeles. Like many children who find themselves dislocated, in a strange city and school with no friends, he hung on to what he knew best – in this case, the guitar. Soon after enrolling in school, however,

he met Fred Conrad Smith, later better known to aficionados as "Connie" Smith, another student who shared his interest in music. Spurred on by his new friend, who played bass, steel guitar and mandolin, Cochran pushed himself ever further on the instrument.

Despite his dedication, however, when he and Connie Smith formed a country trio during 1953, Cochran was relegated to rhythm guitar while another student played lead. It was during this period, playing amateur shows before school and local audiences, that Cochran began developing the style that helped make his subsequent rock career legend. Among the musicians he emulated was Chet Atkins, whose clean, almost elegant sound and complicated picking style became the model for his own playing. His other influences during the early 1950s, before the advent of rock 'n' roll, included a great deal of jazz, most notably records by Joe Pass, Johnny Smith and Joe Maphis. He learned from their records and found their work easy to master.

It wasn't long after that Cochran met Hank Cochran (no relation), a country performer with whom he started playing locally. By 1954, the two had a regular spot on television as the "Cochran Brothers," on *California Hayride* from Richmond, Calif. They played country shows and played as an opening act for Lefty Frizzell, among others.

By the time he was 16, Eddie Cochran was recognized as having lightning-fast hands and phenomenal dexterity. According to Dave Schreiber, who was later the bassist for Eddie's backing group, the Kelly Four, in *Guitar Player*, "Eddie was one of the few guys I've ever seen who actually played guitar with all his fingers. I used to watch his hands: They were very delicate-looking and flexible, as if they didn't have any bones."

As fast as Cochran was gaining new skills with his guitar, however, changes were overtaking music that would cause a split with Hank Cochran. Despite their harmonious relationship, which led to a series of early country duo sides subsequently released on EMI's *Legendary Masters* and other collections, the two had musical differences that were becoming more evident as rock 'n' roll slowly emerged from country music into a style and approach of its own. Hank Cochran was a country player, plain and simple, while Eddie became more and more comfortable experimenting with the new sound. The duo broke up early in 1956 when Hank Cochran decided to move to Nashville while Eddie remained in Hollywood.

Cochran's career seemed set as a session guitarist, owing to the fact that he was not only skilled on the instrument but "multilingual" on it. His playing embraced every style: rock 'n' roll, jazz, blues and country, and he doubtless could've tackled classical as well. In essence, he could play anything. Additionally,

Cochran's mother has said that he could learn any subject or musical piece very quickly, and his contemporaries recall him being able to play pieces perfectly after hearing them only one or two times.

During the waning days of the duo, however, while at the Bell Gardens Music Center, Eddie made the acquaintance of Jerry Capehart, a songwriter looking for someone to record demos of his compositions. With Capehart's help, Cochran quickly moved into the role of session musician, first recording a few demos of Capehart's songs with Hank Cochran. This led to Cochran's intro to the publishing firm American Music during 1956, and the release of his first solo single, "Skinny Jim," on the American-owned Crest label, after a brief stint with Hank Cochran on the R&B label Dolphin as a "hillbilly" novelty act.

The Cochran-Capehart team was one of the most professional in early rock 'n' roll, and reminiscent in some ways of the kind of writing/recording/production cottage industry that grew up around Buddy Holly and, much later, the Beatles. In a few short months the two had worked up a significant body of songs and recordings at Hollywood's legendary Gold Star Studios. Cochran was signed to the newly-founded Liberty label that fall by Sy Waronker, and with Waronker's help, even sooner was engaged to appear in the one-of-a-kind wide-screen color rock 'n' roll movie *The Girl Can't Help It*.

Cochran was signed to appear as an Elvis-style performer in the picture, which was released in 1957. Ironically, although his wild, seemingly untamed image and unique sense of style are evident in the film, as he performs "Twenty-Flight Rock," Cochran was a very different kind of performer from Memphis' king of rock 'n' roll.

A thorough-going professional, Cochran was proficient on piano, bass and drums as well as guitar, and frequently played all of these parts on his demos. With Capehart and Gold Star co-owner and engineer Stan Ross, he began a prolific studio career whose output would long survive Cochran himself. He also excelled in a multitude of rock idioms, ranging from wild numbers like "Twenty-Flight Rock" to gentler, Everly Brothers-style songs like "Opportunity," which sounds more like Don and Phil than Don and Phil do.

One reason for the continued popularity of Cochran's music, apart from the songs themselves, was the sheer vibrancy of the recordings. Whether carrying all the parts himself in his demos, or working with players like Connie Smith and Dave Schreiber on bass, Cochran, Capehart and Ross achieved an exceptionally clean sound, recording with few overdubs in well-miked sessions that captured the action of the instruments with exceptional clarity. Cochran worked out the arrangements and produced his own work, and with Capehart managed the recording sessions.

Of course, it took many listeners nearly 30 years or more to appreciate these elements in his work, owing to the pattern of releases followed by Liberty Records. And then, it was Cochran's British catalog that contained most of the gems.

Cochran filmed his spot for *The Girl Can't Help It* in August 1956 at 20th Century-Fox Studios. One month later he was formally signed to Liberty and, with "Twenty-Flight Rock" featured in the film, that should've been his first single release on the label. Before he had a single song out on the new label, however, he appeared in the teen exploitation movie *Untamed Youth*, in a minor speaking role that also featured him singing "You Ain't Gonna Make A Cottonpicker Out Of Me."

"Twenty Flight Rock" was to be his Liberty debut, and had even been assigned a catalog number (55050, according to Rob Finnis), when Liberty's president Sy Waronker pulled it and instead insisted on Cochran cutting a version of a song called "Sittin' In The Bal-

cony," which had caught numerous industry ears as a regional hit by Johnny Dee. Cochran's version of the song, a pleasant, predictable ballad illuminated by his guitar, became a Top 20 hit. Although it was hardly the musical thunderbolt that "Twenty Flight Rock" would've represented as a debut, it established him on playlists and to audiences, and the subsequent release of his two movie appearances heightened his career's sudden momentum.

He began the obligatory tours early in 1957, on package shows with musicians such as Nappy Brown and Al Hibbler. On one of these programs, in Philadelphia during the spring of 1957, Cochran met Gene Vincent for the first time when the two were booked on the same bill. Their friendship began soon after, amid one-night stands and radio and TV appearances.

Despite his sudden stardom, not all was bright for Cochran during that first year. His second single, "One Kiss," was a failure, as was "Drive-In Show," cut at the same sessions that yielded Cochran's album *Singin' To My Baby*, as follow-up success eluded him.

Part of the problem with both the album and single was a lack of a defined sound, and this had started with "Sittin' In The Balcony." Where Cochran was a multi-talented musician, and one of the few stars of his era who was also a musicians' musician – and thought little of his singing ability – Liberty desperately wanted to push him as a quasi-pop star, crooning coyly when he should've been rocking out. On stage, his shows embraced rockabilly, blues and elements of jazz, and his presence, although not as animated as Elvis Presley, was punctuated by a very, very distinctive dress style, as evidenced in numerous photos. His records, by contrast, were bland, mellow productions more suited to Pat Boone than to any real rock 'n' roller.

His success was sufficient, however, to get Cochran booked on a tour of Australia during the fall of 1957 with Vincent, and his first taste of overseas adoration was even more emphatic than what Cochran found in this country. By the end of 1957, he'd forged friendships with the Everly Brothers and Buddy Holly while appearing on package tours with them, and met his future girlfriend, Sharon Sheeley, after an introduction from Phil Everly.

By 1958, things were looking up for Cochran, particularly after the recording of "Summertime Blues," which was originally released as the B-side of "Love Again" in June of that year. Coming out in the wake of a disastrous single titled "Teresa," "Summertime Blues" caught fire almost immediately as DJs began flipping the single over. The song eventually peaked at #8 on the U.S. charts, but its influence was felt far beyond America's borders – in England, young men (including a teen named Pete Townshend) took it to heart.

Driven by an acoustic guitar sound and thumping bass, it seemed especially appealing to young British skiffle players in much the same way that Buddy Holly's records did. The fact that the voice wasn't the greatest in the world – even if the lyrics were superb – helped even more. This was a fanfare for the common teen, and it immortalized Cochran.

And, for the first time, he had no trouble following up a hit. "C'mon Everybody" (aka "Let's Get Together") was an even better guitar number, without a hint of the schmaltz that had been foisted on Cochran earlier – its infectious beat and chorus carried it to the Top 40 in America and a whopping #6 on the British charts. The song marked the beginning of a string of successful EMI releases on Cochran that were to continue long after his death, under a licensing agreement with Liberty.

During December 1958, Cochran cut a single of "Teenage Heaven" and "I Remember," which marked something of a pause from the hot-rocking hits earlier in the year. He also appeared in the Hal Roach-produced feature *Go Johnny Go*. Although one of the better low-budget rock exploitation pictures of its day, Cochran's appearance is a disappointment, as he mimes flaccidly to "Teenage Heaven," dancing across the stage with his guitar. In 1984, there were stories that Cochran's unused clip of "I Remember" had surfaced and would be included in the film upon its reissue on video, but the lost footage never materialized.

1959 was a year of triumphs for Cochran, highlighted by extensive concerts and the recordings of such songs as "Three Steps To Heaven" – featuring the most delicate guitar playing of his career – and "Hallelujah, I Love Her So." Although considered a major song today, the latter had failed as a single late in the year. By this time, Cochran had also assembled a first-rate band behind him called the Kelly Four, whose membership included drummer Gene Ridgio, pianist Jim Stivers, saxophonist Mike Henderson and bassist Dave Schreiber. His recording sessions included work with both his own group and the post-Buddy Holly Crickets. Holly's death, along with Ritchie Valens and J.P. "Big Bopper" Richardson early in the year, also prompted Cochran to record one of his few overtly topical songs, "Three Stars."

Early in 1960, at the suggestion of Gene Vincent and the invitation of British TV producer Jack Good, Cochran went to London for appearances on Good's new rock 'n' roll/variety television series, *Boy Meets Girl,* and a series of concerts with Vincent. His first two TV appearances were broadcast in January and followed up in February with two joint appearances by Cochran and Vincent together on Boy *Meets Girl*, alongside British rock star Marty Wilde and England's premier rock 'n' roll guitarist of the pre-Beatles era, Joe Brown.

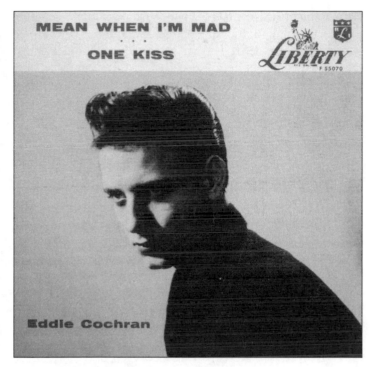

Cochran found audiences in England even more enthusiastic than they were in America, and he and Vincent reportedly relished both the freedom and respect they received in England. Additionally, the two shared the same EMI label in England and it was apparent to all concerned that, whether it was just that British fans paid more attention to music or EMI did a better job of promoting them, their records got heard a lot easier in England.

By mid-1960, it was also clear to both men that American popular taste was moving in a direction distinctly away from the kind of music both of them played. Rock had softened and smothered under a wave of adenoidal schmaltz, and while it is true that Cochran could've – and undoubtedly would've – carried on as a producer, arranger, and session guitarist, and might even have became a teen idol, it is also true that the blues, country and jazz sounds that he favored weren't doing much better than rock 'n' roll.

In England, by contrast, they were considered almost gods by teenagers for doing what they'd always done, and Cochran found his guitar playing respected and appreciated. And well he might have, in a country where a bespectacled ax-man like Hank B. Marvin of the Shadows could become a homegrown hero and Chuck Berry was already worshipped, and where Buddy Holly was still mourned more than a year after his death.

Backed by Marty Wilde's Wildcats, the two extended their British engagements into the spring. By April 17, however, Cochran was scheduled to return to America to record. On April 16, he and Vincent set out for Heathrow Airport at 11 p.m. in a hired car with Sharon Sheeley to catch a 1 a.m. flight. Wrong turns, a resurfaced road and a 100-mile journey all figured in the accident that followed, shortly after midnight just outside of Chippenham, near Bristol.

The rest is a story too well known to repeat. Cochran was still alive after the crash but died very soon after; Vincent was seriously hurt, as was Sheeley. Cochran's burial took place eight days later in Glendale, California.

What followed has been a string of hits in England and other countries but not in the United States. "Three Steps To Heaven," released immediately after his death, shot to the top of the British charts-but was ignored in America, setting a pattern that continues to this day. Liberty Records released one album called *The Eddie Cochran Memorial Album* (LRP 3172) the following month, and another posthumous compilation titled *Never To Be Forgotten* (LRP 3220, with notes by Sharon Sheeley. However, EMI in England issued single upon single over the next several years, all of which sold well and kept Cochran's name alive.

Indeed, EMI's marketing of Cochran in England, capitalizing on the voluminous sessions work and multiple takes left behind by the late guitarist/singer/composer, became a mini-industry in that country reminiscent of the stream of posthumous Beatle bootleg recordings released in America through the 1970s and 1980s. By 1963, some journalists were even questioning the propriety of this activity, and Ray Coleman of *Melody Maker* confronted Liberty label chief Alvin Bennett on the subject in the October 19, 1963 issue.

"I knew Eddie well. He had a great talent," Bennett responded, "and I know that in Britain, especially, he was immensely popular. Every time I visit EMI, they are clamoring for as much Eddie Cochran stuff as I can give them. And no sir, it isn't bad taste – it is catering to a demand."

Bennett knew whereof he spoke. That same year, Heinze Burt, the blond nordic bassist of the instrumental group the Tornadoes, had a hit with a tribute song entitled "Just Like Eddie," patterned very much like the 1960 Mike Berry hit "Tribute To Buddy Holly." Heinz, as he was known, recorded "Summertime Blues" and "Twenty Flight Rock," the latter a song that was covered by Cliff Richard as well.

Also in 1963, Cochran's song "My Way" was released to major success in England. The 1958 vintage track became a favorite of Pete Townshend and company, who were then struggling along as the Detours, and was subsequently recorded by the Who as part of sessions for *The Who Sell Out* in 1967. Although unreleased, the Who's version was later issued on various American bootlegs, whose makers were so ignorant of its origins that they titled the number "Easy Going Guy" and credited it to Pete Townshend as composer. But it was the Who's version of "Summertime Blues," released as a single off *Live At Leeds* in 1970, that revived interest in Cochran in America.

The San Francisco group Blue Cheer also had some underground success with a proto-heavy metal version of "Summertime Blues" in the late '60s.

By the late '70s. there were dozens of Cochran releases extant in England on singles and multiple albums and compilations, including his live performances from *Boy Meets Girl*. Apart from United Artists' admirable *Legendary Masters* two-record collection and reissues of his only full-length album, both of which were out of print by the end of the decade, there was nothing to be found in America, however. MGM/UA's home video *Cool Cats* (c. 1982) raised people's consciousness somewhat, although it was primarily concerned with Cochran's taste in clothes and moves onstage. And a 15-song EMI-Manhattan compact disc called *The Best Of Eddie Cochran* was an adequate first effort.

But EMI in England once again outdid its American counterpart in 1988 with the release of a four-CD set called *The Eddie Cochran Box*, assembling all of his previously released songs in one place for the first time along with numerous unreleased tracks and alternate takes. Coupled with Rockstar Records' release of various Cochran

session tapes, also in England, listeners now have a chance to take in the depth and breadth of Cochran's music and talent. EMI's American arm says it "will probably" release the set here "sometime in the future."

Such is the life of classic American rock.

Most Collectible 45

"Skinny Jim"/ "Half Loved," Crest 1026, $300.

Most Collectible LP

Singin' To My Baby, Liberty LRP-3061, green label, $800.

Recommended Introduction

Somethin' Else: The Fine Lookin' Hits Of Eddie Cochran, Razor & Tie 82162 (released in 1998, this is a 20-song compilation of Cochran's hits and near-hits)

If you want to hear more...

Singin' To My Baby/Never To Be Forgotten, EMD/Capitol 80240 (a twofer containing two of his albums, comprising a good percentage of his released Liberty tracks)

The Early Years, Ace 237 (U.K. import with 20 tracks and demos he recorded before he was with Liberty)

The U.K. box set mentioned in the story seems to be out of print.

Buddy Holly

by Stu Fink

Who could have possibly thought in 1959, when Buddy Holly was lost in that Midwest plane crash, that people would still listen to his music with reverence, or even remember him, some 40 years later? Well, four lads from Liverpool, whose name – The Beatles – was obviously inspired by Holly's group The Crickets, had an inkling. So did the fans, especially in England, who thought highly enough of him that some well-connected ones got British MCA to release The Complete Buddy Holly on LP in 1979. It literally was every known released track from his short career, six vinyl records' worth. And sales of the import later spurred U.S. MCA to issue the same package in an era when box sets for rock 'n' roll performers were rare. Not to mention the thousands who, to this very day, buy his musical output on compact disc and hunger for more. (Much of the material on the vinyl box set remains unissued on CD thanks to legal wrangling.) Obviously, Holly was dead long before there was a Goldmine to sit down with him for an in-depth interview. But many of his closest associates and fans survived. Thus the following piece, which originally ran in two parts, in the July 18 and August 29, 1986 issues of Goldmine. It was called "Buddy Holly: Those Who Knew Him." Of the many pieces on Holly that have appeared in Goldmine over the years, we found this the most fascinating. I hope you agree.

Holly, Valens, The Bopper – all three have certainly attained legendary status since a tragic plane crash took their lives back in 1959. While all three have earned their own individual chapters in the annals of popular music, it has been Holly's unique style and influence that has withstood the test of time and proven to be the seminal fiber woven throughout all of rock 'n' roll.

From his early days as a local performer to his short 18 months as a professional recording artist and entertainer, Holly continually set trend after trend in the music business and introduced a style that became the catalyst for the whole rock era.

For one, Holly was premier in writing and performing his own original material. For another, he was perhaps the first rocker to maintain some degree of technical and musical control over his recording sessions. Holly was also one of the first artists to look into other areas of musical production other than performing (he produced Waylon Jennings' first record). He was not manipulated by any one person or record company, and, to be sure, he was revolutionary in that he called his own shots. Indeed, those were remarkable accomplishments in their day.

Still, during his active years in music, Buddy remained, to all who knew him, a decent, level-headed individual who always maintained a friendly air about him. While writing and producing a Buddy Holly radio documentary back in February 1984, I had the good fortune of speaking with many of Buddy's closest friends and musical associates, people who had spanned his entire career. I was amazed; they all expressed a similar warmth about him, a compassionate feeling felt by only the closest of friends. Although many of these interviewees knew Holly at different times and in different capacities, they indeed conveyed the same image...of a disciplined man set on succeeding, yet who nonetheless always projected a cheerful, happy-go-lucky demeanor to all he came in contact with.

Larry Holley

Buddy's brother, Larry Holley, probably knew him better than anyone else.

"Oh, I just remember him as a common, ordinary young fellow around Lubbock here; he worked for me and I liked having him around. He was a good hand in the tile business and many times we would have him bring his guitar out to the job, and he'd sit on the tile boxes and play for us sometimes while we were working...so he got out of work like that sometimes. I enjoyed going hunting and fishing with him, and we were frequently running around together. He was a bit younger than me but we got along real good.

"About a year before he put out 'That'll Be The Day' we started really realizing that he meant business when it came to music, and he'd play just about every time he got the chance. He had his guitar with him a lot, and we noticed he could sing and play real good just about any song he'd ever heard. It seemed to us that he did them even better than the people who'd put them out. I know we enjoyed hearing him.

"I would say he was an overnight sensation in a lot of respects. Of course, we saw him coming up playing in small places like the fairgrounds or the high school, but then it seemed like he suddenly broke it big the second time 'That'll Be The Day' came out. He recorded it at Norman Petty's place, and I was with him when he did that. We really thought he had a good one. It did take a couple of months before it really broke, but that's pretty quick, really.

"Around Lubbock, no one really caught on to Buddy, except for the younger set that'd heard him play out in the clubs. The older people just took him in stride and didn't think much about it. Actually, he didn't gain a lot of fame here until after the movie *The Buddy Holly Story* came out. So now he has a lot of fans."

What was his reaction when Buddy decided to leave Texas and move to New York City?

"Well, that didn't faze us too much. He had bought a lot here to build his house on, and we were hoping he'd settle down in Lubbock, but he was hardly ever here anyway. He was on tour nearly all the time the last year-and-a-half of his life, and we only saw him once or twice a year. So we didn't mind if he lived in New York or on the road; he wouldn't have been at his home much anyway no matter where it was at.

"Buddy didn't want to go on that last tour, but he was hurting for money. He was about as broke as he'd ever been. His royalties hadn't started coming in; they were all tied up in different ways and he had other things working against him. So he needed the money and I think he was getting paid $1,000 or so a night for that tour. It was offered and he took it.

"I remember listening to the radio the night that he got killed, Feb. 2. I call it the second but everyone says it's the third; that's because the last night they played was the second, and the crash took place a few minutes after midnight on the third. I knew he was up in Iowa somewhere, because I'd seen his itinerary. And I recall the radio saying that a snowstorm was moving into the Midwest, with flash advisories and all that. I remember saying a little prayer that they'd be all right. I didn't know he was flying; otherwise I'd have said a long prayer. I thought they were on the bus.

"The next day I was checking out some of my tile jobs and my other brother, Travis, was working for me. I hadn't had the radio on that morning. It was a

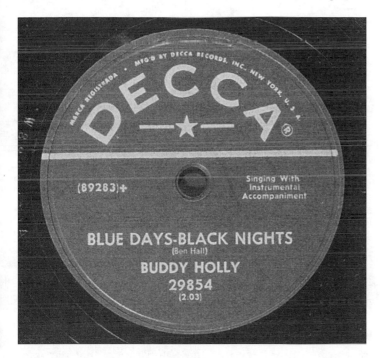

noticed it seemed he was a bit ahead of his time, bridging the gap between country, rock and pop. He blended them together and that caught people.

"I'd like people to remember Buddy as a person who had lots of life to him. He was a quiet sort of person until he got a guitar in his hands, and then he really came alive. He loved music...not just his own, but other people's as well.

"He would have played for free if he couldn't have gotten paid for it; that's how much he loved to play and sing and entertain. He wanted recognition in the world and for people to realize he was a good picker, singer and songwriter. He worked on those three things constantly and I believe he accomplished what he wanted to do."

Jerry Allison

Like Larry Holley, drummer Jerry Allison knew Buddy in his home town of Lubbock. Jerry (now affectionately nicknamed J.I. for his initials), was one of the key players in Holly's musical success; indeed, J.I. co-wrote many of the hit songs and had an active role in the formation of the Crickets. He was also to play on many of Buddy's earliest performances and sessions.

Yet, his musical affiliation notwithstanding, Jerry Allison was also one of Buddy Holly's closest friends.

"I met Buddy probably around 1952 in junior high school; he was older than me by a couple of years. We started making music about '54 or so. I was playing with a group called Cal Wayne and the Riverside Ranch Hands. We played some clubs around Lubbock and Buddy used to come sit in, and that was the first time we'd ever played together.

"Sonny Curtis was around then playing guitar and fiddle; Don Guess played bass fiddle and steel guitar, and Larry Welborne played bass with the group some. When Buddy and all of us first started playing we were more of a country-western band, with Sonny on the fiddle and Don Guess on the steel guitar. Bob Montgomery was singing with Buddy at the time. In fact, he did most of the lead singing and Buddy sang harmony with him in that particular group.

"Around 1956 we went to Wichita Falls, Texas, to Nishman Studios, I believe it was, and did some demonstration records. We sent them to Nashville to some people we ran into in Lubbock who came through on a show. They got in contact with someone who got the record deal, and they just picked Buddy out; Buddy's the one that got the contract. We did some duet records with Buddy and Bob both singing, and then we did some rockabilly, I guess you'd call it, with just Buddy singing. They wanted to sign Buddy and he got the contract.

cold day, and I was wandering around checking jobs, wondering where all my people were. My brother wasn't on the job, and I couldn't find anyone. So I went up to a cafe to eat and the lady there said 'That was sure bad about the boys, wasn't it?' And I said, 'What boys?' She answered, 'Isn't your name Holley?' When I said yes she replied, 'Well, Buddy Holly and them, they had a plane crash.' I told her, 'No, I'd have known about it if they had, it's surely not true.' She said I'd better check with my folks and find out. Then I started getting excited; I knew something must have happened. Sure enough, I found out that the real bad thing had happened. And I thought, Lord, if you'll just help me, if he's still alive, I'll go up there, I'll fight the elements, I'll do whatever. But it was too late.

"For almost 10 years after Buddy died I couldn't even listen to the radio or his records, I was so blue. Finally, that wore off and some years ago I started doing some producing on my own. I'd always been a music critic, so I thought why not try it. I put out an album with me singing some, my son and brother singing a couple. My daughter and I wrote the songs. People have asked me if we were musically inclined at all and that album was my way of answering them. The next question always asked is what was Buddy like? So I wrote a little booklet with pictures for the album telling as much of Buddy as I knew, and what I thought people would want to know about."

Why does Larry Holley think Buddy's music is so much more popular today?

"It's been hard for me to figure that out myself. Buddy had a smooth, sincere quality to his voice. He sang plain where you could understand it, and nearly all of the time his tunes will stick in your mind. I've

"I didn't come on the very first session they did 'cause I was in school at the time. Sonny and Don Guess went on the first trip, I believe it was. Then the next trip we cut the original 'That'll Be The Day' and four other songs...that was in the summer. It was a real in-and-out, three-hour session, a real quick thing. We didn't have any time to fool around with it much. That was at Owen Bradley's studios. I was 17, Buddy was 19.

"After those sessions, we went over to Norman Petty's studios in Clovis and recorded some more demos. We were going to send them to New York because we'd gotten involved with people who knew Buddy Knox (in fact, Buddy Knox's sister lived in Lubbock), and they were going to send the records to Roulette in New York.

"'That'll Be The Day,' the record we did come out with, was one of the demos cut at Norman Petty's studios. It was sent to Roulette but they had already had the Buddy Knox and Jimmy Bowen sounds, so they weren't interested in signing another rock 'n' roll-type group. So Norman sent the records to Murray Deutch at Southern Records, who played them for Bob Thiele at Coral. Thiele signed us and actually put out the demo on 'That'll Be The Day' and 'I'm Looking For Someone To Love.' That was the first record that did anything. It sure got us started!"

After "That'll Be The Day," they made their first tour.

"We played shows with like 20 different acts. In fact, the first tour we played when we left Texas was like 17 weeks long, and I think during that time we only had a week off, not all at one time. We went all over the U.S. and most of Canada. It was grueling but we had a great time. And during that tour 'Peggy Sue' came out and so did 'Oh Boy.' All three records were doing very well while we were on that same tour.

"We had our first booking on *The Ed Sullivan Show* at that time, but we couldn't get off from the tour, so we did *The Ed Sullivan Show* right after that, in December 1957.

"Niki Sullivan left the group after the first tour. He wanted to go out on his own and be a singer, and had gotten a contract with Dot Records. He wanted to be on his own, and I got the feeling that he didn't think he was adding much to the band since Buddy played all the lead guitar. So we decided to go with just three folks, Buddy, Joe B. Mauldin and myself.

"The last tour we did was in October '58. Buddy wanted to move to New York and Joe B. and I didn't. So we were going to try it that way for awhile; none of us were really sure what we wanted to do at the time. Buddy and I had both gotten married, so there was another involvement there. He had married Maria Elena and I married Peggy Sue Gerrow (just like the song); she was also from Lubbock. We were married for nine years."

At the time Jerry Allison had a solo single called "Real Wild Child."

"Yeah, we sort of did that as a joke. We had done a tour of Australia, and there was a fellow there named John O'Keefe. That was one of his big records. So we came back and sort of did it as a joke. I wasn't into singing at all then. Buddy and Norman Petty had the idea for the flip side, 'Oh, You Beautiful Doll.' It was released on Coral by Ivan – that's my middle name."

Which songs did Allison co-write?

"'That'll Be The Day,' 'Not Fade Away,' and 'Peggy Sue.' 'Well All Right' Buddy, Joe B., Norman and I all wrote. We wrote that one 'cause we did some shows with Little Richard and he was always going around backstage and saying, 'Well alright and alright.' I co-wrote 'More Than I Can Say' in 1959 with Sonny Curtis. Bobby Vee did that one. I have most of Bobby's records but I don't have that particular one. We were really tickled when Leo Sayer re-recorded it in 1980."

What happened to the Crickets after the split?

"We stayed in Lubbock where Norman Petty still managed us. Buddy wanted to go to New York and get different management and go in other directions.

"We recorded some other things in Clovis with Norman. Buddy and I agreed that we would be the Crickets and do whatever we wanted to do, and he would just work as Buddy Holly and not use the name the Crickets. We didn't tour at all, so we did some Crickets records for Coral. We cut 'Love's Made A Fool Of You,' a tune that Buddy and Bob wrote. Nothing much happened with it. It was sort of a lull period there.

"Buddy, Joe B., and I discussed that we'd get back together if it didn't work out good, and it *wasn't* working out. So we were all sort of figuring on getting back together again. Waylon (Jennings) was on the last tour with him, and Buddy told Waylon before the crash that he was planning an England tour and wanted Joe B. and I to go with him. And I suppose Sonny, too, since he was working with us at that time. Buddy told him this not two days before he was killed."

Where was Allison on Feb. 3, 1959?

"I was in Lubbock at my folks' house, and Sonny woke me up and told me. I had lost my best friend."

What has Allison been doing since?

"Sonny, Joe B. and I played with the Everly Brothers for a while in '59. We've all done sessions and played with various artists like John Stewart, Johnny Rivers, Ray Stevens, Roger Miller, plus we've written and published songs. We toured with Waylon from '78 to not so long ago."

Do people still remember the Crickets?

"I think they mostly remember the songs, depending on the age group. Of course, *The Buddy Holly Story* movie helped by introducing many younger people to our music. Actually, there's more recognition than I would have thought."

Today, Jerry Allison resides on his own farm just outside of Nashville. Still active in music, he is currently regrouping the Crickets and is planning an upcoming tour with none other than Bobby Vee.

Sonny Curtis

Another west Texas native who has achieved impressive musical status is Sonny Curtis.

Like J.I. Allison, Curtis played with Holly at many of his early appearances and recording sessions. A great musical talent in his own right, he has gone on to many successful solo ventures since playing with Holly and later the Crickets. As a songwriter, he has written such great hits as "Walk Right Back," "I Fought The Law," "The Straight Life," and "Love Is All Around," the theme to television's popular *Mary Tyler Moore Show*.

Now embarking on a solo career and his own record label, Steem Records, Curtis still recalls breaking into music with Buddy Holly.

"I was introduced to Buddy by Bob Montgomery. I lived in a little town south of Lubbock; a little farming community called Meadow, Texas. I was into playing solo. I used to do a TV show in Lubbock whereas I would appear as a guest with just me and my guitar. So I kind of became known in the area. Bob Montgomery wanted to meet me, and a mutual friend introduced us. Then Bob took me over and introduced me to Buddy. I'll never forget that day: it was a cloudy, rainy afternoon, if you can imagine such a thing in Lubbock. Bob brought me to Buddy's house. Just as soon as we met we got our instruments and started playing, and we were all fast friends from then on.

"'Rock Around With Ollie Vee' was one of the first songs I wrote that was ever recorded, and, of course, it was Holly that recorded it. I was always writing but I didn't have much luck. I wrote a song for Webb Pierce, a country song called 'Sunday,' which was done about the same time. It was sort of a country hit. Then 'Walk Right Back' was my next success, for the Everly Brothers.

"I was on most of Holly's sessions in Nashville. There was one session that I wasn't on; I think he went down by himself, or maybe Don Guess went with him. He had a saxophone on those records, and he cut a song called 'Modern Don Juan.' They also recut 'Ollie Vee.' Happily, though, the version I'm on is generally the one they play.

Buddy Holly (center) with The Crickets on stage.

"As I recall, we were all just pretty green kids from Texas, who had no idea of what was going on. We didn't know how to assert ourselves. In Nashville, there was sort of a formula for cutting records, and although we didn't necessarily agree with it, we didn't have an alternative in mind. We knew the sessions weren't quite what we wanted, but we didn't quite know how to go about it. For one thing, I think a mistake was made. Buddy was such a good guitarist and had such a great feel. He didn't even play. He just stood at the mike and sang. I played the lead, and Grady Martin, one of the great guitarists of all time, played rhythm on those dates. We also had a drummer, Buddy Harmon. He was fantastic. But it was sort of us and them. They just showed up to play the sessions, and we just could never get a feel for each other. Nothing against them, 'cause they were great players. Those sessions just didn't have the right feeling.

Nashville wasn't ready for that revolutionary rock 'n' roll sound, but that was just the reason they got us down there. But they didn't know how to draw it out of us. Elvis was making it big right up the road in Memphis, and Roy Orbison was hitting at that time along with Carl Perkins. Jim Denny, then head of the Grand Ole Opry, brought us to Nashville. He'd seen us perform in Lubbock and knew we had that feeling on stage. But when we got to Nashville, they didn't know how to draw that from us, and we, of course, we didn't know either. I don't think it was anybody's fault, it was just the lack of good communication.

"Owen Bradley produced those sessions – unlike the way the movie depicted it. They showed Buddy getting real mad and getting into a fight with the record producer. I'd like to set the record straight on that, if you'll pardon the pun. There was nobody getting into any fights with Owen Bradley. He was a

Southern gentleman and we were on our toes and put forth our best behavior. I guess the movie had to dramatize that a bit.

"We, of course, thought we were going to make it. In those days, we were so naive that we thought all we had to do was get a record out, and then it would be an instant success. I remember seeing one of our songs reviewed in *Billboard* and saying 'Boy, we have arrived!' Needless to say, that wasn't the case. It's hard to describe the first taste of failure; it's just something you have to get used to. We were all pretty down about not having something go No. 1 straight away."

Is that when Curtis left Holly?

"It's hard to describe just what was going on. In Texas, we were all playing in each other's bands. If I got a job, Holly might come play with me. If he got a job, I'd go with him, and so forth. If we made over $15 or $20 a night we were lucky! Waylon Jennings and I used to do things together. He was a disc jockey, and he and I would go over to a movie theater and play in between films for about 15 minutes or so. He'd advertise it on his radio show, and we'd pick up $15 or $20 apiece. I'd do a couple, then he'd do a couple, then we'd play one together and go home.

"So everyone played in everyone else's band. My big break was when Slim Whitman came through Lubbock looking for a band to go on the road. There was a steel guitarist I knew very well who'd recorded with Slim; his name was Sammy Hodges. He approached me and wanted to take me on the road in the band. To me, that was the big time, so I left Lubbock and made the break with Buddy and the guys.

"After that, I went on the road with the Philip Morris Country Music Show out of Nashville. That show starred Carl Smith, Goldie Hill, Red Sovine, and other country acts. I played that show for a while. Then, around December '57, when the Crickets made it real big, I was working in Colorado Springs at a kind of jazz club. I played jazz, country, a bit of everything. And then I left there and went to California trying to get a record deal.

"When Niki (Sullivan) left the Crickets, Norman Petty, who was managing the boys at the time, called me. I'd just returned home for Christmas. Norman called and wanted us to sit down and talk about me picking up where Niki left off. So I drove to Clovis and spent the afternoon talking with the guys, and we all arrived at the opinion that they would be better off with just a trio. They felt more comfortable that way. So I didn't go with them.

"Then the Crickets split with Buddy later in '58, and they called me and asked me to join up and sort of play guitar and do some singing. That's when I became a Cricket on a limited basis.

"After the split, we had heard rumors that Buddy was wanting to get back with the guys, and that he was a little dissatisfied with the way things were going in New York. I can't really speak for his feelings towards the end because I really didn't see him. But I know that for us ... on Feb. 2, 1959, we had driven from Clovis to Lubbock, about a 100-mile trip. All the way there we discussed calling Buddy. When we got to Lubbock we sat up to two or three in the morning at Jerry Allison's mother's house, and we made several attempts to locate Buddy. We finally found him in Iowa, but were unable to reach him. Of course, the next morning we got the news.

"We were very low, of course. When you lose a true friend like that you're awfully far down. As far as the mood around Lubbock, I really don't think that Buddy was all that famous in his hometown, which was even more of a tragedy. Outside of his parents, friends, and people in the music business, I really don't think it made an impact.

What happened to Curtis and the Crickets? Didn't he write several hits like "I Fought The Law?"

"There was a disc jockey we knew from Lubbock named Snuffy Garrett. He also worked in Wichita Falls. He was a real good friend of ours. He later got a job as an A&R person for Liberty Records. Because of our friendship, we signed with Liberty and he produced us. His real name is Thomas Leslie Garrett, and he had some albums on Liberty called *Tommy Garrett And The 50 Guitars*.

"I started writing 'I Fought The Law' while I was still in high school. We recorded it on the *In Style With The Crickets* album shortly after Buddy died. The group consisted of J.I. Allison, myself, Joe B. Mauldin, and Earl Sinx. That was our last album on Coral.

"Bobby Fuller was a kid from El Paso. I hadn't met him till after he recorded the song. He pretty much copied the arrangement of our *In Style With The Crickets* record, although he did enhance it with a

few more instruments. He had the first big hit with it, but it had been done a few times before he recorded it. Some guy from Minnesota – I don't recall his name – almost had a hit with it. That's been one of my major copyrights through the years. All sorts of artists have recorded it: Hank Williams Jr., Lou Reed, the Clash had a hit with it in England, Johnny Rodriguez, Kris Kristofferson and Rita Coolidge, a whole bunch of people did that song.

"I really don't know what happened to Bobby Fuller. It's really a mystery surrounding his death. Some people say he committed suicide, others say he was murdered. I don't think anybody was ever arrested in connection with the crime. He was found outside an apartment building in Hollywood, dead in his car. Evidently, he had ingested some gasoline, and he had a broken arm. I can't understand how somebody would break their arm when they committed suicide."

Where does Curtis think Buddy's career was going?

"I think he'd probably have been in the business end of the music. It's real hard to speculate on that. He'd have probably still been recording, but I think he would have been encouraging new talent, producing records, publishing, and that sort of thing."

Norman Petty

As previously mentioned by Sonny Curtis and Jerry Allison, Holly's hit factor was brought about largely through the assistance of Norman Petty at his Clovis, N.M., studios. Technically as well as musically trained, it was Petty who had the facilities, expertise and good sense to record Holly, while still affording him creative and musical freedom. He was also responsible for successfully marketing Holly's music for worldwide release. Surely, Holly's early hits would not have been possible if not for Petty's patience and involvement.

Upon interviewing him in February 1984, I learned of his unfortunate battle with leukemia. He openly admitted not feeling very well, but was still eager to spend the time reminiscing about his earlier days in music.

At the end of our conversation, we made a tentative agreement to meet the following September in either Clovis or Lubbock, as Buddy Holly Week celebrations would be taking place at that time. That meeting, however, would never take place. This was to be his last interview.

Norman Petty died on Aug. 16, 1984, but his words and memories survive here as a reminder of a musical era long gone.

"Making records was a lot more fun than it is now. I know that sounds like I'm getting old, and I am. But it seemed like the camaraderie among the musicians was really excellent. We had quite a few people coming in and out of the studio, and it seemed like back in those days everybody was interested in seeing that everyone became successful. The fame of the studio probably started with the Buddy Knox recording of 'Party Doll' and Jimmy Bowen's 'I'm Sticking With You,' which the record company later split up and made into two separate hits.

"Actually, the studio was built to record our trio, and we had a few hits on our own as the Norman Petty Trio. We sort of backed into the production business of doing rock records simply because we had good equipment here and then some of the kids didn't know what to do when they got into the studio. I more or less came in the producer's seat at the same time.

"Buddy first came over here to do some demos. He had done some demos in several different places, including our place here, and I got to know him through those sessions, probably around 1956. Even then, he was doing some country-rock things, not all of them being his compositions.

"I think the success of our trio opened some doors for Buddy in New York. One connection helped the other. I think the fact that we were connected to the records we brought to New York helped us place them."

Was "That'll Be The Day" Buddy's first demo at the Petty studios?

"No, that was the first one that *I* had anything to do with, that I took to New York for him. He did some other things here prior to that, but I don't recall the titles at this time.

When it became a hit, "it was a very exciting time for all of us," Petty recalled. "In my memory, it remains one the most exciting times I've ever had. We were like one big family at that time. It was professional, but we had very good personal relationships as well."

What were changes that were to take place among Holly and the Crickets?

"Of course, there have been pages and pages written about that, but it was simply the fact that Buddy was told that he wanted to go to New York, and I think once he got there his mind and ideas changed.

"It didn't make any difference where the record companies were, because we were producing a lot of tape that was released and sold out of here to various record companies all over the world. As far as Buddy was concerned, I think that he and Maria Elena felt they could get better publicity and do better things in New York than they could be staying here with me in New Mexico."

What happened to the book Petty was supposed to have written?

"I started revising. There have been many bitter things written between the time I started writing the book and by other people, and so many vindictive things said, that I decided I wanted to think through and revise some of the things that I had remembered and written down. I wanted to really remember the good things and try not to criticize anybody from the past." (*The book never was finished – ed.*)

Petty fell under some fire in the '60s for adding instrumentation to some of Holly's early tracks and his "apartment" tapes.

"Yes, I've received quite a bit of criticism of trying to impose Norman Petty on those tapes, which really isn't true. Everything we've ever done was done pretty zealously to try to improve upon whatever we thought Buddy would have liked to have on the market.

"I feel I was fortunate to have been connected with so many good things those years, so I don't back away from it, but neither do I like for people to say things that just weren't true. I think if all of us just sit down and stop and think, they were just great years for all of us."

It's been 25 years since Holly's death. Does Petty think people will still remember Buddy Holly in another 25 years?

"I think the longevity of anything is dependent upon how people can use whatever information they have at hand to fit in with what their own lives are. That's been one nice thing about Holly's music: it was not complicated, and it tends to be a good, fun thing for almost every generation that's come along. So I want to be very optimistic and say yes, I think that in 25 years Buddy Holly will still be remembered."

Maria Elena Holly

No move in the life of Buddy Holly has been scrutinized more than was his marriage to Maria Elena Santiago in August 1958. Married for just six short months, she was to bear final witness to Buddy's future goals and aspirations.

Like Holly's initial success, their first meeting was a meteoric one.

"I met Buddy in New York. I was working for Southern Music Publishing Company; I was the receptionist/secretary there. He and the Crickets came in one morning and asked to see one of the executives, Murray Deutch. I asked them to be seated, so they sat down and immediately tried to engage me into a conversation with them. As soon as they found out I was Spanish, they started trying to speak Spanish with me, you know, ending English words with an 'o' or an 'a'. So that was real hilarious, but I just took it that they were trying to be nice and funny.

"We continued talking and then Buddy asked me if I'd join him for lunch. I told him I was sorry, but I was too busy and usually didn't have time for a lunch break. He said he'd come back after his meeting and convince me. So they went in for about an hour or two, and when they came out he said, 'Well, I'll see you later.' And I said, 'OK, goodbye, good luck,' and I thought that was it.

"Apparently, he had talked to Murray Deutch's secretary, and arranged it in such a way that she'd ask me to go to lunch with her that day, and not mention Buddy Holly. So I figured why not!

"She took me to Howard Johnson's, where they had arranged to meet. When we got there, there was a huge line, but off to the side I saw hands waving, and who do you think it was? Buddy Holly and the Crickets, plus Norman Petty, and they were calling for us to come over. So we went and sat down, and that's the first time I really got to know Buddy Holly.

"After that lunch, he asked me to dinner. Of course, I told him no, so he asked me if I would go with him to buy come guitar strings before returning to the office. So we walked toward the music store, and he tried to convince me to have dinner with him.

"Of course, I liked him right away when I saw him, but I didn't take him very seriously in what he was trying to say to me. He told me he was going to marry me, and I said 'Oh, when? Right away?' I didn't take it seriously.

"But after that we worked it out. I asked my aunt and she opposed it right away. I worked on her for awhile and then she consented; she had found out that he was a nice guy. So Buddy did take me to dinner that night, and again he asked me to marry him. 'Oh sure,' I replied sarcastically, 'why not tomorrow?' I didn't know he was *that* serious, but he kept insisting that he wasn't kidding. So I told him to go see my aunt...it was not up to me. I was trying to get him to calm down, and suggested he talk to me when he came back from his tour. But he said, 'No, I don't think so. I want to be sure that, before I go, you say yes.' So I said OK, and made him promise that tomorrow he'd go and talk to my aunt. I thought that he just wouldn't show up!

"But sure enough, Buddy Holly was there the next day ringing the doorbell. He came in and told my aunt that he wanted to get married, that we were in love, and he was sure I felt the same way. He wanted her blessing. And that's exactly how it happened...it all started at Southern Music Publishing Company.

"Buddy was already considering moving to New York City even before we got married. He thought New York was the place to be at that time for the music and his career. He told me this that very first night when we were talking. He was discussing different things about his career and what he intended to do, and I told him he was right, New York was the place to be.

"When we got married we took an apartment in Greenwich Village on 8th Street and 5th Avenue. That's where the Mark Twain House used to be, until they destroyed it and erected an apartment house. We first lived there until we decided what we wanted to do."

In the final months of his life, Maria Elena was with Buddy more than anyone else. Where does she think his career would have gone had he lived?

"Buddy would still be playing rock 'n' roll and he'd still be composing. But Buddy Holly was also a person who was never afraid to look into all types of music. He loved music; it was his whole life, and he was always open to new sounds. So I would say that he would have been involved with country, which he had been all along: the country/rock blend they now call rockabilly. Plus, he would have expanded to other aspects of music, like recording other artists, managing and producing. And I also say that he would still be performing – maybe not as much as he would have wanted to because the other situations would have taken a great part of his time. But he'd still be performing and he'd still be doing rock 'n' roll!

"I'd like Buddy to be remembered for his music, as he's been all along. He was a person who really enjoyed people and wanted them to be happy. That was something he also conveyed through his music: happiness. So I think Buddy will always be remembered as a good composer, a fine musician, and a good human being, just as he was. That's how I see Buddy Holly today."

Currently, Maria Elena is a housewife and mother living just outside of Dallas. A regular attendee of the annual Buddy Holly Week celebrations in Lubbock, she remains Holly's greatest supporter and activist.

Dion DiMucci

Buddy departed Maria and New York in mid-January 1959 to be headline star on the Winter Dance Party tour. Ritchie Valens and the Big Bopper were the co-stars, and both had made spectacular climbs on the charts with their respective hits. Also on that tour was an up-and-coming youngster named Dion DiMucci. He and his group, the Belmonts, were just starting out.

Here are some excerpts from Dion's first interview regarding his rock 'n' roll years in 15 years.

"I was 19 years old when I went on that tour, and it was a tremendous, exciting time in my life," Dion related. "I remember Buddy Holly and I had the first Fender guitars that came out, and we had kind of gotten into competition of seeing who was going to make it ring the longest. He was a bit older than me, 22, and very mature for his age. I was impressed: he knew his mind and what he wanted to do, and that was attractive to me. He made decisions and moved decisively, and *that* impressed me about him, too.

"The tour was real successful. We were playing to thousands and thousands of people each night. Once I think we had almost 24,000 people in this huge civic center.

"We had a lot of fun on the bus, not only with Buddy, but Ritchie Valens was a sweet kid, he was 16 or 17 years old, and the Big Bopper was a joy to be with. I was offered a seat on the plane, because the more people you got to fly, the cheaper it was. But I was kind of frugal and refused it. I was just starting out at the time and was trying to stock up some wood, you know, save some money.

"It was very cold in the Midwest that winter. The way I remember it, at times it was almost 30 degrees

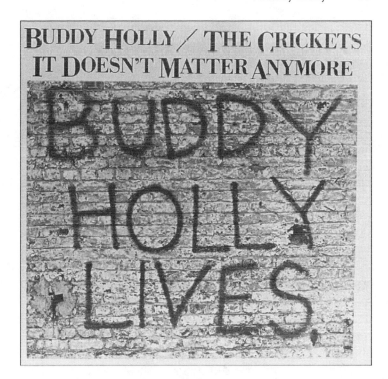

below zero. The bus was breaking down between towns and it was freaking out a lot of musicians and people on the tour. Being a kid, I didn't have that kind of fear in me, so we'd just snuggle under some blankets and tell some jokes.

"I remember Buddy telling me that night they'd take the plane so they could get into town early to do some laundry, get some haircuts, and maybe a little extra rest. They could spend the day getting things done instead of sleeping all night on the bus and arriving exhausted in the morning.

"When we arrived, we heard the plane went down, and it was a tremendous shock for all of us. We had pulled right in front of our hotel. The road manager, Sam Geller, got out of the bus, went in, and came out with the longest face I'd ever seen. And there he announced the news right in front of the bus. He was baffled and saddened. It really cut him to the heart because he loved those guys so much. Apparently, they'd had the TV on, and people were standing around listening to the news. I guess they knew we were coming to town. Again, we were all baffled, but I must say we got support from all over the country. We were in the small town of Fargo, N.D.

"So that day was very puzzling. Yet, that night we got telegrams from all over the country, from Paul Anka and Bobby Darin, from managers and record companies, from friends and relatives. We were all loaded down with support and prayers. It was devastating, yet it was a time for pulling together in God's love and support. I found that very comforting, and we just went on with the tour because we thought that's what the guys would want.

"Bobby Vee came in that night to help us out, he was from Fargo. There was also another fill-in act from Texas, but I forget his name.

"People came out to the shows and were very supportive, and I needed that support. Being that young and having the bottom being torn from under you, it was just too puzzling and baffling."

Tom Anderson

To charter his plane the night of Feb. 2, Buddy called on the assistance of Surf Ballroom manager Carroll Anderson. Anderson made the necessary calls and arrangements to secure the services Holly was seeking. After the Clear Lake show, the three performers were driven to the local air field by Anderson, his wife, and son, Tommy, then eight years old.

Now a schoolteacher living in Chippewa Falls, Wisconsin, Tom Anderson still recalls the night when he was one of the very last people to see Buddy Holly alive.

"The Surf was packed that night; it was just loaded with people, mostly teenagers, of course. I can remember the Big Bopper singing 'Chantilly Lace'; Ritchie Valens sang 'Donna' and 'La Bamba,' And Holly did 'Peggy Sue.' I was pretty young and that's about all I remember about the show. It was a really big event and the place was packed!

"There was very poor visibility that night, with a lot of snow and wind blowing. I can remember them being concerned about whether or not they would be able to fly because of the weather. Just before we left the ballroom, they called and the charter service said yes, they'd make the flight. So my mother and father, myself, and the three entertainers got in the car and drove out to the airport. When we got there they had the plane all warmed up, sitting out on the runway, ready to go. We drove up to the office, and in what seemed like a real short time they finalized any transaction, and so on. The three guys got out in the airplane and we sat there in the car and watched them take off. Of course, with the visibility we couldn't see them for very long. Then we sat there for just a few minutes more, and we turned around and started driving back home.

"The next morning my father got a call telling him that there'd been a crash. He was asked to come out to try to identify the bodies. It had been determined that they crashed immediately, before they could even get out of the airport. The bodies were pretty badly dismembered and it was a pretty difficult thing to try and identify them. Dad had to go by things they were wearing that night when we put them on the plane.

"My father was extremely shocked and sad and upset. He's an extremely kind-hearted person and he really took it pretty hard even though he wasn't extremely attached to any of these people. It was just that situation of having had them there, making arrangements for them, and escorting them to the airport and all.

"I was young but I was pretty impressionable, and I'd realized at the time that these were big rock stars, and I kind of followed that thing. I don't know if I felt the true impact of the crash, but I did realize that it was a pretty serious, sad thing."

Don McLean

No artist today is more representative of Holly's influence than singer/songwriter Don McLean. Although the two never actually met, McLean's 1971 smash hit, "American Pie," immortalized Holly in its opening verses, and has done more to promote interest in Holly's music than any other song to date. McLean also dedicated the entire *American Pie* album to Holly, In later years, Don was to record many different Holly tunes on his various albums, including "It Doesn't Matter Anymore," "Fool's Paradise," "Everyday," "Moondreams," and, most recently, "Maybe Baby."

Today, Don McLean remains a good ole boy from upstate New York. He recently recorded an album with the Jordanaires and toured with Joan Baez. He still cites Buddy Holly as a large part of his musical heritage

"For many years, as I grew up in the late '50s and early '60s, I'd been real crazy about Buddy Holly's music. When an album would come out, I'd get all the different ones, and the effect was, so to speak, totally awesome. Then suddenly he was killed in a plane crash, and it seemed, even back in '59, like a terrible shock; a real trauma for kids. But kids weren't taken that seriously, and their music wasn't taken that seriously, so it was sort of reported on, and that was it. I think a few years later you heard a little novelty record about "Three Stars," or something like that. (*Actually, it was later the same year, and it was a Top 20 hit for Tommy Dee on the Crest label. – ed.*)

"In any case, I was one of those people who kind of kept the faith with Holly's music. I didn't realize, though, that there were so many other people who were doing the same thing. It just dawned on me one day, as a paper boy when I was 12, that I saw this news headline that said Holly had been killed. That was the first time I was really made aware that being a human being was more than just going to school every day.

"So I had this idea for a long time about combining the feeling I had for music and the importance it has, with the way things had gone politically in the United States. I was looking to express the strangeness that'd seemed to take place, more or less. I searched around for a point at which to begin, and one day I just started singing: 'Long, long time ago... I can still remember how that music used to make me smile...' and started thinking about that period, conjuring it up almost. One thing lead to another, and pretty soon I found myself singing in that little thing about the moment when I had seen that newspaper article about the plane crash.

"I had that first little part of the song for about four months. The I wrote a catchy little chorus, and one day I just scribbled out about eight more verses, once I had this 'day the music died' idea. Of course, that was a takeoff on Holly's hit, 'That'll be the day that I die.'

"I don't know if people out there ever knew this or not, but that came from the fact that in '57 or so, *The Searchers* was a giant film by John Ford, and John Wayne, in the film, always said; 'Well, that'll be the day,' every time someone said that he'd get hurt or killed, or something. So Holly and his band saw that flick, and used that phrase to whip off a catchy little hit song. And it was always kind of a sick joke that that was his big hit, and here he was, a martyr.

"But Holly had a fascinating presence, kind of like Rod Serling, more than Elvis did. And I was aware of that, too.

"I had put out an album before called *Tapestry*, which had made me a little bit more than an unknown, and I was headlining with some good people at the Troubadour and the Bitter End. Things were starting to happen for me. When I decided to write this song and tell this story, I really had no idea that anybody even remembered who Buddy Holly was, and that what I felt millions of other people couldn't express. There's been a lot of loss in the United States, and 'American Pie' is a song about that loss, so it keeps being used again and again for the purposes of remembering, which isn't a bad thing to do. The hit part happened because people chose it, related to it, and as a matter of fact, went a little nuts behind it.

"You see, the point is that I make music basically for myself. That's why I did 'American Pie': because I loved the idea of it. And it's been a privilege for me to have been able to shine a little light on the happiness that Holly brought in his music. I think kids today need something that's rocking, yet happy too. It doesn't have to be all cut and slash music. That's why his music will always be with us, because show business has to have a warmth to it, and his music is very warm. This you just don't find in today's music: that real warmth and certain glow that the great

records have. His records are there for everyone to enjoy, and if 'American Pie' got people interested in his music, then that's the most wonderful thing I can think of to happen.

"There are three Holly albums I'm very much in love with. *The Chirping Crickets* record is my No.1 favorite record of all time. But you have to have the original cover, otherwise it just doesn't make it. The sound of that original disc is wonderful; they've fooled with it since. You can really hear the drums and bass and the Latin thing that's in some of the songs like 'Not Fade Away.' Holly was a very interesting musician, and I think to some degree he took a lot of interesting chances.

"What I also found fascinating was the album series called *The Buddy Holly Story*, which was put together after his death. It showed he was making a big transition, not unlike what I've done in my career. If you can sing, you want to sing all sorts of music. So he was moving away from the Bo Diddley/ Mickey and Sylvia/Little Richard axis and more into the Bobby Darin/Sinatra zone with 'Moondreams' and violins and orchestration. It's just as good.

"Of course, I like the first Holly record, too, just called *Buddy Holly*. It had a strange, sepia color, with no glasses. But it's not well engineered. *The Chirping Crickets* really knocked me out because suddenly the sound just leaped out of the speaker, like it wasn't there anymore. That's my definition of radio and of a great record: when that damn thing just comes out in the middle of the night someplace. Just like 'American Pie' did: you have to drive off the road and listen to it!

"Holly is remembered today just as he will always be remembered: by his records and music. He is his own greatest booster in that respect. It's just a matter of getting a little bit of it into some people's ears. What I'm happy about is whenever a radio station would play 'American Pie' they'd very often follow it with a Holly cut, which got a lot of people turned onto Buddy's music. That's music in action: that's my kind of song."

Most Collectible 45

"Blue Days, Black Nights"/ "Love Me," Decca 9-29854, with lines on either side of the word "Decca" at top of label, $600.

Most Collectible LP

That'll Be The Day, Decca DL 8707, black label, silver print, $1,500.

Recommended Introduction

Greatest Hits, MCA 11536 (18 essential Buddy Holly songs; this replaced the 1986 CD called *From The Original Master Tapes*, MCA 5540, which had 20 tracks and, to these ears, sounds better. Find that one if you can.)

If you want to hear more...

The Buddy Holly Collection, MCA 10883 (a 2-CD collection of 50 Holly/Crickets tracks)

Buddy Holly, MCA 25239 (his first album under his own name, originally released in 1958)

The "Chirping" Crickets, MCA 31182 (the other Holly album to be released during his lifetime)

Jerry Lee Lewis

by Colin Escott

It may seem hard to believe today, but Jerry Lee Lewis actually had more success on the country music charts than the pop charts. No, it wasn't the classic Sun Records material that did so well there; it was much tamer material he recorded for Smash and Mercury in the late 1960s and early 1970s, including three No. 1 hits. Most fans, however, have forgotten that, if they knew it at all. He'll forever be known as, to quote this article's original title, "The Ferriday Wild Man," whose biggest hits on Sun still get plenty of spins on oldies radio even today. Colin Escott, who has written some of the most amazing liner notes in the history of CD compilations, did this piece on the rise and fall of the 1950s version of Jerry Lee for the July 14, 1989 Goldmine, *around the time the biopic* Great Balls Of Fire! *was reviving interest in him.*

When musicians sit around and talk about who was the *wildest*, both onstage and off, the conversation usually turns at some point to Jerry Lee Lewis. In a profession marked by excess, Lewis can lay claim to be among the most excessive. Tortured by an unfathomable religion and driven by an ego as big as all outdoors, Lewis has come to believe his own legend. He is the self-created Killer, tempting God to come and reclaim him alive, and tempting every singer who fancies himself a showman to follow Jerry Lee Lewis on stage.

The legend of Jerry Lee Lewis had its humble beginnings when the 21-year-old singer stood at the door of Sun Records, waiting for a chance to sit before the tired studio spinet and ply his wares, a chance that had been conspicuously denied him at other studios. Sun Records president Sam C. Phillips would later look into the singer's eyes and see a craziness that matched his own. More than that, Phillips was an artist who could do all the things that he *would* have done if he could have sung and played. Phillips and Jerry Lee Lewis were destined to come together, and together they defined all that was best in rock music.

Lewis' reputation is founded on the strength of the music he recorded with Phillips. The Top 20 hits were

only four in number. Few legends in popular music have been grounded in such low gross sales. Lewis is prone to brag about the sales of "Whole Lot Of Shakin' Going On," but the fact remains that not merely one, but *two*, versions of "The Banana Boat Song," together with some 30 or 40 other records, outsold "Whole Lotta Shakin'" in 1957. And by the middle of the following year Jerry Lee Lewis' career in the top 20 was over. All of which goes to emphasize that even in popular music, chart placings are not everything. God-given talent, as Jerry Lee Lewis will be the first to tell you, counts for something.

When Jerry Lee Lewis entered Sun Records for the first time, he was 21 years old. He was barely educated, twice married, once jailed and good for nothing much other than pounding the piano, which he had been doing every day since he was 10 years old.

Since his expulsion from the Southwestern Bible Institute in Waxahacie, Texas, Lewis had been playing music in honky-tonks despite incessant carping from both of his wives. Like Carl Perkins and Elvis Presley, Lewis could play music that would make people sit up and take notice. It was that talent that marked him out as unique – and he knew it.

The subject of Lewis' musical influences has been raised but never resolved. When pressed, Lewis will generally say that he had no influences, and it is true that when he walked into Sun Records, he did not sound identifiably like anyone else. Moon Mullican, the self-proclaimed King of the Hillbilly Piano Players, has often been cited as an influence, but Mullican probably did no more than reaffirm Lewis' conviction that the piano had a place within country music. Mullican's music was marked by under-statement, which was never a hallmark of Lewis' style.

Lewis' cousin, Carl McVoy, was probably an early influence. McVoy's mother, Lewis' mother and Jimmy Swaggart's mother were sisters. McVoy was older than Lewis and had gone to New York with his father, who ran a ministry there for a few years. He learned the primitive joys of the boogie-woogie in New York and returned to Pine Bluff, Ark. to work in construction. One summer, Jerry Lee Lewis came to stay. "He worried the hell out of me," recalled McVoy, "wanting me to show him things on the piano. I think I was instrumental in the way his style developed because I got attention when I played. I rolled my hands and put on a damn show. When Jerry went back to Ferriday, he played everything I knew."

And then there was Haney's Big House, a black juke joint outside Ferriday. "My uncle Lee Calhoun, the back-bone of the family of all us mother-humpers, owned Haney's," asserted Lewis to David Booth. "Me and Jimmy Lee Swaggart used to slip in there, hide behind the bar and listen to B.B. King when he wasn't but 18 years old. That place was full of colored folks. They'd been picking cotton all day, they had a 25 cent pint of wine in their back pocket – and they was gettin' with it!"

Jerry Lee Lewis and Jimmy Swaggart habituated the black juke joints around Ferriday. They were later seen as opposite sides of the same disordered personality. However, Swaggart's public defrocking in February 1988 for consorting with prostitutes suggested that they were indeed the *same* side of a disordered personality.

In truth, the influences close to home such as the roadhouse R&B bands who played at Haney's Big House and Carl McVoy were probably more important in the formation of Lewis' style than artists on the radio. However, of the artists whom Jerry heard on the radio, Hank Williams and Jimmie Rodgers exercised a special fascination. Both were what Lewis terms "stylists"; that is, they could sing anything and make it into an expression of their own personality. In addition, Williams had the terrifying intensity of one who is staring the Angel of Death full in the face, and he sang his bleak songs of misogyny and despair every Saturday night on the Louisiana Hayride when Jerry was at a young and impressionable age. Lewis has performed Williams' material throughout his career, and it usually draws the best from him because he knows that he is up against some stiff competition in the form of Williams himself.

Lewis's public debut was at the Ferriday Ford dealership in June 1949. He performed "Drinkin' Wine Spo-Dee-O-Dee" and the sweet rapture of the applause that followed set Jerry on his personal course – initially across the river to Natchez, Miss. and then to Shreveport., La. to audition for a Hayride package show. Lewis was turned down by the Hayride, but before he left he was invited to cut a disc in the KWKH studios. He recorded "If I Ever Needed You" and Hank Snow's hit of the day "I Don't Hurt Any More." He returned to Ferriday in Aunt Stella's car clutching his acetate.

The audition at KWKH probably took place in 1954. That same year Lewis went to Nashville. He toured the record companies, most of whom advised him to learn the guitar. One person to offer him a job was Roy Hall, a pianist and raconteur, who owned an after-hours drinking spot, the Musicians Hideaway. "I hired him," asserted Hall to Nick Tosches, "for $15 a night. He worked from one 'til five in the morning pounding that damn piano until daybreak. Folks would give Jerry Lee their watch and jewelry in case there was a bust figurin' that he would be the one let off on account of his age."

After one bust, Lewis went back to Ferriday and Natchez, where he once again took up residency at the Wagon Wheel. Among his souvenirs from Nashville was probably a song that Roy Hall had sung (and, by Hall's account, co-written) called "Whole Lot Of Shakin' Going On."

At some point in 1956 Jerry Lee Lewis read an article about Elvis Presley in *Country Song Roundup* and decided that his music might fall upon more receptive ears in Memphis. He and his father, Elmo Lewis, sold 13 dozen eggs and drove north to Memphis. Sam Phillips had gone out to work on a new radio station in Marked Tree, Ark. Jack Clement was in the control room.

"I was working with Roy Orbison," recalled Clement, "and Sally Wilbourn brought Jerry Lee back to me. She said, 'I've got a fella here who says he plays the piano like Chet Atkins.' I thought I'd better listen to that. He started playing things like 'Wildwood Flower' and I believe he was playing piano with his right hand and drums with his left. I finally made a tape with him because he was different. We recorded 'Seasons Of My Heart' but I told him to forget about country because it wasn't happening at that time. I took his name and told him I'd let Sam hear the tape when he got back. After Jerry left, I started listening to the tape and I found that I liked it. It really grew on me."

Clement decided to cut a complete demo session on Lewis. He called in the musicians he had met during his brief stint at Fernwood Records. "Jack phoned me," recalled Roland Janes to Rob Bowman and Ross Johnson, "and said, 'Man, I got this piano-player cat from down in Louisiana. He's pretty good. I'm gonna put a few things down on him, Do you want to come in and help us out?' I said, 'Yeah, sure.' He said, could you drop by and get (drummer J.M.) Van Eaton? Think you can get him to come out?' I said, 'Yeah, I'm pretty sure I can.' He (Van Eaton) didn't drive at the time; that's how young he was. So we went down to the session...and cut 'Crazy Arms.' I don't think Jack was even in the control room. He was out in the studio and just left the machine running. Billy Riley had walked in about the time and he picked up my guitar. Right on the end of the song he hit a chord...I came out of the washroom about halfway through the song and picked up an old upright bass and started playing it – and I don't play upright bass. Fortunately, I wasn't close to a microphone. On that song, there are technically only two instruments, drums and piano."

The date was Nov. 14, 1956 when Phillips got back from Nashville, Clement played him the tape. "I don't know if I'd told Jack this," said Phillips to Robert Palmer, "but I had been wanting to get off this guitar scene and show that it could be done with other instruments. They put that tape on and I said, 'Where in hell did this man come from?' He played that piano with abandon. A lot of people do that but I could hear, between the stuff that he played and didn't play, that spiritual thing. I told Jack, 'Just get him in here as fast as you can.'"

Phillips had unwittingly stumbled upon a magic formula. Janes and Van Eaton happened to be friends of Clement, who happened to be running the board while Phillips was away, However, Lewis could not have hoped for two more sympathetic accompanists. Janes intuitively understood Jerry; he knew better than to try and dominate the session; in fact, it was never in his nature to do so. Instead, he supplied rhythmic support and could turn in a solo at a moment's notice. Lewis would usually telegraph the fact that it was Janes' turn to solo by shouting, "Roland, boy!"

Van Eaton quickly developed empathy with Lewis to the point where he had an almost telepathic ability to know in which direction Jerry was heading. The subtle tempo changes and perfectly judged rolls and accents attest to the instant chemistry of Lewis and Van Eaton. Bassists came and went – and were barely necessary anyway – but the nucleus of Lewis' studio band was now in place and would remain until the dawn of the new decade .

Released in December 1956, "Crazy Arms" was not a hit although it sold respectably well. Lewis took work where he could find it. Jack Clement got him a gig in West Memphis with the Snead Ranch Boys. Phillips gave him a little work in the studio backing Carl Perkins, Billy Riley, Johnny Cash and some others. Janes and Riley took him out to some of the dancehalls they played in Arkansas. His uncle J.W. Brown let him sleep on the couch.

On Feb. 23, 1957 Lewis got his first crack at the big audience when he was booked into the Big 'D' Jamboree in Dallas. Two weeks later he was invited back. On March 31 Lewis embarked on a tour that would last until May 5. He was in the company of Johnny Cash, Carl Perkins, Onie Wheeler and others who came and went as the troupe slowly made its way up into the frozen north. From the sub-arctic springtime in Sault St. Marie, Ontario, they trekked across the Prairies, ending up in Billings, Montana.

According to Cash and Perkins, it was during the long haul that Lewis developed his stage act. Upset by the fact that he was chained to the piano stool, Lewis started clowning and expending some of the frightening energy he possessed. Both Cash and Perkins quickly realized that a monster was unleashing itself from the bottom of the bill.

Before he left, Lewis went into the studio and recorded the song that Roy Hall had probably taught him, "Whole Lot Of Shakin' Going On." Phillips initially had little faith in the song, sensing that it was too

suggestive. Lewis had not recalled too much of the original version and, running out of lyrics before the song was barely over a minute long, he slowed the tempo and inserted a talking segment that he had worked up on club dates before storming back for a climatic finale that ended with a triumphant *glissando*.

Phillips had higher hopes for the other side of the record, "It'll Be Me," a song that Jack Clement had concocted on the toilet while contemplating reincarnation. "If you see a turd in your toilet bowl baby it'll be me and I'll be starin' at you..." became "If you see a lump of sugar in your sugar bowl, it'll be me and I'll be looking at you."

Released in mid-March, the record was not fully promoted until Lewis returned from the tour in May. By that time, Phillips had ascertained that "Shakin'" was the side to watch. By early June it was sitting atop the local country charts in Memphis and on June 12 it entered the national country charts. Two weeks later, it entered the Hot 100 at #70.

Sam Phillips' brother, Jud, was almost entirely responsible for getting Lewis off the white trash circuit – and he did it with a bold gamble. "I took him to New York," recalled Jud, "and presented him to Jules Green, who was managing Steve Allen, and Henry Frankel, who was talent coordinator for NBC. I took a real gamble in terms of Sun Records to see whether a mass audience would accept this man. Our distributors made sure that every retail outlet in the United States had copies of 'Shakin'.' That represented a lot of merchandise that could have been returned."

On Sunday, July 28, 1957 Ferriday's pride and joy appeared on the *Steve Allen Show*, one slot behind Ed Sullivan in the ratings. Lewis' appearances on the Allen show are landmarks in the history of rock 'n' roll. He pounded the piano, eyes fixed above with messianic intensity. When it came time to sing, he glared at the camera with a wild-eyed fury. "Whose barn? Mah barn!" It was demonic when set alongside the jugglers and ventriloquists who were the staples of television variety in those days.

The impact of Lewis' first appearance on the Allen show was such that "Shakin'" resumed its upward movement. Before the show, it had started to lose momentum, pegging out in the lower reaches of the Top 30. It eventually rose to the #1 slot on the Country and R&B charts but was excluded from the top position on the pop charts by Debbie Reynolds' "Tammy."

Oscar Davis was quickly brought in to do for Lewis what Tom Parker had done for Presley. Davis had even worked as a front man for Parker. Jud Phillips remained on the scene, as he would for years, in an ill-defined role.

In August 1957, immediately after the appearance on the *Steve Allen Show*, Jerry Lee Lewis was signed as a late addition to the movie *Jamboree*, which was to feature Fats Domino. Lewis had been given a song, "Great Balls Of Fire," by the movie's musical director, Otis Blackwell. The idea had come from a New York writer, Jack Hammer, who had sold the title to Blackwell, in exchange for 50 percent of composer credit. Between October 6 and 8, Lewis labored to produce a releasable version of the song.

"Great Balls Of Fire" is essentially a duet between Jerry Lee Lewis and J.M. Van Eaton. The barely controlled slapback echo almost ranks as a third instrument because it gives such depth and presence to the recording. Phillips had obviously counseled against finesse during the solo, because Lewis starts with four glissandi before hammering away at the same note for six consecutive bars. When the finished product was released on Nov. 15, 1957, there was nothing more that Phillips or Lewis could have done during the production phase to ensure its success.

Jamboree was also released in November and Sam Phillips took the rare and almost unprecedented step of taking out a full-page advertisement in *Billboard* touting "Great Balls Of Fire." The payoff was swift and overwhelming. By December the song was sitting atop most charts. With Elvis halfway into the Army, Jerry Lee Lewis was just about the hottest phenomenon in pop music. However, during that same Christmas season, so different from the one that had preceded it, Lewis also sowed the seeds of his own destruction.

As the year drew to a close, he sneaked off to Hernando, Miss., with a marriage license in his glove compartment. He was going to marry his 13-year-old cousin, Myra Gale Brown, daughter of J.W. Brown, upon whose couch he had slept in leaner times. It was not even common knowledge to Lewis' family for a while, but within six months it would put a 10-year roadblock in his career.

1958 began with a full date book. There was to be an Alan Freed tour, a Phillip Morris tour and a tour of Australia and even England later in the year. Before Lewis started on the promotional whirl he was brought back into the studio to record a follow-up to "Great Balls Of Fire." Otis Blackwell had sent down another song tagged after an exclamation, "Breathless." It was worked up for release in February 1958.

The record moved up the charts with the help of a ploy devised by Jud Phillips and Dick Clark. Beech-Nut chewing gum had sponsored the networking of Dick Clark's Bandstand show. Initial response was unfavorable. Phillips and Clark worked out a cross-promotion deal. Jerry appeared on the Clark show on March 8 and Clark invited the kids to send in 50 cents together with five Beech-Nut wrappers to receive a "free" autographed copy of "Breathless."

The response was overwhelming. Sun's new promotion person, Barbara Barnes, ordered a rubber autograph stamp and everyone in Sun's tiny operation including session musicians and lesser artists was put to work "autographing" and mailing thousands of copies of "Breathless." Clark received half of the proceeds from the sale of the 38,000 records shipped during the promotion. Phillips later asserted that the response had persuaded Beech-Nut to retain sponsorship of the show, although Clark would later abandon Lewis with the indecent haste of a john fleeing a whorehouse during a police raid.

The Alan Freed tour commenced at Freed's old stomping ground, the Brooklyn Paramount Theater, on March 28. Before the tour had started, Lewis had filmed his spot in another abysmal movie. Albert Zugsmith, who would later give the world *The Teacher Was A Sexpot*, had created a quickie exploitation-movie around the teenage drug problem (yes, there was a teenage drug problem in 1958). It was called *High School Confidential* and it starred that old habitueé of the casting couch, Mamie Van Doren. The sole redeeming element was the sight of Jerry Lee Lewis, his road drummer Russ Smith and his uncle/father-in-law J.W. Brown playing off the back of a flatbed truck.

Lewis had rushed back to Memphis to record the final version of the title song during a break in the Freed tour. "High School Confidential" had been concocted by M-G-M artist Ron Hargrove, although

Oscar Davis cut Lewis in for 50 percent of the composer credit. It was shipped only days after Phillips had spliced the ending from an aborted take onto a take that he otherwise considered to be the best. The entire production had another layer of echo added for luck and was released in early May.

On May 23, Jerry Lee Lewis, his sister Frankie and his wife Myra arrived in London, England, to begin a short promotional tour. The opening was in the Edmonton suburb of London. A member of the press picked up a chance remark from one of Lewis's entourage about his wife being rather young. Hounding a rock 'n' roll singer who sported a red-lined black jacket trimmed with ocelot fur was welcome relief for the British press corps. Lewis was hardly a moving target for their big guns, and within days he was greeted with howls of derision at his concerts. The promoter, J. Arthur Rank, took Lewis off the tour and replaced him with a local teenager, Terry Wayne.

Scanning the morning papers as he left England under a cloud, Lewis remarked, "Who is this DeGaulle? He seems to have gone over bigger 'n' us."

Lewis and his entourage had anticipated that they would arrive back in the United States to find that the disclosure of Myra's age, and the accompanying news that Jerry's divorce from his previous wife had not been finalized when he married Myra, would have no impact upon his burgeoning career.

They were wrong.

The first to disown Lewis was Dick Clark, who almost tripped over himself in his hasty cancellation of Lewis' bookings. Alan Freed defended Lewis, saying that jazz musicians and the Hollywood crowd were far worse. "Jerry's a country boy," added Freed, "and Tennessee boys get married quite young." It was courageous of Freed to defend Lewis, although his defense missed the point that no one had complained about the age at which Lewis had married. Elvis Presley, who within a few years would be cohabitating with an underage woman of his own, offered a limp-wristed defense, saying only that "If he loves her, I guess it's all right."

Sam Phillips was dismayed. "It was a stupid damn thing," he said. "I think Jerry's innocence back then, and his trying to be open and friendly and engaging with the press, backfired. They scalped him. It turned out to be a very ghastly and deadly thing. So many people wanted to point a finger of scorn at rockers and say, 'We told you so; rockers are no good.'"

Sun adopted two tactics. The first was to satirize the issue with a novelty record concocted by Jack Clement. Titled "The Return Of Jerry Lee," it used clips from Lewis' records interspersed with questions in the manner of the "Flying Saucer" saga. At the same time, Sam Phillips and Barbara Barnes were composing an ultra-pious and penitent letter for publication in the media. "I sincerely want to be worthy of the decent admiration of all the people who admired what talent (if any) I had..." said the letter in perhaps the most uncharacteristic utterance ever to have Jerry Lee Lewis's name appended to it.

Oscar Davis made matters worse by booking Lewis into the Cafe de Paris in New York as a belated stab at respectability. Almost nobody showed up and the booking was canceled by mutual agreement after two nights. Lewis returned to Memphis to lick his wounds. His first album was shipped at the height of the storm, together with three EPs drawn from it. However, Phillips held off releasing another single for two months, hoping that the furor would die away.

A new arrival at Sun, Charlie Rich, had been promised both sides of the new Lewis single before the scandal. Rich had written "Break Up" and "I'll Make It All Up To You," anticipating that the royalties would keep him in Beefeaters for the next decade. It was not to be. The single climbed uncertainly up to #50 and then died quickly away. The news was doubly bad for Phillips because Johnny Cash's contract had expired just as the storm broke. Jud Phillips also quit Sun to start Judd Records in August 1958, although he took over Lewis' management from Oscar Davis early in 1959.

The effect of the scandal on Lewis' record sales was devastating. There was a virtual airplay blackout, and product out in the marketplace came back by the truckload. However, Lewis' personal appearances were still successful, although without the hit records he could not command his accustomed fees. The scandal may actually have increased Lewis' appeal a little.

Roland Janes said that Lewis never showed that he had been hurt by the scandal. "He's a very deep person," said Janes, who had come to know Lewis from days spent together on the road. "He could be hurting and never let it show. I don't think he ever quite understood why it happened. He's such an honest person, and he didn't think he'd done anything that was unacceptable to anyone. He didn't think the public would be concerned about what he did if it didn't relate to his music which was a total miscalculation on his part. The truth is that you've got the world and you've got Jerry Lee Lewis. He'll do things his way regardless of what anyone thinks. He felt betrayed,. though – and he had every right to – but he held his head up and didn't cry."

Janes continued to play with Lewis in the studio as Sun struggled to find something that would tempt programmers to end their blacklist. However, Lewis rarely wrote his own material, and music publishers were no longer as keen to send him their hottest new prospects. This forced Lewis back to his roots, and there was a heavier concentration of revamped older material in the years that followed his downfall.

Sun's new promotion manager, Cecil Scaife, tried to talk Lewis into adopting a new image, but it was a stillborn idea. Scaife's account of the conversation shows how marginally Lewis comprehended any concept other than those he had already developed independently. "At that time," recalled Scaife, "Jerry had his hair peroxided blond and it was extraordinarily long. That, and his 13-year-old bride, was the image that the cartoonists caricatured. She would be holding a teddy bear in her hand.

"I had a very serious talk with Jerry about his image. We went to the restaurant next door to the studio and sat down in a booth. Jerry had one of his pickers with him. He always had someone with him. You could rarely get him one-on-one. I told him what I thought we should do in as much detail as I thought he could absorb in one sitting. I wanted to get him out of typical rock 'n' roll regalia. Ivy League was in. I wanted him to get a crewcut. I wanted to hold a press conference where Jerry would announce that he was somewhat remorseful. He would take on an adult image.

"We discussed it for over an hour, Jerry was very polite and listened. He would nod every once in a while, but he kept looking at his watch. Finally, he shook it like it wasn't working and he looked at his buddy across the table and said, 'What time is it?' The guy said, 'It's five before one.' Jerry said, 'Oh! The double feature at the Strand starts in five minutes. It's *Return Of The Werewolf and The Bride Of Frankenstein Meets Godz-*

 illa. Then he jumped up and left the table. That was the first time we discussed Jerry's image."

Scaife and Sun's new general manager, Bill Fitzergald, also came up with the idea of releasing an instrumental record by Lewis under a pseudonym on Sun's sister label, Phillips International. However, the results were as commercially stillborn as Lewis' other singles released in 1959 and 1960. His problems were compounded by a dispute with the Musicians' Union over non-payment of dues, which meant that he was unable to record officially – although Phillips proceeded as usual.

The pseudonymous single was probably the low point of Lewis' career. In 1961 be climbed back into the Top 40 with "What'd I Say" and, after years of mounting acclaim overseas, he finally recaptured success at home in the country market. *That*, however, is another story.

Jerry Lee Lewis' earlier sides, especially those made between 1956 and 1960, stand as one of the most impressive bodies of recordings to emerge from a turbulent era, perhaps *the* most impressive. The simple truth is that Lewis would never have made those recordings for a major label. Phillips was prepared to keep the tape running while Lewis plundered his subconscious for barely remembered songs; "Whole Lotta Shakin'" was recorded in that way. Other studios would schedule a standard three-hour session and have four songs ready to record.

"Jerry is an informal person," asserted Sam Phillips, "and the conditions had to be right. You had to have a good song, of course, but atmosphere is nearly everything else. Jerry had to know that the people around him, the people responsible for the session, understood him. He had such spontaneity. With great artists, almost 50 percent of something good they might do happens because of an almost instant reaction to what is taking place around them."

Lewis' early recordings at Sun also exemplified the virtue of keeping it simple. No one else would have dared risk recording Lewis with such a spartan backing. However, any more instruments would have been superfluous.

Lewis was also a born entertainer. He was plying his trade in the studio with an audience of three or four, but the enthusiasm communicated itself vividly on record. "Even when we were going over material," recalled Cecil Scaife, "Jerry would play to you as if you were an audience of 10,000 people. He would sit there and entertain you."

Roland Janes echoes those thoughts. "People are always trying to compare musicians, but I can't find anyone to compare with Jerry. What you hear him doing on records is only a small percentage of what he's capable of doing. I don't think even he knows how great he is. He can take a solo with either hand and sing a song five different ways, every one of them great. I remember when we worked the package shows, Jerry would sit backstage after the show at the piano and all the big stars would gather around him and watch: Chuck Berry, Buddy Holly, the Everly Brothers and so on. Jerry would be leading the chorus and everyone would be having a ball."

Most Collectible 45

"Crazy Arms"/ "End Of The Road," Sun 259, label credit is "Jerry Lee Lewis" with no mention of "His Pumping Piano," $100.

Most Collectible LP

Jerry Lee's Greatest, Sun LP-1265, $250.

Recommeded Introduction

18 Original Sun Greatest Hits, Rhino R2-70255 (has all his 1950s hits on it; essential)

If you want to hear more...

Rare Tracks, Rhino R2-70899 (exactly what it says; Sun-era recordings not available in the US until this CD came out)

All Killer, No Filler, Rhino R2-71216 (two-CD set includes both Sun and later Smash/Mercury country sides)

Classic Jerry Lee Lewis, Bear Family 79005-11542-0 (German import, mammoth box set contains all his Sun recordings)

Little Richard

by Jeff Tamarkin

Even if he'd never come up with anything else, Little Richard forever would be known for his first real hit, "Tutti-Frutti," and its closing line, "A wop bop a loo bop a lop bam boom!" But he didn't stop there – at least not for a while. His follow-ups – "Long Tall Sally," "Lucille," "Jenny, Jenny," "The Girl Can't Help It," "Keep A-Knockin'" (one of my personal favorites) and "Good Golly, Miss Molly," to name just a few – were so frenetic that even the best efforts of Pat Boone and other cover artists could not keep the originals down. The success of "Long Tall Sally" especially helped to bring the end to the era of the cover record. (Covers continued for another couple years, but with diminishing returns, except for the anomalous 1957 hit "Little Darlin'" by the Diamonds, which is a far better record than the R&B original by the Gladiolas.) Well, Richard has had a love-hate relationship with the music that brought him fame ever since. Every few years, he'd renounce "the devil's music" and enter the ministry. Then he'd come back again. As recently as 1986, Little Richard had a hit single with the wild, wonderful "Great Gosh A'Mighty!" from the movie Down And Out In Beverly Hills, which introduced him to a new generation of fans. He even appeared on Solid Gold, the '80s TV show with the sexy dancers. It was on the wave of his new success that the following article was published in Goldmine, in the April 10, 1987 issue.

While interviewing Little Richard, I had to keep from being overwhelmed by the fact that I was actually talking to the guy who made "Tutti Frutti," the guy who was a shoo-in for the Rock and Roll Hall of Fame's first draft, one of the guys without whom there would be no rock 'n' roll.

Interviewing a personal favorite, and someone of such crucial importance as Little Richard, can also be a most frustrating experience. Imagine listening to someone's music all your life, building up a mountain of questions you'd like to ask this person about his incredible life, and then having about a half hour to do it in. No matter how long the interview would have lasted, there still would have been many questions unanswered.

Interviewing Little Richard is frustrating for other reasons though. For a magazine such as *Goldmine*, historical accuracy – and not the sordid tales told in Charles White's authorized biography, *The Life And Times Of Little Richard* – is what is important. And Richard is, like several other Hall of Famers, either uninterested in, or has honestly forgotten, many of the details surrounding his heyday as a seminal rocker some 30 years ago.

More likely, Richard's case is that he's selectively rewritten his own history to fit his present needs. The story of Richard Penniman's roller-coaster ride with religion is well known, and more than once he's denounced rock 'n' roll and his own role in its formation. Thus he tends to avoid recalling his rock 'n' roll days in any detail.

But what is perplexing is that often, Richard simultaneously will choose to ignore some aspects of the early days and to inflate his role in that same '50s rock 'n' roll: On one hand he'll put it down as decadent and go on about how it turned him into an unspeakable nogoodnik, and on the other he'll boast with a rapper's zeal about his being the "originator" and "giving a start" to everyone from Jimi Hendrix to the Beatles.

Trying to sort out the facts from 30 years of rumor and falsification is difficult enough without the best potential source of the truth, the artist himself, evading questions and answering specific questions with general, ambiguous responses. Going into an interview with Little Richard, one expects, despite the man's honest good intentions and all-around righteous manner, a snow job where the history of Little Richard the great rock 'n' roller is concerned.

And that is exactly what one gets. The interviewer is placed in the awkward position of both wanting to spend as much time with the subject as possible, figuring anything he says is worth noting and somewhat useful, and wanting to give him a good swift kick and say, "C'mon, Richard, quit beating around the bush and tell it like it was." When Little Richard goes along disputing and denying the very info offered up in his own "authorized biography" as fact, one can only throw one's hands up, sigh, and hope the truth will sort itself out at some future date.

Compounding the already exasperating situation is the fact that the only reason Little Richard is talking to the press at this time is that he's got a new product to plug. He's released his first album in years, *Lifetime Friend*, on a major label, Warner Bros., and that's what's on his mind (although he doesn't seem especially pleased with it).

While he probably expects a handful of general questions about his notorious past, he's not in any state of mind to participate in a detailed examination of his recording career for a collector's publication like *Goldmine*, especially considering he's just recently returned to the secular world after having spent the better part of the past decade and a half as his alter ego, the Rev. Richard Penniman. Whatever reasons he has for making a contemporary record that's neither gospel nor classic Little Richard rock 'n' roll, but is somewhere in between, it's not because he suddenly wants the world to know what really happened at Specialty Records back in 1955.

So Little Richard has most of his rap down when the questions fly, and he knows how to play the part of Little Richard, and he doesn't get trapped. No, he hasn't turned to rock, this is "message music in rhythm." Yes, he still thinks those early records are great but he'd rather move forward and make records like Prince or "Michael." And no, he won't clear up some of the mysteries still surrounding those records that changed the world 30 years ago, not when he's got to spread his message of love and caring to make up for all those ancient sins – and plan a tour with ZZ Top or maybe "Bruce."

One other thing that's frustrating for the interviewer, however, is that Little Richard sounds so sincere even as he unleashes cliche, ambiguity, misinformation and plain old wishful thinking. He really does mean well, and you can't help but like him.

And whatever his reason for returning this time, he really does miss being in the spotlight. Little Richard wants success again so badly he can taste it, and if he's making some compromises to get it, they aren't so blatant as to negate everything he's been working toward since leaving rock 'n' roll for the ministry the first time.

Sure, Little Richard is full of contradictions, he's mellowed in his middle years, and he seems genuinely at peace with himself, if not his position in the entertainment world. But he also remembers what it was like to be a star, he remembers the applause, and it becomes fairly obvious through talking with him that his recent brush with a comeback, his acting role in the hit film *Down And Out In Beverly Hills* and the hit single that resulted from that, "Great Gosh A'Mighty," are the main reasons for Little Richard being back from the tent shows.

Trying to present a biography of Little Richard in this space would be a waste of every reader's time. That story has been told often enough, and is best told in the Charles White book – once one weeds through the sex and drugs, there's still plenty of rock 'n' roll.

If you want the basics, Richard Penniman, now 54, was born in Macon, Ga., of a large family, sang in church, and won a talent contest in 1951 which earned him a brief record deal with RCA. He next went to Peacock Records in Houston, but in 1955, at the suggestion of Lloyd Price, he sent a tape to Art Rupe of Specialty Records in L.A. Rupe signed him and teamed the flamboyant shouter with producer Bumps Blackwell in New Orleans. The result, of course, was a string of '50s rock 'n' roll classics that have still never been equaled: "Tutti Frutti," "Rip It Up," "Long Tall Sally," "Good Golly, Miss Molly," "Lucille," "Ready Teddy" and many more. You can't know rock In' roll without knowing Little Richard's Specialty sides.

By the turn of the decade, Richard had denounced popular music to enroll in Bible school and become a minister. His new calling would stay with him until the first of several returns to rock in the early '60s. It was during one of these periods that he'd tour Europe and meet up with the not-yet famous Beatles, Rolling Stones, etc., who idolized him. The Beatles, especially, would soon provide a new generation with knowledge of Little Richard via their interpretations of "Long Tall Sally" and the "Kansas City"/"Hey Hey Hey Hey" medley.

All this time, according to legend, Little Richard had led a life of amazing decadence, and he's spend the '70s trying to undo the damage and find himself through religion once again. Although he'd remain popular among rock historians, fans and collectors throughout the years, he vowed never again to return to the evil music. And it seemed he never would. Then, last year, Little Richard was back on the charts with a song that, while no "Tutti Frutti," was definitely not out of character for an aging Little Richard: "Great Gosh A'Mighty," produced for the film by veteran Dan Hartman.

Just when it seemed he was going to enjoy a popular recovery a la Tina Turner or James Brown (also brought back to hitsville via a film), Little Richard wound up in a severe automobile accident, landing him in traction in a L.A. hospital. While there, although details are still unclear, he was apparently introduced to a form of Judaism through Bob Dylan, and it is in this state that we found Richard when the interview took place: full of excitement about his return to entertainment yet equally anxious to spread the word about his latest religious turn. Little Richard is very concerned that he be viewed as a good guy.

Little Richard's responses in the following Q&A are exactly as he spoke them. The grammar has been left intact, the inaccuracies and cloudy runarounds also left alone. Even getting Little Richard to speak about the old days was difficult because, like many artists, he was more interested in what he's doing now. But he did touch on some of the history, and for what it's worth, his perspective is at least interesting.

The interview which follows represents, we hope, as best a brief conversation can, the state of one of the great rockers of all time, Little Richard, in 1987. Sure, there's plenty more we wanted to ask about – *The Girl Can't Help It,* anecdotes about the infamous Beatles tour, how he got his hair like that – but when you're offered an interview with Little Richard you take what you can get, and you relish every thrilling minute of it.

Goldmine: *Do you consider your new album, Lifetime Friend, a return to rock 'n' roll?*

Little Richard: I call it the message sound in rhythm. I liked the job that Dan Hartman did with "Great Gosh A'Mighty" in the film (*Down And Out In Beverly Hills*) and I really wanted to stay in that type of sound. It was today.

What do you really mean by "the message sound in rhythm"?

It's like Bruce with "War" or Michael Jackson's new album. It means that in the world that we live in today, young people as well as the old, in all races, creeds and colors, needs a message. There's so many uncertainties today, the world is so chaotic, everywhere you look is chaos, so I think we need a message now. A message of love, a message of hope. And a message of anti-drugs, to let people know it doesn't pay to be a drug addict like I have been. You need to instill in people that they can make it. Like the homeless, the people on the streets, they have to know that somebody cares, so I have a song on the album called "Someone Cares." My album is anti-drugs, just to let them know that they can make it.

So you don't consider this rock 'n' roll?

I call it a return to recording, a return to entertainment. I want my music to have a message, although it is rhythmic. I stay out of the political arena but there are some terrible things happening, and we need to share – love. I'd like to tour with Bruce and Bob Seger and Paul (McCartney) together. We all need each other, we're all sisters and brothers regardless of race, creed or color. So we need to help each other. In this generation we need to show love. We don't need to pull the clock back, we need to go forward. The album does rock, but it's the message.

Why did you decide to go back into the studio after taking so many years off?

Well, my mother passed away and I had been sitting around so many years without doing anything. Paul Mazursky had brought me back into the studio to do *Down And Out In Beverly Hills*, for which I'm very grateful, and the thing with Dan Hartman, "Great Gosh A'Mighty." So I said it's time, I still have a voice, I still play piano, so I should go and do something while I'm still able to do something. I'm sorry I waited so long. There were other offers.

In the interview you did for your record company bio, you said one of the reasons you wanted to record again was show people like Jerry Falwell and Jimmy Swaggart that rock 'n' roll can have a positive message.

I don't know much about them. What's those names you say?

Jerry Falwell and Jimmy Swaggart. (Author's note: The quote from Richard in the bio reads, "You know, people like Jimmy Swaggert [sic] and Jerry Falwell are comin' down so hard on rock 'n' roll. Maybe clean lyrics can make a difference.")

I don't know much about them. They never booked me or nothing. I don't really know them. I heard that one of those guys is Jerry Lee Lewis' cousin. *(Author's note: Swaggart is.)* I never heard their message. I believe in going to worship on Saturday mornings. I believe in the Sabbath, the seventh day. I believe that the Commandments are just as fine as the day God gave them to Moses. And I believe in Eden. I think it's time we start living by the Ten Commandments and keeping the Sabbath. And I believe that I'm still a messenger for God. I don't know much about those guys, I haven't heard anything about them.

Do you consider yourself Jewish now?

Well, if it's not Jewish it's not you-ish. I think it's time for people to know about the Sabbath and to eat the way God has planned. I don't go bragging about my religion but I believe that the seventh day is the Sabbath. I believe that from sundown Friday to sundown Saturday I don't do anything. Everybody know that's the deal with me. And I believe that you must eat right. I don't stress what I really am but that's my belief. And it's very dear to me, it means a lot to me. When I was in Sinai Hospital and hurt so bad I was just glad I knew God. He opened the Red Sea and my life felt so great.

You've discussed this with Bob Dylan, haven't you?

Bob Dylan is a very good friend of mine. I love Bob, we're very good friends. He came to the hospital and stayed with me almost the whole day. I never know you could have pain that medicine couldn't stop,

but when I felt my leg torn up with all those pins, my bladder punctured, just to hold somebody's hand meant something. He stayed with me for hours.

Getting back to the new record, the version of "Great Gosh A'Mighty" sounds different than the one you did for the movie. Was it re-done?

Yes. The one in the movie was Dan Hartman (producing) and the one that is on the Warner Brothers record, that wasn't even supposed to be on the record. I was just showing them the song that I had did in the movie. They put that on the album and I didn't even record it for that. That really doesn't sound that together. I really didn't record that for them, I was just playing it.

Who picked Stuart Colman to produce the album?

I don't know, but I hope they don't pick him again. He's a nice guy but my preference is Lenny Waronker or Benny Medina, someone today. You want to progress, you want the kids to think this is a new record. When they hear this they're gonna say, "This is not new." You've gotta have the vision. I love Stuart but I think he doesn't have the vision; Lenny and Benny are great producers and they're today. Stuart's a good producer too, but I think he's more in the '50s than he is in the '80s. That's a good way to put it, isn't it? That's not puttin' him down. I don't wanna put him down; I think he's a beautiful guy and I appreciate his interest in me, but I would rather be produced by someone of today. That's not bad to say, is it?

Did the record company try to tell you what kind of music to do?

No, they didn't. I would like to do a rappin' song, one that's really downright rappin'. I think rappin' music is gonna become huge, bigger than what it is. I heard that Michael is comin' out with a thing with Run-D.M.C. and you know what that's gonna do.

The song "I Found My Way" on the new album is kind of a rap song.

I believe that if Lenny and Benny went back into the studio and remixed that, they could make that a rap tune today. If they could pull my voice up so you could hear what I'm saying... in fact, I would like to hear them do that. I think Warner Brothers is the greatest record company in the world; I love Warner Brothers. Mo Ostin and Lenny Waronker are the greatest people I've ever met. They stand for beautiful things.

Was it hard for you to get used to some of the new technology when you went in to record?

Oh, man! I felt lost. I'm not gonna say what I was used to, but you gotta remember when I made "Tutti Frutti" it was three tracks. Now it's all these sounds and drum machines. You don't need nobody but yourself in there. If you know how to program the thing, you got it. I see how a person like Prince, who is a

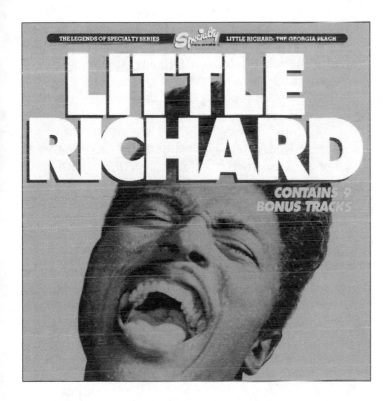

genius in his own lifetime, and a great writer and a great performer, and Michael, who is the entertainer of entertainers to me, I can see how they get that beautiful sound. I'm just learning, but I wanna go back into the studio now and make a better album because I got more hip to everything now. And with my music, the message sound in rhythm, I'd just love to do that.

Does it bother you that some of the lyrics in Prince's songs are suggestive about sex? Wouldn't you consider that negative?

I've never listened to that part of Prince. I just listen to the music. He's so creative. He's an innovator too. He's one of a kind. He's a great musician. And the same for Michael Jackson. He's one of a kind and an innovator, a great musician. He's an emancipator. To me, Michael is the new king.

How long was it before this album since you played the piano?

Oh, a long time. I love the way I'm playing on "Great Gosh A'Mighty" with Dan Hartman. On the Stuart Colman one they didn't bring it up like Dan Hartman did, to get that gut. I have to take off my hat to Dan Hartman, even though I don't wear a hat. I really liked the job he did with James Brown. He resurrected him from the dead. The same as Paul Mazursky did with me in *Down And Out*.

Did you enjoy making the movie?

Oh, yes. I'm just so grateful to Paul Mazursky for giving me that opportunity. That was just once in a lifetime. And to be with Bette (Midler) and Richard (Dreyfuss) and Nick (Nolte), that's good company. You don't have that good company at dinner. I'm

grateful for it. I would love to do more. I'd like to be on a television series. I just did a new video with a group called the Bangles.

What about going out on the road and touring? It's been a lot of years since we've seen you play live.

Oh, yes, I'm going to tour this year. First I'm going to do a few commercials. Then I'd like to do some dates with ZZ Top, one or two things with him (sic). I'm putting everything together now. Then I'd like to do an HBO special.

Will you still do your old hits when you perform?

We're still negotiating about everything. The old hits are in a suit now because I never made any money with my old records. Never, nothing at all. I just wish someone would come forward and make me an offer and give me something for it. We're still in litigation for it. So there's some things I can't say.

How do you feel now about those early records you made for Specialty?

I think they're the greatest I've heard. And they're still popular, more popular than ever. I just talked to one radio station and she said I'm the most requested on the station. ATV bought the music and I just wish they'd make a settlement with me. That's my prayer. I just wish they'd give me $100,000 or two, $200,000 or $300,000. That ain't gonna hurt nobody. If they would do that, I would be grateful. I'd feel compensated a little bit.

Do you consider your music now to be gospel music?

No, I consider gospel to be Shirley Caesar or Al Green, which is not my bag. It's strictly black. I'm not against that but I think you should be for all people. My music is contemporary, it's the message sound. My music does rock. It will always move. I want my music to be full of rhythm. I'm not into that screaming thing. But if I'm talking about love, I want it to be a good message. If I'm talking to people on the street I want to give them a good message. Whatever it is I want to be wholesome. My music isn't screaming like Shirley and all them. That's not my kinda thing. I'll tell you what Id like, I'd like for the stations to be playing my album. They haven't picked it up. I'd like to see the black stations as well as the Top 40 stations play it. "Somebody's Comin'," the new single, and "I Found My Way," I'd appreciate it if they'd play it.

Does it bother you that the record hasn't been on the charts?

Oh, yeah. And it bothers me that it's not being played. It bothers me greatly. You say, "What have I done wrong?" You know, I try to be right with everybody and you have friends on the stations that's your buddies. You eat with them every day, so you don't know what's wrong, and you say, "Oh, my God, what have I done?"

Was it better back in the '50s? Weren't there still black stations and white stations until guys like you and Chuck Berry started getting played on the pop stations?

That's right, but back then you had to get broken on the black stations first. Then the Top 40 stations would pick you up, like Alan Freed, who was a great person and a good friend. Jocks like Dr. Jive, King Bee, Rodney Jones would have to start playing it first. A lot of black jocks and programmers and promotion men didn't get credit back then for what they did. Or black heads of record companies. Now they do and I'm grateful to see it. I just hope they don't forget about their brother Richard.

What kind of radio stations did you listen to when you were growing up in Macon, Ga.?

I used to listen to a station out of Nashville called WLAC. It had a guy named Gene Nobles and I listened to him. That's where I first heard "Tutti Frutti" after I recorded it. My mother didn't know that my name was Little Richard. It came on and I said, "Mother, that's me." I had snuck off and recorded it. That was a big thrill.

You had recorded before that for RCA though.

I recorded for RCA in 1950. (*Author's note: It was actually 1951.*) That was for Camden. If you was black it was called Camden Records, and if you were white it was called RCA Victor. I was with them before Elvis came to them. Elvis came to them in '55. I had already recorded rock for them but they didn't push me. Then from there I went to Peacock Records in Houston and did some work with Don Robey. Johnny Otis was recording for him and Willie Mae Thornton. She did "Hound Dog" about three years after that. (*Author's note: Thornton actually recorded the song in 1952, before Richard came to Peacock.*) When I first got to RCA they were calling me the originator of rock 'n' roll, the king of rock 'n' roll. I was the first person to record that kind of music. I had never heard that kind of music. I was so different there wasn't nobody that would want to touch me. The bands didn't want to play with me because they said, "Man, the way you play, there ain't nobody want to hear that." They wanted blues, and I was rockin'. Even Chuck Berry was playing blues at the time. He was playing stuff like Muddy Waters. I was the only one doin' all that ravin' and screamin' and everybody thought I was a lunatic. So they said, "This man is the architect, he's the originator of rock 'n' roll."

Lloyd Price supposedly told you to send a demo to Specialty.

Right. I was on Peacock, and he said, "Man, why don't you send a record to Specialty?" So I sent a blues. I said maybe I'll just start singing the blues 'cause there ain't nobody listenin' to this other stuff.

So I sang a blues called "Wonderin'" and I sent it to Art Rupe at Specialty. He sent Bumps Blackwell a year later to meet me in New Orleans, at Cosimo's studio (J&M, run by Cosimo Matassa).

Bumps Blackwell arranged all the musicians for the sessions, right?

Yes, Bumps Blackwell got Lee Allen and Earl Palmer and Red Tyler. This same band recorded with Fats, but they recorded a different type thing with Fats. Fats was more like country blues.

There have been rumors over the years that people like Larry Williams and Huey "Piano" Smith actually played the piano on some of those Specialty records.

No, that's not true. They never played piano on my records. I always played. In fact, I didn't know Huey Smith that well. And Larry Williams, I put Larry in show business. Larry, Jimi Hendrix, James Brown, Otis Redding, Joe Tex, the Beatles, Mick Jagger – those people started with me. I started them. I never knew that Larry Williams could play the piano like that. Or Huey Smith. They wasn't famous then and nobody was allowed in the studio. It wasn't but three tracks in like a little kitchen. We had to squeeze in to sing. No, that was a lie, the same as it was a lie that I got my hairstyle from Esquerita. That was a mistake in printing and we went back to the printing company on that. Esquerita copied me. Now I did learn to play some things from Esquerita on the piano. Esquerita just died two weeks ago in New York. (*Editor's note: Actually, Esquerita died October 23, 1990, over three years after this piece first appeared in print. He was probably ill at the time of the interview, but he was not dead. He died of complications resulting from the AIDS virus. He was 55.*)

Billy Wright is another person who was supposed to have influenced you.

Now, Billy Wright is a good friend of mine. He's still alive in Atlanta. He's an older guy but he's still there.

A lot of your songs have co-writer's credit, people like Enortis Johnson and John Marascalco. Who were these people?

Well, back then a lot of the songwriting credits were taken from me. Like John Marascalco was my chauffeur, a white guy out of Mississippi. He came to me with bunch of words and I wrote the songs but I didn't have sense enough to get no crediting. Like "Rip It Up." I wrote the songs, I put the melody to all the songs but I didn't get no credit. I didn't know.

What's the story behind "Long Tall Sally"? Enortis Johnson was supposedly a teenaged girl that walked from Mississippi to New Orleans to get the song to you.

I did that but I didn't get credit I should get, because of Bumps Blackwell. I'm a writer, and when somebody brings a song to me I changes it. All they brought to me was words on paper. Now, "Slippin' And Slidin'," I did that by myself. They didn't have nothing to do with that. (*Author's note: Three other writers besides Penniman are given co-credit.*) Same with "Tutti Frutti." She (Dorothy LaBostrie, who is credited with having changed Richard's obscene original lyrics to the familiar words) shouldn't have gotten any credit for that. But I couldn't do nothing about it. I did the writing. The record company had nothing to do with it (the co-crediting). That was Bumps, the producer, and the writer. Art Rupe had nothing to do with it. At the time I don't think Bumps really knew that much about the business either.

What's your personal favorite of all the old songs?

"Lucille."

Why that one?

Because it sounds like a choo-choo train. The train used to run in front of my house in Macon. I was glad to write about it.

You always had the best scream in rock 'n' roll. It was one of your trademarks. How did you come up with that?

That was from Marion Williams (the gospel singer).

Out of all the covers that were done of your songs, which is your favorite?

I have two favorites. One is Paul (McCartney's) "Long Tall Sally" and the other was Otis Redding's version of "Lucille." And my other favorite was Sam Cooke with "Send Me Some Lovin'."

One last rumor to clear up: that Art Rupe actually speeded up some of the tapes to make the records faster.

If he ever did I never noticed it. We were going pretty fast in the studio. My fingers was about to break. They did a lot of things in the studio but that had nothing to do with the creativity, of making up the song itself or the rhythm.

Did you prefer recording or performing onstage back in the old days?

I liked both. I was like Prince is now. I was a creator in the studio plus I was an innovator. I would take chances and try things. Which I'd like to do in this generation. I hope that some record company will give me that opportunity. And I'm still with God. I'm still a messenger and my music is the message sound and I thank everybody for everything and I would appreciate if they would go and get *Lifetime Friend.*

Would you agree that yourself and some of the other early rockers helped break down the racial barriers in the United States?

Oh yes, we were like the Martin Luther Kings in music. You wouldn't hear people like Michael or Diana Ross if it hadn't been for me. I broke the ice for them and Prince, Whitney Houston, Janet Jackson, Tina Turner. I opened the door. I'd appreciate if I could do a duet with one of them.

One last question before we go: When the history of Little Richard is written, how would you like to be remembered?

As the originator and creator of rock 'n' roll. And as someone who had God and kept the Sabbath. God bless you.

Most Collectible 45

"Taxi Blues"/ "Every Hour," RCA Victor 47-4392, $900.

Most Collectible LP

Here's Little Richard, Specialty 100, $700.

Recommended Introduction

Little Richard: The Georgia Peach, Specialty 7012 (the definitive one-disc Little Richard collection, it has 25 of his original Specialty recordings, including all the most important ones)

If you want to hear more...

Little Richard Vol. 2: Shag On Down By The Union Hall, Specialty 7063 (24 more Specialty tracks)

Little Richard: The Specialty Years (a 3-CD box set containing everything he recorded for Specialty, including alternate takes of many songs)

The Formative Years 1951-53, Bear Family 79005-11544-8 (German import, contains 18 of his pre-Specialty recordings for RCA Victor and Peacock)

God Is Real, Peacock Gospel Classics 12005 (reissue of 10 spirituals and hymns recorded in 1959, during the first time he turned away from rock 'n' roll)

Carl Perkins

by Ken Michaels and Tom Frangione

Carl Perkins will forever be known as the composer and original performer of the 1956 hit "Blue Suede Shoes." But his influence goes far beyond that song, which Elvis Presley quickly covered and made almost his own. On their official releases, the Beatles didn't do a lot of remakes. But they saw fit to do their own versions of three Carl Perkins originals, more than any other composer not named John Lennon, Paul McCartney or George Harrison. Those were "Matchbox," which actually made the U.S. Top 20 in 1964; "Honey Don't"; and "Everybody's Trying To Be My Baby." The Fabs did Perkins' "Sure To Fall" as part of their audition for British Decca on January 1, 1962; they are also known to have performed "Lend Me Your Comb," "Glad All Over" (not the song the Dave Clark Five made popular) and, of course, "Blue Suede Shoes." In later years, Perkins recorded with all three surviving Beatles at one point or another and was widely recognized for his role in popularizing rock 'n' roll. He died January 19, 1998. This interview, among Perkins' last, appeared in the November 6, 1998 issue of Goldmine. And no, there's nothing missing; the two interviewers were chatting off-the-cuff with Perkins before the formal interview started when he broke into song. At that point, they turned on their tape recorder…

Carl Perkins: ...sitting over here in my black leather chair (singing) "I'll be over there while you're over here... we're in love, so have no fear." He said, "Carl, that's a good song!" I said, "Well, hush, and I'll sing it to you! (Laughing) So I did. That's the first song... when I got over to George's house, I sang it for him, and he said, "Wow, man, that's a beautiful song." I had a couple of other things, and I was open for whatever he wanted to do. He kept going back, and he said, "Sing 'That Distance Again,'" and I said, "Sure," and he said "Man, let's do that one." So we buckled down and he played. I played a couple of different guitar parts, he played the piano, he played rhythm, he played slide, he played everything on there. We did everything except the drum, and that boy that plays with Steve Winwood...

Goldmine: Jim Capaldi...

Jim. That's right! Wonderful fellow, he was in the studio with us a couple of the three days I was there. We had a really good time. George worked awfully hard on this thing, he sang all those harmony parts himself, I think he really poured his heart and soul into it. He meant for it to sound great and I'm so proud of that, I really am. I think that there's no question that it's up there with the work that McCartney did on his song that he re-did, you know. Paul and I cut this song "My Old Friend" in 1981, and then he re-sang it again and sent me a newer copy of it about, it could be years ago, and then when I played over in London for the Buddy Holly event for him last year for a couple of days, I told him that I was thinking about releasing it, because through the years he's asked me on several occasions "Man, what are you going to do with 'My Old Friend,' Carl, it's a great song?" I'd say, "I don't know, Paul, one of these days I might release it, so I told him over there that I was thinking about it. I said, "Are you happy with it?" He said, "No, no, I'd really love to work on it some more, I'd like to definitely re-sing my part, and do some more work on the music, and I said well, how about it? So in April, he did that, and sent it to me, and it just blew me away. He sang so great on the thing, he put so much more on it than was there, guitar, it just absolutely a perfect set to me. And I think George's song is right up there with him. I know both of these boys just absolutely gave it 100 percent. They really did.

Carl, on "My Old Friend," you told a story that I haven't told Ken yet, that I think should come from you, about Paul's reaction when you first played that for him down in Montserrat.

Well, it was something that I'll never live long enough to forget. It happened in February of 1981 and as the world all knows, and never will forget, in December of 1980 when John Lennon was taken away from us, and so this was the following year, in February. I wrote the song about and for Paul McCartney. I did it because he was so kind to invite me down to this beautiful island of Montserrat with Stevie Wonder. Ringo was there, just had a wonderful time. I flew down by myself. Paul and Linda met me with a jeep on the (center) airfield with a little single-engine plane and took me across the mountains – we were like kids again, and it was a wonderful time, and I wanted to do... I didn't want to cry when I left after staying down there, and I'm a big crybaby! If something moves me, I'll just choke up... I can't talk about it. I thought that would happen, so the night before, I just wrote how I felt on the isle of Montserrat on every shelf, forget a country boy with a guitar and a song you invited me, and you treated me like kin, and you've given me a reason to go on. So my old friend, think about me every now and then. I sang it for Paul, at about 10 the next morning, I was scheduled to leave flying again in the little single engine aircraft to the island of Antigua where I was flying commercial back to Atlanta and on to Nashville and back to Jackson, where I live here. I sang it, he said "Carl, it's beautiful... would you sing it again?" and I said, "Sure, man." He said "wait just a minute," and he got Linda in there, and they sat on the floor, I sat on his old Fender twin reverb amplifier, with a guitar, I did however notice a microphone over there. I didn't pay that much attention to it, but George Martin recorded it and after I finished singing the song to Paul, he was crying, tears were rolling down his pretty cheeks, and they're pretty to me just like they are to the rest of the world. I think he's a very handsome boy and always did. He's even handsomer when he's crying. And Linda said, "Carl, thank you so much." I said, "Linda, I'm sorry... I didn't mean to make him cry." She said, "But he's crying and he needed to. He hasn't been able to really break down since that happened to John." I mean he stepped outside of the room, out by the pool, and he just had his handkerchief out, and he was going at it. And she put her arm around me and said, "But how did you know?" I said, "Know what, Linda? I don't know what you're talking about?" She said "There's two people in the world that know what John Lennon said to Paul, the last thing he said to him. Me and Paul are the only two that know that, but now there's three and one of them's you... you know it. I said, "Girl, you're freaking me out! I don't know what you're talking about! She said the last words that John Lennon said to Paul in the hallway of the Dakota building were... he patted him on the shoulder, and said, "Think about me every now and then, old friend."

That's just amazing...

And she said, here you are, that's what you just sang, and how did you know? And I said I didn't know it, gosh, I didn't know it. But McCartney really feels that Lennon sent me that song, he really does.

That's truly an amazing story, Carl.

Well, I'll tell you, here's something that's happened since I've told this story. In Nashville. This song, "Distance Makes No Difference With Love," I never wrote that song down. I sat and made it up, looking at my wife. The next day, no more than three days after that I got on a plane, now remember, I have not written this song down, I didn't take it to England written down in my mind. I put my wife on George Harrison's couch and sang it again to her in front of him and it was exactly the same words that I sang. I usually have to write a song down to remember it. I really do. I don't take a chance – if I like it, I'll scribble it down on anything. If I don't have proper paper, I'll write on anything. I'll take a scratch out of my billfold.

Kind of like the "Blue Suede Shoes" lyrics.

There you go – on a potato sack.

On a potato sack that we see in the new album Go Cat Go, which is a fine album, Carl. We'll be talking about that in just a few minutes.

Well, thank you very much, but, I told George about the McCartney happening, I really did, when I saw that he liked the song. Well, Paul has told me he said, "John will come back, there'll be another thing that'll hit you someday and analyze it... don't throw it away... it may have something. I know how you are... you write them, throw them away... don't do it... hold on to it!" Interesting. Well, this "Distance Makes No Difference" is another song that came exactly the same way. I couldn't forget it if I tried! And I never could forget "My Old Friend" – I've never written it down.

That's truly remarkable.

And George said, "Hey man, if John sent it to you, he sent you a good one."

He sent you a dandy, that's for sure. (Perkins laughs.) Well, John Lennon was known to say that the songs he appreciates the most of his own material are the ones that come to him very quickly.

That's true.

That are very inspirational.

That's right

And so these are two fine examples... just like that.

I am never going to be guilty of saying that I don't believe in spirits on this earth, I do. Lennon is gone, we know that, but he's alive on this earth, his spirit is. Elvis Presley is another one – he's alive on this earth, he's deep within the hearts of his fans, they talk to him, so you know I wasn't raised to believe in ghosts in spirits, that's not what this is. This is a power that some people possess, and I wish I could say I could recognize it immediately. I think we recognize it a lot when they have been here and gone, more so than while they're living. But I really got interested and started to read about the mind and people who really have special qualities of being able to speak in a way that it moves people around them, you know? Lennon was one of those people. Paul McCartney is one of those people. Ringo, bless his heart, he's certainly far from being a dummy. This guy plays his role in life and he does a hell of a job with it.

Yeah, we should all be such dummies.

Yes sir...you'd better believe it (Laughing).

Carl, we will talk a little bit more about the album. One of the other things that your fans, myself chief among them, is very excited about this year is the publication of Go Cat Go, your autobiography, written with David McGee. I thought it was a splendid book, and as I say, I do consider myself among your chief fans. And there was stuff in here that I never knew about your personal life, but even about your professional career. There were some things in the book that I want to ask you about.

Sure.

In terms of some of the personal side.

That's the side that's hard to tell. That's the deep secrets you'd like to bury.

We won't be asking for any gory details.

Well, I'll answer anything you ask me. I've told it all in the book, as much as I can remember. I shared a lot about alcohol, that had me beat down and almost into the ground.

That's an interesting story, about the Pacific Ocean element. I wonder if you could share that with us.

I started out playing in honky-tonks around the West Tennessee area, and man, I was well into alcohol when I cut my first record. I never cut a record without drinking. That was part of it. There was a jug sitting on the floor of Sun Records. If you could keep Sam Phillips out of it, you could have a snort every once in a while. I mean, that was a part of it. It wasn't that way with Elvis. He didn't use it, but a lot of the cats down there did. And I guess me, more than anybody, 'cause I came right out of these honky-tonks. I always felt that if I had a big slug out of a jug I was playing better, but I really wasn't. But nevertheless, it got to be a part of me. It was part of my life, I lived it every day, I drank every day, I tried to hide it from people, but it don't write good songs, it can't play good guitar, it does no good on stage, and it will ruin your life, and it almost destroyed me and it wasn't until I started working with Johnny Cash in 1965-1966 and it was being there with the Statler Brothers, Maybelle Carter, rest her soul, and the Carter family, and none of these people drank, so I felt safe. I had a pretty fair job, and I stayed for ten years. Johnny Cash has admitted in his book about his drug problem We quit at about the same time. Within a few days of each other, and propped up on each other. Many nights John would say, "Carl, are you going to take a drink tonight?" and I'd say, "Are you going to take a pill?" "Nope!" "Well, I ain't either." It was a helping situation, I do believe, and we talk about it since then from both of us. It wasn't until I started digging out of the bottle that I realized how far down I was. I was a total nervous wreck, I'd try to go out on the stage, I shook like a leaf. It was terrible, but I got through it. I prayed in the back of his bus. I thought I was dying! I said, "I don't want to die out here and leave my sweet wife and my four little children, please Lord, help me get home, and then you take me, but let me see them, one more time," and I was very sincere about it. And I happened to sit up on the side of the bed in the back of the bus, and I saw my little brown case that I carried my shaving equipment in, and I always kept a bottle of whiskey in there, too – a pint fit perfect in it. I popped that zipper open there was a pint three-fourths full and whoa, baby. And I was so excited, I popped the top, I got it in smelling distance of my nose, and that's where it hit me. Something very clear said to Carl Perkins, "I was going to get you home... you asked me, and I was going to do this. But if you drink this bottle that you're holding in your hand, you're on your own." And I put the lid back on it, crawled out of the bus, and I can remember so well, throwing that bottle into the Pacific Ocean. I walked back, and there were two sets of tracks – the one going towards the ocean, is as crooked as a snake. I was so weak. I was still heavily under the influence of it, but it was dying down, as it will. The tracks coming back to the bus looked like they were laid off with a tape measure, just straight as an arrow. I knew that it was over, and I tell that story in the book, and I tell it for one reason only. I'm not proud. I'm not proud for the world to know that I was weak enough to almost have my home destroyed, almost my life, my music, my friends, hurt because they all knew I was drinking too much but loved me and didn't want to hurt my feelings by telling me. I said that if there's one young boy or girl out there that wants to strap a guitar or an instrument around their shoulder and say I want to make my living, I want them to know what can happen to you, and what almost happened to Carl Perkins. My music suffered as a result of too much alcohol. No question. At one time there might have been several "Blue Suede Shoes" in me, but I flooded them out. And I know I look back at it now, I did it. There's no question about it. So I felt that if I could share that with some of the kids that might read that book, they'd say, whoa! This won't be me.

A couple of other things related to your career that crop up in the book that are addressed in passing are a couple of what I would think are major career milestones for you. I'm thinking specifically of the Rocka-

billy session in 1986, your 30th anniversary special. In the book, you really don't delve that much into how that came about, or what when into preparing that. With all the hoopla that surrounded it, and it was so critically acclaimed, and it holds up. I watch that periodically at this point. It was a terrific show.

There really wasn't a lot of preparation for that. I got a hold of these people, I asked them, they said, "Sure, man, we'd love to." George Harrison said, "I'd love to." Paul McCartney was out of England at that time, and I believe he would have done it. I believe the three Beatles would have been on that show. I honestly, really believe that Paul would have been right on there. He did offer, after it was over, he said, "Man, let's go to the south of France or anywhere you want to go, and we'll film it. And you can put it in there." I said, "Paul, it will look like it was put in there."

It sure would have.

I got on an airplane with my son Stan, and I went to George Harrison's house, we sat down, and we talked about it. He was very nervous. He hadn't done anything live in a long time. I got a lot of help from Olivia, his wife, who said, "George, you'll do great! You'll do great, don't worry about it." He said, "I don't know, I don't know." I said, "I do – you're gonna knock them out!" And he was very nervous about it, but he said "I'm going to do it."

That's great

So what we did, our Cinemax people from New York rented a little rehearsal hall over in some building in downtown London and we didn't rehearse, we started playing, because when Greg and I, we got a

cab from our hotel where we were staying, and we were a little bit late when, walking up the steps, I'm hearing, "Honey, Don't." I'm hearing Clapton's guitar playing. I said, "Hey, Greg, they're already here. We were supposed to meet at 2 p.m., and them cats were hooked up an' pickin' and I just went it and I hugged them, you know, and I don't think they ever stopped playing, and I plugged in going right with them. We sat there and played old Perkins stuff for an hour or two. The Cinemax people, the three cats that came over there, one of them called me off and said, "hey, you need to really get to rehearsing the show." I said "What show?" He said, "the one you're going to film tomorrow night." I said, " Don't you think you're looking at a pretty damn good show here?" And he went berserk. He said, "No way, man... you've evidently never done a professional big show. This is a big show!" I said, "You're damn right. It's going to be big, 'cause I ain't listening to you. I didn't send for you. I made the deal with Cinemax to give them what I call Carl Perkins and friends. I think we're going to call it a Rockabilly session." He said, "That's true, but we're here to see that it's done properly. You've got to give us the times on these songs. You have to rehearse it right down to the minute." I said, "No you don't... not this show you don't."

Have rockabilly what it should be – an exact science.

I did, and they all three got mad, they said, "We must have a meeting." I said, "I don't want to meet with you. I'm going to play with my friends. I came over here to do that. You talk all you want to." He said, "What will they be wearing? It's a must! We want to do this with tuxedos and everybody's got to be fit," and I said, "No you don't. I ain't going to ask my friends – Clapton, Harrison, all these people – I ain't going to tell them what to wear, and I ain't going to tell them what to sing." And actually, nothing was rehearsed. The only time that tape was stopped was when they set the stools up there for them to sit down on. And I swear to you, I had no idea of what I was gonna say, I turned to them and said, "my, my, you look like a bunch of little schoolchildren with your new shoes on," and that was all ad-libbed. Everything about that show was people doing what pickers like to do – smiling, rockin' and cuttin' that music to the bone.

I think that's the best part of the show – that little schoolhouse session in the circle.

There you go!

It comes across loud and clear.

Well, it was not rehearsed. The hellos, the good-byes. They had me sayin' "Hello Ladies and Gen-tle-men... I am Carl Perkins." I said, "Hell, if they don't know who I am they will if they keep that thing on for a minute." I just want to do it my way, and George and the guys

heard me tell these guys that, and they told me later, "Hey man, you just flat stuck to it and we tried to stay with you," and I said, "God bless you, you did." They all played their hearts out. They looked so great. I was always so proud of that. I said more about it than was actually printed. What I did with that book is that David would come down twice a week and he'd turn on a record, and he'd ask me questions and I would answer them. He did, however, tell me, "Don't edit your brain." I said, "I don't know how much I've got, and I sure don't know what you're talking about editing." He said, "If I asked you a question, and you forget the answer, don't stop talking. Go into the shadows of your mind, and that's where the story will be. You'll run into something you've forgotten about." So there was more talk about that particular session than what he took out and wrote about. He took the facts as I would tell them. He'd then condense it cause in the end he had way over a hundred hours of Carl Perkins talking, and that's how I'd talk about my childhood, and he'd write that, and he'd send me proofs of things, and I'd say, you wrote too long here or there. I kind of helped edit the thing. But that special was meant to be, and it was meant to be done the way it was. And I'm proud I was man enough to tell the cats at Cinemax to get out of my way and turn on the camera and that's the way it was going to be, 'cause the other guys – everybody that was a part of that show – appreciated me standing up for them, and saying get the hell out of here, and turn it on or off, I don't care. I'm here with my friends – you want it, get it. And that's what happened.

Certainly no one could argue with the end result. The end result was just truly remarkable.

I really liked the smiles they gave each other, the hugs at the end of the show. How can you rehearse that? It was really off the cuff, and if I do another one, it'll be off the cuff.

One other story I'd like to talk about that's in the book before Ken takes over here and talks a little about the album was The Beatles session back in 1964. Clearly, they held you in high regard. They covered three of your songs which is as many as they had covered by anyone else. The story in there about when you went over to England and kind of found a new audience through the kids listening to the Beatles and John inviting you over to the recording studio – I wonder if you could tell us a little bit about that night. You mentioned something in the book about an after-hours jam session; I was wondering if any of that got committed to tape or if there are songs that you guys worked on that we should know about.

I wish I could surprise you and say, "Man, there's a spool of tape over there that happened." I can't say that. The night that I went to the party and first met those guys at the end of a tour, I'd been over there with Chuck Berry. I knew them, sort of. By that I mean my children were coming home from school "(sings)...I Want to Hold Your Hand...Yeah, yeah, yeah." and I said, "them little boys look like girls." I was pickin' at my boys, 'cause I knew they loved them, and I'm going to say the truth is, Daddy did too. I heard some old Sun Record-quality sound in that song "I Want To Hold Your Hand," the first thing I ever heard from them.

It reminded you of a Sun record?

Yes, it sure did. The George Harrison guitar playing on there. I told them and they acted like they were proud to hear it. I said, "I don't know if you cats are trying to or not, but you sound like...you've got a little roar in your records that sounds a lot like the old Sun records."

What did you think of George as a guitarist?

I thought he was very good. I didn't understand why he ever said he copied anything from me, 'cause if he did, he dressed it up. I never recognized it, I really, truly, never did. And I told him that, and he said, "Well, where do you think this came from?" And sitting together, he showed me some things, and I said, "George, that's not exactly the way I did that." I didn't recognize that as being something I had already done. And I was very truthful with him. I had no reason to tell a lie to him. I just noticed the tone of their records. Paul's bass was electric, but it had a sound like the big old booming bass fiddles did at Sun Studios, on some of the stuff that came out of Sun. To me, it did, and I told him that. They seemed very happy about it. That didn't bother them at all.

OK, so back to the session.

The thing that really got me was that night after we had dinner in somebody's home I was so scared. I said, "Those are the boys that are so hot in America," and I said it looks like the one called Ringo and it was. It was him. There I sat 'til three o'clock in the morning, flat on the floor, and John, Paul, George and Ringo on a couch, and they're asking me about old songs, right stringing, wrong yo-yo, all that stuff, and I said, "How'd y'all know about this?" "We've got them, we've got all your old stuff." I said, "You've got to be kidding." "No man, we've got it. We know what you've done." And I was surprised, yet I was very happy that they had listened to my stuff, knew me, and treated me like somebody they'd known a long time and they really did. They invited me that night to Abbey Road the next night, and I went. And we did play some together before Ringo asked me, he said, "Mr. Perkins, do you mind if I record some of your songs?" and I thought I heard him, and I said, "Did you ask me, you want me to write you some songs?" He said "Well, yes sir, that too, but I sure would like to

do some of your old songs and I just thought I'd ask you." I said, "Man, I'd love for you to!" and he jumped up and said "Hey guys, he don't care!" He went straight to the drums and they kicked off "Honey Don't." I knew they had been playing it before then, because it was so rehearsed. They just hit it, right on the nose, and in between some takes there, I played a few little things – I don't remember. George would ask me about certain runs and I picked up a guitar and showed him. I've never heard anything that we played together in that studio. I just always assumed the button wasn't pushed, because again I say I never heard a record they ever put out during that time that I was on, but it was an experience that I've lived with for a long time. I'll die with it. Few people got to be around these boys in that environment where they were playing their music, cutting their songs, doing some old Perkins things. I was the happiest old man in the world. Let's face it, I was a lot younger then, but I was really thrilled. It's been an honor all the way through for Carl Perkins to say what I feel about these guys, and not because of entirely music. That's not all it. I've found them to be really good human beings. I gave Jamie one of my fine old Fender guitars for his 16th birthday and he is learning to play that thing; I gave Dhani a guitar when he was 16.

These are Paul and George's children.

Yeah, and Paul told me, he said, "Man, he loves it. When he got that guitar, he just started living with it. So he is really blossoming out to be a picker." Paul said, "You know what we need to do? We need to get our kids together in the studio. Jamie loves to hear Stan and Greg play." (He calls his daddy "Pop.") He said, "Pop, them boys can play rockabilly!"

They sure can. I've had the pleasure of seeing you perform at the Lone Star a couple of years ago, which is another story that's in the book that just touched me personally, that you had cited the two gigs that you did in 1993 at the Lone Star as kind of pivotal dates in your recent career. We had the pleasure of talking with you that night, Ken and I, and I gotta tell you, you wowed them that night. There was no doubt about that.

I got some good little guys. I'm so proud of them. They work their hearts out behind me. We just came back. We flew all the way to Geneva, Switzerland. The concert totally sold out. The next night we were in Zurich, Switzerland. We went by train, I requested that. I wanted to see those mountains and that country by train, and then we got back on the plane and flew home. We were tired, but it was wonderful two days. Just absolute standing room only big places we played, and those kids were rocking. It was awesome.

It was awesome. I remember you opened that night with "Got My Mojo Workin'.

Yeah! Yeah!

To put a real perspective on this, you and my dad are the same age, and I just couldn't picture my dad up there singing, "Got My Mojo Workin'"

(Laughter...)

I just don't think it would fly, with all due respect to my dad. That night was truly a great show. Stan and Greg were in fine form as was the rest of your band. There's one other Perkins that shows up on the new album, a DJ Perkins – that's Deborah Joy?

That's my daughter.

We noticed her in the credits, and said, "Wow, yet another." As well as Steve Perkins.

She started writing great lyrics. She's not much on melodies, but she has been writing for years. She's written them, stacked them up, and her mama got to telling me about some of the stuff she wrote. So I think she's going to swing around now to become a really good writer. She's got some good stuff.

Carl, if I may, I'd like to talk about the new album now, and Tom and I are in agreement here, on a scale of zero to ten, we rank your new album about one hundred.

(Laughter)

No, I'm serious about this, because every song just sounds great.

Well, thank you.

And there's a certain consistency to every single track.

Well, thank you very much. I must say I'm proud of that album. You know, I knew Paul Simon like the world knows Paul Simon. I knew he was a super talented boy, I loved his *Graceland* album, I've loved a lot of stuff he's done through the years, but I've never met him until I got him on this album, and went up to New York, spent a couple of days with him, flew him down to Sun Records, him and his son Harper, who played on that album.

Plays a terrific lead guitar.

Boy, he's a killer! Let me tell you something. I told (Paul) something, I said, "Man, you've got an awesome player in this kid." He said "I'm letting him come around, slowly." He really is a fine boy, and he's a heck of a picker, there's no doubt about it. He's very good.

Carl, what I'd like to know, first of all, is was the original concept all along of your new album, Go Cat Go, to be this star-studded album. A lot of people have been calling it your Carl Perkins Duets album. And certainly not every song is a duet, so you really can't call it a duets album, but you have so many great stars on the new album. Did you always want the album to be like this? It's sort of like a continuation of Rockabilly Sessions.

Well, let me tell you about it, and I'm going to be truthful with you gentlemen, because I found out if you tell the truth you can go to bed and forget it. If you tell a lie, you've got to remember it. (laughter) And at my age, that's a little risky. So the truth is that, through the years, and I mean literally ten to fifteen years back, I'd been getting calls from record executives, I don't mean little minor labels, I mean the big boys, that said, "Perkins," and I said, "yeah." "You're really good friends with Paul McCartney and George Harrison," and I said, "Yeah, sure I am." I knew what they were getting at. The grapevine leaked out the message of that in 1981. Well, it wasn't the grapevine. I was on Paul McCartney's *Tug of War* album. I'd say it was about that time that they started calling me, and said, "Hey man, get us a Beatle, and we'll put an album out on you." And I said, "No, you won't! I don't want charity now, and I don't want the public to think that Carl Perkins had to get a bunch of superstars to be on a record. I'd rather do without it, forever. I'm not hankering to get out there and cut a record." And that's the way I felt. Until about a year ago, and this little lady called Valda [came] in my life, just constantly, and has a lot to do with decisions I make. She said, "You know, Carl, I've been thinking about it. You've got a beautiful thing with Paul. Why wouldn't you give George the opportunity to sing with you? You're not being fair to him." I walked around in my backyard, and thought, "Well, this woman's right. I never have talked with George about doing a song with me. And then I thought, "Well, I've never asked nobody. I've been against it. I didn't want to ask them, but I've never given them the opportunity to say whether they wanted to, or whether they didn't want to."

You didn't want to put them on the spot.

And I didn't want to take my friendship and put it on the spot. And say, man will you, and he not really wanting to, but for him to say, that poor fellow, he (almost) died, he may be fixing to die, I can't say no. I just wouldn't have any part of that, and that is the truth. But the way it turned out, I got talking to the record people, and I said, "Look, if you cats want to get in touch with these people, and you want to ask them to call me if they would like to record with me, I'll do that. I will certainly talk to them, but let them know that by calling me, they are consenting to everything – that they like the song, and that they'll record with me. Because I'm not going to ask them." And I made that very clear. One man I asked, and it was the one that my wife mentioned. It was George Harrison. When I was over there (London) with McCartney at about this time last year, and I told him I was going to put that song out, which I had made up my mind that I was going to put it out, I was going to put it out on my own label. Anything, it had laid and gathered dust as long as it was going to, and I was going to put it out I

told him so. Well, when she mentioned that I hadn't given little ole sweet George a shot, George calls, and he'll talk with Valda – he really loves her. He tells me, she is such a Southern charmer, she likes to talk to him, although they've never eye to eye met. But through seeing her pictures, and through her voice on the phone, he really likes her. When she said, "You never give poor little George a chance," poor little George, poor little millionaire George (laughter). It hit me. It hurt me. It really hurt me. And so I popped a fax. Tore me a piece of paper off and said, "Dear George, I am going to release the song with Paul McCartney we talked about before. I'm offering you the opportunity, man, please let your heart give you the answer. Don't for any reason other than if you would love to, man, I'd love to do a song with you. If you're interested, let me know."

That's great.

Gentlemen, that's the way it was done, and here's the kicker, as they always is with me. There's always something strange...

And wonderful (laughter).

And very wonderful. I walked away from the fax machine, I went over and sat down in my chair. I got my little old guitar up in my arms, I was just doodling around, and here comes the (making a fax noise) "doo do do do doo." I ran back over, and in less than a hour, George Harrison had faxed me. I've got it framed in my home. "I would love to do a song with my friend, Carl Perkins...Love, George. Let me know when and where."

So I called him back, and that was it.. He's the one I did ask. The other people, like Paul Simon, said, gosh, are you kidding? I'd love to record with Carl, so they said, "Well call him, here's his home number." He called me one night, and I was actually nervous when Val said, "Carl, it's Paul Simon." I said, "You're kidding." She said, "No, it's him. I can tell by his voice." I told him when I got on the phone, I said, "Man, I don't know what to say, I'm nervous. I'm going to tell you like it is. I'm not always like this, but I'm scared. I'm in awe of your writing and your songs." He said, "I know how you feel. I feel the same way on this end." And he is such a nice fellow. He worked so hard on his song, and on a couple of more songs on there. The same thing with Tom Petty. I never met Tom.

That is a terrific record, that "Restless."

There's one cut, and that's it. He was in the men's room when we started playing that thing. He came out pulling his pants up and trying to get the zipper up, and he got one of his fingers caught in it.

(Laughter)

He came through the studio door – this is true! – he came through the studio door, and we had to cut one of the microphones back he said, cut a damn hit record, and I'm in the damn men's room. He said he'd heard it happening, and he'd said, man, I knew it was in the groove! So that's the track we used, and then he got in there and sang with me. I wrote for him, and he sang while I was there, and then he mixed it. But that's it. There was one cut of that song, and it happened when Petty was getting from the men's room to the studio, and there was a lot of laughing going on. I thought, "Man, we'll do that thing again," but the more he listened to it, he said, "Man, we'll never get that feel on there!" I said, "Yeah, but you've gotta play." He said, "No, I ain't touching it! Perkins, that's it! I'll sing on it, but that groove!" And his band is so good, these Heartbreakers, they're pickers. I said, "Guys, get in G," and I started that little ole riff (singing) don don, don don doun, and they just popped right on it and of course, the melody's simple, and the feel is all there is to it, and it was a one-take thing.

Now with (John) Fogerty, who came a couple of days later, at the same studio I had rented out there, I like blew that one at the very beginning. I had met John once or twice before. I hadn't seen him in a long time, a lot of people hadn't. He's been kind of quiet record-wise, I understand. Sure, I recognized him the minute he walked into that little break room there, and we had our handshakes and our hugs, and I was thanking him for coming, and he said, "Man, I've come to cut...let's get in there!" And there again, I had the Heartbreakers and Lee Rocker playing upright bass, they played on this cut with John. I said, "Well, what you wanna do, boy?" He said, "What do you want to do?" I said, "I don't know. I've got two or three ideas." He said, " I've got one." I said, "What's that?" He said, "Let's do 'All Mama's Children.'" I said, "Are you kidding?" He said, "No." I said, "That's the sorriest song I ever wrote."

That was before "Blue Suede Shoes?"

No, It was after "Shoes," but it was one sorry song. Johnny Cash and I were making fun of the old woman who lived in a shoe, and I said, "let's make it a Blue Suede Shoe." It was a joke thing that we wrote in the back of a car going on the road, and Sam Phillips kind of liked it, and I recorded it and it has been John Fogerty's favorite Carl Perkins song all these years. The minute I said it was the sorriest thing, he kind of had a curious look at me. He wasn't smiling. He wasn't crying, but just kind of stared at me, and said, "You've got to be joking, man." I said, "No, I ain't.. I don't think it's a very good song." He said, "Man, I totally disagree with that." You know, I'm beginning to disagree with myself. (laughter) I said, "It might be pretty good." And immediately I jumped the fence and said, "Oh, yeah, man, it's a great song." He might have turned around and walked out, because he really didn't like me saying that song was absolutely no good. He said, "I've held it in such high esteem and you don't like it?" I said, "I like it better than I did." (Laughter) You know, a man's mouth sometimes speaking the truth can shoot him out of the saddle. But John's a great guy. We had a good time, we made an attempt or two at another song we hit a lick or two on an old thing, "Your True Love," but it never jelled as well as he thought "All Mama's Children" did. All in all, I'll tell you, gentlemen, it was just a magic summer for Carl Perkins. I flew to California three or four times, I went to NY three or four times, I went to London, two or three times, and I went to Austin, Texas, a time or two. I'll look back on it for the rest of my life realizing that I was helping a little bit to put together something that I can truthfully stand and tell the world I'm not ashamed of. I'll never regret that somehow or other I got all these royalties of the music world around me. Once I had George and Paul, George gave me Ringo's private number down at the island of Barbados somewhere, and I called him, and I asked him if he'd like to be on it, and he said, "Yeah, but I ain't going to leave from down here and I ain't got no recording equipment down here." (laughter) I love that dude. I mean, he just tells it like it is. I said, "I ain't asking you to get out of the sun! Hell, I'll bring a guitar and a little recorder and I'll come down there." He said, "No, I don't want you to come down here. (Laughter) I said, "I only asked, bullhead...I'm sorry I even called you!" He said, "No, don't run off mad!" I said, "I'm not mad. I'm interfer- ing with your sunning." He said, "no, I'm just kidding you Carl, I tell you what dude, see if this sounds all right." I said, "Whatever you say." He said, "I've got a cut of "Honey, Don't" that I really like and I did it with the All-Starr Band in San Francisco. What if I have my people just send you that 48-track tape, and you do whatever you want to it." I said, "Hey man, that's great. Anything you say, whatever you want." He said, "That's alright. I'll have my people send you a tape. I'll send you a letter. You do anything you want to it. You can take me off and put yourself..." I said, "No, no I might sing a little harmony with you on that if you don't mind," He said "Do whatever you want to." So I left it like he had it, except I ducked his voice on the second verse, 'cause he insisted that I do. He said, "No, you've got to sing a verse on there now." I said I'll just sing a little harmony with you, but that's how that one came about. It was a cut that he made in San Francisco at a live concert and he's a beautiful man to let me use it and it fits. And then I thought, "Good gracious alive, I've got all three of the Beatles, I'm such a lucky man." I was in Paul Marshall's office when I was up visiting with Paul Simon, when we were writing that "Rockabilly Music" that's on this album, and I knew that Paul Marshall was the lawyer for the Lennon estate. So I talked to him on the phone. He said, "Come over, man, " So I went over there, and I was sitting in his office. I said, "You know, I know that you represent Yoko and the Lennon estate. She's got something I sure would like to use. He said, "What's that?" I said, "The version of John Lennon with The Plastic Ono Band doing "Blue Suede Shoes." I don't know her, I've never met her, he said, well, we'll find out! And he calls her from that office. He hung the phone up, and said, "You've got it!" That was the quickest, easiest thing. She sent me a personal letter saying that she'd appreciate it if I'd leave it exactly the way John recorded it. And that she felt that John would love to be on a Carl Perkins album, and would love to be in the company of the people that I had surrounding me, and said, "Good luck, Yoko." And it's beautiful. That right to knocked me for a loop, because I thought well, I'll just make that request, but that'll never happen.

Back in the Nashville show, I think you had used the term "definitive" in explaining in how you felt about

John, and he's got Eric Clapton on there, and they tear it up. They just really do.

Oh, yeah, yeah... it's great, and then it was Bob Johnson's idea to put Jimi Hendrix on there. I must admit Hendrix wasn't one of my favorite guitar players. I didn't listen to a lot of his music. But he evidently was great. He sold enough records to be categorized as such. I'm very proud that his family let me use it. The idea came from Bob Johnson.

Carl, I find it interesting that you said that John's version was the "definitive version" of "Blue Suede Shoes." For one thing, you had a Number One hit with the song.

Yeah.

And Elvis Presley is so well linked to that song as well. He used to perform it live all the time and include it in his movies.

That's true.

Why would you say that John stood out for you?

Because Elvis did it too fast. Elvis had that song a lot faster. John Lennon did that song almost word for word like I did it.

The same arrangement as well.

Exact tempo that I did, and the only version that I've got a tape over here with about 38 different versions of "Blue Suede Shoes" in Japanese, in German, in everything. Yeah! Bill Haley, Jerry Lee Lewis, Elvis – Lawrence Welk had a version of that! Believe it or not, he really did. And nobody tapped right to the exact beat. Well I did it (singing) "Well, it's one for the money... dank a dank..." I had a pause. A definite stop. John Lennon had that.

Yes, that was specific too. I understand that when they were rehearsing it on the plane on the way to Toronto, John was very specific with the band that they would perform this in the Perkins arrangement, as opposed to the Presley.

(Laughter) Well, I didn't know that. All I knew was when I heard it, I said, "Son of a gun... there is no doubt my record influenced that version of the song.

No question.

There was no question in my mind. And it's the only one that is that close, with identical phrasing. Of course, Clapton's guitar playing is 20,000 miles ahead of mine, but the record itself, John nailed the punctuations right on, he sure did. He even said, "You can do anythang"...he sure did! (laughter)

Carl, getting back to writing material. I know that you discussed "Distance Makes No Difference with Love," a few moments ago, but what I find remarkable about that particular song, which I have to say is an absolute killer for me.

Thank you.

Such a beautiful song... when I heard it, apart from the fact that George is playing his wonderful slide guitar on it.

Isn't that beautiful? God, that tone on that guitar. I was sitting in his studio crying. I bawled. I cried like a baby listening. I had earphones on, sitting just, I could touch his arm when he was doing that, and I was crying. It spoke to me with such soul. That's the prettiest slide guitar on that record that I have heard in my life.

What strikes me about that song is that it sounds like George could have written it.

I think he felt that way too. He didn't say that, but he just kept going back to it. He'd say, "Do 'Distance' again." He was so familiar. He quit saying, "Distance Makes No Difference" He said, 'Distance,' do it again." And without writing it down himself, he'd start singing right along with me after I had done that thing two or three times, he knew it. It's not a hard song to learn, especially if you're as talented as he is, and if you like a piece of material, you catch it pretty quick, and he didn't write nothing down. He knew it, right away, and I knew that he really did like the song. I was in heaven over there with him. I won't ever be able to thoroughly explain the feeling to see him so healthy, to see him happy, to see his little boy bring his girlfriend to the house. I told Olivia, "Oh God, girl, you've meant so much to his life, you've just totaled him out, and it's just wonderful." They're beautiful people. One of these days, in the early part of next year, I'm taking Valda, and I promised him, I'm going with Valda to Friar Park, with George and Olivia. We've set up for three days to talk.

Do they have enough room in that house to put you up?

(Laughter) Man. I've got to tell you. You've got to draw you a map while he's taking you to your room (laughter) or if you're as country as I am, you'll go the wrong way, and you'll never get out. It's a beautiful, beautiful place.

Getting back to a song like that, are there moments, because you have so many talented superstars on this album, when you're writing songs like that, do you ever write with the featured artists in mind? I mean like I said, "Distance Makes No Difference With Love" sounds like George could have done it himself, and "One More Shot" sounds like Tom Petty could have written it.

Well, I had Petty in my mind. I wrote that one just before I went out there, and when I sang it for him, he said, "Wow!" I said, "Is that thing worth thinking about?" he said, "Worth thinking about, nothing, that could be a hit song, Carl!" I said, "Are you kidding?" He said, "No!" So we started doing it. I did kind of have him in mind, (singing) "well, I got a song...do do do...that I gotta sing... Yeah, I wrote it with Petty in mind."

What was it like for you to write with Paul Simon, "Rockabilly Music," which is also a favorite on the album for me.

Well, it is for me too... it really is.

It sounds, again, getting back to matching the style of the other artist, it sounds like it has that Graceland feel, very sparse, guitars, very loose. So I'm wondering, when you're writing this, are you thinking at this is something that would really match Paul Simon, although the two of you did collaborate on that together anyway.

When I talked to Paul on the telephone, he said, "Hey, man, I'd like to look you in the face and talk to you, you're interesting. I always knew you would be." I said, "Well, if we're sitting down, I can look in your face. If we're standing up, I'll be looking at the top of your head (laughter). I said, "Maybe I can get up there, I'll arrange it." So in a couple of days, I called him, and said, "What about Friday," or whatever day it was, and he said, "Sure, man, it would be great." He gave me the address, so I checked into the Plaza Hotel. I spent some of their money. I stayed in the right places. I said, "Well, the record company's paying for it, so I stayed in the Plaza, I got a cab, I went over to the address he gave me, and he had a fella at the door to meet me, elevated me up to the second floor, and all of it's his home, a beautiful place overlooking Central Park. We sat there in his studio, and he said, "Man, tell me about when you started, how tough it was." I said, "It was awful." I said, "Man, I played in places where the bouncer was a linebacker. He had to be to keep them people from fighting." He said, "God, that's great. The bouncer was a linebacker, guarding the doors. Is that what he was doing?" I said, "Yeah," and he wrote it down, and he said, "Well, if they started fighting, what did you do? Did you unplug and run? I said, "No, no, we'd turn it up louder. And you've got that drumbeat, you've got that drummer hitting that fire on the drum and it seems that loud music would settle the fight down if you stopped, everybody in there started fighting." He said, "Man, that's interesting." But he was writing this stuff down, and...

And "Flookie, don't be nervous"... that's got to be a reference to Fluke Holland.

That's him! Paul said, "What was the drummer's name?" I said, "Back then, it was a boy named W.S. Holland." He said, "W.S., huh? Did he have a nickname?" I said, "Yeah, we called him Flookie... He said, "What?" I said, "Yeah." He said, "Damn, that's wonderful!" He said, "That's the greatest name for a drummer, Flookie." I said, "Well, that's what we called him!" and that's how the song was born. He picked up a little ol' tenor guitar, and I had an electric guitar of his, I didn't take one up there, and he

had a room full. So I'm playing, he had a little echoplex thing built in the amp and was fooling with that, and he was (singing) da, da da, on his high string he said, "Do you like this kind of feel?" And I said, "Oh man, yeah." He had electric drums. He set the thing to start drumming, and we were just playing along with it. And he had the first little verse written there, and he said, "Now play something," and I said, "Go to G, man, (singing) da da da da diddle da...that machine was echoing. God, I liked that sound. He said, "I like what you're doing there!" That song was just born in an hour, we were putting a little miniature tape of it down that I brought back home with me. He said, "Let's just work on it in our minds," and then we got to talking about Sun Studios. He asked me if it was still there; I said, "God, yeah... we can record there if you want to." He just really got high over that. He said, "Really?" and I said, "Sure, I don't think the equipment's very good, but I'll get a sound truck and park it out back, and it'll sound like it was cut at the Hit Factory here." So that's what we did, and I told him while I was there, because his son Harper came in, and I could tell that he played, he picked up a guitar for us, and he hit that thing. He hit some licks. And when I started to leave, I said, "Hey, bring that kid with you. That boy can pick!" A big smile broke out on Harper's face, and he was with his dad when we met the plane in Memphis. I insisted that he play. I can tell you this. He made about four passes on that song – by that I mean he took four different takes on it – and the second time that kid did it was much better than what's on that record. I'm gonna tell you the truth, it really is. Paul got it back to NY and he took a part of each one of those four times, and to me it's not as good as what that kid did the second time he made that guitar break on that thing. It was absolutely, and I noticed it. When I went back to NY and we took it to the Hit Factory, after Sheila E put the drums and percussion on it, I said, "Paul, what did you do with Harper's guitar break?" he said, "I mixed it up a little bit. How do you like it?" I said, "I'm going to tell you the truth. I liked the way he cut it in Memphis. I liked that second time he played it." He said, "But listen to this thing now, Perk," he said. "It ain't all that bad. I've got him doing a bunch of little stuff." Of course, it's fine, and I ain't going to argue with nobody that worked as hard as Simon did on that whole thing, but the second cut. You'll be hearing from this boy, he's an awesome guitar player. He really is good. He's got a little bad. He plays a couple of nights a week at some club in NY. Paul said, "I'm just letting him work his own way. When he comes to me and asks, I'll be behind him. But so far, he's been saying dad, when I get good enough, I may ask you to pry the door open for me." Very smart boy.

Moving on to another man named Paul. Earlier you were talking about "My Old Friend," and that Paul had just recently touched up the song. Is the main reason why this song has been held back for so long – we're talking 15 years. Is it mainly because Paul wasn't satisfied with the finished product?

Oh, no, no. In 1981, after I went down there and did that, he took it back to England then, and he asked me, he called me a month or so after I was down there, and he said, "Man, this 'My Old Friend' is a killer song." I said, "Well, thank you, Paul, thank you, man." He said, "Do you mind if I do a little treatment to it?" I said, "I don't care if you put the Queen on there. Do whatever you want to." Well, he did. He put piano, he put bass, he put some electric guitar. But he didn't sing as much on that version that he redid. He sent me a copy of it, and I've had it now for 15 years. I've played it often, I've made copies so I wouldn't wear it out. This last treatment he did to the song, he just nailed the whole thing. He sang so much more on there with me. He is louder than he was on the other one. The music is so perfect on this album here. I immediately called him when I got it, he sent it to me back in April he quit working on projects of his, and I know he worked for four days on it, he wanted it perfect, and that's what he got. The minute I got it, I just sat on the floor and bawled. Valda sat with me. I said, "Have you ever in your life heard anything this pretty?" and I really never have. To think that he would be so great and work so hard... see? I'm at it now, I can't help it. Anyway, I called him, and said, "Man, you shouldn't have!" He said, "What are you talking about, Perk?" I said, "You did so well on that song!" I'm speechless. I'll never get tired of listening to it. It's beautiful. He said, "Well, I'm glad you like it, old friend."

There you go.

And it was just such a wonderful cut of it. He could never beat it. I don't care if he sings it for the rest of his life, he's done it. That song has been nailed and done and he breathed with me on there. My voice was put there in 1981, and he did the final mix on it in April, and I think he did a brilliant job. I think it's wonderful.

You had all those other years, you could have released it.

Oh, yeah, I could have, and I had a lot of people who knew I had it. I've been, as I said earlier, bombarded with people. I said, "Look, just don't call me thinking you're ever going to hear it. Nobody's ever going to hear it. I won't play it for nobody. No, sir." Paul and I were the only people who had heard it. I just wouldn't play it. I'd listen to it every once in a while. I'd go a year or two, and say, "I've got to listen to it again." But when he sent it to me in April, it just absolutely jarred some things loose in my soul that still are a little loose, and may not go back. (Laughter) It was so beautiful to hear him breezin'. This boy was breezin' right with me on those lines and was nowhere near that close to singing right on line with me. He was doing some high humming and different things on the original way we had done it. But this time he really, really nailed it.

That's certainly worth the wait.

Oh God, yeah. I guess I've lived long enough to know... My daddy and my grandpa, when I was a young boy, they'd say, "Son, if it's worth it, it's worth waitin' on. Look at that Sears Roebuck (catalog), and dream about that guitar, and one day you'll get one." And I guess I learned to be patient. Sometimes in waiting, you do get much better results than you would if you ran ahead. I feel clean about this album, because I feel like the public really won't say that these people did it because they felt sorry for Carl. I really hope that nobody feels that, because these people, I tested them. They don't feel sorry for me. They care about me, just like I care about them, and this is a wonderful thing that came together. It may not sell a hundred units, it may not, but it did for me exactly what I could have never dreamed would have happened. Surrounded me with some of the greatest guys I ever knew, and giving the best performances I ever heard. They really did.

Without selling yourself short, Carl, I like to remind people when I play this album for them, and I do do that, that we're talking Rock And Roll Hall of Fame here. We're not talking about anyone doing this out of pity, or anything like that. They all have only the utmost respect for you, in anything I've ever read that Paul George or Clapton, or Dylan, or Johnny Cash, or anyone ever had to say about you, they say all good things.

Well, they proved it all, with this album, and whether they want me as a friend or not, they're stuck with me. (Laughter) That goes for as long as I'm on top of this ground.

One of my favorite recollections is where George is talking about the Rockabilly Sessions, and recalled that he offered you a cigarette, and you said, "Do you mind if I don't smoke it, and just keep it as a souvenir," and he was kind of blown away by that.

I've heard him tell that in front of me, and I heard him say that when I was over at his house to Jim, the drummer, he said, I'm going to tell you something. This dude asked me for a cigarette when I first met him, put it in his pocket, and said, would it be all right if I save it and not smoke it. I said, George, I've got that cigarette, he said, you're kidding. I do. I'm not kidding. It was a British Barclay.

Just to divert for one second, we trust that the cigarette won't be smoked. That the cancer that plagued you a couple of years ago is fully in remission.

Oh, it is, yeah...

That's absolutely wonderful. That's the best news we could hear.

It really is, gentlemen, and it seems like in life, it scares me sometimes to think that it's so wonderful and that I'm so happy, I'm so blessed that it's scary. I don't let these thoughts hang around between my ears very long. I could easily think, well, it's about over, but I really think it's beginning. Every day, I feel good, I realize that I am a blessed old man, and I've never been so ready to get out there and pick, and rock these people who have really given me an uplift. I want to prove to me that I can. I've been lazy. Now I want to rock. I really do.

One thing that I wanted to point out...when I think of this new CD of yours, I also think of the video special The Rockabilly Session, and I recall that when that video was broadcast on cable, on Cinemax, someone on television had reviewed it and said it was like a marriage of people from different generations. The beautiful thing about this CD likewise is that you have people who you grew up with, who are friends of yours from the early years, up through contemporaries of today all paying homage to you. And that's the beautiful thing, that your music can relate to people of so many different generations.

I think that's the good thing about being simple with the music. People can relate to it, people like it, and a whole lot of people can play it if it's not bent out of shape and have too many, I don't know what an octave, or a flat or a sharp is, I just know if the guitar is in tune or not, and I know if my foot's patting on the beat then it feels right, you know? Nothing's ever been fancy about my playing, or about my songs, and I'm very sincere, I don't think there's a whole lot there other than if there's anything there's some- thing that might move you to patting your foot, or popping your finger, I think. That's what rockabilly music is, it's something that you feel, rather than to sit and listen to it, If you don't move something with a good rockabilly song, you run into danger of breaking a bone, from the inside (laughter). It's something you become a part of, you're lost in that groove, you're patting your foot, your head's nodding. I can pull up to a red light, and I can tell if a cat's listening to a rockabilly, because he's patting the dashboard, you know? It is a music that you get involved with. You're listening to it, but it's got to move. I don't think it's something you can lay back and just relax and listen to it. It's got an intense beat, it's up there, you know? I think it's supposed to move you, make you get up and shake.

Your music certainly does that for us.

Well, I appreciate it.

Carl, if I may, I'd like to express an opinion here that has been voiced not only by me, but by many people who have listened to my radio program, and Tom, as well. Certainly after the passing of Roy Orbison, which was a sad event for all of us, many people were thinking about who would make a replacement, if you could ever replace, which you really can't a voice like Roy Orbison's.

That's true.

And a lot of people sent suggestions to me on the radio on who they think would make a good fifth Wilbury, and to me, and Tom, and to so many other people, it seems the obvious choice is that someone like you would fit the Traveling Wilburys so well. These are people who have long admired you, certainly; you know George, and Tom Petty, these are people who look up to you. I wonder if that topic has ever been brought up with you and members of the Traveling Wilburys, or if you have ever contemplated possibly ever being a part of that band.

No, I never was asked. I asked George one time if he ever was going to do that again. He said, "I don't know. I really don't know. We've talked about it some, if we do, I'm not going to be in a hurry to ever do it again." I'll say this... if I heard that they were getting together, and that they were auditioning, I probably would be one of the first in line to get that opportunity. I would love to do that. I don't know how well I'd fit it, but I sure would like to try. I liked what they did, and I think the world loved it. I know it would not be the same without Orbison – as you said, there's no replacing a talent or force like that – but I don't think it would be bad if five of us got together, got us some pretty good songs, and had a pretty good time, and turned on a tape machine. I think there's room for it, and I think there's a lot of people out there that would be happy if George, and Tom, and Dylan, if these people got together and did it. If I heard they were doing it, I'd get in there with them. It would be a great honor.

When you get down to it, the whole idea of the Traveling Wilburys is just to have fun with the music.

That's exactly right...

It's lighthearted and very spontaneous, and I think that certainly given all the stories you've told us so far this evening about what has happened spontaneous with you, you'd fit right in like a glove. I couldn't think of a more perfect choice to be in that band.

Gosh, I appreciate it. You've put me in mighty good company. I certainly appreciate that. Again, I say what an honor it would be to be asked, and I'd work as hard as I possibly could to fit in and I don't know, maybe I'd find a way to fit. Cause I'd certainly try, and I think it would be good. You can't have too much good feeling, happy-go-lucky sounds like these boys were making. I think it's good for everybody. Absolutely hurts nothing. Music is a part of everybody, from the woman cooking with a baby on her hip and one pulling on her apron, to an old lady sitting and rocking on her front porch somewhere with a shawl on her shoulder. I told somebody the other day, and I think we overlook the fact, that music entered our lives first. We were not even old enough to know that when our mamas were humming, rockin' us to sleep, that it was that melody that mama was humming that actually filled our souls, right then. We were addicted to music before we had our eyes open.

Carl, suppose they told you that your audition for the Traveling Wilburys would involve your doing the dance, the Wilbury Twist, that was on their last record...

(Laughter) I'd get in there with them... I'd try it.

Well, I just want to make sure that there'd be no...

I'll be truthful with you. If they said, "You've gotta pass that audition," I'd say, "turn on the machine... that's it."

Ken and I were chewing on the term before, "The Traveling Carlburys," in describing the new album, and saying that gee, it has that same spirit, more than anything. We're not going to say that "this track corresponds to this Wilbury thing." That's defeating the purpose, but in spirit, I think this album reflects that kind of camaraderie, spontaneity, and of course, musicianship that pervades both the Wilburys and the new record.

That's very kind of you to say that, compare it to that. Gentlemen, I can only say to you that you people are the lifeline between the artist and the public. If you weren't there, playing the music, there wouldn't be any. People would move around, cut a record or two, but if somebody never played it, then it probably would never have been heard. You have always been the connection. I want to thank you very much from the bottom of my heart as I speak to you tonight from my den in Jackson, Tennessee, I certainly do appreciate it.

Carl, since you've mentioned life on the road, you've been on the road a good part of your life, you've spent most of the last 40 years performing...

That's right, 42 years ago, I started traveling on the road.

That's amazing.

1954.

What do you do to keep it exciting?

Look at the faces of the people, 'cause people say, "Why are you nervous before a show, you've done it all of your life?" Every time that curtain opens, it's not the same people. They react different. You see smiles some nights; the whole front row is lit up, their teeth are like footlights. And then again, there'd be a dud right in the center of 'em (laughter) You'd say, "What's that fool doing sitting there, he don't like me!" How come he got down front, you know. You experience a lot up there, and it's new every time the curtain opens. There's no two alike. You might say, "Well, I've seen him, and he plays the same way." It might appear that way, but inside of the artist up there, there's nights that he hates to leave, and there's nights that he can't wait 'til the thing is over. They're just not reacting to you. They're not booing you, but man, there's sometimes when the sweat's pouring off of them, and you're tuned in, you've got something happening. There's something between the artist and his audience and when it's there, it's the greatest feeling in the world for both of them. It's like posts on batteries, man, it's like negative and positive, and when it's hooked together, look out, something's going to start, you know. That's the way I feel a lot of times. I'd be nervous before a show, I've always been, gosh, I always will be, that's part of me. I'm just nervous. And people say man, you've been doing this all your life and you're still nervous? Yes sir, I sure am, cause I never saw the same crowd there. Never have. They're always going to be a couple of them duds in the front row. And they're not happy. You say, well, I'm going to look over your head and find me some teeth, man. That's just what you have to do. You've gotta pour it out, but sometimes it's a lot easier than it is at other times, and it was that way for the Beatles, it was that way for Elvis, it was that way for the first one that crawled on the stage. When you're aware of the audience, when you're at your senses, you're not overstuffed on alcohol or drugs, you are nervous. I've never talked to anyone that wasn't until he really got it going with them and then it really flies by. They get out of you everything that you've got. If they only knew that, the audience controls the show. They do. They can move with you, and they cam throw you in another universe. Your band will say, "Man, you played the fire out of that guitar tonight," and I say, I did, I knew that I was enjoying it, but I didn't know. My boys will tell me this, they'll say, "Daddy, you ate it up." I'll say, "Well, it sure did feel good, these guys were pouring it on me." It's magic when it happens. Thank God it still happens, and that's why I'm still out there.

Carl, one other thing about your new album that I wanted to mention is that anyone who looks at all the credits will note that there are songs from the '50s, '60s, '70s, '80s and that there are new songs so this is kind of like maybe what you would view of "the best of..." Are these your personal favorites, or were they a combination of your favorites and the artists that you're working with?

No, I never really thought of it that way. A lot of these things I just wrote, you know, this year, to have something to do with the artist that was going to be on there, like "One More Shot," like "Distance Makes No Difference" like Paul Simon – "Rockabilly Music," "Quarter Horse," so many things. "Go Cat Go," Debbie and my boys and I wrote. "Don't Stop the Music" was written five or six years ago. It's not a compilation of my life, so to speak, or my music. It just happened that way, really.

How do you write new material now? Are there times when it's harder for you to come up with new ideas?

Oh yeah, I've never been one to sit down and say, "I'm going to write a song." I just can't do that. I never could. I diddle around with my guitar, it happens a lot of times early in the morning when I'm fresh, and a lot of times I'm alone in my den, and I'll just start a little ole melody, clicking along, and I'll think of something, and I'll know right away if it moves me, then I'll start working with it. And usually just write it down as it comes. I hardly ever go back and change anything. I've always been that way. A lot of people say, "Man, you don't go back, tighten them up, strengthen them?" I'll say, "I go back and fool with them, and ruin them." Whatever I had, I usually get it but I can't make myself sit down and write. I'm embarrassed trying to sit down and write with people. I really was with Paul Simon. I mean, I wrote the chorus to that thing, I wrote three or four of the lines, but he wrote the biggest part of that song. He'll say he didn't. He's already said that in some interview that he's given, but I disagree with him. He wrote 2/3, and

I wrote about 1/3. He says, "Well, it W.S. Perkins' melody." No, the chorus (singing) "Rockabilly Music" ain't nothing to it, it's just a hopped-up country song. So it happened, and I didn't really have to work on it. I can't pry nothing out of me. If it don't just fly out of there, then I don't know where it's at. I don't know where it comes from, really.

Since you have a few songs on the album where members of your family are writing together, are there times when you just gather around the kitchen table at home or in the living room, and you try to come up with new songs?

I've got a studio at my home here, and we get down there sometimes, my two sons, Stan and Greg, the boys, the two that play. I've got another son that is a draftsman, and never fooled with music. He was a pitcher in Little League and so forth, but he just never got into music. And here lately, my daughter Debbie comes down, and she'd say, "I got this idea last night," and she'll have words typed down, and we'll start knocking around with it and if it feels good, we'll work with it a little while, and then we've got a song. But as far as really sitting down and topping a line to line, Debbie and I have begun to do that. We did one, a religious idea, today she brought it down here. She only lives one door down from us out here, and she came down with a little typewritten page, and she said, "Daddy, I've got something started, and it's called "He Left Us A Song," and it starts out about the boy's daddy, he used to go fishing with him, and now his daddy's gone, but he left him a song. It's a song the old man used to whistle and hum. It's a good idea, I'm going to work on it a while tonight, I guess before I go to bed. I kind of got a melody started on it. It ends up being about Jesus who lived among us, who loved us and taught us all we should need to know about love, and then he too, left us a song to sing. It's got a big hand-clapping chorus (singing) 'We've got us a song to sing!" It's gonna be a pretty good song. So anyway, that's the way it happened.

Carl, one thing I wanted to bring up, and Tom and I have both noted this, is that if you take a look at the last several Beatles releases, from Live At The BBC, to all three volumes of The Beatles Anthology, Carl Perkins is represented somewhere on all those releases. And you're the only artist that one can say that about.

You know, I've had that pointed out to me, and of course, I've noticed that. I'm very, very honored by that in more ways than one. I don't know why these guys did that. I love them, not because of that, but I don't want to know. Really, all I know is that they've honored me so much that I wouldn't tinker with it. I don't want to question them and ask them why did they use my songs.

I think the answer is probably obvious – that they hold you in such high regard. How many other people get asked to be the house band for a Paul McCartney or George Harrison party? How did those things come about? Do you offer? Do they call?

George just called, and I said, "Sure man, I'll be there." Paul called me last year, and I went over, spent two days playing at the Empire Theatre for the Buddy Holly thing. Had a ball.

We actually got to see a clip of the George Harrison Handmade Films Anniversary party. That was in a TV documentary here, and they showed a brief clip of that, and George getting up there and jamming with you guys, and I said, "Boy, there's a house band for you!"

They know that if they need Carl Perkins or want me, they've got my phone number, and if I wanted to talk to George tomorrow, I'd call his house, and if he weren't there, they'd find him for me. I don't bother these guys – I never have. When I talked to them, it's been that. I've gone as long as I want to, I've wanted to find out how they're doing. It's like George would call me and ask me about my health, ask how's Valda doing. He's asked us to join him at this place he goes to near Boston. Later this year, we may do that, I don't know for sure, I haven't heard from him since I was over there, but he mentioned it, he said he would love to have us. That it would do us both good. He goes for about a week to his doctor friend's restful place. He said "It's great, it would do you such good." And I said, "All right, cat, we'll do it!"

That's great. You can tell him some great stories about how people are receiving this work, as we've discussed tonight. It has been a big ad on a number of stations, and I just tell people when they ask me my opinion of it I say, "Gee, what's not to like?" There's just so much good music on here, and it's a record that deserves to be heard.

Again, I certainly want to thank you two guys for spending this time with me. It's nine o'clock here, and we've had a couple of hours, and I've enjoyed every second of it.

Where does the time go?

I don't know, man. It gets away.

Can I ask one last question?

Yes, sir.

Several times when I've spoken to you before, you've talked about a video special that's been in the works that would include you and Paul performing several songs, sitting on a couple of stools together, performing with acoustic guitars...

Here comes an ironic thing – you'll never guess who called me this morning…

I'm reaching here, Paul?!

No. His brother-in-law, Eastman. The lawyer John Eastman in New York called me and said Paul wants to know if you want that tape player. I said, "I sure do!" So he's going after it. See it's been kind of tied up with a guy, a New Yorker, that I was going to do this show with, and he charged too much money to go down to Memphis to film me and Paul, way too much. And I was talking to Paul about it, and he said, "No way. Don't do that. Don't pay him that kind of money. That's ridiculous." He said I did that for you anyway, and I'll take it away from him I'll have the Eastmans tell him he gives it to you. I said, "I might have to do that," So, Paul, out of the clear blue, John Eastman, told me this morning, said "Paul McCartney told me to call you, ask you how you were coming with the video tape," and I said, "Well, I'm right where I was when I last talked to Paul, I can't hear from (the man) him, he refuses to answer my phone calls, he said, he will be talking to you immediately. Paul has put me on it, and so I'll have that tape right away.

That's great.

It's so ironic that you asked about it. He called me this morning, and I fell away from the phone. When he told me it was John Eastman. Naturally, I had heard of him, but I'd never spoken to the man.

There was a passing glimpse of you and Paul jamming, I guess it was backstage on Paul's last world tour, that was included in his last concert film. It was a brief one- or two-second clip that's just kind of in there as documentary footage. Is that part of the same film, or are we talking about two different things?

I don't know that I've seen what you're talking about. I can't say for sure.

In Paul's last concert film, from the Paul is Live Tour, during one of the soundchecks they're showing all kinds of backstage footage, and documentary things...

Oh, well, that happened, no question, at about the same time, as two different pieces of film. Mine was done down in the dressing room, and as Paul says, on the tape, "In the bowels of the Liberty Bowl." (Laughter) I'm going to have that back in my possession, and I don't know exactly what I'm going to do with it. It's 35 minutes long, I'd like to stretch it out to 50, 55 minutes, and I think I'd make a fine special. I don't know, I'm leaning towards maybe sitting down with George and seeing if he wants to do the same thing.

That'd be wonderful.

When you were talking to me about it, you were thinking about having the Judds on the special, Willie Nelson, and a star-studded cast, much like your new CD.

That's true. Yeah, Garth Brooks was going to do it, Wynonna was going to do it, and I was going to really have Paul introduce it for me , but he gave me so much that there was nowhere to cut it, and so Wynonna got pregnant and started having babies, and Garth started traveling around the world, and I then got into it with this fellow that I wasn't going to be able to do business with, he'd charge entirely too much... an outrageous price for flying from NY and renting two cameras – and I just kind of put it on hold and I've looked at it a lot, Paul loves it, he like this thing. He wouldn't be embarrassed its being out. He's said so.

Well, we'd sure look forward to seeing it, that's for sure.

I don't know, I might talk to Paul about it. What I really would like to do is get Paul, George and Ringo, and just sit down with them and pick, and have us in the front yard with one video camera. I don't care. I really would like to do that. Something is kind of saying, "Just hold off, old man, everything comes in its time, you know?" That is something I really would love to do. I'd like to share that with some Beatle fans, and I think that'd be wonderful, because they're together again, they're friends, their harmony is good. I'd just like to sit down and try to write some songs and film it with them. "Hey, George, give me an idea," "All right, 'Old McDonald.'" "They won't buy that, go on deeper." (Laughter) I just think I'd be fun. If we viewed it, and we thought it was stupid. We'd put it out anyway! (Laughter)

The authors' payment for the article was, at their request, contributed to the Exchange Club-Carl Perkins Center for the Prevention of Child Abuse, P.O. Box 447, Jackson, TN 38302-0447, (800) 273-4747, www.perkins-center.tn.org.

Most Collectible 45

"Movie Magg"/ "Turn Around," Flip 501, $1,000.

Most Collectible LP

The Dance Album Of Carl Perkins, Sun LP-1225, $1,200.

Recommended Introduction

Blue Suede Shoes: The Best Of Carl Perkins, Collectables 6011 (23 of his greatest Sun recordings)

If you want to hear more...

Jive After Five: The Best Of Carl Perkins (1959-1978), Rhino R2-70958 (a collection of the best of Perkins' post-Sun label recordings)

Honky Tonk Gal: Rare And Unissued Sun Masters, Rounder 27 (1950s Perkins material from the vaults)

Country Boy's Dream: The Dollie Masters, Bear Family 79005-11559-3 (German import, these are 30 tracks recorded in 1968 for the small Dollie label)

The Classic Carl Perkins, Bear Family 79005-11549-4 (German import, a 5-CD box set of Sun material)

Go Cat Go, Dinosaur Entertainment 76401-84508-2 (Carl's "Duets" CD described in great detail above, this was released in 1996 but appears to be out of print already)

Elvis Presley

by Neal Umphred

You can't have a digest dedicated to the rock 'n' roll of the '50s and early '60s without something on Elvis Presley. But which article to choose? Goldmine *has done well over a hundred pieces on varying aspects of "The King" since the magazine was founded. We finally decided to use one that contains not a single quotation from an associate or anyone else closely associated with Elvis. Let's engage in a bit of revisionist history. What if, when Elvis was drafted in 1958, there had been a real war going on? What if he had been forced to serve in battle? And, even more tragically, what if he had been killed in action? He still would have left behind one of the most amazing bodies of work in music history, all recorded in a five-year period from 1954 through 1958. And that's what this article is about – that music. Because after all the man's idiosyncrasies have been forgotten or parodied to death, the music will remain. And while Elvis certainly made some worthwhile – even some of his best – music after he returned from the Army, he never came close to equaling the sheer consistency of the 1950s material. That's why RCA could put together a box set of the complete 1950s masters – in other words, the released version of every song that he recorded during the decade – and not embarrass either the listener or the artist. This article, analyzing each of Elvis' recordings during his first five years of professional recording, is excerpted from one that appeared in the August 7, 1992 issue of* Goldmine.

Prior to the '60s there was – needless to say – the '50s. Exactly when this particular decade began is moot; for most memories, it began with Elvis. Certainly it was epitomized by the young man with the pelvis that dared to go where no pelvis had gone before. The types of rhythms that Elvis preferred, and that shocked the majority of the American dance population, were already quite common in almost every black dance hall, juke joint or rent party in all 48 states. The music that provided it had undergone several changes, and, as is the wont of music as it embraces a larger, broader (and younger) audience, it simplified its emotions, its gestures more sweeping, less subtle. The rhythm 'n' blues records of the postwar years had succumbed to these effects with certainty and with energy. The ability of black musicians to purchase electric instruments opened up new avenues of expression and let to the type of beat, rhythm and dancing that would be known in a few years as rock 'n' roll.

This music, a hybrid of the black subculture and post-war prosperity, benefited from a handful of daring platter spinners on small AM stations looking for a break. The music attracted younger listeners (i.e., teenagers) in staggering numbers, far beyond the reach of the swing records of their parents' generation. They were, for the most part, white teenagers, responding wholeheartedly to the music of blacks openly and enthusiastically, often to the chagrin of their elders.

This era – the years preceding the meteoric rise of Elvis Presley – is one of fascination for anyone interested in American music. Unfortunately, it is too large, too important, an era to brush off with a few words. There are any number of books that address various aspects of these years; the interested reader is advised to take his or her time and read each one. (And listen to the music. Whatever flaws the digital revolution may have, and there are *many*, it has made a cornucopia of music available at modest prices for the first time in decades. A beginners' library of the late '40s and early '50s rhythm 'n' blues and group vocal music can be had readily at any well-stocked CD store in the country, a blessing indeed.)

So how does Elvis fit in here? There are many misconceptions about the young Presley. It has even been claimed that Elvis took many of his original ideas from Jerry Lee Lewis, this even though Lewis didn't record a single note until Elvis had sold umpteen bajillion records and was quite comfortably a millionaire. More common, and reasonable, is that he lifted his style – singing, moving, whatever – from one well-known (in the South) black performer or another. Presley saw and studied many entertainers of this time, often attending black clubs as the sole white face in

the audience and, while there are marked similarities in various aspects of specific parts of his delivery to a number of other singers, Presley's gestalt – the image projected in the way he sang, the songs he sang, the clothes – is unlike other artists in any other genre.

So, musically, does one begin this "Elvis Decade" with his first recording for Sun Records in 1954 ("That's All Right") and the explosive response of audiences throughout the South who witnessed the Hillbilly Cat before the rest of the world even had a hint of what was in store? Or, do we accept the beginning as his first major successes on nationwide television with RCA Victor Records?

Viewing Elvis' initial television appearances today can still draw a gasp. Whereas a contemporary viewer watching, say, the Rolling Stones on *Ed Sullivan* in 1967 might wonder what the hell anyone found "dirty and unkempt" about Mick Jagger or why a parent would cringe at the thought of his daughter dating said Stone, that same viewer can view Presley in 1956 on the *Toast Of The Town* and stand back in awe. Presley's entire persona overflowed with kinetic energy. There is a look in his eyes that, while certainly not demonic, can be interpreted as possessed. (Folks back then did actually debate whether or not Elvis was an incarnation of the eternally evil one!) But the young singer's enthusiasm, his sense of fun and the "aw shucks, I'm jus' havin' fun" attitude, even when doing his most pulsating pelvic performance, lends the whole thing an air of both levity and surrealism.

On record, all of this did begin in July 1954 when, whatever the explanations proffered by Sam Phillips or others – none of which entirely explains everything – Elvis Presley, with the assistance of Scotty Moore, Bill Black and Phillips, "invented" rock 'n' roll. The best of these recordings do, indeed, appear to possess a timeless personality, as though they could have been recorded a hundred years ago or yesterday.

While the bulk of the 10 sides released by Sun on the five singles are generally regarded in awe (examples: the falsetto-like wail of "That's All Right"; the preternatural assurance of a young man – and a white man at that – in "Good Rockin' Tonight"; the self-conscious but nonetheless wonderful intro to "Milkcow Blues Boogie"; or the awesome "Mystery Train"), the lesser cuts also hold interest. Such pieces as "Tryin' To Get To You," dismissed by many as filler for the first album, is now held as a minor gem; comparing the early 1954 recording with the passionate, howling version that Elvis would give in his 1968 television special is of special note as one of the few times when he dug up an older recording and treated it as something *new*, something that needed the Presley treatment. (Of course, this could be said about much of those June '68 sessions in the Burbank studios, but that's another article.)

Arguably the most revelatory (in light of intervening years) is the alternate, slow blues version of "I'm Left, You're Right, She's Gone," more aptly titled "My Baby's Gone." On this one, many of the devices that would become Presley trademarks are quite evident. This is important due to the fact that many of these vocal tricks – which would devolve into affectations on many later recordings – predate the RCA Victor period, those years the purists have always concluded led to these very mannerisms in the wake of the young singer's waning enthusiasm and the desire of the RCA execs to make some really big money. The young Elvis had a bag of tricks up his vocal sleeves, some of which apparently he or Phillips felt were, er, precocious.

The release of the RCA boxed set *The King Of Rock 'N' Roll: The Complete 50's Masters* heralds a whole new approach from the record company (now owned by BMG, which felt that the Presley catalog was a prime reason for its multi-million dollar purchase of RCA). Four CDs collect everything Elvis recorded in chronological order from 1954 through 1958, with a fifth disc of "rarities," some recently uncovered. The discs offer the best sound that we have heard from Elvis in the digital medium. Thus, *The Complete 50's Masters* necessitates some sort of overview of the man's career, at least during those prime years.

In this article, Elvis' recordings are broken down by session, the musicians involved, discographical and chart data, along with commentary. The recording sessions are noted by date, lumping several together when relevant. Each title is followed by either the catalog number of the RCA Victor 45 RPM single (47 prefix) or the extended play album (EPA prefix) upon which it was released.

The third column indicates the month of release of that 45 while the final column notes the peak position the song reached on *Billboard*'s sales charts (taken from Joel Whitburn's Top Pop Singles 1955-1990). The idea is to show how RCA utilized the dominant medium, the "little record with the big hole," to merchandise Presley, and the success it had – 38 chart entries in a little over four years. Putting that in perspective, only Pat Boone had more entries (39) and he had five years (1955-59), while Fats Domino had 33, also in five years.

July-September 1954

"*I Love You Because,*" 47-6639, 8/56; "*That's All Right,*" 47-6380, 12/55; "*Harbor Lights*"; "*Blue Moon Of Kentucky,*" 47-6380, 12/55; "*Blue Moon,*" 47-6640, 8/56, #55; "*Tomorrow Night*"; "*I'll Never Let You Go (Little Darlin'),*" 47-6638, 8/56.

While the actual origins of Presley's style may predate these sessions by months, July 5 is now the official date for the dawn of the "Elvis Era." The first release, Sun 209, "That's All Right"/"Blue Moon Of Kentucky," was a perfect pairing, establishing the pattern that Sam Phillips would follow with Elvis through his brief stay with Sun, coupling an upbeat black song with a modest country feeling with an upbeat country song with a rhythm 'n' blues feel. The songs, especially the wondrous A-side, still sound exciting and fresh.

Beginning slowly, painfully, Presley sings "I'll Never Let You Go" with utter gentility. Midway through, he breaks form with a long "Weeeeell" and doubles the tempo, ending the song in a rock 'n' roll manner. While this is an unsuccessful master from a technical and artistic standpoint, it is loads of fun and an important artifact, as it stands as a blueprint for the type of vocal gymnastics at which Elvis would later excel.

The four remaining tracks are ballads, forever putting to rest the persistent stories concerning RCA's "forcing" Elvis to soften his image. While it is the Marcels' uptempo, whacked-out doo-wop version that is held near and dear by most early rock lovers, Elvis' version of "Blue Moon," including the banshee falsetto bridge, the arrangement and the production, is quite unlike anything else in Presley's *oeuvre* (nor is there much in anyone else's catalog to compare). Everything about this recording begs attention. Had Elvis attempted some sacred readings in this vein, he might have added a whole new dimension to that genre.

"Tomorrow Night," while less successful, is sung and arranged in a similar ghostly fashion, giving the previous R&B hit a country-ish feel. The relaxed, loping tempo allows him to play with both the song and his nascent style. The remaining tracks hardly work at all: "I Love You Because" shows the very young singer struggling with everything, including a notion of an identity, while "Harbor Lights" is more assured but, like "Because," mainly of historical interest. It should be pointed out that, even here with the majority of the work in the ballad form, at this point Elvis' country and blues roots outweigh his Tin Pan Alley yearnings.

The instrumentation is so basic – Elvis' rhythm guitar, Scotty Moore's lead and Bill Black's bass – that the sound can be disorienting. One listens for other instruments, other voices, something to fill in the spaces, explain the fullness of the sound. When Elvis, Scotty and Bill showed up for early appearances, some promoters were upset that the rest of the band hadn't showed, not believing that the sound on the record had been produced by a three-man unit. While Elvis or Black occasionally resorted to slapping their instruments in lieu of strumming or picking (convincing many that there was a drummer of some sort somewhere), the only "gimmick" is the echo, most noticeable on the singer's voice, and that was the result of the acoustics of the studio.

September 1954

"I Don't Care If The Sun Don't Shine," 47-6381, 12/55, #74; "Just Because," 47-6640, 8/56; "Good Rockin' Tonight," 47-6381, 12/55.

"I Don't Care If The Sun Don't Shine" is possibly the most oddball/wondrous of the whole Sun period, with Elvis taking a piece of fluff from a Walt Disney movie and turning it in on itself and coming out the other end with rockabilly. Elvis is in top form and quite obviously enjoying himself. For some strange reason, when RCA got around to collecting the 10 sides from the five Sun singles onto an LP in 1959, it overlooked this one, using the other nine on two different albums, even though "I Don't Care If The Sun Don't Shine" was the only one of the sides that made the charts as an RCA release (as part of EPA-821, *Heartbreak Hotel*, in May 1956).

"Just Because" is another attempt that doesn't quite gel; the master is available sounds as if the intro has been bitten off. Nice but nothing great. "Good Rockin' Tonight" is classic rock 'n' roll, Elvis doing Wynonie Harris doing Roy Brown, standing quite comfortably alongside each. It was music such as this that allowed white artists to cross over onto black playlists, a feat that is historically far rare than its reverse.

November-December 1954

"Milkcow Blues Boogie," 47-6382, 12/55; "You're A Heartbreaker," 47-6382, 12/55.

Another older blues, "Milkcow" has been recorded endlessly with a variety of title alterations. Presley's version ups the ante, taking chances with the studied "false" start, the breakneck speed at which both the singer and the band rip through the song, and the little gymnastics Elvis puts his voice through. The whole thing is almost too studied, too perfect. Almost. This one, along with "Baby, Let's Play House," provided the blueprint for an entire school of hiccuping rockabilly singers, Charles Hardin (Buddy) Holley the primary exponent.

"You're A Heartbreaker" stands out in approach to the bulk of the Sun material, having a more traditional country sound to the arrangement and the singing. This should have been a huge country hit but was essentially ignored. As Elvis' third single, this coupling was adventurous but the most poorly received of the five Suns.

February 1955

"Baby, Let's Play House," 47-6383, 12/55.

It is almost impossible to hear "Baby, Let's Play House" and not hear the Buddy Holly story. Holly always said without Elvis his career would not have been possible, and this track explains his position. A masterful interpretation and a big hit, this one actually reached the national country charts, selling far more copies than legend (and collectors and dealers alike) would have you believe. Finally, according to the session notes, two other songs were also attempted: "I Got A Woman" and "Tryin' To Get To You." Tapes have yet to surface.

March 1955

"I'm Left, You're Right, She's Gone," 47-6383, 12/55.

This is separated from the above to point out that it was here that a drummer was first used on an Elvis session, one Jimmie Lott. "I'm Left, You're Right, She's Gone" is a typical country cliche used well. The uptempo bridge is clever and whoever thought of it deserves a special pat on the back. An alternate take, technically with the same title but universally known at "My Baby's Gone," is a different interpretation of the more familiar number. Whereas the single was a countrified rocker, this is a slow, almost unaccompanied, blues. Presley glides easily into many of the mannerisms and vocal patterns of the later RCA recordings. Until the dawn of the bootleg era 20 years ago, this one was as much a legend as anything Elvis had ever recorded. And, as noted above, it shows that the style that became the norm at RCA was Presley's, not a product of the decadent big label A&R men.

July-August 1955

*"I Forgot To Remember To Forget," 47-6367, 11/55;
"Mystery Train," 47-6367, 11/55' "Trying To Get To
You," 47-6639, 8/56; "When It Rains, It Really Pours."*

For his ultimate single for Sun, Elvis, Scotty
Moore, Bill Black and session drummer Johnny Bern-
ero scored the first of Presley's many double-sided
hits. Elvis had to be talked into "I Forgot To Remember To Forget," an almost too typical country piece.
Fortunately, once into the sessions, Elvis found the
heart of the song, delivering a bravura performance.
The more legendary "Mystery Train" is arguably the
single greatest accomplishment of Presley's career
(and thus, the single greatest rock 'n' roll song of the
past four or more decades). Both sides reached the
national country charts in late 1955, the A-side reaching *Billboard*'s #1 spot in February 1956, and staying
there for five weeks.

"Trying To Get To You" was again attempted, this
time with some success; while the performance is
good, the final product was deemed unacceptable by
Phillips. Nonetheless, it remains somewhat of a cornerstone for rockabilly. According to Ernst Jorgensen,
the compiler of most of the best Elvis compilations,
Phillips was working on a sixth Elvis single should the
proposed sale of his most important artist not go
through as planned. The sessions in February and July
1955 were both aimed at achieving a suitable version
of "Trying To Get To You" to be set aside for potential
release. Similarly, the following sessions, where Elvis
tackled Billy Emerson's "When It Rains, It Really
Pours," shows where Phillips was trying to take Elvis:

The altered sections in the arrangement give the song
a hipper sound and a little more punch for the pop
audience. Again, not completely a success, this is
nonetheless, a fascinating workout and it's a shame
that RCA did not include this on some album in the
'50s (his first).

At the end of 1955, it was far from clear just how
important these recordings were. Certainly Presley's
fans were aware of them, although fans are often the
least cognizant of the virtues – or failings – of a given
set of recordings, especially at the time. There were
musicians that tuned right in on what Elvis was after;
aside from Holly, an entire genre of music – rockabilly
– was formed from other white Southern singers wearing out the grooves of Elvis' Sun sides. In a way, it's a
shame that Elvis couldn't have stayed a little longer
with Sun; an album issued for the Christmas season of
1955 consisting of the 10 single sides and several outtakes would have been a landmark.

It is difficult to be objective about these recordings: The best of them may be the Rosetta Stones of
rock 'n' roll (and, to a lesser extent, country 'n' western of the last four decades). Except for the exces-
sively maudlin "I Love You Because," every track
has something to offer, and that has nothing to do
with history. This is an amazing talent mapping the
terrain of his abilities. These songs are, in the context
of their time and prevailing culture – a sexually
repressive culture during a notably conservative
period in its history – awe-inspiring. The Sun Sessions, as they have come to be known, are very
nearly the equivalent of Robert Johnson's legendary
attempts to master the demons in his soul through
music. Elvis Presley, the man, would not allow himself to push the perimeters like this again until the
need to salvage his career and reputation led him to
NBC's studios in Burbank, California in June 1968.

January 1956

*"I Got A Woman," EPA-747, 4/56; "Heartbreak
Hotel," 47-6420, 1/56, #1; "Money Honey," 47-6641,
8/56, #76; "I'm Counting On You," 47-6637, 8/56; "I
Was The One," 47-6420, 1/56, #19.*

For Elvis' first RCA Victor sessions, held at the label's
studios in New York City while Elvis was in town to tape
several *Jackie Gleason Stage Shows*, his regular group,
now including D.J. Fontana on drums, was augmented by
the adaptable guitar of Chet Atkins (who as the nominal
producer was, along with A&R man Steve Sholes, in
charge of the session) and a prominent piano. Recent
research through the musician's union logbooks indicates
that Floyd Cramer was the man tickling the keys. Additionally, Elvis was backed by vocalists Gordon Stoker
and Ben and Brock Speer.

Sixty percent of Elvis' first sides for RCA are ballads (more or less). While two of these are unexceptional, "Heartbreak Hotel" is a timeless classic. A huge hit in both the pop and country charts, it is sort of a country weeper sung in a blues manner arranged almost as a melodramatic cocktail lounger. It doesn't really sound like what rock 'n' roll is, or was, supposed to be, but, as it was by Elvis, it now stands out as one of the most recognizable recordings of the entire rock era.

"I Got A Woman" was a staple of the live show for almost two years and, while a credible rocker, the hoked-up ending doesn't really gel. "Money Honey" is a completely different story. Lifting favorite singer Clyde McPhatter's R&B smash of a few years prior, Elvis turns the song into a marvelous rock 'n' roll recording, showing that what was achieved at Sun was possible at RCA. Had the powers that be recognized this – and had the need to place sides where the publishing was owned not been so great – this would have been the better B-side to "Heartbreak Hotel" and would have created a two-sided masterpiece that extended the achievements of the Sun recordings. ("Money Honey" did reach the charts as part of EPA-821, *Heartbreak Hotel*.)

Instead, the conservative ballad "I Was The One" (all mannerism and style with little else to recommend it and RCA's choice for the A-side) was given the nod and a double-sided ballad went out into the nascent rock 'n' roll market. Nonetheless, RCA Victor 6420 sold nearly a half-million copies in its first three weeks of release and had topped 2,000,000 by the end of 1957. (Collectors should note that RCA claimed only 10 percent of those sales were attributed to the 78 rpm version, RCA Victor 20-4720. This pattern would increase – i.e., more of the sales would go to the 45 – with each subsequent release, making the 78s far more rare than the 45s.)

January-February 1956

"Blue Suede Shoes," 47-6636, 8/56, #20; "My Baby Left Me," 47-6540, 5/56, #31; "One-Sided Love Affair," 47-6641, 8/56; "So Glad You're Mine," EPA-993, 11/56; "I'm Gonna Sit Right Down and Cry (Over You)," 47-6638, 8/56; "Tutti Frutti," 47-6636, 8/56; "Lawdy, Miss Clawdy," 47-6642, 8/56; "Shake, Rattle And Roll," 47-6642, 8/56.

These sessions were held to complete Elvis' first long-player, and, of course, to possibly find the second single. Also done in RCA's New York studios, Elvis was able to run through these numbers with his live band – Moore, Black and Fontana – and pianist Shorty Long, as basic a band as any of his RCA sessions would ever have. While "Blue Suede Shoes" was certainly a qualifier for a single – it remains one of Elvis' best all-time recordings and is, for most listeners, the definitive version – Sholes agreed not to release it so as not to step on Phillips' toes and interfere with Carl Perkins' version, which became a massive hit for Sun, justifying Phillips' decision to sell Presley so that he could use the capital to break other artists. ("Blue Suede Shoes" did make the charts as part of EPA-747, *Elvis Presley*.)

"My Baby Left Me," another song from Arthur "Big Boy" Crudup, who'd written "That's All Right," is an extension of some of the Sun sides and was covered by Creedence Clearwater Revival on their *Cosmo's Factory* album in an almost note-by-note copy. (In fact, John Fogerty built a half-dozen Creedence albums around this sound.) "My Baby Left Me" was issued as the B-side of Elvis' second single, with "I Want You, I Need You, I Love You." Ironically, it was the B-side that received the bulk of the initial attention, charting considerably higher than "I Want You." Of course, that only lasted for one week.

The rest of the session(s) are all credible, straight-ahead rock 'n' roll, the best being the reading of "So Glad You're Mine." February 3, the final day of work, saw Elvis deliver two more than competent rhythm 'n' blues workouts: "Lawdy, Miss Clawdy" is as close to unadorned New Orleans R&B as Elvis was to get while "Shake, Rattle And Roll" compares favorably with Joe Turner's immortal recording. A note from Sholes to RCA concerning the two February sides (that they were not single material and should be saved for the second album) indicates that the decision to include the Sun leftovers on the first album had already been made, regardless of what Elvis put on tape in RCA's studios.

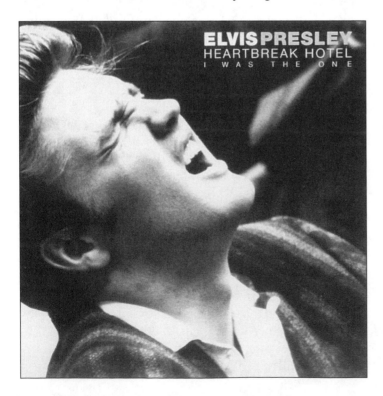

April 1956

"I Want You, I Need You, I Love You," 47-6540, 5/56, #1.

After taping another five Gleason shows (hosted by Jimmy and Tommy Dorsey) and a *Milton Berle Show*, Elvis entered RCA's Nashville studios. A new single was needed (even though four of the preceding sides were available), and Sholes and RCA opted for another ballad. Chet Atkins returns on guitar, Marvin Hughes is on piano and Gordon Stoker and the Speer brothers are on vocals. "I Want You, I Need You, I Love You" is a so-so song given a great reading by Elvis, who, of course, enjoyed the challenge of slow songs (and the legitimacy they gave him as a "real" singer). Plus, the single racked up a half-million in sales in a matter of weeks and was over 1,500,000 by the end of 1957!

July 1956

"Hound Dog," 47-6604, 7/56, #1; *"Don't Be Cruel,"* 47-6604, 7/56, #1; *"Any Way You Want Me (That's How I Will Be),"* 47-6643, 9/56, #20.

In July they were back in the Big Apple to tape the now legendary *Steve Allen Show*. Allen oozed the dilettante's disdain for black-based rhythm 'n' blues music, requiring Elvis to wear a perfectly inappropriate tuxedo and introduce his latest single, "Hound Dog," by singing to ... a hound dog. Few critics of this tactless maneuver bother to mention that the poor dog was forced to wear a hat that made him look a lot more uncomfortable than the young rocker. While there, Elvis and the band were gathered into the New York studios for another session, this time with a new single the goal.

Aside from introducing Elvis to the soon-to-be-irreplaceable Jordanaires (Gordon Stoker on lead along with Neal Matthews, tenor, Hoyt Hawkins, baritone, and Hugh Jarrett, bass), this can be considered the single most eventful session Presley ever had: The single exploded, selling 1,500,000 copies in less than a month, and RCA was claiming 5,000,000 in sales by April 1957, less than a year after release! "Hound Dog," the designated A-side, reached #1 only to be nudged aside by its flip, "Don't Be Cruel." The two sides stayed at the top for three months to become the biggest double-sided hit in the annals of *Billboard*'s charts. According to Joel Whitburn's analysis of those charts, it is the biggest hit of the rock era (1955 through the present).

Legend has it that Elvis was not enamored of putting "Hound Dog" on wax. While it was a rabble-rousing closer for his live show, he felt it was too silly to record. The powers-that-be felt otherwise and we are the better for it. There are no precedents for the sound that erupted from Elvis and the band; this track still sounds like an onslaught, a rave-up of kinetic energy. As noise, it stands as the precursor to the Stones' "Have You Seen Your Mother, Baby, Standing In The Shadows?" and the Yardbirds' "I'm A Man."

"Don't Be Cruel" was offered by Otis Blackwell and was often cited by Presley as the favorite recording of his from this period. Patterning his interpretation on the demo submitted by Blackwell, Elvis' singing is perfect. The entire performance is so smooth, so easy, nearly four decades later this sounds like a perfect record, a hit record, for any generation.

"Any Way You Want Me (That's How I Will Be)" was issued as the B-side of "Love Me Tender." While the appeal of the latter is undeniable, "Any Way" may be one of Elvis' most powerful performances as a ballad singer from the early years of his career. Finally, while Shorty Long is listed as the piano player for the session, Gordon Stoker remembers playing on "Hound Dog."

August-October 1956

"We're Gonna Move," EPA-4006, 11/56; *"Love Me Tender,* 47-6643, 9/56, #1; *"Poor Boy,"* EPA-4006, 11/56, #24; *"Let Me,"* EPA-4006, 11/56.

As these were recorded for Presley's first film at 20th Century Fox in Hollywood using studio musicians who were almost certainly unfamiliar with rock 'n' roll, a lot should not be expected from them, especially given the plot of the film for which they were written, a Civil War period western. Still, the title song, an adaptation of the standard "Aura Lee," was a runaway best-seller (over 1,000,000 moved in a month; 3,000,000 in less than a year) and catapulted the otherwise mediocre film into cinematic history: It remains, 35 years after the fact, the only film to recoup its entire investment and show a profit in its first week of release! (Of course, it was shot on a minuscule budget as a "B" film. *Batman Returns* recently topped $100,000,000 gross receipts in its second week of release and is, technically still in the ledger books in red ink.)

The three other tracks are appropriate to the film; Presley and the musicians turn in better performances than the situation probably justifies. "We're Gonna Move" is a genuinely good song; Elvis should have given it a shot back in Nashville or New York with Moore, Black and crew. The other two are way too uptempo for the film's milieu but are fun nonetheless; the young singer's enthusiasm for the project (Elvis Aron Presley *really* wanted to be a movie star) is obvious and, ahem, infectious. Devoid of many of the

mannerisms with which we have come to associate Elvis, they have aged well.

September 1956

"Playing For Keeps," 47-6800, 1/57, #21; "Love Me," EPA-992, 11/56, #2; "How Do You Think I Feel," EPA-994, 1/57; "How's The World Treating You," EPA-994, 1/57; "Paralyzed," EPA-992, 11/56, #59; "When My Blue Moon Turns To Gold Again," EPA-992, 11/56, #19; "Long Tall Sally," EPA-994, 1/57; "Old Shep," EPA-993, 12/56, #47; "Too Much," 47-6800, 1/57, #1; "Anyplace Is Paradise," EPA-993, 12/56; "Ready Teddy," EPA-993, 12/56; "First In Line," EPA-994, 1/57; "Rip It Up," EPA-992, 11/56.

By September 1956, Elvis had cut 17 sides for RCA, completed his first movie (including four soundtrack songs), appeared on national TV nine times and several *Louisiana Hayride* radio shows, toured from March through August *and* it was only the end of the summer, leaving time to complete his second long player.

Since the guys were all in Hollywood for the filming of *Love Me Tender*, RCA hustled them over to Radio Recorders, and 13 masters were completed in three days. The basic band (Elvis, rhythm guitar; Scotty Moore, lead; Bill Black, bass; and D.J. Fontana, drums) would now include the Jordanaires on every session; for these, Gordon Stoker doubled on piano. Except for the ever-cloying "Old Shep," this is a solid rock 'n' roll album, stating the obvious without stretching any boundaries. Because there are no real chances taken (except "Love Me") there are no real standouts, thus there is a tendency to underestimate the album that emerged, LPM-1382, *Elvis*. Actually, had this album been issued by any other singer of the period, critics would still be singing its praises. However, in the light of Presley's achievements before and after, it has gone down in history as a ho-hum affair.

"Paralyzed," submitted by Otis Blackwell with the hopes of another 5,000,000 in sales and royalties, was not used as a single. Too bad, as it's a wonderful track (and turned up in the Top 10 in Great Britain in 1957). "Rip It Up" is another excellent rhythm number. But the real standout of the sessions is the aforementioned "Love Me." Originally penned by Jerry Leiber and Mike Stoller as a lark – read the lyrics and it is a string of maudlin country cliches – the young singer turns it in on itself, reading the lines with conviction and strength. Elvis has a ball with the now-enveloping Presley mannerisms, making the whole greater than the sum of its less than aspiring parts, much to Leiber and Stoller's amazed delight. (For an example of the song's basic ludicrousness, listen to any other version, including the throwaway readings on countless live Elvis albums from the '70s.)

Although "Love Me" screams – no, pleads – for issuance as a single, RCA opted for a rocker and led the first EP off with it instead. To the surprise of everyone "Love Me" reached the Top 10 on *Billboard*'s singles charts (#2 on their sales charts) as an EP track; there is no doubt that it would have reached #1 as a single and, possibly, could have outsold "Hound Dog." As it was, EPA 992 became the first EP to sell over 1,000,000 copies (a feat duplicated by Elvis and no one else since) "Love Me" is, along with a handful of sides, one of the songs most people immediately identify with Elvis Presley.

The single that was released, 47-6800, "Too Much," a rather grotesquely effective piece that lurched through its verses to an abrupt end without a bridge, backed with the pleading "Playing For Keeps," was issued in the first weeks of 1957, selling a million copies within a month. and approaching 3,000,000 by the end of the year.

Ending 1956 with these tunes on LP and EP, the young king of rock 'n' roll had placed 17 sides on the charts (several of the ones noted above would not actually peak as hits until January 1957), selling nearly 10,000,000 singles. Five titles – "Heartbreak Hotel," "I Want You, I Need You, I Love You," "Hound Dog," "Don't Be Cruel" and "Love Me Tender" – had reached

#1 on the sales chart, a position that Elvis held for 26 of the year's 52 weeks! Both albums reached the top, with the first one becoming RCA Victor's biggest-selling popular album within two months of release and its first to top 1,000,000 copies sold.

January 1957

"I Believe, EPA-4054, 5/57; "Tell Me Why"; "Got A Lot O' Livin' To Do," EPA-2-1515, 8/57; "All Shook Up," 47-6870, 3/57, #1; "Mean Woman Blues," EPA-2-1515, 8/57; "(There'll Be) Peace In The Valley," EPA-4054, 5/57, #25; "That's When Your Heartaches Begin," 47-6870, 3/57, #58; "Take My Hand, Precious Lord," EPA-4054, 5/57; "Party," EPA-1-1515, 8/57; "Hot Dog," EPA-2-1515, 8/57; "Lonesome Cowboy," EPA-2-1515, 8/57; "It Is No Secret (What God Can Do)," EPA-4054, 5/57; "Blueberry Hill," EPA-4041, 4/57; "Have I Told You Lately That I Love You," EPA-4041, 4/57; "Is It So Strange" EPA-4041, 4/57; "(Let Me, Be Your) Teddy Bear," 47-7000, 6/57, #1; "One Night Of Sin."

1957 opened with the now undisputed king of rock 'n' roll back in Hollywood for his second feature film, *Loving You.* New single material was needed, Elvis had decided he wanted to cut a religious EP, and material for the film was necessary; these sessions (January 12 through 24) are about those three goals. Additional musicians included Stoker and Dudley Brooks on piano, Hoyt Hawkins, piano and organ, and, for the soundtrack work, Tiny Timbrell, guitar, and George Fields, harmonica. Fifteen tracks were completed that would be issued in the '50s;

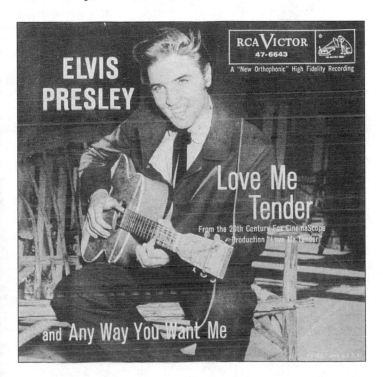

"Tell Me Why" was a modest hit 10 years later while "One Night of Sin" remained an unearthed gem till after Elvis' death.

The first two days were quite productive, and three-quarters of the gospel album was completed. This may seem like business as usual in hindsight, but it was a risky career move at the time, surprising fans and detractors alike. Also cut was one of his biggest chart-toppers, "All Shook Up," while leftovers, especially "Got A Lot O' Livin' To Do" and "Mean Woman Blues," could have served as A-sides at a moment's notice. "I Beg Of You" was unsuccessfully attempted.

February 1957

"Don't Leave Me Now," LPM-1515, 7/57; "I Beg Of You," 47-7150, 1/58, #8; "One Night," 47-7419, 10/58, #4; "True Love," EPA-1-1515, 8/57; "I Need You So," EPA-4041, 4/57; "Loving You," 47-7000, 6/57, #20; "When It Rains, It Really Pours."

As Presley was scheduled to begin his third film in a matter of weeks, he stayed over in Hollywood, returning to Radio Recorders in February to tie up some loose ends. Dudley Brooks helped the band cut another half-dozen tracks in two days "I Beg Of You," not much of a song to begin with, was revived and once again Elvis doesn't really get it perfect, although it does make a good B-side. "One Night" is a bowdlerized version of "One Night Of Sin." Elvis overcomes the censoring by singing this version with more (sexual) ferocity than the original! Wasted as the B-side to the inferior "I Got Stung," "One Night" raced past the designated A-side and placed higher on the charts, although "Stung" received the million-selling credit.

"When It Rains, It Really Pours," one of the songs attempted at Sun, was given a new treatment here; unfortunately, instead of placing this (and others) onto one of the Army albums in 1959, it sat until 1965 before surfacing on *Elvis For Everyone.* The rest of the tracks are of secondary importance. What is notable about all of these 1957 sessions is how much each was scattered to the wind when released: 23 tracks ended up on five singles, two EPs and three LPs over an eight-year period. This would stand as a prototype for the way Elvis would be handled in the future.

In this period Elvis also cut the soundtrack versions of several songs that would appear in *Loving You.* These were, by and large, good recordings but hardly essential (the released studio versions are better). These would not see official release for three decades until the first volume of the *Essential Elvis* series.

April 1957

"Jailhouse Rock," 47-7035, 9/57, #1; *"Young And Beautiful,"* EPA-4114, 10/57; *"I Want To Be Free,"* EPA-4114, 10/57; *"(You're so Square) Baby I Don't Care,"* EPA-4114, 10/57; *"Don't Leave Me Now,"* EPA-4114, 10/57; *"Treat Me Nice."*

Elvis does a soundtrack with Leiber and Stoller – a marriage made in heaven. Jerry Leiber and Mike Stoller were two young white men who had been R&B fans for years and had made a mark for themselves in that field as songwriters (the original of their "Hound Dog" was a hit for Big Mama Thornton years before Elvis touched it) and producers who essentially created the Coasters. Their initial reaction to Elvis' "Hound Dog" was not positive; the very idea of a man singing the lyrics seemed ludicrous. The offer to work with Elvis was acceptable if not terribly exciting. That changed when they met the young singer and found a kindred spirit: Presley was encyclopedic in his knowledge of the music they loved, as passionate in his likes as they were. Plus, as they were to find, he was willing to sing anything. More importantly, once he threw himself into a song, it appeared he *could* sing anything!

Musically, the sessions were interesting for several reasons: Leiber and Stoller immediately took over the sessions, essentially producing the soundtrack (without a contract). Stoller also sat in on piano; it is he who appears in the movie as the unnamed pianist. These were also the first sessions at which Bill Black was using his new Fender bass. At one point he threw the new gadget down in disgust at his inability to get the line to "(You're So Square) Baby, I Don't Care." Elvis picked up the axe and cut the part himself, requiring him to come back and lay the vocal down on an overdub. Unfortunately, the overdub is not perfect and the completed track lacks the feel of his best recordings (Elvis sounds like he's singing in another studio).

While this was Elvis' 15th EP, the bulk of his earlier ones were regurgitations of LP and 45 material. Most EPs were merely samplers from existing LPs, or a hits collection; there have been few attempts to use the medium as a legitimate expression in content and style. Exceptions include the first soundtrack, *Love Me Tender*, acceptable as a soundtrack but hardly great rock 'n' roll; *Peace In The Valley*, the collection of four gospel tunes; and, for the sake of this argument, *Just For You*, four original track from the January 1957 sessions. Unfortunately, these are more or less filler, tunes not good enough for singles (and they were gathered onto the *Loving You* album within a matter of months).

The five songs that make up the EP ("Treat Me Nice" was, for some reason, only issued as the B-side to the title tune) make this one of the handful of truly

great extended play records in the format's history. *Jailhouse Rock* is five strong recordings that sound right together and establish the EP as essential to every Elvis collection of the time. That RCA never really did compile them logically onto LP ("Jailhouse Rock" and "Treat Me Nice" made their way onto *Elvis' Golden Records* in early 1958; "Young And Beautiful," "Baby, I Don't Care" and "I Want To Be Free" ended up on *A Date With Elvis* in '59; "Don't Leave Me Now" was inexplicably ignored) has only stressed its necessity and beauty as an EP.

Jailhouse Rock remains a quintessential '50s film; Elvis handles his role well and this should have shown everyone that there was both talent and desire in the young singer to be a professional actor.

September 1957

"Treat Me Nice," 47-7035, 9/57, #18; *"Blue Christmas,"* EPA-4108, 12/57; *"My Wish Came True,"* 47-7600, 6/59, #12; *"White Christmas,"* EPA-4340, 12/58; *"Here Comes Santa Claus (Right Down Santa Claus Lane),"* EPA-4340, 12/58; *"Silent Night,"* EPA-4340, 12/58; *"Don't,"* 47-7150, 1/58; *"O Little Town Of Bethlehem,"* EPA-4340, 12/58; *"Santa Bring My Baby Back (To Me),"* EPA-4108, 12/57; *"Santa Claus Is Back In Town,"* EPA-4108, 12/57; *"I'll Be Home For Christmas,"* EPA-4108, 12/57.*

Elvis decided to cut a Christmas album. Like the rest of the 1957 sessions, these were held at Radio Recorders, this time with vocalist Millie Kirkham. With the four religious tunes from earlier in the year, eight more songs were needed. A few standards –

including a nice reading of "White Christmas" based squarely on the Drifters' seminal arrangement – were cut along with some original seasonal pop material. The final piece fell into place when Leiber and Stoller, on hand at Presley's request (he was also recording their composition, "Don't," as a single), whipped off a nifty blues, "Santa Claus Is Back In Town," where Elvis gets downright lascivious in the midst of the more genteel holiday offerings. "Blue Christmas," the seasonal song most closely associated with Presley, was not released as a single until 1964, and then on the Gold Standard Series.

For 1957, sales and achievements duplicated the previous year: four #1 singles that spent a combined 26 weeks at the top, "All Shook Up" being the highlight, soaring to 2,000,000 in sales in less than a month; a couple of gold albums; and a special announcement from RCA that Elvis had sold more than 5,000,000 EPs since March 1956.

January 1958

"Danny"; "Hard Headed Woman," 47-7280, 6/58, #1; "Trouble," EPA-4321, 9/58; "New Orleans," EPA-4319, 9/58; "Crawfish," EPA-4321, 9/58; "Dixieland Rock," EPA-4321, 9/58; "Lover Doll," EPA-4319, 9/58; "Don't Ask Me Why," 47-7280, 6/58, #25; "As Long As I Have You," EPA-4319, 9/58; "King Creole," EPA-4319, 9/58; "Young Dreams," EPA-4319, 9/58; "Steadfast, Loyal And True."

King Creole was the fourth and final movie of the decade, made while Elvis was preparing for his induction into the U.S. Army. Again held at Radio

Recorders, these were his most complicated sessions yet. As the movie called for a Dixieland sound, several musicians were brought in to complement the regular band and achieve the desired sound, including tuba, clarinet, trumpet, sax and trombone. Also, Jordanaires Stoker, Hawkins and Matthews lent their skills on bongos, cymbals and bass, respectively. The finished sound was quite good on the rockers; "Hard Headed Woman" was a huge hit and "Trouble" an immediate classic. "New Orleans" and "Dixieland Rock" are great, rousing numbers, incorporating the horns comfortably, while "King Creole" is one of the best – and most appropriate – title tunes Elvis would ever record.

Unfortunately, the ballads suffer: "Don't Ask Me Why" was mediocre by Elvis' standards; "As Long As I have You" lugubrious by anyone's, and "Young Dreams" pure schmaltz. "Lover Doll" is nice, if slight (and, for collectors, the versions on the EP and the LP are different, the EP mix unavailable elsewhere) while "Crawfish" (with vocal accompaniment by Kitty White) remains an underrated gem. Nonetheless, it is an effective session; the soundtrack works and, commercially, a double-sided million-selling hit, two monster EPs (only "Steadfast, Loyal And True" didn't find its way onto a 45) and a gold album were the results. Only "Danny" was shelved (where it rightly belonged) until 1978, where it was part of A Legendary Performer, Volume 3.

February 1958

"Doncha Think It's Time," 47-7240, 4/58, #15; "Your Cheatin' Heart"; "Wear My Ring Around Your Neck," 47-7240, 4/58, #2

Radio Recorders hosted this session shortly after the soundtrack was completed, where Elvis & Co. were joined by Tiny Timbrell and Dudley Brooks. "Doncha Think It's Time" is a good track, rather unlike Elvis' regular repertoire. The released single was actually spliced from three different takes, #40, #47 and #48. When mastering Gold Records, Volume 2, the complete take of #40 was erroneously used. "Wear My Ring Around Your Neck," while a bang-up rocker, was a petty tune that would lead critics to claim Elvis had sold out to the girls. The exact reason for the inclusion of "Your Cheatin' Heart" is mysterious, unless one considers it a demo of sorts; Elvis was dying to land the role of Hank Williams in the much-talked about film adaptation of the country king's life. It didn't show its face until collected in August 1965 on Elvis For Everyone (LPM/LSP 3450).

June 1958

"I Need Your Love Tonight," 47-7506, 3/59, #4; "A Big Hunk O' Love," 47-7600, 6/59, #1; "Ain't That Loving You, Baby"; "(Now And Then There's) A Fool Such As I," 47-7506, 3/59, #2; "I Got Stung," 47-7410, 10/58, #8.

These final sessions of the decade were done while Elvis was on leave from the Army (granted at the Colonel's request) to provide RCA with some singles for release while the King was away. The band was different this time: Elvis played rhythm and Fontana remained on drums but lead guitar was handled by Hank Garland (with Chet Atkins) and the bass was play by Bob Moore. Floyd Cramer returned on piano with Buddy Harman on bongos. In many ways, this band played even harder than Elvis' regular guys. While none of these tracks are outstanding (an argument can be made for "A Big Hunk O' Love"), the sound of the five combined is great and, of course, it's a shame an entire album couldn't have been cut. "A Fool Such As I" shows Presley completely in command of all his now recognizable Elvisisms. Certainly it's self-conscious and at odds with the Sun material; this in no way affects the enjoyment of the recording. It may not be art but it sure is a lot of fun!

A spliced, medium tempo "Ain't That Loving You, Baby" was coupled with an unexceptional ballad ("Ask Me") and released as a single in 1964, giving Elvis a much-needed double-sided Top 20 hit. A faster, complete take was issued in 1985 on *Reconsider Baby*, an album that must stand as one of Elvis' best compilations ever assembled.

Comparing these sessions commercially with the previous two years is difficult. Much of the work was rushed due to Elvis' upcoming Army gig so the quality isn't as high as the previous year (and the songs aren't as strong to begin with). The sessions were broken up and released over a two-year period, 1958 and 1959, with little of the impact that the onslaught of his earlier releases had. Nonetheless, eight of the sides were hits and another five gold records were racked up. By this time RCA could boast that Elvis Presley had 14 consecutive million-selling singles and nearly 10,000,000 EPs sold, several of which topped the million mark. He had also provided RCA Victor with a basic catalog of nine LPs that would remain in print with no changes for over a decade. These albums alone made the company a fortune, selling consistently, year after year. In fact, there would be times that the Presley catalog items outsold current product: During the 1964 Christmas season, *Elvis' Christmas Album* would sell over 300,000 copies, topping the company's year-end sales list!

Most Collectible 45

"That's All Right"/ "Blue Moon Of Kentucky," Sun 209, $4,000-plus (it has twice traded for over $10,000!)

Most Collectible LP

Elvis' Christmas Album, RCA Victor LOC-1035, red vinyl, $15,000.

Recommended Introduction

24 Karat Hits, DCC Compact Classics 1117 (it's a 24-karat gold disc, so it's pricier than the average CD, but it has 24 of Elvis' biggest hits in astounding sound quality)

If you want to hear more…

Sunrise, RCA 67675 (a 2-CD set with all the 1954-55 Sun sessions, early acetates and numerous live tracks from 1955; this collection illustrates succinctly what all the excitement was about)

Elvis '56, RCA 66856 (a single CD that contains 22 of his best recordings from his first year at RCA)

Artist Of The Century, RCA 67732 (a 3-CD set with a generous selection of mostly hit singles from 1954-76 and very little filler)

If you want to hear a LOT more…

The below six releases will give you just about everything you could possibly want by Elvis unless you want to get into some of the *really* bad movie songs, alternate

takes, home recordings, live shows and the like, which go way beyond the scope of what we're trying to do here:

The King Of Rock And Roll: The Complete 50's Masters, RCA 66050 (5 CDs, the contents of the above article and more, it belongs in every collection)

From Nashville To Memphis: The Essential 60's Masters I, RCA 66160 (5 CDs of all of his secular non-movie-related recordings from the 1960s)

Command Performances: The Essential 60's Masters II, RCA 66601 (a 2-CD set with the best of his 1960s movie songs)

Walk A Mile In My Shoes: The Essential 70's Masters, RCA 66670 (a well-assembled 5-CD box that forces the listener to re-assess Elvis' work in his declining years)

Amazing Grace: His Greatest Sacred Performances, RCA 66421 (a 2-CD box with almost all the sacred material Elvis recorded from 1957-71)

If Every Day Was Like Christmas, RCA 66482 (for the first time, all of Elvis' Christmas recordings on one CD, thus making all other Elvis Christmas CDs redundant)

Gene Vincent

by Sue Smallwood

I can still remember the first time I heard the song for which Gene Vincent is best remembered. In my early days of record collecting, my dad's habit was to buy a box of records for some outrageously low price at a yard sale, with no regard to its contents. One of these boxes contained a record by Gene Vincent. I don't remember what I was listening to right before I put "Be-Bop-A-Lula" on my hand-me-down RCA Victor record changer, but my first thought when I heard that drawn-out "Welllll…" was, "What the heck is this?" And I meant that in a good way. This sounded like nothing else I'd heard up to that time. I later found out that this record actually made the top 10 of the national music charts in 1956 – a time when a great record got the attention it deserved. Gene Vincent, though long gone, got his due in Goldmine *with the following article, which appeared November 26, 1993.*

Gene Vincent was a musician decades ahead of his peers. Earthier than Elvis Presley, more sensual than Jerry Lee Lewis, sexier than Buddy Holly, Vincent was the embodiment of the libidinous, defiant tension upon which rock 'n' roll was founded and continues to flourish. In rock iconography, it was Vincent who first donned the all-black leather stage gear that's since become a punk rock and heavy metal hallmark. It was Vincent who first developed the menacing stage swagger (out of necessity; his left leg was crippled most of his life), frenetic delivery and delinquent, rebellious persona still emulated by rockers some 20-plus years after his death. He and his original band the Blue Caps were among the first rock artists to tour Australia and Japan; they've remained an inspiration to generations of music makers – John Lennon and Paul McCartney, Robert Plant and Jimmy Page, Jeff Beck, Eric Clapton, Jim Morrison, Billy Idol, Brian Setzer, Chris Isaak – and music lovers the world over.

Vincent's personal life was informed by the same dictum of rule-breaking, what could arguably be termed a death wish. In 1952, he wangled his under-aged way into the Navy in order to fight in the Korean War. His affinity for fast cars and motorcycles resulted in a horrible motorbike accident in 1955 that left him with a painful, permanent leg injury; throughout his lifetime he continually defied doctors who recommended, then practically demanded, amputation. He had a fascination with guns and knives – often spontaneously pulling them on bandmates, friends and lovers for the sheer thrill of it – and with death, faking his own demise on many occasions for attention and his own amusement. His inability to stay in one place for very long culminated in perilous road treks at his insistence for the exhausted Blue Caps, departing one city for the next within minutes of completing a frenzied concert performance, often the third of the day. His restlessness was a probable factor in the 1960 accident that claimed fellow rocker and close friend Eddie Cochran – Vincent had urged Cochran to leave London ahead of schedule and the pair's speeding taxi ran off the road – a death he no doubt blamed on himself.

Vincent's personal relations were no less rocky. He was married four times, the first to a 15-year-old, and was by turns obsessively romantic, frightening possessive and, as chronicled by biographer Britt Hagarty in *The Day The World Turned Blue*, physically abusive with the women in his life. He fathered three children and was a loving, thoughtful parent when he made time between nearly non-stop concert engagements. A quiet, shy, likable man offstage, a consummate, demanding performer onstage and a perfectionist in the recording studio, Vincent's

revolving band lineups either loved or loathed (or both) the man. The singer's long struggle with alcoholism exacerbated his emotionally excessive tendencies and eventually took a toll on his health, leading to his consequential alienation from friends and family and tragic, premature death in 1971.

Born Vincent Eugene Craddock in February 1935 (the exact date remains in dispute), the native of the bustling military seaport of Hampton Roads, Virginia enjoyed an eclectic soundtrack to his childhood: the traditional Appalachian and bluegrass country stylings heard on the Grand Ole Opry with which he'd entertain his fellow sailors overseas during the Korean War, the gospel spirituals sung by the local black community, the emergent be-bop jazz of the early '50s. Upon his return from the war (and perhaps inspired by Bill Haley and the Comets, whose "Rock Around The Clock" claimed the #1 chart position in July 1955 while he was recuperating in the Portsmouth Naval Hospital from his post-wartime motorcycle accident), Vincent tried his hand at this curious new phenomenon called rock 'n' roll that blended the best of the musics he had always loved. Though stories vary, it is generally accepted that "Be-Bop-A-Lula," his best-known tune, was penned during Vincent's hospital stay by him and a fellow patient.

"Actually, the song was written by a guy from Portsmouth named Donald Graves," states Joe Hoppel, current vice president and former program director for Hampton Roads radio station WCMS, where Vincent's career was launched. "They (Vincent and his eventual manager Bill "Sheriff Tex" Davis, former operations director at WCMS) bought the song from Donald. I believe they paid him $25 for it, which is not unusual. Often artists will buy songs from people who wrote them. They would take the sure money rather than take the risk of not ever getting their song heard. They bought the song from Donald Graves, and Graves' name was replaced with Davis' as co-writer."

After a six-month recuperation, Vincent was released from the hospital and, limited in his career options due to his disfigured leg, decided to give music a go. About the same time, WCMS was initiating a weekly live show and scouring the area for viable talent. "We had decided to put together a live show on the order of the Grand Ole Opry that we would do on Friday night," Hoppel recalls. "WCMS at that time was AM, of course, and we were a daytime station, so what we'd do, we'd tape the show on Friday night, then play it back on the air Sunday afternoon. We called the show *Country Showtime*. We started running some plugs on the air that anyone that wanted to audition for the show to

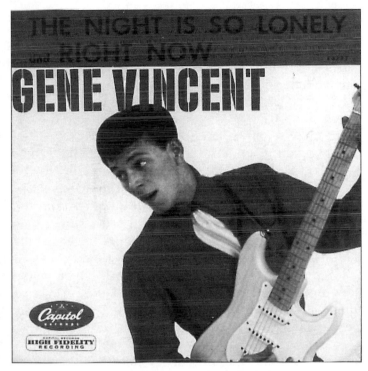

come up to the station on a Sunday. It was a Sunday afternoon in March (of 1956 when Vincent auditioned). The #1 song on the chart at that time was 'Heartbreak Hotel' by Elvis Presley, and we must've listened to that song 50 times that day. Everybody sang it, including Gene. It was easy to remember Gene because, first of all, he had a cast on his leg. He had been in the hospital for quite some time, really, and he was just there while the leg was healing, but it was still in a cast. The cast was all the way up to his hip."

And the voice – sweet, fluid, but with a dark undercurrent of tense energy – was unforgettable.

"So we picked Gene and quite a few other people to be on the show on Friday nights. We first started doing it at a theater in Portsmouth. Then we moved to a theater in Norfolk, it was an old movie theater. We'd do the shows there, it was a live audience. We had a staff band there that backed a lot of the artists that didn't have their own band, and Gene was one of those. (The staff band) was called Wee Willie and the Virginians. So they backed Gene on his appearances on the show. Gene did all Elvis Presley songs – he loved Elvis Presley – on the show," until he decided to try out "Be-Bop-A-Lula" on the Elvis-happy crowds. "It went over like gangbusters, it was a big hit, with the girls, particularly, they went crazy for him. Afterwards they'd all be waiting outside the stage door when he came out to get his autograph and so forth. It went over very well." Sadly, no acetates exist of the *Country Showtime* performances.

Impressed with Vincent's vocal abilities and the always-enthusiastic crowd response, Sheriff Tex, who counted Capitol A&R man Ken Nelson among his close associates, decided Vincent should make a demo recording for Nelson, who was searching for an Elvis-type for the Capitol roster. A backing band was quickly assembled, using personnel from the Virginians and other local acts: guitarist Cliff Gallup, bassist Jack Neal, rhythm guitarist Willie Williams and drummer Dickie Harrell, who was just 15 and still in school.

"Bill said that he had talked to Ken Nelson and they wanted us to make a tape," Harrell recalls. "We said, 'Yeah, I guess it'd be all right.' We didn't have nothing to lose, so we made the tape over at the station one night, and 'Be-Bop-A Lula' didn't sound nothing like it did on the record, nothing. We made it, and I don't even think Bill told (Vincent) what he was going to use it for. A couple of weeks went by...and one night on 'Country Showtime' – that's probably where (Davis) wanted to break the news – (Davis) come out there and he told (the audience) that he had sent this tape to Ken Nelson and Ken Nelson wanted us to come to Nashville to cut this song, 'Be-Bop-A-Lula,' and 'Woman Love' and a couple more. The people just went crazy because Gene was their number one boy then, they loved him. We didn't know nothing about it. Gene about fell out, he almost tripped over his crutches."

On May 4, 1956, Vincent and his troupe of players – including the student Harrell: "I called in sick and played hooky for a couple of days" – entered Owen Bradley's Nashville studio. To the group's surprise, they were not the only musicians present. "We got there and we met Mr. Nelson," Harrell remembers, "and they had another band setting in the place. We came in and I told Cliff, 'Damn, I didn't know they had a session with two bands!' He said, 'I know it. What's going on here?' These guys are all sitting around the wall, and Mr. Nelson was sitting in the control room and Gene came in and introduced the band and everything. So we're sitting around and, I said, 'Mr. Nelson?' and he said, 'Yeah, Dick, what's the matter?' I said, 'Well, what are all these people doing in here?' He said, 'Aw, don't worry about that, you all just play a little bit of the song now.' So Gene got on the mike and did a little bit of 'Be-Bop-A-Lula' and Cliff put the runs on it and then we played a little bit of 'Woman Love.' Nelson said, 'Well, play a little bit more, play a little bit longer.' We played halfway through 'Be-Bop' and then he says, 'Okay, okay. All right, boys, you can leave now.' So these guys packed up and left. I looked around and said, 'Cliff, what's happening here?' He said, 'Well, they're leaving.' And they said, 'We'll see you guys, good luck!'"

Harrell remains nonchalant about the lack of faith Capitol had originally shown in the band. "At first, I don't think (Capitol) wanted the band," he says candidly. "They just wanted Gene and his song because Ken said that it was just what he was looking for, it was the type of voice that he could sing just about anything, which he could. Gene could sing anything, he didn't need all the amplifiers and junk, he could just take the song and just sing it. In other words, when you heard the song, you heard him."

Recording commenced of "Race With The Devil," "Be-Bop-A-Lula," "Woman Love" and "I Sure Miss You." Harrell fondly recalls waxing Vincent's greatest hit, particularly his vocal contributions: "We did 'Be-Bop' and in the middle there, (my) scream was in there. When I did that scream in there they all stopped playing. Mr. Nelson came out and said, 'What's the matter? What happened?' and Cliff said, 'Damn, what's that noise?' I told Mr. Nelson that I just felt like it belonged in there, so he asked Gene, 'What do you think?' and he says, 'Yeah, leave it in there, I like it.' Cliff said, 'Nah, that don't sound good.' Nelson told him, 'Well, let's leave it in there, let's play it all the way through.' And we did the session and everybody was tickled to death. (Nelson) said, 'Oh yeah, boys, it sounds good. You all got something different here.'"

Other highlights of the group's first professional studio sessions, Harrell tells, were Nelson's reaction to the band – "When (Cliff) did 'Race With The Devil' Nelson couldn't believe it because of the runs on it"; Gallup's virtuosity and innovative technique is still admired today – and another Harrell contribution, the band moniker. "We used to all wear caps back in them days and I just had the name the Blue Caps – 'Call it the Blue Hats, the Blue Caps, whatever you want to call it' – and it stuck."

The Blue Caps returned home, Harrell returned to his studies, and "Be-Bop-A-Lula," released as the B-side of the suggestive "Woman Love," quickly scaled the charts. "Next thing I know," Harrell recalls, "Bill Davis says, 'They want you all back to cut an album.' From then on everything just clicked into place." Vincent and his band returned to Bradley's studio in June 1956 – "Be-Bop-A-Lula" had already sold 200,000 copies by then – for four days of recording, tracks which would comprise their first album, *Bluejean Bop!*, released in September of that year. Upon completion of recording, Vincent and the Blue Caps hit the concert trail for a nearly non-stop schedule of performances, including a stint with the Johnny Burnette Rock 'N' Roll Trio, and the beginning of the group's hellfire reputation for its frenetic, kinetic live act. Vincent and the Blue Caps made their first live concert appearance at Folly Beach, just outside Charleston, South Carolina; Harrell, however, recalls more vividly a show in Shamokin, Pennsylvania.

"It was in this little theater and I think the price to get in was like 85 cents," he says. "We went out there and played, they had some rock movie playing. We had just bought these brand new clothes. They were tan jackets and we had cream-colored pants with black shirts and white ties, I'll never forget it. That show, I don't know what happened, but (the crowd) went crazy, they knocked the bandstand over. They tore everything up. The lights went out, the bandstand toppled over, all of us were underneath the stage. One or two jackets were saved, but the rest of them they just tore up. When I got up I went out the front and all that I had on was the imprint of the jacket in the front, all of the sleeves were gone, the buttons were gone. Gene was sitting there going, 'I don't believe it.' And Bill Davis says, 'You know how much money it cost for them jackets?' It was so funny. From then on, everywhere, that was just the way it was."

According to Harrell, Vincent, a dedicated entertainer, was a bit of a pill when it came to live performances, confounding fans and bandmates alike. "Only bad thing about Gene," he says, "you couldn't get him to sing his songs on the tours. He would sing everybody else's songs; he'd sing 'Be-Bop' and he might do 'Dance To The Bop' or 'Bop Street.' Most artists when you go to a show, especially if they have a brand new album out, they'll do the whole album. But he didn't do that. All you would hear the whole night (from the crowd) was "'Be-Bop-A-Lula,' we want 'Be-Bop-A-Lula,' we want 'Woman Love!'" He'd say, 'We'll get it in a minute,' and then he'd sing Little Richard, Chuck Berry, Bo Diddley. We'd sit there (prior to a concert) and he's say, 'I'm going to do this, I'm going to do that, I'm going to do this,' and next thing you know, he'd come out there and he'd start singing 'Long Tall Sally' and he didn't even have it on the list. This is what he did because he did what he liked."

Shortly before *Bluejean Bop*'s release, "Be-Bop-A-Lula" had made its way to the top 10 on both the country and pop charts and the Top 20 on the U.K. chart. The song's A-side, "Woman Love," had since been banned from radio airplay in several states and by the BBC, its slap-echoed moans and pants deemed obscene. "Race With The Devil" b/w "Gonna Back Up Baby" was released in August 1956, peaking at a dismal #96, and "Blue Jean Bop" b/w "Who Slapped John" followed in September, along with *Bluejean Bop!*

The rigors of the road took their toll on the Blue Caps. Shortly after the album's release Willie Williams quit the band, replaced by fellow Hampton Roads native Teddy Crutchfield, who was replaced by country picker Paul Peek, and Cliff Gallup gave his notice as well. "Cliff always said it was just too much for him because he was married," Harrell says. "It ain't no place if you're married. Today, if you're married you bring your wife with you and your kid and they sleep on the big bus with all the modern conveniences, but we didn't have all that stuff. We had an old '56 station wagon, the windows were broke and the heat didn't work. We were working so doggone much, I think that Cliff – well, it wasn't what he wanted. It got to the point that we were playing three jobs a day in three different places. In six months time, which I think might have been why Cliff (quit), and Willie also, I came home one day. It was on Christmas. I go home Christmas morning and I had to go back out Christmas night to Milwaukee to play."

Vincent and the Blue Caps landed an appearance in *The Girl Can't Help It,* one of the earliest rock 'n' roll movies, starring Jayne Mansfield and also featuring performances by Eddie Cochran and Little Richard. Russell Willaford, yet another southeastern Virginia native, filled in for Gallup for the brief but rousing film fragment of "Be-Bop-A-Lula," but did not accompany the band into the studio shortly thereafter for recording of the second Vincent and Blue Caps full-length outing, which again featured Gallup's cutting-edge technique. Returning to Nashville, Vincent and the band spent four days recording what would become their eponymous LP before trekking to Las Vegas for a two-week engagement of historic significance.

"When Elvis played (Vegas), I think he had the big band," Harrell explains, "but when we went out there we were the first rockabilly band. We played the Sands lounge, the midnight shift, 12 to 6. "We played 40 (minutes), we were off 20, something like that. They didn't put us in the main ballroom because we were a fill-in act. The Sands had all these jazz groups, which at the time was the thing. So we played the first night and couldn't believe it. (A Sands staffer) came up to Gene and said, 'Man, you all are going to have to tone that stuff down, the people have stopped gambling!' You didn't see a whole lot of crazy stuff going on back then – Gene was known for his (wild) stage show – so I told Jack, 'Throw your bass up in the air like you do.' He threw it up in the air and when he did the strings or something came loose and it all just came off, the bridge just came off completely. We had to stop the show.

"The next night Liberace came in, and his brother. Liberace came behind the stage and the smiles were just going. He was a shrewd operator, he was a businessman. He came back there and I'll never forget what he told Gene. He said, 'Let me tell you some-thing, son, if you do what these people (the audience) tell you, you'll work the rest of your life right here in this place. If you're not going to do what they tell you, you'd just as well pack your bags and go back to Virginia.' So Gene says, 'Uh, well, thank you very much.' For a whole two weeks it was jammed in there, every night it was jammed. They'd just never seen anything like that before; I used to get down on the drums and just jump right off the bar and land on the ground and Jack would get on top of that and the people would eat it up because they never had seen anything like that.

"In the big (room) they had a big show coming up, it was Sinatra, Eddie Fisher, Debbie Reynolds, Peter Lawford, Sammy Davis, but that was the big thing in those days. They were playing one night we played, they had their show and we had ours. A lot of the people that came out from their show were coming to sit and watch ours. Next thing you know, here comes (gossip columnist) Hedda Hopper, she came in and sat down. A guy comes over and tells Gene, 'I don't know if you know it or not, but Hedda Hopper's over there,' and Gene said, 'Well, who's that?' He said, 'Don't worry about who it is, you just go out there and do a good show.' And she wrote a nice article. After that there were four or five places out there that wanted Gene to work," plus the Sands, which wanted to renew its option for another few weeks. "But I really didn't think that Gene liked playing the clubs because, it's not like playing the concerts. He liked to hear them kids screaming. When you play the clubs, they enjoy the show, but it's more of a tentative audience and that didn't go down with him."

Things turned tenuous after Vegas: Bassist Jack Neal quit and Vincent and Davis severed their business relationship. In January 1957 "Crazy Legs" b/w "Important Words" (featuring Vincent backed by the Jordanaires, Presley's vocal group) was released without fanfare, and protracted litigation with an agency connected with WCMS kept the band from performing. During the downtime, Harrell helped Vincent gather together a new version of the Blue Caps, rounding up Johnny Meeks, originally a country guitarist, and electric bassist Bill Mack in Peek's hometown of Greenville, South Carolina. Tommy "Bubba" Facenda, a longtime pal of Vincent's and Harrell's joined as well, becoming one-half of Vincent's backing vocal duo, lovingly dubbed the "clapper boys" by the British.

"I've known Dickie all my life," says Facenda. "We grew up together. It was through Dickie that I met Gene when Gene was down at *Country Show-time.* We all just started hanging around together. I was still in high school and Gene used to come to the ball games; I played basketball. We just all became friends and back in those days we used to sing under the streetlights and those type of things. At night we'd just hang out, even then, and Gene remembered that when he was looking for background singers. Elvis had the Jordanaires; it was just the thing, he wanted some background singers and he wanted them to go on the road with him.

"That's when he first approached me. I was kind of hesitant at first. I really had not thought about this as a career; I was always kind of looking for a military career or something. I was kind of doubtful about it, but I did it. Everybody else had left him except Dickie – Cliff and Jack and Willie had all left. Gene was really not happy, he wanted a show band, a bunch of young guys who would do stupid, crazy things like he would want them to do. We went through a barrel of people trying to find someone (to sing) opposite me.

"Finally, we just got Paul (Peek). Paul was playing rhythm guitar and we just decided, to heck with it, me and Paul were going to do it. So that's how me and Paul became clapper boys, and clapper boys was a term given to us by the British; we never heard that term over here. The only good thing about being a clapper boy was that Paul and me were the original, and the only, clapper boys Gene ever had. He went through a lot of guitar players and bass players and everything else, but he never had but us as the clapper boys. We did all Gene's background work, singing, and it was a show band and we loved it."

Gene Vincent And The Blue Caps was released in March 1957 and featured some of the band's most groundbreaking work, from Gallup's eerie echo-doubling on "Catman" and the rollicking group free-for-all "Double Talkin' Baby" to Vincent's mellifluous, downcast vocal work on the standard "Blues Stay Away From Me." The raucous rockabilly mover "B-I-Bickey-Bi, Bo-Bo-Go," which showcased yet another jaw-dropping Gallup performance, b/w "Five Days, Five Days," another Jordanaires-backed outing, was released the same month, but surprisingly found little audience. Vincent and his new band (the lineup remained ever-changing: Bill Mack left at this time, replaced by Bobby Lee Jones) were back on the road, playing a 10-day stint with Roy Orbison, Carl Perkins and Sanford Clark; co-headlining with Eddie Cochran the "Rock and Roll Jubilee of Stars," a 50-act bill in Philadelphia; and performing in front of 30,000 rioting teens during an appearance on Chicago's Howard Miller Show between tour legs.

By June, Vincent had engaged new management, Ed McLemore of the Big D Jamboree in Dallas, and had moved his family to Texas. The Blue Caps per-formed a bit around Texas, including the "Top Record Stars Of 1957" bill in Beaumont featuring Sonny James, Johnny Cash, Jerry Lee Lewis and fellow Capitol recording artist Wanda Jackson, with whom the Blue Caps would perform on her 1960 single "Let's Have A Party," before heading to California for more sessions, this time at the Capitol facilities.

"The Capitol studio was a big huge studio at the Capitol Tower in Hollywood," Facenda remembers. "Capitol Records wasn't really set up for recording rock 'n' roll songs, they were really into the Les Brown-type sound, Frank Sinatra, that type thing. They have these huge studios so we had to kind of close them off with partitions and things to get the sound we wanted. Our recording session back then was almost like our shows. We almost did a show: I'm moving, moving around and (Nelson) would have to stop us – "Don't get too far from the mike!" – because we were kids and we felt it. But Mr. Nelson understood and he was great. And we were primitive; my God, we just had little Fender amps. One mike was all that we used when Paul and me were on each side of Gene. A lot of times Paul and me never had a separate mike, we'd use the same mike as Gene and work right up close to him. This was how we got the routine that's known as the clapper boys overseas, of being right next to Gene, face to face, with our hands clapping on each side of him."

In July 1957, "Lotta Lovin'," the first single featuring the newly-added backing vocals and handclaps, b/w "Wear My Ring," a Bobby Darin/Don Kirshner ballad, both cut at the Capitol sessions, was released while the band criss-crossed the United States and Canada. "Gene might be playing a funk-butt Chicago all-black revue in Chicago one week," Facenda remembers, "and the Grand Ole Opry down in Nashville the next week, I ain't never seen nothing like it. And we were constantly booked. If we weren't booked, we were at the Capitol Tower recording, it was just steady."

By September, with both "Lotta Lovin'," which peaked in August at #13, and "Wear My Ring" doing well in the charts, Vincent and the Blue Caps embarked on yet another performance milestone, the first rock tour of Australia, accompanied by Eddie Cochran and Little Richard. "Gene and Richard would always argue about who was going to do this and who was going to do that," Harrell chuckles. "They were the best of friends, but you know how it is in this business. Richard would come out there and say, 'Well, Gene, how long you gonna sing tonight?' And he'd say, 'Oh, I ain't gonna do too much, I don't feel too good.' So Gene would go out there and he wouldn't do too long, maybe 20 minutes, then Richard would come out and do an hour and half. The next night, same thing: (Richard) would say, 'What are you going to do tonight?' and Gene would say, 'I don't know,' then he'd go out there and do an hour and Richard would go out there and do two hours.

"One night we was playing, the place was triple-packed, and I jumped up on this baby grand piano with my drum and the leg broke. When the leg broke, the piano went up in the air, I came off the piano and went over off the stage into the band pit. The crowd loved it. They had it in the paper over there. And they didn't charge us for the piano!"

Upon the Blue Caps' return from Australia, Harrell handed in his resignation. He was replaced by Dude Kahn, who'd played with Sonny James, and another Texan, 17-year-old Max Lipscomb (a.k.a. Scotty McKay), was also hired, functioning first as a backing vocalist, then a rhythm guitarist, then pianist.

Harrell says of leaving the band: "I just got tired of it and said, 'Aw, the heck with it, too much moving around.' When it gets to the point when it's no more fun, then it's time to get out." After a brief respite, Harrell rejoined his friends, just in time to tape a performance on The Ed Sullivan Show of "Lotta Lovin'" (which peaked at #13 in September 1957) and new single "Dance To The Bop," released in November b/w "I Got It" (the A-side eventually rose to #23 on the charts). "Gene called and asked me if I'd do it," Harrell says, "and I told him, yeah, I'd go ahead and do it. That was the thing in those days, if you were on Ed Sullivan, you had it made. I guess (Gene) was a little scared, but first time for everything."

Bolstered by Vincent's renewed popularity, Capitol booked the Blue Caps back in the studios again for four days in December to record 15 more songs. Perhaps influenced by Jerry Lee Lewis, one of his favorite artists, Vincent insisted on adding piano parts, supplied by Lipscomb. While the band was ensconced in recording, "Dance To The Bop" cracked the Top 100 at #43. After the sessions, Vincent trekked to Philadelphia for a solo appearance on American Bandstand, where he lip-synced, as was customary at the time.

At the commencement of 1958, things were progressing quite positively for Vincent and the Blue Caps. "Lotta Lovin'" and "Dance To The Bop" both held healthy, though not Top 10, chart positions and the galloping "I Got A Baby" b/w "Walkin' Home From School," a likable puppy-love rock ballad, was released. Tommy Facenda and Paul Peek decided to part company with Vincent, however, both wishing to focus on solo vocal careers. Lipscomb also departed, replaced by pianist Clifton Simmons.

The band pressed on, though, touring the South and Midwest with the likes of Ferlin Husky, the Champs, Bill Justis, Sonny James, Jerry Lee Lewis, Buddy Knox and Jimmy Bowen, picking up guitarist Grady Owen along the way, and touring back down to Texas, after Vincent had made his second solo appearance on American Bandstand, lip-syncing once again. Harrell, homesick and missing his girlfriend (Facenda's sister), finally decided to hang up his drumsticks for good and Dude Kahn was once again brought in as replacement. Vincent, no doubt wistful for his former lineup of close, trusted friends, approached Peek and Facenda about rejoining him, using the lure of an upcoming movie appearance and new LP release to cement the offer.

March 1958 proved to be productive month for Vincent and his Blue Caps. The group's third full-length effort, Gene Vincent Rocks! And The Blue Caps Roll, hit the stores; Juvey Gomez, a drummer who shared a similar style with Harrell, was hired; another album was recorded and Hot Rod Gang was filmed. Vincent and the band entered the Capitol studios toward the end of March, where they were joined by Eddie Cochran, by now a fast friend of Vincent's, who contributed backing vocals to the sessions (which went uncredited). Vincent's sound had changed somewhat, with even more emphasis put on keyboard parts; most of the 16 songs from these sessions feature prominent piano solos from Simmons. On March 30, 1958 Vincent and the Blue Caps began production of the B-movie Hot Rod Gang, performing "Baby Blue," "Dance In The Street," "Lovely Loretta" and "Dance To The Bop."

In May 1958 Capitol released the soulful, sensual single "Baby Blue" b/w "True To You," which was recorded in June 1957 sessions, to tepid response. Peek and Facenda excited once again and Meeks and Jones gave their notice as well. "Gene's drinking got a little heavier and he was taking a lot of medication for the pain in his leg," Peek told biographer Hagarty in The Day The World Turned Blue of Vincent's slow-but-sure darkening metamorphosis. "He got to be more of a recluse and he didn't want to sign autographs or do interviews. He'd stay in his hotel room and brood, and he got to thinking the world was down on him."

But the road was where he was most comfortable, so Vincent, eager to continue touring, recruited Texan Howard Reed as his new lead guitarist. Owen switched to bass and Lipscomb returned to play rhythm guitar. Dude Kahn also returned briefly, replacing Gomez, who was still in school, but soon quit and was replaced by ex-Presley timekeeper D.J. Fontana. Simmons remained on piano. Mid-tour, Vincent, forever fine-tuning, fashioned a new version of the clapper boys consisting of former bassist Bill

Gene Vincent (center) in action with one of his many groups of Blue Caps.

Mack, Owen and Lipscomb. The (once again) new lineup toured across Canada, then trekked its way south, losing Fontana along the way, who was replaced by Gomez.

Vincent, evidently not pleased with his clapper boys resurrection, axed Lipscomb and Owen. Vincent was also displeased with Reed and persuaded Meeks to rejoin. The group continued to tour, playing the Pacific Northwest, the Southwest and back into Texas. Gomez exited at the conclusion of the tour, replaced by Butch White.

In July 1958, "Rocky Road Blues," a Bill Monroe classic, b/w "Yes I Love You Baby," was released, followed by "Git It," featuring Eddie Cochran's classic, basso "well oh well oh wop, wip, wip, wip" intro under Vincent's falsetto, b/w "Little Lover" in September. Neither single even dented the charts. Butch White then left the band and Clyde Pennington, a longtime friend of Meeks', was hired and Vincent once again put the band out on the road, traveling through the Midwest and West, stopping in Los Angeles for five days of recording at the Capitol Tower. Again, Vincent altered the sound markedly, this time adding tenor saxophone from Jackie Kelso and delving into a more R&B-inflected rock 'n' roll tenor. A prime example of the new sound, the rollicking, Meeks-penned "Say Mama" was released in November (b/w "Be Bop Bookie Boy"), almost simultaneously with Vincent's fourth LP, *A Gene Vincent Record Date*, wholly composed of tracks from the March sessions with Cochran.

"Say Mama" stiffed and, after a year of creative, credible but non-selling singles supported by non-stop touring, Vincent snapped. The Blue Caps disbanded, equally as frustrated and unwilling to tolerate Vincent's increasingly volatile temperament. "Gene couldn't keep a band together because he was hot-headed and the guys just wouldn't take it," his second

wife Darlene confided in *The Day The World Turned Blue*. Pennington, also quoted in the biography, confirmed, "Gene didn't get along with anybody!"

To add to Vincent's woes, he and his wife lost their Dallas home to the government in a tax dispute (according to Hagarty, McLemore's agency did not tend to Vincent's taxes while he was on the road; Vincent consequently left McLemore) and relocated in the Pacific Northwest, eventually setting up in Oregon. Vincent, the quintessential entertainer, continued singing with pick-up bands around the area. In January 1959, Capitol released "Over The Rainbow" b/w the energetic rocker "Who Pushin' Your Swing?" followed by "Right Now" b/w "The Night Is So Lonely" and *Sounds Like Gene Vincent*, his fifth LP in June. They, too, met with lukewarm reaction.

Vincent had been playing with guitarist Jerry Merritt, a longtime fan of the singer's during the early months of 1959 and the pair soon garnered a reputation for a wild, woolly live show replete with near-acrobatics. Despite the emergence of teen idols such as Frankie Avalon, Fabian and Bobby Rydell, demand overseas for a bona fide rock 'n' roll show was so great that Capitol sent Vincent on yet another landmark junket, the first-ever rock tour of the Orient. Ten thousand eager fans greeted Vincent and his sidekick Merritt at Tokyo International Airport and a parade was held in downtown Tokyo in the musicians' honor. Over five days at Tokyo's Nichigeki Theater, Vincent and Merritt, backed by a Japanese band, performed three times a day for throngs of 20,000 each show. It wasn't long, though ,before Vincent, a restless soul, wanted to return to the States; in fact, he departed Japan four days early and Merritt was forced to impersonate the singer for the remaining engagements.

After Merritt's return to America, the pair entered the Capitol studio for four days of recording backed by players furnished by Capitol: drummer Sandy Nelson, bassist Red Callendar, pianist Jimmy Johnson, saxophonist Jackie Kelso and backing vocal trio the Eligibles. Vincent continued to tour the West Coast throughout 1959, either with Merritt or Clayton Watson and the Silhouettes. By December, as the notorious payola scandal had cast a deadly pall over the once maverick music industry, Vincent was preparing to leave the country, embarking on a British tour arranged by his new manager.

Vincent arrived at Heathrow Airport early December 5. Despite three years without hits, swarms of fans, reporters and celebrities were on hand to greet him, the warmest reception he'd received since his Japanese jaunt. The next day Vincent made his U.K. live debut, performing on *The Marty Wilde Show*. The crowd went crazy, especially the girls, British guitarist Joe Brown remembered in *The Day the World Turned Blue*. Later that week Vincent, accompanied by Brown, traveled to Manchester to tape 11 songs for Jack Good's popular television program, *Boy Meets Girl*, which was divided into three separate segments for three different broadcasts. Vincent spent the rest of the month performing in France and Germany, where he was enthusiastically received.

Despite hardly making any impression in the U.S., "Wild Cat" b/w "Right Here On Earth" had climbed to #21 on the U.K. chart by mid-January, with Vincent's pal Eddie Cochran's "Hallelujah, I Love Her So" close behind at #28. Toward the end of January, Cochran arrived in the U.K. to co-headline a 12-week Vincent tour, which commenced in Glasgow, Scotland. While in Manchester, England, the pair taped segments for *Boy Meets Girl*, this time with Vincent clad in all-black leather regalia, reportedly at the suggestion of Jack Good. Along with his characteristic limp and histrionic stage antics –Vincent would often writhe about the stage, twist himself around his mike stand, sing while thrashing on his back, leap over pianos and bash in drums – his leathered, rebel-rocker persona, adopted and imitated by legions of greasy Teddy Boys in the '60s strife between the punky Rockers and the mop-topped Mods, would make an indelible mark in the rock lexicon.

Vincent and Cochran spent most of February and March playing mobbed shows in London, Cardiff, Manchester and Leeds. In March, Vincent appeared twice on the BBC radio show *Saturday Club*, once accompanied by Cochran.(The British Rockstar Records has released *Rock & Roll Heroes – Gene Vincent & Eddie Cochran* [RSR-LP 1004], comprised of the *Saturday Club* tapes, including interview segments.)

On March 10, the Johnny Burnette-penned tracks "My Heart" b/w "I've Got To Get To You Yet," never released in the U.S., cracked the U.K. charts, eventually ascending to #16. *Crazy Times,* Vincent's album with Merritt, was also released in March. Vincent and Cochran continued touring the first few weeks of April, finishing up the trip with a week-long engagement at the Hippodrome in Bristol.

On April 17th, the pair, along with Cochran's girlfriend Sharon Sheeley, hired a car to take them to Heathrow Airport for their return trip to the States for a brief vacation. In the town of Chippenham in Wiltshire, the driver, reportedly speeding, lost control of the car and skidded into a lamp post. Cochran was thrown out of the vehicle and died later that day of massive head injuries. Vincent, asleep in the back seat, suffered a broken collarbone and fractured ribs and sustained further damage to his crippled leg.

By all accounts, Vincent was devastated by Cochran's death. "Eddie didn't want to leave that night from the Hippodrome in Bristol, he wanted to stay overnight," Facenda says, "but not Gene. I can see him right now, he wanted to leave, get to London right then. We know, because we remember so many times on the road that we wanted to stay overnight after our show and Gene would have us to pack everything up in that station wagon and drive all night. Gene kind of blamed himself for Eddie's death, I know he did. Eddie was like a brother to all of us, he was an honorary Blue Cap."

"I think the 'schizophrenia' set in when Eddie Cochran died," Vincent's U.K. road manager Henry Henroid told biographer Hagerty. "Gene was lost. They were like brothers."

Second wife Darlene added, "Gene was really shook up. He and Eddie were very close. He talked a lot about Eddie and sent flowers to the funeral. But he didn't go because he didn't think he'd be able to handle it."

After a short convalescence, Vincent returned to the U.K. and continued touring. On May 11, he entered EMI's London studio where, backed by the Beat Boys with Georgie Fame on piano, he cut the country standard "Pistol Packin' Mama" (using Cochran's arrangement) and the ballad "Weeping Willow," Vincent's first foray into orchestration. In June, Capitol released both tracks in the U.K. "Pistol Packin' Mama" climbed to #15 on the U.K. charts in July; *Crazy Times* peaked at #12 the same month, while in the U.S., "Pistol Packin' Mama" became the B-side to "Anna-Annabelle" released in September. After a few more weeks of touring, Vincent returned to the States under possibly self-created circumstances: At a performance on June 18 in Nottingham, a tearful Vincent announced to the crowd that he had just been informed that his infant daughter had died of pneumonia and he was going home; though Vincent would say months later he was the victim of a hoax, wife Darlene told Hagerty that she felt Vincent had fabricated the entire story.

In January 1961, Vincent recorded eight songs in Hollywood, exploring string accompaniment even further with backing from the Jimmy Haskell Orchestra. After his long rest, Vincent was eager to perform again and returned to England, where he still enjoyed substantial popularity. Upon his arrival, he learned that, without his knowledge, Capitol U.K. had released several of his older songs: "Jezebel," waxed in 1956, b/w "Maybe," recorded in 1958, and, later "Brand New Beat," from 1957, b/w "Unchained Melody," a 1956 track. Neither of the singles broke into the charts. Vincent continued to do what he did best – live performance – touring extensively as Capitol released the string-laden "Mr. Loneliness" (which Vincent performed live on *Saturday Club*) with "If You Want My Lovin'" as its flip.

After a quickie trip to the States, to appear in a Pat Boone/Connie Francis movie, *State Fair* (Vincent's part ended up on the cutting room floor), and to discover that his wife Darlene had deserted him, Vincent returned to England and threw himself into performance once more. Backed by Sounds Incorporated, he hit the concert trail again, appearing on the television show *Thank Your Lucky Stars* in May before trekking to South Africa, where "Mitchiko From Tokyo," recorded in 1958, was a hit (the song was not released in any other country).

In South Africa, Vincent was backed by Mickie Most and His Playboys. Vincent returned to England to learn that "She She Little Sheila" b/w "Hot Dollar," another non-U.S. release, was a hit, reaching #22 on the charts in July. He continued touring – in Liverpool headlining the Cavern Club, where a popular local group called the Beatles opened for him – until July, when he and Sounds Incorporated entered EMI Studios on Abbey Road and recorded several songs, two of which featured producer Norrie Paramor's orchestra. "I'm Goin' Home" was released shortly thereafter and peaked on the U.K. charts at #36. Vincent and Sounds Incorporated resumed touring.

In March 1962, Vincent joined Brenda Lee for his seventh tour of Britain. "Lucky Star," his current release, was part of his live repertoire, but he had traded in his black leathers for an all-white leather wardrobe. Both backed by Sounds Incorporated, Vincent and Lee's performance at the London Palladium was televised. Vincent, clad head-to-toe in white, and the band also appeared in the movie *It's Trad, Dad*, performing "Spaceship To Mars," recorded in July 1961. Vincent then re-entered the EMI studio and recorded four songs, including "Be-Bop-A-Lula '62" with Charles Blackwell's orchestra, then embarked on tours of Italy, Germany (backed by the Beatles, according to Hagarty, at the Star Club in Hamburg, as Sounds Incorporated's train arrived late) and Israel.

In 1963, after two operations on his leg and marriage to his third wife, Vincent had a startling revelation: Beatlemania had engulfed the U.K. and Capitol declined to renew his contract. His drinking had worsened dramatically and his behavior was becoming more bizarre and erratic, including as described in *The Day The World Turned Blue*, his drawing guns on friends and associates, attacking his road manager, and instigating violent arguments with his then-pregnant wife.

In December 1963, Columbia Records, Vincent's new U.K. Label, had released "Where Have You Been All My Life" b/w, "Temptation Baby," followed by "Humpity Dumpty" b/w "Love 'Em Leave 'Em Kind Of Guy" in early 1964. Though neither entered the charts, Vincent did perform "Temptation Baby" in the movie *Live It Up*, titled *Sing And Swing* in the U.S. Hapless when not performing, Vincent recruited a new backing band, the Shorts – Sounds Incorporated had landed its own deal with Columbia – and again hit the concert trail. Despite his lack of hits and personal tribulations, Vincent was still a phenomenal live draw and his performances were not lacking.

British rockabilly star Graham Fenton, who toured with the reunited Blue Caps last summer, described a 1964 Vincent show in *The Day The World Turned Blue*: "We got inside and there was this big build-up, 'Now, ladies and gentlemen, from the U.S.A., the one and only, the amazing, the fantastic, the man in black...Gene Vincent!' The crowd just went berserk! Gene started with 'Say Mama,' then threw his leg over the microphone, then held the whole stand over his head. When he did 'Baby Blue' he jerked his body to the beat and pushed the mike stand back and forth at the drummer during the guitar solo. At the end of the show he teased the audience by going offstage. They all screamed for him to come back, so he reappeared and did 'Be-Bop-A-Lula' and the crowd went mad. They were all pushing and shoving and going crazy."

Vincent and the Shouts entered the studio in London in early 1964, recording Vincent's most rock-oriented effort since his work with the Blue Caps, *Shakin' Up A Storm*. Columbia released "Private

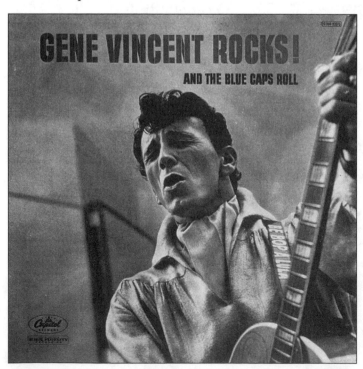

Detective" b/w "You Are My Sunshine," which Vincent and the Shouts had performed in the movie *Don't Knock The Rock,* but the single stiffed. Vincent resumed touring, then took time off toward the end of 1964 to spend it with Jackie Frisco, Mickie Most's sister-in-law, whom he'd met on his 1961 tour of South Africa. The two flew to the U.S., vacationing in New York before visiting Vincent's parents in Albuquerque, then traveling to Mexico, where Vincent obtained a quickie divorce from his third wife and married Frisco. In March 1965, after surgery at the Royal National Ear, Nose & Throat Hospital in London, Vincent was eager to return to music. He was no longer using the Shouts and entertained ideas of getting his old friends in the Blue Caps back together.

"He was in the hospital over there (in England)," recalls Dickie Harrell, "he had an ear operation. I called him one night and talked to him. The nurse went down and got him out of bed and brought him to the phone. We were talking and he said, 'Man, I would sure love to get the band together and bring them over here.' We were willing to go," but strict rules regarding work visas prohibited the reunion. "When he came home (on vacations), he'd come over and see us a couple times ... and we talked about it, but that was it, it never materialized."

Instead, Vincent teamed up with the Puppets, touring the U.K., France and Germany before landing a summer-long engagement at the seaside South Pier in Blackpool, Lancastershire. In September 1965, Vincent was forced to leave the country due to financial disputes with manager Don Arden, which had left him with many angry creditors and child support demands from his third wife. In addition, his damaged leg had developed osteomyelitis, an inflammation of the bone and marrow, and required medical attention. En route to Albuquerque, where Vincent planned to undergo treatment, he and Frisco stopped in Hampton Roads, visiting Harrell and Facenda in Portsmouth.

"Gene always idolized my mother and father," Facenda recalls. "Me and Gene used to go over there and spend nights at my house because he loved my mother and father so much. So my mother called me one evening and said, 'You're never going to guess who's here!' I said, 'Who?' She said, 'Gene.' I said 'Gene who?' and she said, 'Gene Vincent!' Man, I just couldn't believe that! So Gene got on the phone and I told him – I just lived a block or so away – 'Man, you have got to come over!' He had this South African girl, Jackie, with him. He'd heard about 'High School USA' (Facenda's biggest single as a solo artist), but he just couldn't believe that was me. We talked and that was the last time I saw him alive. He looked puffy and he talked with a British accent

from living over there, a lot of 'actually's and things of this nature. But he was still hyper, he wouldn't stay long, he was up and down."

Vincent entered the Veterans Administration Hospital in Albuquerque in February 1966. When amputation was prescribed, Vincent exited. In May, Vincent, who had remained in touch with Dave Burgess, an old friend who now ran Five Star Music and Challenge Records, journeyed to Los Angeles to do some recording for Challenge, including "Born To Be A Rolling Stone," written by Jerry Merritt. Challenge released the country-styled "Bird Doggin" b/w "Ain't That Too Much" in September, followed by "Lonely Street" b/w "I Got My Eyes On You." In the fall of 1967, Challenge released an LP, *Gene Vincent,* in the U.K., and EMI put out *The Best Of Gene Vincent,* also a U.K.-only release featuring mostly Blue Caps-era tracks, including non-album cuts such as "Be-Bop-A-Lula."

A tour of France followed, marred by hassles with promoters and backing bands, then Vincent returned to the States, performing in clubs throughout the Pacific Northwest for most of the winter of 1967 and spring of 1968. In May, Capitol U.K. re-released the original "B-Bop-A-Lula" b/w "Say Mama"; neither side pierced the charts. Toward the end of June, Vincent recorded two tracks for Playground Productions, "Story Of The Rockers," a musical primer of early rock 'n' roll, and "Pickin' Poppies," co-penned by Vincent and Frisco, which were released on Forever Records to little success.

Vincent and his fourth wife moved to a large house, ironically located on Cochran Street in Simi Valley, just outside of Los Angeles, in September. In November, Capitol U.K. released "Lucky Star" b/w "Baby, Don't Believe Him" from the October '61 sessions, followed in February 1969 with *The Best Of Gene Vincent, Volume Two,* which, again, captured several non-album tracks. In May, Vincent produced his own session of four demo tracks – "Green Grass," "Roll Over Beethoven," "Mister Love" "Rainy Day Sunshine" – later released as an EP, *Rainy Day Sunshine,* on the British Magnum Force label. BBC disc jockey John Peel, a longtime Vincent fan, got hold of the demo, was duly impressed and signed Vincent to his fledgling Dandelion label. With Kim Fowley producing, Skip Battin (later of the Byrds) on bass and handling arrangement, and Johnny Meeks on guitar, an album was recorded in about a week.

"I just admired him immensely and wanted to be able to say that Gene Vincent had recorded on my label," Peel told Hagarty in *The Day The World Turned Blue. I'm Back And Proud,* featuring classic

'50s covers, country tunes and remakes of "Be-Bop-A-Lula" and "Lotta Lovin'," was released in U.K. in January 1970 on Dandelion/Elektra.

Vincent had performed in Toronto in September 1969 as part of a rock revival festival. Jim Morrison, a friend Vincent had made during the Dandelion sessions in Los Angeles, and the Doors were, according to Hagarty, scheduled to back the singer, but they were late in arriving and the Alice Cooper Band filled in instead. John Lennon's Plastic Ono Band, Chuck Berry and Jerry Lee Lewis were also on the bill. Not long after Vincent's return to the U.K., "Be-Bop-A-Lula '69" b/w "Ruby Baby" was released. The singer completed a mini-tour of France, then dove directly into a U.K. tour, a jaunt Hagarty intimates was nearly sabotaged by threats from associates of Vincent's former manager Don Arden to a BBC-TV film crew, shooting the tour for the U.K. documentary *The Rock 'n' Roll Singer.*

By spring of 1970, Vincent had acquired new management, Tom Ayers, former bassist for Johnny Burnette, and a new label, Kama Sutra Records. Backed by the Sir Douglas Quintet, Vincent recorded an LP, *If You Could Only See Me Today,* fat with exorbitantly lengthy instrumental breaks and – aside from a few country-styled tracks – strained, forced vocals from Vincent. The singer performed selected dates in the U.S. and Europe throughout most of 1970, then returned to the studio in October to record *The Day The World Turned Blue,* his last album, comprised largely of rock and R&B standards, ballads and country tunes. His fourth wife, who could no longer tolerate his drinking and increasingly violent mood swings, left him shortly thereafter.

The road had always been a tonic for Vincent, so he launched yet another U.K. tour in January 1971, backed by the Houseshakers, Graham Fenton's band. Vincent did a Peel session for his BBC radio program, performing "The Day The World Turned Blue" with the band. With creditors, the tax men and Don Arden's cohorts harassing him, even on the road, Vincent's performances, typically spectacular, began to decline. He returned to America, where Kama Sutra canceled his contract because of two tracks, "Say Mama" and "I'm Moving' On," he had cut for the British B&C Records during the U.K. tour. Vincent waxed four tracks – Sam Cooke's "Bring It On Home To Me," Little Richard's "Hey-Hey-Hey-Hey," Buddy Knox's "Party Doll" and his own "The Rose Of Love" – for Rollin' Rock Records before going back to England for another tour. Upon his arrival in London, the singer was served a writ by his second wife demanding alimony and child support. He fled the country. Returning home, he discovered his current girlfriend had deserted him, taking all his furniture and much of his belongings from his home in Simi Valley, according to *The Day The World Turned Blue.*

Worried about their son, Vincent's parents, then residing in Saugus, California, trekked to Simi Valley to find him drunk, brokenhearted and disoriented, Louise Craddock (Vincent's mother) told Hagarty. They decided to take Vincent to their home in Saugus and, upon entering the house, Vincent tripped and fell, bursting his chronic ulcers, and began vomiting blood. He was taken by ambulance to Inter-Valley Hospital where he passed away about an hour later. "After he died, he had the sweetest smile on his face," Craddock said. "He wanted to die. He was glad to think that he was getting out of the mess he was in."

All these years later, the singer's impact on the music world remains enduring, evidenced by a current resurgence of interest in rockabilly from record makers and consumers. Jeff Beck released a disc of all-Vincent gems earlier this year, former 'billy belter Johnny Cash recently signed with the hip rap/metal label American, rockabilly crooner Chris Isaak's releases consistently crack the pop charts. Demand for authentic rockabilly overseas has been so great of late that the '58 Blue Caps - Harrell, Facenda, Peek and Meeks plus Merritt – reunited this year for a whirlwind summer tour of the U.K., France, and Germany, where Vincent is still revered.

"I've never been around anyone else that could sound just like their records," Facenda says of the secret to Vincent's perpetual appeal. "Gene was like he had a built-in little echo-chamber in his throat, he needed no dressing up in the studio. Elvis and everybody, they would make Gene sing when they were around him. He had the voice of an angel."

Most Collectible 45

"Story Of The Rockers"/ "Pickin' Poppies," Playground 100, $200.

Most Collectible LP

Crazy Times, Capitol ST 1342, stereo, black label, rainbow rim, logo at left, $500.

Recommended Introduction

The Screaming End: The Best of Gene Vincent & His Blue Caps, Razor & Tie 82123 (20 of his classic rockabilly sides, recorded in 1956 and 1957)

If you want to hear more...

Capitol Collector's Series, Capitol 94074 (more than 20 of his biggest and best hits)

Bluejean Bop!/Gene Vincent And His Blue Caps, Collectables 2712 (two of his original LPs on one CD)

Gene Vincent Rocks! And The Blue Caps Roll/A Gene Vincent Record Date, Collectables 2714 (two of his original LPs on one CD)

Sounds Like/Crazy Times, Collectables 2720 (two of his original LPs on one CD)

Ain't That Too Much!, Sundazed 12004 (recordings he made for Challenge in 1966-67)

Link Wray

by Steve Roeser

I had heard of Link Wray's biggest hit, "Rumble," before I actually heard it. It was supposed to be one of the great instrumentals in rock 'n' roll history. Well, sometime in the 1970s, I found an original copy of the 45 on the old Cadence label, better known for the Everly Brothers and Andy Williams. Once I got that disc home, I put it on the turntable. And what an amazing sound! It was still a powerful, almost scary performance. I couldn't imagine what it must have been like to hear that series of power chords over and over in 1958! Then, toward the end, Wray added some echo to the record. Amazing. Even today, on those rare instances it gets played on oldies radio, you can't help but stop everything, turn up the volume and do your best air guitar. Well, Link Wray did an awful lot more than "Rumble," but even if that was the only record he ever made, he'd be remembered today. This interview with the guitar legend first appeared in the February 13, 1998, issue of Goldmine.

If there is one man left standing whom hardcore rock 'n' roll fans ought to salute, or at least tip their hats to, that man is Link Wray. And if there's a guitar player remaining out there before whom aspiring rock guitarists should kneel and bow down – and many, unashamedly, have – that man is also Link Wray.

And this is true even among Generation X rock 'n' rollers. Richie Lee of the band Acetone, recently signed to Neil Young's indie label, Vapor Records, was heard to comment, "We all agree that Link Wray is it, if there was anything like one overriding influence."

Wray only had one Top 20 hit in his career, and it happened 40 years ago, but it was a monster. It also happened to have been an instrumental, and its name was "Rumble." Wray's guitar playing on that one record was so powerful, so tenacious, edgy and unforgettable that its impact has reverberated down through the ages of the rock world ever since.

Link Wray created the power chord, and it was good. And as the awesome, super-charged intensity of "Rumble" echoed in the minds and imaginations of discontented, disconnected male youth around the world for years afterwards, Link Wray's sound begat determined rockers by the hundreds and by the thousands.

Just as in the world of comedy, there would never have been an Eddie Murphy had there not first been a Richard Pryor, without Link Wray most likely there would not have been a Pete Townshend. Or, at least, not the Pete Townshend that imagined and then realized a band called the Who. (Towser wrote the liner notes for Link's 1974 Polydor LP *The Link Wray Rumble*.)

Furthermore, it is heartening to know that Link Wray never went away after he was first heard from in a musical context. He just moved to Europe, where he's been living happily for nearly the past two decades. In 1997, partly in support of his album *Shadowman* (recorded a couple of years back, but now out on Hip-O Records in the States), Link returned here for a nationwide club tour on which fans young and old(er) hailed him for his sonic genius and went nuts for his performances. He's due back early in 1998 for more shows at the House Of Blues clubs in various cities and other venues.

Closing in on age 70, there seems to be no stopping the phenomenal Link Wray. While trendy punk rockers half his age have already burned out and hung it up, too jaded and tired to move on to the next phase. Link Wray, the burning flame, carries the rock 'n' roll torch and takes it to a new generation. Godhead.

Born Frederick Lincoln Wray (named for his father, though he was the second son) May 2, 1929 in Dunn, North Carolina, Link and his brothers (Vernon, the older, rhythm guitar and vocals and Doug, the younger, drums) formed their first band while World War II was still going on. Do the math, as they say. Link Wray has been playing in bands for over 50 years.

Later adding a cousin, Shorty Horton, on bass, they played a mixture of country and rockabilly until Link was required to serve his country in the Korean War. He returned in the mid-1950s and he and his brothers moved up to the Washington, D.C. area to continue with the music.

Link's continued good health and energy in the 1990s is all the more miraculous for the fact that he survived a serious bout of tuberculosis in the Fifties, was hospitalized for a year and had to have one of his lungs removed. He has lived most of his life with that remaining lung and it never seems to have set him back.

What it did do was make singing less of a priority, and caused him to concentrate that much harder on his guitar playing. The results are on numerous recordings, which came out on a plethora of labels, that have materialized over the past four decades.

In addition to the excellent *Shadowman,* there is no shortage of Link Wray music available today on CD. As good a place to start as any is by picking up *Rumble! The Best of Link Wray*, a 1993 Rhino collection of 20 tracks that begins with the guitarist's most renowned tune from 1958. It has a bunch of his 1960s recordings and a few things from the Seventies.

Once you get hooked (and chances are good that you will, if you aren't already), further suggested Link listening leads us to the "Missing Links" series on Norton Records, four volumes that take the faithful through the early work of the brothers, billed as Lucky Wray and the Palomino Ranch Hands (Lucky was brother Vern, who later took the stage name Ray Vernon), then Link Wray and the Raymen, and various other recordings done under band names like the Spiders and the Fender Benders. (When the Beatles and the other British Invasion bands started making noise, Link and his brothers tried to stay competitive as best they could.)

Speaking of the Beatles, also of no small interest to Link Wray fanatics are the many recordings he did for the Swan label, and Norton has also collected those (63 tracks in all) on a double CD titled *Mr. Guitar.* (Some of these, like "Run Chicken Run," "Deuces Wild" and "Batman Theme," are also on the single-disc Rhino compilation.)

For the hardcore fan, Norton has the "Link Wray Jukebox Series" available on seven-inch vinyl 45s, 10 of his Swan A-sides backed with something equally delectable.

In the 1970's, Link made a couple of albums with neo-rockabilly singer Robert Gordon and, basically, has always been doing something musically his entire life.

The following interview with Link Wray took place over the phone on November 15, 1997, just as he had completed his U.S. tour. The previous evening, a Friday night, Link had wrapped up a two-night stand at a club in Atlanta, where worshipful fans had gathered to see him do his "gee-tar" (as he says it) thing, before he was scheduled to fly back to Denmark with his young wife Olive, who was accompanying him on tour. They have a teenage son.

For more information on Link Wray and his recordings, one could track down a copy of *Goldmine* issue #292 from October 4, 1991. This was a "*Goldmine* Goes Guitars" issue that featured a story/tribute written by guitar player and Link Wray disciple Cub Koda.

Goldmine: Have you always felt a strong identification with your Native American heritage!

Link Wray: I wasn't born on a reservation, you know. I was born to a little Shawnee lady, that was my momma. And my dad was in the army. My mother was born in North Carolina, about four miles from Dunn. Dunn is about 30 miles from Raleigh. She was Shawnee, and my dad was a war hero in the first World War. And he was half-breed Shawnee. His momma was brought up by the Chippewas. The Chippewa nation captured her mother, and I think killed her dad, and took her and raised her. And this here white guy, name of Florentine Van Edgar – I think he was from Holland – came and married her. This was in the 1800s, during the uprising of the James Gang, and the Daltons and everyone. And (Van Edgar) was like a farmer. And my dad was born to the Shawnee mother, and this Van Edgar guy. And because they were hidin' the James Gang, and the Daltons and the Youngers, he had to change his name – this is my granddad – from Van Edgar to Wray, to escape the Pinkertons. Those assholes, you know? They were railroad cops. To escape bein' hunted down by them, my granddaddy just changed his name. And that's how I got the name Wray. My mom brought me up no mixin' with anybody, even though we lived around the Cherokees. When I was 13, we moved to Portsmouth, Virginia.

Both your parents were preachers?

Yeah, street preachers, exactly right. My momma, she'd get out on the streets of Dunn and Benson and Raleigh and Lillington, and preach to blacks, who was drinkin' and not livin' the good life. They was killin' each other, knifin' each other, gettin' drunk – you know, low morals. She preached to them, and preached to poor whites (too). The poor white people was livin' right beside of 'em, you know? They were downtrodden people, too. Even though, in the South, the blacks and the whites didn't mix. She was still preachin' to all of 'em, to try to live a better life. And she was crippled, my mother was a cripple lady. She had to wear braces since she was 16 years old. She was walkin' home from school one day and (some

kid) stuck a knee in her back, and broke my mother's back. And she was a cripple all of her life (thereafter), until she passed away. But even though she had a weak body, she was strong in spirit. And that's the way she raised us boys.

How early on did you and your brothers get some instruments and start playing music together?

Oh, well, I'll put it to you this way; I started off playin' guitar at eight years old, (thanks to) an old black man called Hambone, Right? This was in Dunn, North Carolina. Well, when I was 12 or 13 years old, my daddy got a job in the Portsmouth navy yard, you know. And we moved from Dunn to Portsmouth, right? And then my brother Doug, who played drums on "Rumble" and all the other hit records, he was still too young. And I started sittin' in with bands in Portsmouth, Virginia, learnin' how to play the guitar, you know? And finally we got in a five-piece jazz combo with my brother Ray (aka Vernon). He played drums and I played guitar, and we had sax, horns and piano. Traditional jazz, you know what I mean? And then I got bored, quit that, and went to a 40-piece band, like a Tommy Dorsey band, where I played guitar with them. I was the only one in the band that couldn't read music. And then that got boring to me. Then me and my brothers opened up (with) a thing, what was called "western swing." Elvis hadn't appeared on the market. It was only (at that time) country music, and jazz, and pop music. There was no rock 'n' roll.

Right.

But there was western swing, with Hank Locklin, and Pee Wee King, and all those cats, you know! Down in Nashville and Memphis, doin' the western swing stuff. I got into (it) and I started playin' western swing in Portsmouth, Virginia. And while I was livin' (there), my brother Ray got friends with the sister of Hank Williams. Her name was Irene. And she invited us to Hank's memorial, when he passed away (in '53). So we went down there, and played the western swing in Mobile, Alabama (during) the wake. They were havin' music all over Mobile, in respect of Hank Williams. It was like a wake, you know? All over Mobile, I mean *all* the country stars, like Ernest Tubb, Jim Reeves, Little Jimmy Dickens...That's where I met Curtis Gordon. And Curtis Gordon jumped up on stage with me, and started jamming on the old country songs, like "Tennessee Waltz" and stuff like that, jammin' 'em up, you know? Like Elvis did (later) on "Mystery Train" and "That's All Right, Mama." But Curtis was doin' it in 1953. He was jamming with me and my brother Doug, and my brother Ray, and Shorty on bass, in '53, in Mobile. And that's where I got the first glimpse of the kids screaming and hollering over this *beat* my brother Doug was doing. He was doin' this here real D.J. Fontana kind of beat behind Curtis Gordon doing the old country songs, with a rockabilly type of a feeling. You know what I mean?

Sure.

But then it was called western swing. We did that, and then we played all over Portsmouth and Norfolk, Virginia, backing up the country & western stars – people like Lash LaRue, Roy Rogers, Gabby Hayes, and all those people that'd come to town, right? They'd shoot their guns, and we'd play the music while they were out there on stage. This was at fairgrounds. Then in 1955 I moved from Portsmouth to Washington, D.C. That's where I broke down with tuberculosis, because I was in the Korean War. And I went right into the hospital, and my brother Doug got to play with Jimmy Dean – (Link sings in low voice) "Big Bad John." You know that guy?

Right.

Jimmy Dean. My brother Doug got a job playin' drums with Jimmy Dean. Roy Clark was the lead guitar player. This was in 1955 and '56, when I was in the hospital. And then Elvis came, and was on the Jimmy Dean Show (on TV, out of D.C.), because Jimmy Dean was the number one country star in Washington, D.C. He had a (local) daily program on channel 7 in Washington, D.C. And Doug was playin' drums behind Jimmy. While I was in the hospital, I was watchin' television, *The Jimmy Dean Show*, with my brother Doug playin', and in walks Elvis, as a guest on the show. And he did some singing with Jimmy Dean. And then he went and did a live gig, I think, with Scotty and Bill – I don't think D.J. was with him then – on a boat, like a riverboat, in Washington, D.C. And then, when I came out of the hospital in 1957, I got back with Doug and Shorty and Ray, and started doing record hops with (local deejay) Milt Grant. He was a deejay on channel 5. And I started doin' these here record hops, all over about a 125-mile radius from Washington – all over Virginia, Maryland...Buddy Dean was over in Baltimore, doin' the same thing as Milt Grant was in Washington. And Dick Clark was doing it nationwide (out of Philadelphia) – you know, kids dancin' on the show, and they'd play records. And the big rock stars would come on the television show. And that's how "Rumble" was born. One night in Fredericksburg, Virginia in 1957 – about 125 miles from Washington – in this here hot rod building, which was about 5,000 kids dancing while we were playing this music, Milt Grant got up on stage and said, "Play a stroll." And I said, "I don't know a stroll." My brother Doug said, "I know the beat to a stroll." And he started playin' the "Rumble" beat. And then God zapped "Rumble" right in my head, and I started playin' "Rumble." And it was a four million-seller for me (in the studio version). When I say "God zapped 'Rumble' in my head," I mean, I'm not religious, but I'm really spiritual, from my Shawnee momma. She loved every minute of my music.

Speaking of Elvis, do you have a favorite Elvis story?

(Thinks a moment) Mmmm...no, not really. Because I didn't really (get to) be that much friends with Elvis. You know, I just met him occasionally. My brother Doug introduced me to him. But, ah, I got a Colonel Tom Parker story.

OK.

He was in vaudeville, right? And this was the rumor that was goin' around in Nashville and Memphis, when I was travelin' there. That Colonel Tom Parker, before he had Elvis, or any of the country stars that he was managing, even before he did that, he was doing vaudeville. And it was called "Colonel Tom Parker and his Dancing Chickens," you know? He had a hot plate under the chickens, and the chickens would jump over the hot plate. But I didn't know Elvis that much. I loved his music, because he opened the door for people like me, and rock 'n' roll. He sort of like opened the door for everybody.

You're somewhat like Chuck Berry and Bo Diddley, in that you emerged as a rock 'n' roll star at a relatively advanced age.

I was 30 when "Rumble" was born because, like I told you, I was in the hospital. I mean, if you were 30 years old in '58 or '57, you was over the hill! Because Elvis was what (when he began)? 19 or 20 years old. So I was sort of like an old guy when "Rumble" came out. You know what I mean?

Have you ever thought of yourself as being a similar type artist to Chuck Berry or Bo Diddley?

No, not really, because, you know, (even though) Chuck was playin' rockabilly, the standard Jerry Lee Lewis, Elvis, Chuck Berry, Fats Domino, Little Richard – they were all doin' rock 'n' roll. When "Rumble" came out, it wasn't rock 'n' roll at all. It was like pre-heavy metal, you know? I was stickin' holes in my speakers to get my fuzz-tone. I was searchin' for sounds, because I had a lung taken out. I couldn't sing, I couldn't *do* the Elvis, I couldn't *do* the Jerry Lee Lewis, I couldn't *do* the Chuck Berry and the Little Richard...I couldn't do *all* that shit, even though I wanted to. If I'd had two lungs, and I was healthy, man, I'd have been boppin' along with the rest of 'em, you know? There would have been no "Rumble." So I just put all of my heart and my soul into my *gui*-tar, and searchin' for sounds. Because I knew I could never play like Chet Atkins, even though I tried to. And I couldn't play like Les Paul, and I couldn't play like Grady Martin, Hank Garland, Tal Farlow and Johnny Smith, Barney Kessel, and all the really great guitar players. I could never *play* like them. And so I said, "OK, if I can't play like them, I'll play like *me*, and search for sounds." Like I said, I punched holes in my speakers to get the distortion with "Rumble." And I bought an old off-brand guitar called a Danelectro. Sixty dollars. It was in a guitar magazine. I bought four of 'em. Now they cost like thousands of dollars for those guitars.

Did you invent fuzz-tone?

I think I did, with the holes in the speakers, right? Because nobody'd thought of it. Ha, ha, ha, ha! *I* didn't even think of it. I was just tryin' to get a distortion, you know? When I made "Rumble" up that night in '57, my brother Ray took the vocal mike and put it to my amplifier. And these little mikes, it was shaking all over, rattling all over, because I had my guitar amp turned all the way up to 10, you know? And when I went to the studio to record it, it was too clean. And I couldn't get that distortion. So I said, "Well, I'll take the heads off of the speakers and I'll punch holes in the speakers, and get that distortion." So, I guess I did sort of like invent the fuzz-tone (laughs) accidentally. Well, no, it was *deliberately*.

Back in those days, I didn't know they were gonna make the boxes, right? I didn't know they were gonna later on make the fuzz boxes and everything.

Among that bunch of guitar players you mentioned, is any one of those your favorite?

I tell ya, like Tal Farlow, Grady Martin – Grady Martin, he played behind Red Foley. He (also) had a jazz group, and he was one of the fastest guitar players I ever heard in my life. And Tal Farlow, I mean, when I heard him, I just couldn't keep up with his guitar playing. You know? It was so fast, when he did "Tea For Two" (for example). Then I briefly met, and heard, Speedy West and Jimmy Bryant. You know those cats? Oh, man! I mean, they was *out* of this world. I love all those cats, but I never could play like 'em. I admire 'em, because I admired what they did. And I get scared when I hear Jimmy Bryant and Speedy West play, man. It's so *unique*, the way they do it. Speedy West playin' with his thumb pick, right? And this is on the *steel*. He plays faster on the steel than most lead guitar players can, you know?

Did you listen to a lot of blues artists in the late '40s and early '50s?

Ah, not really. I loved the Jimmy Reed stuff, but I got it off of Elvis. I heard "Baby What You Want Me To Do" and "Ain't That Lovin' You Baby" (but) I heard Elvis do it first. And then Jimmy Reed came out with these here *hits*. And I started listenin' to Jimmy Reed after he had his hits. And then John Lee Hooker, and ...uh, what's the name of the guy? I recorded one

of his songs – (Link drops into lowdown voice) "I'm a *tail* dragger" – I forgot his name now. *(Willie Dixon - ed.)* But, anyhow, after I got listenin' to all these guys, then I started pickin' up on it, you know?

Did you regard your brother Vernon as the studio genius, and therefore just let him produce your (early) records?

No, I produced my own records. He produced other people. He produced Ronnie Dove. But he never produced me. He just played rhythm guitar on "Rumble." I did my *own* stuff. I created my own sound, and I produced my own stuff. But Ray was a good, ah, assistant to me. I'd say, "Ray, hook up this here to my amplifier," and he'd say, "Aw, you're *crazy*. What're ya doin' *that* for? Like, why are you punchin' holes in speakers, Link? You're insane, you know? Why are you puttin' outdoor speakers to your amplifier?" He didn't understand (that) I was tryin' to create my sound, you know? But, I mean, I didn't know how to do all that. I knew how to play, but I wasn't a good technician. So, he was a good technician. He helped me get my sounds for *me*.

Your original recording of "Rumble" might sound tame to some people today, but your guitar playing actually upset a lot of people back then.

Yeah, because it related to gang fights. Because of the title. And it was a menacing type (record) for those days. They'd say, "Link is not Jerry Lee Lewis, he's not Elvis, he's not Chuck Berry..." These deejays were tryin' to put a handle on me, what to call me. They didn't know what to call me back in those days. So I think one of the journalists in a big paper, or Dick Clark or somebody, said, "Well, Link Wray is just another James Dean with a *gui*-tar." Because I wore leather jackets, and everybody else wore fancy suits, you know? They was wearin' ties, and bowties and tuxedos and really lookin' fancy, but I was comin' out in shades and leather and long hair. And I looked really, completely *weird*, you know? Back in those days, that was unheard of. So they didn't know what to call me.

Some people might forget this now, but back then people really believed that rock 'n' roll could corrupt the morals of young people, isn't that right?

Well, that's the churches. You know the old sayin', they call it "the Devil's music." And the Devil sure as hell didn't give me "Rumble," man. It was God. I mean, I'm *very* spiritual. I came out of the death house, when the doctors told me I was gonna die, right? And I got a 14-year-old son (named Oliver Christian) with my wife Olive Julie in Denmark, you know? Well, when Oliver was around six years old – and I always try to teach him like my mother taught *me* – I say, "Who we love, Oliver?" He says, "Jesus

God." You know? And he said, "Daddy, does God love rock 'n' roll?" I said, "Well, Oliver, I was sick, and the Devil tried to kill me in the death house, and tried to destroy me, and the doctors took out my lung. And then God took me out of that death house, and gave me "Rumble." I said, "Don't you think God loves rock 'n' roll?" And he says, "*Oh*, yeah! God loves rock 'n' roll – He gave you 'Rumble.'" (laughter) When he was six years old he told me that. That was really lovely. But that's the truth! I mean, that was just pure truth. I heard Johnny Cash say, in an interview on European television, "I'm not religious, but I'm very spiritual. And, as far as I'm concerned, God gave me rock 'n' roll – He gave me my music. So it's not the Devil's music." He didn't mention my name, but I guess he's heard it, and saw the way I say it – I don't know if he did or not. But he was speaking the words I usually speak. This is what Johnny Cash was sayin' on a European (broadcast) about two years ago. And I been sayin' this ever since "Rumble," you know? About how God gave me rock 'n' roll.

Was the reason "Rumble" was banned (from the airwaves) in New York and other cities around the country...

That was because of the gang fights.

It really was?

And Archie Bleyer's daughter, Archie Bleyer who had Cadence Records, it was his daughter naming (it). She named the instrumental "Rumble." You know, from the gang fights in *West Side Story*. And so the song was (linked) to the gang fights. So they banned it in New York, they banned it in Boston, they also banned it in Detroit. And then Jocko, a disc jockey in Jersey who used to wear a space outfit – just on a radio show he was wearin' a space outfit. Nobody could see him, but he was still wearin' this here space outfit and it looked cool, you know? 'Cause he had so many journalists, and artists, and people comin' in to see him on his radio show. And he player "Rumble" every 10, 15 minutes. Until he was pumpin' it into New York City. (Link breaks into Wolfman Jack kind of voice, impersonating Jocko): "It's banned in New York City, but Jocko's gonna play '*Rumble*'!" And he played the *shit* out of it. And it was like #1 in New York, #1 in Boston, it was #1 in Detroit – all places it got banned it was still #1.

Milt Grant was actually your manager at one time?

No, he was my brother Ray's manager. Ray was on record before I was. He was on Cameo-Parkway. Bernie Lowe owned the label. The only other artist (then on Cameo) was Charlie Gracie. This was 1957. In fact, I was still in the V.A. hospital and I had to get a leave. I had to ask for a leave to go to Philadelphia to record with my brother. I hadn't even come out of the hospital then. I was still in. And I went to Phila-

delphia on a train, to record with my brother Ray on the Cameo-Parkway label. And it was in a basement in Bernie Lowe's house. They had no studios back in those days. All the studios was in radio stations... So, Bernie had his studio in the basement of his house. And this here guy who wrote "Teddy Bear" for Elvis wrote this here song for my brother Ray to do on Cameo, called "Remember You're Mine." So we went in there with the Ray Charles Singers, and a drummer and bass. Bernie had it all set up, and we went in and recorded it, right? And about a week or two weeks later, Pat Boone comes out on Decca Records with the very same arrangement – with the way I played on the guitar and the whole thing. Only it was with Pat Boone singin' and not Ray, on Decca Records, "Remember You're Mine." And, of course, Pat Boone had the big hit on it. (Note: Boone cut his version at Radio Records in Hollywood on June 17, 1957, with Billy Vaughn arranging and conducting. It actually came out on Dot Records, for whom Boone did all his recordings in the 1950s. Label owner Randy Wood produced it, and Bernie Lowe got a co-writing credit on the tune. It was a Top 10 pop hit.)

What was the Washington, D.C. music scene like in the late 1950s?

It was country. It was all country. Jimmy Dean was the "King of Country" in Washington, D.C. He had a daily show on channel 7, and of course, you had the little country bands all over there. And Ben Adelman had this little studio in Washington, D.C. (True Tone on Georgia Avenue). He recorded Patsy Cline, he recorded Jimmy Dean, and Roy Clark – they were locals, you know, at that time. And Dick ("Dickie") Williams, the brother of Bob Williams, who wrote "Tennessee Waltz." In fact, I played on a 1955 recording with Dick Williams in that little Ben Adelman studio, called "Robber." And Steve Sholes bought it and put it out on RCA Victor in 1955, just before Elvis went on RCA. He was still on Sun then. And I got a letter from Steve Sholes, remarking how good the *gui*-tar sounded on this here record called "Robber." It wasn't a hit, but anyhow Steve Sholes just wrote a nice letter to Ben Adelman, praising the gui-tar playing on this here single called "Robber." And then later, 1959, this here Ben Adelman studio, he sold it to a guy called Ed Green. And that's where "Raw-Hide" was born. The same studio where Patsy Cline did recordings, and Jimmy Dean and all the country stars down in Washington, D.C. when Ben Adelman had it. And then Ed Green bought it, right? And I cut "Dixie Doodle" and "Raw-Hide" in that little studio. And (that single) was a million-seller for me on Epic Records.

Did it ever trouble you that you were forced to share writer's credit, on your early songs like "Rumble," with Milt Grant?

Well, they just stole it. I mean, I hate to bad-mouth my brother (Ray), but I didn't know anything about the recording business. My brother took "Rumble" and (published) it in my dad's name. He put it in my dad's name instead of mine. My dad (couldn't) even play a guitar.

OK, that's where the credit "F.L. Wray, Sr." (came from)?

"F.L. Wray, Sr." My brother Ray could control my dad. To keep the control, he took it completely away from me, you know? I hate to bad-mouth my brother, but that's the truth of it. He put it in my dad's name, takin' it away from me in 1957. And then Milt Grant took half of the writer's (share), because Milt Grant had this big (radio) show, and Link Wray was a nobody. You know, who was Link Wray in 1957, with this here little instrumental? It didn't even *have* a name, until Archie Bleyer's daughter named it. I was like a nobody there in Washington, D.C., doin' these little record hops on (Grant's) show. So he had the power to just take it – take half of the writer's. And then him and Ray shared publishing. So me and Doug got *shit*, off the publishing *or* the writer's. It was shared by my brother Ray and Milt Grant. And I just got (screwed) there, you know? Cause I didn't know the business.

Did you know Gene Vincent personally?

No, but in 1948 and '49, he came and was sitting in, and listening to us play, when we were doin' live country music on this here radio station in Norfolk. And the disc jockey (there) was the guy who wrote "Be-Bop-a-Lula" (with Vincent), Sheriff Tex Davis. And he was just hangin' around there, you know? But I didn't personally know Gene, no.

When you were starting out, did you see yourself becoming more of a country artist, like a Hank Williams?

You mean in Portsmouth?

Yeah, really early on.

No, not really. Not really. I never thought I'd reach that limit. No, I was still learning how to play. I was just happy to be on the stage playin' behind the B-movie western stars! You know, like Roy Rogers and Lash LaRue. I was just happy to be playin'. I didn't ever think about bein' a country star. I never thought I'd ever reach that high a level. I never even *dreamed* of it. Even until I made "Rumble," I mean, Link Wray, I was just a gui-tar player, playin' behind my brother. *He* was the star. And I was just a gui-tar player, playin' behind him, and Doug was a drummer. God kept that a secret from me, right? When God gave me "Rumble" that night in '57, God kept it completely a secret and *zapped* it in my

head. And here's this little three-chord instrumental that *any* gui-tar player can play, right? He just zapped it in my head. I had no *idea* that it was gonna be a big, huge hit. I was on Buddy Dean's show in Baltimore with "Rumble." And he said, "Link, how does it feel to have a hit?" I said, "Tell me what a hit is, and then I'll tell ya!" And he laughed so hard, he fell off the chair, you know? I was so ignorant in the business. He was laughin' – he was a nice guy, Buddy Dean.

After the end of the 1960's, did you continue to work in the studio with your brothers?

Uh... When President Kennedy got shot, right? I did "Jack The Ripper" in 1960 and put it out. I thought it was gonna be mine and Ray and Doug's label, and I ended up again gettin' screwed. It was Milt Grant and Ray's label! Right? Called Vermillion. "Ver," Vernon Wray, and "million," Milt Grant. "Jack The Ripper" was on that label, and I thought it was ours. You know, I just trusted my brother Ray, 'cause I still didn't know the business in 1960 and '63. So (Link Wray music) came out on Vermillion Records until 1963. Swan Records bought it and put it out, and ("Ripper") was a million-seller for me in 1963. And then the president got shot, and the whole Elvis/Chuck Berry/Link Wray/Jerry Lee Lewis type o' music *died* with President Kennedy. You know? And then, when music arose again, it arose with the Beatles and the British rock 'n' roll, and (later) FM stations...and the Allman Brothers and the Grateful Dead, and Frank Zappa, and Quicksilver Messenger Service, and all those guys started risin' up again, with the American type music.

Among the rock guitar players who've made it big over the past 20 to 25 years, whose style do you really like?

I like all of 'em! I mean, I like Pete Townshend. Pete Townshend's a genius, right? He became a superstar. (laughs) He said Link Wray gave him his start, but anyhow he just took it and became rich over it. And David Gilmour, and Eric Clapton, you know, I could sit here and name 'em...I dedicated a song, not to Dicky Betts, but to the other Allman brother that died... Yeah, I dedicated a song to him, off of one of my Polydor albums. (*The song was "I Got To Ramble" from* The Link Wray Rumble *– ed.*) Because I liked the way he played "Layla" with Eric Clapton, and I liked the way the Allman Brothers played. They played for 30 minutes, one song! I mean, just keep *goin'*, And I'm goin', "Wow!" Because I'm a gui-tar player, and I can understand that kind of (philosophy): "Keep right on *playin'*." You know? Like Cipollina (John, the late Quicksilver guitarist), and Nick Gravenites (and) Quicksilver Messenger Service, and all those cats, man. I mean, I loved every *minute* of it. Even though I wasn't up there doin' it, because I didn't want to play to the LSD crowd, right?

Uh-huh...

And so I just (dug it). Even though I was listening to 'em on radio, I was never goin' out playin' to that audience, 'cause, you know, I don't mess around with any kind of drugs. Like I told you, I'm very spiritual. I drink Heineken, I drink beer, you know? So what I did, when that type of music, with the LSD audience and everything arose and started bein' popular, I just started playin' in this redneck club, down in Maryland, called the Two Thieves Club. Down by the waterfront, you know? And I was playin' down in this club, playin' CCR, and Elvis and (roots rock). And that's what I was doin' until Polydor...Actually it wasn't Polydor. The Beatles wanted me to be on Apple Records. And so they sent this here representative from New York City down to talk to me, (to see) if I'd record for Apple Records. I said, "Well, I guess, you know..." (The rep) says, "Aw, the Beatles love Link Wray. They want Link Wray on their Apple label." So, they talked me into it, anyhow. After hours, after I get through playin' my redneck club, then I can go into the studio and do a little bit of recording. And I thought I was recording for Apple Records. But between the time I was recording and it got all mixed down, then some producer out of New York City goes up to my brother Ray, and all of a sudden I'm not on Apple Records. I'm on Polydor Records. You know, I still think there was money involved there. I don't know how. But anyhow, I just told my brother Ray, I said, "Well, you're not gonna cheat me this time. The songs this time's gonna be called 'Link Wray.'" So, that's when I signed with BMI on the Polydor stuff. That's the first time that I put my foot down and said, "OK, *my* writing is gonna be called 'Link Wray' from now on." Even though they still stole the publishing from me. At least I got my writer's.

So that material that you thought you were recording for Apple, that ended up coming out on Polydor?

Polydor, yeah. I thought it was gonna be on Apple Records, and there was a lotta money involved there, you know. My brothers, and these producers and everything you know? And, of course, he kept the money. And Polydor put it out. And the Neville Brothers recorded two of the songs off of that album (*Link Wray*, 1971). I think it was "Falling Rain" and "Fire And Brimstone." The Neville Brothers. I never met 'em, but a journalist, like you, in Denmark said, "Link, do you know the Neville Brothers recorded your song?" I said, "No!" So this journalist sent me this tape...

I imagine Creedence Clearwater (Link covered CCR's "Run Through The Jungle" on Shadowman) was a band that you liked.

Oh! They were fuckin' *great*, man. I love John Fogerty. He got cheated out of his money, too, you know? I heard that Fantasy Records took it and just kept it. They didn't give him shit. I heard, for a long time, Fogerty wouldn't even sing his songs. He got the same shaft that I did, you know? I recorded "Run Through The Jungle" because I love CCR so much. I just thought they were great. I thought John Fogerty was a genius with a gui-tar. The way he played that gui-tar on those songs? Oh, man, it was great.

When did you become aware that Pete Townshend and other British rockers idolized you?

When I met him in '71, when I was on Polydor Records. I was over at Polydor Records and Pete Townshend was doing some overdubbings on *Live At Leeds* at the Record Plant, you know? And he told my brother Ray, he said, "I wanna meet Link Wray – I'm a true fan of Link Wray." So Ray comes over and gets me, right? And I go over there, and the place is jammed and packed with journalists, like you, and photographers, *Rolling Stone* (magazine), everybody was there, you know? At Record Plant. And I walk in, shook hands with Pete: "Hi Link Wray, I'm glad to meet 'cha." You know? And, all of a sudden, somebody jumps in and grabs me from behind, and just picks me up and starts whirlin' me around, hollerin' "Rumble!" just as loud as he could. And finally he let me down, and I almost fell when he let me go. And I turn around, and the guy didn't have a *stitch* of clothes on – he's completely naked. That was Keith Moon. that was amazing. I was a little embarrassed, but I said, "OK, is this the way it is now? Is this the new type of rock 'n' roll?" You know? Ha! Ha! Ha! Ha! Ha! 'Cause it surely wasn't that way in the Elvis days, you know? When (Presley) couldn't even shake his hips. And now they're takin' their clothes off. So I sez, "Is this the way rock 'n' roll is today?" And Pete Townshend's laughin' his ass off. It was a great night. I mean, I had a real good time talkin' to those people.

What has your music career been like since you moved to Europe?

Oh, it's great! I'm very happy, man. I live very happily on a farm in Denmark. I play all the time. But just no bookers would bring me back to America. I couldn't get (U.S. bookings, until recently), because I wasn't on these here big labels. You know, I wasn't on Polydor anymore, or CBS. So the bookers wouldn't bring me back over here. Not until "Rumble" and "Ace of Spades" and "Jack The Ripper" started hittin' the charts (again). I mean, started hittin' the movies – *Pulp Fiction, Independence Day*... Well, in 1988, I did a CD for a little label out of London called Ace Records. And on this here CD there was three songs: one called "Viva Zapata," and "Hotel Loneliness," and "Don't Leave Me." And they ended up in the *Johnny Suede* movie in 1988, but it didn't make it. It was like a hit in France, I think. It was a hit all over Europe, but it wasn't a big bang like *Pulp Fiction* and *Independence Day* and *Desperado*. It wasn't that big.

What kind of diet should a rock 'n' roller eat to stay young and energetic, like yourself?

Believe in God. Get a guardian angel, like I got. I got a guardian angel that protects me. Of course, I'm a vegetarian, too. I got common sense with it. I take 4,000 (milligrams of) Vitamin C every day, I take Vitamin E, I take all the Vitamin Bs, I take zinc. I just go into the health food stores and buy all the vitamin tablets. I eat eggs, omelets, and I drink milk, but I don't eat meat. 'Cause I think meat gives you cancer. I really do. Just once in a while, I go into a Burger King and get a fish sandwich. I eat a lotta potato chips, 'cause it's good for my throat, so I can sing. Plus, potato chips has got a lot of fiber in it. And you need fiber, right? If you don't (have it), you get colon cancer. I eat a lotta popcorn...I guess, if you want to say, I eat a lotta *junk* food. That's what I live on: junk food and vitamins. I'm 68 years old, and I'm still *rumbling,* you know?

How long you been a vegetarian?

All my life. Never ate no meat.

Really? You never had any problem finding substitutes for meat in your diet?

No, no, I never worried about it. I mean, I was raised *poor.* (laughs) Hey, man, I went for days and *days* in North Carolina without (any) food. No shoes (either). Me and my mother would go to bed crying, you know? Praying, "God, please help us with food." I mean, there was plenty of times I went to bed hungry. No food at *all*. I'd go to school, and when the kids went to the place to eat, I had to go outside and set in the swing, until dinner time was up. Until lunch time was over. 'Cause I didn't have no food to eat. And this one little girl in school, she was totally in love with me. So she'd come out and give me a peanut butter sandwich that she had, that her mom and dad gave her. She'd divide her peanut butter sandwiches with me. Otherwise, when I'd come home at night, there was no food at all. My daddy was a war hero, but he was like a casualty. He couldn't go out and work and everything. So we were very, very, very, *very* poor.

So I didn't worry about diet, I just worried about survival. I was a vegetarian, not touching any meat, but I would eat eggs. And I would drink milk, when I could get hold of it. And eat bread, and pinto beans, and navy beans, and black-eyed peas, and turnip greens, and collard greens – every time I'd get hold of stuff like that, I'd eat it.

People would assume, especially people who've seen you play in 1997, that you believe "you're never too old to rock 'n' roll." True?

Never. Never! I'm 68. I say to the audience, I make a little joke, I do an Elvis tune (that goes): "You're so young and beautiful, but I'm so *fuckin'* old!" And then I go into "Run Chicken Run." And they just laugh, and start jumpin' up and down. I'm old, right? But I still got my black hair, and I'm still skinny, and I can jump around on stage, you know? In fact, I fell *off* the stage in San Francisco. I was running (along the edge), and all of a sudden, there was no more stage! And I fell into the monster pit (sic) and hurt my leg. But it's OK now. I played the House Of Blues in L.A. and I had to finish off (the show) sittin' on a stool. They had to carry me off stage. But the kids went wild – 18, 19, 20-year-old kids, bangin' on the stage (shouting), "We love you, Link!" I played two nights in Atlanta and it was sold out. I went to the edge of the stage, and let (this) kid bang on my guitar, and he started bitin' it like Jimi Hendrix, with his teeth. A 19-year-old fan. I was in church (at that moment) – I was just next to God then. That's the way I think about these kids. I'm very happy to come over to America and play to these beautiful young kids who come out to see me. When they come out with love like that, with rock 'n' roll, I'm just close to God then, man. These here young kids, in these young bands, they come out and have me carve my name on their gui-tar with a knife or a pen, or a pencil. Sometimes they pull out a switchblade knife, and I have to carve "Link Wray" in the gui-tars, you know? Ha, ha, ha, ha! And sometimes they just want me to do it with a pencil, you know? These little rock 'n' roll bands. They play all Link Wray music. And all over America now, ever since I been comin' (back over) to America, these little bands has been comin' out, with the bangin' on the stage, and really with the (true) rock 'n' roll spirit. To me, that's like bein' in church. You know what I mean? The rock 'n' roll spirit, man, to me it's just like bein' in church. I couldn't get no closer to God, man – these little kids with the rock 'n' roll spirit. You know, man?

Most Collectible 45

"I Sez Baby," Kay 3690, $100.

Most Collectible LP

Link Wray And The Wraymen, Epic LN 3661, $250.

Recommended Introduction

Rumble! The Best Of Link Wray, Rhino R2-71222 (20 of his best and biggest, including, of course, the classic title song)

If you want to hear more...

Mr. Guitar, Norton 242 (a 2-CD set consisting of the best of the material he recorded for the Swan label, mostly in the 1960s)

The *Missing Links* series: *Hillbilly Wolf,* Norton 210; *Big City After Dark,* Norton 211; *Some Kinda Nut,* Norton 212; *Streets Of Chicago,* Norton 253 (various recordings Link made in the 1960s and 1970s, many of which were previously unreleased)

Shadowman, Hip-O 40069 (recorded in 1995 but not issued in the U.S. until 1997, you can hear how he sounds in more recent times)

Part III
The Teen Idols

Fabian

by Wayne Jancik

One could argue that Fabian was an important pop pioneer. Every manufactured rock and pop act since, from the Monkees to Milli Vanilli, owes him a debt, as Fabian was the first to prove that it could be done. This brief interview with the most maligned, yet one of the most durable, teen idols of the late 1950s first appeared in the December 28, 1990 Goldmine, when he was 47. The comedy series he refers to in the interview never has happened, but there's still time. Believe it or not, Fabian is younger than every Beatle except George Harrison, and that by only 19 days!

He has been called the "archetypal manufactured teen idol." The butt of many a joke, Fabian Forte went on to sell millions of recordings. There was, in rapid succession, "Tiger," "Turn Me Loose" and "I'm A Man." And then, "Hound Dog Man" and "This Friendly World." When his contract and career were in his own hands, the hits stopped, but a chain of TV spots and 30-plus films followed. He appeared with Bing Crosby in *High Time* and John Wayne in *North To Alaska.*

"It was terrible," Fabian recently said. "I was out in front of people, lip-syncing my record, feeling very strange, and very awkward. I was never really comfortable with myself until about five years ago."

Currently, Fabian, now 47, runs Rattlesnake Productions, a documentary and movie-making concern. The Fab One has toured with Bobby Rydell and Frankie Avalon as "The Golden Boys of Bandstand" and is constantly appearing with or setting up endless caravans, featuring musical peers Lou Christie, Little Anthony, Lesley Gore, etc., billed as "The Fabian Goodtime Rock 'n' Roll Show."

Goldmine: *Before that serendipitous discovery event, what did you want to do when you grew up?*

Fabian: Do you remember what you wanted to do when you were 14? All I wanted to do was get laid a lot. I liked football and school, I remember that. I had some idea that I wanted to get into engineering.

And your dad, what did he do?

He was a cop.

Ever consider it?

Nah. I respect the force though.

Had you done any singing?

Oh, all the time, with the radio. I was a red-blooded youth. I was glued like all the rest to rock radio. I was brought up on it; that and all the a cappella groups that were all around in my neighborhood. it was all I ever heard every night, in the summer.

But you never sang with any?

No. Nothing official as a group.

Tell us the "discovery story."

My father had a heart attack. I lived in a row house in South Philadelphia; a house much like you'd see in Brooklyn. Anyway, I called an ambulance. He was being rushed out. I was sitting on the steps. I wanted to go but my mom wouldn't let me. I had to watch my two younger brothers. I'm sitting there. There is a lot of people around, and this fellow, Bob Marcucci, who owned Chancellor Records, was driving by. He had a great friend – now if you can picture it, the stair stoops are like glued together and the friend lived right next door to us and his wife was pregnant. Marcucci thought that it was his friend's wife who was being taken. So he stopped. That's how we met.

He introduced himself. He was rude enough to say, "Are you interested in being in the singing business?" I told him to go to hell. I remember that, real well. I mean I couldn't believe the balls on this guy.

Did he know the situation?

Obviously. Then, he kept bugging. And then as the weeks and months went by and my father came home and couldn't work, things were getting very desperate at our house. Compensation on disability was only $45 a week. My mother didn't work and I only brought in $6 a week, that I got as a delivery boy. Marcucci started asking the friend next door to ask me again if I was interested. I kept saying no. When we got more desperate, he showed up at our door. I loved rock 'n' roll. All I ask him was that I made some money for my family. This is what I'm interested in. If I can do that, I'll be glad to go along with this. That's how it started. It was part love of rock 'n' roll, but mainly it was to help my family. I never made any bones about it. And the wonderful effect was I did get involved in making rock 'n' roll.

The movie The Idolmaker *was supposedly about Bob Marcucci and you and Frankie Avalon?*

I sued. Avalon, for some reason, didn't want to get involved. I don't know whether it was because he didn't want to put the money up front or what. But I won.

On what grounds did you sue?

It was fraud. They were claiming that it wasn't about me and Frankie.

But everyone with a smidgen of pop history knowledge saw it that way.

Of course. So I sued for five years and received a major settlement with them, which I can't disclose. The main thing that I like is that I refused to sign the settlement unless they did a major public relations thing in which they apologized. I wanted a full page ad on the back of both the [*Hollywood*] *Reporter* and *Variety* with an apology to my family. And I got it.

How much input did you have in the making of your records?

I picked the songs, most of them. There was a couple of albums – hah – of those old standards where I didn't get to pick a thing. I didn't want to do those. I was coerced, forced into that. None of that was of my choosing. The rock things were mine. "Turn Me Loose" was mine. "I'm A Man" was mine. "Tiger" was mine. Those things came off half decent, I though.

How much influence did Dick Clark have in your making it?

None. Oh, no. Except for being a good friend now and an acquaintance then, Dick didn't have anything to do with it, except that he did put me on his show. I don't mean to demean that, but you're talking about something darker.

Yeah.

He had nothing to do with Chancellor, as far as I know. Hey, It was a Philadelphia label, that's it. In those days, I didn't know he was involved in anything else.

All the surrounding Beatlemania-like hysteria must have been scary.

No question about it. It was very unique. Very few people, prior to me, went through it. I mean, Sinatra and, going back further, Rudy Vallee went through the experience. But this response was all new, you'll have to remember. I mean, I couldn't imagine me going through it. And it was quite an experience. You'd think it would be flattering, but it was unwielding. It's so out of control.

I've heard of you being smuggled into a venue in a policeman's suit. And another time a window was broken and you got glass in an eye during one of those fan encounters.

Yah. I was coming out to do a film. The plane landed and they rushed a cart out onto the field to get me, but they broke through and I got goddamn glass in my eye. The film had to be delayed for three weeks.

The price of fame. Another price you had to pay was that music critics were hard on you. I think you caught the brunt of it more than the other teen idols.

Yeah, yeah. And I know why. I've had time to think about it and now and again people ask me of those crazy days and I've had to piece it together in my mind. I had a manager who was an egomaniac. He was a frustrated dancer/performer. And he put it in the press this way: He wanted all the credit for manufacturing me and Avalon. So he presented it to the press that I was taught what to do. Consequently, the press

got a hold of that and really killed me. It's like being stabbed in the back by your own. I didn't realize it at the time. I was too busy to read reviews and shit like that, you know what I mean.

But as I go back and look at the quotes of his – and I've double-checked it with him – he said it all. He set it up. Now, maybe there were critics out there who actually didn't like me, too. But that's fair. You can't please everyone. But the major thrust of it came from Marcucci's ego.

I used to be bitter, but no more, I've finally come to terms with it. But, believe me, I would do it all over the same way, if I could. I would have liked it if I had been older and more experienced. I wasn't prepared and it was all like a dream world.

Was it just you and Frankie that he managed?

No, there was the Four Dates. I used them on the road for a lot of dates. They were great. I see them all the time when I'm back in Philly. And there was Jodie Sands. She was very good, by the way. I'm not sure what became of her.

You had a real string of hits in a two-year period. Any favorites?

Ah, "String Along," that's the best. When that time was up, I bought out my contract. Everybody wants respect. I was 18 and went and did some things for Dot, but that didn't work out. I guess I just wasn't interested.

You stopped recording in 1962, except for a recording for Cream in 1977.

Yeah, but that last one was just play-time. We were just goofing off. I don't know what that was. We were all in the studio and I said, "Hey, give it a shot." The things that were never released, those are the things that I like the most. They were done eight, 10 years prior. I had done four sides with Lee Hazelwood and Billy Strange. These things were just great. I guess they were never intended to be put out.

You then switched over to movies and you've been in a string of them. Was there ever a time when you laid back from the business totally?

No. If I'm not working on some feature, I'm putting together some tour or on the road myself.

Any plans of returning to the recording studio?

Ah, no. I mean, I don't have any say. But I doubt it. It would be great, but I'm not going to do it because I doubt that any record company would back me. That is just the reality for our age group. I'm not angry about it but there is a sense of disappointment. I don't even think about it now because I'm more or less a businessman. Not that I understand it, but I understand where the record companies are coming from. The demographics ain't there. My age group will come to see the show. They'll put down anywhere from seven to 25 bucks for the concert, but they won't go buy an album of new stuff.

Bobby Rydell is spending his own money putting something together. And Chubby Checker, his last album was great. It had such a drive and was fresh. Some of these guys are sounding better than ever. I'm not going to do it just for my ego – excuse me, I don't mean that these guys did it just for their egos – so that I got another album cover to put on the office wall. That would be ridiculous.

What does the future hold?

I'd like to do a comedy series. Maybe that will come up. I'm going to keep producing and packaging shows, and touring. We did like 350 shows as the "Golden Boys of Bandstand," me and Frankie and Rydell. I don't know if there's a reason to do that again. I guess anything is possible.

Most Collectible 45

"I'm A Man"/ "Hypnotized," Chancellor S-1029, stereo single, will be clearly marked as "STEREO" on the label, $50.

Most Collectible LP

Hold That Tiger!, Chancellor CHLS-5003, stereo, pink label, $150.

Recommended Introduction

The Best Of Fabian, Varese Vintage 5577 (his best American compilation ever)

Rick Nelson

by Jeff Tamarkin

It's hard to believe today that at one time, Rick Nelson's music was not taken very seriously. He had been just another "teen age idol," to quote one of his many hit songs. He was in the same category as Pat Boone or Frankie or Fabian or the rest, or so it seemed. Those who claimed that, however, hadn't listened to the music. Sometimes it takes an artist's death, unfortunately, to realize how outstanding their records really were. Nelson's stature has only grown in the nearly decade and a half that has passed since his plane went down after a New Year's Eve gig in 1985. He rarely wrote his own material, but he astutely chose which songs to record, and he had some of the best musicians in the business behind him, most notable among them James Burton, who would later play in Elvis' band. Finally, as opposed to many of his peers, he had hit after hit after hit. He's the only of the so-called "teen idols" whose music stands tall enough to allow him a spot in the Rock and Roll Hall of Fame. This rare interview with Nelson appeared in the February 14, 1986 issue of Goldmine *and served as a final tribute.*

"**R**icky" he was called, and if you grew up in the 1950s you knew him. Maybe not personally, but you watched his life story unfold every week on national television. Ricky Nelson was the youth of America in the '50s – or at least the clean-cut, wholesome alternative to the black leather jacket types that adults figured as the culprits behind rock 'n' roll.

So it took some of those adults by surprise when Ricky himself turned into a rock 'n' roller, although they might have begrudgingly accepted him as tolerable compared to that greasy Elvis and the wild men who followed him. What few of the screaming teenage girls or their parents could have realized at the time, though, was just how serious Rick (he dropped the "y" in his 20s) was about his music. Ricky Nelson, after all, was a TV star, not a rock 'n' roll singer, and before he set the precedent, the twain never had met.

Sure, Elvis had appeared on TV to sing his hits. But never before had the relatively new medium been used to break an actor *as* a singer. It wasn't until Nelson sang Fats Domino's "I'm Walkin'" at the end of a 1957 episode of *The Adventures Of Ozzie And Harriet* that anyone realized quite the amount of power the tube in the living room had; literally overnight, Ricky Nelson had turned into a rock 'n' roll star. Perhaps Ricky was as surprised as anyone by this; he'd only tried singing on the show to impress a girlfriend who liked Elvis Presley.

Nelson had already been popular among teen girls, but as an actor. His boyish looks – even as he entered his teens – were classic "cute," and his weekly presence on his family's TV show made him seem both accessible and harmless. Who knew what Elvis did on a date? But Ricky you could watch as he went through his day-to-day existence in front of you.

It was that believability, perhaps, that extended to his music career. Rick Nelson was obviously not a manufactured talent; he had already been familiar both to radio and TV audiences for some eight of his 17 years before he picked up a guitar. And whereas TV kids like "Beaver Cleaver" and "Bud Anderson" were actors playing roles, Ricky Nelson played Ricky Nelson. There was no reason to believe he wasn't sincere.

What developed in the following years was unpredictable, though. No one, probably least of all Nelson, knew he had such a natural flair for a song. And he never seemed less than completely in control. Where even Elvis Presley allowed himself to be manipulated to often embarrassing extremes, Rick Nelson probably recorded very few songs in his 28-year musical career that would force him to blush. Nelson was a natural and he had a good ear – he even knew when he heard a great musician right from the start (his choice of guitar great James Burton being a prime example). And if

Nelson was subdued next to Presley, Lewis, Berry and Vincent, he was certainly leagues ahead of his fellow "teen idols": Fabian, Frankie, etc.

Even if someone was a skeptic in the '50s, Nelson's commitment to his music was unquestionable by the late '60s. Even after *Ozzie And Harriet* went off the air in 1966, Nelson continued to make music – if anything, the cancellation of the program freed him to put his career into overdrive. Years after the hits – "Be-Bop Baby" (No. 3, 1957), "A Teenager's Romance" (No. 2, 1957), "Stood Up" (No. 2, 1957), "Believe What You Say" (No. 4, 1958), "Poor Little Fool" (No. 1, 1958), "Lonesome Town" (No. 7, 1958), "It's Late" (No. 9, 1959), "Travelin' Man" (No. 1, 1961) and "Hello Mary Lou" (No. 9, 1961) – had dried up, Rid Nelson kept on writing and singing his music. And he grew with the times.

The mid-to-late '60s were tough years for Rick, like they were for any American artist who had made it in the '50s. Times had changed and most of the old guard had been evicted. It remained one of Rick Nelson's greatest frustrations for the rest of his life that he could not be accepted for what he was after he and his music grew up – and outgrew being a pin-up boy for squealing pubescent girls.

These feelings culminated in the early '70s and ironically provided Nelson with his best-selling record in more than 10 years. "Garden Party" was written after an audience at New York's Madison Square Garden, there to see a "revival" of '50s rockers, found the "new" Rick Nelson – long hair, the Stone Canyon Band behind him, new material – alien to its expectation. The fans wanted Ricky Nelson, teen idol. What they got was Rick Nelson, musician. He didn't have to be revived.

Not much was heard from Nelson during the rest of the '70s. He did countless live concert dates, happy to play for anyone who'd accept him for what he was. He learned how to live with the unshakable Ricky image, but he continued being Rick to the end.

That end came New Year's Eve on a private plane after leaving Guntersville, Ala., where he had played his final show to a crowd of 250 in a place called PJ's Lounge. The engine kicked smoke into the fuselage and the plane went down, somewhere near DeKalb, Texas, on the way to another gig. Like Buddy Holly, Otis Redding, Lynyrd Skynyrd, Jim Croce and too many others, Rick Nelson was lost in a plane crash on his way to work. His fiancee, Helen, Blair, and five members of Nelson's band, some of whom had complained about the safety of the airplane, perished as well. The two pilots survived. Nelson is survived by his mother, Harriet, his brother, David, a daughter and three sons (from a marriage to Kristin Harmon that ended in divorce).

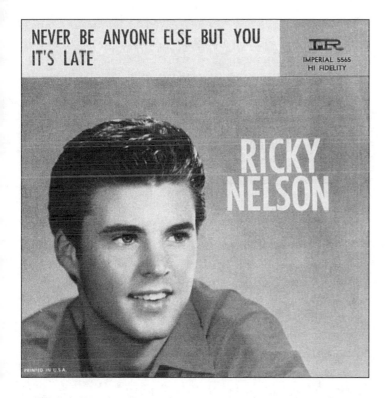

NEVER BE ANYONE ELSE BUT YOU
IT'S LATE

IMPERIAL 5565
HI FIDELITY

RICKY NELSON

The following interview was conducted in 1981 at a hotel in New York City. Rick Nelson was in Manhattan to play a show at The Ritz, in support of his first and only Capitol album, *Playing To Win*. He was justifiably proud of the record, which found him returning to his rock 'n' roll roots after years of performing country and ballad type material. Portions of this interview – printed verbatim, and for the first time, in *Goldmine* – were used in an article for a local newspaper, but by and large most of it has never been published. Nelson was soft-spoken, polite, cooperative and honest – a good interview subject and a nice guy.

Eric Hilliard Nelson, 1940-85, may or may not be truly appreciated as the talent he was. As David Hinckley of the *New York Daily News* said, "Ricky Nelson was not the difference between rock 'n' roll surviving and failing. Nonetheless, his role was real and today, in an age when rock songs have become a calculated part of TV's marketing package, easy to overlook ... (But) Rick Nelson was one of the reasons rock 'n' roll did not fade away with Pat Boone's white bucks. To all the singers who do that, we owe something; in this case, Rick, we owe a little more." Well put.

Goldmine: A lot of child actors are isolated from the outside world. Did that happen to you?

Rick Nelson: No, I think just the opposite happened to my brother and me. It wasn't like we had stage parents. We were kind of born into it, so that was our normal existence. We were exposed to a lot of things. I know the early shows we did on radio and then TV, when I was about seven or eight, were written around real things that happened to us.

What do you remember most about your childhood? Was most of your time spent doing the shows?

No, I remember going to school – we always went to public schools – and the friends that I had. I had a lot of friends outside of show business, so I had a life outside of that. The show business part was just a job that we were doing.

You were always portrayed as a clean-cut kid, sort of an antidote to the crazy rock 'n' rollers. Was that just an image that was given you or were you really that innocent?

I think that was just a thing about the '50s. Those were just the values of the '50s. So it's kind of hard to stand back now and look at it, to judge those things.

How did music enter the picture? Had you been wanting to sing or did someone decide to see what would happen if they put a guitar in your hand on the TV show?

I had always been around music. My dad started with a band and my mom was a vocalist, so we were always listening to music and I was always a fan of different music people. It started when I was in high school; that's when I started to actively pursue it.

When you first went into the studio to record for Verve, what was it like?

It was scary. I remember all these people there, and I had gone straight from singing in my bathroom to the recording studio. There was nothing in between. Things were all in mono then. Then it went up to two tracks and then four, and everyone was saying "Four tracks! Why do you need four tracks?"

When the show ended in 1966, what made you decide to choose singing over acting as a career?

I think they're related in a certain way, but the thing that's not there with acting, unless it's a play, is that live experience. It's really a good feeling to go out there and make somebody feel something, and get that direct response.

Going back to the '50s again, what was it like being branded as a teen idol? Were you concerned yet at that point that your music wasn't being taken seriously?

No, it was a great time for me. It was really the beginning of rock 'n' roll and I was fortunate to be around then. We played places that had never heard electric guitars.

It wasn't until much later that people realized what great musicians you had working with you on your early records. In particular, how did you find James Burton?

I had just signed to Imperial and I was looking for a band. I heard an audition coming from down the hall and I just heard this great guitar playing. A guy named James Kirkland was the bass player, just playing slap bass. He came up with Bob Luman of the *Louisiana Hayride*. So I went in and subsequently got to know

James (Burton) and we started doing some things. Then I asked them if they wanted to be in a band. We stayed together for over 10 years.

When the Beatles era came along you stopped having Top 10 hits. Do you think that was a direct result of the changes in music or were there other factors involved?

Well, a lot of people who had been around just stopped getting airplay. You had to be English to get things played for awhile. But I was still under contract and it gave me a chance to do things, recording-wise, that I might not have had a chance to do otherwise, to experiment. I did production-type albums and country albums.

The Stone Canyon Band, which you formed in 1969, was heavily country oriented. Why did you decide to head in that direction?

It was a different kind of thing to try, to use a steel guitar in rock 'n' roll and use those types of harmony. It was an idea I got when I saw Buck Owens on the old *Jackie Gleason Show*. There was something about it, that feel, that made me think it would work. So I contacted Tom Brumley, who was Buck Owens' steel player, and he hadn't been on the road for about a year and a half. He didn't want to go on the road at first, then all of a sudden he changed his mind because he never had the chance to play music like that. Then I heard Randy Meisner with Poco – they were just getting together and doing the same thing I wanted to try, and it sounded great. I heard them at the Troubadour and Randy, at that time, wanted to do something else, so I was fortunate enough to get him. It made me feel really good that he went on to the Eagles, because he's so talented.

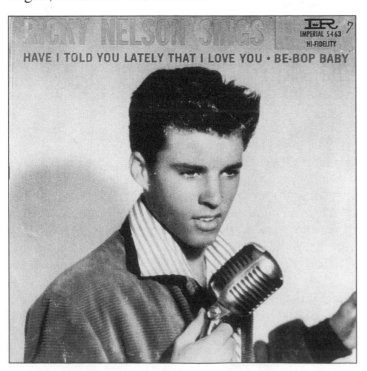

Moving up a few years to 1972, you had your biggest hit in years with "Garden Party." What was the actual story behind that song? You were jeered at a concert?

It was actually kind of confusing at first because we had done all our songs in chronological order – we had to go back and learn them. At the time I was involved in writing new songs; I had to talk myself into being there (the Madison Square Garden '50s revival concert at which his show was poorly received). I felt weird being there; I thought, I knew I shouldn't have done this. It wasn't a frightening experience, it was more of a weird one. We had just come off of doing a lot of colleges where there was no problem playing new songs, so it was weird getting that non-acceptance. But now when I look back at the pictures, my hair was real long at the time so physically I guess it was a whole different thing than they expected. I had never been to one of those before. I don't get that so much anymore. Now I think people are more willing to accept new things, and we do a show in which we incorporate some of the older things.

You were signed to Epic Records in 1977 but only one album, Intake, came out of that. Apparently you weren't very satisfied there.

It just got to be an unworkable situation because there were so many people giving their input in the recording that it got to be out of hand. Nothing was right after awhile.

Moving along to the present, how did you come to sign with Capitol?

I was looking for a company that wanted to sign me for myself, and not to try to work me into a certain thing that was supposedly happening at the time. I was so glad to find Capitol because their people have musical backgrounds; it's not like attorneys running a company.

On your album for Capitol, Playing to Win, you cover a Graham Parker song, "Back To Schooldays." Was that your idea or was that a case of the company thinking it would be hip for you to do material by a popular new-wave artist?

Jack Nitzsche brought me that one. I heard it when we were up in Canada and I thought it was amazing; it really sounded like a (Johnny) Burnette song to me.

How about the John Fogerty song, "Almost Saturday Night"?

I had gone to see John where he was living, in Oakland, and we had thought about him producing. But it didn't work out because he was going through a period where he was trying to get his own thing together. But in talking to him, he mentioned that song and played it for me. I've always wanted to record it.

You do a Burnette Brothers song, "Believe What You Say," which you've already done successfully once before, in 1958. Why the remake?

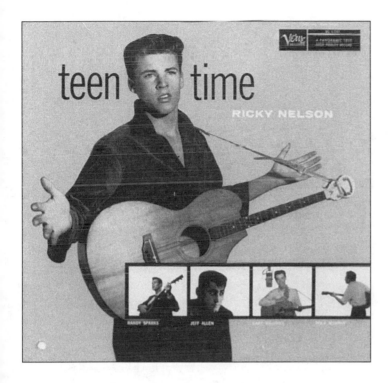

We've always done it in the show and it's always gotten a real good response. It didn't seem dated; it's just a basic rock 'n' roll song. One night when we were recording, we were trying a few things just as a warmup. We played it and liked the way it sounded; it had a live feel to it.

Jack Nitzsche also produced this album. What was he like to work with?

We got along well. We started together back in the '50s, really.

You've recently turned 40 and you've been singing professionally since you were 15. Did you ever imagine when you were making records for Imperial and Decca that you'd still be doing this 25 years later?

Not at all. At first, I just wanted to record, to be able to walk around and show my friends a record. I thought nothing beyond that. We did it on the television show as an afterthought. All of a sudden that exposure helped a lot faster than anybody ever thought it would – in about a week's time we sold a lot of records.

What do you want to do next?

Keep playing. In the last year we averaged about 200 dates on the road. But it's been paying off for me, because the album is actually doing fairly well sales-wise without having a single; it's always been the opposite for me. It's always been that if anything, I'd have a single going.

This new album is almost a tribute to your own roots. You haven't recorded such a basic rock 'n' roll album since the early days.

I just feel much closer to rock 'n' roll, and if anything, it's getting back to what I started out doing. It's something that I know about, and I really enjoy recording that way. That's what seems to be happening now, with new wave and smaller bands and that type of thing. They're like garage bands and that's what I started doing. That's what I really like.

Looking back over your whole career, what stands out for you?

I've just thoroughly enjoyed doing the things I've done. And it's so important to really like what you've been doing. It's never been work for me at all. It's always been a necessity for me to do what I do. Even when I'm home alone, I always end up doing something that has to do with music.

Most Collectible 45

"Lonesome Town"/ "I Got A Feeling," Imperial X5545, red vinyl, $600.

Most Collectible LP

Teen Time, Verve MGV-2083, also includes songs by other artists but Rick is pictured prominently on the front cover, $500.

Recommended Introduction

Legendary Masters Series: The Best Of Rick Nelson, Volume 1, EMD/Capitol 92771 (approximately two dozen of the songs he made famous on the Imperial label from 1957-60)

The Best Of Rick Nelson, Volume 2, EMD/Capitol 95219 (26 more Imperial hits, these from 1960-63)

If you want to hear more...

The Best Of Rick Nelson, 1963-1975, MCA 10098 (15 recordings he made for Decca and MCA, including all the significant charted hits)

Stay Young: The Epic Recordings, Sony Legacy 48920 (material he recorded for Epic in the late 1970s, much of it unreleased until this CD came out)

Bobby Rydell

by Wayne Jones

He's usually grouped in with the "teen idols." And he certainly was as big as almost anyone in the early 1960s, though his star faded with Beatlemania. He did actually record the John Lennon-Paul McCartney tune "A World Without Love," and it came out in the States at roughly the same time as the familiar hit by Peter and Gordon, but the British original won out. That was, more or less, the end of his hit-making career. Unfortunately, because of the ongoing lack of Cameo-Parkway Records reissues, his original recordings have been out of print for over 25 years. An entire generation has missed out on the fun material Rydell recorded, except for the all-too-rare times an oldies station spins "Wild One" or "Wildwood Days" or one of his many other early-1960s hits. When this interview ran in Goldmine, in the August 1979 issue, his hit-making years were already 15 years past. Two decades on, Rydell still performs the old hits, especially on the East Coast, where he never really went away.

Goldmine: *Today, we're speaking with one of the top teen idols from the '50s, and also one of the finest entertainers around today, Bobby Rydell. Bobby, does that term "teen idol" bother you?*

Bobby Rydell: No, not at all Those were great days and you kind of like to go back to them once in awhile. "Teen" really sounds nice now, especially since I'm into my thirties. So, "teen idol" never really affected me.

I understand that your first break into show business was because of Paul Whiteman. Is that correct?

Actually, that was the first thing I had done professionally and I was very young at the time, maybe about 8 or 9 years old. At that time in my career I was basically doing impersonations, people like James Cagney, Edward G. Robinson, James Stewart, and others… I was on Paul Whiteman's show doing these types of impersonations, and then became a regular for about 2 1/2 to 3 years. Then the show lost its ratings and went off the air – so at about 11 or 12 years old, I was out of work. But that was my first break.

Then, as I understand it, a fellow named Frankie Day, who was with a group called Dave Appell & The Applejacks, happened along and took an interest in your career. Right?

That's right. Although it was only in print that he was with Dave Appell & The Applejacks, which sounded better – because the group had a couple of hit records like "Rock-A-Conga" and "Mexican Hat Rock." Frankie Day was a local bass player from Philadelphia, who was working for a group called Billy Duke and the Dukes at a place in Somers Point, New Jersey, just outside of Atlantic City. This was a summer resort mainly for college kids to go in and have a good time. Now, about that time I had been working with a group called Rocco and the Saints where Frankie Avalon was playing trumpet and I was playing drums and singing. Whatever Frankie Day saw in me, he liked. I must have been about 13 or 14 years old and he wanted to manage me. I really knew nothing about management because I was too young, so we all got together with my Mom and Dad and finalized things just on a handshake. We lasted together for a good 14 years. He was a hell of a good man and a fine manager, but things do happen, so in 1970 we split on a handshake, still friends. And as I say – he was one hell of a manager and a good person.

Your first record was on the Veko label, a song called "Fatty Fatty." This tune also showed up on another obscure label called Venise but with a different flip side. What was the background behind this song appearing on two different labels?

The only thing I could imagine was that after I met Frankie Day, he, in turn, had met a couple of people from the Baltimore-Washington area who we later found out had no money. They left Frankie Day and my Dad stuck with paying the recording costs, studio time, musicians and tape, etc. , from a session I had done. At the time, my Dad was only making about $70 a week as a foreman at a place in Philadelphia, so we got stuck with all of these bills. The label itself was called Veko. We recorded "Fatty Fatty," "Happy Happy," "Dream Age" and a few other things. Then these other cats that were involved all of a sudden just split with the tapes and as I said, we were left with all of the recording costs. We finally paid off all of the bills and as far as I can remember the reason why there were two different labels was that those people who split with the tapes – after I became successful with a few hit records – decided to jump on the bandwagon by coming up with some cockeyed label called Venise or whatever the hell it was called and put out those songs that were recorded some years earlier. So, that's about the only thing I could recall about how that happened.

How did you get involved with Cameo-Parkway Records?

I auditioned for Cameo-Parkway, and as a matter of fact, I auditioned with another singer from Philadelphia whose name I can't remember. But we sang a song together called "Buddies." The song went something like this... (Bobby then proceeds to sing a few bars of "Buddies.") So we recorded that and put it down on tape. I later found out that Bernie Lowe of Cameo-Parkway liked me but didn't like the other kid and that he also wanted to sign me to a recording contract. That's exactly, of course, what Frankie Day was looking for. Up to that point, we'd already been to Capitol, RCA, Columbia and other major record companies, but they all said no – mainly because they didn't feel that another teenage idol-type could make it. But Bernie Lowe took a shot, and I signed with him, I think in the latter part of 1956. I had a few records that absolutely bombed and did nothing whatsoever. I was about ready to give it all up and go back to playing drums for some groups. Then Bernie Lowe, Kal Mann, and Dave Appell came up with a song called "Kissin' Time." This became my first hit, which had taken about three years after I had signed. It was released in the summer of 1959 and that's basically how that happened.

You mentioned that up to the point recording "Kissin' Time," your first releases weren't successful, so I'm wondering then after you recorded "Kissin' Time," did you have any special feeling that perhaps this song could have been the one with hit potential?

Who knew, really? I must have been just 16 or 17 years old at the time and couldn't tell what would be a hit any more than anyone else could. I guess if any-body could predict something like that he'd make a million dollars a week, just picking out hit records. "Kissin' Time," though, sounded good to me. It had a lot of gimmicks in it, like mentioning quite a few cit-ies in the U.S., for example; it had a handclap-heavy beat to it. So when we recorded it, it sounded great. Actually, we recorded it with a local Philadelphia group that worked a lot of the Shore resorts called Georgie Young and the Rocking Box. I put my voice on it, Bernie Lowe, Kal Mann and Dave Appell wrote it, and we put it out. Then, a disc jockey in Philadelphia named Harvey Miller started playing the record on WIBG, which was at the time, *the* radio station in Philadelphia. He played the record three, four, five times in a row, just back to back to back. The record started taking off in Philadelphia – at which time Dick Clark became aware of it, and that sales on it were up to 100,000, 200,000 copies. This led to a guest appearance on his show, and from that appearance on *American Bandstand*, the record just took off nationwide.

Then about a year later, you redid a standard called "Volare." Whose idea was it to re-record that song and were there any hopes for that one?

Up to the point of "Volare," we had hits with "Kissin' Time," "Swingin' School," "Wild One." I remember we were doing an album which was to con-tain songs like "Sway," "That Old Black Magic" and "Volare," but as it turned out the rest of the songs on this recording session for this album really didn't come off well. I remember there was a song called "Chemistry" and a few others, but on the whole, it didn't come off so good, so we shelved it. But then we needed a single to follow up "Swingin' School" with. We sat down and listened to the tapes from this shelved album, particu-larly "Volare." Bernie Lowe picked it and my mother loved the song, too. My mother suggested to me that "Volare" should be released as a single. I explained to her that it wasn't up to me. Bernie Lowe, though, did take the tape of "Volare" back to the studio and sweet-ened it up, adding whatever they had to add to it. It was mastered, then released.

To me, it sounded good, but my God, I thought, Domenico Modugno had already sold over a million copies with it, Dean Martin also had a million seller with it, so how many times can one song really be a hit? Ours, of course, had a completely different sound with the "Wo-Wo's" and the "Yea-Yca's" – the Rydell sound. We put it out and, sonofagun, it became another million seller. But again, it all came about from an album that was never released. Then, the songs that followed "Volare" happened to be some of the other songs from that same recording date like

"That Old Black Magic" and "Sway," which became hits as well.

Shortly thereafter, you had a short musical associa-tion with Chubby Checker, and recorded a great album together. As a matter of fact, when I spoke to Chubby Checker a while back, he told me that he thought the album you had both done together was one of the best things he had ever done. From this album came a hit sin-gle, "Jingle Bell Rock." Was the idea of teaming up with Chubby arranged by the people at Cameo-Parkway?

Yes, it was arranged by them and also my manager and Chubby's manager at the time. It was around Christmas time when the album was released, although it wasn't specifically a holiday LP. There were a couple of holiday songs on it like "Jingle Bell Rock" and "What Are You Doing New Year's Eve." It was meant to be marketed, though, at that time of year. Chubby and I had an absolute ball doing the album. It was a lot of fun. The tracks had already been recorded and we both sat with Dave Appell, Cameo's A&R man at the time; learned everything; went into the studio; and overdubbed our voices on the tracks. We had a fantastic time and I agree with Chubby, it was a fun album and a good album. It didn't knock you down sensationally music-wise but I have to repeat it was a fun album to do.

In the early 1960s, you got involved with motion pictures. You appeared in the movie version of the Broadway show Bye Bye Birdie *with Ann-Margret. I also saw you appearing in another film called That Lady From Peking. Was there much of a transition from going into a recording studio or making stage appearances to filming a movie?*

It was a completely different experience for me. When you're a kid and you think about motion pic-tures, it's almost like Disneyland. In other words, is there really a place like that somewhere? So that's what Hollywood meant to me. It was like fantasyland.

But, anyhow I went out and screen-tested for *Bye Bye Birdie* with Ann-Margret. Of course, she had done a couple of things but really wasn't all that hot as a star at the time. Whatever they saw in me they must have liked. Evidently, a lot of people screen-tested for the part of Hugo Peabody, but they liked the way Ann and I came off together on screen. We both had done the screen test in February, then in April I received a call from the William Morris Agency, who I was signed with, saying that Columbia Pictures wanted me for the part of Hugo Peabody. I was ecstatic about it.

So I went out to the West Coast and spent six months making *Bye Bye Birdie* and it was fantastic, although it was a lot of hard work. Making motion pictures is not easy, by any means. It's almost like the Army – "Hurry up and wait!" There was a lot of hanging around and days where I had to get up in the morning at 4:30 or 5, be in makeup at 7 a.m. and just hang around until 7 p.m. without doing anything. That's not the hard work involved, but you can get very bored just hanging around and wish you could at least be doing something. Those happened to be the days they just couldn't get around to the parts that I was in. But the picture did take six months to make and the hardest part for me was the "Lotsa Livin'" number. Now, I'm not a dancer per se, although I could do a few moves, so I worked for two weeks with a choreographer named Anna White, who was simply marvelous. At the time she worked with me, her leg was in a cast and she was on crutches. Evidently, she had fallen down, broke her leg and had to teach me all the proper dance steps all the while on these crutches. It took two weeks to learn the steps and another two weeks to shoot the scene because they were building special mounts to shoot it from all kinds of different camera angles.

But what can I say? It was a great picture to be in, a big Broadway success and it meant a lot of prestige for me as well. It did well in America and even better for-eign-wise. I went to Tokyo shortly after the release of *Birdie* overseas and although I had been there before, it's amazing what a film can do because when I walked down the street in Tokyo, people automatically turned around and recognized me from the movie. The recognition was really amazing! For example, I did an appearance there at a leading department store and all hell broke loose! They were expecting maybe 500 people and 3000 showed up! Record departments fell

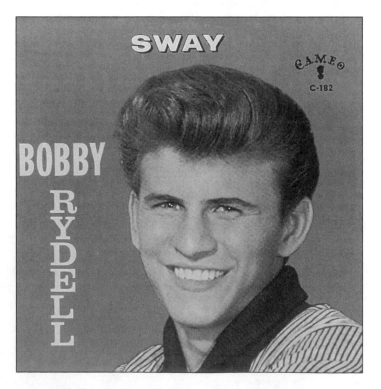

down, TV's went crashing, police were everywhere. (Laughing) But it was a lot of fun.

I just did *Bye Bye Birdie* again, by the way, this past summer in stock. I didn't do the part of Hugo Peabody, though. I played the Dick Van Dyke part in the film of Albert Peterson. It was marvelous, I had a ball, and we ended the last six weeks in Philadelphia, at the Playhouse in the Park. We got super reviews on it.

Bobby, I mentioned too, another film you starred in called That Lady From Peking. *Were there any others?*

The Lady From Peking was a bummer. It was filmed in Australia, and also starred a marvelous actor, Carl Betz, who died not too long ago, and also starred Nancy Kwan. It was a spoof, tongue-in-cheek, James Bond-type spy picture. The plot was dumb. The lines were dumb but we did it. Why did we do it? I don't know, because the money wasn't all that fantastic. You figure with people like Carl Betz and Nancy Kwan how could it miss? The picture just didn't have any balls to it.

During the '60s, we had the British Invasion, which, of course, hurt the careers of many American recording artists. But it wasn't The Beatles that hurt your career as much as Uncle Sam did. Is that right?

Yes, that's right. This was right after *Bye Bye Birdie*. I was in England and my manager received a letter sent from the States. He read it and the letter started off with "Greetings!" Well, I said, "Uh-oh, here we go." I got back home and went to the draft board in Philadelphia with hopes of trying to get out of the service because of a hardship case. Now that may sound awfully silly to you, but at that time, my father was working for me, and I was supporting not only my mom and dad but also my grandparents, who were living with us at the time. So I went to the Selective Service board with what I thought was this legitimate reason: For if I were to be drafted, there would be no money coming into the family, and of course there would be bills to pay, etc. So they told me, "We can understand that, Bobby, but it didn't do Eddie Fisher any harm, so..." Well, I said, "OK, fine," and resigned myself to the fact that I would have to go away for two years. Then, after thinking about it, my manager and I decided that it might be better if we looked for an alternative. I started looking around for a Reserve unit because the two-year bit began to scare me. Initially, we found all of the units full up until I went to this one Reserve unit on 32nd & Lancaster in Philadelphia which was a Combat Engineer Reserve Unit. In other words, bridge builders! They had one slot open, so I signed up with them and in 1964, I went away to Fort Dix in New Jersey and put in my basic training for six months. From there, the next 5 1/2 years were spent in the National Guard building bridges.

Had you opted to take the two years in the Army, would you have been placed in Special Services because you were an entertainer?

If I had gone away for the full two years, I would imagine they would have put me into a Special Services area but we thought that being away for a solid two years would probably hurt anything we had going for us at the time, the career and all. That's why really we opted for the National Guard. To this day, I have to say my days in the Reserves were fantastic. I look back on my basic training days as the fondest memories in my lifetime because I wasn't surrounded by people in the entertainment industry. I was back with the type of guys I was born and raised with, guys from Brooklyn, the Bronx, Newark, New Jersey –tough guys really, who hung out on the corner like I did when I was 13, 14, and 15 years old. They were fantastic although we worked our asses off.

I'll never forget basic training and I've never felt as good as I did when I came out of there. When I went into the service, I weighed only 96 pounds. I thought they wouldn't take me! My God, I thought, the Army boot weighed more than I did! I went in at 96 pounds and came out at 125 pounds. Today, I'm at about 145 pounds and that's where I've been for the last few years. Great times, though. it did hurt things a little and it's a long way of answering your question, but the British Invasion also hurt a lot of the artists a lot harder than the Army hurt me.

I would like to back up a little and ask a question about a Lennon-McCartney song you recorded, called "A World Without Love." This song was also a hit for Peter & Gordon. Was your version first or a cover?

What had happened there was, I had recorded a song called "Forget Him," which became my third million seller for Cameo. We released a song after "Forget Him" that I can't recall the name of. (Author's note: It was "Make Me Forget.") But we had recorded, and were prepared to release as the second record after "Forget Him," the song "A World Without Love."

One day, my manager and I were driving to New York City and we were listening to WABC on the radio when all of a sudden we heard Peter & Gordon's "A World Without Love." We looked at each other in disbelief and said, "What's that?" "It's not me but it's our new record that was supposed to be released. "Well, evidently something happened in England where one of the Beatles (Paul McCartney - ed.) was going out with the sister of Peter Asher of Peter & Gordon so they gave the song to them. I really don't know all of what happened but it left my manager and I with a decision to make. Do we sit on our version or do we release ours and fight with Peter & Gordon's version – which is what we ended up doing.

It was funny because some radio stations wouldn't play my record because Peter & Gordon's had about a week and a half jump on it and they thought mine was a cover, which it wasn't . Then other stations wouldn't play Peter & Gordon's version, preferring mine. Pittsburgh, I think, never heard their version at all and mine would be the only one that they played. Then again, some radio stations were so disgusted with the fight over the two versions between Capitol and Cameo that they played neither one. But we had a hit with it, although not as much the hit it would have been had we put it out right away.

You switched labels and began recording for Capitol Records, a major label. While with them, you had about seven or eight singles released without enjoying any major success. What do you attribute that to?

Well, first, they had me doing country and western, which I'm not. Then they had me singing R&B, which I'm not. They went every way but the right way. We did a couple of things with a big band sound, which I really enjoyed. I remember one song called "You Gotta Enjoy Joy," which was the theme song of the *Milton Berle Show,* where I had been a regular for six months. We recorded it with a big band, Louie Bellson on drums and all of the All Stars were there. It was great. Capitol also put me with different producers And no one seemed to know what direction to go in.

We did have one song on Capitol called "Diana," which was a remake of Paul Anka's first hit. We did it, though, as a ballad and it was a great record. So we released it and it immediately sold 15,000 copies the first week in Chicago and 19,000 copies in Miami, By any standards, that's a hit record. Now, at the same time Wayne Newton, who was also with Capitol, came out with a cover version of Vic Dana's "Red Roses For A Blue Lady." Whenever a cover version comes out, the record company has to try to beat the original version that it's competing with. Capitol immediately dropped any promotion that they were doing on my record, "Diana," and went to work on "Red Roses For A Blue Lady." "Diana" then slowly sunk and Capitol blew it! I think it they had stayed with the record, I might still be with Capitol Records.

It was just a misfortune so after three years with them, my manager and I offered to buy out of the contract. They were paying me a hell of a lot of money for those three years but I wasn't going anywhere record-wise. They kept telling me not to worry and that they'll get one (a hit) but 'it' never materialized. So, it hurt but again they really blew it with "Diana"!

I appreciate hearing the background on that because your version of "Diana" happens to be one of my favorites and I've often wondered why the record never made it.

There's no doubt it was a good record. The quality and sound on it was great. The background girls' voices sounded angelic and it had the "Unchained Melody" ending to it. It was a totally different sound for Rydell, more of a soft and breathy thing as opposed to some of the other things that I have done.

From Capitol Records you moved to Frank Sinatra's label, Reprise. A couple of things you recorded for Reprise ironically went on to become hits for other people.

(Sarcastically) There's another label that really helped my career a lot! The first song I recorded for Reprise was "The Lovin' Things." We recorded it in California and on the recording date, Glen Campbell was playing guitar. At the end of the session, all of the musicians stood up and applauded. After having been in a recording studio many times before, something like that had never happened to me. All of the musicians said, "Bobby, it's a great sound and it looks like you'll be back on the charts again." Well, when you get that kind of feedback from the musicians you really feel good about it. The engineers were also happy with it, as was the A&R man.

Then came nothing! Absolutely nothing! Reprise didn't do one thing for the record. If they put one ad in either *Cash Box* or *Billboard*, that was about it. No promotion, whatsoever. Lo and behold, The Grass Roots recorded the same song and it went top ten! [No. 49 in *Billboard* in 1969 – ed.] Not that theirs was a bad record but mine was a better record.

Then we did a thing called "The River Is Wide". Again it did nothing – so what happens? The Grass Roots record this one too and it went top twenty! [No. 31 in *Billboard* – ed.] In the can, we had another song called "It's Getting Better" which Reprise never released [It actually was released, but as the flip side of "The Lovin' Things" – ed.] Mama Cass comes along, records the same song and it went number one! [No. 30 in *Billboard* – ed.] After all of this I had to stop and ask myself, 'Am I doing something wrong? Am I blowing it?'

All of this happened within a year's time. Three potential hits that Reprise blew! But what can you do? Just chalk it up to experience and treat it as water under the bridge, I suppose.

You also had one record released for RCA, a song called "Chapel On The Hill" backed with "It Must Be Love." What happened there?

Yeah, that's right. Just the one for RCA and that was a good record.

By the way, Bobby, can you date that for us?

I think it was around 1970. That all happened with a guy in Pittsburgh named Joe Rock. Some time earlier, he had been a promotion man when I was with Cameo. He had managed The Skyliners and also another group called The Jaggerz. Anyhow, the Jaggerz wrote a song called "It Must Be Love." Teddy Randazzo wrote the B side, "Chapel On The Hill." It was really a good record with a good sound. The B side, "Chapel On The Hill" had a very different Rydell sound, much different than anything else I had ever recorded. It starts off as a ballad, but at the end picks up with some shouting and screaming – and I was never known to be a screamer. Joe made some sort of deal with RCA. They liked it but nothing ever happened with it. Why? I don't know.

Bobby, many of the performers from the '50s and early '60s had serious problems receiving monies due them from record royalties. Did you experience any problems along those lines?

No, I was lucky. We may have gotten some wrong counts but not all that much. I think that all goes back to management as well. Frankie Day was a super guy and a super manager who stayed on top of everything. He would go in every day and check the books on record sales. I would say that Cameo-Parkway as a company treated me with respect as an artist for the label and I don't think I ever got screwed on a royalty. Again, they may have missed a couple of thousand here and there. Whatever they did with it, who knows? But I made a lot of money with Cameo and they paid the royalties.

During the late '60s, we saw the resurgence of early rock 'n' roll with oldies revivals and the Richard Nader shows and of course, they're still going on today. I don't seem to recall if you have done many of the revival type shows at all. Have you?

Yes, I've done quite a few shows for Richard Nader, mainly at Madison Square Garden. As a matter of fact, I did the show that Rick Nelson was on. I closed the first half, and that was the same show you may remember that Ricky sang his "new" bag and the kids didn't want to hear that, preferring his older things. You can't blame the guy for doing what he wanted to do, although I think he probably picked the wrong time to do it. This was where he got booed off the stage which prompted him to write "Garden Party" that went on to become number one and a million seller.

But anyway, I have done a few of those shows. The Nader shows always had good quality . . . and I've done some other shows that were produced very, very badly - where the musicianship was absolutely terrible and rotten. As a role, they' re fun to do if they're done right and produced well. Other than the Nader shows, I can't think of too many "Oldies But Goodies" shows that I would do. Not that I put down those songs, but let's face it, I'm 37 years old and my career right now is nightclubs like the Playboy circuit, the Hyatt Regencys, the Waldorfs and things like that. I really can't

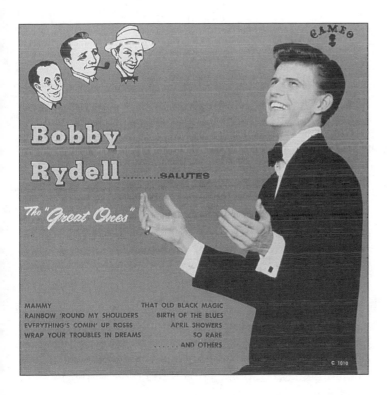

bank on "Wild One," "Kissin' Time," "We Got Love," "Volare" and "Sway" to keep a career going. It was good for its time and of course, I still do some of those songs in the nightclub act today; but again, one can't sustain in the business by just doing things that were done ten to fifteen years ago.

Do you regret being classified as an "oldie but goodie"?

No. I think it's tremendous because one thing that really knocked me out was one time I was working in New York City and a guy who was a truck driver, somewhat grubby, with a heavy Brooklyn accent came up to me telling me what a big fan of mine he was. Now, he had with him a shopping bag full of everything I ever did. I mean this guy had the Veko single, the obscure Cameo releases, albums, pictures, and you name it. I just couldn't believe it. I could understand the girls when I was a teen idol being in love with me, proposing marriage . . . but here's a guy that had gone bananas over my records. It really was a joy for me to meet and talk to this guy and to know that some of my records meant something special to him. So, being known as an "oldie but goodie" is great, although as I said, you can't bank a career on it. But I do know I can't get away from my "roots."

In recent years, you had released a disco version of your earlier hit, "Sway." Was this prompted by the fact that Frankie Avalon had redone "Venus" disco-style?

No, because as a matter of fact, the label Frankie was on was called De-Lite, which was a subsidiary of Pickwick. So Frankie had come out with "Venus"

(disco) and I got a call from some guy at Pickwick who said they had recorded a music track of "Sway" with a disco beat. He also told me that they checked *Billboard* and discovered that I had the hit with it many years earlier. He asked if I would like to come in, listen to it and to put my voice over the track. I went to Hempstead, Long Island where they were and thought that the music track sounded fantastic. I then signed a contract with Pickwick, went in and put my voice on it. "Sway," I thought it was a damn good record but I think at the time it was released a lot of the DJ's were getting bugged with remakes like Frankie's "Venus" and others like "Baby Face," "Goody Goody," etc. My record came in on the tail end of all of that. Although "Sway" (disco) did become the No. 1 disco record in Canada and even without it breaking into the "top 100" in *Billboard*, we still sold 150,000 copies. It also got up to No. 26 in the "Easy Listening" charts in *Billboard*. So we just missed on it. I feel because it was on the tail end of that tide that was running at the time . . . the funny thing is that now everybody's starting to do remakes all over again, so you never know.

You've done quite a few shows and gigs over the years. Is there any one particular show that stands out where something unusual or memorable happened? I do recall the early Dick Clark TV appearance of yours where there was some sort of a problem with the spotlight on you.

Oh yeah. Well, that was a long time ago. That was the Dick Clark *Saturday Night Show* and it was right after I had recorded "Kissin' Time," which was my first hit. To get reaction from the kids I would try to get closer to them. Of course, while doing a TV show, they always put a mark on the floor where you're suppose to stand while singing. So, on this show, I was walking away from my mark and going to the kids in the audience where they were all screaming. The director was going crazy in the booth screaming at me to get back where I was supposed to stand. Of course, I was going out of the lights into the dark and the cameras couldn't follow me.

As far as thrills are concerned, though, Red Skelton would have to be on top of my list. I did twelve TV shows for him in three years which averaged out to four appearances a year. He was like a father to me and treated me like a son. TV-wise, he was probably the most instrumental in my career, just a super man to work for.

Are you recording nowadays?

No, although I just completed filming a pilot for my own TV show produced by the Osmonds in Provo, Utah. The show is called "One More Time" starring Bobby Rydell. It's a situation-variety show that deals with a little nostalgia, production numbers and comedy. We' re hoping that the show sells. If the TV show is picked up, and because the Osmonds are a big conglomerate in Utah, I would imagine that I would be signing a recording contract with them. That's all up in the air right now. I'm also going to be talking with Don Kirshner, who has expressed an interest in recording me. So that looks pretty good, too.

If someone ever writes a definitive book on the history of rock music, how would you like to see Bobby Rydell remembered?

That's kind of a hard question. I guess, happy. I think that most of my records related to a happy feeling, the guy-next-door kind of thing. Basically remembered as an average around-the-corner type of guy who enjoyed what he did and is still doing today and wouldn't change it for all of the money in the world. I think I made a lot of people happy with the songs I recorded, so I feel being remembered for that would be nice.

Most Collectible 45

"Fatty Fatty"/ "Dream Age," Veko 730/731, $120.

Most Collectible LP

All The Hits, Cameo C-1019, red vinyl, $150.

Recommended Introduction

Unfortunately, the ongoing lack of compilations from the vaults of Cameo-Parkway forces us to recommend an import that may or may not be a legitimate issue:

Bobby's Biggest Hits, FG 971004 (German import with 30 tracks that appear to be the original recordings, probably mastered from vinyl sources)

If you want to hear more...

Best of Bobby Rydell, Dominion 3378 (re-recordings of 12 of his hits)

Born With A Smile, Plum 1418 (1976 recordings, including disco remakes of several older songs)

Part IV
The Early 6O's
Rockers

Chubby Checker

by Wayne Jancik

Not until the Macarena was there anything again like the Twist. And even with the Macarena, you didn't see macarena clubs open up around the country. You didn't have singers begging a special girl to "come on to my macarena party." You didn't have respected soul singers "macarena-ing the night away." No, that 1990s dance craze was basically restricted to one song. The Twist – now, that was a phenomenon. Even Ol' Blue Eyes, Frank Sinatra, recorded a song called "Everybody's Twistin'." Hank Ballard may have written the song and first recorded it, but Chubby Checker of Philadelphia popularized it and turned it into his own. (Unfortunately, only the very earliest pressings of the Parkway 811 single credited Ballard as composer.) It also spurred a nearly half-decade-long string of mostly dance-related hits that didn't die out until the British Invasion swept him and most of his contemporaries off the charts. Today, Chubby Checker still sings and twists, like he did last summer, and the summer before that, and the summer before that... Thanks to oldies radio, which gets the chance to play Checker's original recordings that American consumers can't buy except in used record shops, many of his dance hits are as popular today as ever. "Let's Twist Again," in fact, was used in an ad campaign when the movie Twister was released on video cassette. And "Limbo Rock," thanks to its use in the 1980s TV series Moonlighting, actually did make a CD appearance on that program's soundtrack – one of the few Cameo-Parkway tracks to have made it to compact disc so far. The following interview with the 1960s dance king appeared in the December 28, 1990 issue of Goldmine.

Come on baby, let's do the Twist." With those words, Chubby Checker created the most popular dance of the rock 'n' roll era, and guaranteed himself both steady work and a permanent place in rock history.

Rock 'n' roll has always been dance music, from its primordial beginnings as an underground black music in the '40s into the present. There had been dances before the Twist, and some of them had names. But the Twist was revolutionary: it freed the dancer. No longer was it necessary to hold onto your partner. Just grind your feet into the ground as if you're putting out a cigarette butt, and move your body left and right as if you're rubbing your backside with a towel. That was the Twist, and it caught on in a big way in the early 1960s.

Chubby Checker didn't write "The. Twist." Hank Ballard did that, in 1959, but even he admitted basing it on a 1955 Clyde McPhatter song, "What'cha Gonna Do." Ballard's "The Twist" was released as a B-side and did next to nothing until Chubby Checker covered it (and invented the dance to go with it – Ballard hadn't thought of that part).

Chubby Checker was born Ernest Evans on October 3, 1941, in Philadelphia. A former chicken plucker, his music career didn't take off until he was signed to Philly's Cameo-Parkway label in 1959. Dick Clark's wife, Bobbie, seeing Evans playing a Fats Domino tune at the piano, came up with his new name.

Checker's first singles for Parkway could hardly be called hits. His first single to chart, 1959's "The Class," found him imitating not only Domino but Elvis and the Chipmunks. It wasn't until the following summer that his remake of "The Twist," originally intended is a B-side, clicked, riding all the way to number one.

Despite its impressive sales, the Twist dance phenomenon did not follow immediately. It simmered slowly, the dance eventually catching on not only with the teenagers who watched Checker do his gyrating on *American Bandstand* but with adults. Suddenly, the Twist was "in" among the fashionable – even First Lady Jackie Kennedy was caught in the act of twisting.

Checker scored a second number one record in 1961, "Pony Time," and two more Top 10s, "Let's Twist Again" and "The Fly," all in 1961. In the fall of that year "The Twist" returned to the charts, buoyed by the dance craze, and ascended to number one a second time. It remains the only single of the rock era to reach that height twice with a gap of a year or more between placings.

Checker's career remained in high gear throughout the early '60s. "Slow Twistin'," "Limbo Rock" and "Popeye The Hitchhiker" were all Top 10 records and his albums – including one cut with fellow Philadel-phian Bobby Rydell – sold well. With the arrival of the British Invasion the records still charted but failed to create the sensation they once had.

In 1969 Checker moved over to Buddah Records, scoring a minor chart single with a cover of the Beatles' "Back In The U.S.S.R." in 1969. He has continued to record for other labels sporadically through the ensuing years, making one album for MCA, *The Change Has Come*, in the early '80s.

By and large, though, Checker has forsaken the recording scene for that of the revival circuit. Still agile enough to stomp out a cigarette butt and rub his rear with a towel, Chubby Checker continues to Twist again, like he did all those summers ago, into the '90s.

Goldmine: Mr. Checker?

Chubby Checker: Come on, Wayne. I'm a rock singer. Knock off that Mister.

You know the set-up. Goldmine readers would like to know who Chubby Checker, or more importantly, who Ernest Evans is. Any musical background?

I sang in church. I was born in South Carolina in a small farming community called Spring Valley. My whole life then was around the church. We were a Baptist kind of people. All we ever did was work the fields or sing, endlessly. The church and singing were everything to us.

Any training on an instrument?

I came to Philadelphia when I was 10. I bought a piano from my shoeshine money. I went to the Settlement Music School where I studied under Dr. Purchek. I didn't want to do classical music. I had my own ideas. But it was very good training for me. The things I learned, they are still very much with me. That was the only training I ever received. I made up my own songs and I sang with my group on the streets. We were the Quantrells.

Like Quantrell's Raiders?

Yeah. Exactly. We were bad boys.

Little Ernie Evans was a bad boy?

Ah, nah. Not me. I'm a South Carolina church boy, through and through. But we did sing at school, once, and at contests and we got popular. We were hot. There was Rivers, who sang bass. Lytsy was baritone. Ray was the tenor. And me, Fat Ernie, I did the leads. We didn't get the chance to sing that much at our school, South Philadelphia High. I was in the tenth grade. We brought the house down that day. I'll always remember it. I mean it. There was such an uproar in the auditorium. I'm told that was why they didn't let us sing anymore. Everyone was going nuts. It was the biggest live thrill of my life. And it was so disappointing for me that they made us stop.

What songs were the Quantrells singing that day?

We had this song, "Miss Ann" – the Little Richard number – but we had our own rendition of it. It really was hot. There was this song called "Bacon Fat." It would go like this: (Here Checker breaks into an acappella slice) "Wop wop pa do dee wop wop..." I took that backdrop and had "Miss Ann" laid on top. "Oh, oh oh, Miss Ann...Ah, it was good.

Did you ever get to record "Miss Ann" like that?

Nah. That was then, the Quantrell days. It all ended when I went into the eleventh grade.

Did the Quantrells ever record with you? Was it ever even considered?

No. There was some friction in the group. Lytsy sang flat. And Rivers, who was very talented, was already a star. It didn't hold. It takes a lot to make it, a lot to get here, and just a little bit to leave. That spark I was talking of that I had with the Quantrells – that fire caught on. I've carried it with me. It lives on into this day. When I'm on stage, it's got to be the best. It has to be.

How did you get your foot in the door?

Persistence. Dick Clark needed someone to do a singing card for his family. And the kind of Christmas card he was putting together involved the sounds of different artists of the day doing "Jingle Bells." He needed someone doing impressions. The word got back to him that I could do that sort of thing. Now, I had gone to that record company like a hundred times, many people don't know that. They kept throwing me out! But I kept going back.

Cameo was the only record company in town who could do anything for me. I'd be wasting my time to go elsewhere. So I kept going back and getting tossed out. There are times in this life that you have got to pick yourself up and go back, just to be put out again and again. Persistence pays. It may take that to get recognition. A lot of people with potential give up before they have even started. They never come back. They can't take the rejection, but you must. I just kept going back and when that opportunity came they knew about me.

Now, I was in the studio doing a Fats Domino hit at the piano. I was rehearsing and was so excited about my chance. I was excited, but it was in a quiet way, 'cause this is the music business and you never should get full-out excited about anything. Things they say will happen don't always. So inside of me there was this light of hope, but there was so much darkness in me too. So, I was calm doing my Domino and Dick Clark's wife Barbara comes in. She says, "You're Chubby." I'm chubby, yeah. "You're Chubby Checker, like Fats Domino, 'cause you're doing one of his songs." After she said that the company got interested in me. Then they wanted me to do something like this "Jingle Bells" thing. And "The Class," my first record, was a clone of that. My life changed. It changed everything. I was 16 years old.

How did you feel about being labeled Chubby Checker?

I didn't like it. No. But there were no Chubby Checkers around. It was kind of unique.

There were two other records before "The Twist."

Yeah. "Samson And Delilah" and "Dancing Dinosaur." I liked that one. Then, "The Twist."

How did you feel about "The Twist" when you were first asked to record it?

Well, I knew it was a Hank Ballard song. I'd seen him perform it. But he didn't do the Twist. Ever seen in the old movies where the Indians catch the settlers and then they dance around them? Well, that's what Hank Ballard would do to the song on stage. But, you know, there were kids in the ghetto doing this Twist thing and a little slipped on to *Bandstand*; it was some other tune. And it inspired me, and when my "Twist" came out we decided that the Twist would be like putting out a cigarette with both feet, or like coming out of the shower and wiping your butt with a towel.

Now, let me tell you that little bit of instructions was like the guy who invented electricity, the guy who thought up the wheel, the guy who created the telephone. What happened – it was a great discovery – kids could now dance apart. It's been going on ever since. Before that no one danced apart, except for those line dances, like the Stroll. People now dance apart to everybody's music and don't realize that it was because of "The Twist" and my little instructions.

Bernie Lowe made "The Twist" the B-side (much as Syd Nathan made "The Twist" the B-side of Hank Ballard's release).

Yeah. "You got the cutest little toot." Hah. "Toot" was the top side. It should have been the hit. But, there was this guy in Pittsburgh named Porky Chedwick. He was on WEAM, or something. He said, "I don't give a damn about no 'Toot.' I'm doing 'The Twist.'" At that time, if a record broke in Pittsburgh or Youngstown, Ohio, it was going to be a hit. And "The Twist" took off right there in that town.

From "The Twist" people made up anything, as long as they were dancing apart and having a good time. "The Fly." "The Pony." I did it all for them. It's been 30 years now and I'm still doing it for them.

When you first recorded it, did you have any feeling about it, that you liked it or didn't, that it was special?

It was cool. It's always been a cool song. I needed a song where I could expend my energy and make people nuts. I've always liked physical action that approaches that of a religious revival. A going crazy is what I was looking for; where the music is so good you lose control. "The Twist" did that. I heard it on the radio today. I don't turn it off, 'cause, boy, it still sounds good. It's the coolest song that I've ever done.

Did you consider yourself a dancer?

No.

Did this force you into considering yourself as such?

Not really. I was just doing what everybody else did. I just did whatever I did. I preceded that whole hippie idea of doing your own thing. It was in the air and it was time for "The Twist." Now, my grandfather, Grandpa Fred, said, "Boy, you're going to hell for doing that." "Why?" I said. "Well, you know what you just did? That stuff is going to go on forever. You started it and you're my grandson and when I die I got a lot to explain." And I said, "But I have fun." He said, "Well, just look at that, look at that! You see those women, they're half naked." I said, "I did that?" "Well, it's all about that Twist." He said, "Why, 20 years from now, they're gonna be naked and doing that." And he was right. When I look at the videos today, and *Soul Train* and the *Bandstand* show, they're naked."

Did he change his views?

No. He said, "God never changes." When I was singing in Myrtle Beach, about 1980, I saw this man sitting in the back of the club with this big black hat on. It was my grandpop. "No," I said to myself, "I'm going to hell. I know it. He's comin' to get me." I saw him after the show. He came to my room and said, "You're gonna get it. I told ya. Boy, you're gonna get it good." I said, "Ah, come on Granddad, didn't you like it?" He said, "You got talent, but you know what's gonna happen to ya." He's gone, but that always stays with me.

A couple of Twist trivia questions. Is it true that Dick Clark initially wanted Danny and the Juniors to record it and that Freddy Cannon turned it down before it was offered to you?

Who knows?

Is that the Dreamlovers in the background?

Yeah! Nice people. We were always friends. We were all good buddies. It was the Dreamlovers on "The Fly," "The Hucklebuck," all of them.

Have you and Hank Ballard ever discussed you covering his "Twist"?

Yeah. I'm so happy that man was born and I tell him that. When I see him, I run and hug him. "Man, what ya huggin' me for?" I say, "I love ya, you son-of-a-bitch. You made all of my dreams come true." I'm his best friend. Look what I did to his song. Think of all these years that I've kept his song alive and that his song has kept my thrill alive.

If "The Twist" had not happened – and "The Twist" started a whole chain of successful dance discs – what would have become of Fat Ernie?

Well, I was well on my way to the big nightclubs in Vegas. After "The Class" they said, "This guy's got talent, let's give him some Broadway stuff and groom him for the nightclubs." I was on my way. I was studying to do just that. Then "The Twist" came and screwed up my life. It did! I had to work years and years before people noticed that I had any talent.

More to the present, what was the story on your hard-rockin' 1982 album for MCA, The Change Has Come*?*

Heartbreaking situation. Heartbreaking. At that time, people weren't ready to hear Chubby Checker get current. Thirty-year-old DJs who only wanted to remember me for what I sounded like then didn't know how to take it. Here I was laying down music that was able to fit in with what they were playing. It fit with the sounds on the radio that they were playing. They either didn't want to play it 'cause Chubby Checker is just supposed to be an oldies act, or they'd have just played it and said here's a new record by Chubby Checker, I think it would have done alright. They didn't and it died. I'm not making records anymore! I'll keep doing "The Twist." I love "The Twist."

How about that mysterious LP for 51 West, in 1984?

You got me. Ah, that could've been the release of some early '70s stuff I had done. I wrote all the songs on the album. I wrote 'em cold. There was "Don't Get Hung Up In The Love Tunnel," "Goodbye Victoria," "No Need To Get So Heavy." I did the stuff during a period where I had just got a band together. It was '68, I dumped the charts, got a van and hit the road, starting all over, playing these rock 'n' roll clubs. I had just met all these really raunchy and rotten musicians. They were just jerkin' me around. Jealousies. Little games and other crap. It was a whole new life for me. I was affected by it and wrote these songs.

Now the Buddah stuff was also strange. They had bought into Cameo/Parkway. There was this tune called (here he breaks into song) "Hey mama wake up/and look around/your gold and tinsel idols have fallen to the ground/Your credit card has been canceled/you have milked the sacred cow/and we're looking at tomorrow right now . . ." I love that song. That was a single.

I wrote "The Rub" for Amherst. Now that was a great song. It was really dirty dancing. "Welcome to the club/I've been lookin' for ya/I've been wanting to do this new dance with you/Now that you're here/Come to me my dear/And rub me baby/Let's do the rub/I want you to rub me baby/Let's do the rub." Great, great song. My grandfather would really get off on that one.

You've had 35 charting singles, sold maybe 100 million records . . . and during the Beatle era things just tapered off. What happened?

Ah, that's life. Talent stays alive. Popularity wanes. The media can be real unfair. But that is the record business. It's a crazy business and I'm afraid there is really not a lot of nice people in it. It looks good on the surface, though. Under it all can be very rough. Getting to be a record star depends on many, many things. Like the Milli Vanilli thing. Let's face it, those two guys sold the records. It was because of them that those records sold. Someone needs to speak up for them. Without that visual presentation that they presented, I don't think that they would have sold half a million of 'em. That physical appearance was needed in front singing those songs. Without it those girls won't have gone crazy and bought all those records.

People are overlooking that part. The producer knew what he was doing, why, all of a sudden, is he changing his mind? They sold seven million albums! I'm not saying it's right, but if we put the ugly face on the cover you might not want to hear the damn record. It shows ya how stupid the public can be.

I'm a survivor, though. When the Beatles were everywhere, I was still here. When everything was Motown, I was still here. When it was singer/song-writers and disco, I was still here. In 1988, the Fat Boys came to me saying, "Hey Chubby, I wanna do 'The Twist.'" So I said, "What do you want with me?" They said, "Well, you know, we don't sing. We rap. We got the track and all, so come on down and sing. We don't wanna do it with nobody else." We did it and we made the charts.

I thought that after that and all the concerts, and the videos, and MTV, and commercials for BVDs and Nabisco's Oreo cookies, and that movie that flopped, She-Devils, where I did a new song on the soundtrack called "Party Up" – well, I thought maybe we could get to do something. Maybe everybody was ready for Chubby to do something new.

I've been working on some stuff for 18 months. I'm different. It's contemporary and I hope we'll have something out by April or May (1991). I'm excited, but it's a quiet excitement. There's that light of hope. But there's a darkness and I don't know how many valleys and rivers I have to cross before I'll have something to play again on the radio.

Most Collectible 45

"You Just Don't Know"/ "Two Hearts Make One Love," Parkway 965, $200.

Most Collectible LP

Twist With Chubby Checker, Parkway P-7001, all-orange label, $40.

Recommended Introduction

Unfortunately, the ongoing lack of compilations from the vaults of Cameo-Parkway forces us to recommend two import CDs that may or may not be legitimate issues:

Twist With Chubby Checker, BOW 8420 (contains roughly 30 of his original recordings from 1959-61, including all the early biggies)

Loddy Lo, Hooka Tooka And 28 More Hit Songs, BOW 8437 (30 more original recordings from 1962-64, almost all in true stereo!)

If you want to hear more...

Best Of Chubby Checker, Madacy 2135 (re-recordings of 19 of his hits with two extended mixes; the most readily available collection of Checker music and often selling for under $8)

Lesley Gore

by Dawn Eden

There's not a lot to add to this article, which originally appeared in the November 11, 1994 issue of Goldmine. A rather obvious victim of the 1964 British Invasion, casual readers might be surprised to learn that she's still in the business and never really left it. As recently as 1980, she was on the music charts – as a composer with her younger brother Michael on the soundtrack from Fame. The original headline was "She's No Fool," which is an apt way to sum up this survivor.

Before Barry McGuire growled "Eve Of Destruction" all the way to #1, the closest that the Top 40 got to serious social commentary was via messages encased in ostensible "love songs," like "Uptown" and "He's A Rebel" (both sung by the Crystals) and, most significantly, Lesley Gore's "You Don't Own Me." In these modern times, it is nearly impossible to imagine how jarring the lyrics of that song sounded when they first drifted from car radios, transistors and hi-fis nationwide.

The concept of the hyphenated, capital-T "Teen-Ager" was still new and the baby-boomers were just beginning to rumble. Lesley Gore's musical expression of independence and rebellion – "I'm Young, and I Love To Be Young/I'm Free And I've Got To Be Free" – struck a chord with youths who had survived the frustrated 50s and were ready to break loose. It wasn't just Hayley Mills wannabes who heard the call, either. While "You Don't Own Me" was riding the charts, Lesley Gore was invited to sing it at a Carnegie Hall benefit for NAACP, where she was one of the only whites present. The 17-year-old singer was rewarded with a standing ovation.

Although Gore did not write "You Don't Own Me," she went on to become one of the first female singers to write her own hits. After her own hitmaking career had peaked, she then turned to writing for outside artists, earning a Grammy nomination in the process. Beneath that flip hairdo lay real talent.

She was born Lesley Goldstein, the first child of Leo (owner of a swimwear company) and Ronny Goldstein, in Brooklyn, New York, on May 2, 1946. At the time, her father was in the process of changing the family name back from Goldstein, which his father had adopted at U.S. immigration center Ellis Island, to their original Russian name, Gore.

The room that Ronny made up for her young child was immaculately clean. Everything was white, from the bevy of stuffed animals to the shiny toy piano. By 1950, about the same time that Schroeder started tinkling his plastic ivories in Charles Schulz's "Peanuts" strip, Lesley, too, was making her own music.

Shortly after Lesley entered kindergarten, the Gores did like many upwardly mobile 50s families and moved to the suburbs – Teaneck, New Jersey, where they lived until their new house in nearby Tenafly was finished. The toy piano also made the move. It would soon have to do double duty, as Gore's only-child status was invalidated by the arrival of a baby brother, Michael, four and a half years her junior.

Lesley Gore's earliest musical memories are of her parents' dance music. "They loved to ballroom dance," she recalled recently. "It was very trendy at the time. They even had a couple who used to come to the house, called Manolo and Ethel. If it was Tuesday night, Manolo and Ethel would come in. I can remember when we moved to Teaneck, and my brother and I used to sit on the steps and look through the banister at my mother and father and Ethel and Manolo doing the cha-cha!"

At the same time, she was building a fascination with records. "I remember rainy and snowy days in Teaneck, when Michael and I couldn't go out and play, or we had been out long enough, and I used to literally lock myself in the spare room in the house, which was, like, our den, and I had a 45 record changer, and I had probably a couple of hundred 45s. At this point, I was just beginning to read, so I really couldn't even read the labels or the names. I just knew from the color what the song was, or if I saw a 'P' I knew it was Patti Page, and so on. So I listened to hundreds of records. Sometimes I would get addicted to a record, until my family was ready to tear the door down; I'd play the same record 40, 50, 60 times, til I could lip-sync literally every breath."

Her favorite singers at the time were the great female pop vocalists of the day, such as Page, Doris Day and Teresa Brewer. By the time she reached junior high school, she added some rockers to her list, including Elvis Presley. For teenage fans of rock 'n' roll, Tenafly was three steps to heaven. Every Friday night there was a hop and, yes, Gore did wear bobby sox and a poodle skirt on the dance floor.

As Gore recalls, she was not Tenafly's only home-grown rock singer. "Interestingly enough, Tenafly was the original home of Ozzie and Harriet Nelson. When we used to watch (the TV show) Ozzie And Harriet, around Christmas time Ozzie would get on the phone and he'd call his family, the Nelsons in Tenafly. The Nelsons in fact did exist – he had a brother – and one of their sons was a young man by the name of Willie Nelson, who is not the Willie Nelson that you know very well, but it is a Willie Nelson who managed his cousin Rick's career for a number of years, during the last part of Rick's life. Willie was a great-looking guy, blonde, and he had a voice.

"Willie was kind of our in-house celebrity, so he became the M.C. of the rock 'n' roll shows. He was it. Everyone wanted to get close to Willie. You'd go to wherever you had to go after school to see him. He was cool before cool was 'cool.'

"I don't think anyone knows this," she added, "but at one point, when I was in about seventh or eighth grade, I joined a girl group. This group was headed by Mary Lombardi, and all they did was Shirelles songs. I think this is the first time I've ever discussed this. I did two shows with them, on rock 'n' roll shows with Willie Nelson, when I was in junior high."

When Gore was 15 and enrolled in Englewood, N.J.'s Dwight School for Girls, her parents agreed with her that her vocal talent deserved professional training. "Because I did show some promise and I was interested, I started studying with a vocal coach in New York," she recalled. "He was in the Ed Sullivan building. What I would usually do was take the bus in from school on Monday afternoon. I'd get on the bus on Palisades Avenue and go across the George Washington Bridge, and then I would take the subway down."

One should note that, despite stories about Gore being a child of privilege, her parents could not afford to send her downtown and back by taxi. (Additionally, New York City was safer then. Gore admitted that she won't take the subway today.)

Gore said that she enjoyed the lessons "very, very much. I worked with a man by the name of Myron Earnhart, and everyone called him 'Pappy.' He was a kind of heavy-set man, and he worked with his wonderful wife, Mathilda, who played piano. I have to say that in all the years I've studied, and I've studied with a lot of different people over the years in different places, his was the best advice and his was the best technique. Whenever I have a problem, I always come back to someone who teaches his technique, which is basically classical operatic singing."

One of the vocal qualities which Gore sought, and which Pappy Earnhart helped her achieve, was the use of "head" voice rather than "chest" voice. "That's what these ladies I admired were doing," she explained. "They weren't strictly singing from the chest, or beating it out. They had lovely voices and they let them kind of just come out and ease a bit. I mean, when you grew up with the Perry Comos and the Dean Martins, what you got was this sense of – it wasn't forced. Use a little finesse. Make it look easy. Make people enjoy watching it, instead of thinking you're gonna have a heart attack.

"I was sort of caught in that funny little place, because I was a rock 'n' roller at heart, but with a kind of umbrella of something a little bit more pop, and I definitely had jazz leanings. When Sarah Vaughan and Lena Horne and Dinah Washington came into my life, well, granted, Patti Page was a wondrous thing, but when the world opens up and Ella Fitzgerald steps out, oh my gosh."

A multitude of stories exists as to how 16-year-old Gore was signed to Mercury Records. One tale which can be completely discounted is that which appears in the liner notes of her first album, stating that she was "discovered" while singing at a friend's birthday party. Other stories sound more possible, but still conflict with one another, i.e., she was spotted while singing at a

New York hotel, or a friend of the family got a demo disc of her to a booking agent who got it to Mercury, or her vocal coach suggested making a demo which got to Mercury. Gore obligingly set the record straight:

"My cousin Allan Albert was a darn good drummer, and he was in a band with guys who were working their way through college. It was Sal Bonafetti's band. I got to sing with them because one Sunday morning Allan was out at our house in Tenafly having brunch and he got a call that they were supposed to do a gig in Queens at a catering house, an Italian wedding, that night, and the singer was sick and couldn't sing. Allan said, 'Leslie, you wanna go?' It was a Sunday night, which meant Ed Sullivan at eight and nine o'clock, 'to bed, young lady!' So I looked at my parents and my parents looked at each other, and they said, 'You're with Cousin Allan,' who was all of 18, 'Go ahead, go see what it's like.'

"They put us at a table, and the whole band and I would stare at the big pitchers of beer and wine. It was the first time I'd ever eaten really wonderful Italian food, and every 20 minutes I'd get up and do two or three songs.

"Later on, this band went to play at the lounge of the Prince George Hotel, and I just happened to be there on that evening. This was a (showcase) gig for the boys. And I got up and sang, and (Mercury president) Irving Green heard me sing live that night for the first time, when I did two songs with the band.

"After that, I went in with Myron Earnhart and I went upstairs to a little studio in his office building and we recorded, with piano and voice, four demos, quickly, just one after the other. These demos then went to (booking agent) Joe Glaser through Allen Albert's brother. His brother was a businessman in New York and his pastime was that he managed fighters. Prizefighters. Joe Glaser was a major fight fan. Joe used to be Louis Armstrong's manager. He was a very legendary figure in the entertainment world. Allan took my demos to Joe, Joe heard them, sent Irving down to see me sing again, and boom! Meet Quincy."

Mercury A&R man Quincy Jones was only the second black person to direct talent for a major record label. (His predecessor at Mercury, Clyde Otis, was the first.) He and Gore were copacetic from the start, and the singer recalls that he helped her bring out the best in herself. To this day, she has nothing but praise for him: "Quincy is one of the most charismatic people you will ever meet. The beauty of him is that he was just a superstar in talent long before he helped create (the sound of) Michael Jackson. He was genuine. When you talked to this guy, he looked into your eyes. He *heard* you.

"Quincy was an adult figure for me, but he wasn't as old as my parents. He was much hipper than my parents. He talked a whole lot straighter, and one of the things I always admired about Quincy was that he always had his own language. In a way, I kind of picked that up from him. He's got a pen name for everyone and it usually has to do either with a physical characteristic or a special something about who they are. His name for me was Li'l Bits.

"What Quincy did and does so well, because of his warmth, is that he can bring a group of people into an enclosed area and say, 'This is what we're gonna do.' And then what he does is leaves room for everyone to do their thing. He brings a lot of love, and he gives you the security to try. I was not a tremendously secure kid. I mean, I had all the hangups that other young teenagers have. I surely wasn't able to just get out onstage like 'that'; that was very nerve-wracking for me.

"But to go into a studio was very different, because you weren't going to be judged. I mean, you were going to be judged, but if you didn't like it you could do it over again. So it gave a lot of latitude and it was very challenging. Quincy really showed me what it was like to get in there and challenge yourself, to listen to something and see if you could do it better."

In February 1963, after Irving Green had paired the producer and singer, Jones came over to the Gore family home to select a song for the first single. The Gores were impressed to see Jones arrive in a chauffeured car. (Lesley Gore didn't learn until later that the reason for this was that Jones had never learned how to drive.) He was weighed down with boxes of acetates which he had auditioned and thought were possibilities, 200 in all.

However, Gore believes that Jones knew all along that she would choose "It's My Party."

"He was carrying these big boxes in," she recalled, "and we set them in the den, and he put on 'It's My Party.' It's the first time I've ever done this, so I said to him, 'It's not half bad. I like it. Good melody. Let's put it in the "maybe" pile.' And we went through the entire 200, and it was the only song we had at that point. Then we went back to the drawing board. Paul Anka wrote a couple of songs at that point and I think a publisher found us one more, but Quincy knew exactly what he was doing."

While Gore was thrilled to be making a record, she tried not to be overly optimistic about her chances of success. Odds were that the disc would follow the fate of most singles and flop, or even remain in the can. If it didn't succeed, Gore was prepared to do as many suburban young women of the era did – go to college, get a degree in a "feminine" profession like education, marry a nice young man and have the average 2.5 kids.

"No one wanted to get my hopes up," she says. "Quincy didn't, Irving didn't, my parents didn't. My parents thought it would be good experience, but they didn't want me to suffer from it if it didn't work out. So their mold for me was basically, 'OK, this is something you want to do. We're behind you, we'll support you, but you must understand that very often you record these things and they're never released.'

"I said, 'I understand, but I would love the opportunity just to go into a professional studio.' That pretty much was my approach to going in. I never really figured we'd come out with a hit record, and I don't even think it was something I cared about at the time."

Gore said that her parents deserve credit for allowing her to sign to Mercury, but she added that she had proven herself to be ready to take on new responsibilities. "If I was a really flighty kid and seemed kind of emotionally unstable," she noted, "I don't believe they would have made that choice."

March 30, 1963 is a day that Lesley Gore will never forget. It is the day that she recorded her all-time biggest hit, as well as the day that she entered a professional recording studio for the first time. Since she had never seen an orchestral score before (and could not even read music), Quincy Jones helped her through the experience.

"He had this huge score on the table," she recalled, "and he said, 'C'mere, Li'l Bits, let me show you what a score is.' And he knocked it out for me; showed me the instruments on the left, showed me how the melody would be running horizontally, letter 'B' was eight bars into the song, and he really took me right through. Then he pointed to the top and said, 'Here *you* are. You're the "lead vocalist," OK?'"

Gore describes Jones as a true artist who created elegant recordings that were free from the extraneous, over-the-top flourishes that characterized pop music at the time. "I remember Quincy could do things like, he would come in on the 'It's My Party' session, and I believe that the intro that (arranger) Claus Ogermann had on 'It's My Party' had a seven-beat vamp before my voice came in. Quincy came in and said, 'Cut that away and make the intro only two beats.' That's very telling. That's the essence of pop song recording right there."

In Bob Shannon and John Javna's *Behind The Hits* (Warner Books, 1986), "It's My Party" co-writer Wally Gold claims that Gore's version of the song preempted one which Phil Spector planned for the Crystals. Gore confirms the story. "It was Saturday, March 30, 1963," she said, "the day that we had recorded 'It's My Party,' and Quincy was at Carnegie Hall, representing Mercury as an executive, because Charles Aznavour was in concert there that night. Phil Spector got out of his limo at Carnegie Hall with his black cape with a red lining, he comes *flying* at the steps like a vampire and tells Quincy about this great song he's cutting with the Crystals. The Crystals were just coming off of 'Da Doo Ron Ron.' 'Da Doo Ron Ron' was the number one song in the nation at that moment." [Writer's note: According to *Billboard*, "Da Doo Ron Ron" did not hit until one month later. Even so, the Crystals were still enormously successful at that point, coming off of "He's A Rebel" and "He's Sure The Boy I Love."]

"Quincy realized that one of the publishers had given Phil an exclusive and the other had given Quincy an exclusive for me, so what he did was, he went to Bell Sound, where we had done the recording, that very night, and he picked up the master tape. Then he called (engineer) Phil Ramone and they met down at A&R Studios, and Quincy and Phil ran off one hundred acetates themselves, on a lathe, right in the room, one at a time. They had to make a hundred 'passes.' Quincy put them in the mail to every top program directory in the United States.

"I'm driving home from school on April 6, the Friday after we recorded that. So it's maybe 20 minutes after two, and I'm listening to WINS, which at that time was the station that Murray the K was on, and there it was. I heard it for the first time driving home from school, going right across Engle Street. At first, I actually didn't think it was *my* record. I thought, 'This is the song I *recorded*.' And then I realized. I had to make that leap between what it sounded like on those big speakers in the studio, to this little tiny radio speaker in the car. And then I realized, somewhere around the first chorus, that it indeed was my recording."

It is hard to shed any tears for the two-timed Spector, as he had just done the same thing to Liberty Records, pre-empting the label's release of Vikki Carr's "He's A Rebel" with a version on his own label by, once again, the Crystals.

Although Jones oversaw most of Gore's recordings through early 1966, the person with whom the singer spent the most time planning recordings was noted German conductor, arranger, and songwriter Claus Ogermann. Gore recalled that, in more ways than one, "Claus was instrumental...When I think about these sessions, I really think of it as a triumvirate of three souls: Quincy, Claus and Lesley.

"Claus and I actually worked most closely together before the sessions. After we got started and it was suddenly time to do an album, Claus and I would spend most of the time together. We would screen material, much the way Quincy did do for me originally. Then we would bring writers in and work with them on new concepts for songs. That whole writing staff at Screen Gems was there and available to us.

"So it was a very exciting time creatively. You could almost turn around and say, 'I want another such-and-such kind of song,' and Neil Sedaka would pop into the room four days later with a new tune. So Claus and I were privy to a lot of these first-time-ever kind of things. He was also responsible for the simplicity of the arrangements. His job was to choose the instruments to successfully find the right sounds.

"There's no taking away from Quincy as an incredible producer, but most of Quincy's really fine, superb work happened in the studio, whereas Claus and I basically did the framework. We would sing these songs over and over and over together at the piano. He would play, I would sing, until the arrangements were so locked in that there was nothing else we could do; every note and every modulation was meant to be and there was nothing extraneous.

"Claus was a wonderful combination of science and soul. He was a very clear-thinking, focused German brain with a wonderful sense of whimsy, but as a result of his scientifics about music, we would go through things quite simply and find out where the best harmonies were and how to treat things. Claus taught me some major lessons in how to analyze a song and how to think about producing a record. His arrangements are very lean, and they're very to-the-point, which is also how Quincy liked to work. He really cut away the fat."

"It's My Party" entered *Billboard*'s Hot 100 on May 11, 1963. Things began happening quickly for Gore, who had only just turned 17. On May 14, Mercury rushed her into the studio to record a follow-up that was written to order, "Judy's Turn To Cry." By mid-June, "It's My Party" was #1. The song was still in the Top 10 in July, when "Judy's Turn To Cry" came out. The two songs shared the Top 40 for a time, until "It's My Party" slipped and "Judy" shed her tears on #5.

The appeal of "It's My Party" was not limited to white listeners. It actually topped *Billboard*'s Hot R&B Singles chart for three weeks, one week longer than it topped the Hot 100. "Judy's Turn To Cry" likewise hit the R&B Top 10. "It's My Party" also made it across the ocean, hitting #9 in England. In short, during that final summer of John and Jackie, it was impossible to turn on a hit radio station without hearing about Johnny and Judy.

Unfortunately, the image of Lesley Gore which was fed to teen magazines was not the same as the real Tenafly teen. Gore credits Mercury publicity head Jean Linehauser with coming up with the image of the singer as a poor little rich girl. She also recalls one event which occurred shortly after the release of "It's My Party" which fed the rumors of her being a child of privilege: "I was up in Detroit. The weekend was my birthday, and I did an 'American Bandstand' kind of show at WXYZ. The station was done in a colonial style. My father was sitting in the lobby, in front of a very large fireplace, and so they had me stand next to him and take some pictures. The station also had a big driveway, and they sent a limousine to pick us up. So, suddenly I look in a teen magazine and this became 'My House,' and here was my father and I in 'Our Den.' So the wealthy image always felt a little uncomfortable for me." Ironically, that same fireplace photo still gets mislabeled today. In the book that accompanies Bear Family Records' Lesley Gore boxed set *It's My Party*, the photo appears with the caption, "Lesley At Home."

From the beginning, Lesley Gore was associated with the "flip." The hairdo with gravity-defying ends was the favored style of '60s teenage girls, as well as adult style leaders such as Jackie Kennedy. Gore took the 'do on the advice of her fashion consultant, also known as "Mom."

In retrospect, she wishes she had chosen a different reference point. Although she forsook the flip in 1966, it haunts her to this day, giving her an undeservedly sterile image in some people's minds. At the very mention of the hairdo, she mimics an assault rifle. Her defining memory of the flip is from the first time she visited Chicago: "You remember how windy it is on State Street, where they literally have what looks like ballet bars on the edge of the street? Well, Lesley was practically parallel to the sidewalk, but my hairdo was perfect. It never moved."

As most women who grew up in the 50s know, a flip required can after can of Aqua-Net or some other hair spray to keep it in place. Gore is not unaware of the toll that her trademark style took on the environment, as she said, tongue-in-cheek, "All of that stuff I put up into the ozone, I don't know how I'm ever going to pay society back. I work every day at it. That's what keeps me going."

The influence of Gore's parents upon her career, while well-intended, made life uncomfortable for the young singer at times. She later told the *Village Voice*, "My parents did make judgments about my career and bookings, but not for the normal reasons. They would not say, 'Don't play the Garden because it's not the right career move,' but rather, 'Don't play Michigan because they're having a snowstorm and you might get sick.' You must remember that when I started at 16, I was still a kid. I had led a very isolated life. So, at 16, I traveled with my mother or father. If I had come from South Philly and I was used to scrounging around the streets, then perhaps it would have been different. I mean, Connie Francis didn't travel with her mother."

Today, when asked about the way her family handled her career, Gore is forgiving. "I don't think I necessarily made the best management choices at that stage, but I also don't think I was really keen on what was going on. My father became my business person kind of by default, because he was in an office and had a telephone and dealt with the agents and the producers and that kind of stuff. He was a business person, but frankly, he didn't know show business. I think I would have been better off going with someone who had a more professional understanding of the business, but I think he did the best he could under the circumstances."

June 1963 saw the release of Gore's debut album, *I'll Cry If I Want To*, which would be her highest-charting album ever, reaching #24 on *Billboard*'s Top 200. It was a "cry"-themed album, filled with more melodramatic tears than a Roy Liechtenstein exhibition. If one got past the overkill of saline, the album proved that Gore's talent extended beyond the style of her hits. "Cry Me A River" showed her affinity for jazz-pop, while "Just Let Me Cry" showed that her range and verve could turn what would otherwise be an lachrymose album cut into a real charmer.

While *I'll Cry If I Want To* was entering the charts, Gore was in the studio recording her next single, "She's A Fool." A shimmering piece of Brill Building-style ear candy, the song became Gore's third straight Top Five hit, reaching #5 in the fall of 1963. Meanwhile, the singer was on her first-ever tour, criss-crossing England on a package with Dion, Mercury labelmate Brook Benton, Trini Lopez and Timi Yuro.

One night, while in London, she went to the White Elephant Club, where she met the band that was taking the country by storm, the Beatles. Although Gore does not recall anything special about the meeting, the group must have been impressed to see her. A few months earlier, when they first heard "It's My Party," they had told producer George Martin that they wanted their vocals to sound like Gore's, double-tracked, reverb-laden, and BIG.

Gore ended 1963 with an armload of industry awards, including the National Association of Record Merchandisers' Most Promising Female Vocalist, the American Disc Jockeys' Most Promising Female Vocalist, and *16* magazine's Best Female Vocalist. "It's My Party" received a Grammy nomination for the year's Best Rock and Roll Record. When the New Year hit, she had one more reason to celebrate, a new song on the charts, "You Don't Own Me."

Those who consider "You Don't Own Me" a proto-feminist anthem may be surprised to learn that, as with John Stuart Mill's *The Subjection Of Women*, it was actually written by a man – two, in fact: John Madara and former Danny and the Juniors singer David White. (As members of the Spokesmen, the duo would go on to write and record one of the era's most notorious right-wing hits, "The Dawn Of Correction," an "answer song" to "Eve Of Destruction.")

Gore first heard "You Don't Own Me" during the summer of '63. "I met John Madara and Dave White up at the Catskills (New York) hotel Grossinger's. I was up there doing a record hop, gratis, for a disc jockey by the name of Gene Kay at WAEB in Allentown. I was sitting at the pool on, I think it was Saturday, the day I was going to perform, and John and Dave came up to me with a guitar, took me into a cabana by the pool, and played me 'You Don't Own Me.' I told them they had to meet me in New York on Monday, to see Quincy and play him the song, and we were in the studio probably a week and a half later.

"It is much to Quincy's credit that he could see what was really involved in that song, because his edict, as far as I know, was to keep me in 'It's My Party' territory, keep it light, keep it frothy, keep in young. You can't hold back a 17-year-old woman – she has got to find a way to spread her wings – and this was a song that allowed me a little bit more freedom vocally.

"The beauty of that song is that the verses start in a minor key, and then, when you go into the chorus, it goes into the major and there's such a sense of lift and exhilaration. After seeing how powerful that is, it became method I've used on a number of occasions, such as the title track of my A&M album *Love Me By Name*."

"You Don't Own Me" was as unstoppable as its protagonist. Arriving right at the start of Beatlemania, needless to say a difficult time for American singers, it raced to #2 on the Hot 100. It stayed there for two weeks, held off from the top by the Beatles' own "I Want To Hold Your Hand." The Fab Four, with their first U.S. hit, had beaten the singer whom they wished to emulate.

However, as Dreamers leader Freddie Garrity had noted the previous year, at that unique time in history there were really two pop music charts, one for the Beatles, and one for everyone else. Lesley Gore had topped the "other" chart. However, the beginning of the Beatles' era was the end of an era for her. Although she would continue to hit the charts until 1967's acid-drenched Summer of Love, "You Don't Own Me" was her last Top 10 hit.

Although Gore was not as successful on the charts in 1964 as she was the previous year, she was, if anything, *more* visible on the pop scene. In the spring, as soon as "You Don't Own Me" fell off the charts, she had a smash hit with the notably less assertive "That's The Way Boys Are." Later that year, she was invited to appear in the movie *The Girls On The Beach*, for which she lip-synced the single's B-side, "It's Gotta Be You," as well as her own composition "Leave Me Alone."

Gore recalled that, by the time she was through playing her part in the film, the crew wished she had left them alone. "I believe that the production crew of *Girls On The Beach* will remember me very well. I was on the set for one entire day. That's all I was there for, starting early in the morning. I think we shot something like three scenes. Somewhere around one o'clock in the afternoon, I began to develop these kind of red blotches all over my face. By about three o'clock, I had a raging fever. By 4:30 I was practically in need of paramedics. I went home with German measles and then learned that everyone on the set got sick. I think they remember me really well."

In May 1964, Lesley Gore entered the charts with "I Don't Wanna Be A Loser," the follow-up to "That's The Way Boys Are," penned by the "She's A Fool" team of Mark Barkan and Ben Raleigh. Unfortunately, the title was prophetic, as the song charted lower than all of Gore's previous singles, #37 on the Hot 100.

Over the years, the Beatles and their compatriots have received the blame for the chart decline of American acts like Gore. In many cases, the British Invasion merely provides a convenient scapegoat for U.S. artists who were on the decline anyway. However, in Gore's case, the argument has some merit. When "You Don't Own Me" peaked at #2, in February 1964, there were only two British acts in the Top 40, the Beatles and Cliff Richard, with three songs between them. Four months later, when "I Don't Wanna Be A Loser" peaked at the disappointing #37, over one-fourth of the Top 40 was British – eight acts, 11 songs. The changeover wasn't complete – an act like the Serendipity Singers could still score big with "Beans In My Ears" – but it took place so rapidly that American artists and their record labels were at a loss for what, if anything, they could do.

Lesley Gore was still a presence on the album chart in the summer of '64, this time with her third effort, *Boys, Boys, Boys*. The album is noteworthy for being the first one to showcase Gore's writing talents, with "Leave Me Alone" and "I'm Coolin', No Foolin'."

Gore admits that "Leave Me Alone" was a response to the pressures of the music business: "I think I started writing it in a car on the way to a gig or something. The melody stayed in my head and when I got home it was still there, so I transferred it to tape. I think it was very much a feeling of already being claustrophobic by fame and feeling a little closed in."

At the time that Gore wrote "Leave Me Alone," in early '64, she was also preparing to graduate high school and enter the prestigious Bronxville, New York women's college Sarah Lawrence (also the alma mater of Linda Eastman McCartney and Yoko Ono). Although college fit in perfectly with Gore's straitlaced, All-American image, it seemed strange for a star whose name still had cachet with radio stations. Gore was well aware of what it might do to her career.

"I was questioning whether that was the right decision. I think that, deep in my heart, I knew it was, but I also knew that the same career would not be out there when I finished in four years. So it was a difficult time. On the other hand, Sarah Lawrence offered me a little bit of solace at a time when, frankly, celebrity had become something of a burden."

Despite her reservations, once she arrived on campus that September, she became increasingly certain that it was altogether the best thing for her, both personally and professionally.

"Sarah Lawrence had a kind of idyllic campus setting, yet I was still able to get into New York, because it was only 30 minutes outside of Manhattan – and actually record with Quincy or do television shows, that kind of stuff. It did afford me a way of being able to back out a little and get some perspective on the whole thing. I really did have the sense that if I continued with my career, I would never go back to school. You know what that pattern can be. Then there were so many things that I yet wanted to study; in fact, to this day, when I think about the things I haven't had a chance to study, it saddens me. I could have been very happy spending the rest of my life in school. I found it a very nurturing and wonderful way of life."

Although Gore enjoyed her studies, her fellow students, meeting her for the first time, viewed her more critically than had the ones at the Dwight School, who had grown up with her. "College was different," she later told the *Village Voice*, "because I arrived and I was already a personality. I was also a rock personality, which was not considered at all chic. People at Sarah Lawrence were either into classical or folk music. Had I been tall with blonde hair, had I been Mary Travers, I would have gotten along fine. However, I was short... well, at least my flip hairdo was gone by then. If I had kept my flip, I probably would not have gotten through my four years at Sarah Lawrence."

The very week that Gore entered college, she was back at #14 on the Hot 100 with her biggest hit since the British Invasion, the Ellie Greenwich-Jeff Barry tune "Maybe I Know." The haunting melody, replete with tempo changes and minor-major modulations, and Gore's convincing reading of the disturbing lyrics, made it one of her most memorable hits.

Gore's next single was a complete change of pace: "Hey Now" coupled with "Sometimes I Wish I Were A Boy." "Hey Now" was the kind of record that she and Quincy Jones had wanted to make for some time, with a droning, percussive, almost bluesy sound, a far "cry" from "It's My Party."

The flip has since become legendary among connoisseurs of camp. Surprisingly, Gore says that it has *never* been on her personal hit parade. "That's one of Quincy's faves," she groans, "and one of my *hates*. I *still* hate it! Oh, God! That was one of those songs that we negotiated. Quincy must have let me do 'Secret Love' or something in exchange for singing that. Oh, God, I hated that song – that one and 'I Struck A Match.' I think it was really just the subject matter. It was just the way that the story was told; I felt it was really dorky. I thought, 'I've gotten past this.'"

Dorky or not, it was an undeniably strong song – at lest for novelty value – and many disc jockeys picked it up, diluting the airplay of the A-side, "Hey Now." As a result, neither side was a hit – "Hey Now" peaked at #76, while the flip peaked at #86.

Interestingly enough, in light of Gore's mention of Quincy Jones' skill at "negotiation," she did record the Doris Day tune "Secret Love" at around the same time that she did "Sometimes I Wish I Were A Boy." It remained in the can until this year, when Bear Family located it for its *It's My Party* box.

In fact, a scan of Gore's session records reveals that she recorded several pop standards, such as "When Sunny Gets Blue" and Charles Aznavour's "You've Let Yourself Go," that never saw the light of day. Usually, such songs were done at the end of a session, either with the musicians sticking around or with Gore just accompanying herself at the piano. Since Mercury rarely saw fit to release them, it appears that they were done only to pacify the singer, who loved the songs and wanted very much to expand her range of styles.

In December 1964, producer Shelby Singleton took Gore into the studio to record nine songs. It is unclear why the bulk of the tunes was not released. One lone single from the sessions appeared two years later and promptly became Gore's rarest recording, "I Just Don't Know If I Can," which she wrote with Carole Bayer [later to be known as Carole Bayer Sager – ed.].

Listening to it today, the reasons for the junking of that session are even more of a mystery. Both the song and its production combine the best elements of early L.A. folk-rock, the type of trebly sounds pioneered by Jack Nitzsche and Jackie DeShannon. The only possible answer that comes to mind is that, with "I Just Don't Know If I Can," Gore and Bayer were just a few months ahead of their time.

For the follow-up to "Hey Now," Mercury wisely pulled out another Greenwich/Barry tune from the "Maybe I Know" session, "The Look Of Love." The single, recorded the previous July, came out at Christmas time, and its sleigh bells were no accident. Quincy Jones had them added on when he learned the date of the release. The new year began with smiles all around as "The Look Of Love" returned Gore to the Top 40, reaching #27 during a nine-week chart stay.

March 1965 saw the release of "All Of My Life," written by Helen Miller ("It Hurts To Be In Love," "Foolish Little Girl") and fellow Brill Building great Tony Powers. If "Hey Now" was a change, "All Of My Life" was even more jarring, a mature number that finally earned Gore the title of "soulful."

Radio programmers were not impressed, and the single only reached #71. As Gore says today, it deserved to be heard by more than the youthful Top 40 audience: "Isn't that a wonderful song! I love that song so much. It was a pretty sophisticated record for that time and, boy, it took some chops to sing it. I loved that song because of what I was able to vocally accomplish with it. It was way too good to hit."

The next single, "Sunshine, Lollipops And Rainbows," had originally appeared two years earlier, on the singer's second LP, *Lesley Gore Sings Of Mixed-Up Hearts*. Gore says that the idea for it came from a sparkling individual. "There was a gentleman who came to Mercury by the name of Morris Diamond, who was head of their promotion department, and Morris always loved 'Sunshine, Lollipops And Rainbows.' Two years after it had been recorded, he insisted it come out as a single. He used to say, 'Let's have Mor(e) Diamond and Les(s) Gore!' A slogan man. I'll never forget that."

Although producer Jack Nitzsche recorded a new version of the song with Gore in March 1965, the version that came out on a single was the original 1963 recording. It is possible that the Nitzsche version, which has less reverb than the original one, was used to give it a "live" sound when Gore lip-synced the song in the 1965 teen flick *Ski Party*.

"Sunshine, Lollipops And Rainbows," one of the first songs to bring composer Marvin Hamlisch into the spotlight, hit #11 in the summer of 1965. For teens, it must have seemed like Lesley Gore was everywhere that summer. Not only was she in *Ski Party*, but she also appeared in the groundbreaking concert film *The T.A.M.I. Show*. The movie, which also featured the Rolling Stones, the Beach Boys, James Brown, Marvin Gaye and many others, was best described by David Ehrenstein and Bill Reed in *Rock On Film* (Delilah Books, 1982), as "the greatest gathering of rock performers ever assembled for one film, *Woodstock* and *Monterey Pop* notwithstanding."

As the summer of 1965 wound down, "Sunshine, Lollipops And Rainbows" fell off the charts and was replaced by the first A-side to bear Lesley Gore's name as a writer, "My Town, My Guy And Me." Gore recalls that the song was originally presented to her by co-writers Paul Kaufman and Bobby Elgin.

"We worked on it a bit together, and when it was finished, I recorded it. We had our hands slapped for saying 'Frisco' instead of 'San Francisco.' We discovered that people who lived in San Francisco don't like to hear their town referred to as 'Frisco.' That was interesting; they wouldn't play it in San Francisco as a result."

The song may not have washed in the Bay Area, but it did respectably on a national scale, reaching #32 in two months on the Hot 100. It was the last recording of Gore's to be personally overseen by Quincy Jones, who moved to Los Angeles shortly thereafter to focus on the movie industry.

Gore was handed once again to Shelby Singleton, a Mercury executive who is better remembered as an industry mover-and-shaker than as a producer. His best move with Gore was to give her a top-rate arranger, Alan Lorber (Claus Ogermann had moved on), who was largely responsible for the sound of the ensuing album, *Lesley Gore Sings All About Love*. The highlights of *All About Love* were two songs that Gore wrote with her brother, Michael, who was then only 15 years old, "I Won't Love You Anymore (Sorry)" and "We Know We're In Love."

"We always spent a fair amount of time at the piano together," Gore says. "It was sort of like having an in-house orchestra. Michael was very musical at a very early age, and we were on the same level somehow. It was great to just say, 'Let's sing this or that.' He had these 'fake books' and we would just pick out songs. We spent a lot of time doing that. That just naturally got him into writing different melodies at the piano, and that naturally got me into lyricizing his melodies."

Both "I Won't Love You Anymore (Sorry)" and "We Know We're In Love" were strong songs, and Mercury released them as singles, one after the other. Despite their evident commerciality, neither one approached the Top 40. By the time that "We Know We're In Love" stalled at #76, in February 1966, Gore was far less visible than she was at the same time the year before, and that surely hurt sales.

Although her disappearance from the performing scene was due in large part to her focusing on school, Gore admits today that she also had cold feet: "I did as little performing as possible because, frankly, I was scared to death of it. I didn't have the chops, it made me nervous. The studio was a 'safe' place for me and a good learning experience, so I was comfortable in the mode."

In March, 1966, Mercury pulled one more song from *All About Love*, "Young Love," and was rewarded with a #50 chart item. It would be Lesley Gore's last Hot 100 entry for nearly a year, until "California Nights" brought her back. During the meantime, she released two excellent singles, both of which made the *Billboard* Bubbling Under chart.

The first, "Off And Running," was written by Carole Bayer and Toni Wine and was also sung by the Mindbenders in the hit movie *To Sir With Love*. When the songwriting duo presented the song to Gore in early 1966, Gore loved it, but she most wanted to record another of their compositions.

"Carole and Toni brought me 'A Groovy Kind Of Love.' When I heard that, I took Toni and Carole by the hand up to Shelby Singleton's office, at 745 Fifth Avenue. We played him the song, and Shelby actually stood there and looked at Carole Bayer and said, 'You gotta change the world "groovy."' Carole looked at me and I thought she was gonna cry. I said, 'No, I don't think she really has to. I think that's great.' So the Mindbenders wound up recording that song, on a Mercury subsidiary [Fontana]. I probably would've had a fairly good-sized hit with that one."

After "Off And Running" flopped, Mercury paired Gore with producer who had a better idea of what to do with her, Bob Crewe. Crewe was one of a handful of producers who were true artists. His work with the Four Seasons helped define the sound of '60s hit radio and influenced countless other producers here and abroad, including Rolling Stones avatar Andrew Loog Oldham. His first effort for Gore was a song which he wrote for her with Gary Knight, "Treat Me Like A Lady."

Although the disc failed to hit, Crewe did not give up. His next Gore disc, "California Nights," was more a creation than a mere slab of vinyl. The singer, who calls Crewe a "genius," is very proud of that record, largely because it reminded her of the jazzy sounds on which she grew up. "It's a good Lesley Gore record because it's so unlike anything else. It also had a slight Jazz/R&B feel. It was back to those kind of funny roots that I had. You don't lose those things."

While "California Nights" reached #16, the follow-up was an artistic success and a commercial flop. The gorgeous "Summer And Sandy" went over like a beached whale in the Summer Of Love, stalling at #65. From there, Gore's commercial fortunes plummeted with surprising speed. The unfortunately-titled "Brink Of Disaster" was her last Hot 100 single, hitting #82 at the tail end of 1967.

Gore continued recording for Mercury and releasing singles for the label through the end of the '60s. One of her last sessions, done on October 3, 1968 in New York City, was with producers Kenny Gamble and Leon Huff, who would soon attain worldwide fame as the architects of the Philly Soul sound.

At the time that they paired with Gore, they were just getting rolling, having masterminded hits for the Soul Survivors, Jerry Butler and the Intruders. One of their arrangers on the Gore session was also a master producer in his own right: Thom Bell, who was then coming off of his first hits for the Delfonics.

Today, listening to the three tracks done at that session – the Bell compositions "Look The Other Way" and "Take Good Care (Of My Heart)" and Gamble and Huff's "I'll Be Standing By" – the beginnings of the Philly Soul sound are obvious. However, the public or Mercury Records may not have been ready for such a soulful Lesley Gore, as the singles from the sessions failed to hit the charts.

Gore's last Mercury release was the Laura Nyro number "Wedding Bell Blues." She recalls that when she brought it to Quincy Jones, who was overseeing her again at that point, she had no idea that it was already being recorded by the Fifth Dimension.

"My brother Michael and I were just made for Laura Nyro, and I would continually bring Quincy songs of hers that I wanted to record. Finally, I brought in the most benign of all her songs, 'Wedding Bell Blues.' Then the Fifth Dimension literally pre-empted us; they must have put their record out two days before we were ready with ours."

At the end of the decade, Gore was wooed away from Mercury by Crewe, who wanted her for his new label, Crewe Records. Unfortunately, while Crewe had high hopes for the label, his financing fell through, and the label went bankrupt within a year.

Before the label folded, four singles by Gore emerged, one of which was a duet with Oliver that was credited to Billy and Sue. By this time, Gore, at the ripe old age of 23, was well past singing in an innocent voice about Judy and Johnny. Her voice had deepened, and her songs, more often than not originals, had more in common with Liza Minnelli than Shelley Fabares. She demanded to be accepted on her own terms, as a growing, developing artist, and she was not tied to 1960s musical sensibilities.

For fans of the shimmering, double-tracked vocal sound of Gore's hits, this was a bitter pill to swallow. Nonetheless, it was an understandable move for an artist to take in a musical climate which had moved on to such modern innovations as 8-track tapes and quadraphonic sound.

In 1972, after Crewe Records folded, Gore released the album *Someplace Else Now* on Mowest, a division of Motown. Despite a rave review in *Billboard*, the album flopped and Gore turned to non-musical projects.

Two years later, finding that there was a resurgence of interest in her music, she returned to the stage. In 1975, she signed to A&M and reunited with Quincy Jones to make the album *Love Me By Name*. It is her last album of all-original material to date. Since then, besides becoming a top-drawing oldies act, she has become a commercially successful songwriter.

In 1980, her song "Out Here On My Own," written with brother Michael, was on the million-selling soundtrack of the movie *Fame* and became a Top 20 hit for Irene Cara. It earned both Oscar and Grammy nominations and marked a remarkable turnaround: Lesley Gore, the woman who had made her name as a singer of other writer's songs, had written a critically acclaimed song for another woman whose career was that of singing other writers' songs. All in the recording industry could finally see that the voice in front of the creativity had become the creativity behind the voice.

Today, Gore continues to keep up a heavy writing and performing schedule. She is ever-thankful for the support she receives from fans, which has pulled her up from difficult times. "For a lot of years, I didn't make a living as a singer. In the '70s, I started recording again, but in terms of personal appearances I wasn't in that much demand. What happens as the years go by is, if you're lucky enough to still hang in and live through it, your work will sometimes become appreciated."

On the vocal front, Gore, already well-versed in the technical aspects of singing, is thrilled at the results that she is getting with her current coach. "I'm working with a woman now who's given me a whole new vocabulary and a whole new way of singing. Right now, because of what she's teaching me and the vocal quality I'm getting now, I'm actually reaching the peak of my abilities for the first time. It's really exciting for me. I find that vocally I can do almost anything; I don't even know where to start!

"I am first and foremost a singer, and I am then a composer. If I can't do those things, then it doesn't pay to get up and eat and sleep and drink, because those are the things that are important to me. So that's what I try to be every day. I try to be a musician."

Most Collectible 45

"Je Ne Sais Plus"/ "Je N'ose Pas," Mercury 72245, $20.

Most Collectible LP

I'll Cry If I Want To, Mercury SR-60805, stereo, no blurb on cover for "It's My Party," $40.

Recommended Introduction

The Golden Hits Of Lesley Gore, Mercury 810 370-2 (18 of her biggest hits)

If you want to hear more…

Sunshine, Lollipops and Rainbows: The Best of Lesley Gore, Rhino R2-75325 (20 hits and LP tracks; much overlap between this and the Mercury CD above)

It's My Party: The Lesley Gore Anthology, Mercury 532 517 2 (2-CD set of 52 of her Mercury recordings)

It's My Party, Bear Family 79005-11574-2 (German import, 5-CD box set)

Wanda Jackson

by Bruce Sylvester

This interview with "Rockabilly's First Lady," as the article's original headline dubbed her, appeared in the March 1, 1996 issue of Goldmine. *Not as well-known to the general public as she ought to be, she was a pioneer female rocker, back when female singers were supposed to be, as Tina Turner once put it, "nice...and easy." As with many rockers who stopped having hits, she eventually turned to country music and was a consistent presence on the C&W charts from 1966 through 1972. But even before "Let's Have A Party," she had made the country charts as early as 1954.*

Wanda Jackson's signature song "Let's Have A Party" alone wins her a place in the pantheon of rock 'n' roll. Born in Maud, Oklahoma, on October 20, 1937, she started in country, moved into rockabilly at her friend Elvis' urging, returned to country and then sang Christian music. In 1995, Rosie Flores (her long-ago guitarist) invited Jackson to sing on her *Rockabilly Filly* album and took Wanda with her on tour. At age 58, Jackson still has the throaty growl and frenzied whoop that made "Let's Have A Party" a cult classic.

Besides reissues on Rhino, Curb and Hollywood plus a four-CD box on Germany's Bear Family label, her vintage songs are reprised on *Wanda Jackson*, inaugurating Capitol's new "Vintage Collections" series.

Goldmine: *How did you get started?*

Wanda Jackson: My father put a guitar in my hand when I was six and began teaching me chords. I would accompany him while he sang. My folks loved to ballroom dance. All the couples would bring their kids. I'd stand at the bandstand and listen. I especially enjoyed hearing the girls sing in the big bands like Bob Wills and Tex Williams. They yodeled and dressed in pretty sparkly clothes. Rose Maddox was an influence. From about age six I told everyone that I was going to be a singer.

Rockabilly had very few women.

In those days there were very few females even in country music. Kitty Wells opened doors for all of us in 1952 with "It Wasn't God Who Made Honky Tonk Angels." Jean Shepard was the next one that I remember. I was about the third on the scene. There weren't many females played outside of pop, Broadway and the movies.

Why? Have you seen the book Finding Her Voice: The Saga of Women In Country Music? It tells of women performers like Goldie Hill walking away from careers in country music to raise families.

Back then the mindset of women, which I still don't see anything wrong with, was, as soon as I'm out of school, if I don't get married, I'll work until I get married. I certainly wanted to be a singer. I wanted fame and fortune and everything, but the thought was always there, 'Just until I get married.' Then I was fortunate and married a man who wanted to help me in my career and not take me away from it. My parents helped raise my children, so it's been great for me. It didn't work that way for everyone.

We have a daughter and a son in their thirties and three beautiful granddaughters. When I'm home, I get the grandchildren whenever I want them as long as I want them. We have a business with our son. Our daughter works for us in it so we're a close-knit family. It's part of a national franchise, Alta Mere, automobile window tinting and alarms. We own three franchises in the Oklahoma City area. That keeps my husband busy when we're home, not only booking my dates, but working with Alta Mere and my son.

We wanted to help our children some way and neither of them chose music as a career – there was nothing I could do to help them – so we found what rang the bell. Our son had always loved cars and had trophies out the gazoo for all his car shows. We've been in his business about 12 years.

You're the woman, who has everything: career, travel, family.

And Jesus too. Heaven when I die. You can't beat that.

Reading the liner notes to the Country Music Foundation's Jean Shepard reissue, I saw a lot of parallels with you. Both of you as teenagers were taken under the wing of Hank Thompson. Both of you were very young when Capitol discovered you. I guess because of all the troubles Capitol ran into when Jean was number one on the charts but sill a minor, they hesitated to deal with you.

They wouldn't sign me until I was 18. That's why I went with Decca for two years first.

Did you encounter any problems due to your youth?

No. My parents were right there involved with me. I'm sure that helped.

What was your first big break?

Hank Thompson moved to Oklahoma and heard my radio show and invited me to sing with his Brazos Valley Boys. My first record was with his bandleader, Billy Gray. Hank's publishing company had a song for a man and woman, "You Can't Have My Love." Hank helped us get the Decca contract so we could release the song. One thing that sold it was we said "cain't." A lot of people say it nowadays just like everyone uses "ain't" and no one raises an eyebrow, but back then in music you didn't have accents like that. And I just sang, "But you cain't, no you cain't have my love." Everyone told me that may have gotten attention for the song.

Plenty of other singers would have moved to Nashville or Los Angeles, but you stayed in Oklahoma. Why didn't you move to an industry center?

In those days I was primarily working the Midwest dance spots. I recorded in Nashville and the West Coast quite a bit, but I just never saw the need to move. In retrospect it might have been a good move so I could have had a chance at the songs a little faster. I'd kind of get the colds, but I had a lot of sources for music. I wrote a lot myself. Hank helped me and friends in Nashvile would send me things, so I never really hurt for good material. But I did miss some great songs because they want to write them today, have them recorded tomorrow and be on the charts next week. Since I was in Oklahoma, it took a little longer than that for songs to reach me, but I really don't regret staying there. I'm proud to be an Okie, not from Muskogee, but from Maud.

They say your one Grand Ole Opry show ruffled some feathers.

It was probably 1955, even before I was out of high school. I'd been brought up on the Opry so it was exciting for me to play there. I was designing my own clothes. I didn't like cowboy boots or the girls wearing hats and big old full skirts. I wanted to see some glamour. I was quite a movie buff. Still am. I liked Marilyn Monroe and Elizabeth Taylor. So I began designing straight skirts with soft fringe and rhinestones. I had high heels and long earrings and long hair. That was the persona I wanted. So when I went to do the Opry I designed a special dress. My mother made it – she was a professional seamstress. She made all my stage clothes. And Ernest Tubb said I couldn't go on the Opry stage in that dress. I'd have to cover my shoulders. It really threw me for a loop. So I had to go back into the dressing room and get the coat I'd worn, a white leather one with long fringe. It worked OK, but it made me very upset.

A lot of things about the early days of the Opry I didn't go along with so I didn't join. I had been working with Hank Thompson, and he is a professional's professional. I knew the difference in staging people and your presence on stage and lighting and so forth and the Opry had none of that to offer.

Alton Delmore's autobiography Truth Is Stranger Than Publicity makes WSM radio and its Grand Ole Opry sound like total exploitation.

That's exactly what it was and I could see it for that. The bigger you got, the more the Opry expected you to be there on Friday and Saturday nights, the biggest nights of the week when you could make money elsewhere and realize something out of your work. I said, "That isn't right. I don't want any part of that."

Why were you billed as "too hot to handle"?

Well, I don't know. I think it meant that Capitol Records and Jim Halsey (my manager) and the American public didn't really know what to do with me in those days. I was my own person and I had my own style and nobody was going to change me. I didn't cause problems or anything, but if they didn't want to do something my way, I just found someone who did. I wanted to be presented properly and do a proper show. I wanted to look different than people in the audience. My manager would say, "You should dress like a normal lady would dress." And I'd say, "No. I don't go out for entertainment to see someone dressed the way I'm dressed. I want to see them look different." He never could understand that. I think the reason the expression started was they couldn't put me in a pigeonhole. I wouldn't let them. I was sort of a renegade. I was on the cutting edge and they could do it my way or they could forget it.

How do you explain the fact that your songs like "Fujiyama Mama" and "Riot In Cell Block Number 9" didn't do particularly well on the pop charts then but now are considered cult classics?

I think the public is finally ready to hear it from a woman. Without realizing it, I was blazing a trail for the ones who've come along since. I was just doing my thing.

What do you think of the women's movement?

It's caused a whole lot of problems, I think. But I'm glad to see women coming into their own.

Did Elvis encourage you to do rockabilly?

Very much – he and my father. But it took a while for me to get the courage, I guess because no other woman was doing it. But suddenly I found "Let's Have A Party." If my life were a song, it would be "Let's Have A Party." I got it from Elvis's movie *Loving You*. He did it in a different style. I started doing it at dances and people loved it. Then I put it on my first Capitol album and it was two years before it was released as a single and became a hit.

What was a date with Elvis like?

Well, we dated just when we were on tour. My father traveled with me and I wasn't allowed to go in the car or travel with Elvis from job to job or anything like that. But we both loved movies so when we were in town early enough, we'd catch a matinee and maybe have an early supper together and then do our show. After the show maybe Bill (Black), Scotty (Moore), Elvis, my father and I would have a bite to eat. Or we might go to a drive-in and get a hamburger and Coke and drive around. You know how teenagers talk all the time. We just spent time talking and having Cokes. He would always have me back to the room when my father said I had to be there. We liked each other a whole lot, but we were both career-oriented.

What songs did he introduce you to?

I don't remember exactly. He did take me to his home in Memphis, the little house before he built his mother Graceland, and played me songs from his record collection and showed me how to make a blues song into a rockabilly and take a country song and change the beat and things. My father was a fan of the black blues so I'd heard it all my life and loved it. Elvis would take the record off and say, "What if you did it like this?" Of course it would sound great when he did it. I'd say, "Well, I just don't know if I can get the feel for it." And he'd just keep saying, "Well, you can do it. That's what you need to be doing. You've got the voice for it and you love it, so try it."

It's been said that only children tend to bond with each other. Could that have affected your friendship with Elvis?

I'm sure. We both respected and revered our parents. It wasn't anything we had to be taught. It was the mindset of the whole nation then. I wish it were that way again.

I revered my father at that point in my life because he was the one traveling with me, influencing me and teaching me things I should and shouldn't do. He let me know right quick what I could and couldn't do. I could never sit on anyone's lap to have a picture made. If I got sleepy, I couldn't lay my head on someone's shoulder because he wanted my reputation to be held up. He knew that if he didn't guide me closely, me just

being a kid, my reputation could get ruined. And I'm grateful because as far as I know I've had a good reputation throughout this whole career.

I've always had a man traveling with me. My father traveled with me until I was married. And then about two weeks after I was married, my husband gave up his career with IBM and began traveling with me. I'm the kind of female who needs a man and don't mind admitting it. I love men.

How do you feel about being invited to tour with Rosie Flores, whom you influenced so long ago?

It's fantastic. I get to introduce her to my fans from my generation and she's introducing me to some of the younger generation, even though most of them already know about me. I feel very lucky that it's happening.

Most Collectible 45

"You Can't Have My Love"/ "Lovin' Country Style," with Billy Gray, Decca 9-29140, $60.

Most Collectible LP

Rockin' With Wanda, Capitol T 1384, mono, black label, rainbow rim, Capitol logo at left, $400.

Recommended Introduction

Vintage Collections, Capitol Nashville 36185 (20 tracks recorded from 1956-61)

If you want to hear more...

Right Or Wrong, Bear Family 79005-11562-9 (German import, 4-CD box set, more from the same era as *Vintage Collections*)

Tears Will Be the Chaser For You, Bear Family 79005-16114-2 (German import, 8-CD box set)

Brenda Lee

by Sue VanHecke

Fans of classic rock probably hear Brenda Lee's name at least once every couple weeks. She's mentioned by name in Golden Earring's 1974 hit single (and hit LP track) "Radar Love" – "Brenda Lee, comin' on strong." "Coming On Strong" was one of her last major hit singles, in 1966, but long after that she continued to record, right into the 1990s. Of course, she's best known for her string of mid-tempo and ballad hits from the early 1960s. "I'm Sorry." "I Want To Be Wanted." "Break It To Me Gently." "All Alone Am I." Even before that, she began by singing upt-empo rockabilly material in a voice that belied her young age (her first record came out when she was 12). And, of course, she did "Rockin' Around The Christmas Tree," which gets her back on the air every holiday season, even on stations that don't specialize in oldies. Goldmine caught up with "Little Miss Dynamite" for an interview that appeared as a cover story in the March 15, 1996 edition.

Brenda Lee's voice is as big as all outdoors, and her genre-spanning catalog and roster of accomplishments is nearly as vast. From her early rockabilly sides like "Dynamite" – which earned the pre-teen songstress the apt handle "Little Miss Dyanmite" – and the now-classic "Rockin' Around The Christmas Tree" to her sorrow-sodden ballads such as "I'm Sorry," "I Want To Be Wanted" and "All Alone Am I," Lee's knowing way with almost any song has brought her countless awards, worldwide sales of close to 100 million and a devoted international following that keeps her as active today as she was at the dawn of her career in the early 1950s.

The incomparable Lee's throaty alto is arresting, her interpretive skills without peer; she's able to bring deep emotional resonance to the simplest of songs. As her longtime producer Owen Bradley put it, "She knows how to communicate, how to get to you, how to make you understand what she's talking about. It's something you're just born with."

Brenda Lee was born Brenda Mae Tarpley on December 11, 1944 in the charity ward of Grady Memorial Hospital in Atlanta. The second child of semi-pro baseball player and carpenter Ruben Tarpley and his wife Grayce, she was a musical tot who spent hours listening to the radio "when we had one," Lee recalled. "We didn't have a radio or a television or a record player. I've always said I was on television before I had a television. We didn't have all of those things, so most of the music that I heard was through the church. My (two) sisters and brother and all sang in church and stuff like that, but I'm the only singer. And my mother can sing, my mother used to sing to me when I was little and teach me Hank Williams songs and things like that."

By age three, the toddling tyke was chirping back entire songs she'd heard only once or twice. Her first full-length favorite was the tearful Eddy Arnold ballad "My Daddy Is Only A Picture." Gospel music, particularly as sung by Mahalia Jackson, was a huge influence on little Brenda Mae, and at age five she gave her first gospel performance at church, testifying alongside the Master Worker's Quartet.

In 1950, older sister Linda entered Brenda in a local talent contest in the Tarpley hometown of Conyers, Georgia, just outside Atlanta. The event was an annual spring festival open to kids from three counties. "I wasn't even in school," the singer recalled in Paul Kingsbury's biography *Brenda Lee*, included in last year's Bear Family Records boxed set *Little Miss Dynamite*, "but my sister was in the first grade and they used to have a talent show every year between schools, and whatever school won, won the trophy for that year. They got to keep the trophy for that year. She entered me as the talent for the school."

For her first secular singing performance, the freckle-faced five-year-old donned a tiny homemade evening gown and sang "Take Me Out The Ball Game," taking first prize for talent and runner-up honors in the beauty contest. "The school was given the trophy," she told Kingsbury, "and I got a box of King Edward peppermint sticks." Her voice, as astonishingly muscular wallop from a girl so very small, was so striking that she was invited to perform on a popular local Saturday morning radio show, *Starmakers Revue*, by the sponsors of the festival. Lee's parents allowed her to decide. "We thought that if Brenda wanted to sing, we should let her sing," her mother told *Esquire* in 1962. Brenda didn't have to think twice; she was belting it out on the airwaves, knocking down "Too Young," a few days later.

Little Brenda was a big hit and quickly became a regular on *Starmakers*, where she appeared for the next year. She was paid no money for her work on the show, which was sponsored by Borden's Ice Cream, "but you could get all the ice cream you could eat," Lee recalled in her official artist's bio. "Looking back, I felt very proud of her then," Grayce Tarpley told *Esquire*. "I had the feeling that perhaps maybe it was only a dream or a hope that perhaps someday she would be a great singer."

Mother's dreams matched daughter's, in fact. In the autumn of 1951, the going-on-seven-year-old Brenda announced that she intended to perform on the Atlanta television program *TV Ranch*. The show was hosted by local musician John Farmer and aired on WAGA. She auditioned with the Hank Williams hit "Hey, Good Lookin'," and when the uproarious audience demanded an encore, followed up with "Too Young." Again, Brenda, her dramatic voice seasoned with the cracks and slides of a singer thrice her age, was soon a regular performer, appearing each Saturday with Boots Woodall and the TV Wranglers, again for no money, this time not even for ice cream.

Her non-paying local radio and television appearances led to the first of countless professional concert engagements: performing at a Shriners' Club luncheon for $20. Income from her appearances went toward family bills, as Ruben Tarpley didn't make much from his occasional carpentry jobs. "We were so poor we didn't have a record player," Lee said in a 1981 interview with *Us* magazine. "And at Christmas time all we'd get was, maybe, some candy or hand-made toys."

The family's financial woes worsened in spring of 1953 when Ruben Tarpley was injured in a bizarre accident at a construction site. While working on the ground floor of a two-story house, he was hit on the head by a hammer that dropped from the upper floor. He was knocked unconscious and died several days

later. "He was an alcoholic," Lee recounted to Alanna Nash in her 1988 book *Behind Closed Doors: Talking To The Legends of Country Music*. "I was goin' on nine when he died."

After Ruben's death, Lee's mother toiled 18 hours a day at a local cotton mill to feed her family. Little Brenda pitched in, taking paying singing jobs wherever she could find them. The third grader's extracurricular work was almost as grueling as her mother's, the late weekend hours affecting her school performance. "I'd be so tired Monday morning," she told Kingsbury, that her teacher, Miss Norton, would "let me put my head down on the desk and sleep until about one o'clock."

In 1955 Grayce Tarpley remarried, to Buell "Jay" Rainwater, who moved the family to Cincinnati, where he worked at the Jimmy Skinner Music Center. While in Ohio, Brenda performed with Skinner at the record shop on two Saturday programs broadcast over Newport, Kentucky radio station WNOP. The family soon returned to Georgia, however, this time taking up residence in Augusta, where Brenda appeared on the *Peach Blossom Special* on WJAT-TV. While there, the

show's producer, Sammy Barton, re-christened the little singer Brenda Lee, believing that Turpley was just too difficult to remember.

Rainwater opened a record store in Augusta, the Brenda Lee Record Shop, where station WRDW originated a weekly program, hosted by disc jockey Charlie Raiford "Peanuts" Faircloth, who was once a fellow frequent *TV Ranch* guest. The enterprising Brenda composed her own theme song for the show: "Brother, if you want to get the lowdown/Come along and let's all have a hoedown/ At the Brenda Lee Record Shop Saturday at 3/ On the Brenda Lee Jam-bo-reeeeeeeee!" Again, Lee received no money for these shows, but the exposure led frequent live paid bookings.

On February 23, 1956, Lee got her first important career break. A radio station in Swansboro, Georgia had asked her to be a guest on its *Peach Blossom Jamboree* program. Although it had offered $30, she turned the job down, to see one of her favorite entertainers instead, country music star Red Foley, known for hits like "Chattanoogie Shoe Shine Boy" and "Peace In The Valley" and an early host of the Grand Ole Opry's NBC radio network show. Foley was appearing with the cast of the ABC-TV show *Ozark Jubilee* at Augusta's Bell Auditorium.

"We got into Augusta late and Red had about five minutes to get dressed," Foley's manager Dub Allbritten remembered in *Brenda Lee*. "This local DJ (Faircloth) grabbed us as soon as we walked through the stage door. He kept saying, 'You've got to hear this little girl sing.' 'Yeah, yeah, yeah, we know,' we kept sayin'. You know, we heard that kind of stuff everywhere we went. But his guy was insistent. He all but grabbed Red by the collar and dragged him out to hear her."

Foley relented and agreed to put Brenda on the show. "I still get cold chills thinking about the first time I heard that voice," Foley remembers in Lee's bio. "One foot started patting rhythm as though she was stomping out a prairie fire but not another muscle in that little body even as much as twitched. And when she did that trick of breaking her voice, it jarred me out of my trance enough to realize I'd forgotten to get off the stage. There I stood, after 26 years of supposedly learning how to conduct myself in front of an audience, with my mouth open two miles wide and a glassy stare in my eyes." When Lee sang "Jambalaya," Foley recalled, "I'm tellin' you, she did bring down the house. She was a sensation."

Foley had Allbritten sign Brenda immediately to appear on the next *Junior Jubilee*, the monthly edition of the Springfield, Missouri-based *Ozark Jubilee* that featured younger entertainers. On March 31, 1956 Lee made her first nationwide television appearance, singing "Jambalaya" on the *Junior Jubilee*. She left quite an impression. The show's producers received three times their usual fan mail, almost all requesting another Lee appearance. Jack O'Brien, a columnist for the *New York Journal American* newspaper, led off a TV review saying, "I didn't catch the name of the 9-year-old singer on last night's *Ozark Jubilee*, but she belts a song like a star."

Shortly after her formidable national TV debut, Lee and her family took up residence in Springfield. She appeared on the *Ozark Jubilee* from 1956 to 1959 as a regular, then as a guest. "From that show I went on to do the Perry Como show and Steve Allen and things of that sort," she remembered matter-of-factly of her early network TV years. "And also, before I'd even done those things, I had been doing local television and local radio. So I was just kind of used to it."

Foley and Allbritten had great confidence in their petite prodigy and shopped Lee to all of the record companies. "It was hard to 'sell' a child in those days," Lee told Nash. "Nobody wanted a child on the label. I was turned down by RCA Victor and by just about every label." Finally, Foley and Allbritten took the youngster to Foley's label, Decca. Paul Cohen, Decca's head of country A&R, took one listen to little Lee and signed her to his label on May 21, 1956. She was just 11 years old.

By that time Elvis Presley, who'd moved from the tiny Sun label to RCA, was burning up the charts, selling 50,000 singles and 8,000 LPs and EPs a day of his hip-swiveling rockabilly, according to *Billboard*. It was a revolutionary sound, an adventuresome hybrid of "race music"– the gospel and beat-heavy rhythm 'n' blues of the black community – and the melody-driven, Anglo-derived idioms of traditional Appalachian and bluegrass country.

Predictably, the era's official arbiters of taste, including the Nashville establishment, were thoroughly outraged by the provocative racial and sexual taboo-scoffing new music. But the rebellious sound had captured the interest of open-minded producer Owen Bradley and he'd had some success dabbling with it. In January 1956 the 40-year-old pianist and former music director for Nashville's WSM station (home of the Grand Ole Opry) had recorded Buddy Holly at his Nashville studio. Gene Vincent, Capitol's answer to Elvis, had also cut tracks there in May 1956, and in July, Bradley had recorded Johnny Burnette and the Rock 'N' Roll Trio's boisterous rocker "Train Kept A Rollin'."

In August 1956, Paul Cohen, with Bradley at the piano, oversaw Lee's first recording sessions at the Bradley Film and Recording Studio. With her country-leaning roots and throaty gospelish growl, it wasn't easy to pigeonhole the young songstress into any single category. Consequently, her first session featured a variegated repertoire, from Hank Williams hits ("Jambalaya," "Your Cheatin' Heart") to a novelty noodle ("Doodle Bug Rag"), a pair of crisp holiday tunes ("Christy Christmas," "I'm Gonna Lasso Santa Claus") and a toe-tapping rockabilly romp ("Bigelow 6-200").

"I'd been singing a long time, I was used to singing, I was used to that atmosphere," Lee recalled, denying any first-time studio jitters. "I think when you're that young, too, you just don't get nervous about things. I don't think you know the bigness of it, or the drama of it at the time. You're just little and you're singing.; that's what you know how to do and that's what you're used to doing."

"We were all astounded at this little girl who had such a big voice," Bradley remembered of the first time he heard Brenda Lee sing. "Everybody was real impressed that somebody that small could make such a big note. In retrospect, after awhile, I just didn't think about Brenda being a kid so much."

Bradley never needed to give Lee much direction, he said, because "Brenda's always been real well-prepared. (But) I'd say, 'That was a good take there, Brenda, let's play that back.' We'd play it back –and I would have probably kept it – and her mother'd say, 'Now Brenda, you could put more into that. Let's do it one more time!' And her mother was usually pretty right about it. So she'd sort of build a little fire under Brenda and get her to put a little more into it, add a little zip to it. Whatever it was, I give Grayce credit for doing her part. We were all trying."

As their little star-in-the-making's first single, on September 17, 1956 Decca released the twangy "Jambalaya," backed with Lee's hiccuping "Bigelow 6-200." Though she was 11 at the time, Decca billed her on the label as "Little Brenda Lee (9 years old)," a not-too-unbelievable fib in the name of marketing as Lee was unusually small for her age (and today stands only four feet, nine inches). *Billboard* gave the single an enthusiastic thumbs up, gushing prophetically, "This nine-year-old country chick has the projection, voice and sincerity that can skyrocket her to great heights, not only in the country field but in the pop field as well. On this strong two-sided disk she also has the material for a most impressive debut on wax. 'Bigelow,' with her bright-eyed rendition, is a tune that could catch, while on the flip she takes the Hank Williams oldie for a real ride."

Despite the endorsement, neither song broke into the charts. Decca followed up in October with a seasonal single, "I'm Gonna Lasso Santa Claus" paired with "Christy Christmas." *Billboard* again glowed, crediting Lee with having " a lot of style and know-how for her age, and so this holiday opus will have to be watched."

Again, her age was fudged, further emphasizing the amazing contrast between little Lee in her gingham pinafores and that great big voice.

Lee continued her *Ozark Jubilee* appearances and became a regular on the package tour circuit, traveling with heavyweight country stars like Mel Tillis. "Mel's wonderful," Lee said of the man who has penned some of her biggest records. "He used to drive us to the shows. I used to sit in the back seat. He used to say I kept him up talking all night long. I'd stand up in the back seat, because I could, I was so little, and talk to Jim and Faron Young or George Jones or whoever was on the tour at the time. He said I was a very precocious little girl."

Precocious indeed. In December 1956 the tiny 11-turning-12-year-old made her Las Vegas debut, a three-week stand at the very adult Flamingo Club. "I sang 'Tutti Frutti,' 'Jambalaya' and other songs all through the show," she told *Country And Western Jamboree* in 1957. "For about 10 days I had bad trouble with my throat but kept on singing. Don't think we'll go back there any more, but I think they want me." Lee has since become a Vegas mainstay, regularly playing multi-night engagements.

The young Lee did not read music, relying on careful listening and memorization to build her repertoire. And obviously, she had no intentions of cultivating a strictly country music career, as her inclusion of the Little Richard hit in her show indicated. "Brenda is the quickest study I've seen in 25 years in this business," Foley told *Folk And Country Songs* in 1957. "It's fascinating to watch her sit alone in a corner and make changes in both words and music to suit her own style."

New York City's Pythian Temple, a huge ballroom-turned-recording studio, was the site of Lee's next session in January 1957. Milt Gabler, who had helmed Bill Haley's history-making hit "Rock Around The Clock" in 1954, produced. Decca's house band, the Jack Pleis Orchestra, accompanied Lee, along with the Ray Charles Singers. The tiny songstress polished up a pair of tunes, the kid-oriented dreamer "Fairyland" and the hip-shaking, hand-clapping, pop-gospel inspirational "One Step At A Time," given a commanding rockabilly treatment by little Miss Lee. Not long after its release, "One Step At A Time" strode to #15 on Billboard's country chart and also landed on the pop chart, peaking at #43 in the spring of 1957.

Lee's bold single fit in perfectly with the prevailing pop sound: rock 'n' roll. The music industry had found a voracious new market – teenagers – who were buying up 80 percent of the records sold in the U.S. And the preadolescent Lee, the cherub with the husky howl, was the perfect teen songbird. Not sur-

prisingly, her next session, at the Bradley studio in April, focused on a rock 'n' roll sound.

As with "One Step At A Time," chorus vocals were used again, provided by the Anita Kerr Singers, one of the most popular vocal quartets on the Nashville session circuit. Led by singer/arranger Anita Kerr, the foursome would become a fixture on countless Brenda Lee releases. Material for this session included the teen-targeted "Love You 'Till I Die" and "One Teenager To Another," a swinging retread of the Ray Charles R&B hit "Ain't That Love," and "Dynamite," an all-out rocker that delightfully showcased Lee's shouts, pouts and purrs. But paired as a single with "Love You 'Till I Die," the rambunctious rollicker, which earned Lee the appropriate tag "Little Miss Dynamite," hardly dented the pop charts, peaking at #72 that summer.

In late May 1957 Lee toured briefly with Patsy Cline, who was enjoying pop success with her six-month-old crossover hit "Walkin' After Midnight." Despite their considerable age difference, the two belters immediately hit it off. "Patsy was great," Lee remembered fondly. "She was a big-hearted, wonderful broad, in the nicest sense of the word. I went on a tour with Patsy when I was about 12, I believe. She just took care of my mom and I. Just such a sweet person. But, I mean, she gave as good as she got, she didn't take much off of people. She was her own person and knew what she wanted to do and that's what she did. But she sure was good to people along the way."

Encouraged by her two chart placements, Lee and her family moved to Nashville in July 1957. Dub Allbritten assumed exclusive managerial duties and Charlie Mosley, a Nashville accountant and co-owner of the Ernest Tubb Record Shop, became Lee's legal guardian by order of judge Beverly Briley (later Nashville's mayor from 1963-1975). Thanks to the "Jackie Coogan laws" designed to protect child entertainers from exploitative adults, Lee's income was put into a trust fund until she reached age 21. Lee found herself at the center of litigation, though, when Crossroads TV Productions filed suit in Nashville to keep the singer from departing *Ozark Jubilee* and working for anyone else.

Depsite the five-year contract between Crossroads and Lee, Chancellor Ned Lentz could not find for the plaintiff, citing fears of derailing Lee's burgeoning career if an injunction was granted. Lee and Crossroads settled out of court for an undisclosed amount, though clearly, with Lee's reported earnings then at $34,000 a month, the sum was no doubt substantial. The little singer had come a long way from the days of entertaining for ice cream.

Not surprisingly, with her pint-size charm and astonishing vocal talent, Hollywood soon came a-callin'. Twentieth Century Fox wanted Lee for a proposed biopic of Shirley Temple, but Lee's mother was cautious. "I don't want them trying to turn Brenda into something she's not," Kingsbury reported Grayce Rainwater as saying. "Twentieth Century-Fox wanted Lee for a proposed biopic of Shirley Temple, but Lee's mother was cautious. "I don't want them trying to turn Brenda into something she's not," Kingsbury reported Grayce Rainwater as saying. "Twentieth Century-Fox has a good script which fits Brenda real good, but I sort of hate to think what could happen to her if she made movies which didn't fit her." Lee did not appear in the film, pursing instead a childhood of some normalcy.

In the fall of 1957 Lee was enrolled in North Nashville's Maplewood Junior High School. The 12-year-old led a typical schoolkid's life, enjoying extracurricular activities like the debating squad, and co-editing the school newspaper. "I went to public school and I was a cheerleader and I did all the things that you do in public school, up until my last two years when I went to a private school in California," Lee reflected on her childhood. "But my mom sort of seen to it that I was pretty normal, and I think I was about as normal as you can be doing what I was doing. I got punished if I did wrong. I wasn't allowed to get away with much. I had two sisters and a brother and I wasn't pampered or spoiled. Of course, yeah, I think I missed some things. I'd be probably dishonest if I said I didn't. But I also gained a lot from being able to do what I was doing. I was able to give my family a better lifestyle, help my sisters and brother through school and college, help my mom. So I think all the rewards certainly made up for anything that I missed.

"I had gone to this school for a long time in Nashville and I was just one of the kids. They thought it was great when I had success, they were very supportive, but I wasn't any different than I'd always been to them. I thought that was great, I really enjoyed that. Of course, Nashville, there are so many entertainers, they're used to that."

Lee returned to the Bradley studio in November, waxing a pair of mid-tempo rockers, "Rockabye Baby Blues" and "Rock The Bop." A braying, bluesish sax similar to those used in Fats Domino and Little Richard hits became a prominent feature on Lee's tracks, but her signature rock 'em, sock 'em vocals remained the unmistakable centerpiece. So where did the wee lass learn to belt out rockabilly like the big boys? "A lot of people ask me that and I really don't know," Lee said. "It's just something I've always done, I don't know where it came from. It's just a gift."

Even professionals recognized this and refused to tamper with the girl's innate abilities. Lee told Nash, "My mother took me to a vocal coach when I was 14, and he said he wouldn't touch it. He said, 'If I even tried, she'd lose what style she has. She doesn't need any vocal training. Maybe breathing and learning to sing correctly, but no voice lessons.'" Her hearty growl hardly came from listening to Elvis, Carl or Jerry Lee, either, Lee swears. "Actually, those people really weren't out until I started doing stuff," she said.

She might not have listened to much Elvis, but she was swept off her feet by the comely rocker when they met in December at the Grand Ole Opry. Lee was making her first Opry appearance, singing "Bill Bailey, Won't You Please Come Home" at the historic Ryman Auditorium. Presley, in Nashville to consult with manager Colonel Tom Parker after receiving his draft notice, had dropped by the Opry and sang "That's All Right," according to a 1987 issue of *Life*. "I just thought, 'Boy, he's sure a good-looking guy,'" Lee told the magazine, "and he sure sings good and he sure is nice." Presley glad-handed backstage, posed for pictures and gave the 13-year-old a big hug. They remained friends until his death.

"He was a really nice kind of a shy southern boy," Lee remembered, "cared a lot about his mother, his family, his roots. But very shy, and very gentlemanly. Through the years we corresponded and I ran into him a couple of times. I was invited to his home in Memphis and various places, but I never really wanted to infringe on his private time because I knew he had so little of it. I felt like that was his time and I didn't need to be there. But I did have the invitations and he was a friend of mine."

The close-knit relationship between Lee and Owen Bradley, who had arranged most of Lee's material to this point, was cemented in April 1958 when Paul

Cohen left Decca's country A&R position to head pop A&R for Coral, a Decca subsidiary. Bradley, with whom Cohen had worked closely for a decade and held in the highest esteem, was appointed to the country post. He would produce almost every Brenda Lee recording session until 1976.

Lee and Bradley visited the studio again in May 1958. Impressed by the lush sonics of the new stereo sound, Bradley had outfitted his place with the latest stereo recording equipment. Again, Lee was joined by the usual A-list session players, including Hank Garland on lead guitar, Grady Martin on second electric bass, Floyd Cramer on piano, Bradley's younger brother Harold on electric bass, Bob Moore on standup bass and Buddy Harman on drums. The players behind what would eventually be called the Nashville Sound, country given a smooth pop gloss, they backed Patsy Cline, Roy Orbison, Elvis and myriad other country crooners who recorded in Nashville. Some of the men – Cramer, Martin and Garland – would go on to successful solo careers themselves. Presley's vocal backup, the Jordanaires, were also present.

Lee had had a modicum of success with her rockabilly stylings and continued largely in the same vein during the May sessions. She belted out "Ring-A-My Phone" in feverish hepcat fashion and turned out a smoking performance on the irresistible slide-heavy boogie "Little Jonah (Rock On Your Steel Guitar)," featuring nimble young steel guitarist Buddy Emmons. The two crackerjack songs were paired for Lee's seventh single, released in June, but amazingly, neither side pierced the charts. On October 19, the 13-year-old junior high school student returned to the studio with Bradley and the band for a marathon session that stretched well past midnight. Included in the material that evening was what would become one of her biggest hits.

Bradley had a new tune in hand by New York songcrafter Johnny Marks, who'd also written the Gene Autry hit "Rudolph The Red-Nosed Reindeer." Given the success a year earlier of another Decca artist, Bobby Helms, with another seasonal song, "Jingle Bell Rock," Bradley believed Marks's "Rockin' Around The Christmas Tree" might just be right for Lee. "That song came in with about 20 other songs from Johnny," Lee told Kingsbury, "and that was the only Christmas one, and it was the only one I liked of all the songs. I thought the song would be successful. I never dreamed that it would be the Christmas standard that it is." With Lee's warm and welcoming vocal, the bouncing bass line and perfectly placed guitar and sax accents, Lee's "Rockin' Around The Christmas Tree' was downright charming.

The night session also included "Papa Noel," another Christmas ditty set on the bayou, Lee's jumping retread of the old standard "Bill Bailey, Won't You Please Come Home" and the rippin' rockabilly hummer "Let's Jump The Broomstick," a nod to the mountain marriage tradition of hopping over a broomstick. Decca coupled "Rockin' Around The Christmas Tree" and "Papa Noel" a month later, but, astonishingly, the single stiffed, eluding any chart action.

"Everybody said, 'Boy, that's really a good record,'" when he first played "Rockin' Around The Christmas Tree" for the Decca brass in New York, Bradley remembered. "But we didn't sell any, because nobody really knew Brenda very well. You don't send out a million records on somebody that's not well-known. I think we sold 5,000 records" that season. But the song was far from finished.

With no big movers since "One Step At A Time" and "Dynamite," by the close of 1958 Lee's manager Dub Allbritten was scrambling to prop up her limping career. Though she continued to be salable, making television appearances and touring with the country package shows, she was lacking hits. Now at the awkward, in-between age of 14, Lee could hardly be pitched as a moppet marvel, yet she was still too young to work the sexy diva angle. With interest in Lee's recordings waning stateside, it came as blessed news, then, that her sales were booming in France.

Decca quickly ordered Lee back into studio in January 1959, where she waxed an album of pop standard remakes. Though still in school, the teenager again worked deep into the night, infusing new energy into classics like "Just Because" (which Elvis had resurrected while at Sun) and Tin Pan Alley stalwarts like "Pennies From Heaven" and "Toot Toot Tootsie Goodbye." Decca released the 12-song disc, amusingly titled *Grandma, What Great Songs You Sang!*, in August to lukewarm reception from American music buyers. But the label would make the most of its investment, later repackaging, resequencing, and retitling the album as *Brenda Lee Sings Songs Everybody Knows* in 1961 and *Here's Brenda Lee* in 1967.

Taking full advantage of Lee's European popularity, Allbritten, his tiny charge and a pair of schoolteachers jetted to Paris for a performance at the Olympia Theater. Lee's French debut was shrouded in a bit of sensationalism, as rumor had spread across the country that the singer was actually a 32-year-old midget. "They had never seen me in France, they'd only heard me," Lee remembered for Nash. "And when we were gettin' ready to go over there, they wanted publicity pictures, and we sent 'em like I looked, you know, 12. But they didn't believe it, they thought we were lying. So they printed the story."

The outrageous publicity didn't hurt, however, and Lee's brash performance was a winner. *Vogue* magazine reported, "Brenda Lee, the 14-year-old American rock 'n' roll singer, is relaxed and shows off her pro airs well. The French were quite impressed by her showmanship and ease."

Le Figaro gushed, "Never before since Judy Garland has anyone caused as much clapping of hands and stamping of feet." What was originally a two-week stand stretched to a full five weeks, with Lee making television appearances in Brussels, Milan and London. Her concert jaunts abroad would become, and remain today, frequent, as she is as loyal to her European fans as they are to her.

"I'm lucky," she said. "I started courting that market around about 1958 because I wasn't doing anything in the States. We went over there, we had an offer to go over there and work. It just so happened I had some hits over there, 'Let's Jump the Broomstick,' 'Dynamite' and those rockabilly songs that were not hits in the States. So I became known over there and started working over there and I've continued to court that market all these years. They've been very supportive of me and my music. To this day I think that that audience has such a respect for the beginners of rockabilly and rock 'n' roll. You can go over there and you can tour and you can have packed houses even if you haven't had a hit record since the '60s, because they really revere that music and the pioneers that started it."

A month-long tour of Brazil followed. The diminutive dynamo, whom the South Americans came to call "The Explosive Girl," made such an impression that the tour netted 51 front-page newspaper stories and feature spreads in nine magazines. Brazilian President Juscelino Kubitshek de Oliveira dubbed Lee "the best goodwill ambassador the U.S. ever had."

Back home, Lee, Bradley and the A-Team reconvened in the studio in August 1959. They were eager to record a song Lee, Bradley and Allbritten had chosen, "Sweet Nothin's," penned by a young rockabilly singer named Ronnie Self whom Lee had met on the Ozark Jubilee. It was a frisky teen tune which Lee and Bradley gave an unusual twist, a brief spoken-word intro of whispered telephone talk and distinctive psst-psst-psst backing vocals. The ear-catching embellishment was certainly experimental for its day, but indicative of Lee's and Bradley's willingness to take chances on something a little off the beaten path. "Owen always tried to use different instruments to get a different sound, maybe on intros," Lee explained. "Different little things to make my records different. We weren't afraid of experimenting and we did that quite often." Bradley recalls, "The disc jockeys used to have a little fun with that. See, they could put that on and then they could talk to Brenda, say something and then let the record go. It gave 'em something to talk about."

Lee's lustful read of the song is also notable, in that "I didn't even know what a boy looked like" at the time, she confessed to Nash. "I don't know where that came from. I really don't. Because you didn't even talk about it when we were that age. I guess I fantasized in that song. I probably wished that I was in that situation, and sang it like that, but I hadn't had any experience, that's for sure."

Billboard didn't seem to notice, calling the sassy song in September 1959 "a rocker...sung with spirit by the thrush over a tricky ork (sic) backing."

"Sweet Nothin's" entered the pop charts by Christmas that year; in late April 1960, it peaked at #4. Seizing on Lee's sales momentum, Decca swiftly released a four-song EP in April, the first of 14 Decca EP compilations of available singles, B-sides and album tracks. Across the Atlantic, "Sweet Nothin's" became Lee's first chart success in England, where the song climbed to #4, and her first charter in Germany as well, topping out at #34. It would be the first of many Top 10 hits.

In March 1960 Lee and Bradley re-entered the studio, rejuvenated by the success of "Sweet Nothin's" and ready for some more creative experimentation. For the first time in Nashville recording history, Bradley brought in a string section, a distinctive component of the Nashville Sound, which he intended to use on a couple of mature ballads, "I Want To Be Wanted" (an English translation of the Italian "Per Tutta La Vita") and "I'm Sorry," another Ronnie Self winner.

"We had three strings," Lee recalled (though other sources say four). "I'm Sorry" was a song that I had had a couple of years. I had met...Ronnie Self, who was quite a rockabilly singer in his own right, and writer. I had met him and had had given me two songs, 'Sweet Nothin's' and 'I'm Sorry.' I had held on to those songs and believed in them. I wanted to cut 'I'm Sorry' and the record company really was kind of skeptical of it because they said it was such a grown-up song for my age at that time. But we finally recorded it, we did it on the tail-end of a session in about five minutes in two takes. It was really something, I'll tell you."

"We used four strings," Bradley recalled in *Billboard* in 1966, "now we use 10...On 'I'm Sorry,' Anita (Kerr) had the voices going along well and everybody else was faking along, but the fiddle players were A-team and needed something very specific to do. We decided to let the fiddles answer when Brenda sang 'I'm Sorry,' the fiddles would answer 'I'm Sorry,'. So Bill (McElhiney, arranger) came up with some notes for them and wrote them down and we were off and running."

Also distinctive is the recitation of lyrics midway through, originally not part of the song. "We added that because it was only like an eight-bar song, so we had to add that to make it long enough," Lee recalled with a laugh.

Of course, Lee's aching vocal truly made the tune. The teenager's voice had attained a smoldering huskiness that emanated sheer emotionality, and she had acquired an impeccable feel for phrasing. "Owen said that it was always uncanny the way I could read lyrics at that age and sound believable," Lee told Nash. "I don't know how I did it except that I love lyrics. And I was raised on Edith Piaf. Piaf and Judy Garland and Tony Bennett and Frank Sinatra. And I guess Bessie Smith and Billie Holiday and Charles Azanvour. These are the people that I cut my teeth on. Everybody says, 'Chuck Berry, Elvis Presley...' I had those records, but my manager would always bring these other people to me and say, 'Listen to this.' So these are the people that I learned my phrasing from. And, of course, they were all innovators, so they helped me a lot. I particularly learned a lot of my phrasing from Sinatra, who I think is the greatest phraser in the business. Bennett, as Sinatra said, might possibly be the greatest *singer* in the business. I don't know. But these are the people I listened to."

Lee and Bradley crossed their fingers that they might have a smash on their hands with "I'm Sorry." "I think we did," Lee said when asked if she and her producer could tell when they'd cooked up a winner. "I think when we chose (the songs that became hits), we knew. We knew they were great songs. We didn't necessarily know that I could have a hit on them. But we knew they were great songs and we knew that somebody would. We hoped that I would."

Several uptempo numbers were also waxed during the March sessions, including stereo remakes of "Jambalaya" and "Dynamite" and a revved-up read of "That's All You Gotta Do," written by guitarist Jerry Reed, who would become a star himself a decade later. Obviously swayed by the success of the rocker "Sweet Nothin's," Decca buried the stellar "I'm Sorry" as "That's All You Gotta Do's" B-side. *Billboard* didn't miss it though, writing of the single, "The little lass with the big voice comes thru (sic) with a sock reading of a rhythm tune on the top side, and then sells a ballad with wistful tenderness."

Decca's judgment proved canny, however, as "That's All You Gotta Do" vaulted up the pop charts, reaching the #6 spot in just five weeks. It was surely to Decca's surprise, though, when "I'm Sorry" shimmied up the charts right behind its A-side, then passed it, presiding at the #1 position for three weeks in July. The quavering ballad beat out the Hollywood Argyles'" Alley-Oop," Connie Francis' "Everybody's Somebody's Fool," Roy Orbison's "Only The Lonely" and Duane Eddy's "Because They're Young." Lee's first #1 smash remained in the Top 100 for more than six months, garnered her a Grammy nomination and became the singer's first gold record, selling over one million records. It remains her biggest-selling single , with worldwide sales of over 15 million. Promptly following up on Lee's impressive string of hits, Decca issued *Brenda Lee*, the singer's second LP, in August 1960, just one year after release of her full-length debut. *Brenda Lee* crashed the album chart party within three weeks of its release, climbing to #5.

Decca put Lee back in the studio six times during the last two weeks of August, where she cut 21 songs. True to Lee-Bradley form, the repertoire was expansive, including personal Lee favorites like Ray Charles's "Hallelujah, I Love (Him) So," Fats Domino's "Blueberry Hill" and the Ink Spots' "If I Didn't Care." Unproven material included tame rockers like "I'm Learning About Love," "The Big Chance" and the nonsensical "Crazy Talk." Ballads included the Mel Tillis-Ramsey Kearney composition "Emotions," an English translation of an Edith Piaf song, "If You Love Me" (recorded by Kay Starr in 1954 and LaVern Baker in 1959), and another string-steeped stab at the Italian tune "I Want To Be Wanted."

The latter became Lee's next single, backed with "Just A Little," as Decca wasted no time, issuing the record in September. Little Miss Dynamite just couldn't miss; "I Want To Be Wanted" became her second #1 hit in late October, knocking the Drifters' "Save The Last Dance For Me" from the top slot. Two weeks before her second chart-topping success and just two months after the release of her last album, Decca rolled out Lee's third long-player, *This Is Brenda*. That album also rocketed up the album charts, peaking at #4.

Wringing all things possible from Lee's winning streak, Decca dusted off the two-year-old "Rockin' Around The Christmas Tree" for the 1960 holiday season. It, too, was chart-friendly, becoming a Top 20 hit. The record would go on to become a much-loved Christmas standard and holds #4 honors in the Top 10 All Time Christmas Songs. It remains Lee's second-biggest-selling record, having moved more than eight million units by 1995. In 1991, Lee re-recorded the song for her Warner Brothers album *A Brenda Lee Christmas...In The New Old Fashioned Way*.

A five-week tour organized by Dick Clark, host of ABC-TV's popular *American Bandstand* series, followed. The only girl on a bill with Duane Eddy and Chubby Checker, Lee was accompanied by a chaperone at all times. But it was hardly necessary. Lee told Kingsbury, "I was always the baby, the little sister. It was tough when Duane Eddy and Fabian became my pals. And I wanted them to flirt with me, but all they did was tell me their troubles."

By the beginning of 1961, Lee's newest single, the big ballad "Emotions," that again featured a creamy string echo of Lee's chorus, was on its way to hit status, eventually making the Top 20. Its B-side, the likable easy-rocker "I'm Learning About Love," made the Top 40.

In early January 1961, Lee returned to the studio, putting her rock 'n' roll sound on hiatus to again wax a bushel of old standards, including "Georgia On My Mind," the Hoagy Carmichael tune Ray Charles had made a chart-topper the previous November, Judy Garland's trademark "Zing! Went The Strings Of My Heart," the 1932 Louis Armstrong favorite "You Can Depend On Me" and the 1924 Vernon Dalhart million-seller "Someone To Love (The Prisoner's Song)." Lee also gently covered the Shirelles' hit of the day, "Will You Love Me Tomorrow."

Lee's move away from rock 'n' roll reflected the trend of the times as softer, gentler pop sounds were peddled full force. By then, the music industry's payola scandal and unyielding parental pressure had fostered the rise of clean-cut, sanitized teen idols like Fabian and Ricky Nelson, and girl-next-door balladeer. Brenda Lee fit right in. Lee's record label was eager "to disassociate (Lee) from the stigma of rock 'n' roll," Lenny Salidor, then Decca's New York director of promotions, told *Esquire* in 1962.

But Lee would not completely forsake rock 'n' roll, writing in a one-page editorial for the March 1961 edition of *Music Journal*, "Americans have constantly criticized the current trend in popular music, claiming that it is responsible for low morality. I, being both a teen-

ager and pop singer, naturally disagree. I feel the musical taste of the young people in this country is a healthy one. We can dance to the music, sing it, tap our feet to the rhythm, and identify with the lyrics...If radio stations would be listened to fairly our critics would find that many current hits are ballads, and some very lovely ones, too. I know, myself, that my albums are bought by adults (as well as by people my own age) who are very surprised when they learn that I am just sixteen years old. As long as the public listens to this type of music and likes it, I will continue to perform it as best I can."

Decca released the sad-'n'-slow, string-filled "You Can Depend On Me" in April 1961, coupling it with the percolating Jim Seals ballad "It's Never Too Late," recorded during the August 1960 sessions. The A-side quickly went Top 10 and *Billboard* glowed of the single, "Two very moving sides by the young thrush. The first is the old standard done with exceptional warmth and heart at an unusually slow tempo. The flip is another ballad sung with great emotion by the gal, embellished effectively by a wide string background." Decca continued the momentum with the release of Lee's fourth album, *Emotions*, composed mostly of Lee's renditions of standards ("Crazy Talk" is the LP's only rock 'n' roll track).

After more touring abroad, including a chaotic jaunt through Australia where hundreds of hysterical fans trapped Lee in a room at the Melbourne Airport for three hours, Lee was back in Bradley's studio. Again, the emphasis was on a safe pop repertoire: standards like "All The Way" and "How Deep Is The Ocean," R&B hits like "Kansas City" and "Talkin' 'Bout You," gentle rockers like "Dum Dum" and grand, heart-wrenching ballads like "Eventually" and "Tragedy." The Hammond organ-garnished finger-snapper "Dum Dum," penned by Jackie DeShannon (later of "Put A Little Love In Your Heart" fame) and Sharon Sheeley (rocker Eddie Cochran's ex-girlfriend who also wrote Ricky Nelson's "Poor Little Fool") was chosen as the next single, backed with "Eventually," another Ronnie Self number. Both sides made the charts; the flirty "Dum Dum" cracked the Top 10 in the U.S. and climbed to #22 in the U.K.

Lee waxed all-new songs in August 1961. One of these was a country weeper, "The Biggest Fool Of All," introduced to Bradley through a demo done by Nashville new-gal-in-town Loretta Lynn. Lynn and the song's composer, Kathryn Fulton, were represented by country stars-turned-publishers the Wilburn Brothers; in a deal to obtain the song for Lee, Bradley was compelled to sign Lynn to Decca. Other notable material recorded at the sessions included the capering "Here Comes That Feeling," co-written by Joe Osborn and Memphis rockabilly Dorsey Burnette; the bluesy mover "Anybody But Me," another Ronnie Self number; and another DeShannon-Sheeley rocker, "So Deep." The sessions' standout, though, was another sweeping ballad, "Break It To Me Gently," which the teenaged Lee filled with torn-from-the-chest passion and world-weary soul.

Many of these tracks comprised Lee's fifth LP, *All Of Me*, released in August 1961. Decca chose to issue "The Biggest Fool Of All" as the album's first single, retitling it "Fool #1" and pairing it with "Anybody But Me." The A-side quickly hurtled up the charts, peaking at #3, Lee's highest charting since the #1 "I Want To Be Wanted" a year earlier. Continuing her string of double-sided hits, "Anybody But Me" went Top 40 as well.

Lee's terrific hit run as well as Patsy Cline's remarkable crossover success prompted *Billboard*, in October 1961, to dub Owen Bradley its Country and Western Man Of The Year. "He is very proud of the success of both Brenda Lee and Patsy Cline," the magazine reported, "who are now among the top thrushes in the country both in the pop and country fields." Lee said of her longtime producer, "Owen Bradley is absolutely one of the most intelligent people I know, especially regarding music. He's one of the sweetest, nicest, most gentle people. He has a real love for what he does and for the artists he's been associated with, a real caring about them and their career, not just for commercialism's sake. He really cared about his people and the material that he got them and what they did with their lives and their careers. He still keeps up with all of his artists. He's a friend to all of us, our dear friend. We socialize with him personally and work with him professionally. He's just very unique, there are not many people like him around.

"He knows his artists. He knows what they're capable of, he cares about them. They're not just a product to him. They're real people and they come in there with real wants and real needs and he tries to give them what they need. And he has just a real love for what he does and a real caring, and he wants to make it right."

By the time "Fool #1" was released in September 1961, Lee and her family had forsaken Nashville for sunny Southern California. Hollywood had been pushing hard and both Lee's mother and her manager Allbritten felt it was time to explore a film career. Lee was enrolled in the private Hollywood Professional School and started work on an Eddie Albert-Jane Wyatt film, *The Two Little Bears*, for Twentieth Century Fox. "It was cute," Lee told Kingsbury,"...but I just really was not interested in movies. It wasn't something that I wanted to pursue. I was interested in my singing." She did perform two numbers in the film, "Honey Bear," crafted by Jay Livingston and Ray Evans of "Mona Lisa" renown, and "Speak To Me Pretty," a tune she'd recorded in May 1961 and featured on the *All The Way* LP. "Speak To Me Pretty," which went unissued as a single in the U.S., became Lee's most popular U.K. side, charting at #3.

Her dispassion for acting did not go unnoticed, with *Variety* writing in December 1961, "Miss Lee, a skillful vocalist who warbles like a little league Kay Starr, has much to learn about acting. Her vocals are out of place in these proceedings, but she renders them with assurance and enthusiasm."

Though the movie was a bomb, Lee's musical star was still on the rise. She returned to Nashville in October for more recording, once again cutting standards for her sixth album, *Sincerely*, which would see daylight in February 1962.

Again, tried-and-true classics were the order of the day, with "I'll Be Seeing You," "Lazy River," "You Always Hurt The One You Love" and more recent hits like the Platters' "Only You" and Little Richard's "Send Me Some Lovin'" benefiting from the brassy but sensual Brenda Lee treatment.

Lee rode out 1961 in Las Vegas with a three-week stand at the Sahara Hotel, backed by the Louis Basil Orchestra and her own longtime road band, the six-piece Casuals from Nashville. *Variety* was in attendance at her December 5 opening and wrote, "Brenda Lee had the adults in her opening night audience on her side from the very first song...The tiny vocalist has not yet developed a consistent style of her own, but she radiates personality and sells a song like a vet, adding a certain winning tonal trickery. She's at her best as a belter."

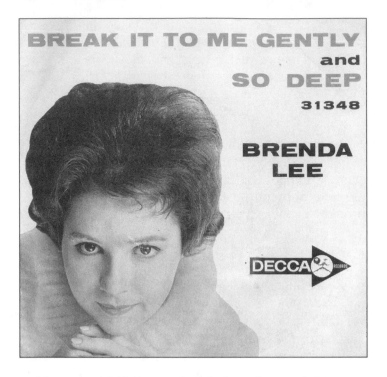

The year 1962 dawned with the release of the soaring "Break It To Me Gently," backed with "So Deep." The A-side entered the charts within a week of its release, eventually grabbing the #4 spot on the pop chart. In testimony to the song's timelessness, 20 years later singer Juice Newton's nearly note-for-note version of "Break It To Me Gently" nabbed the #11 pop chart position and peaked at #2 on the country chart. Lee sang (or, more likely, lip-synched) both sides of the single during her February 12, 1962 *American Bandstand* appearance.

She trooped back to the studio in March, armed with new material from Ronnie Self (ballads "Everybody Loves Me But You" and "It Takes One To Know One"), the DeShannon-Sheeley team (the slow dance "Heart In Hand") and Jerry Reed (the uptempo "Sweet Lovin'"). For Lee's next single, Decca rolled out "Everybody Loves Me But You," backed with "Here Comes That Feeling" from the August 1961 sessions, in early April. By May, the A-side had crested at #6 on the pop chart. Meantime, a two-week concert tour took Lee to England where she joined rockabilly pioneer Gene Vincent, also wildly popular abroad.

"Gene Vincent was wonderful," Lee recalled. "I started working with him overseas. We were known as the King and Queen of Rock 'n' Roll in Europe. We used to do these long tours. He was just a wonderful, wonderful entertainer and just a very sweet, gentle person. He had a very troubled life and the last several years, because of his accident (the taxi crash that killed Vincent's best friend, fellow rocker Eddie Cochran, and aggravated Vincent's already crippled left leg), was in a lot of pain and all. I was young at

the time, a teenager, and I really didn't know all that until after he died. I wasn't aware, I knew he wore a leg brace but I didn't know why and I didn't feel it was my place to ask. But then later on I learned through his family and through other entertainers about the accident and how much pain he was always in." In December, the British music paper *New Musical Express* voted Lee Most Popular Vocalist of the year, as it did annually from 1960 through 1965.

Many other artists would appear with Lee on her European tours, including a four-piece rock 'n' roll band from Liverpool, England. "The Beatles used to open for me in the early '60s, throughout Europe, Germany especially," Lee remembered in *Behind Closed Doors*. "Right before they hit it big in the States. They were crazy. John (Lennon) was always pulling practical pranks. One night he threw a smoke bomb into the audience. And people just went nuts, thought the whole place had been bombed. But he was always doin' somethin' like that. He was just a funny, funny guy. When Dub (Allbritten) and I came back to the States, we begged Decca to sign 'em. And they wouldn't. Musically, they were very raw, you know, but they were great. You could see that talent, and the depth."

Lee scored her ninth consecutive Top 10 pop hit with "All Alone Am I," another throbbing ballad cut in August 1962. Again, Bradley was an innovator, embellishing the song with Nashville's first electric harpsichord. The torrid tune lofted to #3 on the American pop charts in November and to #7 on the U.K. chart the following March. At the time she had recorded it. Lee may have felt just like "All Alone Am I"'s lovelorn lady; romance was apparently not on Lee's docket, despite rumored linkings with the disparate likes of Fabian, Yul Brynner and Hugh O'Brian of television's *Wyatt Earp* program. That changed in October 1962 when Lee met the love of her life, Ronnie Shacklett, at a Jackie Wilson concert in Nashville. The two married in the spring of 1963 and are still happily together, the proud parents of two grown daughters.

Other changes were in store for Lee as well. As 1962 drew to a close, so too did her string of consecutive Top 10 pop singles. "Heart In Hand," released in June, peaked at #15. Then tragedy struck on December 31, when the home Lee shared with her mother outside Nashville burned to the ground. Except for Lee's pet poodle, which was lost to tbhe blaze, no one was hurt, but many valuable keepsakes were destroyed, including Lee's gold record for "I'm Sorry." The new year would commence in a more positive direction, however, with Lee landing a 20-year contract with Decca with a $775,000 advance and guarantee of payment for two movies with Universal-International Pictures, whether she appeared in them or not.

Lee's next hit came with "Losing You," yet another torchy ballad, this time colored with clarion trumpet from Don Sheffield. In May 1963, the song went Top 10 on both the U.S. and U.K. pop charts. That success was followed by respectable showings from the sing-song. "My Whole World Is Falling Down" and sultry, slow song "I Wonder," paired as a single in July and kicking off a three-year run of Top 20 hits. In August, "My Whole World" rallied to #24 on the pop chart, with "I Wonder" tailing it at #25. Across the Atlantic, "I Wonder" ascended to #14 on the U.K. chart as the single's A-side.

In November, "The Grass Is Greener," a Barry Mann ("You've Lost That Lovin' Feelin'") ballad recorded at the same time as "Losing You," reached #17 on the American pop chart, followed by the broken-hearted country crooner "As Usual," which peaked at #12 in the U.S. in early 1964. "As Usual" was one of Lee's few ballads that fared better internationally than domestically, reaching the #5 position on the U.K. pop chart. "Too Many Rivers," written by Harlan Howard ("I Fall To Pieces") and featuring Grady Martin on one of Nashville's first 12-string guitars, maxed at #13 stateside in 1965 and reached #22 in the U.K. (The Forester Sisters, who would provide backing vocals for Lee's 1991 eponymous LP, made a Top 5 country hit of the song in 1987.)

While on a U.K. tour in September, 1964, which included a Royal Command Performance before Queen Elizabeth II, Lee recorded "Is It True," with hotshot British producer Mickie Most at the console. Most had helmed the Animals' international smash "House Of The Rising Sun" and had just commenced work with British teen-dreams Herman's Hermits. For the hot-rocking "Is It True," Most gathered some of London's best session players, including a young Jimmy Page on snaggling lead guitar. The single was rush-released in the U.K., where it careened to the Top 20; it also went Top 20 stateside. Lee's London rock sessions with Most were her only tracks from early 1957 until 1968 which were not produced by Owen Bradley.

Back at home in August 1966, Lee, Bradley and the trusty Nashville A-Team emerged from the studio with "Coming On Strong," a near-Top 10 hit. The horn-garnished, country-pop platter, issued in September, reached #11, her last Top 20 pop chart placing. Now a long-established pop star loved as much for her explosive stage show as her emotion-plucking records, Lee toured tirelessly, appearing at concert halls and nightclubs across the United States. She traveled abroad extensively, shrewdly cultivating her devoted fandom in England, Germany, Italy, France and Japan.

Back in the States in October 1968, under the direction of producer/A&R man Mike Berniker, Lee cut a pop rendition of Willie Nelson's country side "Johnny One Time" in New York. Written by long-time country collaborators A.L. "Doodle" Owens and Dallas Frazier ("Elvira," "There Goes My Everything"), Lee's easy-listening rendition just nipped at the pop Top 40, peaking at #41 in April 1969, but brought Brenda Lee her second Grammy nomination.

As the 1970s dawned, the musical climate was in a state of flux, and so was Lee. She was now a new mother and was also having serious throat problems, due to overuse of her vocal cords. And though she had recorded albums in New York, Los Angeles and Memphis – without Owen Bradley, at the urging of Decca, which was searching for a new image for Lee – she'd been without pop hits for a few years.

"There was no real demand, first of all, for female vocalists," she reflected in *Behind Closed Doors*. "Female vocalists have always had a rough time of it, because females are the record buyers. And there was no place for me. Any my health had been bad. I didn't want to just keep on putting out product that wasn't going to sell. I felt it could only hurt me. So I just stopped for a while."

The respite gave Lee, who was not yet even 30 years old, valuable time to reevaluate her career and reflect on her next move. She decided to go with what she knew best, and in 1971 reunited with Owen Bradley and his session players at his new studio, Bradley's Barn in Mount Juliet, Tennessee. Her gamble paid off with her lush rendition of Kris Kristofferson's "Nobody Wins"; the song sprinted to capture the #5 slot on the country charts in early 1973. It was the start of yet another winning streak for Lee. Between 1973 and 1975 she scored a half-dozen Top 10 country hits with her "story-songs," including "Sunday Sunrise," "Wrong Ideas," "Big Four Poster Bed," "Rock On Baby" and "He's My Rock."

Though Lee was now labeled a country artist, she believes it was more a matter of musical genres being reclassified than her sound changing much. "I was still sort of recording the same way I'd always recorded," she said. ("Nobody Wins") was recorded the same way as "Fool #1," "As Usual," all the songs that I had that were pop and rock before. But I think music had changed so much, and what we knew as rock was no longer rock or even pop at that time, it was going through a drastic change and phase. I think that I was just considered country then, that I started selling to the country audience, categorized in the country field. I think that's what happened. I didn't go into the studio and say, 'Well, I'm going to try and make a country record and get into the country feel.' I never did that."

After an ill-advised stab at country-disco for one Elektra single in 1978, she returned to Decca and once again conquered the country Top 10 with a strong string of hits. Decca was now MCA, with new management and A&R direction from Jim Foglesong and Ron Chancey. Label head Foglesong was a long-time Brenda Lee fan, having first seen her perform in the mid-'50s on the Ed Sullivan television show, where he'd worked as a backing vocalist. And Chancey, also a fan, was ecstatic to be producing her. Lee's voice was still in phenomenal form – her 1979 Top 10 country hit, "Tell Me What It's Like," brought Lee her third Grammy nomination. She followed up in 1980 with "The Cowgirl And The Dandy," then "Broken Trust," again produced by Chancey and featuring backing vocals from country harmony group the Oak Ridge Boys. Both songs went Top 10 country.

In an odd aside, according to Jimbeau Hinson, "Broken Trust"'s composer (who also penned the Oak Ridge Boys' "Fancy Free"), Lee recorded his song because, "As a child, I saw Brenda on TV and became one of the first male Brenda Lee impersonators appearing in clubs, honky-tonks and fairs in my home state of Mississippi," he stated in the liner notes to *Brenda Lee Anthology Volume Two 1962-1980.*

Other notable collaborations have included a 1983 duet with Willie Nelson, "You're Gonna Love Yourself (In The Morning)" and a 1983 album with Nelson, Kristofferson and Dolly Parton, *Kris, Willie, Dolly & Brenda: The Winning Hand*, a 1984 Top 15 country hit with George Jones, "Hallelujah, I Love You So," and a 1989 Grammy-nominated track from post-modern country crossover songstress k.d. lang's *Shadowland: The Owen Bradley Sessions* LP, "Honky Tonk Angels Medley," featuring Lang, Lee, Loretta Lynn and Kitty Wells.

"I was doing the Calgary Stampede in Canada," Lee recalled of how she met the controversial lang, undoubtedly the only openly gay, androgynous, animal rights-advocating vocalist in country music. "I forget who told me, but they said, 'There's a girl that's playing in town that you really need to see. She's really good, she's kind of unorthodox, but she's really good.' So after my show that night I went over and saw this girl and couldn't believe it. I really wanted to meet this girl, so I went backstage and we met. At the time she was doing some stuff in Canada, but nothing in the United States. She was just working the clubs, I guess wherever she could work, and she was wearing the strange clothes, the whole nine yards of what she was doing when she first came here.

"So I met her and she said, 'You know, my biggest dream is to record with Owen Bradley.' I said, 'Well, you know, he's retired now, but if you really are serious about it, I'm going home, I'm going to see him and I'll tell him.' So I went home and I says, 'Owen, there's this girl named k.d. lang from Canada and she's about to die to record with you.' He said, 'Well, OK, I'll check it out.' Next thing I know, I'm being called to do a song on the session with k.d. and Loretta and Kitty Wells, the 'Honky-Tonk Angels.'"

Today, Lee still maintains a rigorous work schedule. In addition to extensive touring across the U.S. and abroad, the singer headlined two Broadway-scale productions at the Acuff Theater at Opryland USA, *Music! Music! Music!* in 1988 and 1989 and *Spirit Of America* in 1990. And no stranger to the camera – in 1980 she appeared in the Burt Reynolds-Sally Field flick *Smokey and The Bandit II* – Lee was one of the TV hosts for Willie Nelson's Farm Aid benefit concert in 1985, was featured in a Cinemax cable special, *The Legendary Ladies*, in 1987, and has hosted cable channel the long-running TNN (The Nashville Network) program "Nashville Now," in addition to a plethora of appearances on TV specials. The singer has also hosted her own syndicated radio show, *Brenda Lee's Country Profile*, and has confessed ambitions of one day having her own talk or variety show.

In 1991, her new label, Warner Brothers, released *A Brenda Lee Christmas...In The New Old-Fashioned Way* and *Brenda Lee*, a critically hailed return to her rockabilly roots helmed by veteran country producer Jim Ed Norman. Currently, Lee, Bradley and many of the players from her early Decca years – including pianist Floyd Cramer, sax man Boots Randolph, drummer Buddy Harman, guitarist Harold Bradley and arranger Bill McElhiney – are hard at work on updated remakes of two dozen of Lee's former hits.

"We're having a lot of fun doing it," Bradley said, "and Brenda, her voice, is just as fantastic as she ever was."

After more than 40 years in the spotlight, Brenda Lee remains one of the most versatile and enduring artists in music history. And her ranging repertoire, which proves she's equally at home performing rockabilly rave-ups, chest-heaving ballads or tear-stained country laments, still makes her difficult to categorize. That suits Lee just fine.

"All of us entertainers hate labels," she said, "though we realize that we have to have them in the record business. I would just like to be known as Brenda Lee the singer, because I like to sing it all, and I always have. I've always been able to incorporate (rock, pop and country) into my shows and my recordings and I've enjoyed it. I'm just proud to still be around, to be able to be doing what I'm doing."

Most Collectible 45

"Christy Christmas"/ "I'm Gonna Lasso Santa Claus," Decca Children's Series 9-88215, $50.

Most Collectible LP

Grandma, What Great Songs You Sang, Decca DL 78873, stereo, black label, silver print, $50.

Recommended Introduction

The Brenda Lee Story – Her Greatest Hits, MCA 4012 (22 of her top 1950s and 1960s hits for Decca)

If you want to hear more...

Anthology, MCA 10324 (a 2-CD set of 40 hits from the 1950s to the 1980s, with the biggest emphasis on the 1960s)

In The Mood For Love: Classic Ballads, Hip-O 40111 (an interesting CD of Brenda singing mostly standards, few of which were released as singles)

Jingle Bell Rock, MCA Special Products 20728 (10 of her Decca Christmas recordings including "Rockin' Around The Christmas Tree"; her 1964 LP *Merry Christmas* has yet to be issued on CD in its entirety)

Little Miss Dynamite, Bear Family 79005-11577-2 (German import; 4-CD set that covers all her recordings from 1956-62)

Roy Orbison

by Colin Escott

As can be expected, most of the attention given to Roy Orbison is focused on his golden years with Monument Records. Almost all his best-remembered recordings were done for that small label from 1960 through 1964. But before that, Orbison had been in a frustrating relationship with the famous Sun label of Memphis. He had one hit single, the fine rockabilly raver "Ooby Dooby." But later events would prove that Orbison was much more than a rocker. In the May 5, 1989 issue, not long after his death in late 1988, Goldmine published this article on the ill-fated attempts to make him a rock 'n' roll star in the 1950s. An interesting side note not mentioned in the following article: Orbison briefly recorded for RCA Victor in the late 1950s, and one of the tracks he made then was the original recording of "Sweet And Innocent," which, years later, would become the first solo hit for none other than Donny Osmond!

The sight of Roy Orbison playing with George Harrison, Tom Petty and Bob Dylan in the Traveling Wilburys, shortly before his death, served to remind us that Orbison survived better than most. Surprisingly, his lately-acquired pony tail was his only concession to the changing times; the character of his music remained remarkably consistent. In fact, one can make a strong case for saying that the most anomalous music he ever cut was during his brief fling with rockabilly.

Between early 1955 and the end of the decade, Roy Orbison tried – with varying degrees of conviction – to become a rock 'n' roll singer. By his own admission, his heart remained elsewhere. Despite the fact that Orbison made periodic forays back into the country and rock music of his youth, his uniqueness was rooted in pop ballads.

Roy Orbison was born in Vernon, Texas on April 23, 1936. His parents, Orbie and Nadine, gave him a guitar for his sixth birthday and taught him the chords to "You Are My Sunshine." Orbie was an auto mechanic in Vernon but, during the war, he moved the family to Fort Worth to work in the defense plants. "My first music was country," Roy Orbison recalled to rock historian David Booth. "I grew up with country music in Texas. The first singer I heard on the radio who really slayed me was Lefty Frizzell. He had this technique which involved sliding syllables together that really blew me away. When I was about six, I used to sing Bob Wills' 'Dusty Skies.' Ernest Tubb used to advertise milk back in those days, singing off the back of a truck in Fort Worth when I was there." Every Saturday, Orbison would cycle down to the local radio station for the talent hour and, when he was 10 years old, he played his first paying gig at a medicine show, where he sang "Jole Blon."

Orbison was sent back to Vernon because there was an outbreak of polio in Fort Worth. After the war, his parents also moved back to Vernon briefly before moving on to Wink, in west Texas, fairly close to the Mexican border. Wink was an oil boom town and Roy grew up there. When he was 13 he formed his first band, the Wink Westerners. His talent was never in doubt. He had his own radio shows from the age of eight and his own television shows from the age of 13. The character of his music can be judged by the name of his group and the Roy Rogers-styled bandanas tied jauntily around their necks. "I remember we played a free gig for the principal of our school," he recalled to the BBC, "and someone came up to us and asked if we'd play a dance. I was going to say that we only knew about four or five songs when they said, 'We'll give you $400.' I said, 'Yes, sir, we'll make the date. We'll be on time and you'll love us.' That was the first time I realized that I wanted to be an entertainer. I enjoyed it and you could make money at it."

After graduation, Orbison worked for a while in the oil fields, playing music at night; then he went to college at North Texas State and subsequently transferred to Odessa. While at North Texas State, Orbison would visit the Big 'D' Jamboree in Dallas. It was there that he saw Elvis Presley for the first time. "First thing," he recalled to Nick Kent, "he came out and spat out a piece of gum onto the stage. He was a punk kid. A weird-looking dude. I can't over-emphasize how shocking he looked and sounded to me that night. He did 'Maybellene' and the kids started shouting. There was pandemonium 'cause the girls took a shine to him and the guys were getting jealous. Plus he told some real bad crude jokes. Dumb, off-color humor. His diction was real coarse – like a truck driver's. But his energy was incredible and his instinct was just amazing."

Back in Odessa, Orbison had a television show sponsored by the Pioneer Furniture Company. In 1955 Johnny Cash appeared on the show and implanted the idea of recording for Sun. Ever conscious of security, Orbison continued to study geology, preparing to follow his father into the oil fields if all else failed. One of his contemporaries at North Texas State was Pat Boone, who had been raised in Nashville but had eloped to Texas with Red Foley's daughter (the one certifiably wild-ass move of his life). After a false start on Republic, Boone resumed his recording career for Dot shortly after he arrived in Denton.

"All these people were doing what I wanted to do," recalled Orbison to Dave Booth, "but it seemed as though I was in the wrong place at the right time. I wanted to get a diploma in case I didn't make it in the music business. In the end, though, I decided I didn't want to do anything halfway, so I jumped into the music business."

Orbison and his new group, the Teen Kings, armed themselves with "Ooby Dooby," a song Orbison had acquired from Wade Moore and Dick Penner at North Texas State in Denton. Moore and Penner had written the song in 15 minutes on the flat roof of the frat house at North Texas State. It appears as though it was first recorded in late 1955 during a series of sessions at Norman Petty's studio in Clovis, N.M., together with 12 or 14 other songs. A little later "Ooby Dooby" was re-recorded in Arlington, Texas. An acetate was submitted to Columbia, which later gave it to Sid King. By that point, though, Orbison's original version had appeared on Je-Wel Records.

The exact circumstances by which Orbison was affiliated with Je-Wel are still far from clear. "Je-Wel" was a sort-of-acronym for JE-an Oliver and WELdon Rogers. Rogers was reportedly the first mandolin

player with the Teen Kings. Jean Oliver was his girl-friend and Jean's father, Chester Oliver, underwrote the first Teen Kings session at Petty's studio with some of his oil dollars.

Even stranger was the fact that Orbison recorded "Trying To Get To You" for Je-Wel. Never a real lover of rhythm 'n' blues, Orbison had latched on to an obscure song by the Eagles (that ironically was the first production by Fred Foster, who later owned Monument) and recorded it at roughly the same time that Elvis Presley recorded a version for Sun that remained unissued until 1956. A possible scenario is that Presley sang the tune on one of his forays through Texas and that Orbison learned it from Presley. Orbison used Presley's shuffle rhythm and made the same minor lyrical change as Presley. An additional wrinkle was added to the story when Orbison's Je-Wel cut was leased to Imperial for a B-side to a Weldon Rogers single in 1956.

At the suggestion of Johnny Cash, Orbison approached Sam Phillips at Sun Records, but Phillips rebuffed him, saying, "Johnny Cash doesn't run my record company." However, Orbison had a stronger ally in Cecil Holifield, who operated the Record Shops in Midland and Odessa and had booked Elvis Presley into the area. Holifield sent a copy of the Je-Wel

record to Phillips, who heard something unique in the strangely fragile voice. "My first reaction," recalled Phillips many years later, "was that 'Ooby Dooby' was a novelty type thing that resembled some of the novelty hits from the '30s and '40s. I thought if we got a good cut on it we could get some attention. Even more, I was very impressed with the inflection Roy brought to it. In fact, I think I was more impressed than Roy."

Orbison and the Teen Kings arrived at Sun during March 1956. They re-recorded "Ooby Dooby," but Phillips wanted one of his own copyrights on the flip side, so they cut "Go! Go! Go!," a composition by Orbison and his drummer, Billy Pat Ellis. The coupling was released in May 1956. *Billboard* praised its "spectacular untamed quality" and surmised that it would "cash in for plenty of loot in the rural sectors." In fact, it did good business everywhere, eventually reaching #59 on *Billboard*'s Hot 100 and selling roughly 200,000 copies.

Orbison and the Teen Kings hit the road as part of package shows assembled by Bob Neal. He and Warren Smith, Johnny Cash and Carl Perkins would form a caravan of Cadillacs and tour the mid-South for $100 each a night. "We played all these unbelievable little towns," recalled Orbison to Booth. "We were trying to make stage shows out of one hit record – which is very difficult – so we jumped around onstage like a bunch of idiots. We even had this song called 'The Bug' where we had an imaginary bug we would throw on each other. When it hit you, you had to shake." Trying, as he said, to make a show out of one song, Orbison would begin his segment by playing everyone else's hits and would close with "Ooby Dooby."

By that point, Orbison had developed a fascination for studio work. He moved to Memphis and played sessions at Sun and performed on commercials and radio spots that Sam Phillips continued to engineer just in case the rock 'n' roll craze blew over. Orbison had also started to write prolifically: "I'd write in the car when we were on tour," he recalled to *New Musical Express*. "Even when we'd take a break alongside the road I'd jump on the fender of the car and play the guitar and sing. Then we'd go back (to the studio) and get somebody to turn on the machine and we'd play this thing in some form or another to see if it would make a record." To Orbison's amazement, some of those demos started appearing on Sun anthologies (and have been collated with all the finished Sun masters for a CD on Bear Family).

Like Carl Perkins, Orbison was unable to find a follow-up. He took "Rockhouse," a song that Harold Jenkins (a.k.a. Conway Twitty) had worked up as a theme song for his group, the Rockhousers, and coupled it

JE—WEL
Records
Hi-Fidelity

JE-101-B
BMI - Time: 2:21
Pub. T. N. T.

Vocal
Roy Oribson

OOBY DOOBY
(Moore & Penner)

THE TEEN KINGS

with "You're My Baby." The latter was a Johnny Cash song, originally titled "Little Wooly Booger," that Cash later characterized as "the worst thing I ever conceived in any field." *Billboard* was once again effusive in its praise of Orbison's "sock showmanship" and "Rockhouse" possibly deserved greater success. Released in September 1956, perhaps it was already too countrified and primitive.

Orbison sought to rectify that problem when he returned to the studio to cut his third single, "Sweet And Easy To Love" b/w "Devil Doll." Taking his cue from Elvis and the Jordanaires, Orbison had brought a vocal group, the Roses, in from Texas for the session. "Devil Doll" also allowed Orbison's true musical soul to come up for air for the first time. By this point, Orbison and the Teen Kings had parted company and Roy was working with session musicians and Sun's new engineer, Jack Clement. The change in direction was not a harbinger of renewed acclaim, so Sun's new musical director, Bill Justis, gave Orbison one of his first efforts at rock 'n' roll composition, "Chicken Hearted." It was a novelty song, the quintessential nerd's lament. Released in December 1957, it was Orbison's swan song on Sun.

Orbison was disillusioned at Sun. He was being force-fed a steady diet of rock 'n' roll songs and, with hindsight, came to look askance at the garage mode of recording. "We had to make do," he asserted. "I had to write the songs, sing the songs, arrange the songs and play the guitar. However, out of necessity grew something that has since become very important – music-wise. I'm glad now there was no one to call on." In particular, Orbison delighted in telling the story of

how Sun's engineer, Jack Clement, told him to stay away from the ballads because he would never make it as a ballad singer.

Orbison returned to Texas shortly after "Chicken Hearted" flopped with his new bride, Claudette. She had joined him in Memphis and – for a while – they chastely slept in separate rooms at Sam Phillips' house before their marriage in 1957. However, when the records stopped selling they returned home, although they did so in the "Ooby Dooby" Cadillac.

At Sun, Orbison was one of the many young rockabillies, easily lost in the shuffle after his first surprise hit. It was a legacy that Orbison was hasty to disown but one to which he returned in subtle ways throughout his career. "Neither Elvis nor I thought our work for Sun was any good," he was fond of saying. "Then around 1970, the era of instant history came along. Everybody saw it as a beginning." In one of the least commercially astute moves of his career, Sam Phillips had kept Roy Orbison on a steady diet of rock 'n' roll. Phillips' uncanny ear told him that he had heard something distinctive and unique; arguably, he did not know what to do with it. However, Orbison knew that his talent was being wasted at Sun and events proved him demonstrably correct.

As he returned to Texas though, Orbison was beginning to question whether he wanted to continue as a performer. He admitted to a measure of jealousy over the fact that Buddy Holly had started to score heavily while his own career seemed hopelessly roadblocked. At Sun he had started writing quite prolifically and had scored a fleeting Hot 100 hit for Warren Smith with "So Long I'm Gone" and done considerably better when Jerry Lee Lewis revamped what he could remember of "Go! Go! Go!" as "Down The Line." Orbison also submitted a few songs to the departing Johnny Cash, who refused to submit his own songs because he would receive a higher writer's royalty at Columbia. Cash recorded "You Tell Me" during the final crush of sessions that marked his exit from Sun. And Ken Cook, a protege of Orbison's, from Odessa, Texas, recorded "I Fell In Love," which also sported Orbison's unmistakable harmony vocal.

However, it was the success of "Claudette" that made Orbison's thoughts turn towards writing. "I was back in west Texas," he recalled to *New Musical Express*, "and I stopped by Memphis to put it on tape. Bill Justis was there and he's been a lifelong friend so I expected to get the tape but never did." Two versions of the song were taped. The first (initially released on *The Sun Story*, Phonogram 6641.180) was recorded with only his guitar. Orbison fluffs the lyrics and can be heard muttering "Crap!" to himself. On the second version (released on

Problem Child, Zu-Zazz Z 2006) there is a drummer but Orbison's vocal is still very tentative.

"I'd just about stopped performing but I'd gone to Indiana to do a show with the Everlys," he recalled to *Crawdaddy*, "and everyone was pitching songs to them. I wouldn't do that. I just said hello and was headed for the door when they asked if I had any material. I said I had one song and played them 'Claudette' and they said, 'Write the words down, Roy.' So I tore off this cardboard box top and wrote down the words to 'Claudette.'"

Orbison bought himself out of his Sun contract by signing over all of his copyrights (excluding "Claudette") and went to Nashville to work with Acuff-Rose. It was probably Wesley Rose who secured Orbison his one-year term with RCA that resulted in two singles hitting the market to minimal acclaim. The final session featured two songs, "Paper Boy" and "With The Bug," that went to New York for approval. The head office nixed the single and Orbison was cast adrift once again.

One option that was considered was for Rose to place Orbison on his own Hickory label, but Orbison apparently refused because he saw Hickory as a country label. In the event, he landed on a label with an even lower profile than Hickory. During the last RCA session, Orbison had a conversation with the bassist, Bob Moore, who was buying himself a stake in Monument Records, a small Washington, D.C.-based label. "Roy said RCA was not going to renew his contract," recalled Moore, "so I called Fred Foster, the owner of Monument, and said, 'You know what I heard today? RCA is letting Roy Orbison go.' Fred took the bull by the horns and the next thing I knew we had Orbison signed." Wesley Rose insisted that they re-cut "Paper Boy" as the first single but it did little business.

Back in Texas, Orbison had started writing with Joe Melson, who led a local group called the Cavaliers in Midland. "A mutual friend, Ray Rush, was dealing around in management," recalled Melson, "and he loved my songwriting. I played him a song called 'Raindrops' one night and he said, 'I want you to meet Roy Orbison.' I think Ray wanted to show Roy that someone in that area could write songs besides him. I went to Odessa where they lived with Claudette's mother. They had just released his first record on Monument, 'Paper Boy.' He loved 'Raindrops' and got a dub of it.

"When I was leaving I said, 'Roy, I really love your singing,' and his whole face just brightened up. We became friends right then.

"One night I was at the drive-in and Roy drove up in his Cadillac. I got in his car and we had the normal musicians' conversation. Finally, he said what I wanted him to say. He said, 'You write a pretty good song and I write a pretty good song. I believe if we put it together we could write some great ones.' I said, 'Let's do it.'

"I was studying rhythm 'n' blues at that time and I was studying themes that were selling in the market. We'd ride around in the car and play the pop stations and try to write. We tried for a year." One of Orbison's and Melson's first efforts, "I'm In A Blue, Blue Mood," was later recorded by Conway Twitty and pre-dated much that Orbison later accomplished with its bolero rhythm and melodramatic construction.

After some more false starts, Orbison and Melson came up with the song that would set the stage for his unprecedented success. "We were in adjoining motel rooms in Odessa, trying to write," recalled Melson. "I hit a melody line on the guitar and Roy really liked it. He said, 'That's a real uptown melody. Uptown. Uptown.' We wrote 'Uptown' that night. We moved from rock 'n' roll to class rock right then."

When he came to record "Uptown," Orbison asked Foster if he could use strings. Foster agreed and got Anita Kerr, who arranged strings for television commercials, to write the string parts. They brought in three strings, paired them with Boots Randolph's tenor sax and a vocal chorus led by Melson and Kerr. In order to get clarity and presence on Orbison's voice, Foster's engineer, Bill Porter, placed Orbison behind a coat rack which served as an isolation booth. "When we listened to the playbacks," recalled Melson, "we looked at each other and almost wept because the strings were so pretty."

"Uptown" sold well, peaking halfway up the Hot 100. Looking for a follow-up, Melson showed Orbison a fragment of a song he had been working on called "Only The Lonely." They honed the song to perfection over a period of weeks. "We wrote late at night because that was the lonely time," recalled Melson. By the time they went back to Nashville to record, they had crafted an epic, the first song that truly used the frightening potential of Orbison's voice. Melson led the chorus on a vocal counter-melody, "Dum-dum-dum-dummy-doowah," then Roy Orbison came soaring in with "Only the lonely..." and, in so doing, found his true voice.

Reviewing the *Billboard* charts in 1960, Sam Phillips found three of his departed proteges doing exceptionally well: Johnny Cash, Warren Smith and Roy Orbison. Phillips was already assiduously recycling his Cash repertoire and Orbison's success convinced him that it was time to look through the tape vault and get a little mileage from another departed star.

To his chagrin, Phillips found tape boxes filled almost exclusively with rockers, which had been cut at his behest. He gave the entire stash of tapes to Vinnie Trauth and Scotty Moore, who added some extraneous instruments and a chorus to the masters. They came up with a revised edition of "Devil Doll" for a single and a complete album of doctored masters titled *At The Rockhouse*.

The album justifiably infuriated Orbison, and he went to see Phillips in 1961 and demanded all of his unissued tapes. The tapes that remained at Sun have been prolifically recycled by the Singleton Corporation and their licensees. With hindsight, we can see future success presaged by Orbison's phrasing and delivery on slower songs such as "Trying To Get To You," "This Kind Of Love" and "It's Too Late." However, Phillips' lack of foresight in insisting that Orbison stay with rock 'n' roll is quite undeniable.

Recalling his 1961 meeting with Phillips in a conversation with Nick Kent, Orbison said, "Sam looked at me and smiled and said, 'You'll be back.' His brother Jud was in the room – he just looked at me, rolled his eyes and said, 'The hell he will!'"

Most Collectible 45

"Ooby Dooby"/"Tryin' To Get To You" by the Teen Kings (Vocal, Roy Orbison), Je-Wel 101, $4,000.

Most Collectible LP

Roy Orbison Sings Lonely And Blue, Monument SM-14002, stereo, $600.

Recommended Introduction

For The Lonely: 18 Greatest Hits, Rhino R2-71493 (in addition to 16 of his Monument sides, it has two of his Sun recordings, thus giving the listener a taste of what he was doing in the 1950s)

The All-Time Greatest Hits Of Roy Orbison, Monument/Columbia 45116 or DCC Compact Classics 1118 (a reissue of a 1972 two-LP set, this contains 20 of his greatest Monument recordings)

If you want to hear more...

Roy Orbison: The Sun Years, Rhino R2-70916 (20 of the tracks he recorded for Sun in the 1950s)

The Classic Roy Orbison 1965-68, Rhino R2-70711 (18 tracks he recorded for MGM after his Monument era was over)

The Legendary Roy Orbison, Sony Music Special Products 46809 (a 3-CD set with 75 tracks he recorded for a variety of labels from 1956 through the early 1980s)

Roy Orbison Sings Lonely And Blue, Sony MasterSound/Legacy 66219 (a 24-karat gold disc version of his very first album, one of the great early stereo rock 'n' roll recordings)

Mystery Girl, Virgin 86103 (his last album, finished just before his death, it's a worthy swan song)

Traveling Wilburys, Volume One, Wilbury 25796 (almost criminally, this is out of print, but as it sold 3 million copies, this shouldn't be too hard to find in a used CD shop; Roy's "Not Alone Any More" is one of his finest recordings ever and alone is worth the price)

Gene Pitney

by Dawn Eden

I'm not sure which Gene Pitney song I heard first, but I sure know which one grabbed me and never let go – "It Hurts To Be In Love," his Top 10 hit in 1964, in the midst of the British Invasion. First of all, it starts with those pounding drums. And then the plaintive way he sang that opening line – can any teenager (or adult, for that matter) not relate at some point in their lives? "It hurts to be in love/When the only one you love/Turns out to be someone/Who's not in love with you." Then more drums. This was one of the great records of the 1960s. Exploring deeper into Pitney's repertoire, you find even more gems, including the best song about a movie that should have been its theme, "(The Man Who Shot) Liberty Valance." Goldmine paid tribute to this underrated, under-appreciated talent, who is still around and entertaining thousands, if not millions, of fans around the world, in the October 1, 1993 issue. In 1998, I had the chance to vote on the inductees into the Rock 'n' Roll Hall of Fame for 1999. Gene Pitney was on the ballot. Voting for him was a no-brainer. Unfortunately, it wasn't for enough others, so he's still on the outside. But the guy belongs. Pick up the recommended music at the end of the article and hear why.

In today's necrophiliac rock culture, where reissues by stars like Elvis, Roy Orbison and Del Shannon are far more available now than they were during the artists' lifetimes, Gene Pitney has the dubious honor of being rock's last Great White Singer. No other surviving singer from Pitney's generation can claim his list of successes, which includes:

- Writing major songs for outside artists, including Ricky Nelson, Roy Orbison, Bobby Vee and the Crystals.
- Simultaneously hitting the U.S. pop charts, the English pop charts and the Italian pop charts - with four different songs.
- Playing the Grand Ole Opry with such country greats as Buck Owens.
- Working closely with a wide range of talented writers and producers, including Phil Spector, the Rolling Stones, Burt Bacharach and Hal David, Dmitri Tiomkin, Randy Newman, Al Kooper and all of the Brill Building greats (Mann/Weil, Goffin/King, Miller/Greenfield, etc.).
- Racking up gold records around the world, including two in the last five years (for the 1989 duo with Marc Almond "Something's Gotten Hold Of My Heart" and the 1990 U.K. compilation album *Backstage – The Greatest Hits And More*).
- Taking both the #1 and the #2 spots on the *Billboard* Hot 100 for one week – one with a song he sang, the other with a song he wrote.
- And, finally, earning the adulation of intensely devoted fans around the globe, who keep his fan club busy and keep him on the road six months out of every year.

The man with the sensuous lips, quavering voice and powerful pop sense was born Gene Francis Allan Pitney on February 17, 1941, and grew up in Rockville, Connecticut. His family loved music, and music was always present in his house. Especially talented in that area was his mother, who played piano by ear and was a world-class whistler. (That must be where Pitney acquired his own talent for whistling, which he later displayed on "Only Love Can Break A Heart.")

Although Pitney studied music at parochial school and sang in the church choir, he never intended to become a performer. As he later related to Spencer Leigh in the liner notes for his See For Miles disc *The EP Collection*, "I was pretty much a loner, and if you had told me that I was going to end up singing to millions of people, you would have seen the dust as I was running down the road away from you."

Pitney elaborated on his youthful shyness to *Goldmine*: "When I was a kid, I used to sit out on the front porch with a copy of *Hit Parader,* the magazine that printed the lyrics of the hits of the day, and I used to sit there and sing, just in my natural tenor. I later found out that people used to sit outside and listen. I didn't know it, because they wouldn't let themselves be seen. If I had known it, that would have been the end of it – I would have been gone!"

By the time Pitney entered adolescence, in the early 1950s, he was hooked on pop radio. "When I really started loving music," he recalls, "was when the black groups came about in the '50s, with what I think was the fusion of R&B with country that made the original rock 'n' roll. It was groups like the Flamingos, the Orioles, the Spaniels and the Penguins."

Music was not Pitney's only hobby. He was also an avid trapper, catching minks and other small game. Perhaps it was his abundance of experience with rodents that prepared him for the music business types whom he would encounter later on. Unfortunately, this experience gave him no defense against his most difficult predator at the time, yardstick-wielding nuns. "I remember being in the playground at the parochial school I went to," Pitney says, " and the nun from my class came over to me and she said, 'You've been selected to be one of the four altar boys for the rest of the school year.' I knew this was coming, I had an inkling. I said, 'I'm sorry, Sister, but I can't do that because I have to check my traps. It's a law; I have to check my traps at four o'clock in the morning. I can't go to Mass.' She broke her yardstick in half right over the top of my head." Obviously, she was not a fan of the Trappist order.

It wasn't until Pitney entered high school that he began to toy with the idea of performing. He bought a guitar, took some lessons, and formed a band. Gene Pitney and the Genials, who performed at local record hops. A manager spotted Pitney at a Genials gig and offered him a recording deal. Since duos were popular at the time, Pitney was paired with a female singer, Ginny Mazarro (later Ginny Arnell of "Dumb Head" fame), and the two released two singles on Decca in 1959 under the name Jamie and Jane.

After the Jamie and Jane singles flopped, Pitney was briefly pressured by a manager to adopt another pseudonym, Billy Bryan, under which he recorded his first four solo numbers. (After Pitney became successful, those songs – "Cradle Of My Love", "Please Come Back To Me Baby" and "I'll Find You" – turned up on several budget compilations under his real name.)

After the Billy Bryan venture fared no better than Jamie and Jane, Pitney decided to concentrate upon songwriting. In 1960, he quit the University of Connecticut, where he was studying electronics, and made the first of several trips to New York City to find a music publisher. He found a simpatico ear in publisher Aaron Schroeder, who took Pitney under his wing and helped him enter the field of professional songwriting. The Kalin Twins were the first to record a Pitney song, with the 1960 disc "Loneliness." Several major recordings soon followed, including "Tomorrow Is A-Comin'" by Clyde McPhatter, "Today's Teardrops" (the B-side of the million-selling "Blue Angel") by Roy Orbison, "Rubber Ball" (which Pitney originally wrote as "Rubber Band") by Bobby Vee, and "Hello Mary Lou" by Ricky Nelson.

In January 1961, Gene Pitney finally had a hit of his own with a recording that was originally intended as a song demo: "(I Wanna) Love My Life Away." To save money, Pitney played nearly all of the instruments on the song, as well as overdubbing his own voice on it several times. While the song edged into the U.S. Top 40 at #39, it also began Pitney's British career, reaching #26 on the U.K. chart.

"(I Wanna) Love My Life Away" was released by Musicor, a label created by United Artists especially for the promising young singer. In fact, Musicor had such faith in Pitney that, after his second single, "Take Me Tonight," missed the charts entirely, it paid for a pull-out-all-the-stops orchestral session for his third single, to get him back in the spotlight. The result of the session was the Gerry Goffin/Carole King song "Every Breath I Take," one of the first chart records produced by Phil Spector, and one of the earliest examples of Spector's Wall of Sound.

Pitney followed "Every Breath I Take" in the fall of 1961 with his biggest single yet, "Town Without Pity," the theme from the film of the same name, written by noted movie composers Ned Washington (words) and Dmitri Tiomkin (music). While that song was nominated for an Academy Award, Pitney's next single, "(The Man Who Shot) Liberty Valance" wasn't even used in the movie for which it was written. Nevertheless, "Liberty Valance" continued Pitney's upward chart trend, hitting #4 in the spring of 1962.

Gene Pitney positively ruled *Billboard*'s Hot 100 during the week of November 3, 1962, when he was at #2 with "Only Love Can Break A Heart" and the Crystals were keeping his disc from the top spot with his own composition, "He's A Rebel." Like "(The Man Who Shot) Liberty Valance," "Only Love Can Break A Heart" was penned by Burt Bacharach and Hal David.

As 1963 rolled around, Pitney remained near the top of the American pop charts with hits including "Mecca" and "Half Heaven – Half Heartache." However, his U.K. sales were slipping, so in November he went to England to promote his latest single, the Bacharach-David tune "Twenty Four Hours From Tulsa," which was already succeeding in America. While in England, Pitney's U.K. publicist, Andrew

Loog Oldham, introduced him to a group Oldham was managing, the Rolling Stones. The group and Pitney became friendly, and Pitney agreed to record the Mick Jagger/Keith Richard composition "That Girl Belongs To Yesterday." The single, released in January 1964, reached the U.K. Top 10. While it only hit #49 in the States, it made rock history as the first Rolling Stones composition ever to hit the American charts.

At the same time that Pitney's recording of "That Girl Belongs To Yesterday" was making its mark in America, Pitney was back in England, sitting in on piano at a session for the Rolling Stones' first LP, which was also attended by Phil Spector and, reportedly, Graham Nash. Pitney played away on "Little By Little," which became the U.K. B-side of "Not Fade Away," as well as several impromptu jams which were not released.

Years later, he told the story of the session in the January 1983 issue of *Goldmine* (his only other *Goldmine* interview to date): "I was on my way back from Paris and stopped over in London for one day. Andrew Loog Oldham called and asked if I could come to the recording studio where the Stones were working on a follow-up to 'I Wanna Be Your Man.' He was in a little bit of a panic because Decca had wanted the song, like, yesterday.

"Andrew told me that he had the guys in the studio, but it was one of those days when nobody was talking to each other. So I told him that I would try to help out. I jumped into a cab and got to the studio on Denmark Street. Now, who's outside in his big Rolls-Royce? None other than Phil Spector...Anyhow, Phil and I both ended up inside. As I recall, I had five fifths of cognac with me, which was the duty-free limit. We made up some fabricated story about it being my birthday and that it was a characteristic thing in my family to celebrate with a glass of cognac. In the end, they all got a little tipsy and made up with each other. I believe Phil played on an empty cognac bottle with a half-dollar."

During this, Pitney's most productive period, he succeeded in a dizzying variety of markets. Not only did he record his hits in foreign languages such as Italian, German and Spanish, he also recorded material that was specifically written for those countries' markets. In addition, at the encouragement of Musicor, he recorded successful duets with two of the label's country acts, George Jones and Melba Montgomery.

Although the British Invasion set many American acts grumbling, Pitney continued to have hits throughout 1964, including the Top 10 smashes "It Hurts To Be In Love" (written by New York talents Howie Greenfield and Helen Miller) and "I'm Gonna Be Strong" (written by Barry Mann and Cynthia Weil just prior to composing "You've Lost That Lovin' Feelin'.") One of the reasons that Pitney was able to get such top-rate material was that, whenever he had a recording session approaching, he made it a point to go into publishers' offices himself and have them present songs to him. He sought nothing short of perfection.

Although "I'm Gonna Be Strong" was Pitney's last American Top 10 hit of the '60s, he continued to make the Hot 100 chart through the end of that decade, occasionally hitting the Top 40 with songs including "Last Chance To Turn Around" and the 1968 R&B/rocker "She's A Heartbreaker" (written by Charlie Foxx and Jerry "Swamp Dogg" Williams). Contrary to the liner notes of Rhino Records' Pitney CD, he never sunk to recording the Shirley Temple number "Animal Crackers (In My Soup)." The liner-notes writer was probably thinking of Pitney's 1967 single, written by "Happy Together" authors Gary Bonner and Alan Gordon, "Animal Crackers (In Cellophane Boxes)."

In England and elsewhere around the world, Pitney's records were still going strong well into the '70s. One song, "Something's Gotten Hold Of My Heart," actually hit twice, first in 1967, when Pitney took it into the U.K. Top 10, and then in 1989, when Soft Cell member Marc Almond re-recorded it as a duet with Pitney. The 1989 version sold three million copies, hitting #1 in England and just about everywhere else in the world – except for the U.S., that is, where Almond's label, EMI, inexplicably refused to release it.

Although Gene Pitney has always maintained a strong presence in Europe, Australia and Asia, he has toured America comparatively little since his '60's heyday. This unintended obscurity caused him to become the subject of "Where Are They Now" pieces, as well as a brief entry in Norm N. Nite's purportedly authoritative tome *Rock On* describing Pitney as a hermit. Earlier this year, Pitney performed at New York City's Carnegie Hall, intending to both end the hermit confusion and test the waters for a large-scale American comeback. Concert promoters had long been pursuing Pitney to play the Big Apple, but he held out until a gig at Carnegie Hall could be arranged. His instincts proved wise, for the show that he put on there sounded far better than the type of arena or high school auditorium package concerts to which oldies fans have become resigned. It was Pitney's first time at the venue, and his first area show that anyone could recall in at least two decades. It sold out.

The following interview with Gene Pitney was conducted in June 1993.

Goldmine: A journalist would be hard pressed to find another major hit maker who has been involved in as many different cross-currents of rock 'n' roll as you.

Gene Pitney: I think that's been beneficial and a problem for me. I went out purposely to do that, because I love the challenge of just trying all those different avenues. But I think when you do that, sometimes you spread yourself very thin.

But it seems that over the years you've managed to find a kind of balance.

Oh, it's been terrific for me. What I mean by that, like, let's say with the foreign language thing: When you go into a country and you create a market for yourself in their language, that's all great when you first do it. But then you realize that in order to keep it up, that added another LP, another set of material that I had to go through, a whole new set of producers and writers and people that were creating the product for only, say, Italy. It just added on top of everything else you had to do. A lot of the successes I had in Europe were the songs that were different than the songs that were in the States. As a result, the same thing happened (as in Italy).

According to the liner notes of the 1968 double album The Gene Pitney Story, at one point you had four different songs on the charts in three different countries.

Yeah, that's right. It's great, until you realize what a workload that adds. By the time I would get back from some of those foreign tours – which would be back-to-back, I'd go around the world and come back – when I got back to New York, I'd be, like, two LPs behind. So that made it tough.

When I mentioned cross-currents earlier, I was also thinking of how, unlike a lot of other pop singers of your era who mainly did songs that were brought them by their producers, you picked most of your writers, and among them were so many greats. A collector perusing your albums will find songs by not only Randy Newman and Al Kooper, but also Mike D'Abo – before he hit with Rod Stewart's "Handbags And Gladrags" – and even one song you did, "Lips Are Redder On You," by legendary English producer Joe Meek (writer of "Telstar").

That was a really weird choice. I had no idea who Joe Meek was. I never, ever, saw the guy or ran into him. I remember him sending a very nice note thanking me for recording the song, and that was it.

I was very lucky, because the majority of these people were just fledgling songwriters – they were out there, just trying to make a name for themselves – and they've all since become names. But at the time when I was looking for songs, the Mann and Weils and Goffin and Kings and the Meeks and D'Abos and people like that were all just struggling songwriters.

How did you come to be on the Musicor label?

After I recorded "(I Wanna) Love My Life Away," Aaron Schroeder listened to it and said, "You know, I think this could be a hit just like it its." I had listened

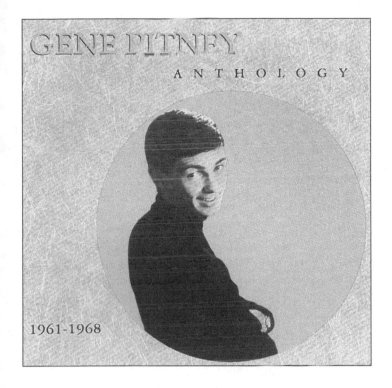

GENE PITNEY

ANTHOLOGY

1961-1968

to it purely as a demo to present to somebody to record. Aaron set up an appointment with Art Talmadge, who was the president of United Artists, and I went over with him, sat down, played some songs for Art, and we played him some of the songs we had cut as demos. That afternoon, Art asked me, "Would you feel more comfortable being signed to United Artists, where there are a lot of other people in the stable, or do you think it would be better if we created a label to cater to yourself?" So that's why Musicor came about.

Looking at the albums you did for the label, it seems like Musicor put a low priority on such things as programming and design.

They weren't very good packagings. The only thing that I can say for my side of it was that I worked really hard to make sure that the songs weren't just filler, that they all had some strength to them. For an example of how the label operated: I had an apartment for quite a few years at the top of Seventh Avenue, right on Central Park, and the guy that I shared it with was from the William Morris Agency. I was in the apartment one night, and he was roaring laughing. I said, "What are you laughing at?" He said, "Have you listened to your new LP?" He had just gotten it that day from Musicor. I had heard it, so I said, "What's wrong with it?" It was a phony live LP, and they'd hired a guy like Murray the K to say, "And here he is now –" Well, when he did this whole spiel and introduced me, the crowd started to roar. My roommate played it for me and said, "Did you ever hear the bell?" I said, "What bell are you talking about?" He put the record back on. They didn't have a crowd noise

tape in the studio, so they used a fight crowd! The gong for the round goes off, and then you realizes it's all the guys in the background going, "YUHHHH! Hit him again!" It's kind of indicative of the packaging that Musicor did.

Upon listening to records like "If I Didn't Have A Dime (To Play The Jukebox)," it seems that, although you liked tunes that have a dramatic build, you also liked material that had a haunting, inexorable type of rhythm.

Oh, probably more so. I loved the big builds, but things like "If I Didn't Have A Dime" just had a great little hook about them. The guy who wrote that song, Bert Berns (a.k.a. Bert Russell), came in to my office and sang that song to me. He had an acoustic guitar, and when he strummed the guitar, he also hit the box of the guitar – with his ring, I think it was – and it was the greatest sound. I said, "Look, I'll record it, but you gotta come and play," and that's him playing on the session.

Your 1964 smash "It Hurts To Be In Love" is similar to your first hit, "(I Wanna) Love My Life Away," in that you managed to overdub your own voice so many times, without losing sound quality.

You have a good ear, because both songs were done at Dick Charles Recording Studios in New York City. You know, I never ever thought of that – that they were done at the same place and they do have the same sound. "(I Wanna) Love My Life Away" was originally intended as a demo. There were two or three studios that we used for demos, and Dick Charles was one of them because of that great sound they had.

Why was there no production credit on most of your '60s records?

Aaron Schroeder, being a half-owner of Musicor and also my publisher, was the overseer of everything. He had producer's status, but it was not necessary for him to have a credit.

Did you have an influence in choosing the musical arrangers for your recordings?

Oh yes, I had an awful lot of input, probably more than anybody around at the time. I've always said that I think 95 percent of the time that we spent on a session was pre-production. The other five percent was when we got into the studio. It was all thought out and all laid out and hashed over and over again on piano, guitar or whatever.

In relation to the arrangers, there were certain people that I felt very comfortable with, and they got to know me very well. Garry Sherman did an awful lot of things, one of them being "I'm Gonna Be Strong." He was just the right guy. Before the session, I would sit down with Garry – or, if I was out of the country, I'd get on the telephone with him – and I would go over the whole song and explain to him how I thought it should be done. And then, the majority of the time, we would click mentally and he would be able to put what I was looking for down on paper so that it would come out well in the studio. But there were certain times when I had great songs and the minute you heard them played in the studio you knew they didn't have a chance.

There were certain times when it was really terrible, because there were songs I knew were out-and-out winners. One was "Follow The Sun." It was an LP track, but the reason it was that was because it was relegated to an LP track. It should have been a single, and it should have been a great song. Another was a song that I wrote, "Save Your Love." Sometimes, it would really go so wrong.

One the other hand, Garry did brilliant things with songs that nobody really liked at all. I had to fight so hard to get a Randy Newman song called "Just One Smile" done. Randy Newman used to make these horrible demos. He was a very eccentric guy, and they couldn't get him into the studio, so he would always do his own demos on a tape recorder at home. When he did them, he would leave several bars in between each line of the song and it stretched everything out so bad. I heard "Just One Smile," and I kinda lived with it, and I got it down pat on the piano, and I started to condense 'cause I knew there was something there, and everybody hated it. The producer hated it. The arranger hated it. Everybody tried to talk me out of it, and I put my foot down and I said, "No. There's a great song here somewhere." And when I got into the studio, Garry Sherman again had transferred it into an arrangement and got all the right pieces.

It seems like, as well as having an ear for melody, you really had an ear for lyrics. There was something very intense going on lyrically in that song.

I did a show in London with Randy Newman a couple of years ago and he asked me, "Do you ever sing my old songs?" I said, "They're two of the best things I ever do on stage ("Just One Smile" and Nobody Needs Your Love")." I have them in most every show, in the countries where they were successful. That was his best period of time, because, like a lot of writers that write novels and things like that, when you're hungry and when you're depressed, anguished, whatever it is that drives you – that's when you write your best things, and he definitely was at that period of time.

Speaking of great songwriters, it's surprising that you've never done any of Jimmy Webb's songs, considering how his material seems so well suited to your style.

Well (chuckles), I can only go back to relate a story to you. When Richard Harris hit with Jimmy Webb's "MacArthur Park," I happened to have been in Europe on a tour. The *Sun* newspaper group called me from London. They were calling up any artists that they could get their hands on and asking them the question, "Why do you like 'MacArthur Park'?" Well, I told them I never did like it. And they said, "Oh, well, you're no good to us then." They only wanted positive answers!

I give Jimmy Webb all the credit for what he's done and all the success he's had, but it's just like – I remember the day that I was out cutting the grass and someone said Australia was on the telephone. I came in, I huffed and puffed up to the phone, and it was a guy that I knew very well, calling from Melbourne, Australia, and he said, "What did you think of Elvis?" and I thought, what a strange thing for a man to ask, calling me from Australia in the middle of the afternoon. And I said, "Y'know, I was never really that impressed. I was not a great Elvis fan." And then all of a sudden he stopped me and he said, "Do you know what's happened?" And I said, "Well, I've been out cutting the grass for about three hours. No, to be honest with you." He said, "Elvis had died."

The two people that you're mentioning – Jimmy Webb's songs, and Elvis as a performer – never had the depth of the people that I liked, a lot of people who were obscure. Clyde McPhatter was one of my favorites, just a unique individual, in his own pattern, not following after anybody else.

Both Webb and Presley had a lot of substance, but it got drenched in hype. I think that you're probably so turned off by hype that it turns you off from whatever substance is there.

Yes, you're exactly right. You can quote that part from yourself.

Thank you! In 1965, you told Melody Maker *that you recorded the single "Princess In Rags" because you were tired of the "big climax" productions for which you were known and wanted to do something different before returning to formula with your next single. It's fascinating that you took the reins of your career to such an extent, that you could actually predict the public tastes and not follow up a hit song with another that sounded exactly like it.*

I had to do that, because all of a sudden those big ballads became a trademark that was totally associated with me, to the point where, if I asked somebody who was writing songs for a session, "Have you got everything," every song I got was something with big, huge notes in it and it would climb. They were all the same type of thing and I hated that, because I hate to get stereotyped like that.

"Princess In Rags" was one of the hardest times I ever had trying to get a single out. I was in Australia doing a tour, and I finished the tour in Perth, which is at the far west side of Australia. I had to get back to New York in order to do the recording session that

"Princess In Rags" was on as quickly as I could so that they could finish the session, master it, and get it over to England where I was going to start on tour within 10 days or so. When I checked about getting back to New York, the quickest way to go was not the normal way, through Honolulu, because the flight had a one-day layover somewhere. The easiest way was to go through the Far East, through Europe, through London, and back to New York. It would only save me 17 hours, but it was worth it.

The flight took off and the pilot came on the loudspeaker. We were flying over the Australian desert, and he said, "Ladies and gentlemen, this is your captain speaking, and I have no idea where we're going." Two wars had just started – one was between Malaysia and Indonesia, and the other was elsewhere in Europe – and he had to be told where he could land without being shot down. We went to Columbo, Ceylon; Jakarta, Indonesia; up the Adriatic to Vienna, from there to Frankfurt and from there to London. All this time, we're losing the 17-hour gain that I was supposed to get. By the time we got there, I was into my second day of flying. From London, I got to New York. Thank God, a guy from my management agency met me there. He took a look at me and said, "What the hell happened to you?" I was a crumpled wreck. He took me into the city and put me in a hotel by Seventh Avenue. Every other room in the city was taken up by conventioners, and this was the only place they could get me into. "Look, I don't care what kind of place it is, just get me a bed!"

I got into the room, and it was the old style architecture, where my window as directly across from another window that was probably no more than 15 or 20 feet away. As I went to pull my shade down, I looked out and there in the window looking across at me was a woman about 25, stark naked, standing up in the window. I thought I'd snapped. I couldn't figure this out at all. I was so tired, but I had to figure out why she was doing that. She had a man over, and I could hear the conversation from her room. What had happened was that she had tried to pull the window shade down, and it snapped, and she had to get a chair to pull it down, so she was standing on that chair when I looked out.

The next morning, I got up and went to Mira-Sound studios. When I got there, they were taking out the engineer, Brooks Arthur, and putting him into an ambulance. I couldn't believe it. I asked the producer, "What happened to him?" He said that Brooks had an inner ear infection and couldn't sit up. Every time he'd sit up, he'd throw up. I said, "Man, you've got to do something. This is an important session." They actually got Brooks to go back in again and try to do the session, but he was just a wreck. So now I had all these musicians, all these songs, and no engineer, in a studio that Brooks designed.

They brought a guy in from the Columbia Studios. As we recorded the songs, we listened back to them, and I wondered why I couldn't hear certain instruments. It turned out that those instruments weren't even connected to the board! So, "Princes In Rags" was the best of what came out of the session. It's very thin – not because the musicians weren't there, but because they never got on tape!

How did you get your next hit, "Backstage"? Its writers, Ansfield and Denson, are pretty obscure.

Freddy Ansfield came in and played that song for me and I loved it. I thought, boy, that really does depict the situation backstage; it's exactly what happens. I wanted to record it, but right after that Freddy had a mental breakdown and when he did, everything that he owned or controlled became inaccessible – you couldn't use it. Years later, I saw Freddy walking down the street. He looked great. I said to him, "Hey, how ya doin'? You still got that song?" and he said, "Yup." That's when we jumped in and recorded it. He wrote another song which I loved, "Where Did The Magic Go," which I recorded at the same session as "The Flower Girl."

When you performed last February at Carnegie Hall, your first New York City performance in 20 years, audience members wondered beforehand if you could still hit the high notes.

I love that, because I know what I can do. Actually, I think, in some ways, I can do better now than I could ever do in the '60s.

I felt that way when I heard you live, because your voice sounds fuller. It's lost some of the...I hate to say this –

I know what you're gonna say: the high-pitched nasal sound.

Yeah!

Definitely! I love it, because I used to hate that myself. It's rounded out, which I much prefer.

Would you like to express a message to your fans who will be reading this interview?

Just say, even though a lot of people in this country think so, I've never, ever been away. I've always been out there performing. Thank God everything still works; the pipes are probably better than they were before.

I'll be back out on the road soon with new original songs, not to capitalize on anything that was successful before. This is purely the tough route, because this is purely going out there to compete on a contemporary basis with what's out there today, and it's difficult – doubly difficult if you've got a track record that dates back to the '60s. A lot of disc jockeys will listen to something that's new material that you're putting out to compete in the contemporary market, and they'll say, "Yeah, it's very, very good, but it doesn't sound like what I know Gene Pitney to be like." But if you do something that sound like Gene Pitney, they'll say it sounds dated. It's an interesting game to play. I think we're going to beat it completely, because I knew that the only way I could go out and compete is to do it with songs that are so strong that *anybody* could record them and have a hit with them.

You've got a unique vantage point from which to measure things. Being a rock star is like being Peter Pan; the public wants you to be a child forever, not just in terms of looks, but also in terms of romantic outlook, because they don't want to grow up. Although you've been placed in that role, you balance it with the side of yourself that is grown-up and sees things from an adult perspective.

Fortunately, I agree with everything you're saying, you're right on the money with all of that. The only thing that I think that I still have is what an old friend of mine, the English songwriter Roger Cook ("Something's Gotten Hold Of My Heart") used to always say: "I've still got a little bit of the boy in me." I think that's important. You have to retain that.

Most Collectible 45

"Going Back To My Love"/ "Cradle Of My Arms," by Billy Bryan (early alias), Blaze 351, $30.

Most Collectible LP

The Many Sides Of Gene Pitney, Musicor MM-2001, mono, brown label, $50.

Recommended Introduction

For the absolute minimum at a bargain price:
Best Of Gene Pitney, Laserlight 12421 (list priced at $5.97, it has 10 of his biggest hits, and they are the original Musicor recordings)

If you want to hear more...

Anthology 1961-1968, Rhino R2-75896 (16 tracks, issued in the late 1980s, this has been largely superseded by the next entry on the list)

25 All-Time Greatest Hits, Varese Vintage 6002 (issued in 1999)

More Greatest Hits, Varese Vintage 5569 (19 tracks not on the Rhino *Anthology,* including the 1989 U.K. hit with Mark Almond, "Something's Gotten Hold Of My Heart," which is rarely heard in America)

For even more, the Sequel label from the U.K. has reissued most of his original 1960s albums on CD as twofers; at least nine of these exist.

Del Shannon

by Dawn Eden

Who says that rock 'n' roll was dead in the early 1960s? Just listen to Del Shannon's music sometime. "Runaway," with its eerie proto-synthesizer sound and paranoid lyrics, was one of the spookiest No. 1 songs ever. Shannon also had a keen ear for a good song: When he was in England in 1963, he was on a bill with The Beatles. He heard their new single, as yet unreleased in America, and decided to make it his next. That song was "From Me To You." It briefly made the Hot 100, outdoing the Beatles' own version, at least until full scale Beatlemania broke out in 1964. He was highly influential to the next several generations of rockers; it's said that Mark Knopfler of Dire Straits decided to take up the guitar after seeing Del Shannon perform, and there was some talk that he would replace Roy Orbison in the Traveling Wilburys after Orbison's passing. Finally, Shannon was inducted into the Rock and Roll Hall of Fame in 1999. Alas, he did not live to see the honor he so richly deserved. Goldmine did one of the last interviews ever with Shannon, and the result was this piece that appeared in the March 23, 1990 issue, just over a month after he took his own life.

When Del Shannon died, on February 8, 1990, countless people felt that they had lost a kindred soul. Anyone who has ever been rejected by a loved one can identify with the timeless sentiments that Shannon expressed in such hits as "Runaway" and "Little Town Flirt."

Shannon's suicide was also felt as the loss of one of the last original self-contained rockers. Popular rock singers from his era commonly subsist by doing lounge-style performances of their own and other artists' hits. Unlike those performers, Shannon's live shows were dominated by fiery versions of songs that he himself made famous. He strived to remain true to himself, keeping old fans at the same time that he converted new ones. In this way, he avoided a time-warp mentality, always remaining true to the original spirit of rock 'n' roll.

This writer, an avowed fan of Shannon's music, interviewed him on May 13, 1989, on the night that he performed at an oldies concert in Fairfax, Virginia. At the time, Shannon was trying to escape from a quandary in which he had been trapped for nearly 30 years. It all began with "Runaway," his first and most successful single. "Runaway" hit #1 on the *Billboard* chart in April 1961 and stayed on top for four weeks. Its haunting chord changes influenced countless other musicians, from the Beatles on down. Cover versions of the song number in the hundreds and still crack the Top 100 periodically.

Unfortunately, as happens all too often in the music business, Shannon's biggest success became an equally large jinx. His post-"Runaway" career was spent trying to convince audiences that he still had something to say. He was different from the pre-fabricated "Bobbys" of his era (Rydell, Vee, et. al.) in that he was a "singer-songwriter" before there was such a term. The thought of him in recent years, playing oldies tours with those same Bobbys, is almost as insane as if Paul, George and Ringo headlined a Richard Nader "Garden Party."

At the time of this interview, Shannon was once again trying to escape his fate as an oldie performer, this time via his most exciting musical collaboration in years. He was recording an album produced by Tom Petty's Heartbreakers guitarist Mike Campbell and receiving generous musical help from Petty and ELO's Jeff Lynne. He had previously worked with Lynne and Petty separately, but never with the two, of them together. Now, after the duo's success with the Traveling Wilburys, and with Petty's Lynne-produced *Full Moon Fever* racing up the charts, the timing of their collaboration with Shannon seemed ideal. The first fruits of their labor, the superbly commercial "Walk Away," had just been released in Australia (RCA/BMG Records), and Shannon hoped to soon obtain an American deal.

The interview began backstage as Shannon waited for his call to perform. He was visibly pleased to discuss his musical history with someone who was familiar with more than his biggest hits. As the interview progressed, it became more like a conversation. This was, in this writer's opinion, partly because he wanted readers to have a deeper understanding of him, and partly because he simply enjoyed discussing his music. Considering how many interviews he must have done, he was surprisingly non-jaded.

That night, in appearance as well, Shannon looked more like he was about to open for John Mellencamp than close an oldies show. His image, like his music, was that of the eternal rocker. His full head of brown hair (mysteriously thicker than in his younger days) trailed almost to his shoulders, with not a hint of grease. Although he was nearing 50, when he got excited about a subject his face would take on an expression of childlike wonder. His wide eyes and wider smile projected an aura of innocence that was almost disarming. It was easy to picture him as the 21-year-old kid who wrote "Runaway."

About a half-hour into the interview, Shannon was called on stage. One would have assumed that this would have spelled the end of the interview. However, because of Shannon's aforementioned willingness to share his story, he continued the interview after the show. For a performer who had just played for a crowd of several thousand, this was above and beyond the call of duty, and was even more proof of his dedication.

Del Shannon was born Charles Westover on December 30, 1939 (according to most official accounts; others list the year as 1934), in Coopersville, Mich., the son, of a truck driver. He began singing and playing guitar while in his teens. He honed his musical skills while stationed in the U.S. Army in Germany, where he performed on the *Get Up And Go* radio program. Upon his return to his home state, in 1959, he formed his first band, the Midnight Ramblers. They soon took residence at Battle Creek's Hi-Lo club. "It seated 400 people," Shannon said. "We had a regular gig – four nights a week." The band played mostly country songs by the likes of Lefty Frizzell and Carl Smith.

At the time that Shannon was in the Midnight Ramblers, he worked by day as a salesman in a carpet store. He admitted that he didn't give his all to that job: "I didn't sell too many carpets. I hated to do anything but play music, and to survive I had to do a night job with the band and work in the day trying to sell carpets. But the carpet job was easy, really, because customers would come in and then they would leave, and the guy sold them bad carpet anyway. (When customers came in to complain) the boss would hide under the desk. He said, 'Don't tell them I'm here!' I was so embarrassed working there."

One patron of the Hi-Lo club claimed that he was going to be a famous wrestler – "Mark Shannon, the wrestler." Charles Westover liked the surname and decided to use it as his own. "Del" is a contraction of Coupe DeVille, a car he liked at the time.

Shannon married his first wife, Shirley, while both were still in their teens. "It was a secret," he said. The marriage lasted 27 years. Shannon briefly explained why the two did not stay together. "She left about four years ago (1985); said she didn't know who she was. But now I'm happily remarried to a girl, LeAnne. She loves rock 'n' roll. See, (when) my first wife married me, she didn't know that I was gonna be ... she always thought I had these dreams, but never thought I ... (she thought), 'Aw, he's just a guitar player in Coopersville, and he'll grow out of it.'" During the Midnight Ramblers' residency at the Hi-Lo, Shannon was discovered by local disc jockey Ollie McLaughlin, who helped launch his recording career. "Ollie found me," Shannon recalled. "Strange how you get started in the business. First your mother likes your music. Then you go get a band and the drummer falls off his stool one night. It was some song I was writing and he said, 'My God, I can't believe this song. It's unbelievable!' And he threw up his sticks. That was a great inspiration, because no one would ever say, 'Love your music,' and drop their drums! Then he said, 'I know this guy, Max Crook, and he plays this weird, funny machine; get him down here.' I said, 'I don't want a piano player, man.' He said, 'Just try him.' So (Crook) came in and played that silly machine, and I hired him right away."

Crook's Musitron was a forerunner of the synthesizer, an unusual kind of organ whose trebly notes contributed substantially to "Runaway's" success. (Crook also played keyboards on Shannon's most successful outside production, Brian Hyland's 1970 hit "Gypsy Woman.")

Shannon recalled that Crook's father was a brain surgeon. "Max was a classic," he said. "I never saw him take a drink in his life. He used to drink Kool-Aid with cookies. He was a great baseball freak. He'd listen to the ball game in one ear and play the piano with the other. (When on stage) he had this big box of Kleenex. Every 10 songs, he would blow his nose. He hated smoke. He was just unbelievable, but he loved to play music.

"We did a little gig for a friend of ours' birthday party about a year ago (1988). Max came and we had a drummer and a bass player. He played the same old keyboard – still got it.

"(Crook) knew Ollie (McLaughlin). He said, 'Let's get Ollie down here (to the Hi-Lo) to record your songs.' I said, 'Well, we better bring him on a Saturday afternoon,' because he was black and there were no blacks (allowed) in the club."

McLaughlin produced demos of Shannon's songs and played them for Harry Balk and Irving Micahnik, who signed Shannon to their Big Top label. Balk and Micahnik quickly sent Shannon to New York to record his material. However, after these recordings failed to yield suitably commercial songs, Shannon soon was back to playing the Hi-Lo. It was there, in front of an audience, that he unexpectedly composed the music to what would be his first single.

It was a scene worthy of Hollywood. Crook happened across a chord progression that struck Shannon's fancy. Shannon asked Crook to keep playing it over and over, while Shannon worked out a melody. "We played it for about 15 minutes," Shannon said. "Got in trouble with the manager, too, who finally came up on the stage and told us we were nuts: 'Stop playing this! What are you doing?'"

Shannon completed the song's lyrics the next day while working at the carpet store. The inspiration came from closer to home than one might assume, "I ran away from myself, just wanting to get out of that town," he explained. "I think everybody wants to run away. That's why that song seems to live on.

"I wanted to run away from the environment. I always want to run away from A to B, and then I get to B and I wanna go back to A. I suppose everybody's like that, so that's probably why – I write songs sometimes as neurotics. People are neurotics – the batch of new songs I'm just writing now are still neurotic songs. I still write (in) the same, simple form of writing.

"... A lot of my songs come from past experience, but then I'll add some flair to make them commercial so they sell. I don't really write songs so (that) they don't sell. I like to write songs that will sell. I'm a businessman. But still I know some won't. But I really strive to be commercial. I love pop, Top 40 music. Like hooks – I love bridges and hooks."

Possibly Shannon's largest contribution to the evolution of modern rock hits was his usage of the A-minor key. Most of his original hits, from "Runaway," began in this haunting key and shifted into a tension-releasing G-major key for the chorus. (For proof of how this style was influential, there are countless examples; one need look no further than the Beatles' "I'll Be Back.")

When asked why the key of A-minor held such a special appeal for him, Shannon replied, "It's sad, and it can set up a mystery. 'Stranger In Town' is kind of a mystery song ... I like minor chords. I learned it from

Hank Williams, who went from minor to major in 'Kaw-Liga.' I don't think I was more inspired by a song by Hank Williams than 'Kaw-Liga.'"

After the lyrics to "Runaway" were complete, Shannon and Crook headed to New York to record the song. Unfortunately, during the long drive to the city, the two had to suffer for their art. Shannon recalled the drive with distaste. "It was about 10 degrees below zero, and the heater broke, and the muffler fell off. It was awful. I smoked cigars then, and Max hated smoke, so I had to leave the window open and blow the smoke out. We had our wives with us.

"We were totally broke. I had to borrow 60 dollars from my manager. I thought he was gonna knock my head off."

Despite these adversities, they arrived in town safely, recording "Runaway" and its B-side, "Jody." Not long after Shannon returned home, the single hit big and things began to happen all too quickly for the new star.

"It was insane," Shannon said. "I didn't get to enjoy it, really. I was too anxious about the future. All of a sudden, you get what you want, and it isn't really what you expected.

"My first (touring) gig was on Broadway and I'd make more there in a week than I was gonna make all year at the Hi-Lo club. It was unbelievable. I was in total shock. I walk in and I'm working with Jackie Wilson, Johnny Burnette, Ray Peterson, Dion, Bobby Vee.

"And here's my first gig on Broadway: 'Wow, this is amazing,' after all these (Hi-Lo gigs where there was) bottle-throwing and knife throwing. And I go to New York and here's these young, screaming kids, and five shows a day, and this little dressing room. I thought (that when I'd) go to Broadway, I'd have this Hollywood dream (dressing room), with lush, purple carpets and white ceilings. I came in and it was cold and the window wouldn't shut.

"Dion was there and I stepped on his foot! He said, 'Hey, what are you doing? Where did you get those ugly pants? Look at those bad pants.'

"I said, 'Well, that's hip.'

"He said [because Shannon's pants were baggy], 'That's not hip! Pegs are hip!' I had red socks and a red tie, and a black suit. He said, 'I can't believe what I'm seeing.'

"He talked New York, a real strange voice. It sounded like Mars to me. It was like when I met John Lennon. I thought, I'm meeting another Dion, another foreign, very outspoken, frank fellow here. Dion and John Lennon would have gotten along together if they had been at the same age. They would have been amazing together, because they were both very talented."

Shannon's next hit, "Hats Off To Larry," followed closely on "Runaway's" heels and was nearly as successful, reaching #5 in *Billboard*. His next five singles had considerably less impact (one, "Ginny In The Mirror," failed to chart at all), but in December 1962, he was back on top with "Little Town Flirt."

When asked if "Little Town Flirt" was inspired by a real person, Shannon answered, "Possibly. The idea came to me from Robert McKenzie, who was a black fellow I used to write with in Detroit. He came to me and he said, 'I have this great idea, man. It's called, 'Here she comes, the little town flirt, down the street, and' – and I said, 'Wait, Bobby,' 'cause he always talked fast.

"I said, 'I know a little town flirt. Her name was Karen. She used to live near my hometown, and I went out with her. She was very young at the time. I was older than her. She went to a dance one night and I tried to find her. I went to the dance and she was with another guy. I couldn't believe it.

"I tried to follow them. They ran out of the dance and got in a car, I tried to chase them and I didn't catch them. But I went to her house the next day and got my teddy bears back and dumped her."

(For those wondering who were the background singers on that record, Shannon revealed that they were a Detroit group called the Young Sisters.)

Despite the success of "Little Town Flirt," Shannon's next two singles failed to reach the Top 40. One, "From Me To You," was the first recording of a Lennon-McCartney song to ever reach the U.S. charts, peaking at #77 during the summer of 1963. He had learned the song while in England, where the Beatles not only performed with him but also came backstage at his own gigs.

In late 1963, Shannon felt that he would have a better opportunity to both hit the charts and see his royalties if he broke from Balk and Micahnik's wings. He formed his own label, Berlee, and released two singles. Recalling the way in which the Big Top owners treated him, he said, "I knew what they were doing, but I was afraid. I kept fighting them and fighting them – mainly Micahnik. Though they were in business together, (Micahnik) was the manager and (Balk) was the producer.

The Berlee releases fared no better than Shannon's last Big Top output, and he soon returned to Balk and Micahnik, who secured him a contract with Amy Records.

Shannon described the way in which he and Balk recorded his hits: "I played the guitar on most of them and I arranged most of them, including the harmonies. I would work with the band and (Balk) would go into the studio. I definitely needed him at the time." He felt that Balk's experience recording Johnny and the Hurricanes showed him to be a capable producer. "You can't beat that experience. I hadn't a clue about studios at all. I wouldn't have known what to do.

"So it all worked out, except that I didn't get paid what I thought I should be paid. What I (eventually) did was sue them, and then I got all my copyrights back. Dan Bourgoise – my manager now, who's been taking care of business for me for years – takes care of all my publishing. We got together and he said, 'You ought to have your publishing back.' About 12 years ago (1977), we got them all back, everything."

Unlike Shannon's albums on Big Top, his Amy albums were centered around cover versions of other artist's hits. One consisted entirely of covers: *Del Shannon Sings Hank Williams*. For the most part, the covers were songs that were personal favorites of Shannon, such as the aforementioned album and Roy Orbison's "Crying." (This would change later, when he was on Liberty and covers were stuffed down his throat.)

Not long after Shannon was on Amy and back with Balk and Micahnik, the hits returned. A streak of four successful singles began with his sped-up covers of "Handy Man" (June 1964) and "Do You Wanna Dance" (September 1964, months ahead of the Beach Boys' similarly fast arrangement). The hit streak continued with "Keep Searchin'" (November 1964) and ended with "Stranger In Town" (February 1965).

While Shannon's career was on the upswing, his physical and emotional life was the reverse. Shannon, whose father drank, was beginning to suffer from an alcohol problem that would continue to trouble him through the 1970s. Recalling the period when his problem intensified, he said, "It was a strange time of my life. I remember how I was drinking heavy in those days. I wrote 'Keep Searchin'' and 'I Go To Pieces' within a couple of weeks. Then I wrote "Stranger In Town." It's kind of foggy, in a way, as my writing goes. I would just sit down and get boozed up and write."

"I was sober when I wrote 'Runaway.' (At the time of) 'Hats Off To Larry,' I was sober, I think. Then, when I got three or four hits, I got to drinking heavy. When I found booze, I went crazy for it. I didn't write 'Flirt' boozed, because Robert (McKenzie) was boozing and I had to be straight. But after that, when I wrote 'Keep Searchin', that's the period when things get a little foggy." (At another point, he put it bluntly: "I wrote 'Keep Searchin'' totally bombed.") "That's when I was hitting the juice pretty bad. Booze can be good for you for a while if you're a writer. After it takes you over, and you have no control over it, it's over, man. I mean, in the end of my drinking 11 years ago (1978), I'd sit down for three minutes, try to write a song, and I'd be up drinking again.

"But all that's changed now," he added. "I don't drink at all anymore."

In early 1965, as Shannon's latest string of hits was coming to an end, Peter and Gordon recorded his "I Go To Pieces." He had introduced the duo to the song while on tour with them in Australia. The sad ballad, quite different from the rockers for which Shannon was known, became one of the group's biggest hits.

While discussing "Jody," the lushly orchestrated B-side of "Runaway," Shannon revealed his reasons for writing "I Go To Pieces." "I wanted to give ('Jody') to Johnny Mathis," he said. "See, I always wanted to be a crooner. I always want to sing slow songs, but, like (when) I wrote 'I Go To Pieces,' and I said, 'Oh God, finally I wrote a slow song that I could really sing," and my manager says, "Aw, you gotta write uptempo songs, man. 'I Go To Pieces,' it's really not you." At the, same time, I had also written 'Keep Searchin'" so they said, 'Do "Keep Searchin'". 'and I gave the other song to Peter and Gordon."

Listening to Shannon's songs from this period, and knowing of his alcoholism, one might assume that he was continually depressed. On the contrary, Shannon claimed that he wrote his saddest songs at the times when he was happiest. "When I wrote 'I Go to Pieces,' I was in a great place," he said. "I usually write when I'm in a great place. When I'm depressed I don't usually write. So I take all of when I'm depressed and throw it into (songs) when I'm feeling good. Weird, I guess.

A photo on the back cover of Sire Records' *The Vintage Years/Del Shannon* depicts him singing from sheet music. When asked if he could actually read the notes, he responded without pause: "No, no, I couldn't read (music), and I never did. I tried it once and I wish, I would've, because it is so simple. If you try to figure out something you can just go (flutters his fingers), just like a typewriter.

"I think I'm glad I didn't (learn). because I think it takes away, from the – it's like Dolbying your records, you know what I mean? It's too high-tech. Just like some of today's records are too high-tech and they lose their thing. Back to hiss, please! Give me hiss on records. Don't clean it up so much. Oh, God. it's pathetic."

Shannon's next two singles after "Stranger in Town" – "Break Up" and "Move It On Over" – each had a progressively harder edge. Driven more by fuzz guitars than his hits' trademark organ sound, the songs sounded more like the work of a group than of a solo artist.

Shannon admitted to *Goldmine* that he had tried to make his songs sound more like those of the groups that were hitting the charts. He added that he believed that this conscious effort to blend in with the crowd cost him his popularity. "When your a leader, you're OK," he said, "but when you start to be a follower, then it's not good. Harry Balk always told me, "Always be a leader. Don't be a follower.'

"There were times in my career when I would try to write songs like Bob Dylan; 'wow, that's hip.' There I am following, and me trying to write songs like Bob Dylan is like Bob Dylan trying to be Beethoven. Same stupid thing! But artists get hooked up in that. To be a follower, you lose. Can't win being a follower. And Harry was always right about that."

"Break Up" stalled at #95, and "Move It On Over" missed the chart completely. Discussing "Move It On Over," the image that came to Shannon was one reflecting his state of mind at the time of the song's release. "I had bought a house on the lake in Whalen, Mich., one of only two houses on the lake," he said. One day, frustrated by his placid surroundings, he took a box of "Move It On Over" singles and sailed them, one by one, on the water. "I got very depressed ... it was cloudy, and I hated living there. I had bought this cottage (because) my ex-wife liked it, and I said, 'Why am I here? I'm so depressed. What am I, retired?' I said, 'I can't believe I'm in this horrible place,' and yet it was beautiful. Those peaceful places are great for me for a while, but rockers gotta have telephones and guitars."

(In view of this, one might note an observation made by some of Shannon's friends upon his death. They said that, at the time of his death, he was having difficulty adjusting to his new home of two weeks.)

"Break Up" and "Move It On Over" were both very commercial songs. Their failure may be attributed to the fact that their garage punk sound was not what audiences expected of Shannon at the time. Lack of promotion was probably a factor too, for after those singles failed, Shannon decided that he could do better at Liberty Records. In early 1966, Shannon finally broke free of Balk and Micahnik and signed with Liberty. Although the label allowed some of its acts creative "liberty," Shannon was lumped in with their Los Angeles stable. Liberty gave him the same producers and songs as labelmate Gary Lewis and the Playboys. The incompatibility was obvious.

Ignoring the fact that Shannon's biggest hits were self-penned, producer Snuff Garrett made Shannon churn out cover after cover. These included his first Liberty single, a version of Toni Fisher's "The Big Hurt," and continued with "Under My Thumb" and "She" (which was soon upstaged by the Monkees' version).

When asked about his version of "She," Shannon said, "It isn't that good of a record. See, I gotta be very careful when I do other people's songs. If somebody writes a song for me, I have a hard time with it. Like, 'The Answer To Everything' was successful as far as (my getting) a lot of requests (to perform it), but it took 23 takes to get it, and I never was happy with it."

In the midst of these cover versions, in July 1966, came an excellent original single, "Show Me" b/w "Never Thought I Could." However, the "Stranger In Town" momentum was long gone, and this too went ignored.

In early 1967, Shannon connected with Rolling Stones producer/manager Andrew Loog Oldham. Sorely in need of a break from the Liberty production treatment, he asked Oldham to produce him. Oldham used his Immediate Productions stable of musicians (including Billy Nicholls, Nicky Hopkins and John Paul Jones) to back Shannon, and the resulting album was called *Home And Away*.

Greg Shaw, in his liner notes to The Vintage Years/ Del Shannon, called *Home And Away* "an unbelievable triumph." It was definitely a product of the psychedelic era, far removed from anything Shannon had done before. However, despite its polished production and strong material, Liberty refused to release it. Only a couple of singles from the recording saw the light of day. When asked why the label would not put out the album, Shannon said, "'Cause they were Liberty. 'Cause Liberty was a little wazy-hazy there.

"Al Bennett, who just passed away, was the president of that label. When he was in London, I called him and I said, 'Andrew Loog Oldham wants to produce me. He's expensive, He goes into the studio with top cats.' We had 25, 30 musicians on (*Home And Away*). (Bennett said) 'Fine, do it, man.'

"So, for three of four weeks, I had the time of my life with Andrew. He'd let us use his Rolls. I liked him because he was very adventurous. He wasn't in a good place in those days, 'cause him and the Stones weren't getting along too well, but I liked him and I liked working with him musically.

"He did it all. I just said, "Take over.' And that's another dangerous thing for an artist to do, unless the guy really knows what you're doing and knows your style, I mean, you just can't do it. Jeff Lynne said to me, years ago, 'Del, you seem to be lost a bit and you don't know which direction you're going in.' Now, the last time I worked with him, there was no doubt. We just sat down and we just did it. I'm not afraid to risk now at all. I don't have to follow, 'cause if it isn't successful, it's OK. It's successful to me. And my ma loves it, and my wife loves it, so what do I care? I care, but I mean ..."

In 1968, chastened by Liberty's rejection of *Home And Away*, Shannon recorded his next album, *The Further Adventures Of Charles Westover*. It was the first album on which he wrote or co-wrote all but two songs. By using his real name in the title, he was following the lead of other artists like Bobby Vee who were going "contemporary." Although many Shannon fans admit to liking the record, it definitely sounds contemporary for its time, in that late-'60s psychedelic singer-songwriter vein. Although most of the songs were kept to three minutes, with no extended acid guitar solos, the material was unlike that for which Shannon was known. It was less intense and more atmospheric. It was not a commercial success.

Following the *Charles Westover* album, Shannon left Liberty for ABC/Dunhill. The label released two singles of his, both of which were songs written with old friend Brian ("Sealed With A Kiss") Hyland. Neither was a hit. When asked about one of them, "Sister Isabelle," Shannon said that it was one of his best. He explained why it didn't hit: "It was out of its time. Plus, it was about priests and nuns, and in those days you didn't talk about that."

By this point, in 1969, it was four years since Shannon's last hit. He wisely turned to producing ouside artists, arranging the version of "Baby It's You" that was a hit for Smith and producing Brian Hyland's *Gypsy Woman* album. The title cut from the Hyland album reached #3 in *Billboard*.

As the '70s rolled around, Shannon's recording and production career slowed down considerably. Between 1969 and 1980, his only new album was *Live In England* (United Artists, 1974). Although the record was strong, it contained no new material (unless you count "Coopersville Yodel"). He did release a few singles between 1972 and 1976, including the Dave Edmunds-produced "And The Music Plays On" (United Artists UK, 1974), and the Jeff Lynne collaboration "Cry Baby Cry" (Island, 1975). None of these

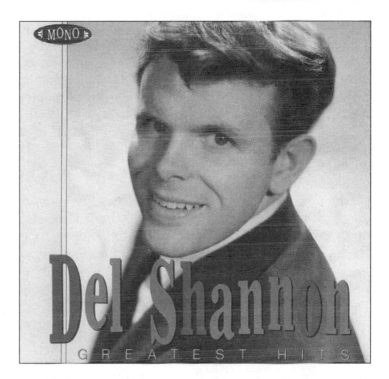

releases were major hits in the U.S.. or elsewhere. Despite the lack of a hit, Shannon retained his substantial power as a tour draw.

In the mid-'70s, Shannon plunged further into the depths of alcoholism. Discussing the years between 1976 and 1979, he said, "I was gone, man. Booze took over totally and I was in my room, a soundproof room with no windows, and I would sit there and just play Waylon Jennings' 'MacArthur Park' all night, for eight hours, sometimes, with a candle – I like candles – and a jug of whiskey or whatever I had, and I'd just drink all the time."

Asked if people tried to pull him out of his habit, Shannon replied, "Everybody tried to. They always try to stop a drinker, but they really can't. It's up to you. They can have power over you if they leave you alone and let you stand on your own. If they keep helping you, you probably may not ever stop drinking. They wanna save you and they kill you. But my ex-wife said one time, 'You're finished, man. I'm leaving and I'm getting outta here.'

"I didn't know what to do. I was all by myself in my little dungeon, and I said, 'Oh, my God, hmm, wow. Maybe I'll go to a hospital.' So I went to a hospital, only because I didn't want to stand by myself. Dried up at a hospital and never drank since, and I don't want to."

This writer asked Shannon if his faith in a higher power enabled him to quit drinking. "Well, I think faith helps you to do all kinds of things," he answered. "That's probably why we're alive, is because of a little faith someplace. I mean, so many people want to kill themselves today, yet they don't. Why? Because something inside says, 'Don't do that.' I believe that."

In 1978 as Shannon was becoming sober, he itched to pick up where his career had left off. His first impulse was to go to Nashville and record country music. However, an inspired person at MCA Records suggested that Shannon collaborate with label artist Tom Petty. The result was Shannon's first studio album in more than a decade, *Drop Down And Get Me* (Elektra, 1981).

Shannon was attracted to using Petty as a producer because he "loved (the Heartbreaker) guitars. 'Cause all of a sudden, guitars weren't too hip then. Petty was rockin' and I said, 'God, it's great to hear guitars again!' So I got with Tom and I said, 'I was thinking of going to Nashville,' and he says, 'You're a rocker, Del. You can sing country music when you're 70 years old.' Then I said, 'Let's do it.' So we did that album, and it took two years.

"The biggest mistake I ever made with Tom Petty – still can't believe it – (is that) I never asked him if he had any songs (I could use). It's just amazing, what a great writer he is. (I was) stupid."

While describing how Petty maneuvered him away from Nashville, Shannon revealed for the first time his current feelings about recording country music. "I grew up with country music, and I always wanted to be a country singer," he said. "I don't today. Even though I sing country music and write it. I don't really have that desire, I used to, but I've been in Nashville and I see what's going on – I'm successful in my own era now. I don't want to bother with (country). I really have never said that to anyone, but I'm saying it to you now."

Shannon said that the lyrics of the title cut of *Drop Down And Get Me* reflected his chaotic emotional life at the time. "That definitely was, 'Come on and get me outta here!'" he explained. "See, I never could get out of that place, which is really – it's only because I wasn't happy in the place I'm in, and I'm trying to learn now to live today, to be happy, not then or in the future, 'cause you can't make it (that way). We all are (learning that), and I'm learning it better now. I'm accepting what's coming down a lot better. Like, cutting a new record now doesn't scare me like it used to. 'If it don't (hit), my God, I'll die; if it does, I don't know what I'll do, it'll be great!' ... Stupid way to live your life, but when you're programmed as a kid with fear and money – 'You can't have that electric train 'cause we don't have enough money' – it's a drag, man. A real drag."

Drop Down And Get Me spawned Shannon's first Top 40 single in 14 years, a cover of Phil Phillips' "Sea Of Love." The album was less successful, only reaching #123, but it succeeded in re-establishing Shannon as a current artist.

After his comeback album, Shannon recorded a couple of country singles for Warner Brothers. Soon, his career began to stall, and this was once again due partly to problems in his personal life. When asked what he had been doing during the years since 1984, besides touring, he answered, "Getting my life together. My ex-wife left me, and that was devastating. And now I'm glad she left, because some times you're blind to what's going on, and the other partner sees this ain't making it, and yet you think it is because you're locked into it. It's called, 'You don't miss the ex-wife, you miss the structure, the comfort zone.' That nearly destroyed me. I didn't want to drink, but it nearly drove me to the nuthouse.

"But I got through that, and now I think I'm on a spark of writing. Whether it's successful or not doesn't matter. Now I have it in much more control than when I was a kid writing. I don't get frustrated. I know when I can say, 'That's it, lay that song down, and forget it.'"

At the time of the interview, the "Walk Away" single had just been released, but only in Australia. Shannon said that his manager wanted to test the foreign waters before pursuing a domestic label deal. When this writer offered to put in a prayer for Shannon to get an American deal, Shannon said, "Oh, you don't wanna do that! I think it's dangerous for me – you don't have to pray for me. You can pray for his will for me. That would be great. 'Cause what if we got (the deal), I go up in an airplane, and it goes and crashes! Forget it! Hit record with a crash!"

As the interview wound down, Shannon spoke of wanting to direct all of his energy into completing his new album. "I turned down Japan this year," he said. "I turned down England. I don't wanna tour extensively this year. The reason why is because I just wanna be recording."

The Associated Press' obituary for Shannon quoted friends saying that at the time of his death he was uncomfortable about embarking upon a scheduled tour of England. Perhaps this was because of his desire to concentrate on finishing his album.

When writing about Shannon's death, it is all too easy to say that it was simply consistent with the feelings of loneliness that he expressed in his songs. His remarks in this interview show that, despite his bouts with depression, he knew in his heart that he must keep faith. In fact, his lyrics and his remarks show that, if he were not a believer in faith, his life would have ended much earlier. He wouldn't want to be remembered as one, who gave up, but rather as one whose struggle against adversity encouraged others, not to give up. A listen to nearly any one of his compositions, from "Runaway" to "Walk Away," reveals that he was a fighter from the beginning to the end.

Most Collectible 45

"From Me To You"/ "Two Silhouettes," Big Top 3152, $60.

Most Collectible LP

Runaway With Del Shannon, Big Top 12-1303, stereo, $1,600.

Recommended Introduction

Greatest Hits, Rhino R2-70977 (20 of his 1960s recordings, including the essential early ones)

If you want to hear more...

Runaway/One Thousand Six Hundred And Sixty One Seconds With Del Shannon, Taragon 1022 (a twofer that contains two of his greatest albums in hard-to-find true stereo)

Del Shannon 1961-1990, Raven 51 (Australian import, a 2-CD collection that goes from "Runaway" to the Australian hit "Walk Away")

Drop Down And Get Me, Varese Vintage 5927 (his fine 1981 comeback album produced by Tom Petty)

Part V
Behind The
Scenes

Dick Clark

by Jeff Tamarkin

Saturday afternoons at 12:30 p.m. Not very much could get in the way of that time for me when I was young. For that was when American Bandstand *aired on the East Coast. I still remember the "other" theme song, the one from the late 1960s and early 1970s, before Barry Manilow revived Les Elgart's original "Bandstand Boogie." I also remember when the Jackson Five took over the show – any time Dick Clark could nab the biggest act in the country, which the brothers Jackson certainly were among* Bandstand's *core audience in 1971, it was a big deal. Of course, Clark became a media mogul thanks to such things as the American Music Awards,* New Year's Rockin' Eve *and* The $10,000 (later $25,000 and $100,000) Pyramid, *one of the more intelligent and fun game shows in TV history. But it's for* Bandstand *that he'll be remembered by rock 'n' roll fans. The following interview with one of the key non-performing figures in the history of the music appeared in the December 28, 1990 issue of* Goldmine. *Since the article appeared,* AB *briefly appeared on cable with a new host, reruns of old* Bandstands *aired on VH1, and Clark himself, despite wondering aloud why he'd be worthy of such an honor, was named to the Rock and Roll Hall of Fame in 1993.*

The most amazing thing about Dick Clark is not that "America's Oldest Living Teenager" still fits that role at age 61. It's not that he's one of the most successful (and wealthiest) people in show business. It's not even the fact that nearly all the great (and plenty of not-so-great) artists in the history of rock 'n' roll have appeared on his *American Bandstand*. The most amazing thing about Dick Clark is that he can't dance. He's admitted it. Dick Clark has two left feet.

Beginning August 5, 1957, the Monday afternoon when he took over as host of the longest-running variety program in television, Dick Clark brought dancing into millions of American homes, first on a daily basis and then weekly. For over three decades, thousands of well-scrubbed kids appeared before the *American Bandstand* cameras to dance the Stroll, the Twist, the Bump, the Fly, the Jerk, the Hully-Gully the Frug, the Loco-Motion, the Philly Dog, the Madison, the Monkey and the who-knows-what to many more thousands of records. But Dick Clark never joined them. Not that he had the time to; he was too busy creating an American icon. And an empire.

In 1990 *American Bandstand* no longer exists. Clark finally took himself off the show more than a year ago and describes its current status as "in limbo." That hardly makes him an idle man, though. His Dick Clark Productions puts its stamp on dozens of television, radio and film projects every year and Clark's pace is no less hectic than it was during Bandstand's heyday: he hosts specials, such as the annual *New Year's Rockin' Eve* and the *American Music Awards*, a nightly *Jeopardy*-like game show (*Challengers*), and his ever-smiling face graces myriad other programs. He has a lot to smile about – his hard work has paid off to the tune of a personal fortune estimated at more than $100,000,000.

While his story isn't quite rags to riches, Clark didn't get to where he is through luck or laziness. Always an ambitious workaholic, his career has been marked by smart moves, his eye sharply focused on trends in popular culture and how best to package them for the masses. Clark has often said that he doesn't make culture, he sells it. And no one in the entertainment industry is a better salesman.

Richard Wagstaff Clark was born November 30, 1929 in Mount Vernon, New York, the son of Richard Augustus Clark, a sales manager for a cosmetics company, and Julia Clark. An older brother, Bradley, was killed in action during World War II. "For almost a year," Clark later wrote in his autobiography, *Rock, Roll & Remember*, "I dealt with it by eliminating the outside world as much as possible." One of the ways he escaped was by listening to the radio. "It seemed so romantic to stay up all night and play records and get paid for it," he wrote.

After graduating from A.B. Davis High School in 1947, Clark and his family moved to Utica, New York; his uncle had purchased the nearby radio station WRUN and the elder Richard Clark was hired as sales manager. At the same time, Dick Clark was hired – he ran the mimeograph machine, stuffed envelopes, distributed memos. Before long, he was reading weather reports and the news.

When the summer ended, Clark began attending Syracuse University, taking radio and advertising courses. He quickly landed a spot on the campus radio station, WAER, and, in his senior year, moved over to local station WOLF.

Clark graduated college in June 1951, a B.S. degree in business administration in hand, and promptly discovered television, taking a newscasting job at the small WKTV in Utica. Even then, there was no doubt where he was headed. "He was full of ambition," station manager Michael C. Fusco told the *New York Post* years later. "When I hired him he told me frankly he only intended to stay a year. I hated to lose him, but he was much too good for a station our size."

Clark kept his promise and in 1952 relocated to Philadelphia, working first as a summer replacement announcer at radio station WFIL, where he hosted *Dick Clark's Caravan Of Music* program. That June he married his high school sweetheart, Bobbie Mallery.

In September of that same year WFIL's television outlet, Channel 6, launched a new program, *Bandstand*, to replace its afternoon movie program, which had been bombing. Bob Horn, a DJ on WFIL radio, had been hosting a program called *Bob Horn's Bandstand* and convinced the TV station management that the concept could transfer well to the budding new medium. With Tony Mammarella producing, *Bandstand* hit the TV airwaves in October 1952, Horn introducing guest Dizzy Gillespie and cutting to musical film clips between artist interviews.

It wasn't quite the right formula, though. Horn took a cue from a radio program called *The 950 Club*: bring in kids to dance to the music. The station bit, assigned Horn a partner, Lee Stewart, and the program became an instant success. The kids would dance to current hits, introduce themselves and say what school they were from, and critique the records they heard.

Bob Horn is credited with having introduced the Rate-A-Record segment of *Bandstand,* and it was during his tenure that the immortal line, "It's got a good beat and you can dance to it," was first heard. (Trivia note: the lowest-rated song ever on American Bandstand was "The Chipmunk Song," which rated a 35, the lowest score a record could earn on the show. It went on to sell a million copies.)

Stewart left the show in 1955 and Horn was dismissed the year after that, following an arrest for drunk driving. In July 1956, Mammarella offered the job to Dick Clark, whose radio program, not so coincidentally, had also taken on the *Bandstand* name in the meantime. Clark debuted on July 9, 1956. One other thing had also changed: the music. Now kids were dancing to something called rock 'n' roll.

The number one song on *Bandstand*'s "Teenage Top Ten" the day Dick Clark took over as host was "Stranded In The Jungle" by the Jayhawks. Clark was by no means a fan of rock 'n' roll music, admitting he didn't "understand" it at first. But he grew to enjoy it and, in short time, to be able to smell a hit.

As the program grew in popularity, so, too, did Clark's power within the music industry. Radio stations jumped on records that the *Bandstand* kids liked, and promo men from record companies constantly shoved 45s in his face. Clark didn't allow himself to be bullied into playing a record, though. And more importantly, he didn't allow airplay on the show to be bought, a point that would save his career a few years later.

Bandstand was not strictly a rock 'n' roll show, however. Pop singers such as Tony Bennett and Al Martino were just as likely to make a guest appearance as any rocker, and country and jazz artists were featured as well.

Nor was *Bandstand* segregated. While black artists had been featured on the show literally since day one, the dancers were all white kids until Dick Clark insisted on integrating. "Look, it was just too painfully obvious that rock 'n' roll – and by extension *Bandstand* – owed its very existence to black people, their culture and their music," he told Michael Shore in the book *The History Of American Bandstand*. "It would have been ridiculous, embarrassing *not* to integrate the show."

Bandstand had become more popular than WFIL had ever imagined; what began as a time-filler for afternoon off-hours had become a magnet for local teenagers. Some of the kids who danced regularly on the program were becoming well-known in their own right. They received mail at the station. Lines formed outside the studio doors every day, kids hoping to make it inside to appear on the show. *Bandstand* was now the highest-rated afternoon TV show in any American city. Clark thought the show might be of interest to viewers outside of the Philly area. He wasn't the only one: clone shows sprang up in other cities.

Clark's enthusiasm wasn't immediately shared by network execs, one of whom was heard to proclaim, according to Clark himself, "Who the hell would want to watch kids dancing in Philadelphia?" But the numbers spoke the truth and in June 1957 the ABC-TV network agreed to give Clark and his program a five-week trial run, allotting 90 minutes a day. On August 5, *Bandstand* became *American Bandstand*.

Some 67 stations carried *American Bandstand* that first day as Dick Clark played records, introduced guests Billy Williams and the Chordettes, and the kids danced.

The critics were not impressed. "As a sociological study of teenage behavior, the premiere was a mild success," said *Billboard*. "As relaxation and entertainment, it wasn't ... A local smash, the series isn't going to help Philadelphia's reputation nationally as a quiet town."

What resulted, of course, was not only the national success of *American Bandstand*, but the elevation of Philly's status to that of a barometer for national music trends. Not only was it important which records Clark played and the teens liked; being a performer from Philadelphia could guarantee a measure of success. The so-called teen idols – Bobby Rydell, Frankie Avalon, Fabian, et al. – became teen dreams immediately, largely due to their exposure on Bandstand. Local black performers such as Chubby Checker, the Orlons and Dee Dee Sharp (many of whom were signed to the Philly-based Cameo-Parkway labels) would later find national success. But just being on *American Bandstand* was a boost, and virtually every important early rock 'n' roll artist, save Elvis (and later the Beatles), appeared on the show.

So, too, did more than a few who didn't find success. Shore's *Bandstand* history book contains a complete listing of Top 100 songs lip-synched by the original artist on the show (artists never sang live until much later in the program's history, and even then nearly all mouthed the words to their records), but

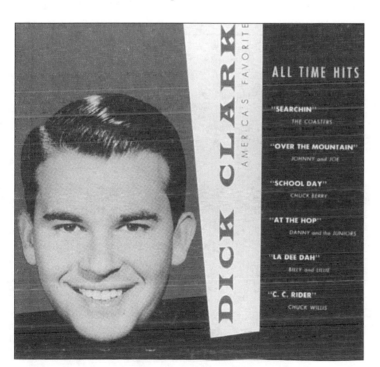

DICK CLARK AMERICA'S FAVORITE

ALL TIME HITS

"SEARCHIN'"
THE COASTERS

"OVER THE MOUNTAIN"
JOHNNY and JOE

"SCHOOL DAY"
CHUCK BERRY

"AT THE HOP"
DANNY and the JUNIORS

"LA DEE DAH"
BILLY and LILLIE

"C. C. RIDER"
CHUCK WILLIS

there are plenty of air dates where no artist is listed, generally meaning that day's guest's record wasn't greatly aided by the artist's appearance.

Dick Clark has always maintained that there was nothing he – or anyone else – could do to make a bad record a hit, that it was in the grooves; the kids either liked it, and bought it, or they didn't.

That didn't stop some of his colleagues in the broadcasting industry from trying to "help" a record along, accepting a little payola in the form of green paper or material goods from someone with a vested interest in seeing the record do well.

The payola scandal of 1959-60 was one of the darker episodes in rock music's history. For reasons that remain somewhat unclear, yet all too clear, the U.S. government decided to crack down on the practice at that time. It was rampant, if illegal, and the government wanted it stopped.

The roots of the payola hearings can be traced to the establishment of BMI (Broadcast Music Inc.) in 1939 and its rivalry with ASCAP (American Society of Composers, Authors and Publishers). Although too complex a situation to be discussed within the confines of this article, the culmination of the war came in the mid-'50s when BMI became the target of criticism (and lawsuits) not only from ASCAP but various songwriters' associations, whose old-line Tin Pan Alley songwriters felt threatened by the new rock 'n' roll industry, which relied on its own writers.

That, and the perceived threat of rock 'n' roll in general by the nation's adults, led to the antitrust subcommittee of the House Judiciary Committee in Washington investigating the so-called payola practice. Looking for a way to stop rock 'n' roll – and, they hoped, BMI – the subcommittee began holding hearings on payola, a common practice in the music industry for a hundred years. If they could prove the rock 'n' roll disc jockeys were accepting gifts in return for playing records, they could get rid of that national threat led by Elvis Presley and his greasy-haired legions.

The scandal brought down more than one broadcasting career, most notably that of pioneering rock 'n' roll disc jockey Alan Freed. Freed, then working for powerful New York radio station WABC, had refused to sign an affidavit saying he'd refused to accept payola, or bribes, for playing records over the air. He was convicted, fined and given a suspended sentence but his career was virtually ruined by the incident. He died a broken man in 1965.

Clark says in his book that he had, of course, been approached by promo men eager to hand him cash in exchange for favors. When called before the subcommittee, he even admitted that he had accepted gifts, including cash, a fur and jewelry for his wife – but never as a payoff to push a record. In addition he had invested a sizable chunk of his even more sizable income in music business-related concerns since his career took off in 1957. Clark was already a multi-millionaire by the time the payola hearings came about, and as far as the House was concerned, there had to be some shady business behind his good fortune. There had to be something wrong with a guy making all that money off that disgusting "music."

On May 2, 1960, it was Clark's turn to go to Washington. Grilled by politicians with little schooling in music or the industry, he answered one absurd question after another. Basically, what their poking around boiled down to was that Clark had to be accepting bribes or he wouldn't be playing such trash; he'd be playing Frank Sinatra, or Mantovani, anything except rock 'n' roll.

Clark held his ground. He played what the kids liked, he played hits, he didn't take money. He defended his business interests, listing 33 of them from music publishing to stuffed animals. "You say you got no payola, but you got an awful lot of royola," said Rep. Steven B. Derounian (R-N.Y.). "I seek to provide wholesome recreational outlets for these youngsters whom I think I know and understand," Clark said. When it was all over, Clark was cleared. He divested himself of all music-related business interests, throwing away an estimated $8 million in the process. One congressman called him a "fine young man."

American Bandstand prospered throughout the '60s. In 1964, as the Beatles – Clark missed the call on them, didn't see any potential – and their British compatriots came along, the show moved to Los Angeles. Eventually, the daily show was dropped in favor of a weekly program.

Clark, who had established Dick Clark Productions early in his career for the purpose of diversifying, created new TV programs, including the music shows *Where The Action Is*, *Happening* and *In Concert*, and funded films, among them *Because They're Young* and the 1968 San Francisco hippie exploitation classic *Psych-Out*. Later films (many of them for television) included *Elvis* and *The Birth Of The Beatles*. He's hosted the successful radio programs *The Dick Clark National Music Survey* and *Dick Clark's Rock, Roll And Remember*.

Clark has been enormously successful outside of the music arena as well, creating the game show *The $10,000 Pyramid* (later doubled to $20,000 and then raised another five grand), *TVs Bloopers And Practical Jokes* and *The American Music Awards* and obtaining the rights to broadcast the Golden Globe Awards, the Country Music Awards and countless specials. He's been known to have regular programs running on three networks simultaneously.

And Dick Clark has lent his name to records, books and videos (culled from old *Bandstand* episodes). The bottom line is the bottom line for Dick Clark: will it sell? If it will, and it falls within the scope of what he considers good entertainment, Clark is likely to take on the project. Not everything his hands have touched has turned to gold, but enough has to keep him from worrying where tomorrow's dinner will come from.

In 1959 he began taking artists on the road on "Caravan of Stars" tours, promoting dozens of top names of the day and bringing integrated concerts to some places that had never seen any – in Atlanta, the Ku Klux Klan dropped by to see if they could stir up a little trouble when Sam Cooke was presented on an otherwise all-white bill.

Clark's open-mindedness toward music has never faltered. While he admits falling out of step during the late '60s – the San Francisco era left him on the outside looking in – Clark has always embraced the new. His personal taste has never played a part in any decision determining the music he's booked – if there's interest in it, he'll book it. Looking over the listing of Bandstand guests during the '70s and '80s, one marvels: disco, punk, pop, jazz, rap, everyone from Aerosmith (1973) to Janet Jackson (1982), Los Lobos (1985) to the Sugarhill Gang (1981), Bobby Sherman (1971) to Madonna (1984), have appeared on the show.

Dick Clark isn't a man who dwells on the past. Although he admits in the following interview that of all he's done he is proudest of *American Bandstand*, he is an entrepreneur with an eye on what's next, not what's come and gone. He is acutely aware of his own place in the history of twentieth century popular culture. and modest in spite of it. "The greatest thing about the '50s was that nothing happened," he once told a reporter.

That, of course, is not true. Rock 'n' roll happened, and Dick Clark's American Bandstand was there to bring it into millions of American living rooms, making sure that it would never go away.

Goldmine: At this point in your career you could obviously take it easier than you do. Yet you're still involved with a multitude of projects at once. What keeps you going at this pace?

Dick Clark: It's always challenging and interesting. It isn't always great, but it does keep life interesting and I suppose that's all you can ask out of any line of work. Once you lose interest in it you probably shouldn't do it anymore.

Which part of the entertainment business do you prefer, the entertainment or the business?

I think they're so intermingled to the point that you can't separate them. Everybody's in show business, that's what makes it fun.

You once said that you don't make culture but sell it. Does that still apply?

I think there's a tremendous amount of truth in that. I think culture and the art comes from the artists. The people who merchandise it, make it available, sell tickets to it, put it on television, send it to venues, are merely the tool with which it reaches the public.

What does Dick Clark Productions encompass today? How many projects do you take on in a given year?

There are probably 30 or 40 under development right now, in active stages of development, several hundred flying around the airport just trying to land. It runs from radio, television, motion pictures and theatrically for television.

Before you made your name in television, you worked in radio. What attracted you to the medium of radio initially?

I don't know. I looked in a diary I had the other day and every other page was "I listened to the radio." As a sub-teen I was hooked on radio. There wasn't any TV at that time; when I first entered the business it was all radio. I was in television about the time it was created. I started in radio about 1947 and by '49 or '50 I was appearing on television, regularly in '51.

Rock 'n' roll wasn't really around yet at that time. When it did come into the mainstream, what did you think of it? Did you foresee yourself as someone who might play such a key role in its development?

I don't know how to answer that. I was just there at the right moment in time.

Bandstand, when it was just a local Philly show, was first hosted by a man named Bob Horn. What do you remember about him?

He was a very famous and popular disc jockey on radio in Philadelphia and when the station was unable to get Joe Grady and Ed Hurst from *The 950 Club* to transform their show into a television program they hired Bob Horn and Lee Stewart to host it.

Why do you think Bandstand happened in Philly? Could it have happened elsewhere?

Bandstand went on the air in 1952 and was an immediate success with two other hosts so it could've happened in Cleveland or Buffalo or Dallas or Dubuque. It just happened to be in Philadelphia, which is propitious because not only was it in the east, it was close to New York, it had its own music industry. It did well probably because in those days I think Philly was the fourth or fifth largest city. It might not have happened in a tiny little town.

Were the anti-rock 'n' roll critics on you from the beginning?

First of all, you have to realize that from '52 to '55, there wasn't a great deal of controversy. Once rock music, rhythm 'n' blues and country music entered the field, then the heat was on because the people who were attuned to another world and whose purse strings were attached to it got very upset that newcomers were maybe going to take the money away, which eventually they did. So in the process, they tried to kill the art form.

When did you realize that you were starting to gain power in the industry as someone who could break records?

Well, the secret was that every one said that *Bandstand* was a powerful promotion vehicle for music when in truth we did have a huge audience and what caused the power was most of the ... I don't even know if they called them Top 40 radio stations in those days, but the ones who played the popular music of the day would copy the (*Bandstand*) playlist, then immediately jump on (the records played on the show). So you got this double whammy where the radio and television were playing the same songs and they hadn't even entered the charts yet. So it was tremendous clout and we were the folks who got the credit, and not totally justifiably.

You must have had the pushy promo men on your back every day. How did you learn to handle them and keep your distance?

I was very young and innocent and cordial and they were my friends and they just lived at the television station. They would fly in from all over the world.

When did the Rate-A-Record concept come into the show?

That was from the beginning. It was there from the first day and was there in 1956 when I took over.

You've been quoted as saying you were puzzled by the whole idea.

I'm still puzzled by it. They still talk about "I like the beat and it's easy to dance to." They've been saying it for 37 years. It never seemed to affect the outcome of the success of the record because some of them that were just butchered by the kids went on to great success, while others that were praised to the skies disappeared.

You always said that there was nothing that could make the kids buy a record if it wasn't in the grooves.

That's been proven right into the '90s. That's always been a truth. A lot of people don't believe it but it happens to be true.

Were you thinking in terms of going national with the show even before the network approached you to do so?

Oh yeah, that's the story of how, in my youthful enthusiasm, I went with a representative of WFIL, which is now WPVI, to New York to present a kinescope – we had no tape – of the show, which was getting 67 percent of the audience in Philadelphia. We

said this could work nationally and their response was "Who the hell would want to watch kids from Philadelphia dancing to records?"

So they sent a guy down to investigate the phenomenon and he said, "I don't understand what they've got here but I think they're right and you oughta do it." They eventually gave us a five-week trial. It worked.

I missed the point though. He wrote me a letter which inasmuch as said don't call us, we'll call you. The letter is in my office. I ran up there (to New York) and in my enthusiasm said, "You're gonna love our show," and I guess we must've overwhelmed them.

You developed a lot of personal friendships from among the guests on the show. Who were some of the performers you became personally close to?

There were all kinds of people. I still work with people I knew 35 years ago, which is the greatest joy of my life. I'm now into exchanging photos of their grandchildren and talking about their personal lives, and that rarely ever happens in the entertainment business. I just got an invitation to Rod Stewart's wedding. It goes from the '50s to the '90s. It's kinda nice. You hang on to the people you run into along the way.

Because of the show's roots in Philadelphia, you were often associated with the so-called teen idols, the Frankie Avalons and Fabians. History hasn't treated them kindly. How do you feel about the Philly teen idols of the '50s and early '60s now?

You know, the shameful part of that is, they always speak disparagingly of teen idols, forgetting that Elvis Presley was a teen idol, the Beatles were teen idols, Bing Crosby and Frank Sinatra were teen idols. It's a stupid journalistic thing to be critical of artists who are appreciated by the young.

Do you see a continuum from Elvis and Fabian through the Beatles on up to New Kids on the Block?

Sure. The Osmonds and the Jackson Five were teen idols. Everybody gets painted with that disparaging crush. It's an easy, cheap shot to take if you're a writer.

We recently received a letter from Pat Boone at this magazine, and he thinks he got a bum rap in the history books. Do you agree?

Yeah, well, he's intelligent enough to handle it so I don't worry about him, but what I worry about is people who are not in the business anymore or are constantly criticized. I ran into Fabian on an airplane the other day. Now, here's a guy who's still out there working, gainfully employed, working with his tongue in his cheek, and enjoying every moment and reflecting back on his good fortune. I'm sure he knows, and he's admitted in public, that he hasn't got the greatest set of pipes in the world, but the man is an entertainer and the people who go to see him want to go see him and enjoy him and what he does. So what in the devil is wrong with that?

Do you feel you also got a bum rap from being associated with those people?

The easiest thing to write, for the most part in the late '60s and early '70s – young people who had no touch with the business and hadn't grown up with it – was that all we ever did was play Philadelphia artists, not realizing that two-thirds of the people in the Rock and Roll Hall of Fame made their debut on *American Bandstand*. They paid no attention to the Chuck Berrys, the Little Richards, the Platters, the Penguins, all the roots people who were on. They always said it was the white teenage idols.

If I were a writer I guess I could tie into that, along with all of the roots people and all of the country people and all of the jazz people. Yeah, we had some teen idols and we had some Philadelphia people.

You also had a lot of mainstream pop people, Frankie Laine...

Tony Bennett was with us for years. And (Johnny) Mathis, for goodness' sake. So to put us in a pigeon-hole, that really bugs the daylights out of me. It' makes me very annoyed because that was an open store for all kinds of music, whatever sold.

I can remember one day in Los Angeles we had Herbie Alpert, Billy Preston, I'm trying to think of who else .... incongruous guests on one show. And it was acceptable and it should always be acceptable. It's unfortunate that we've gotten so segmented in music now.

What was the response when the show became integrated?

The show was integrated in terms of artists from the first day in 1952 or '53. They didn't have artists on the first day but that happened within a week or two. One of the earliest was Dizzy Gillespie. Blacks were always represented. They were not in the audience till '55, '56.

When I was involved with the show in '56 we began to integrate with a greater purpose in mind, because it was obvious that was going to happen. Before that it was obviously a segregated show – it had a white audience, a white dancing audience. And the fact of the matter is that when it became integrated, there wasn't a ripple. Nobody cared, there were no outcries, there were no nasty letters, there were no fist fights. It just happened. The whole world should've happened like that.

Yet when you went out on the road with the Caravan of Stars tours, and you hit the south, it wasn't like that at all.

Oh yeah, I wrote about that in my book (*Rock, Roll & Remember,* Thomas Y. Crowell Co., 1976) if you want to look up the horror stories. That was not one of the more pleasant days of my life. There's a poster here on my wall – I collect things – that says "Notice. Stop. Help save the youth of America. Don't buy Negro records." It goes on with some more wonderful racist remarks that, in the '90s you say, God, I can't believe these things were hanging around on lampposts. We would trail into town and be confronted by one of these things. It's scary stuff.

Right under that I have a picture of the first integrated concert in Atlanta, Georgia, that we put on, with Sam Cooke as the black artist on an all-white bill. He was playing in front of an integrated audience, which had never happened before.

Even a lot of the Philly artists you presented were black, Chubby Checker being the most prominent example.

And the Orlons. And Solomon Burke. It's all nonsense.

You're probably sick to death of talking about the years 1959 and '60 (the years of the payola scandal)...

No, never. Those were good years.

In spite of having to testify before Congress at the payola hearings?

That's the dark side.

You've said that the payola hearings were an issue of greed, not morality. How did you mean that?

Absolutely. It's not like what we're facing now, which is a controversy over the meanings of the words and people being able to say dirty words in public. This was absolutely founded upon, here's a

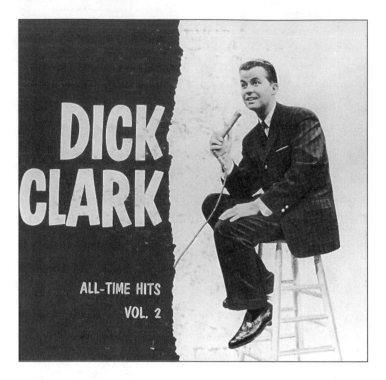

threat to my pocketbook. And the people who held the pocketbook strings in those days, the music publishers, the old-line writers, the artists, the record companies, they were concerted in their effort to squash this new form because they were going to lose money.

And they used as their excuse, and bamboozled enough people into thinking, that this was going to cause the moral decay of American youth. And a lot of people were swept into that, including a lot of prominent Broadway actors and actresses, writers, popular singers of the day: Mitch Miller, Frank Sinatra, Helen Hayes. Here's a wonderful quote from 1960 (reads): "Congressman Tip O'Neill demands that the FCC investigate payola and protect America's youth from rock 'n' roll, which he calls a type of sensuous music unfit for impressionable minds."

Do you see a correlation between that and the censorship issue of today?

No, I think it's a little different. People understand but perhaps don't want to face the problem of do you undermine the right to free speech just because dirty words bother you? It's a very hairy issue. You might not subscribe to the lyrical content or the thought process that goes behind it, and regard for women is also mixed up in this whole thing, but that's a whole other issue. Whether you want to do that yourself or support it is questionable.

The problem is, you cannot governmentally censor it because then you're in the world of the Nazis. We fought too hard to get the First Amendment and freedom of speech and you can't take it back now.

The courts don't even seem to be able to come up with a consensus. One says 2 Live Crew's album is illegal to sell but another says it's OK for them to perform the same music in front of an audience.

It'll sort itself out. It's a real easy issue to get people stirred up about because if you quote some of the current-day lyrics, to one mindset it's the most outrageous thing in the world. There are words that, in the old days, you didn't say in public. What these people don't understand is that the language has changed, the mores have changed, the world has changed. It's probably the reflection of a great number of people who are out there finding no problem with this.

Do you see the censorship battle as a racial issue?

Oh, I'm sure it's probably mixed up in there somewhere, along with the feminist issue. Again it isn't necessarily as it was back in '59 and '60, one of money.

When you moved American Bandstand to L.A. in 1964 was it hard for you to leave behind all of the kids who had become regulars on the show? How did that move affect you and the show?

As a matter of fact, that's a premise for a motion picture that may get made one of these days. We had Barry Levinson financing it at one point before *Rain Man* hit. The whole world changed that year. Kennedy was assassinated, the English came and took over the music world, the *Bandstand* moved from Philadelphia, Californians were rising to the top of popularity in music and the whole world turned around. Then the Vietnam War came on not too long after that.

There's a story in your book about the first time you played a Beatles record, "She Loves You," on Bandstand, and it just didn't click. The kids didn't think it was anything special and you didn't see what was coming.

No, I couldn't figure that at all. I was at the dentist this morning and he said, "Dick, you always had a good ear for hits and know when people are gonna be stars," and I said, unashamedly, "Yeah, I'm pretty good at it." I don't point out the two or three I'd like to forget. That's one I certainly missed.

And logically, too, because most of that music that was coming to us from overseas was a reworking of stuff I'd already been through and I couldn't understand. But it was new to the public. And if they hadn't looked that way, if the German girlfriend of Stu Sutcliffe hadn't cut their hair that way and had them dress in leather initially, would it have been as impactful at that moment? Probably yes, but it certainly didn't hurt. Even today, someone like Sinead O'Connor, looking bizarre is one of the ways you get attention.

Were you disappointed that the two great acts that never made it onto Bandstand were Elvis and the Beatles?

Not disappointed because they were already huge. We settled for second best: we'd get telephone calls from Presley and videos from the Beatles.

Did a record ever skip on Bandstand?

There are a lot of stories like that but I don't remember any of them. There have been stories written about artists who say it happened to them so I presume it did. The only one I remember distinctly was Jimmy Dean appearing and we played the wrong record; we played a Dee Clark record. Paul Anka tells a story that he came on once and the record skipped. I'm sure an artist would be much more aware of that than an onlooker or even I. I might've been turned away or talking to the control room or whatever.

Why did the show get scaled back to once a week? Was that your decision or the network's?

That was ABC's decision, certainly not mine. My guess is that station managers wearied of the format and thought that they could put something else on that would prosper. The truth of it is that they lost the time period.

In the mid-'60s you started taking on new shows such as Where The Action Is and Happening. What was behind that decision?

Where The Action Is was developed as a CBS summer replacement for Jackie Gleason. It had been turned down for a variety of reasons and a guy at CBS asked if we'd do it five days a week as a half-hour and we said yes. It was a wonderful vehicle for a lot of the English artists and American artists. We took it out of doors and did skiing sites and beach sites and parks and nightclubs. It was quite an undertaking.

I associate it more with the American groups, like Paul Revere and the Raiders, than with the English groups.

They were regulars but we had the Yardbirds, the Who, the Moody Blues, Billy J. Kramer.

You've said that you started losing touch with the music in the '60s. Which music did you not take to?

That was during the first psychedelic period. I couldn't figure it out. I wasn't into drugs so it left me behind. We still presented the artists but I couldn't tie into it because I didn't know what the hell they were talking about.

Yet you produced a movie at that time called Psych-Out, which was a classic '60s hippie movie.

Yeah. Jack Nicholson wrote the original script. It was not accepted but he became a star. It was originally called *The Love Children* and they changed the title to *Psych-Out* because they thought the movie would be about bastard kids when they sent it out to the exhibitors; they tested the title and when it came back they didn't know what it meant.

Did you feel even more alienated from the music when disco and punk came along in the '70s?

Once the drug thing took its position everything was fine. I had no trouble understanding disco music; it's dance music. Punk was just a further extension of Little Richard and Screamin' Jay Hawkins.

The show's ratings didn't really jump when disco came along. That's surprising.

We lived through the folk period and the psychedelic period when dancing wasn't all in vogue. The show wasn't really based on whether you liked dancing or not; it was whether you liked people of that age. What were they wearing, what were they doing?

Do you recall an appearance on the show in 1980 by a group called Public Image Limited? It was one of the more noteworthy moments in rock 'n' roll television in the early '80s.

Oh sure, (former Sex Pistol) Johnny Rotten, Johnny Lydon. He wasn't feeling well, he was tired, so he said "I'm not going to do a lip-sync, I'm just going to run around the studio and cause mayhem," and we said fine. It was a very bizarre appearance but typical and memorable.

Any other latter-day appearances that stand out?

Oh, the Beastie Boys were pretty memorable. The first time Madonna was on was pretty exciting. Same with Cyndi Lauper. The first time Lionel Richie appeared as a solo artist. Prince was of course memorable.

Are you a fan of today's music?

You don't stop being a fan. Being a fan of music doesn't necessarily mean you're a fan of all music. What your own personal taste is has nothing to do with what you're called upon to present.

There's a controversy in the music industry today involving lip-synching by artists at supposedly live concerts. A few states are considering laws banning it. What's your feeling on that?

I don't think it makes a bit of difference because obviously the fans of Madonna and New Kids and Milli Vanilli don't care. (*Editor's note: This interview was conducted before the recent revelations regarding the two men known as Milli Vanilli not actually being the singers who made the record.*) As long as the people who like the music are happy to be there and enjoy the occasion, they're the ones who have to worry about it. If it bothers you then the easy solution is you don't go. That's another one of those phony premises for whipping people into a frenzy. The world may blow up in the Middle East tomorrow; this isn't something to spend time worrying about.

What made you decide to drop out of the show?

I was approaching my 60th birthday and the show was going to go to cable, and I thought now's the time to pass over the reins.

What's the current status of the show?

It's in limbo at the moment. I'm hoping that in the next year or so it'll come on in some form. We've had some interesting inquiries about it. It's one of the most recognizable names; it's an icon of sorts. I think it'll be back on television in one form or another.

Do you miss it?

Yeah, very much. You don't hang around something for that many years and not miss it.

If it comes back would you want to host it again?

No, I don't think so but I'd like to be asked back on occasion to do something.

Earlier you mentioned the Rock and Roll Hall of Fame. What's your feeling about it?

I sincerely hope they get it done. It's been a long, hard fight; it's long overdue.

Are you upset that you haven't been inducted yet?

I don't think there's any reason that I should be.

Last year you wrote a mystery novel, Murder On Tour (Mysterious Press, 1989).

No, that was ghost-written. There was a book producer who called me and asked me did I want to do a mystery on a game show? I said, "No, no, no, what you want to do is get Pat Sajak or Merv Griffin." He then said, "Well, how about a rock 'n' roll tour," and I said that'd be fine.

Was there anything you ever undertook in your career that you wish you'd never done?

Oh, I'm sure there are a lot of them but I don't dwell on those. Some things, you think, why did I ever do that? It's like having every tooth in your head extracted at the same time.

How have you changed the most in your 40 years in the business?

I guess like everybody you mature a lot. I wish I'd had a little more maturity when I started but you don't get that when you're in your twenties.

But could you have done what you did if you'd been 10 years older at the time?

Probably. I don't think that had anything to do with it because my predecessors were older. The only thing that would've helped me had I been a little older and more mature, I might not have made some of the mistakes I made in friendships that I had. There were some people around me that I couldn't realize weren't really my buddies.

How does it feel still being called "America's Oldest Living Teenager" at age 61?

It's like being America's oldest living Civil War veteran. That was first written in *TV Guide* over 20 years ago, as a dig, no less. I said that's a great piece of business. It works very well in introductions, whether you're giving a speech or making a personal appearance. It brings a smile to people's faces; it's obviously tongue-in-cheek and the silliest thing, so it breaks the ice.

Of everything you've done in your career, of what are you proudest?

I'm proudest of *Bandstand* because it proved a point, it stayed on the longest, it's the longest-running variety television show in history – that's in the *Guinness Book Of Records*. It's been a part of almost four generations. You can't get much better than that.

Alan Freed

by Jeffrey L. Rutledge

It's said that Alan Freed was the first to take the new sounds of urban rhythm 'n' blues and give them a name – "rock 'n' roll." Certainly the term existed before Freed first used it to describe the music – Bill Haley implied it in an early recording, and as far back as the 1930s the Boswell Sisters had a hit record called "Rock And Roll." But few did as much to bring these "forbidden" sounds to the ears of white America than Alan Freed in his role as a disc jockey, first in Cleveland, then in New York. In fact, it's Freed's work in Cleveland that gives the city its somewhat tenuous justification as a worthy home of the Rock and Roll Hall of Fame. Alas, he was an easy target during the payola scandals of 1959; he was never the same thereafter, as within five years he was dead. The original title of this piece, which ran in the February 1, 1985 issue of Goldmine, *was "The Fall From Grace Of A Forgotten Hero."*

It was to require more than a routine check-up when Alan Freed, the first king of rock 'n' roll, entered the Desert Hospital in Palm Springs, Calif. He had been living a few miles away from the hospital for the past four years or so, seeking refuge from the furor which had disrupted his career back in New York. Christmas of '64 had just passed, and although he enjoyed the company of his family, it was a very lean holiday. It pained him not to be able to provide his children with more, but he had little income and the IRS was after him for alleged back taxes. Now his own health was in danger. Most of his friends didn't even know he was sick. Then on Jan. 20, they found out – a little too late. Alan Freed was gone.

The official cause of death was uremia, though many would say Freed died of a broken heart. At the time of his death, just about all the fight had gone out of him. The rock music world, which he helped build, had all but forgotten him. Death brought no nationwide tributes, no emotional vigils outside of his Palm Springs home. He left this world characterized as a criminal and an alcoholic, neither of which was a part of his personality. Why did it end that way?

Now that 20 years have passed since his death, it seems that few really knew Freed. From the myths and even lies that have been repeated over the years, it appears that many people are content in letting his story remain untold. To date, his story has been less than flattering: famous New York disc jockey deceived all those around him, including his fans, and finally got caught. This depends, of course, on who's telling what story.

"I've always resented those people who speak cruelly of Alan," says Jo-Ann Campbell, a friend of Freed's who performed regularly on the many Freed programs. She knew him well, thinking of him almost as a second father. She and many others adamantly claim that Freed was no bad guy, but rather a loving individual who gave his life for the good of others. He was deliberately victimized, they insist.

"People don't want to know the Alan Freed story," stressed one music industry executive who insisted on anonymity, "especially in this business where it is better, for whatever reason, to believe that Freed got what he deserved." Even 20 years after his death, Alan Freed – a mere disc jockey to some – brings uneasiness in the industry he left behind.

Freed was making news long before he arrived in New York in 1954, beginning with WAKR in Akron, Ohio. There, Freed began to play black music, mixing so-called "race records" with the popular white artists of the day. It was 1944, and racial prejudice was an accepted part of society. WAKR was a family owned and operated station. They had their own ideas on how a station should be managed, none of which included a black audience. But Freed's show was remarkably popular. WAKR relented for a while, giving their star a raise in salary and even providing a new car as a bonus. That was in 1946. A year later, Jackie Robinson would break the color line of major league baseball.

In late 1948, Freed was fired from WAKR, stemming in part from his insistence on having full control over his show. For the next year, he would have control over no show, as a clause in his WAKR contract kept him from joining any rival station.

In 1950, Freed set forth in a new direction. He now had a manager, Lew Platt, who was a friend from back home in Salem, Ohio. Platt was a well respected talent agent and promoter, and secured Freed's return to radio. He started at Cleveland's WJW, where he continued to play formatted music – which meant more Perry Como and Dean Martin records. It was his goal to return to playing the music that earned him a great deal of attention in Akron. Soon he would get his wish.

Leo Mintz was an advertiser on WJW radio. He owned a record store in the heart of Cleveland that Freed often visited. Legend has it that Mintz pointed out some youngsters who were buying the rhythm 'n' blues records Freed was fond of. As the story goes, Freed was amazed, and went back to WJW management and suddenly got a show playing these race records, which he soon called rock 'n' roll.

Legend is wrong in this case.

Mintz played a role in Freed's success at WJW, but he didn't need to convince Freed that there was an audience for rhythm 'n' blues music. Freed was only waiting for the time when he could again play the music he loved, and Mintz catalyzed that opportunity by agreeing to sponsor a show on WJW dedicated strictly to R&B records. WJW allotted a second time-slot for their soon-to-be star. The name of the show was "Moondog's Rock 'n' Roll Party"; Freed was Moondog.

Moondog was not a name that Freed adapted in order to hide the fact that he was a white disc jockey playing black music; his audience knew very well who Moondog was. It was a gimmick, a great gimmick. It enabled Freed to stand out and, by calling the music "rock 'n' roll," he gave it a new, universal identity. His radio show went over exceptionally well, but that was not enough for him. He wanted to bring these rock 'n' roll artists to Cleveland for a live show set at the Cleveland Arena. The "Moondog Coronation Ball" was set to take place on March 21, 1952.

What was to be the first-ever rock 'n' roll concert was a career risk for Freed as well. It could make him a national star, or it could bring his career to a premature end. The anticipation lingered up to the night of the show. No one could have predicted the disaster that would soon occur as fans began to gather outside the gates of the arena. Some fans already had their tickets, others planned to purchase theirs at the door. The crowd grew larger and larger, and soon the impatient group broke through the arena gates. The "Moondog Coronation Ball" was over before it started. Stories would arise that claimed Freed had oversold the arena, while another mentioned that an anti-Freed group had printed up counterfeit tickets. None of them were true, and public threats to bring legal action against Freed were quickly forgotten. That fateful evening Freed got an idea of the power of his rock 'n' roll.

New York would be the turning point in Freed's life and career. He had always wanted to go to New York, to be a star and live happily ever after. In September 1954, he set out to make his dream come true, taking his rock 'n' roll show to WINS radio in New York.

WINS was hardly at the top of the ratings, but they were not content to stay down. To gain new listeners, they agreed to pay Freed $75,000 a year plus a percentage of his advertising. Along with the hefty salary, he asked for – and got – an air-conditioned office and (more importantly) full control over his show. WINS would also construct a studio on the property of Freed's newly acquired home at Wallecks Point, near Stamford, Conn.

Freed was proud of his new home. Salem, his hometown back in Ohio, was small, and his family worked hard for even the necessities of life. His new home was a monument, even requiring a full-time security force. He and his second wife, Jacqueline, would install a huge fence around the house and build an outdoor pool in the back yard. For a while, he talked about bringing his mother and father out to live with him. It was a new course in his life. Alan Freed, king of the newly discovered rock 'n' roll, was an indisputable success.

New York may have been the fulfillment of a dream, but it was also the beginning of a nightmare. The entertainment industry is a world of its own, an often harsh world not swayed by the admiration of its fans. The New York entertainment industry had its own set of rules. Freed, however, lived and worked by his own standards. It was he who had taken the risk of promoting black music, enduring the criticism he had fully expected. By his own admission, Freed did not get along with station management: they expected him to conform to their standards. The recording industry reserved the right to decide when a musical change was in order, not some disc jockey from Ohio. Radio stations would be pressured, because Freed's ever-growing popularity would enhance the rock 'n' roll craze. Either these stations would meet the demand, or the audience would turn to one that would. Thus, in September 1954, Alan Freed had enemies on all sides.

"I think there were people who were planning his downfall even before he got to New York," one broadcasting official now claims.

As expected, Freed ruled the ratings during his tenure at WINS. Occasionally, he would broadcast from Wallecks Point, where WINS had built a studio in a cottage adjacent to his home. There were personal appearances – including a TV show hosted by Eric Sevareid in which Freed served as the faithful spokesman of rock 'n' roll, defending the young institution against the opposing forces.

In 1956, Freed was approached to star in a rock 'n' roll movie entitled *Rock Around The Clock*. Many of Freed's friends were already lined up to star in it, including his buddy from Ohio, Bill Haley. Freed wanted $15,000 for his appearance, but the producers were working with a tight budget and offered a compromise. Freed finally accepted $10,000 and. a percentage of the movie. *Rock Around The Clock* was a smash hit. In the next three years, he would make four more pictures and screen them during his live shows in New York. Within the first two years in New York, Freed had the top-rated show on radio, made a smash hit of a movie, and set attendance records with his live stage show.

Freed was successful because he knew how to parlay music into a sensation that everyone would embrace. His manager and friend, Lew Platt, was as instrumental in that success because he complemented Freed's weaknesses with his knowledge of the inner workings of the entertainment industry. He knew when a deal was right, and he knew when it was wrong. Aside from being a strong business associate, Platt was a friend that Freed could count on through good times and bad. With all this in mind, it is hard to understand why the two would split up. But they did, and it was under less than friendly circumstances. Freed really had little to do with the split; the problem was that too many people around him were talking for him. Understandably, Platt objected.

In what one source claims occurred after a heated argument, Platt was told in no uncertain terms to go back to Ohio. Years later, Freed would be sitting in a New York restaurant, nursing a drink, and lamenting over the loss of his lifelong friend and business associate.

Things were not to get much better. Aside from his other activities, Freed spent a great deal of time with his live stage show, and in March of 1958 he took a leave of absence from WINS. His stage show was booked for an extensive six-week tour of the country, and Freed had lined up a bill which included Buddy Holly and the Crickets, Chuck Berry, Jerry Lee Lewis, and Jo-Ann Campbell, among others. The tour played to packed houses throughout the Midwest with few, if any, incidents, to hamper the show. Then the Freed entourage arrived in Boston for the fate which awaited them.

"I was there the entire time," recalls Jo-Ann Campbell, "and there were never any stabbings or anything else that people had said happened." The kids in the balcony were rowdy though, and Freed had to stop the show three or four times in order to keep things under control. "He said, 'Look, if you don't behave yourselves, we're going to have to stop the show altogether,'" Jo-Ann recalls. "After that, everything went fine." But someone threw on the houselights, giving the obvious impression that the show had been stopped. Concerned about the incensed audience, Freed tried to get the lights out so he could go on with the show.

The show did finish, and most assumed that all was well. It was not, at least as far as the city of Boston was concerned. Three days later, as the Freed show was completing a swing through Canada, Boston officials announced they were indicting Freed for inciting a riot and attempting to overthrow the government. For the latter charge, the officials dug up an anarchy law from the 19th century, meshed between other laws forbidding citizens from leaving their horses unattended. A state senator claimed that Freed's audiences were using drugs, a charge which had no basis in fact. It made good politics, though. The F.B.I. conducted its own look at the events which occurred that night in Boston, eventually issuing a memo that provided their own version of what happened. It was the beginning of a long, sincere interest that the F.B.I. and other government agencies would have in the life and career of one Alan Freed.

When Freed began a nightly TV show on WNEW, he lost his job on WINS radio. Publicly, he stated that he resigned because they had failed to stand behind him over the controversy from the Boston incident. In reality, Freed was fired because WINS management had heard the rumor concerning Freed's rowdy audiences and were concerned about their own interests. Freed signed on with WABC for a considerable cut in pay. Instead of making a $75,000 base salary, he was making $44,000. However, the cut in pay would only be a small part of his many problems. Though he would sign a five-year contract with ABC, many contracted changes along the way made it clear that he was held in less than high esteem by station management. Down the road, a nationwide investigation into how various jocks such as Freed supplemented their income was brewing. The industry would know it as "payola."

"Let me tell you something," says Cleveland disc jockey Carl Reese. "It was no big secret that Alan Freed was getting paid by record companies and the like. So what?" Reese was a friend and admirer of Freed's who would later work at many of the Ohio stations where Freed got his start.

Freed was at WNEW and ABC for about a year and a half before word hit the broadcasting industry that a major investigation was under way which would uncover how their stars were making money on the side. Freed and others were accused of accepting bribes in return for favoring certain artists' records. Another victim was Detroit disc jockey Tom Clay, who became the focus of a cynical *Time* magazine article. Alongside the Clay story was a report on Freed's alleged involvement, entitled, "Now Don't Cry." It was a lurid article describing Freed's fans as they were making their sad farewell to Alan Freed as he did his final show on WNEW. It was November 1959, and within that same week he would also lose his job at ABC. Freed would be the primary focus of the New York payola investigation, which was being directed by assistant district attorney Joseph Stone.

The payola scandal would be the final blow to Freed's career. Though he would not admit accepting money as bribes, it was indeed common knowledge that he and others had outside sources of income. This did not mean bribes, Freed insisted, but few were listening. Mel Leeds, Freed's program director from WINS, would be found innocent of payola involvement after proving that his employees were aware of his additional income. Freed could not furnish such proof.

Asst. D.A. Stone recalls how Freed's employers abandoned him: "Freed meant nothing to them," he says. Stone, now a retired New York judge and a recognized expert on "commercial bribery" (the legal term for payola) now says he holds some compassion for what happened to Freed, though he's quick to insist that "Freed betrayed himself." Freed promised to "tell all," but was convicted nonetheless in late 1962.

The payola scandal wrecked Freed's career, but in 1960 he left New York with every hope that he could put himself back on top once again. His third wife, Inga, insisted that he take a brief rest from the pressures of the business. He took a job at KDAY radio, where Mel Leeds was now employed as the general manager. Freed was making $25,000 a year, and he and Inga resigned themselves to starting life anew in California, moving into a home on Desert Holly Circle in Palm Springs. His two children from his previous marriage, Siglinde and Alan Jr., were with him.

After only a short time at KDAY, Freed was fired and replaced by Tom Clay, the velvet voiced disc jockey from Detroit. According to Clay, Freed's ratings had not impressed station management. Thus he retreated to his Palm Springs home, where he would contact Clay a short time later.

"He was listening to me in Palm Springs," Clay recalls. "He wanted to compliment me on my show. He said things like I was the most exciting DJ he'd ever heard, and predicted that I would own L.A. in a short time. We became friends on the phone, and he even put his wife on to substantiate what he had said."

KDAY would be sold within a few months and Clay would take a job back at CKLW in Detroit. At the same time, Alan Freed would go to work as a promotions man for Mercury Records.

By this time, Freed was depressed at the state of his career, and had turned towards alcohol for consolation. As he toured the country for Mercury Records, he met up with Tom Clay again, now the No. 1 jock in Detroit. It was "record day," and Freed had hoped to get some of the Mercury releases on Clay's show.

Clay now recalls:. "He was drunk, and when he opened up his briefcases I could see that it had a couple of half pint bottles of whiskey in it. It didn't matter to me. He was a legend, and I respected him for what he had done for radio, not condemning him for what radio had done for him."

Other record promoters visiting the station were making fun of Freed behind his back. Clay lashed out at them, then abruptly tossed their records in the garbage. Clay was disheartened. "It was like he was a beggar making a plea for his records. Maybe I hated that more than the record guys making fun of him." Freed's association with Mercury soon ended as well.

Miami's WQAM would be Freed's final job in radio. It would not be a memorable one as Miami would only host a Freed show for a few months. He left WQAM, returned to New York briefly to answer the payola charges in New York, and then went back to his Palm Springs home. He was in financial ruins, and Inga would go to work in order to help support him and his two children.

By 1963, Freed had suffered many defeats, degrading defeats which could have killed a weaker man. It is almost impossible to separate his personal defeats from his professional, as they reflected on each other. Still, into 1963, Freed did not have a defeatist attitude. During the year he visited Jo-Ann Campbell and her husband Troy Seals at a New Jersey nightclub where they were performing.

"He was with Inga, and he seemed to be happy," Jo-Ann recalls. "He was very nice to Troy, and he complimented us on our show and all." In mid-summer, Freed received a visit from his younger brother David, a prosecuting attorney in Ohio. He talked to David about going into syndication, leasing his famous rock 'n' roll show to stations around the country – much like he did when he was back in Cleveland. Alan Freed lived on the hope that there was still room for him in the world of rock 'n' roll.

In mid-1964, Freed paid what was probably his last visit to New York. He visited briefly with Glen Moore, a close friend and songwriter who had collaborated with Freed back in Ohio. Now, as they sat in a New York restaurant, Freed needed someone he could talk to. He began to have more than his share of drinks from the bar. Although he didn't discuss it much with Moore, Freed had plenty to worry about. A grand jury in New York had just indicted him for income tax evasion.

Freed was hardly surprised at the indictment. As early as Oct. 31, 1958, he was paid a visit by an agent of the IRS who presented him with a demand for back taxes. The next year, as he lost big jobs at WNEW and WABC, IRS agents garnished wages owed him by these employers. Now, it was alleged that he owed over $37,000, a large part of which stemmed from the reported payola income. He enlisted New York attorney Richard Steinhaus to help defend him against the charges. Steinhaus, with the assistance of attorney Bruce Hochman on the West Coast, would live to see many of the evasion charges dismissed. Alan Freed would not.

"I don't know if I can take it any more," Freed stated after he was informed of the tax evasion indictment. He was speaking to a friend from a pay phone in New York City, shortly before he was to meet with attorney Steinhaus. The friend, insisting on anonymity, recalls that Freed sounded different than ever before. "He was disillusioned," the friend now recalls. "He wasn't drunk or anything, I don't think, but he didn't sound too good. He was real quiet; you know, and if you knew Alan, you knew he had a robust, excited manner. I said to him, 'Alan, where's Inga at?' He didn't answer me. I didn't know what to do. He didn't ask for help or anything. I more or less felt helpless. I guess he felt the same way." Soon Freed returned to his home in Palm Springs. Litigation concerning his income tax evasion charges moved to Los Angeles.

In October 1964, the tax evasion charges were officially filed in a Los Angeles court. However, Freed was granted a delay in answering the charges a month later. He would be expected to appear before the district court in Los Angeles on Jan. 10, 1965. However, there would be one final delay.

Thus Alan Freed had little to be festive about on Christmas Day. Deep in debt, there was much to worry about with more legal hassles staring him in the face. Then the worst happened. Freed's stomach had caused him many problems through the latter part of his life, particularly after a serious car accident he had after his late night radio show back at Cleveland's WJW. As Christmas passed, Freed was suffering from serious pain, complicated further by the hemorrhaging that finally put him in the hospital.

He entered Desert Hospital in Palm Springs a few days before the New Year, and it appeared from the start that something was seriously wrong. As one week passed, little improvement had been made. Within the next week, he grew sicker. On Jan. 20, while Lyndon B. Johnson was being inaugurated for his first full term in office, Alan Freed died.

That was 20 years ago, and since his death everyone but Freed himself has reaped the glory of rock history. There were others who gave of their talents to revolutionize rock 'n' roll, but every revolution needs a leader, and Freed served with more pride and dignity than he was permitted to leave this world in.

This is but a small part of the Alan Freed story. Most people are interested in myths and legends. For those interested in the fictionalized version of Freed's career, there is the 1978 movie *American Hot Wax*. While it did much to further speculation about Freed's life and career, it also managed to capture some of the excitement of his stage shows at the Brooklyn Paramount.

Most of Freed's friends, though, were highly critical of the movie. Jo-Ann Campbell: "I didn't even go to see it, because I knew it wouldn't do him justice." Screamin' Jay Hawkins, one of the movie's performers, called it "nonsense." Yet Freed's widow, Inga, voices a positive note about the movie. "Well," she recently said, "a lot of people liked the movie."

Whether or not Freed was guilty of wrongdoing should not affect our remembering a man who gave his life for a sensation that has brought happiness to so many people – and made many others multi-millionaires. If we are to be judged equally, as we all claim, then Freed is as great as any rock legend living or dead.

Back in Salem, friends and family still wonder aloud whether their native son was the man history has claimed. They, like many, have their doubts. "I often felt that Alan wasn't guilty of those things," states a cousin of Freed's. A former classmate, Laura Mae Whinnery, who recently died, stated: "Poor Alan took the brunt of everything, while everyone else seemed to get off scot-free."

"The thing I liked about Alan," states Tom Clay, "is that he was never afraid to pay a compliment. He was a legend." Screamin' Jay Hawkins calls him a "martyr" for all his efforts for the obscure black artists of the past. Another DJ, Carl Reese, is equally sentimental about Freed: "There's no doubt in my mind that many of the black artists of the time would not have had the chance they had if Freed did not come along to do all that he did."

And the Alan Freed legacy? Well, Freed never left any legacy per se. He did, however, pave the way so rock 'n' roll superstars yet to come could leave theirs on their own terms. For them, the consolation is in knowing that someone close to them worked for something that will last longer than any of us.

"I'd give anything to have him back, I swear it," say Jo-Ann Campbell. She thinks of Freed's four children, including his son Lance, who is now an executive with a major record company. "They were all pretty young, and with everyone picking on their daddy, they probably thought the worst." She pauses, holding back tears. "But their father was a great man, and I just loved him so much. Now they'll know the truth."

We'll take no tearful leaving
We'll say no sad goodbyes
For though our hearts are heavy
The world before us lies.

Quaker Annual
Salem High School Class of 1940

Leiber & Stoller

by Harvey R. Kubernik

Jerry Leiber (on the right in the above photo) and Mike Stoller were not renowned singers or instrumentalists. Yet, if not for them and other tunesmiths such as Otis Blackwell, Gerry Goffin and Carole King, Neil Sedaka and Howard Greenfield, Jeff Barry and Ellie Greenwich, and many more, the early days of rock 'n' roll would have been much less rich. Many of the early stars, and that includes Elvis, did not write their own material, so they had to get it from somewhere. Leiber and Stoller filled the bill so well that they've been inducted into the Rock 'n' Roll Hall of Fame for their songwriting. The play Smokey Joe's Café, *based on Leiber-Stoller compositions, continues to play worldwide. The two were interviewed by* Goldmine *for this article, which appeared April 28, 1995, not long after* Smokey Joe's Café *opened on Broadway.*

If they'd only written, say, "Hound Dog," "Kansas City" and "Stand By Me," they would already deserve their place in the Songwriters Hall of Fame and the Rock and Roll Hall of Fame, both of which have inducted them. But Jerry Leiber and Mike Stoller were also the tunesmiths who gave us "Jailhouse Rock," "Treat Me Nice" and "Loving You" by Elvis Presley, "Ruby Baby" and "Dance With Me" by the Drifters, "Only In America" (Jay and the Americans), "Saved" (LaVern Baker) "Drip Drop" by Dion, "I (Who Have Nothing)" (Ben E. King) and "Love Potion #9" by the Clovers. Not to mention the Cheers' "Black Denim Trousers And Motorcycle Boots."

They also co-wrote "Spanish Harlem," "There Goes My Baby" and "On Broadway." And did we mention they also wrote (or co-wrote) virtually every hit record by the Coasters and their predecessors the Robins: "Charlie Brown," "Poison Ivy," "Along Came Jones," "Searchin," "Young Blood," "Yakety Yak," "Smokey Joe's Cafe," etc.?

That last classic of '50s rhythm 'n blues, in fact, just happens to serve as the title of a new Broadway musical that celebrates the songs of Leiber and Stoller. It opened March 2 in New York, after a successful run in Los Angeles that had critics falling over themselves to come up with phrases such as "must-see" and "electrifying entertainment."

Leiber and Stoller's songs hardly needed Broadway to become legitimized, of course. Having been recorded by everyone from the Beatles and the Stones to Peggy Lee and Edith Piaf, their work has stood as a cornerstone of the rock 'n' roll songbook since – well, since there has been rock 'n' roll. A fine collection of their compositions, *There's A Riot Goin' On: The Rock 'N' Roll Classics Of Leiber & Stoller,* featuring most of the above names, can be found on Rhino Records.

As if their rock 'n' roll songwriting credentials weren't enough, Leiber and Stoller have also written for film and stage, and were also successful record producers and record company proprietors. Now in their sixties, they've been a partnership for 45 years, and they're still going strong.

Let's talk about Smokey Joe's Cafe.

Jerry Leiber: This show started in Seattle and Mike went to see it.

Mike Stoller: It wasn't this show as it is now. They licensed our songs for a show at the Empty Space Theater. They wanted to put on a show, so we figured, "It's Seattle, it's not New York or L.A., let 'em do it." However, they got a very good review in *Variety* and they were selling out. They originally had a deal for five weeks and they extended it and it had repeat business. I went up to see it. It had great spirit, people were dancing in the aisles.

The thing that kind of hung it up, was the thing that hung up *Yakety Yak,* that was put on in a little theater in the East End of London, which was very exciting. It moved from the East End to the West End and somehow the show got lost in the move. And earlier, in 1980, there was another show, *Only In America,* but what they all had, to one degree or another was a book. And it was the book that hung it up because you were trying to use songs that were not written for books, songs which were only stories in and of themselves.

And shoehorning these things and squeezing them into a book, and making the book take turns they shouldn't in order to accommodate different songs, was the major problem. And that problem has been solved with this production. *Yakety Yak* was done in London, three or four years after the other show, by Ned Sharon's production at the Roundhouse, and the guy who did it, who is a very interesting fellow, and a very good director and writer, who had done a lot of dramas for the stage, had no idea that you had to license songs. And so he put this whole show together, and after, he found out that you had to go and get a license. And it wasn't too difficult, as it turned out.

How did the current director, Jerry Zaks, who did a latter-day version of Guys and Dolls, *become involved?*

JL: He saw the show in Chicago. It started in New York earlier where two workshops were done. The workshops didn't really work well enough to suit Mike. He called me and told me some of the songs were really good, but not enough to make a show. It was shelved for a while. I was a little nervous it would be indefinitely. I was afraid the momentum would be lost. 'Cause I spoke to this director and kind of promoted him to do a workshop and I convinced people to give me a chance to get this going. One showing. They really went crazy over it. Nine songs, instead of 40. They bought it. It was very exhilarating. The Chicago production evolved from *Baby That's Rock 'n' Roll,* directed and choreographed by Otis Sallid.

We all went to Chicago. We got quite far, there was a lot of good stuff, about 30 minutes or so, and somewhere in Chicago, between 30 and 45 minutes, it seemed to run out of gas. Someone came in, pulled it together in two weeks, made it happen, added new stuff and she got it going. And the reviews we got in Chicago were incredible. Previews, incredible. At some juncture they told us they were going after a New York director and they were going to talk to Jerry Zaks. It was really remote because he was so busy.

Well, Jerry came to see the show and loved it. He told us he fell in love with the show. He was a fan of the music. He knew it all. He bounced about five songs, added half a dozen others, and completely reshaped the show.

MS: I've always admired his work. We were thrilled that he had interest in doing it. We went to every casting call. The show has a little of everything. You get a feel of the time and a sense of continuity, but it's something you can't always put your finger on. It just feels good.

With the recent reissues of your work, as covered by a lot of artists, plus boxed sets, repackages, tunes in soundtracks, who is your audience?

MS: My response to the show has been one of amazement at the audience response. I am carried along and buoyed by that audience response and it's a wonderful thing to behold. Really, it's very exciting and the audience ranges from kids who come with their parents to 80-year-olds who are there rockin' and rollin' and clappin' their hands in time. So, there's the "Disney audience," and at the same time people 40 and 50 who lived these songs.

How was the song selection made?

JL: Mike sent them 80, 90 songs. Forty are in the show now. And they picked what they wanted. I told Mike at one point, I think I said, "Man, we shouldn't have done that because they are gonna pull out all these B-sides that all these record buffs love to pull out, and feel this is a gem that we overlooked." The song "Don Juan" was added to the show in Chicago and it's one of the show-stoppers. In Chicago, after a couple of songs, the whole audience got up, dancing in the aisles. And these were not kids. Some of these melodies and lyrics have become part of the public consciousness.

You guys have three songs on the new The Beatles Live At The BBC set, "Kansas City," "Young Blood" and "Some Other Guy."

JL: Did you read the review in the *San Francisco Chronicle*? It mentioned who the Beatles owed debts to, and we were the very last on the list, which makes it look real good.

"Some Other Guy" was heard on the very early film clip of the Beatles performing at the Cavern.

MS: I heard years ago a tiny bit of "Some Other Guy" from the Cavern and it has been in a documentary. I could barely hear it.

What does it feel like to pen something 30, 35 years ago and hear artists like the Beatles do your work?

JL: I'll tell you what it's like. I have no sense of the passage of time and it's like they cut it last night, and someone said, "You want to hear a Beatles cut?" "Yeah, Great." I don't have this long sense of distance and time and history and baggage. I don't have it. I think we both experience time and history differently. I think the two of us are in some kind of time warp 'cause...

MS: I'm in time and he's warped. I've never heard the Beatles do "Young Blood." I know Leon Russell did it at the Bangla Desh concert.

How was it written?

JL: That's the only song in that whole raft of rhythm 'n' blues, rock 'n' roll songs that was written in this fashion. Jerry Wexler was taking me to his house in his green convertible Cadillac that he was ready to trade in 'cause the bumpers were falling off of it. He lived in Great Neck (New York) and his wife Shirley was gonna cook this great dinner for me that night. And he was taking me home. On the way down to the garage to get the car, Jerry said, "Doc (Pomus) has this great title that he's having trouble writing. Would you like to take a crack at it?" I was smart, but very naive at the same time. I didn't know I was being hustled into a thing. (laughs)

So I said, "Sure, I'll write it, that's fine," and Wexler said, "When do you think you can do it?" "On the way out to your house." Which is the way we used to write all the time. And he thought I was joking. He thought maybe I sat down at a desk and put on a kind of visor and started making copies of things. I used to write almost everything to some kind of dummy rhythm that I would cook up and yell lyrics. Once I had two or three verses it deserved the yellow tablet, but until I had some of the verses paper was not used.

And I got in the car with Wexler, started singing the song, by the time we got to his house, it was pretty much written. Of course, not the melody, but the structure of it was pretty much written. And Wexler was crazy about it. He called up Doc from his house and said, "Sing it to Doc."

MS: We were later sitting in Atlantic's recording studio and we were mixing something else and Jerry gave me the song on a legal pad and I wrote the music. I started singing it and that was it. Doc, and this is not to take anything away from Doc, who was a great writer, Doc wrote the title. We recorded it in L.A. We wrote it in New York. We came to L.A. and had "Young Blood" and wrote three others, including "Searchin'" and we went to Master Recorders on Fairfax Ave.

I remember that one of the Coasters, one of the original members, was unable to come to the studio that day, so as a ringer we got Young Jessie. And so Young Jessie is one of the voices.

"Some Other Guy" was a song you wrote with Richard Barrett, who you worked with at Red Bird Records. He was a musician and producer.

MS: We were recording Richard. He was involved with the Chantels. He produced them, and I guess he wrote a lot of their songs, I don't remember. He was a very capable record producer and writer on his own.

He wanted to do a session as an artist. We produced that, and we were going to put it out on our own label, I can't exactly remember what year it was, but we ended up, I think, leasing it to Atlantic. Two sides, that's all we did with him, "Some Other Guy" and a thing called "Tricky Dicky," and, I guess it found its way to Liverpool. It was not a hit.

And then you wrote "Kansas City"/"Hey! Hey! Hey! Hey!"

JL: When we did it with Little Willie Littlefield, it was all right. Later Wilbert Harrison's version came out, it sounded right.

MS: Between the Beatles' records and Paul McCartney's recordings there is a vast array of versions, but the first version was taken from Little Richard's version, which came out in the U.S. right after Wilbert Harrison's record came out. It just said "Kansas City." Little Richard did the four "Hey heys."

I liked Paul McCartney as a vocalist, and especially loved him on those very melodic things that he wrote. Between him and John Lennon that was the '60s as far as I'm concerned. And I loved the way he sang our songs. Beautiful.

The Rolling Stones did a version of "Down Home Girl" that Jerry co-wrote with Artie Butler.

JL: I saw Artie last night, Mike is not happy with that ("Down Home Girl"). I understand why, and if it happened to me I would be unhappy too. Somebody we love, one of our oldest friends, Artie Butler, came to me, and this is not a put-down, or anything like that. Anybody can be influenced by anybody's work. And, Artie (then) is gonna be influenced by the guy he admired more than anybody else, Mike Stoller, right? And he starts to write a couple of songs in the mode of Mike Stoller. He brought one to me and wanted me to write it with him. It was a track.

(Mike) had a couple of requests from lyric writers. And he did some, like Bert Berns came to Mike. And I would try to keep our people; I didn't want them to think I was blowing them off, that they were not good enough. I did one with Phil Spector ("Spanish Harlem"). I did it with Artie, who was a sweetheart. I did it with a couple of people. Some of 'em turned into good songs, some of them never saw the light of day. But I'd write one song with them. So "Down Home Girl" was the one song I wrote with Artie.

I think Mick Jagger learned a lot of things about phrasing from "Down Home Girl."

MS: He might very well have. We might have taught him the form if he'd have asked! (laughs)

And the Stones did another Coasters song of yours, "Poison Ivy," which another English group, the Paramounts, also covered. That group included future

members of Procol Harum, including Gary Brooker, the vocalist.

MS: And we produced Procol Harum in the mid-'70s.

What was it like writing for Elvis Presley? He covered 20 of your songs, including "Hound Dog," "Jailhouse Rock" and another Coasters song, "Little Egypt." How did Elvis get your material?

MS: I almost didn't hear any of his versions! (Author's note: Stoller is alluding to a boat disaster. He was on a cruise ship and 50 people perished in an accident. Stoller and his first wife reached shore on a lifeboat and were met by Jerry Leiber, who brought a new set of clothes and was raving about their hit single from a singer named Elvis Presley. "Hound Dog" was initially written at the request of Johnny Otis, the band leader and A&R man for Big Mama Thornton, who wanted Leiber and Stoller to listen to his acts and to see if they could write some songs for them.)

"Hound Dog," Elvis knew the record, Big Mama's record, because he was a student and, in addition, his first records (pre-RCA) were on Sun Records. And Sun Records did an answer version, which they were sued for by Don Robey (Peacock Records' owner). They did "Bear Cat" with Rufus Thomas, it was a big record on Sun.

And it was a woman's song. Jerry wrote the lyrics for Big Mama and I think we recorded it in 1952 and it came out in early '53 by Big Mama and it was a big R&B hit. Segregated radio, segregated charts, etc. But Elvis heard a lounge act doing it in Las Vegas and they had corrupted it so they could sing it because they were guys. They put in this rabbit thing that wasn't in the original 'cause the original is Jerry's lyric, where a woman is singing to a gigolo and this is kind of meaningless, but it still has the hostility in the line. "You ain't nothin' but a hound dog." Elvis heard them sing it. I think the group was Freddy Bell and the Bell Boys, so he recorded it the way they had done it lyrically.

Did you see Elvis over the years in Las Vegas when he was performing?

MS: I did. He was big. He was parodying himself and he was poking fun at himself.

What were your first impressions when you met him and worked with him?

MS: Jerry and I had actually produced, without credit, the records, our songs in particular, that were in the film *Jailhouse Rock*. And he had asked for us to be there. We had never met him before. He was a very good-looking young man, very energetic. I mean, he just kept going and going in the studio. He'd say, "Let's do another one." And it would go on and on until he felt he had it. The studio was booked for the day and we were used to three-hour sessions.

JL: He loved doing it. He wasn't someone who was doing it and wanted to go home, like a lot of people. He had more fun in the studio than he did at home. He was very cooperative and was a workhorse. He had the "Memphis Mafia" around him. They were his boys. He would be nice to other people but he did not interact that much. We met him in the studio. He had seven or eight guys hanging around. He had his entourage, Lamar, Red, his cousins. He traveled with his environment. And the Colonel was smart, he let him travel with his entourage and it kept him insulated. And nobody could get to him, by the way, if you tried to lay an idea on him just because he was there.

MS: I ended up spending a little more time with him than Jerry because I played the role of his piano player in *Jailhouse Rock*, which Jerry was supposed to play but he had to go to the dentist that day.

What did you enjoy most about his talent, especially his vocal abilities?

JL: I thought he was the greatest ballad singer since Bing Crosby. I loved to hear him really do a ballad. 'Cause there weren't too many people who could do our ballads to our satisfaction. We didn't have people like Tony Bennett and Frank Sinatra because we were writing rhythm 'n' blues, torch ballads and they didn't do those things, you see. They did Sammy Kahn songs, Sammy Fain, they did those other kind of structures that we, by the way, admired very much and loved, and still do. We wrote a couple, and Frank finally did one. It's unreleased. The thing is, that was what we were writing and that's what he sang better than anybody. As far as I'm concerned, nobody cuts Little Richard on rhythm tunes. You have to go far and wide. But Presley is the ultimate in the ballad.

Was it microphone technique? Instincts?

MS: No. It was just singing. It was singing. Pure talent. Later, in Las Vegas, when he was so large, he was poking fun at himself and he would do this thing with the scarf, tossing it back to the audience. He would do 20 of those. That was the show. Sure, he could still sing, but it wasn't like it was before and it was clouded by all this show biz. I mean, there is nothing wrong with relating to an audience but it was mannered.

JL: He'd become somewhat of an imitation of what he was, coupled with some show biz schtick that he thought, and his managers thought, and the club-owners thought, would go down.

In the '70s, did you ever re-submit any tunes to his people after you quit writing songs for the scripts a couple of decades before?

MS: We wrote a song with Doc Pomus. The three of us sat down together and wrote a song called "She's Not You," and submitted it. We had stopped submitting songs to him other than if we had a record. If it was a good song and it didn't happen, we'd sometimes throw it at them and he frequently did it. For example, "Girls, Girls, Girls" was a Coasters record that just didn't happen like the prior four or five. "Bossa Nova Baby" was a record we made with Tippi and the Clovers on a short-lived label we had, Tiger, and we didn't have any distribution, so nothing happened and we submitted it. And he liked it.

Mike, you studied with the great piano player and teacher to Fats Waller, James P. Johnson. What kind of impact did he have on your playing?

MS: At that time, all I wanted in the world to know from him or anybody else, was how to play boogie woogie. Now, had I been maybe four or five years older, I could have learned so much about music from him because he was a brilliant composer. I lived in Sunnyside, which was part of Long Island City. Johnson lived in Jamaica, which was a subway or two subway rides away, and I was 10.

The first couple of times my mother took me. Then I went alone but I'd had a slight accident and walked with a cane. I dove into a swimming pool. It happened to coincide when I was taking these lessons but first what happened, there was a guy in the neighborhood who was a cartoonist, actually, who loved jazz. And he heard me when I was eight or nine playing boogie woogie piano. And he said, "That's amazing. You should study." He's the one who set me up with James P. Johnson. I also listened to Albert Ammons, Meade Lux Lewis, more of the boogie woogie players, not stride players like Johnson and Willie "The Lion" Smith. I can't put my finger on the kind of influence they all had on my piano playing but I knew what blues singing and blues accompaniment was because I bought boogie woogie piano records, and on the B-side, really the A-side for me, had people singing on it, which wasn't that interesting to me.

I moved to L.A. with my parents in 1949. You mentioned that James P. Johnson had his own musical the same year at the Las Palmas Theater. What happened in my evolution in my musical tastes was when I was three years old, all I wanted to hear was old RCA records of Strauss, and the next major influence on me was when I went to an interracial summer camp when I was seven in 1940. I heard older kids, teenagers, a few of them playing upright piano in the bar, which was our recreation hall. I wanted to do what they were doing. I loved what they did. I used to watch them and when they'd leave I'd try and make my hands do what they were doing.

I can't play the guitar, maybe one or two chords. The only other instrument that I played really competently was the tuba. I was drafted out of study hall at Forest Hills High School because they needed a tuba player for the marching band and for the orchestra. And I played it pretty good. I played "God Father" by Miles Davis on it. But when I graduated from high school, I couldn't afford a tuba. They were like a thousand bucks. I haven't touched a tuba since I was 16.

Why has this friendship and business collaboration worked so well with Jerry Leiber for over 40 years?

MS: I don't know. In a jocular way I often say because we are both masochists. (laughs) It's a habit.

You guys were probably the first independent production and record company.

MS: We were the first, I'm told, by the guys at Atlantic. We got into that by doing that. In other words, we used to get a phone call from Ralph Bass at Federal Records, "Hey guys, Little Esther is cutting with Johnny Otis's band over at Radio Recorders on Tuesday. So go to the studio and bring some songs." We would teach the song to Esther in the studio and we'd have some ideas on how it might go and Johnny was busy doing head arrangements because his band was so tight that he could pull out a riff and, boom, a harmony. And we'd go back to the four chord. The arrangement was written in about five minutes and it was recorded. We'd bring four songs in, and on a break would go out and write a fourth one. So we got to get a hands-on situation and we learned from watching Johnny Otis.

We learned a lot from watching guys like Maxwell Davis, who was wonderful. Johnny was a major talent scout. I learned about arrangements just like I learned from Maxwell Davis. Maxwell could do an arrangement, and frequently wrote out his charts, whereas Johnny's were mostly the ones where I experienced it when Jerry and I were in the studio. We'd bring in a song where there couldn't have been an arrangement on it, because nobody could have seen it, and we would teach it to Esther, and Johnny would listen. We might have an idea as to one thing or another in a chart. He could just yell out one riff and the band would go into it in harmony, the horn section would play it. They were so used to working together that it was a fascinating thing.

JL: After a while we learned styles of songs that led to styles of arrangements. And it was shorthand.

MS: Johnny would yell out, he'd give you half a title or something: "That style in the third verse. Go into that lick." We had the same kind of shorthand. If we wanted a certain pattern, we'd say "Yancey," or "Long Gone."

Jerry, were you a good student?

JL: I met Mike when I was still in high school. I was very good in English and literature. That may have had something of an influence on my writing. What you absorb has something to do with what you know. I've thought about it once or twice, and one of the reasons I became so meticulous with words was because English was not my first language. Yiddish is my first language. And one tries so hard as a child to master the language because one wants to be accepted at school as an American. In kindergarten it was kind of funny. Not taunting, but a teacher would hold up a fork and my hand would be the first up and I'd answer in Yiddish what a fork was.

With the records you wrote from the Robins like "Framed" began a style of narrative-oriented composition, which later evolved into the things you did with the Coasters. What were the influences and where did that come from?

JL: The multiple narrative voice I had heard before. Jimmy Ricks and the Ravens. He'd come in with a bass line...I must say, I didn't really think about the songs I was writing. They were natural sort of evolutions of a state of mind. I'd be walking down the street and start singing a line. I didn't think of it. It would happen. These things happened. The only time that I started actually actively thinking was when I started to edit the work and make it fit better.

I've heard the legendary story that one of your school teachers told a friend of yours that due to the music you were listening to in the late '40s, you were going to end up in the electric chair. Also, Paul Coates, on local television in the mid-'50s, said that you were leading innocent teenagers into every negative place. He cited your parody of Brando in The Wild One, "Black Denim Trousers" by the Cheers.

JL: That came from my third grade teacher. We were into regional blues. Memphis Slim, Smokey Hogg, Bullmoose Jackson, "I Want A Bow-Legged Woman." The music was sexy. It was a lot of fun. It was on the radio. I used to work in the summertime as a bus boy in sundry restaurants, and one of them I worked with had a lot to do with getting me focused on this type of music.

I was brought up on the perimeter of a black neighborhood in Baltimore so it wasn't new to me. It was renewed. There was this Filipino short-order chef who was stoned constantly. I didn't know what he was doing until later on when I found out he was smoking joints. He used to chop food as fast as a latter-day sushi chef. He kept the radio going listening to a Hunter Hancock-type rhythm 'n' blues station constantly and I loved it.

I didn't know what he was listening to, and he could hardly speak English but he loved it. I listened to that and at the time I was planning on being an actor. I had studied in Baltimore and had planned on being in the productions in school. At age 15, out in L.A. I joined the Circle Theater started by Charlie Chaplin and Constance Collier. I took tickets and

CHARLIE BROWN

Words and Music by JERRY LEIBER and MIKE STOLLER

As Recorded by
THE COASTERS
on ATCO RECORDS

sold Cokes and swept up and cleaned sets and did that for two summer seasons. I was going to be an actor. And one day I was watching Sherlock Holmes and later schlepping dishes and on the radio I heard "Bad Bad Whiskey" by Amos Milburn. That was the end of my career as an actor.

How did you meet Mike?

JL: I went down to the Orpheum to see him a couple of times where he worked as an usher. I was writing songs at 16 at Fairfax High with a drummer. His name, I think, was Jerry Horowitz. He was a carrot-red-headed kinky-haired guy, a really nice guy. He had written a couple of songs and he wasn't able to make two or three sessions. And I hadn't seen him for a while. I ran into him in the school hall at Fairfax I said, "Hey man. Are you gonna write songs, or what?" He said he had to contribute to the family's economic situation. So he said, "You know what? I've been saving this for you. I got a gig last Saturday night in East L.A. and the piano player was real good and struck me as somebody that I thought might want to write songs. I got his name.

I wanted to ask you about Lester Sill, formerly with Jobete Music, Screen Gems, involved with ASCAP, co-founder of Philles Records, and a mover in the L.A. R&B community via his work as a sales manager and promotional man with Modern Records. He just died recently and I know you guys were very close to him and he was very helpful in your early career.

JL: If you are talking about the music business, the "era," that's one discussion. If you are talking about him subjectively as a person that's another discussion. Because they don't come together. Lester's presence and encouragement... First of all, Lester was a surrogate father. My father died when I was five. I met Lester when I was 15 1/2. Lester became a surrogate father, and to some degree a surrogate mother. I mean, he was a real momma-daddy. He did an awful lot of nourishing, on all fronts. He was a man who was filled with an infinite amount of generosity. He was the first to see my abilities. He saw it before anybody. He did a lot for my confidence, and Mike's to some degree, but Mike was more independent and not as dependent on outside factors, outside of me. Mike's mother and father were intact, educated, they were both literate. They were both refined people. They went to college. Lester was the source of my confidence.

He came into Norty's (record shop on Fairfax Ave.) one day. It's very simple. I looked at him and I said to myself, "I've never seen a better looking suit." He was wearing a brown suit and was the head of promotion and national sales for Modern Records. And he came in and wanted to know how certain numbers were moving. I worked there, which is hardly the place to be checking numbers because all they wanted in there was Frankie Laine's "Mule Skinner" and the rest of them wanted "Hava Nagilah" for bar mitzvahs. And he took the time, and he was in no rush and he was interested in people first. And then information. It's not the same.

He asked me, "What are you going to do when you grow up?" Which was a real straight-on question. I thought he might laugh at me. I said, "I want to be a songwriter," and he asked me to sing him a song. Right in the store. I sang "Big Ugly Woman," that Jimmy Witherspoon cut years later. After I did 16 bars he said, "Do you have that on a lead sheet?" I said, "No, but I can get one." I lied. "Get me a lead sheet on that song, I'll get it recorded." He said, "That's a good song."

He took us around and we met the little independent record labels. That was a *secret world*. Modern Records. Aladdin Records. They were in Beverly Hills. We walked up the street waiting for a meeting with the Bihari Brothers at Modern Records. They were late, and Mike said, "Let's get out of here." And we walked up the street to Aladdin Records and sold them four songs. Lester took us to the right music people, the places where they made rhythm 'n' blues. Capitol wasn't. If we went to other labels with anyone else instead of Lester Sill it would have been all over. But he knew. He knew the difference between songs for Eddie Fisher and songs for Memphis Slim.

You know who else knew the difference? He took us later, and was great. He was not the monolithic support system that Lester Sill was, but he was a good publisher and a lot of fun, and he knew what he was doing: Harry Goodman, Benny's brother. He ran ARC Music. He had Eddie Boyd and Willie Mabon. They had everything. Lester and later Harry Goodman reinforced our blues vision. Harry was lethal. We'd go into Harry's office on Selma in Hollywood and he'd be in a three-piece suit that cost more than the buildings on the whole block. He was so elegant. He was loaded sometimes, but he could function. He'd sit there with his feet up on the desk. Cary Grant didn't dress better than Harry Goodman. And he'd say, "Play me some shit, boys." And Mike would go to the piano, and I'd rip off a song from my legal pad and start singing... "Wait a minute. That's a piece of shit," he'd say. "Throw it away. Play me something else." I'd sing another. Throw it away into the waste paper basket." He'd then lean over and then smooth the wrinkled paper with the lyrics that were tossed. I'd say, "What are you doin', Harry? You said that was just another piece of shit." He'd say, "Yeah, baby, but that's the kind of shit I can use." We formed Spark Records later with Lester Sill and put out the Robins.

MS: Back in the early '50s, like '52 or '53 or whenever, those disc jockeys were banning records and saying rock 'n' roll is over. In fact, around 1953, or maybe '54, *Billboard* magazine, which was on newsprint at the time, came out in the year-end issue and saying "rock 'n' roll is over." And I remember Lester Sill saying, "No way, man. This music is here. This is going to last. This is here for a long, long time." He was right. Jerry and I moved to New York later in the '50s so we kind of separated our partnership with Lester. In terms of the music business, Lester was our dad. The business now is a different game. And Lester, it's interesting. He was such a sweet man, such a human being. And he kept up with all the changes in the business.

Leiber and Stoller were later partners in Red Bird Records, started in 1964 with George Goldner. In 1966 you sold out your interests. Were you not seeking talent for the label? I know you were busy in administration and in the recent Jerry Wexler book written with author David Ritz, Wexler mentions you guys scouting the Young Rascals at a club in New York.

MS: We scouted talent very rarely, very rarely. I mean, the only act that we ever signed because we heard them live was in, like 1952, Linda Hopkins, who we heard singing at the Champagne Supper Club in Oakland, or San Francisco. Jerry and I were up there and Lester was up there. We went to this set-up club. They served you ginger ale and club soda, you paid your 50 cents and you brought your own liquor. She was performing there. We later brought her down to L.A. and out of our pockets, which were not very deep, we paid for a session and we waited to get paid back because we had cards printed up that we were A&R men for the rhythm 'n' blues division of Crystalette Records.

Here's what happened. After a while at Red Bird, numerous things led us to just give it up to George Goldner, and turn it over to George Goldner, who had helped to build it because he knew how to sell records, how to promote records. We knew nothing about that. We only knew how to make 'em. And one of the things was we were bored. And around this time, I said to Jerry, "If we get one more hit act we're gonna be stuck here for another 10 years." We had the Ad Libs, Shangri-Las, Dixie Cups, Alvin Robinson. What happened around that time, a few acts came to see us who were waiting outside and never got in to see us. One of those acts was the Young Rascals.

Recommended Introduction

There's A Riot Goin' On: The Rock & Roll Classics of Leiber & Stoller, Rhino R2-70593 (contains Leiber & Stoller hits as sung by Elvis Presley, the Coasters, Dion, Big Mama Thornton, Ben E. King, Wilbert Harrison and others; unfortunately, this appears to be out of print)

If you want to hear more...

The Very Best of the Coasters, Rhino R2-71597 (all 17 tracks were written and/or produced by Leiber and Stoller)

Smokey Joe's Café (original Broadway cast album), Atlantic Theatre 82765-2

Sam Phillips

by Hank Davis & Colin Escott

    In the formative days of rock 'n' roll, no producer was more important than Sam Phillips. If all he'd ever done was get Elvis Presley into his Sun Studios in Memphis for those incredible 1954-55 recordings that still resonate today, Phillips would be remembered. But he also had a hand in the success of Johnny Cash, Carl Perkins and Jerry Lee Lewis; he recorded Charlie Rich early in his career; and even before he had his own record label, he worked with such R&B and blues pioneers as Ike Turner, Jackie Brenston ("Rocket 88") and B.B. King. The following are two parts of a three-part series of articles that ran in Goldmine *back in 1987. The two parts we have opted to reprint were originally titled "Sunrise," covering the formative years of the Sun label up to the release of Elvis' first 45, and "Golden Sun," the glory days of the label from 1956-58, which ended when Johnny Cash left for the greener pastures of a major label, Columbia. After 1958, Sun never had another major hit, and Phillips eventually closed down the label around 1967, selling the rights to the label's catalog to the Shelby Singleton Corporation of Nashville. Before this, Phillips rarely gave lengthy interviews. These two pieces, which we have melded, first appeared in the July 31 and August 14, 1987, issues of* Goldmine.

Only a handful of non-musicians have significantly shaped the course of rock music. Only a handful of record company presidents have combined solid commercial judgment with artistic integrity. Even fewer have had the courage to damn the torpedoes and release what they knew to be fine music against the prevailing current of public taste and still make money.

Samuel Cornelius Phillips, president of the Sun Record Company of Memphis, Tenn., fits these criteria. He was one of the first, possibly *the* first, record producer in the modern sense of the word. In recording Elvis Presley, Jerry Lee Lewis, Johnny Cash, Charlie Rich, Carl Perkins, Roy Orbison, Howlin' Wolf, B.B. King and others, he decidedly influenced the course of rock 'n' roll.

For a few years, from the mid- to late '50s, Phillips released records that were both artistically valid and surprisingly successful. In other words, he was a success on his own terms and his success helped break down many of the barriers which had previously existed between black and white music.

Phillips has seldom granted extensive interviews so we were surprised and, yes, flattered when we heard that he would talk to *Goldmine*. Between the two of us it had been a 40-year wait and we had enough questions for a six-month interview: factual questions and general questions. Would he remember anything or had the past receded into a blur? Would he remember a bad debt from 1957 more clearly than a session with B.B. King?

Phillips greeted us in the lobby of his radio station. He has a piercing stare that had riveted Elvis Presley and all the others before us. He looked surprisingly youthful for his 58 years. A full mantle, a beard of long reddish-brown hair and a ponderous drawl. And he does remember both the sessions and the bad debts. The man has a photographic memory for sessions held in his stifling little studio 30 years ago. Not just the great names (most of whom were only household names in their own households when Phillips first met them), but also the lesser artists who cut one record and went back to farming or pumping gas in rural Arkansas.

Phillips is acutely aware and proud of his achievement. There are occasional traces of self-effacement but one thing is quite clear: Sam Phillips knows what he has accomplished.

"I'm a very uncommercial person," he told us. "At no point in my life did I approach this thing from a standpoint of commercialism. I knew that I was put on this earth for some purpose. As things worked out, I was able to do it and not starve to death. I was monetarily rewarded but, more than that, my rewards have been on the side of doing something I believe in fully when not too many people believed in it at all.

"I knew I was going to be up against a society which required that some fortune come in or you wouldn't be in business for very long. For some reason that freed up my mind so that I didn't feel pressured from inside or outside into making commercial compromises."

Sam Phillips grew up dirt poor in Florence, Ala. The Depression was in full swing, but he wanted to be a lawyer. Bowing to economic realities, Phillips pointed his verbal skills into a more practical application. Preaching and politics seemed to be out of the question, so he went into radio. As the initial excitement wore off, Phillips yearned for something new.

It was at this point that he started the Memphis Recording Service. From an inauspicious beginning recording weddings and sermons, he started documenting some of the blues music still to be heard in Memphis and pitching the masters to small record labels. From that springboard he eventually started his own record company.

This interview offers a glimpse into the complex psyche of Sam Phillips and, in the process, an inside look at the early years of the post-war record business and the emerging careers of some of its giants.

In particular, Phillips is proud of the manner in which he treated his artists. Most of the independent record companies in the late '40s and early '50s were notoriously rapacious, especially those that specialized in black music. Their margins were slim and they economized where they could: royalties and advances. An artist was often paid a few dollars in cash as a flat recording fee. If the record did well, the artist's only recourse was to hike his personal appearances and subsequent recording fee. On the other hand, Phillips maintains that he always treated his artists fairly.

"If I've got any forte at all, and certainly I didn't do everything right, it's my honesty and integrity. They're everything to me. They were back then, too. There were just very few people that I knew in the business that were as honest in their accountings as I was."

In running his operation, Phillips was essentially a loner.

"When I sold Elvis to RCA, one of the best human beings in the world was Steve Sholes (the country artists and repertoire director of RCA who finalized the deal to secure Presley). Steve really wanted me to go to work for RCA. I said, 'Steve, the worst man you've got up there, he'd be a hell of a lot better than me.' There was no way I would have worked under that formula thing. I would have been unhappy and I couldn't have helped them."

Even when Sun Records was at its peak in 1956-59, its staff was minimal. There was a secretary/receptionist and a publicist/press officer. Jud Phillips, Sam's brother, was sales manager and Jack Clement (later producer of

Charley Pride and Waylon Jennings) was the engineer. Bill Justis was the musical director. Justis later recorded the massive hit "Raunchy" for Phillips and eventually moved into session work for Kenny Rogers and many others before his death last year. Most of the orders were shipped directly from the pressing plants. Everyone, including the artists, helped with mailing the promotional copies. In the very early days, bluesman James Cotton, another of Phillips' discoveries, remembers hand-carrying records to jukeboxes in rural Arkansas.

Phillips recalls, "It was such an interesting thing with me that there was no way I would have a bunch of people around. I didn't want it to get too mechanical and I didn't want to get too far away from any phase of it. I'm like that right now with this radio station. They say a smart man is one who can delegate authority, so I must be a dumb son-of-a-bitch!"

Was the man responsible for so much memorable music a musician himself?

"I'm an artistic person emotionally. I played music from the sixth grade to the 11th grade in school. I never was a very good musician. I was a good conductor. I could always see the people that did have the talent and get it out of them. And they would know that I was getting it out of them."

Phillips retains a curiosity today about how he came to do the things he did. What were the factors which made him make a borderline decision to quit two secure jobs and go into the R&B record business? He can still recall the details with photographic clarity but it's the motivation which appears hazy.

"I think that the names and dates have been represented fairly well. I'm more interested in the psychology, the psychological aspects of what made me and what gave me the gift that I had. What made me take this very brave step? Looking at it from a strictly business standpoint, I'm not sure anybody in their right mind should have done it.

"I had obligations all my life. I was the youngest of eight kids, lost my father early on, I had a deaf-mute aunt... Anyway, I was trying to raise a family myself. I was at WREC and I had worked hard to get there. A little country boy that wasn't too good of an announcer, I guarantee you that."

However, Phillips started his tiny studio at the junction of Union and Marshall Avenues in Memphis.

"I opened in January of 1950 and went into a little storefront there. There was a vacant building and I worked on it from October of 1949 and we opened it up in the first week of 1950. I quit my two regular jobs in June 1951. I knew what I had in mind. I was recording weddings and funerals and I was taking care of the PA system of the Peabody Hotel, which was a big convention center for the whole of the mid-South area. (I) was doing the Peabody broadcast every night at 10:30 and then back at work at 7:30 in the morning and even doing the Sunday Symphony and concert orchestra. I was working seven days a week then. I was an 18-20 hour a day person.

"Then I went home and told my wife one night, 'Becky, I can't stand it.' I'd already had a nervous breakdown. This was psychologically, mentally and emotionally exhausting so I told her, 'I've just got to make a decision. I've worked awfully hard to get where I am. I've got a second job. I like it but it's not what I want to do. But I do have a great responsibility here.' So she said, 'Whatever you want to do, we'll be there,' and June of 1951 is when I resigned. I had no income except what I could hustle up."

When Phillips entered the record business, there were hard and fast demarcation lines between pop (Rosemary Clooney, Perry Como, etc.), country music (Eddy Arnold, Hank Williams, etc.), and black music (Roy Brown, Wynonie Harris, etc.). The market was dominated by the major companies: RCA, Columbia, Decca and Capitol. These were being chased by three newer companies, MGM, Mercury and London, which had all started since the war, and a host of smaller independent companies, or 'indies,' which included Atlantic, Imperial and Chess.

The indies mostly specialized in urban black music because the majors largely ignored it. Very few artist and repertoire directors at the major companies understood or cared for black music, and they had little reason to, either. Surprisingly, according to a 1952 survey in *Billboard* magazine, R&B accounted for barely five percent of total sales, roughly the same as kiddies' products.

One of Phillips' most obvious achievements was the almost unbelievable number of major artists who made their first recordings for him in that tiny piece of real estate at 706 Union. The list has often been repeated and it is still endlessly impressive: rockers like Presley, Carl Perkins and Jerry Lee Lewis; country superstars like Johnny Cash, Conway Twitty and Charlie Rich; blues legends like Howlin' Wolf, B.B. King and Bobby Bland. This list goes to such length that one surely expects to learn that behind it lay a crack team of scouts who systematically combed the countryside auditioning everyone in sight.

In reality, there were no talent scouts. No one but Sam Phillips himself. Pure and simple, the talent found him. Once word got out that there was a man in town making records there were, if not exactly lineups, then certainly a steady stream of hopefuls of all colors and musical persuasions.

This is not to take anything away from Phillips. Surely, word of his personal style and integrity also spread and encouraged some who might have stayed home. But even more to his credit was his ability to screen out the promising artists from the derivative and mediocre. Sometimes the promise was pretty thin, but Phillips still heard it. How many label owners and A&R men turned down Jerry Lee Lewis before Phillips smiled and drawled his approval? How many would have accepted Presley as he sounded in April 1954? Hindsight makes successful A&R men of us all, but what Phillips did, he did on minimal bearings with history yet to be written.

Phillips began by pitching his masters at the Bihari brothers in Los Angeles. The Biharis operated a television distributorship and a record label, Modern, which was soon joined by RPM. They recognized that the mid-South was an important source of product, and Phillips operated the only studio in the area. Among the first artists to walk in the door were B.B. King and jazz pianist Phineas Newborn, both of whom Phillips recorded for the Biharis.

After one year, Phillips acquired two hot properties: Ike Turner with his cousin Jackie Brenston and Howlin' Wolf. He signed them to personal contracts and abruptly switched his allegiance to the Chess brothers in Chicago. Leonard and Phillip Chess had begun by recording local nightclub acts but their unexpected success with Muddy Waters encouraged them to move into commercial blues. They quickly became Phillips' major customer. He gave them two massive hits, "Rocket 88" by Jackie Brenston and "Booted" by Roscoe Gordon, together with some strong sellers by Howlin' Wolf. At that time, Wolf was a DJ on KWEM in West Memphis, Ark., and

laced his tortured blues with weather and farming information. Phillips regarded Wolf as a giant.

"He had no voice in the sense of a pretty voice but he had a command of every word he spoke. When the beat got going in the studio he would sit there, and sing, hypnotizing himself. Wolf was one of those raw people, dedicated, natural. His message was definitive. Wolf, Jesus Christ, he was a guy I hated to lose."

By 1952, the Chess brothers were accepting fewer of Phillips' submissions. In addition, one of the Bihari brothers was opening up a label on Phillips' doorstep. By this point, Phillips had seen that he could make hits for others and he felt that he had been short-changed in many of the deals.

"I knew what it was like to be cheated. Just flat cheated. I knew that I was emotionally not prepared for that."

With all of these factors in mind, Phillips started Sun Records in March 1952.

"I honestly feel that I can say I know what it is to have a baby. I literally mean this. This is what Sun Records was to me. Thank God I didn't let anybody abort me. Tenacity is one thing and I have that. Also a great insight into other people. I read people well. If I hadn't read them as well as I did, I would not have been able to do what I did. Now, I know that it wasn't just musical knowledge that did it. It was communication. It was the viability of stuff that people had rejected for social reasons that the world needed to hear. To me, a lot of that stuff did not become legend overnight."

The first two releases were barely distributed outside of Memphis and Phillips folded the label for almost a year while he looked for some partners and settled a lawsuit over the name "Sun" (there had been at least two previous Sun record labels).

When the label was revived, Phillips had a small roster of local talent including WDIA deejay Rufus Thomas, who later went on to national fame with animal dances like the Dog and the Funky Chicken. It was Thomas who gave Phillips his first hit with an answer disc to Big Mama Thornton's "Hound Dog." It was too close to the original and it landed Phillips with another lawsuit, but it garnered a little attention for Sun Records.

Despite the notoriety and some good sales on the Rufus Thomas disc, Sun Records was still a sideline to the Memphis Recording Service. Phillips would load his equipment into the car and record weddings, sermons, speeches... In fact his company motto was "We record anything, anywhere, anytime."

These were difficult years but Phillips' reputation was growing. Phillips is convinced that the creativity he tapped into could not have been found anywhere but Memphis.

"The thread," as he puts it, "runs back to the delta. The only other place you see it is Chicago. But even in Chicago the creativity runs back to the delta. This is borne out by the fact that almost every top blues musician in Chicago grew up in the delta: Muddy Waters, Sonny Boy Williamson, Little Walter, Howlin' Wolf."

Blues artists came trekking to his door. Many of them had preconceptions of how they would be treated.

"I had to overcome the feeling that these people had when they came to me that I was going to take them for some kind of money, that they weren't going to owe me something when they left that studio, a charge for an audition. They still thought that there was some kind of hook. I had a hard time to convince them that there wasn't any obligation. I don't mean that I sat there arguing with them for hours trying to convince them. I mean, in my demeanor, my manner. And even after they came back time after time, many of them felt that they were going to get a bill, get sued, for services rendered."

By the end of 1953, Sun Records had not seen a hit for a few months. The returns were coming back and many of the best blues artists had headed north.

One of Phillips' last hopes was a vocal group that was not heading north – or anywhere, for that matter. They were the Prisonaires who, as their record label said, were "Confined to the Tennessee State Prison, Nashville." Their first record, "Just Walkin' In The Rain" was a small hit and was later revived by Johnnie Ray, who took it to the top of the pop charts in 1956. Ironically, Ray had to fight his way up the charts past Phillips' discoveries, including Elvis Presley and Johnny Cash.

Occasionally, Phillips would go to the penitentiary to record the Prisonaires but, more frequently, the group would come to Memphis. The guards would sit next to door sipping coffee in Taylor's Cafe while Phillips wrestled with the group's complex harmonies.

After a few issues, the novelty of the Prisonaires was wearing thin and Phillips began turning to white country artists in an attempt to keep his little label afloat. The first white artists Phillips recorded were the Ripley Cotton Choppers.

The Choppers borrowed their name from a group of Tennessee musicians who had performed widely during the Depression. Although they had never recorded, they were known locally for their broadcasts over WREC in Memphis. The Cotton Choppers group that Phillips recorded in July 1953 was headed by Raymond Kerby, a house painter, contractor, guitarist, rancher and jack-of-all-trades. The group performed in a traditional, basically non-electric style. They recorded with a guitar, fiddle, mandolin, string bass and included a host of local musicians and family members. The record sold dismally, although it remained on the jukeboxes in Ripley until 78s disappeared.

Phillips looked for something in his white artists that he had seen in the black musicians. The artist who personified the feeling that Phillips was trying to capture was hanging around Lauderdale Courts in Memphis with unfashionably long and greasy hair and a battered guitar which he played in two keys. It was Elvis Presley, young, hungry and disarmingly humble…

The story of Elvis Presley's 18 months on Sun Records has been copiously, if not always accurately, documented. The major point that Phillips wants to make is that he never said that he wanted to find a white man who could sing like a Negro.

"That's not what I was looking for. I'm not the smartest person in the world but I knew that wouldn't have worked. Even if it had, I wouldn't have wanted it. Not imitator. I was looking for the feeling.

"I have been misquoted so many times on this. For example in Jerry Hopkins' damn book (*Elvis: A Biography*, Simon & Schuster, 1971). And I told him so! Why didn't he just put it in the *National Enquirer*? Would have been just as well."

When Presley began his experiments for Sam Phillips at Sun, the first requirement was to find a backup band. Early in his recruiting attempts Phillips approached Raymond Kerby of the Ripley Cotton Choppers. He had been impressed with Kerby's playing when the Choppers had recorded their only Sun record in late 1953. Kerby talked the possibility over with his group but they decided against it. Presley was an unknown, a little weird at that, and besides, the Cotton Choppers already had a vocalist. It made little sense to replace Kerby's uncle Jesse Frost with Elvis Presley.

The next hillbilly band to record for Phillips was Doug Poindexter and the Starlite Wranglers. Again, after the session Phillips gently raised the possibility of the group backing up Presley. Poindexter decided that if his sidemen Scotty Moore and Bill Black were interested, he wouldn't stand in their way. Poindexter himself wasn't too impressed with Presley's talent – at least its country side.

"We were strictly a country band. Elvis worked hard at fitting in but he sure didn't cause too many riots in them days."

Nevertheless, as Poindexter recalled, "Scotty and Bill had the chance to go to Shreveport with Elvis (for a regular job on the *Louisiana Hayride*) and they wanted to go ahead with it. I stayed in Memphis. Eventually, Sam forgot about me. I guess it was all for the best. There was no way of knowing that success would come to Presley. Frankly, I thought the boy would starve to death."

But he didn't. By the end of 1955 Presley was the only act keeping Sun Records in business. Johnny Cash and Carl Perkins were starting to sell well locally, but only Presley was attracting large orders outside the tri-state (Tennessee, Arkansas, Mississippi) area.

Phillips had been approached by several companies, including Mitch Miller at Columbia and Ahmet Ertegun at Atlantic, to buy Presley's contract. One Saturday night in November 1955 Presley gave up his regular gig at the *Louisiana Hayride* in Shreveport and played the Annual Disc Jockey's Convention in Nashville. Steve Sholes and Ann Fulcino of RCA were watching closely and closed a deal with Phillips within days.

When Phillips sold Presley's contract to RCA in November 1955, he had few real alternatives. Presley would have left when his contract expired, and Phillips did not have the money to pay back royalties or promote Presley in the manner which RCA could. Presley was sold as a hot country artist but RCA saw that he had the potential to cross over into pop and immediately started to line up television slots.

Hard as it is to imagine when one sits opposite all the confidence and prosperity that is Sam Phillips today, in 1955 the man was scrambling, actually on the verge of packing it in: no more Sun Records. In turn, this might have meant that there would be no "discovery" of Carl Perkins (forever to remain an unknown with just two hillbilly records to his credit); no "discovery" of Jerry Lee Lewis (who was still two years away from walking into 706 Union demanding an audition); no Roy Orbison, no Charlie Rich, no "Blue Suede Shoes," no "Folsom Prison Blues," no "Whole Lotta Shakin'," no "Great Balls Of Fire." How different would rock 'n' roll and the '50s have been?

For Phillips, every day had been a struggle to stay afloat and the sale of Presley had given him what he needed most: 35,000 pre-inflation dollars in operating capital. Within a few weeks Phillips parlayed this into hundreds of thousands as "Blue Suede Shoes" hit the charts, while RCA was still wondering if they had just wasted $35,000.

The real loss is ours. Presley was never recorded in more favorable circumstances than in Phillips' little studio. RCA tried at first, but their productions got increasingly fuller and more mechanical. RCA is still sitting on a few vintage Sun outtakes and there might have been even more if Phillips had not been so short of money and recorded over some of Presley's rehearsals.

At this point in Sun's history, Phillips began to record more white artists. Thus began Sun's inevitable move away from rhythm 'n' blues.

"Keep in mind that there were a number of good rhythm 'n' blues labels on the market but the base was not broad enough because of racial prejudice," says Phillips. It wasn't broad enough to get the amount of commercial play and general acceptance overall – not just in the South."

When Phillips started peddling Presley records throughout the mid-South, he came face to face with the full force of Southern bigotry. He was selling white music played with a distinctly black feel.

"Even though I may have started recording (white) country music, I never left the kinship with the black man altogether. When you're on the road 65,000 to 70,000 miles a year as I was in those days, you get a lot of input from the ground. On Monday and Wednesday when the jukebox operators, and Tuesday and Thursday when the smaller retail outlets came in to buy their week's supply of records, I'd be there at the distributor. They'd tell me, 'These people (the blacks) are ruining our white children. These little kids are falling in love with the niggers.' These were basically good people, but conceptually, as to what life is all about, as to the kinship between the blacks and whites, it was just not apparent to them at all."

Sun Records' golden days began in 1956 with a string of hits by Carl Perkins, Johnny Cash and Roy Orbison. For the first time the major record companies were losing their grip. The independent labels controlled 70 percent of the singles market in 1956. Sun joined Dot, Imperial, Cadence and Atlantic. Phillips recalls this period with pride.

"The major labels laughed at the independents. They figured 'These damn people will go away and what percentage of the market are they going to get? One percent? Two percent?' So, while their eyes were closed to us who were hungry and knew what we were doing and weren't shackled by corporate routines, we grew beyond what they had expected.

"We took in an awful lot for a small company and we didn't take many returns. My good friend Randy Wood started Dot Records at almost the same time. He put out so much product and we had practically the same distributors in most cities. I'd go in and there would be no returns for us. Anyway, Dot would have warehouses full of records to come back and you could hardly find a Sun return. We used to have to check the returns when they came in twice a year. We'd sometimes find different labels, other people's product they had used to fill out a box. I didn't pre-ship or hype product. I think we must have set a record for the lowest returns ratio against sales. We could have probably sold twice what we did but the returns would have been up and we would have started getting careless. I didn't want to operate that way."

Sam's brother, Jud, who ran sales and promotion, represented the antithesis of this approach. It brought the brothers into constant conflict. As Bill Justis recalled, "When you had Sam, who was the Ebenezer Scrooge type, and Jud, who was lighting cigars with dollar bills, then it just didn't work out." In 1958, Jud left Sun to start his own label.

Phillips was also careful to maintain the high standard of his releases. The prevailing theory was to sling as much mud at the wall as possible in the hope that some of it would stick. Phillips took the opposite approach.

"We made it plain that if we put a record out we gave it a chance, although certainly with our limited staff we missed on some that we could have brought through. The distributors and jocks were always waiting for the new Sun release because we didn't abuse them with a bunch of releases that we weren't pretty damn confident in."

Sun's enduring reputation is based on the success of its major artists. Along with Presley, no history of Sun Records would be complete without recognition of Carl Perkins, Johnny Cash and Jerry Lee Lewis.

For 25 years it was hard to find a detailed account of Lewis' life. Now there are four biographies, including Nick Tosches' masterwork, *Hellfire*, and Murray Silver's insider's portrayal, *Great Balls Of Fire,* written in conjunction with Jerry's child bride Myra, now edging 40.

Very briefly, Lewis was born dirt poor in backwoods Louisiana with a family history of craziness. Married twice before his 15th birthday and tormented by religious demons, Lewis was destined for fame or notoriety if he possessed any talent at all. And he had it in abundance. No one in Nashville saw it when he went there in 1955. They all advised him to learn the guitar. But Sam Phillips saw his talent and snapped him up: "I knew if he could do anything at all, even toot a mouth organ, I had me my next star."

After one flop and four nationwide smash hits, scandal erupted when Lewis and his child bride went to England. Phillips had poured all of his resources behind Lewis only to see it fall apart literally overnight.

"Believe me, before that happened, Jerry was the hottest thing in America. The press tore him up in England over his marriage to Myra and it rebounded back home. It was a devastating, unnecessary, stupid damn thing, but what could we have done about it? I think Jerry's innocence back then and his trying to be open, engaging and friendly with the press, it backfired. They scalped him. There's no question about it. It turned out to be a very ghastly thing. So many people wanted to do in rhythm 'n' blues, rock 'n' roll, and this was just what they were looking for, to point the finger of scorn at a rocker and say, 'I told you so, rock-

ers are no good.' They picked on the first one they could. I don't say the press were entirely at fault, but they made so much of it... It should never have played a role of such significance in Jerry's life."

A few months after the scandal Lewis was a supporting act for Cookie and the Cupcakes, playing the small halls in Louisiana and Mississippi.

Lewis stayed with Sun until 1963. There was one more major hit, "What's I Say," in 1961, some fine music and a triumphant return to England during these years, but Lewis had to wait until 1968 before he was a headliner once more. Phillips had this to say about his contribution to Lewis' career:

"Jerry Lee Lewis has a superb talent. In my estimation he is one of the greats that left Sun, I don't think Jerry has been able to achieve product-wise what he could have done. There's very few people that have the ability to take a great artist like Jerry and really maximize the man's versatility and ability in the recording studio. I just believe I was one person who could do that."

It smacks of immodesty but Phillips is indisputably correct. Lewis would never have made those great recordings if he had been snapped up by a New York label and force-fed songs about teenage angst from the songwriters' pool in the Brill Building.

"It has an awful lot to do with the atmosphere under which the artist is working. This is generally true of any artist, but Jerry, particularly, is a very informal person and the conditions have to be just right. You have to have a good song, of course, but atmosphere is nearly everything else. Jerry has got to know that the

people responsible for the session, even the people that do the mixing, understand him. He had such spontaneity. Great artists, all of them, almost 50 percent of something good they might do happens because of an almost instant reaction to something around them."

By comparison, Johnny Cash provided Sun Records with a steady string of top selling product from 1955 until long after he left the label in 1958. Cash is almost an institution, which obscures the fact that he revolutionized country music back in the 1950s. Until that point, country music hits had been covered for the pop market by the crooners like Tony Bennett. But Cash forged a sound that was able to crash into the pop charts on its own terms while never losing sight of its hillbilly soul.

Cash had first auditioned for Sun as a gospel singer but was turned down by Phillips, who told him, "I love those hymns and gospel songs too, John, but we have to sell records to stay in business. We're only a small company and we can't afford to speculate on a new artist singing gospel."

It almost goes without saying that "Old Time Religion" was firmly etched into the character of most of the good ol' boys Sam Phillips recorded. One certainly doesn't have to look far for evidence of Elvis's religious roots. Gospel warm-up sessions, although never legally issued, are known by collectors to have evoked more emotionally charged performances than the pabulum Presley typically recorded during subsequent sessions. Likewise, Johnny Cash and Carl Perkins, both members of the Million Dollar Quartet, have proudly displayed their devotion to Jesus on national television, best-selling albums and international tours. Even Jerry Lee Lewis, the archetypal hard-living rocker, has been battleground for skirmishes between his fundamentalist heritage and carnal ways.

Sam Phillips's reluctance to record gospel music was hard wrought. He was no stranger to the Bible himself, and recognized this side of his artists and experimented with gospel music during Sun Records' infancy. His first attempt at recording gospel had involved the Prisonaires.

When it came time to think of a follow-up record to their modest hit "Just Walking In The Rain," Phillips surprisingly chose two religious songs. If Phillips was looking for "feeling" he had come to the right place. *Billboard* magazine admired the uptempo reworking of "Softly And Tenderly," but despite critical attention, the record sold poorly. For their final two Sun releases the Prisonaires reverted to secular music. Phillips learned quickly and must have regretted squandering an opportunity to capitalize on the group's pop music potential.

If Phillips made a vow to stay away from gospel music, it seems to have lasted only until January 1954, when a black quartet known as the Jones Brothers held a gospel session at Sun. Although he was rather quick to record this session, Phillips vacillated for nearly a year before releasing the results. "Look To Jesus" and "Every Night" sold dismally and further solidified Phillips' judgment that, whatever his faith or that of the artists, there was little point in releasing religious music. Record buyers, at least those reached by Sun's distribution system, were not responding.

While he debated over the Jones Brothers' fate, a young white singer from Manila, Ark., appeared in Phillips' studio. Howard Seratt had been stricken with polio before his second birthday, and was confined to a wheelchair when he first met Sam Phillips. Seratt played the guitar and harmonica and sang in a painfully simple and affecting style. He had been to the 706 Union studio once before, to make a private recording of two religious songs that were released on the obscure St. Francis label. Now, in April 1954, he was back and Phillips again recognized something very special about this young man. Sitting with us 27 years later, Sam Phillips remembered Seratt clearly. Of all the musical giants we discussed that afternoon, none evoked the praise or admiration Phillips reserved for this unknown crippled singer.

"Oh, that man! I have never heard a person, no matter what category of music, who could sing as beautifully. The honesty, the integrity, the communication, the unpretentious quality. It just had a depth of beauty about it in its simplicity. Just him and his harmonica and guitar. Oh, God almighty! That was a sad thing because I could have just recorded Howard Seratt *ad infinitum* and never gotten tired."

But Seratt never gave Sam Phillips the chance. They recorded two titles in April and Phillips dutifully released them. Predictably, the record barely sold. Nevertheless, "Troublesome Waters" and "I Must Be Saved" are among the most affecting Sun recordings for exactly the reasons Phillips offers.

It's fascinating to think of what Phillips might have done with Seratt's talent had he been able to mold it as he did Presley's and Cash's. But the chance never came. It was Seratt himself who drew the limits that Phillips could not transgress. The depth of Seratt's religious convictions proved one of the few barriers that Sam Phillips could not cross.

Needless to say, Howard Seratt was not alone in offering this impediment to Phillips. Phillips knew he had to take the religious feeling, perhaps even the style, the abandon, and secularize it. This, of course, became the formula for successful black music during the late '50s and '60s, for artists like Ray Charles and James Brown. In fact, it virtually summarizes the entire field of soul music.

Among white artists, it perhaps describes no one better than Jerry Lee Lewis. Jerry Lee came by his religiosity honestly: former student at the Waxahachie Bible Institute, occasional preacher at camp meetings in his hometown. Ferriday, La., and recipient of seemingly endless sermons from his cousin Jimmy Lee Swaggart on the evils of just about everything Jerry Lee lived for and dreamed about.

Among over 150 titles Lewis recorded during his seven-year tenure at Sun, there are relatively few actual gospel songs. Exceptions, such as "When The Saints Go Marchin' In," appeared as early as Jerry Lee's first album in 1958 and were treated seriously enough by Phillips to be overdubbed with vocal chorus and eulogized in his liner notes.

But the real key to Jerry Lee's religious fervor comes in his reading of secular music. His religion shows through in the quiet intensity of the country standard "Night Train To Memphis" or the rocking frenzy of hits like "Great Balls Of Fire."

What heresy! Wasn't it bad enough to mix religious and secular music? Did he have to "choose 'Great Balls Of Fire'"? This remained the ultimate irreverence until a year later, when Ray Charles turned a Wednesday night prayer meeting into an orgy in "What'd I Say."

Surely, Lewis knew this, and it was at the "Great Balls" recording session that provoked the now legendary theological debate that occurred between himself and Sam Phillips. While other musicians wandered away in boredom, Lewis bared the agony of his soul to Phillips, who tried to smooth things over to little avail. Yes, it's true the session continued (a final version of "Great Balls" was recorded almost immediately) and Lewis did not abandon his career as did other periodically tortured souls like Little Richard.

But in all fairness, it doesn't sound as if Sam Phillips can take much credit for easing Lewis' mind on the topic of religion. This was one of the few debates that Sam Phillips, aspiring country lawyer from Florence, Ala., did not win.

Sam Phillips: Now, look, Jerry. Religious conviction doesn't mean anything resembling extremism ... Now I've studied the Bible a little bit ...

Jerry Lee Lewis: I have too. I've studied it through and through. I know what I'm talking about.

Sam: You mean that you can't do good by being a rock 'n' roll exponent?

Jerry Lee: You can do good, Mr. Phillips, don't get me wrong. You can have a kind heart and help people.

Sam: I don't mean a kind heart. You can save souls!

Jerry Lee: No! No! How can the devil save souls? Man, I've got the devil in me! If I didn't, I'd be a Christian.

Sam: The point I'm trying to make is if you believe what you're saying, you've got no alternative ...

Jerry Lee: It ain't a matter of what you believe, Mr. Phillips. It's what's written in the Bible. It's what's there!

Sam: No! No! If it's not what you believe, then how do you interpret the Bible?

Jerry Lee: Man alive! There's some people. You just can't tell 'em 'cause they just don't listen. You can talk and talk ...

Like Lewis, Johnny Cash offered some resistance to Phillips' secular musical plans.

"Johnny Cash was another one I had similar problems with, but that was strictly on the first, maybe second visit. He had some exceptionally good original spiritual songs and he did them well. But I had to tell him that I knew I just could not merchandise them at all. I saw a thing in Cash that was so distinctive. I knew we had to go in a direction that allowed him to include some of his religion in a secular approach."

When Cash arrived for his audition at Sun, he brought a three-piece group. However, the steel guitar player froze in the studio, leaving Cash and his two buddies to carry the audition.

Phillips took this stripped-down sound, applied a formidable amount of tape echo to bring Cash's lonesome baritone into sharp prominence, and build a unique sound around the painful limitations of the group.

"The best country music in the world was being produced in Nashville," said Phillips. "I knew I couldn't do that well at producing country music ... but those guys didn't leave enough to the imagination. Can you hear 'I Walk The Line' with steel guitar added to it?"

When Cash's contract was close to expiring, the offers started coming in. Cash had some amazing consistency in the country charts and was a strong contender in the pop charts, too. It was obvious that the man had staying power and the majors were sniffing around.

Cash eventually signed with Columbia, which also claimed another of Phillips' early hitmakers, Carl Lee Perkins from Lake County, Tenn.

Perkins provided Phillips with his first taste of national success. Perkins' record of "Blue Suede Shoes," released in January 1956, rose to the top of all three charts: pop, country 'n' western, and rhythm 'n' blues. It was the first record in history to do so.

People like to say that Perkins could have been bigger than Presley if he had not suffered an auto accident just as his career was taking off. The truth is that Perkins was selling supercharged hillbilly music to bobby-sox crowds.

Perkins was a country boy who, along with his brothers Clayton and Jay, honed the edge of their music playing the bars and honky tonks in Jackson, Tenn. Like many of Sun's artists, they got nowhere trying to interest the major labels in their curious hybrid of blues and country 'n' western. After hearing Presley on the radio, Perkins was sure Sun Records would lend a sympathetic ear. He was right.

The truth is Perkins was lucky to have one massive hit. He was married, balding, and his music was firmly rooted in the barrooms and honky-tonks of west Tennessee. Some of the things that counted against him in 1956 make his music sound so good today. It was undeniably authentic music that was in a different orbit from "Poor People Of Paris" and "Lisbon Antigua," songs that shared the pop charts with "Blue Suede Shoes."

Sam Phillips' first reaction on meeting Perkins?

"I saw Carl Perkins as one of the great plowhands in the world. There was no way Carl could hide that pure country in him, but that means an awful lot of soul too."

More than anything else, Perkins was an influence. Rick Nelson has often said that he wanted to be Carl Perkins. More realistically, he succeeded in watering down Perkins' sound until it was bland and easily digestible. John Lennon and George Harrison virtually learned how to play guitar from Perkins' solitary Sun album, and the Beatles recorded three of his songs in addition to an unreleased jam session with Perkins. A few years later, Creedence Clearwater Revival blended Perkins' sound with some other primary influences and imaginary bayou folklore during their stint at the top of the charts. Perkins himself has not seen a Top 10 record since 1956.

Just as Cash, Perkins and Lewis all came to Phillips, they all left him. Why did they leave or, more to the point, why did he allow them to go?

There's no simple answer although it often had something to do with money. Phillips was never a big spender. To make things worse, by the late '50s he was competing with the big boys. How do you offer advance money to compete with major labels or international conglomerates? The simple truth is that you don't. At least if you are Sam Phillips.

But it wasn't just impractical frugality. Apart from his personal feelings, Phillips may have reasoned, "Let him go. I'll find another one." If and when he had this feeling it was more than sour grapes. Phillips' track record may have led him almost to a point beyond arrogance, to a belief in the same magical streak of luck that had guided a nonstop procession of raw superstar material to his door. Why should the luck stop in 1955 when Presley left? Why should it stop in 1958 when Cash, Perkins and

Orbison left? Why should it stop in 1963 when Jerry Lee Lewis and Charlie Rich bid their goodbyes?

The answer is simply that by the early 1960s the record industry had changed radically and so had Phillips' role with Sun. The Beatles were on the horizon and English foursomes were unlikely to come marching down Union or, by then, Madison Avenue in Memphis looking for an audition. And if they had, they were unlikely to have found Sam Phillips. By that point he was no longer listening to hopefuls as he had 10 years earlier. That job had been relegated, a gesture that took a toll on Sun's fortunes.

Most interviews have asked how Phillips found all that talent. We asked about the other side of the coin. What did it feel like to lose the talent he had not merely found, but nurtured? Didn't it have meaning far beyond the potential loss of income? Without being overly sentimental, wasn't it a bit like losing family?

As it turned out, Phillips had some pretty strong feelings in this regard. He revealed some hurt that a quarter of a century had done little to erase.

"It hurt when each one of 'em left. The one that hurt me the most was Johnny (Cash). I had heard that Johnny was going, first to Capitol. My distributors had called because word was out and I didn't know it.

"I had put Bob Neal in charge of booking these artists. Incidentally, I never got a penny in my life off these bookings. My brother Jud and I always booked our artists, set up all the bookings and never took a penny. In fact, we set up Stars Incorporated with Bob Neal for booking all the unknown artists while they were getting started.

"Anyway, Johnny was out of town so I called Bob Neal and asked him, 'What's happening?' I said, 'This isn't fair to the distributors because they played an integral role in bringing Cash through just as they had with Elvis.' If there were negotiations for me to sell another artist I wanted to tell them. When they called, I told them I had no plans to sell Cash. With Elvis, it was different. I just desperately needed the money. When the distributors had called back then I had said, 'Look I'm not going to tell you I want to sell Presley's contract. But I'm in desperate need of money. Even though we're selling records, it's expensive. I've got pressing costs, matrixing, telephone bills, overhead...' When they called me about Cash I said, 'No. But let me check this out for sure now.'

"I called Bob Neal back. Now here is my friend that I put in business in Stars Incorporated. Nice offices, nice secretary to take care of things ... and he said 'I don't know a thing about it.'

"Now some days or weeks later I called Bob again. I said, 'I'm getting too many reports. My distributors are becoming disturbed. These people have helped me. They desire to know the truth. When will Cash be back in town?' Bob told me and I said, 'When he gets here I want an appointment with you. I'll come by and we'll go out and see Johnny. You let me know when he's here.'

"Well, the phone didn't ring. Then I found out that Cash was back in town. I called Bob Neal again and said, 'Where's Cash?' He said, 'Oh, I meant to call you. He's at home.' I said, 'I'll be down to pick you up. Meet me in five minutes downstairs. You call Cash and tell him we're coming out now.'

"Well, I went out there and looked Johnny straight in the eye and I said, 'John, I understand you have signed an option to go to another label at the expiration of your contract with Sun. I want you to look me in the eye and tell me, have you or have you not? Bob Neal here says you haven't. Now which is the truth?'

"I knew when he opened his mouth that he was lying. The only damn lie Johnny Cash ever told me that I was aware of before or after. He said, 'No sir, Mr. Phillips, I have not.'

"I said, 'Well, I have evidence through the American Federation of Musicians that an option agreement is in the office of the President of the Union in New York right now. Is that not so?' He said, 'No sir, I haven't signed.'"

Why did Cash lie to him in the face of conflicting evidence?

"He couldn't face me because I'd been so damn honest with him. I had always told him the truth and he was not prepared. Baby, when I come to you, I ain't lookin' at no walls. I'm lookin' you in the eye 'cause I always told you the truth ... He couldn't handle it right at that time. Later it was documented that he signed in November of that year and this talk we had was sometime in January of the following year. That hurt! That hurt! It hurt that he would even leave, but that he would lie ...

"I mean, Johnny was doing real well at the time. Money wasn't really it. His and Carl's reason for leaving at that time was ... see, I had given each of them a lot of time getting started. Then I gave Jerry Lee Lewis a lot of time. But they saw it as if we were petting Jerry Lee and devoting too much time on him. They had forgotten that we had brought them along the same way. They were young people and there was an awful lot of jealousy ...

"Still, even with these hurts, even losing all of these people, I cannot say that there was an artist who worked with me whom I disliked. Even though some of them have said things about me that were untrue. But I cannot say that there's one of them ... and if there were one I thought was a damn shitass I'd tell you! But even if there was, it still wouldn't have anything to do with me thinking that if he had talent it deserved to be expressed."

Recommended Introduction

The Sun Story, Rhino R2-75884 (20 of the more rockabilly-oriented tracks from the label's history, including Elvis, Carl Perkins, Johnny Cash, Jerry Lee Lewis and more)

If you want to hear more...

Spotlite On Sun Records Vol. 1: Doo-Wop & Rhythm And Blues, Collectables 5809 (14 of the group recordings that were issued on Sun)

Spotlite On Sun Records Vol. 2: Doo-Wop & Rhythm And Blues, Collectables 5810 (14 more group recordings that were issued on Sun)

The Sun Records Story, Rhino R2-71780 (3 CDs, 74 singles from the original Sun Records, including some of Elvis' Sun recordings)

The Complete Sun Singles, Vols. 1 through 6, Bear Family (German imports, six 4-CD sets of the A and B sides of all the singles released on Sun during Sam Phillips' time at the label; truly an amazing collection)

Phil Spector

by Michael Aldred

In the first paragraph of the below story, which originally appeared in the June 17, 1988, issue of Goldmine, *mention is made of a pending Rhino box set of the best of Phil Spector's work. In fact, a related story with this article gave the complete rundown of the track listing for the upcoming box Less than a year earlier, in the fall of 1987, Rhino had become the sixth different label to release Spector's classic Christmas album, and the first since the originals on Philles Records to restore its original cover and title (well, close enough – the original was called* A Christmas Gift To You From Philles Records; *the Rhino version was* A Christmas Gift To You From Phil Spector). *As it turned out, the Rhino box never happened. Spector instead ended up with Abkco Records, the label of notorious manager Allan Klein. The box set, rechristened* Back To Mono, *did finally arrive in 1991, and it's certainly a worthy overview of Spector's career, but it was almost an anticlimax, arriving, as it were, three years late. Spector remains an enigmatic figure; his most recent attempt at producing were some abortive sessions with Celine Dion in 1996 that have yet to be released. But the power and importance of the material he produced from the late 1950s to the mid 1960s cannot be denied; he remains often imitated, but never duplicated. Listen to the productions of Brian Wilson, Jeff Lynne and Jim Steinman, just to name three, and you can tell they listened to Phil Spector's work first. The piece below ends just as Spector was at his commercial peak, in 1965, with his otherworldly productions for the Righteous Brothers.*

Phil Spector created his own sound in pop music in the '60s, one which reverberates even now. As a record producer and writer, he created a string of pop classics that left an indelible impression on the collective cultural consciousness of an era. Not only did he become one of the most successful producers of his generation – certainly the most famous – but in so doing, he orchestrated a legend that continues to serve him very well. Although his productions bore such names as the Ronettes, Crystals and Righteous Brothers, they are still usually called Phil Spector records today. Of the 40 or so records that charted and are credited to him, a handful can be counted among the greatest pop records ever made. Rhino Records' release later this year of *Wall Of Sound: The Essential Phil Spector*, a boxed set of 60 favorite Phil Spector tracks, affords us the opportunity to once again audition those legendary masters, this time in as near perfect a replication of the original recordings as technology permits. Now we will finally be able to hear, in their truest detail, the sounds that only Phil Spector and those immediately involved in the recording process have been privy to.

In a business renowned for mediocre imitation, Phil Spector stands apart as an original, an enigma that some have dubbed genius and others crazy. Thirty years after his first #1 smash, the Teddy Bears' "To Know HIm Is To Love Him" – which was also, incredibly, one of his first production efforts – the name Phil Spector retains a very special magic and awe, not only to collectors, but to the industry which at one time seemed, regrettably, to have turned against him.

Harvey Philip Spector (born Dec. 26, 1940, in the Bronx, N.Y.) attended Fairfax High School in Los Angeles after moving from New York with his mother, Bertha, and sister, Shirley, in 1953. (His father died when Spector was nine.) Like many other teenagers, Phil Spector dug rock 'n roll. By his 13th birthday, when he was given a guitar for his bar mitzvah, his interest in music bordered on passion. He had a particular interest in black music stations, and was intrigued enough to find out who put some of the records together. He admired the work of two local writers, Jerry Leiber and Mike Stoller, who were having their tunes cut by artists like Jimmy Witherspoon on Modern Records and Big Mama Thornton on Peacock. They had written "Hound Dog" for her, before Elvis covered it and took it to #1. Rock 'n' roll had its roots in "race music," as it was then called, and Phil Spector loved it.

By the time he was 17, Spector was trying to write his own songs. He formed his own group, the Sleepwalkers, with future Beach Boy Bruce Johnston and drummer Sammy Nelson, who became Sandy Nelson. Later on, he recruited two other friends, Marshall Leib and Harvey Goldstein, and formed the Teddy Bears. For whatever reason, Goldstein dropped out, and was replaced by someone his girlfriend Donna knew: Annette Kleinbard. The new combination clicked, and they started rehearsing regularly. It was Spector's intention to make a record of his songs and get it released somehow.

Annette Kleinbard is now known as Carol Connors – the writer, along with Bill Conti and Ann Robbins, of the *Rocky* movie theme; she has been nominated for two Oscars, four Emmys and a Grammy. Recently, Connors recalled the group she had with Spector.

"The Teddy Bears came about because my girlfriend was dating Phil Spector," Connors said. "Her name was Donna and we were in junior high school. I used to sing all the time – in the halls, wherever. He (Spector) asked me one day if I had $10, and I said, 'No, I do not have $10 but I think my parents have $10.' I got the $10 from my mom and dad, and we went in and we cut the flip of 'To Know Him Is To Love Him,' called 'Don't You Worry My Little Pet,' the most dreadful record in the history of records.

"But what happened was that my voice kept shining through, because I was the girl. It was Phil Spector, Marshall Leib and myself, and Phil said to me one day, 'I want to write a song for your voice.' He fell in love with my voice. His father's epitaph said, 'To have known him was to have loved him' and that became the title of the tune, which was 'To Know Him *Is* To Love Him,' and that's how that song was born.

"I was still in junior high school, Louis Pasteur Junior High School, and they were in Fairfax High School. We recorded it at Gold Star, with Stan Ross, the engineer. We did it in 20 minutes, two takes. Sandy Nelson played drums. It was the first (studio) thing he ever did in his life. One of the DJs once said to me, 'Well, who were you thinking of?' And I said, 'My father,' because I was too young to have a boy friend.'

"It literally did not sell one record (at first), but it was the most requested record in Southern California, because every junior high school and high school was calling to request it. A disc jockey named Lou Reigert in Minneapolis, KDWB, flipped it over one night. He just happened to put it on, and he fell in love with my voice; he's told me this. And he played it, and the lines lit up, and Dore Records got an order for 100, 300, 1,000, 3,000 10,000, 20,000, within, like, two to three weeks. And we said, 'My God! We've got a #1 record. Get to Dick Clark!' We performed it on Dick Clark's *American Bandstand* as the #1 record in the country, and the rest is history. It sold millions and millions of records.

"Phil was one of the singers. He did the Voh, doh, doh, doh's.' That is Phil, and Marshall and he did backup, and I did it in two takes. One take for balance, one take on tape. That was it, and we rushed out of the studio. This was like a high school get-together type of group. I was interested in music before this, but this was obviously the first thing any of us had ever done in our lives.

"Then I had a terrible accident. When I had enough money to buy a car – even though we got ripped off for a lot of the money – I went off a 350-foot cliff, and it really ended the group. I had bought an MG, and I went off a cliff. I lost control of the car. Twenty-six stitches to put my nose back on my face. I was pretty much of a mess. But in the long run, everything has turned out OK. I'm very grateful."

By 1958, the sound of rock 'n' roll was changing. Honking saxes had given way to twangy guitars, and Duane Eddy became America's biggest rock instrumental star. His records were produced in Phoenix by Lee Hazlewood, who became partners with Lester Sill. Sill had worked with the Modern Records group of companies and was associated with Leiber and Stoller. As a manager, a publisher, a promotion man, and sometimes a producer, Sill established a strong base of operations on the West Coast, and had many contacts in both Philadelphia and New York, which at the time was considered the main hub of the music industry. Spector met Sill in L.A., and after the Teddy Bears' follow-up records on Dore and Imperial flopped, he hooked up with him. (Also notable from this period is a Spector instrumental record, "Bumbershoot," cut for Imperial as Phil Harvey.)

"I had seen Phil in a studio on Fairfax Avenue, when he was recording the Teddy Bears," says Sill. "I knew the record would be a hit, even though I didn't have the time to really stay and listen. I was there mastering some Duane Eddy records. Anyway, Phil was in there working with the Teddy Bears, and I asked the fellow, Bunny Robine, who ran the studio, who he was, and he said, 'He's fantastic!' And I said, 'Gee, I love the record'; sure enough, it came out, and it was a hit.

"I was on Argyle at the time. Some time went by, and I guess Phil got unhappy with the record company, and he came up to see me because he knew I worked with Leiber and Stoller years before. And we signed him to our company as a writer and as a record producer. That's how it happened. I can't give you a year, but shortly after that, Phil traveled with us to Phoenix when we were producing Duane.

"Phil came along with us a number of times, and he also produced a couple of things for us: somebody by the name of Kell Osborne, and some other acts. He did the Paris Sisters for us. He did 'I Love How You Love Me,' which wasn't our song, and we had a hit with it, and then he did 'Be My Boy,' which was a hit, and we owned it. And then we started Philles Records.

"Lee and I parted ways. We still owned the company, but Lee and I went on our own, and I went with Phil and we started Philles Records. That's basically what it is. Then Phil and I had some misunderstandings about certain people. I set Phil up in New York with Leiber and Stoller and Atlantic Records. After that, he and I just parted ways, and I sold my interest to him.

"I had signed Phil to the publishing company, a writer's contract and a production contract. See, Phil was signed to us as a producer, to Gregmark Music Company, and we came out with a label called Gregmark Records, which was distributed for us in the beginning through Era. I could not get anyone to buy the master. I went to Snuff Garrett and some other people, and that's it basically. Jack Nitzsche worked with Lee then. He did some production, but basically he did a lot of arrangements for Phil, and he worked with Lee. It was a publishing company, and when I sold it out – well, I didn't sell it out, we kept it, but Lee and I parted ways. He stayed with Duane, and I stayed with Philip, and Philles Records came into being, which came off Phil's first name and my first name. I felt that he (Spector) was a monster, He was a fantastic piece of talent. It's a shame that he's so neurotic.

"Gradually, things started to change. You had the so-called British Invasion; the jocks were maybe looking for a different sound. Who knows? I think that was all part of it. But I think that Phil was young enough to bend with it, and to adjust, but he just ... I don't think that he would accept anything that was not original, that he didn't come up with, you know. He had an incredible, enormous kind of an ego, and also a very, very insecure feeling about himself, and that made him a little shaky sometimes. I would say more than a little shaky; I would say about 50 percent off center. But, oh, what a completely tremendous talent!"

The Spectors Three was the name of one of the projects that Phil Spector undertook for Trey Records, the company owned and operated by Lester Sill and Lee Hazlewood. Warren Entner, later a founding member of the Grass Roots, was, for all intents and purposes, a member of that group, although Russ Titelman and Annette Mirar – the first future Mrs. Phil Spector – did the recordings.

"It was probably the only project that was not successful for him during his little heyday," remembers Entner. "The record came out on Trey Records, owned by Lee Hazlewood and Lester Sill. It was when the Fleetwoods, two guys and a girl, were popular with the real soft, breathy type of sound. We were going to be the next. Phil had already graduated by the time all of us went to Fairfax. So he was sort of the 19-year-old legend, while we were 15 or 16.

"God knows who it really was on the record, but there we were in the photos, and we did a couple of TV shows, and it was an all-Jewish Fairfax High School trio, you know, a second-generation Teddy Bears. It was a Phil Spector record; what can I tell you?

"He was intriguing. He knew he was hipper than hip. I'd seen him earlier, and he was very shy. I don't know if shy is the right word, but maybe a little guarded. Then I remember him picking me up in a new Jaguar that he had bought. He was back from New York and he was super-hip, it seemed like. Very hip dialogue; the first time I heard some certain slang out of New York.

"He did something with the Paris Sisters around the same time. He'd done other stuff in between, I believe. Then he really concentrated on the songwriting thing, with the other songwriting teams. That's how he got involved with the Goffin and Kings, the Jeff Barrys, the Ellie Greenwiches. Everybody wanted to be the next Frankie Avalon or the next Connie Francis or whoever. How many wanted to be a great record producer? I guess Phil Spector did, because he went out and did it. I think he just went to New York and said, 'Here I am; I've got a hit record,' and found his way into the Brill Building. And that was it."

In the early part of 1960, Spector decided that the New York scene was where the action was, and that Atlantic Records, and the production team of Jerry Leiber and Mike Stoller especially, were what was happening. For some time, Leiber and Stoller had been producing acts for the Ertegun brothers. LaVern Baker, Ruth Brown, the Drifters and the Coasters were all enjoying great success with their material. As producers, they were without peer; in fact, they were quite innovative. They were the first to use a string arrangement, written by the underrated Stan Applebaum, on an R&B record, the Drifters' "There Goes My Baby," and were an undeniable influence on the work of Phil Spector and others, Burt Bacharach among them.

It was arranged for Spector to be put on the Atlantic payroll, work under the aegis of Leiber and Stoller and assist Jerry Wexler and Ahmet Ertegun in the studio. Spector's apprenticeship with the producers included him playing guitar on some of their sessions, sometimes contributing to the arrangements and writing songs. Ben E. King's "Spanish Harlem" was written by Spector with Jerry Leiber, and King's "Young Boy Blues" was written with Doc Pomus. Spector also had a hand in several record dates with Bobby Darin. Although "Spanish Harlem" is credited to Leiber and Stoller as producers, there is no doubt that Phil Spector was heavily involved in its creation. (*Editor's note: Even more intriguing is a never-confirmed rumor that Spec-*

tor worked on the production of Elvis Presley's first post-Army album.)

As a producer, Spector already knew the importance of a great song in making hit records; just like many others involved in the music business in New York, he began to hang out with publishers and their writers, people like Don Kirshner and Al Nevins, who ran Aldon Music, and writers such as Gerry Goffin and Carole King, Barry Mann and Cynthia Weil, and Howard Greenfield and Neil Sedaka.

Spector's collaboration with Jeff Barry and Ellie Greenwich began during this period of searching. As a team they wrote many of Spector's biggest hits: "(Today I Met) The Boy I'm Gonna Marry," "Da Doo Ron Ron," "Wait 'Til My Bobby Gets Home," "Be My Baby," "Then He Kissed Me," "Baby I Love You" and "River Deep, Mountain High." Neither writer is willing to discuss their involvement with Spector, Jeff Barry stating that he no longer does interviews about "the Spector thing," and Ellie Greenwich declining for "personal reasons."

However, in view of the fact that Spector's fame overshadowed theirs and that they were both, separately, involved in several successful projects of their own, it is perhaps understandable. They had a "first refusal" agreement with Leiber and Stoller, and they originally turned down "(Today I Met) The Boy I'm Gonna Marry," which was played for Spector by publisher Aaron Schoreder. The song was written by Greenwich and her collaborator before Jeff Barry, Tony Powers.

Spector liked the song enough to want to cut it with Darlene Love, but would only do so if he could cut a deal that gave him writer's credit also. It represented a practice which many writers even now are frequently required to submit to if they want to have their songs recorded. Of their later hits together, Greenwich offers that Spector did make a contribution to the process, although whether to the actual writing of the song or its eventual success is not made clear. It would seem, however, from the way that he works, that Spector would have to have had considerable input into the songs that he chose to record.

Spector's tenure with Leiber and Stoller and Atlantic Records produced no hits for which he was credited, although he'd produced records by Ruth Brown, LaVern Baker and others. Leiber and Stoller had more work than they could handle, and so when they were approached in 1960 by Dunes records to cut Ray Peterson, they recommended their protege, who left their organization to freelance for the job. "Corrina, Corrina" became a Top 10 hit, and Spector followed it up with a hit for Curtis Lee, another Dunes artist, "Pretty Little Angel Eyes," in 1961. Lester Sill called him back to the West Coast for some dates with the Paris Sisters, and "Be My Boy" scored as a medium hit in early 1961. The follow-up, however, "I Love How You Love Me," was a Top 5 smash, and became Spector's biggest hit since the Teddy Bears "To Know Him Is To Love Him" three years earlier.

By now, Spector was considered a hit producer. Gene Pitney was a singer-writer signed to Aaron Schroeder; Schroeder believed that Pitney had the potential to be a hit-making artist, and had formed Musicor Records to promote him as such. Schoreder wanted Spector to produce Pitney, confident of success. The sessions were incredibly expensive, as Spector spent hours and hours trying to create something different and unique. Commercially, the record "Every Breath I Take," did not do as well as hoped, peaking at #42, and financially, just about broke even. Still, it charted, and so did Curtis Lee's next record, "Under The Moon Of Love." Spector also produced a single for Johnny Nash (who went on to have reggae hits in the '70s) for ABC Records, and tracks for Connie Francis, Arlene Smith and others.

While his stature as a producer was growing, Spector was learning something about the financial side of the business, including a few things from his mother, who had worked as a bookkeeper for a company called California Record Distributors. He was not altogether satisfied with his current situation. Technically, he was still working for other people, even as an independent producer. He wanted more for himself. When, in the summer of 1961, he was offered the opportunity to record a group of girl singers who were doing a demo session for Hill and Range Music, he agreed – on the condition that they would be signed to his own newly formed company, Philles Records. "There's No Other (Like My Baby)" became the new label's first release, and a Top 20 hit for the Crystals. Mann and Weil's "Uptown," which followed, was even more successful for the Crystals, and, despite a few Philles flops not produced by Spector, Philles Records was in business. Its slogan: "Tomorrow's Sound Today."

Although he was a partner in the company and the raison d'etre for its existence, Spector was not the sole owner, so he was not in control of its fortunes. The situation evidently rankled him. He had very strong ideas about how he wanted to run his enterprise, and was determined to have his own way. So, in 1962 Spector accepted an offer from Snuff Garrett to become the head of A&R in New York for the West Coast-based Liberty Records, which would pay him $25,000 a year and still allow him to continue working with the acts he was producing. It gave him independence. While at Liberty, he cut the A-side of a Troy Shondell release and a couple of singles with Bobby Sheen and Obrey Wilson. None were hits, and within months he was back to devoting all his time to Philles. Bobby Sheen recalls, "I was signed to Liberty when I first met Phil. People thought I had the Clyde McPhatter sound, and Phil evidently liked my voice. I went to New York and we cut some things. The studio was in a hotel somewhere; midtown, I think. Anyway, we worked together then, and later when he started his own company, Philles Records, we worked together again. I was singing on sessions with Gloria Jones, who was in the original Blossoms. Sometimes we'd do backgrounds together, demos and things like that. "Zip-A-Dee-Doo-Dah" was just a demo originally, and then someone at Cash Box told Phil that he should release it just the way it is.

"It was different then. It was cheap to record, and quick. You could go in and out and not have to spend too much money. It was good if you were an artist, but not so good if you were a writer. Some places you could go in with a song, and come out with less than when you went in. People would jump on a song if it was any good, and the writer would lose out.

"Phil, I remember, was young, energetic and enthusiastic. He was out to make a name for himself, and records were the way he was going to do it."

At Liberty, Spector heard the demo of a new Gene Pitney song which was intended for Vikki Carr. Spector loved it. He told Snuff Garrett he was thinking of quitting the business and was taking an extended European vacation to think things out. Instead, he jumped on a plane to Los Angeles, and cut "He's A Rebel" for the next release by the Crystals. He bought out his two business partners, Lester Sill and Harry Finfer, and announced to the press that he had "acquired complete and absolute control of Philles Records, Inc."

Until that time, Barbara Alston had sung lead records on the Crystals records. Spector felt that her voice was not right for "He's A Rebel," however, so he had Darlene Love from the Blossoms sing it.

"I had my own group, called the Blossoms, and we did a lot of session work in L.A.," says Love. "We were always very busy and would sing background on every record that was ever being made at the time, or so it seemed. We knew Phil because we had already done some work for him on a few things.

"He called me up and asked me to sing the vocals on this new song he had, which turned out to be 'He's A Rebel.' It was just another session for me, and I didn't think too much about it at the time. I was paid double or triple the scale, I can't remember now, and that was it. I didn't see any royalties from the records; bonuses, yes, but royalties, no. In those days, if you had your name on a record, you thought that was good enough. Years later, after we had been recording together and I was Darlene Love instead of part of a group, Phil did put me on a retainer of $300 a week while he was getting ready to record again. I would get a check every week waiting for him to record me. He was doing some things with John Lennon and with Cher. I did 'Lord, If You're A Woman' and something else, but I don't think it ever came out.

"I did quite a bit of recording with him. They were always sessions, though. We'd record something and then it would come out, and you'd never know whose name was on it. Sometimes it was the Crystals – I did a few under their names – and then we did Bob B. Soxx and the Blue Jeans, and I had no idea who they were until I heard it, and I did my own records, of course. Sometimes I'd wonder which one I was supposed to be. I don't think it mattered, really, because they were always Phil's records. If he thought the voice didn't sound right when the record was finished, well, he'd take whoever was on there singing, and do it all over again. He had to have it perfect."

"He's A Rebel" hit the #1 spot. Spector soon released records on Philles by Bob B. Soxx and the Blue Jeans ("Zip-A-Dee-Doo-Dah," featuring Darlene Love and Bobby Sheen), the Crystals ("He's Sure The Boy I Love"), The Alley Cats (featuring Billy Storm, who Spector had produced earlier as a solo, on lead) and Darlene Love ("[Today I Met] The Boy I'm Gonna Marry"). The name Phil Spector was becoming synonymous with hits. By the time the Crystals' "Da Doo Ron Ron" came out, released on Philles 112 on April 27, 1963, each new Phil Spector record was regarded as an event.

The song was another smash for the Crystals, and on this record, there was another new singer, Lala Brooks.

"I was on 'Da Doo Ron Ron' and 'Then He Kissed Me' and that's about all," she recalls. "Oh yeah, I was on 'Little Boy' and 'All Grown Up,' too. I think Phil withdrew them. He was always doing that. One minute the record was released and then it wasn't.

"It was crazy. We were on the road, and we didn't know if we were supposed to sing the songs or not. I think we did anyway; I know we did 'Da Doo Ron Ron,' and 'Then He Kissed Me' and the other hits, like 'He's A Rebel,' and 'Uptown.' We'd have to sing those songs five times a day sometimes. Can you imagine singing, 'Met him on a Monday and my heart stood still, da doo ron ron ron, da doo ron ron,' five times a day? I got sick of it in the end. I felt 'Da doo ron ronned' to death.

"The Crystals started out just fooling around in schools and doing little clubs and things like that. We started doing backgrounds for some company, I think, although it was mainly getting known from school. In those days you used to do a lot of things in schools, singing and things like that. So we met Phil Spector and he wanted to record us because he was opening a company – Philles – with Lester Sill; he needed some artists, and he just tried us.

"Darlene and I did most of the tracks. Some of the girls only did the first ones, like 'There's No Other (Like My Baby)' and 'Uptown.' After that Phil took me to California when he knew I could sing. All of us were on 'There's No Other (Like My Baby)' and 'Uptown' because we did it in New York. But then Phil moved to California. After that was recorded, he didn't take everyone to California.

"When I did my tape, Darlene would come and do the background with other people. Cher would do the background. She would just sit there waiting to do backgrounds. It's true! I remember when I got off the plane one time, Sonny was a valet for Phil, and she had to go look for an apartment and she didn't have enough money to pay for the apartment. I thin the apartment was like $300 a month, and she and Sonny didn't have a place to stay, so she and I went to look for an apartment. It was too much money in California, because she couldn't afford it, and then I went to her house, and she was living in this flat that was really cheap.

"She was always dying to be on Phil's backgrounds. She used to sit in that studio for hours, waiting to get a chance to sing. I'll never forget it, and then as soon as we put the lead on, she would ask Phil if she could go in there and sing with Darlene and them, and he'd say, 'Go ahead, go ahead!' But she always waited for that opportunity, because she would be sitting on the side all day. They'd pick me up, maybe 11 or 12 in the morning, and we wouldn't finish until at least maybe 8:30 at night. Sometimes the tracks weren't done. The men would do them first, and then when they finished the track, we would go in there after, and we'd be sitting around looking at them.

"Phil was always nice to get along with, and I think my first gift from him was a poodle. He took me in this limousine, and he gave me a poodle, a gray poodle, and I was so happy for it. And he gave us luggage, whatever. But he never paid us royalties. So my poodle came out to be a royalty. Yeah, royalty was my poodle, and luggage that I could put him in and travel with. (Crystals member) Dee Dee Kennebrew and him didn't hit it off, plus ... he was just weird. He liked everything in the dark, and he always turned out all the lights. He was very health-oriented. Sometimes he could treat people kind of raw, though. Sometimes people would come in and say, "Phil, can I listen a minute?', and he would say, 'Get out of here, goddammit!' When he was busy working, he'd sometimes tell people, 'Shut this door and don't come back!'

"I'd stay out in California about a couple of weeks, and when he was finished, I'd come back home. Then when he wanted to do another track, I'd go out there just by myself, with my manager. The Blossoms used to sing on the record, and Bobby Sheen sang on Phil's things a lot. I think he (Spector) was mostly souped up on himself, you know. He thought that he made the sound. He didn't realize that me and Darlene and talent, and we were shortchanged. But Phil loved himself, to the point it was like sickness.

"The only reason I didn't do 'He's A Rebel' was because at that time Barbara was the lead singer, an Phil didn't know that I could sing. I came in last, and when I popped up, I was the youngest. I sang background on 'There's No Other (Like My Baby),' but what happened was when we performed on stage, Barbara got hoarse and I sang 'There's No Other.' I could sing so well, I started singing all the leads, but Phil Spector wasn't aware of it, because Barbara was always the lead singer. So he knew that when he got this record from Gene Pitney, 'He's A Rebel,' that Barbara's voice was too light to sing it. I was too new in the group to be recognized, an Darlene was recognized because we had been doing record dates with him, and so he recorded Darlene on 'He's A Rebel.' I could do it as well, but Phil didn't know it.

"We were all getting frustrated. Mary and Pat just dropped off because of Phil Spector, because we weren't getting paid. We weren't really making that much money. I mean, we were making nothing from the record company, and then when we started working with the tours – James Brown, Diana Ross and all of them – we were making $75 a week, each of us. That's all we made. And my money was supposed to be in a trust fund until I was 18. When I got to be 18, there was nothing there. The lawyers had been taking it, so I ended up with nothing."

In 1963 alone, Philles couldn't be stopped. There were chart hits by Bob B. Soxx and the Blue Jeans ("Why Do Lovers Break Each Other's Hearts?" "Not Too Young To Get Married"), Darlene Love ("[Today I Met] The Boy I'm Gonna Marry," "Wait Till My Bobby Gets Home"), the Crystals and, still to come, the Ronettes. Phil Spector and Philles Records were now big business, even for a small, independent company, and Spector's reputation as a phenomenon, albeit an increasingly eccentric one, was growing rapidly.

Danny Davis was the national promotion director for Philles Records. He remembers those chaotic times:

"I joined Phil on the East Coast. Phil was never a promotion man himself; he wasn't good at promotions; that's why I came on board. Sonny Bono handled the promotion for us on the West Coast. Sonny Bono I fired. I fired the mayor of Palm Springs! Sonny was already there. Phil and I had established a great friendship when I was at Hill and Range. A lot of business was done with publishers in those days, more so than now, I would say. He brought in "Zip-A-Dee-Doo-Dah," as a matter of fact, and we established a great friendship and cultivated it.

"When I left Kirshner, it was to go with Phil. He's a great song man. He knows good songs, and he's been involved for a long period of time. Some of the best songwriters in the country he numbers as his great friends. I mean, Barry Mann and Cynthia Weil, Mort Shuman and Doc Pomus Gerry Goffin, Carole King, Jeff Barry and Ellie Grenwich. They're all great writers, and Phil recognized that right away. And, of course, they all saw the same kind of thing in him.

"An awful lot of people regard anybody who worked with Phil, or who knows Phil, or whatever, as a very special kind of person, and I've been greeted with that time and time again. I can't tell you anything but the truth: It's a nice feeling. The business was run in a different kind of way when I was working at Philles. You had to rely on the distributors to pay you for selling the records. There were no returns. An awful lot of distributors did not pay, and even if they sold the records, they didn't pay. I mean, that was always a problem. You could have a big record – I mean a big record – and there was always the chance that you could go down the drain.

"We were still what would be considered a small company. We had a receptionist, a sales manager, we had myself, and we had a bookkeeper. Phil was never there. But gradually the disc jockeys weren't as enthusiastic about some of the things he was putting out. To say that he had fallen on hard times is a little harsh. I'm sure he wouldn't like that. I mean, we weren't gaining the same kind of acceptance that we once enjoyed.

"When he set up Phi-Dan (another spinoff label, established in 1965), we had a record called "Home Of The Brave" by Bonnie and the Treasures. It was a record designed to gain play through my own regard at the radio level. Phil thought that if the jockeys knew, if the programmers knew, that I was involved with it, we'd have a better chance for success. I was winning every award known to man: Promotion Man of the Year, *Billboard*, the *Gavin Report*. Anywhere it was, I was always top of the heap as far as promotion was concerned, and he wanted to capitalize on that. I really do believe that was a gesture to me, to either keep me happy or say thank you, one of those, and he gave me a piece of the action.

"Had it met with success, I would have had a real score, or been able to have a real score. I view it as one more chip, so to speak, in a great mosaic of my experience with Phil Spector, which has served me well for a long period of time. Phil has provided me with unending stories, and he has contributed to my stature in the business.

"I think that producers outdo themselves sometimes. I think that – and this is not meant to be a deprecating remark – it's just that his time came and went. If you doubt what I tell you, then explain to me why the Ramones' session (in 1980) wasn't a hit. Phil enjoyed a great run while he had it and while it was running. And life goes on, records go on, music moves forward, and the public is extremely fickle.

"A lot of people had paid him homage: the Beatles, the Rolling Stones, Dylan, but it was another time, another place. His time had come and gone. It's as simple as that. I really do believe that's exactly it. It's nothing he had control over. I think he still has hit records in him. I just don't think that he works at it any longer. But when he did, boy, those records were something, weren't they? I can still hear a cut by the Ronettes or 'You've Lost That Lovin' Feelin'' and still get taken by it. But everything old is new again. There's an awful lot of people trying to recapture his sound at the moment. They won't do it. Only Phil Spector can make that 'Phil Spector Sound.'"

Indeed, much has been made of the Phil Spector "Wall of Sound." It's also true that sound was often imitated, although it was never duplicated.

Ray Pohlman played bass on many of the Spector hits. He remembers what those sessions were like: "Nearly everything I did with Phil was cut at Gold Star. I'm not sure if it was three- or four-track at this point. Larry Levine engineered. They weren't rhythm tracks that we did; those were the tracks. Horns and everything. I think only strings were added later. We generally worked on one song per date. That was not uncommon.

"Phil knew what he wanted, and he would mold it as he went. He had very good songs, and very good artists, and good taste. The sessions were hard work, very hard work. There wouldn't be many takes, but there'd be a lot of rehearsal. Not so much for the band, but for the mix. The tracks were a performance thing. The entire room had a feel.

"Gold Star had a lot of innovation. Stan Ross and Dave Gold were the owners. At that time, studios were homemade; they were hand-built. The room, the echo chambers, were designed by Dave Gold. Probably, they were some of the finest chambers around, and they had their own unique sound. Much of the electronics was designed by Dave Gold.

"Most of Phil's dates were done on a Sunday afternoon, because the (studio) band wasn't available for him. We were too heavily booked. It was a lot of hard work, but we had a good time. We laughed a lot. It was sort of like going on a Sunday afternoon party and playing."

Nino Tempo first met Phil Spector in New York, when he was recording with his sister, April Stevens, for Atlantic Records. He, too, has vivid recollections of those sessions for Philles.

"I started coming to sessions on 'Zip-A-Dee-Doo-Dah,'" he says. "I was not scheduled to play, but he said to me, 'Nino, do me a favor; go out and play the lower part of the piano next to Leon (Russell).' So I was playing the bottom end of the piano, just a chunka-chunk-type piano. Leon was playing the top.

"Like I say, I wasn't scheduled to be there, but there was like two extra hands that he hadn't counted on, and when I got there, I guess he liked the overall sound that everybody was making, so that's what happened.

"There were a few accidents that happened. For instance, when Darlene sang 'yeah, yeah, yeah' at the end, that was an accident. When we listened back, everybody said, 'Oh man, that's great! Leave it in!' Phil said, 'You're right, I love it!' That was not intentional.

"When Billy Strange played the first guitar solo, it was like he was finding his way; he wasn't quite sure what he wanted to play, but was playing it safe. On the next track run-through, Billy knew exactly what he wanted to do and he started playing more and more and more. All of a sudden, it got to be too much, and I said, 'Phil, that first solo is the best one, man, it's like he wasn't trying too hard.' Phil went back to listen to the first take and he said, 'You're right. I like it.' So that was that.

"At the end of 'Da Doo Ron Ron' we were about to leave. Nobody was in the studio except Phil, myself and Larry Levine. And you know that bass drum that you hear – 'Bom-boom-boom ... Yes, my heart stood still ... bom-bom bom-boom'? I said, 'Phil, you know, the whole track suggests that there be a kick drum there. Whether it's there or not, it feels like it's there. Why don't I try and put it on?' And he said, 'No, no, no. It's like four in the morning. No, no. Let's leave. OK, Larry, just put it on.'

"So I went in there. The drums are still set up and I sat right on the floor, and that's me going 'boo-boo-boom' on 'Da Doo Ron Ron.' I remember he said it would be OK if he didn't lose too much quality on the pass, because he was going from mono to mono. Maybe it didn't make the record a hit, but it was a nice touch."

In 1963, the Crystals had another monster hit with "Then He Kissed Me," and then Spector released the debut record on Philles by a new group he had a special interest in. "Be My Baby" by the Ronettes was even bigger hit than the last record by the Crystals had been. The group consisted of three girls: Veronica and Estelle Bennett, who were sisters, and their cousin, Nedra Talley. All three worked around the dance clubs in New York City and became regulars at the Peppermint Lounge, and went on tour as dancers with the Clay Cole Revue.

When they met Spector, they had been doing session work around New York and had recorded several sides for Colpix Records, which later issued an album, *The Ronettes Featuring Veronica*. Spector fell in love with Veronica's voice, and the songs he began to write told his story: "Be My Baby," "Baby I Love You," "Born To Be Together." It can even be argued that the amount of time Spector spent on records for his future wife damaged the careers of his other artists. Darlene Love's "A Fine Fine Boy" barely cracked the Top 50, and the Crystals' "Little Boy," by Spector's standards, was a bomb. It barely made the Top 100. But "Be My Baby," "Baby I Love You," "Walkin' In The Rain" and some of the Ronettes' lesser hits stand not only as some of Spector's most spectacular productions, but some of the finest music of the '60s. And their LP, *Presenting The Fabulous Ronettes*, is one of the most coveted Spector collectibles.

However, Spector's greatest artistic and commercial triumph was still to come. "You've Lost That Lovin' Feelin'" was one of *the* top hits of 1964-65. The Righteous Brothers sang their way into posterity when the song became an anthem of '60s pop. Spector's creativity was reaching new heights, although at the expense of early Philles acts such as the Crystals and Darlene Love, who were dropped from the label by 1965. "You've Lost That Lovin' Feelin'" is one of the greatest songs that Mann and Weil — or anyone — ever wrote, and Spector's recording of it was brilliant, spectacular, dynamic. It remains an unsurpassed masterpiece.

The follow-up, "Just Once In My Life," written by Spector, Gerry Goffin and Carole King, was just as awesome, perhaps more so, although the song did not have the same emotional impact than "Lovin' Feelin'" had, and did not follow it to #1, peaking at #9. Two more Righteous Brothers tracks, "Unchained Melody" and "Ebb Tide," made Top 10 before the duo and Spector split. Ironically, the duo's Verve debut, a Spector sound-alike called "Soul And Inspiration" outperformed "Lovin' Feelin'" on the charts, hitting #1 for three weeks.

Recommended Introduction

Unfortunately, there is no legitimate single-CD compilation of "the best of Phil Spector" available. Among currently available CDs, the following is the best introduction to the sound:

A Christmas Gift For You From Phil Spector, Abkco 4005 (quite simply the greatest rock 'n' roll Christmas album ever; "Christmas [Baby Please Come Home]" is worth the price all by itself)

If you want to hear more...

Back To Mono (1958-69), Abkco 7118 (a 3-CD box set of most of Phil Spector's key productions, plus a bonus fourth CD contains the Christmas album)

Part VI
To The Present

25 Great Rock 'n' Roll Movies

by Paul Kennedy

Almost as old as rock 'n' roll is the rock 'n' roll movie. In fact, one could argue that without the right song in the right movie, rock 'n' roll might never have taken off. "Rock Around The Clock" was Bill Haley And His Comets' first single on Decca, a forgotten non-hit that had been eclipsed by his cover of Joe Turner's "Shake, Rattle And Roll" and, later, "Dim, Dim The Lights." Then the producers of Blackboard Jungle *opted to use "Rock Around The Clock" in the opening credits of their movie. Suddenly, the forgotten song gained new life and helped start a phenomenon. Ever since then, as writer Paul Kennedy, the acquisitions editor of Krause Publications' book division, notes, rock 'n' roll and film have had an uneasy alliance. In 1999, Goldmine published a series of "25" lists to commemorate its 25th anniversary. In that spirit, exclusive to the* Roots Of Rock Digest, *here are the top 25 rock 'n' roll movies, from the '50s to the present. Would my choices have been different? Sure. But that's part of the fun of a subjective "top 25" list.*

The marriage of film and rock 'n' roll has, to say the least, been interesting. When done right, as in *The Buddy Holly Story* starring Gary Busey, the two go together as nicely as a Stratocaster and three-chord shuffles. But when this union of rock and film goes awry, as in *Sgt. Pepper's Lonely Hearts Club Band* featuring Peter Frampton, we are reminded of just how awful the cineplex in hell is going to be.

Sifting through the good, the bad and the downright painful (rent *Xanadu* with Olivia Newton-John sometime), the editors of *Goldmine* have arrived at a list of their favorite "Celluloid Heroes." The list is as diverse as the music yet the movies do have one thing in common: Rock 'n' roll plays a starring role, whether in the central theme of the movie or simply the soundtrack.

And now, *Goldmine's* 25 Best Rock Movies of All Time:

1. Woodstock (1970): Directed by Michael Wadleigh; features Joan Baez, Richie Havens, Country Joe and the Fish, Jimi Hendrix, The Who, Joe Cocker, Sly and the Family Stone, Ten Years After, Crosby, Still and Nash, and thousands of hippies. A brilliant film that captures the music, the spirit and the mud of the most famous concert in rock history. Academy Award winner for Best Documentary Film.

2. The Last Waltz (1978): Directed by Martin Scorsese; stars The Band, Bob Dylan, Neil Young, Joni Mitchell, Van Morrison, Eric Clapton, Paul Butterfield, The Staples, Ronnie Hawkins, Muddy Waters, Emmylou Harris, Ringo Starr, Ron Wood, Neil Diamond and others. This incredible documentary about The Band's Thanksgiving farewell concert in 1976 is about as good as it gets. Director Scorsese also assisted in the filming of *Woodstock*.

3. Don't Look Back (1967): Directed by D. A. Pennebaker; stars Bob Dylan. Dylan, the person and the musician, makes this candid documentary of his 1965 England tour remarkable. Also showing up are '60s icons Joan Baez, Alan Ginsberg and Donovan. Dylan performs "The Times They Are a Changin'," "Don't Think Twice, It's All Right," "It's All Over Now, Baby Blue," and "Subterranean Homesick Blues."

4. The Buddy Holly Story (1978): Directed by Steve Rash; stars Gary Busey. Not only did Busey play Holly masterfully, but he performed the vocals as well, giving the film an authentic feel and sound rarely found in rock movies. Just how good was Busey? Put it this way, he was so good he even made those nerdy black horned-rim glasses look cool.

5. American Graffiti (1973): Directed by George Lucas; stars Richard Dreyfuss, Ron Howard, Cindy Williams, Harrison Ford and Wolfman Jack. A coming-of-age classic set in the summer of 1962, the film features cool cars, drive-in car hops on roller skates, and the lost art of "shooting the moon." Oh, yeah, and perhaps the greatest movie soundtrack of all time. Featuring Chuck Berry, Fats Domino, The Beach Boys, the Big Bopper, the Platters, Bill Haley, Del Shannon and a host of others, the soundtrack spent 60 weeks on *Billboard*'s Top Album Chart.

6. Saturday Night Fever (1977): Directed by John Badham; stars John Travolta and Karen Lynn Gorney. Travolta did more for white leisure suits than any other man in the history of polyester. Say what you will about the Bee Gees, but the Brothers Gibb helped define a musical era. Unfortunately, that musical era happened to be disco. But still, the *Saturday Night Fever* soundtrack charted No. 1 on Billboard for 24 weeks and stayed on the charts for more than two years. Oh, and it sold 25 million copies.

7. Jailhouse Rock (1957): Directed by Richard Thorpe; stars Elvis Presley. Along with *King Creole*, easily Elvis' best film, which may not be saying a lot. The King is caught in all his nostril-flaring, hip-swiveling, pre-Army glory. Great soundtrack featuring "Treat Me Nice," "Don't Leave Me Now" and the title song. Elvis choreographed the "Jailhouse Rock" dance number.

8. The Decline of Western Civilization Part II: The Metal Years (1988): Directed by Penelope Spheeris; stars Joe Perry, Steven Tyler, Gene Simmons, Paul Stanley, Chris Holmes, Lemmy, Ozzy Osbourne, Megadeth. Heavy metal documentary that pulls no punches. May be your only chance to see Ozzy Osbourne cook breakfast.

9. The Decline of Western Civilization (1981): Directed by Penelope Spheeris; stars Black Flag, Circle Jerks, Fear, Germs, Alice Bag Band and X. It's no coincidence that much of the cast of this powerful documentary about the L. A. punk scene at the end of the 1970s is dead. A revealing, yet funny, story with a breathless soundtrack

10. The Big Chill (1983): Directed by Lawrence Kasdan; stars Tom Berenger, Kevin Kline, William Hurt, Glenn Close, Joebeth Williams and Jeff Goldblum. Great music from the 1960s helps make a reunion of former college radicals now gone mainstream an entertaining picture. The soundtrack, featuring songs by Marvin Gaye, Temptations, Young Rascals, Three Dog Night and Procol Harum, spent more than three years on the *Billboard* charts.

11. Yellow Submarine (1968): Directed by George Dunning; stars animated Beatles. Story has the Beatles trying to save Pepperland from the Blue Meanies. Silly? You bet. But who cares? This surreal, pop-art film is as much fun to watch as it is to listen to. Songs include "Lucy in the Sky with Diamonds," "When I'm Sixty-Four" and "All You Need is Love."

12. Stop Making Sense (1984): Directed by Jonathan Demme; stars Talking Heads. One of the greatest concert films ever made, thanks to the presence of a major filmmaker and the mesmerizing David Byrne. Byrne's spastic performance of "Once in a Lifetime" is electrifying.

13. This Is Spinal Tap (1984): Directed by Rob Reiner; stars Michael McKean, Christopher Guest, Harry Shearer, Tony Hendra, June Chadwick, R.J. Parnell, David Kaff and Reiner. Dead-on parody of rock documentary with Reiner playing director Marti Di Bergi, who chronicles the American tour of an aging British band. Among the best gags: an amplifier that goes to "11" and drummers who spontaneously combust.

14. Purple Rain (1984): Directed by Albert Magnoli; stars Prince, Apollonia Kotero and Morris Day. Granted, the story line is mushy and the characters tend to be sexist and not all that likable. Still, the concert footage is dynamite. The soundtrack topped *Billboard* for 24 weeks during its seventy-two-week stay on the charts.

15. Truth or Dare (1991): Directed by Alek Keshishian; stars Madonna. Love her or hate her, Madonna knows how to market herself. And this not-always-flattering yet revealing backstage/performance film markets the heck out of the Material Girl.

16. A Hard Day's Night (1964): Directed by Richard Lester; stars the Beatles. A visual delight about a typical day in the life of a Beatle. Sort of. Super soundtrack features "Can't Buy Me Love," "And I Love Her," "I Should Have Known Better" and the title track.

17. The Kids Are Alright (1979): Directed by Jeff Stein; stars the Who. A bit overblown and disjointed, this documentary on the Who is still quite good. Wild interviews with Townshend, Daltrey, Moon and Entwistle, along with such tunes as "Magic Bus," "Happy Jack" and others from *Tommy* help capture the chaotic spirit of the group.

18. Wayne's World (1992): Directed by Penelope Spheeris; starring Mike Myers (Wayne) and Dana Carvey (Garth). The movie plays out every teenage boy's fantasy: to host a cable access rock talk show from his basement in Aurora, Ill. OK, so maybe Aurora isn't part of the fantasy, but Wayne's love interest, Tia Carrere, certainly is. Schwinnng! Classic scene: The boys lip-synching Queen's "Bohemian Rhapsody" while cruising in the Garth Mobile. A most excellent movie.

19. Dazed and Confused (1993): Directed by Richard Linklater; stars Jason London, Rory Cochrane, Wiley Wiggins and Milla Jovovich. If you've ever wondered what it was like graduating from high school in 1976, then wonder no more. Amazingly accurate portrayal right down to the clothes, the hair, the language, the bongs and the music. The soundtrack, featuring songs by Ted Nugent, Black Oak Arkansas, Nazareth,

War, Kiss, Foghat and Rick Deranger, spent 71 weeks on the *Billboard* charts.

20. The Blues Brothers (1980): Directed by John Landis; starring John Belushi and Dan Aykroyd. Forgive the excessive car chases and the automobile carnage, this movie is packed with great tunes. It's worth the price of admission alone to catch Aretha Franklin and the late, great Cab Calloway in action. Besides, the boys' deadpan covers of "Stand By Your Man" and the theme from "Rawhide" are a hoot.

21. The Commitments (1991): Directed by Alan Parker; stars Andrew Strong, Angeline Ball, Robert Arkins, Maria Doyle, Bronagh Gallagher. A band of Irish misfits come together to play American rhythm and blues and just about hit it big before imploding. Funny with a extremely danceable soundtrack laced with such standards as "Mustang Sally," "Take Me to The River," "Try a Little Tenderness," "In the Midnight Hour" and "Destination Anywhere." The soundtrack charted for 76 weeks.

22. Grease (1978): Directed by Randal Kleiser; stars John Travolta and Olivia Newton-John. Yeah, we know, another John Travolta movie, and this one co-starring Olivia Newton-John, for crying out loud. Well, let's not forget that rock is built for summer fun, and this was a summer hit. And you have to admit that Olivia did look pretty hot in those tight, shiny black pants. The soundtrack, featuring the title song by Frankie Valli, was No. 1 for twelve weeks on Billboard. All told, it spent 77 weeks on the charts.

23. Dirty Dancing (1987): Directed by Emile Ardolino; stars Patrick Swayze and Jennifer Grey. Spoiled girl (Grey) learns a little something about life and dancing when she meets dreamboat dance instructor (Swayze) on summer vacation. Soundtrack topped the charts for 18 weeks, thanks in part to "(I've Had) The Time of My Life," which won an Academy Award for best song.

24. National Lampoon's Animal House (1978): Directed by John Landis; stars John Belushi, Tim Matheson, John Vernon, Tom Hulce, Karen Allen and Donald Sutherland. OK, so perhaps not your classic rock 'n' roll movie but a heckuva lot of fun nonetheless. Features a wonderfully sloppy – and sloshed – cover of "Louie Louie." And let's not forget the goofy floor dancing done to "Shout."

25. Rock 'n' Roll High School (1979): Directed by Allan Arkush; stars P. J. Soles, Vincent Van Patten, Dey Young and the Ramones. High-school kids rebel against tyranny of new principal. What, you were expecting *The Graduate*? The movie never takes itself seriously and the soundtrack is a ripper, featuring "Teenage Lobotomy," "Blitzkrieg Bop," "I Wanna Be Sedated," "Sheena Is a Punk Rocker" and the title song.

The 45 — In The Beginning

by Tim Neely

The following article did not first appear in Goldmine *magazine. It was originally meant for publication in March or April of 1999, to commemorate the 50th anniversary of the 45 rpm single. Instead, it first appeared on the Goldmine web site, www.goldminemag.com, in the spring of 1999. Another version of this article appeared in the introduction to the* Goldmine Price Guide To 45 RPM Records, 2nd Edition, *which was published in the spring of 1999. The rise of the 45 coincided with the rise of rock 'n' roll in the mid-1950s; more copies of "Rock Around The Clock" changed hands in the big-holed 7-inch size than the small-holed, more fragile 10-inch size, and by 1959, the 78 was basically extinct.*

Fifty years ago this year – March 31, 1949, to be exact – the 45 rpm record was introduced to an unsuspecting world that didn't yet know it needed its second new record format in as many years.

Basically, there's no really good reason why 45 rpm records exist in the first place. They were created out of a combination of rivalry and spite in the heady post-World War II era. In June of 1948, Columbia Records announced its new microgroove 33 1/3 rpm album, which it called by the trademark "LP." (It would later lose the trademark because the term had become generic.) As a courtesy, William Paley, chairman of CBS (owner of Columbia Records), demonstrated the new format to General Robert Sarnoff, president of NBC (which owned RCA Victor Records), several weeks before the public announcement. The hope was for RCA to join in with Columbia – they were the two major players in recorded music at that time – to ensure the success of the new format.

Instead, according to Howard "Scotty" Scott, one of the Columbia staff who was part of the invention of the LP, "When Sarnoff heard the demonstration, he was furious and chewed out his entire staff in front of Paley and (Bill) Wallerstein (the true inventor of the LP). Sarnoff left in a huff."

Columbia was so eager to have its new system accepted as the standard that it didn't even patent the technology. It was willing to let other record companies use it without paying a royalty. But refusing to admit that they'd been beaten by a competitor, the RCA Victor engineers immediately went to work on their own "new and improved" system. RCA, in fact, would be the last of the major labels to finally release its own 33 1/3 rpm albums, possibly not doing so until 1951.

"RCA decided that they were going to come out with a new system because they thought that they were powerful enough to get away with it," said George Avakian, another of the team involved in the 33 1/3 rpm LP, in an interview with Michael Hobson of Classic Records in 1998. "In 1962, when I was at RCA, someone finally told me where 45 rpm came from. They apparently took 78 and subtracted 33 which left them with 45, which they went with out of spite."

And the "Battle of the Speeds" was on.

Some claim that the 45 was introduced earlier in the year than March 31, but Norm Katuna's study of actual RCA Distributor's Record Bulletins from the era pinpoint the exact date.

Katuna, a long-time record collector from southern California, annually posts his research into RCA Victor's introduction of the 45 in several Usenet newsgroups. He notes, "In the March 21, 1949 issue of the Bulletin, ALL record listings are with the 20 and 21 prefix. These were 78 issue prefixes. Also, nowhere in the Bulletin is there ANY mention of 45s, past or future. The back page shows some of the prior three issues' releases, and they all have 20, 21 and 22 prefixes---all 78s. So there were no 45 rpm record issues from RCA as of this issue. Also, in the March 28, 1949 Bulletin, even though it is in part a special issue dealing with the upcoming (that week) unveiling and beginning of the 45, none of the new issues for that week were on 45 either. They all had the 20, 21 and 22 prefixes. So as of this date, no 45s had ever been commercially issued."

RCA ran a four-page ad in the April 2, 1949 *Billboard* magazine, directed at RCA Victor dealers, trumpeting their "50-year marketing achievement."

"To them must go much of the praise for these two newest and finest examples of research and engineering – the best automatic changer ever built – the finest record ever made," read the ad. "The new RCA Victor record and changer constitute the sensible, modern, inexpensive way to enjoy recorded music. The product is ready... the public is ready. A demonstration, more than ever before, means a 'close.' Its advantages will eventually make it the only way to play music in the home."

The introduction to the new records spent as much time talking about the new record changer as it did the records itself. RCA must have realized one of the big improvements of the Columbia system – the consumer didn't have to get up and change sides every four minutes anymore. Thus the need for a fast, reliable automatic changer so that their records could play continuously as long as an LP did.

Thus, also, the large center hole. As RCA intended for its system to be an alternative to Columbia's, it had to have a way for consumers to put many records on its changer at once and not have to worry about handling. RCA probably measured some workers' hands and came up with a size at which most people could grab the record's edge and the inside of the large hole without touching the record groove.

The ad finally did get around to praising the new records, but oddly never once mentioned the speed of the records. Among other things, it hailed the "CONVENIENT 7-INCH SIZE! More than 150 single records or 18 symphonies fit in one foot of bookshelf space. No storage problems for your customers. You can display a wider, more complete selection without sacrifice of space." (Anyone who collects 45s today realizes the truth of this. It's amazing how little space 1,000 45s consumes.)

And the other item of note to collectors today: "Sparkling identifying colors!--Record classification is simplified because a different color is used on the entire record... not just on the label to denote each classification. This helps you to determine the type of record at a mere glance."

Yes, one of RCA's marketing gimmicks was to make each type of music correspond with a different color of vinyl – black for pop, red for classical, midnight blue for "light classics," green for country-western, yellow for children's, sky blue for international, and "cerise" (not orange) for rhythm and blues. That lasted for a couple years; by 1952, all of RCA's 45s were on black vinyl.

On debut day, March 31, RCA Victor released 76 albums and 104 singles on 7-inch, large-hole, 45 rpm records. "Albums" were three- or four-record (sometimes more) boxed sets of 45s meant to be stacked on a changer for continuous play. (That's why, in a four-record box, Side 1 was backed with Side 8, Side 2 with Side 7, Side 3 with Side 6, and Side 4 with Side 5.) Most of these were reissues of material first made available on 78s.

Among the promotional items RCA used to sell its new system was a custom display for record stores. It consisted of a rotating, elevated carousel, which had seven different color threads hanging from it, one each for the colors of RCA Victor records. The base of the display was a 45 rpm turntable that played something called the "Whirl-Away Demonstration Record" over and over as the carousel rotated above it. It was named for Whirlaway, the famous horse that won the Triple Crown of thoroughbred racing in 1941. Only two copies of the record, probably the first 45 ever made expressly for promotional purposes, are known to exist today, though others likely survive.

After the initial burst of 45 rpm releases, RCA Victor began releasing the hits of the day on the new format. The first song to hit the top of the *Billboard* charts that was available on 45 at the time was "A - You're Adorable" by Perry Como (RCA Victor 47-2899) in the May 7, 1949 issue. That was followed the next week by the year's biggest hit, "Riders in the Sky (A Cowboy Legend)" by Vaughn Monroe (RCA Victor 47-2902).

Columbia, meanwhile, didn't sit idly by as RCA made its splash with the new format. It introduced its own single format in April 1949, the microgroove 7-inch single. These had a small hole and played at 33 1/3 rpm, so they were incompatible with RCA's one-speed, wide-spindled changers. But Columbia never marketed them with much zeal; microgroove 7-inch singles were a failure and were discontinued in early 1951. Attempts were made in the early 1960s to reintroduce them to the public without success, though certain segments of the jukebox trade used stereo 7-inch 33 1/3 rpm small-holed singles into the 1970s.

As RCA was on the way to winning that battle, it was going to lose the war. Its 45 rpm albums were no match for Columbia's long-players. Who was going to listen to a movement of a symphony on four 45s, complete with interruptions every 4-6 minutes, when one could listen to the entire thing without a break on an LP? Because of this, there were strong rumors early in the 45's lifetime that RCA was going to pull the plug.

But something quite unexpected happened. Kids caught on to the 45 and began to make it the format of choice for singles. RCA quickly used that as a selling point. Quoting the RCA Distributor's Record Bulletin from November 14, 1949: "…(F)rom coast to coast – teen-agers are lining up for bargain player attachments. The whole thing's on key with their allowances – neat little records they can slip in their pockets, with a first-class band playing their favorite hit--for 49 cents. Times are like the 30's, the early 40's again, when the youngsters made up the big biz in the pop market. …(T)hey go for the lowest priced at the new speed, they go for the little disc that fits on the shelf beside their paper-backed novels, is unbreakable, and has quality of tone that can't be matched."

By this time, a second label – Capitol Records of Hollywood – had begun manufacturing 45s. Its earliest 45s, peculiarly, had a "54" prefix before the catalog number. Perhaps this was because at the time RCA's own 45s had prefixes from "47" through "53." Capitol also added a "57" prefix to its 78s of the last few months of 1949. But it quickly abandoned that system; by early 1950, its 45s had an "F" prefix and its

78s had no prefix. MGM also began manufacturing 45s in 1949 using numbers in the 8000s; among its first was the year's biggest country hit, Hank Williams' "Lovesick Blues" (MGM 45-8010), and the big R&B hit, Ivory Joe Hunter's "I Almost Lost My Mind" (MGM 45-8011), the latter the first No. 1 R&B hit to be on both 78 and 45. MGM quickly abandoned the separate numbering system, instead putting the letter "K" before the five-digit 78 rpm number.

In early 1950, other labels began joining the 45 parade one by one. The first non-RCA chart topper to be available on 45 at the time it hit the top was "The Cry of the Wild Goose" by Frankie Laine (Mercury 5363-X45). Two on semi-independent labels followed, Eileen Barton's "If I Knew You Were Comin' I'd've Baked a Cake" (National 9103-X45) and Teresa Brewer's "Music! Music! Music! (London 45-30023).

The Decca/Coral/Brunswick labels were among the last majors to make 45s. The Ames Brothers' "Rag Mop" (Coral 60140) was the last No. 1 hit on the Billboard Best Sellers chart to be available only on 78, and it was never issued on 45 with that number. Two earlier 1950 Decca No. 1 hits were later released on 45 with their original numbers – the Andrews Sisters' "I Can Dream, Can't I?" (Decca

24705) and Red Foley's crossover hit "Chattanoogie Shoe Shine Boy" (Decca 46205).

Finally, in late 1950, Columbia bit the bullet and started making its own 45s. They originally had a "6" prefix followed by a three-digit number, but that was quickly abandoned for a "4" prefix before the same five-digit number that adorned the 78.

The independent labels were much slower to embrace the 45. Aladdin and Savoy were among the first, as each had a handful of 7-inch singles available in late 1950. King/DeLuxe/Federal began in 1951, as did Swing Time, Specialty, United and RPM/Modern. Atlantic, one of the key R&B labels, began in mid-1951 by reissuing two of their biggest hits onto 45s, Ruth Brown's "Teardrops From My Eyes" (Atlantic 919-45) and Joe Morris' "Anytime, Any Place, Anywhere" (Atlantic 914-45). Surprisingly, the last Billboard No. 1 record on the R&B chart that was available only on 78 when it was on top was the classic "Rocket 88" by Jackie Brenston (Chess 1458) in June 1951. Only three years later were a small number of 45s pressed in Los Angeles with the same label and number; these are among the world's most valuable 45s.

Chess/Checker didn't begin full-scale production of 45s until 1952, and neither did Imperial. Most new labels of the era, such as Vee Jay, made both 45s and 78s from their first release. An exception was Sun, which started in 1953, yet had four 78-only releases before doing records both ways. Many of the early 45s on independent labels are among the rarest and most sought-after of all 45s.

By 1955, the 45 was firmly ensconced as the dominant single format in the United States. That was the year that 45 sales surpassed 78 sales for the first time. Perhaps not coincidentally, that's also the year that a rock 'n' roll song hit No. 1 on Billboard for the first time. Within another two years, several major labels already were on the verge of discontinuing 78s, including Capitol and Columbia. By 1959, only a few 78s were being made in the U.S., though they continued to be made elsewhere well into the 1960s. (Beatles singles from 1964 are known to exist on 78s made in India!)

And despite periodic challenges, the 7-inch 45 with the large hole remained the dominant American singles format for the next 30 years.

2OOO Fan Club Directory

The following is a selected list of clubs and fanzines dedicated to recording artists. For more information about the clubs listed here, most require that you send them a self-addressed stamped envelope. For more information about fan clubs in general, including clubs formed in honor of actors, non-recording artists, sports figures, etc, we recommend that you contact the excellent National Association of Fan Clubs at 818-763-3290 or visit http://fanclubs.eonline.com/. The information contained here comes, more or less, verbatim from the clubs or their publications and is not individually verified by *Goldmine*. *Goldmine* cannot accept responsibility for any claims made by the clubs. Costs noted with $ should be paid for in U.S. funds; prices noted with £, in British pounds sterling.

A

JOHN AGAR

The John Agar Fan Club
Scott Hughes, president
7901 Iroquois Court
Woodridge IL 60517-3332 USA
Phone: 630-985-4714
Best time to call: Weekdays after 6 p.m.
Web address: www.tou.com/host/johnagar/index.html
E-mail address: joagar@ameritech.net
Cost: $5 USA; $6 Canada; $8 overseas
Frequency: Twice a year
Special features: Members receive an autographed snapshot.
Description: This is the only fan club officially authorized by Western and Sci-Fi film hero and recording artist John Agar. *The John Agar Newsletter* tells the latest news from and about John Agar.

THE ALLMAN BROTHERS

Hittin' The Note — **The Quarterly Almanac For Allman Brothers Band Fans**
Kid Glove Enterprises
2305 Vineville Avenue

Macon GA 31204 USA
Phone: 912-746-4615
Cost: $21 USA; $25 Canada; $30 overseas; back issues, $6 each

DAVE ALVIN AND THE BLASTERS

American Music: **The Blasters and Dave Alvin Newsletter**
PO Box 210071
Woodhaven NY 11421 USA
E-mail address: davistb@aol.com
Cost: $8
Frequency: Quarterly
Special features: Interviews, stories, tour dates, contests
Description: This official newsletter/fanzine gets all its information directly from the band members.

B

SYD BARRETT

Late Night — **A Magazine About Syd Barrett**
Jon Allan II
Box 499
Barrington NH 03825 USA
E-mail address: jon@elmers.net
Cost: $5 per issue
Frequency: Twice a year (Apr. & Oct.)
Special features: Interviews, news, reviews, in-depth research

THE BEACH BOYS
See also Dennis Wilson

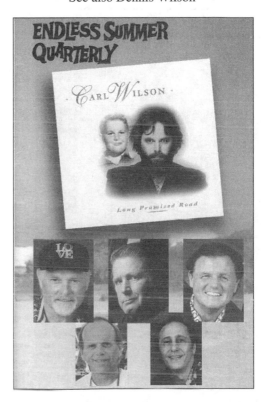

Endless Summer Quarterly (ESQ)

David Beard/Lee Dempsey
PO Box 470315
Charlotte NC 28247-0315 USA
Web address: http://members.aol.com/esqeditor/welcome.html
E-mail address: esqeditor@aol.com
Cost: $24 USA; $26 Canada and Mexico; $30 Australia, New Zealand & Japan; $28 other overseas
Frequency: Quarterly (March, June, Sept., Dec.)
Description: ESQ was founded in 1987 and is considered to be America's premiere Beach Boys/Brian Wilson publication. Each issue (40 pages or more) features exclusive interviews, audio and video reviews and up-to-the-minute news regarding Brian and The Beach Boys.

THE BEATLES

Beatlefan

PO Box 33515
Decatur GA 30033 USA
Fax: 404-321-3109
Cost: $17 ($21 first class) USA; $23 Canada and Mexico; $25 ($31 printed matter airmail) U.K., Western Europe, Latin America; $27 ($33 printed matter airmail) overseas; credit card orders accepted
Special features: Exclusive interviews, photo-packed tour issues, retrospectives; sample issue $4 USA; $5 overseas; back issues also available;
Frequency: Six issues per year
Description: Been around 20 years; readership of 15,000+

Beatlefan/Extra!

PO Box 33515
Decatur GA 30033 USA
Fax: 404-321-3109
Cost: $35 USA; $37.50 Canada and Mexico; $38 overseas; SASE for sample
Frequency: 18 issues
Special features: Fax subscriptions available for additional charge
Description: Our subscribers get the news while it's still news!

Daytrippin'

Trina Yannicos, editor and publisher
PO Box 408
Beltsville MD 20704-0408
Phone: 301-490-2118
Fax: 301-490-2118
Web address: www.daytrippin.com

E-mail address: editor@daytrippin.com
Cost: $14
Frequency: Quarterly
Special features: The most Fab magazine for Beatles fans!
Description: From the fresh perspective of rock journalists, celebrate The Beatles with exclusive interviews and in-depth articles on the latest Beatles news, events and people, as well as columns by Martin Lewis and our own auction and memorabilia experts. Plus, book/CD/video reviews, calendar of events, artwork, convention info, contests and reader contributions.

Good Day Sunshine

Matt Hurwitz
PO Box 661008
Mar Vista CA 90066-9608 USA
Phone: 310-391-0778
Fax: 310-390-7475
Best time to call: 8 am to 5 pm PT
Web address: www.gooddaysunshine.net
E-mail address: info@gooddaysunshine.net
Cost: $15 USA, $24 for first class; $18 Canada; $24 overseas
Frequency: Five issues
Description: The biggest, most detailed Beatles magazine in the world! Lots of behind-the-scenes facts and photos, plus information on Beatles record and memorabilia collecting from some of the country's experts.

Liverpool Beatlescene

Bill Logan
Cavern Walks
Mathew Street
Liverpool L2 6RE England
Phone: 0151-207-0148
Fax: 0151-207-0148
Web address: http://come.to/Liverpoolbeatlescene
E-mail address: Jcatha1@aol.com
Cost: £12 U.K.; £15 Europe; £17 worldwide
Frequency: Quarterly
Special features: Postcards, pen pal service, reports on Liverpool Beatles convention, regular articles by Alistair Taylor
Description: The only fan club in Liverpool since the early 1960s. Our aim is to bring together those who enjoy the music of the world's greatest musical phenomenon, The Beatles.

Octopus' Garden

Beth Shorten
21 Montclair Avenue
Verona NJ 07044 USA
Web address: http://members.home.net/hlnwheels
E-mail address: Beatles94@aol.com
Cost: $12 USA; $15 overseas
Frequency: Quarterly (March, June, Sept. Dec.)
Description: We are a quarterly Fanzine registered with the National Association Of Fan Clubs. We've been around for nine years and are dedicated to putting out a fanzine for all age groups. Our readers keep us alive with their input, short stories, news, opinions, games, etc… Whatever our readers want is what they get!

Tokyo Beatles Fan Club

Kenji Maeda & Otohei Shima
4-6-14-304 Toyotama-Kita Nerima-ku
Tokyo 176-0012 Japan
Fax: +81-48-773-6320 (24 hours)
Cost: $27

Frequency: Quarterly

Special features: Our magazine is written in English

Description: We are the largest nonprofit Beatles fan club in Japan, established in 1991 to celebrate The Beatles' 25th anniversary of their visit to Japan.

THE BEE GEES

Bee Gees Quarterly

Renée & Beverly

PO Box 5340

Lighthouse Point FL 33074 USA

Web address: www.beegeesquarterly.com

E-mail address: renee@beegeesquarterly.com

Cost: $20 USA; $22 Canada and Mexico; $25 overseas

Frequency: Quarterly

Description: I am employed (free-lance) by The Bee Gees and started this club in 1989 when I was a full-time employee of The Bee Gees.

PAT BENATAR

Pat Benatar Fan Club

Mary Wiesner

Web address: www.BenatarFanClub.com

E-mail address: MaryW@BenatarFanClub.com

Cost: $0

Description: The Pat Benatar Fan Club provides accurate and current information about Pat and the band. It offers fans the opportunity to share information and exchange views and opinions in a friendly, open forum. Other benefits include: late-breaking news, timely tour information, discography, lyrics, photos, access to members' pages and more.

MARC BOLAN

Rumblings — The Marc Bolan Journal

Paul Johnson, editor

PO Box 297

Newhaven E Sussex BN9 9NX United Kingdom

Phone: +01273-208414

TOMMY BOLIN

Tommy Bolin Archives, Inc.

PO Box 11243

Denver CO 80211 USA

Web address: www.tbolin.com

MICHAEL BOLTON

Bolton Bulletin

June Allen

9 Palm Close

Witham Essex CM8 2PJ England

Fax: +44(0)1376-500059

Best time to call: Anytime

Web address: www.imagcom.demon.co.uk/bb/index.htm

E-mail address: June//bb@imagcom.demon.co.uk

Cost: $3.20 per issue or $19.20 for six issues, includes post and packing

Frequency: Bi-monthly

Special features: Gallery, wants & swaps, concert write-ups, full color front page

Description: We are a U.K.–based fanzine, dedicated to singer/songwriter Michael Bolton. We keep fans informed of concert tours/CD releases and Michael's sporting activities and charity work.

PAT BOONE

National Pat Boone Fan Club

Ms. Chris Bujnovsky, president

1025 Park Road

Leesport PA 19533-9594 USA

Phone: 610-926-1099

Best time to call: 12:30 to 2:30 p.m; 4:30 to 8:30 p.m.

E-mail address: chrisb926@juno.com

Cost: $10 USA; $12 Canada and overseas

Frequency: Quarterly

Special features: Letter from Pat Boone, memorabilia on Pat

Description: I've been President of Pat's national fan club since 1960. I am a quadriplegic confined to my home since 1953 (polio victim). The fan club has become a hobby for me. Love & enjoy promoting Pat!

ERIC BURDON

The Eric Burdon Connection
Phil Metzger, editor
448 Silver Lane
Oceanside NY 11572 USA
Web address: www.liglobal.com/~ebcn
E-mail: ebcn@i-2000.com
Frequency: Six times per year
Cost: $20
Special features: Hotline, tour dates

DAVID CASSIDY

Just David — International David Cassidy Fan Club
Barbara Pazmino, copresident
979 E 42nd Street
Brooklyn NY 11210 USA
E-mail address: Bpazmino@worldnet.att.net
Address for U.S.A., Canadian, South American fans
Tina Funk, president
Bueltbek 20
22962 Siek Germany
E-mail: tina.funk@t-online.de
Address for European, Australian and Asian fans
Cost: $10 USA and Canada; $15 Asia and South America, checks sent to Barbara Pazmino; European: $5 plus five international reply coupons sent to Tina
Frequency: Quarterly
Description: The club was started by Tina in 1974 with the approval of David's record company at that time, RCA, and it has been going strong ever since. David made the club official in 1975. Tina handles the European/Asian branch and Barbara handles the US/Canadian/ South American branch. The newsletters are filled with information we get from David's manager, associates, David's mother Evelyn Ward, and when we see him, David himself. The club has David's approval, and he is always willing to help us when he is able to. Ocassional handwritten printed message from David.

CHEAP TRICK

Cheap Trick Official Fan Service
Trick International
1957 86th Street Suite 149
Brooklyn NY 11214 USA
Web address: www.cheaptrick.com
E-mail address: oneonfour@aol.com

CHICAGO

Chicago True Advocates
Bob Dillon
PO Box 195
Landing NJ 07850 USA
Phone: 973-398-5050
Web address: http://members.aol.com/CTATickets
Cost: $20 USA; $22 Canada and Mexico; $30 overseas
Frequency: Quarterly
Special features: Special ticket availability to fan club members.
Description: Chicago True Advocates is the official fan club for the rock group Chicago. We offer exclusive concert tickets to fan club members and have an annual convention that includes a meet and greet with the band.

LOU CHRISTIE

Lou Christie Official International Fan Club
Harry Young, president
PO Box 748
Chicago IL 60690-0748 USA
Web address: www.geocities.com/SunsetStrip/Palladium/9229/christie.htm
Web address: http://members.aol.com/DennisKQV/christie.htm
E-mail address: egshum@hotmail.com
Cost: $11
Frequency: Twice per year
Special features: *Lightning Strikes*, the Lou Christie newsletter contains photos, news, reviews, articles, details, etc., all aspects of Lou Christie, past, present & future.
Description: The Lou Christie Fan Club was founded in 1977. The club has contributed to Lou Christie reissue CDs on Taragon, Varèse Vintage, Rhino, Sequel & Collectables.

PETULA CLARK

The International Petula Clark Society
Bonnie Miller
50 Railroad Avenue
Madison CT 06443-3123 USA
E-mail address: ipcs_us@hotmail.com
Cost: $20
Frequency: Quarterly
Description: The original and definitive organization, established in 1971. This official publication offers accurate news on Britain's most successful female recording star.

EDDIE COCHRAN

The Eddie Cochran Connection
W.H. Beard
15 St. Clements Court, Mardyke Park
Purfleet Essex RM19 1GL England
Phone: +01708-861505

BRUCE COCKBURN

Gavin's Woodpile — **The Bruce Cockburn Newsletter**
Daniel Keebler
5925 107th Avenue SE
Snohomish WA 98290 USA
Web address: www.seanet.com/~danjer
E-mail address: danjer@seanet.com
Cost: $10 USA; $12 Canada; $15 overseas
Frequency: Six times a year
Special features: Tour dates
Description: *Gavin's Woodpile* is provided information by Bruce's management and record label, including tour dates. The newsletter also features interviews, photos and articles.

ELVIS COSTELLO

Beyond Belief — **The Elvis Costello Newsletter**
Mike Bodayle
110 Granburg Circle
San Antonio TX 78218 USA
E-mail: mbodayle@txdirect.net

Mark Perry
6 Hillside Grove
Taunton, Somerset TA1 4LA United Kingdom

E-mail: mark@perrys.prestel.co.uk
Cost: $16 USA; £12 U.K.; $20 Japan and Australia
Frequency: Quarterly
Description: A 24-page glossy newsletter devoted to the life and times of Elvis Costello.

COWSILLS

Cowsills Fan Club

Marsha Jordan, president
PO Box 83
Lexington MS 39095 USA
Web address: www.cowsill.com
E-mail address: cowsillfan@aol.com
Cost: $10
Frequency: Quarterly

CREEDENCE CLEARWATER REVIVAL

Creedence Clearwater Revival Fan Club

Peter Koers, editor
Schoppershofstrasse 74
90489 Nüremberg Germany
Phone: +0911 563647
Fax: +0911 563647
Web address: www.ourworld.compuserve.com/Homepages/Peter_koers
E-mail address: Peter_Koers@compuserve.com
Special features: Interviews, reviews, photos
Description: Founded in 1981.

WARREN CUCCURULLO

See Duran Duran

THE CHARLIE DANIELS BAND

The Charlie Daniels Band Volunteers

Ginger Ambrose
17060 Central Pike
Lebanon TN 37090 USA
Phone: 615-453-9888
Fax: 615-453-9888
Best time to call: 8 a.m. to 5 p.m.
Web address: www.charliedaniels.com
E-mail address: cdbfanclub@aol.com
Cost: $10
Frequency: Three times per year
Special features: Newsletter, guest pass, yearly fan club family reunion, photo, discography, bio
Description: Fan club president, coordinate guest passes, merchandise, etc.

NEIL DIAMOND

The Diamond Connection

June Allen
PO Box 2764
Witham Essex CM8 2SF England
Fax: +44(0)1376-500059
Best time to call: Anytime
Web address: www.imagcom.demon.co.uk/tdc/tdc.html
E-mail address: June//tdc@imagcom.demon.co.uk
Cost: $5 per issue or six issues $28 includes post and packing
Frequency: Bi-monthly
Special features: Write-ups, articles supplied by fans, photos, memorabilia
Description: We are a U.K.–based fanzine dedicated to singer/songwriter Neil Diamond. We keep fans connected worldwide with all the latest news and information on Neil.

DURAN DURAN

The Icon Duran Duran Fanzine

PO Box 158
Allen Park MI 48101-0158 USA
Phone: 313-928-3368
Fax: 313-928-7755
Best time to call: 24 hours
Web address: www.theIcon.com
E-mail address: Nancy@theIcon.com
Cost: $8
Frequency: Quarterly
Special features: Occasional interviews with band members, the latest news & photos.
Description: We are the longest-running U.S.A.–based Duran Duran fanzine, having been publishing for more than eight years now. We also run a Duran Duran convention once per year.

Privacy — The Warren Cuccurullo Fan Club

Cyndi Glass
PO Box 593
Vincennes IN 47591 USA
Phone: 812-888-5806
Web address: http://159.218.20.79/privacy.html
E-mail address: cglass@vunet.vinu.edu
Cost: $0

Frequency: Updates at web site
Special features: Web site, information about Missing Persons (Warren's former band)
Description: Web sites — Warren Cuccurullo: http://159.218.20.79/wc.html
Missing Persons: http://159.218.20.79/mp.html
Michael Des Barres: http://159.218.20.79/mdb.html
21 Jump Street: http://159.218.20.79/21index.html

E

ELO

Electric Light Orchestra Fan Club

Face The Music Germany
Wiener Platz 6
7730 Villingen Germany
Web address: http://userpage.fu_berlin.de/~dmhoff/ftm.html
Cost: Outside Germany cost on request
Frequency: Three issues per year
Special features: E.L.O., Jeff Lynne, Roy Wood, more
Description: We publish a 48-page A4-sized fanzine plus fan club CDs and have also published the E.L.O. book, *Unexpected Messages* (still available).

THE EVERLY BROTHERS

The Beehive—The Official Everly Brothers Fan Club

John Hosum, editor
PO Box 3933
Seattle WA 98124-3933 USA
Phone: 206-783-1798
Janet Dalgliesh
11 Cottesmore Road
Doddington Park
Lincoln LN6 3RH England
Phone: +01522-884643
Cost: $15 North America; $20 or £12 overseas
Frequency: Six issues per year, plus updates
Description: The official and only international Everly Brothers Fan Club recognized by Don and Phil Everly; founded in 1995.

G

LESLEY GORE

Lesley Gore International Fan Club

Jack Natoli, president
PO Box 305
Pompton Plains NJ 07444-0305 USA
Phone: 973-616-1233
Fax: 973-616-0484
Best time to call: 6 p.m. to 9 p.m.
E-mail address: jacknatoli@prodigy.net
Cost: $8
Frequency: Quarterly
Description: This club is Lesley Gore's only official fan club and has been in existence since 1965 with the same president. New members receive a packet of photos, biography and complete discography.

THE GRATEFUL DEAD

Relix

PO Box 94
Brooklyn NY 11229 USA
Phone: 718-258-0009
Web address: www.relix.com
E-mail address: relixrec@aol.com
Cost: $37 — eight issues
Frequency: Six times a year
Special features: Specializes in The Grateful Dead
Description: Classic rock publication with emphasis on Grateful Dead, also covers jam band scene, blues, country-rock, etc.

H

HALL AND OATES

Rock And Soul International

Lori Allred and Diane Vaskas
PO Box 450
Mansfield MA 02048 USA
Web address: www.hallandoates.com
E-mail address: lori@hallandoates.com
Cost: $10 USA; $15 overseas
Frequency: Quarterly
Special features: Issues feature exclusive photos, stories and contests

JIMI HENDRIX

Jimi Hendrix Information Management Institute

Ken Voss
Box 20361
Indianapolis IN 46220 USA
Phone: 317-257-JIMI
Fax: 317-255-4476
E-mail address: kenvoss@iquest.net
Cost: $15 USA; $20 overseas
Frequency: Quarterly
Description: Archives and fan club designed to accumulate and disseminate information regarding the life and music of Jimi Hendrix. Publish *VooDoo Child* newsletter.

BUDDY HOLLY

The Buddy Holly International Fan Club

Jim Carr
45 Westfield Road
Tickhill Doncaster DN11 9LB England

ENGELBERT HUMPERDINCK

Engelbert's Goils Fan Club

20201 Lorain Road # 406
Cleveland OH 44126 USA
Phone: 440-331-5601
Best time to call: Anytime
Cost: $18 USA; $20 overseas
Frequency: Bi-monthly
Special features: Current information, itinerary, releases
Description: We are a club that dispenses information on the life and career of Engelbert Humperdinck. Schedule of appearances, record releases, traveling information and much more as available.

Engel's Angels In Humperdinck Heaven

Jean Marshalek
3024 Fourth Avenue
Baltimore MD 21234-3208 USA
Phone: 410-665-0744
Fax: 410-665-0744
Best time to call: 10 a.m. to 9 p.m.
E-mail address: Jean3024@white-marsh.aim-smart.com
Cost: $10, $5 husbands USA; $13 overseas
Frequency: About seven issues per year
Special features: Itinerary, new releases, reviews
Description: I am the president and editor for the club and have been for 28 years. I keep record of all incoming information on Engelbert and put it together in newsletter format. All memberships begin July 1 of each year.

I

JULIO IGLESIAS

Friends Of Julio International

Isabel Butterfield, president
28 Farmington Avenue
Longmeadow MA 01106-1433 USA
Phone: 413-567-0845
Fax: 413-567-9530
Best time to call: Evenings
Cost: $18 USA; $20 Canada; $25 Europe; $28 Asia and overseas
Frequency: Quarterly
Description: We are a fan club honoring singer Julio Iglesias. Newsletters chronicle his career, his tour dates, reports on concerts, including photos. Brings news of his life to fans.

IRON BUTTERFLY

Iron Butterfly Information Network

Rick Gagnon
9745 Sierra Avenue
Fontana CA 92335 USA
Web address: www.Geocities.com/SunsetStrip/pit/2041/
E-mail address: Rickgagnon@DreamSoft.com
Cost: $0
Description: I. B. information, fan relations, Q & As

J

MICHAEL JACKSON

MJ News International

Web address: www.mjni.com

JAN & DEAN

See also Dennis Wilson

Surfun — The Official Jan & Dean Fan Club

Lori Brown
328 Sumner Avenue
Summer WA 98390 USA
E-mail address: surfun1@aol.com
Cost: $8 USA; $9 Canada and Mexico; $10 overseas
Frequency: Quarterly

Special features: Concert information, current events and memorabilia.
Description: In cooperation with Jan & Dean, this club was founded in 1986 with main goals of informing fans of concerts dates, current events and album releases as well as a network for collectors.

ELTON JOHN

Hercules International Elton John Fan Club

Sharon Kalinoski
PO Box 398
La Grange IL 60525 USA
Phone: 815-293-3843
Best time to call: 24 hours
Web address: www.eltonfan.com
E-mail address: HerculesUS@yahoo.com
Cost: $30
Frequency: Quarterly
Special features: Laminated membership pass, frequent member-only special offers.
Description: Hercules has departments worldwide: U.K., Germany, Benelux, Italy, U.S.A., Canada and contacts in many other countries. We publish a professional fanzine quarterly with lots of news and photos of Elton John. Also have frequent fan conventions worldwide.

AL JOLSON

International Al Jolson Society

Mrs. Delores Kontowicz
11520 W James Avenue
Franklin WI 53132-1134 USA
Phone: 414-529-2868
Fax: 414-529-2868
Best time to call: 10 a.m. to 4:30 p.m.
E-mail address: dkontowicz@aol.com
Cost: $18
Frequency: *Jolson Journal* twice a year, Spring and Fall, plus three to four newsletters
Special features: Stories on Al Jolson, members' exchange, news on members
Description: Currently secretary of society, also run collectibles dept. where members can purchase Jolson CDs, records, sheet music, misc. memorabilia. Also am the founder of society, which began April 1950 (before Jolie died in October 1950). Will celebrate 50th anniversary in 2000. Also served as president for approx. 15 years. I also have edited more than 50 *Journals*. We have just published *Jolson Journal* #90.

DAVY JONES

Davy Devotees — The Official Fan Club Of Davy Jones

Abby Alterio
8142 Amble Way
Indianapolis, IN 46237
Web address: www.geocities.com/Hollywood/Lot/4213/dd2.html
E-mail: DavyDvotee@aol.com
Frequency: Six issues

SHIRLEY JONES

Shirley Jones Int'l Fan Club

Martina Schade
2295 Maple Road
York PA 17404 USA
Phone: 717-764-9517
Web address: www.shirleyjones.com
Cost: $15 USA; $18 Canada; $22 overseas

Frequency: Quarterly
Special features: 8x10 photo, 2 4x6 photos, bio fact sheet, membership card
Description: Keep fans abreast of Shirley's activities, personal appearance schedule.

K

JOHN KAY
See Steppenwolf

KINGSTON TRIO

Kingston Korner
Allan Shaw
705 S Washington Street
Naperville IL 60540-6654 USA
Phone: 630-637-2303
Best time to call: Late mornings
Web address: www.folkera.com
E-mail address: allan@folkera.com
Cost: $0
Frequency: Five to six times yearly
Description: We are a pseudo fan club for the Kingston Trio and other popular folk acts of the Folk Era. Through our *Rediscover Music Catalogue* (which is really a magalogue), we keep folks up-to-date on their favorite '60s folk acts.

KISS

KISSONLINE
Sony Signatures
Web address: www.KISSONLINE.com
Cost: $4.95 per month or $48 per year
Special features: Will provide exclusive news, photos, video streaming and audio reports, live chats, reports from backstage and trading post for collectible merchandise
Description: Founded in 1993, Sony Signatures is an industry leader in merchandising, licensing and marketing, representing high-profile concert touring artists, celebrities, the Sony Pictures film and television properties and other entertainment properties.

L

ERNIE LANCASTER

Ernie Lancaster Fan Club
Vicki Newton
PO Box 629
Harre de Grace MD 21078 USA
Phone: 410-939-5864
Best time to call: 6 to 10 p.m.
Web address: www.geocities.com/sunsetstrip/stadium/7622/
E-mail address: newtdog@webtv.net
Cost: $0
Frequency: Quarterly
Special features: Cassette and video availability, current club dates.
Description: Ernie Lancaster is the best-kept secret in America! Guitarist extroidanaire. Poet and composer of 99 percent of Root Boy Slim's music, now solo, also heard on lots of Ring Snake recordings.

LEAD BELLY

Lead Belly Society
Sean Killeen, president
PO Box 6679
Ithaca NY 14851 USA
Phone: 607-273-6615
Fax: 607-273-4816
Best time to call: 9 to 5 M-F
E-mail address: sk86@cornell.edu
Cost: $17
Frequency: Quarterly
Special features: Fresh articles, rare photos, music reviews
Description: Mission of Lead Belly Society is to foster the appreciation and celebration of Lead Belly and his music.

BRENDA LEE

Brenda Lee International Fan Club
Bob Borum
4720 Hickory Way
Antioch TN 37013 USA
Web address: www.brendalee.com
E-mail address: brenda@voy.net
Cost: $0
Frequency: Bi-monthly internet newsletter
Special features: Web site contains not only fan club, but also publicity information

THE LETTERMEN

The Lettermen Society
3860 S Higuera Street D-16
San Luis Obispo CA 93401 USA
Phone: 805-547-1365 (concert line)
Best time to call: 24 hours
Cost: $13 new memberships; $10 renewal

HUEY LEWIS AND THE NEWS

NEWSline II
Debbie Parry
PO Box 99
Payson UT 84651 USA
Web address: www.geocities.com/Hollywood/Set/3884/
E-mail address: newslineii@e-mail.msn.com
Cost: $10 basic, $13.30 deluxe USA; $12 basic, $18 deluxe overseas, plus 10 SASEs or IRCs and/or an e-mail address
Frequency: Two large newsletters, monthly updates
Description: We are the fan club for Huey Lewis & The News. We have a rather large group of folks from all over the globe within the Newsline Family. We are also happy to say we enjoy an affinity with the band's office as well as with the band.

LOWEN & NAVARRO

Lowen & Navarro Fan Club
PO Box 19285
Alexandria VA 22308 USA
Web address: www.lownav.com
E-mail address: fanclub@1X.netcom.com
Cost: $15
Frequency: Two per year
Special features: Autographed photo, bumpersticker, fan club cassette

BARRY MANILOW

Very Berry Kentuckiana Connection

Ann Harris
409 N 28th Street
Louisville KY 40212-1905 USA
Phone: 502-261-5104
Fax: 502-772-3849
Best time to call: Nights
E-mail address: takersgal@webtv.net
Cost: $0
Frequency: When there is news
Description: We celebrate the man and his music… Barry Manilow.

JIM MARLBORO

Jim Marlboro Fan Club

David Kelly
2011 State Avenue SW
Decatur AL 35601 USA
Phone: 256-351-8353
Best time to call: Anytime
Cost: $8
Frequency: Quarterly
Special features: Picture and newsletter
Description: I am the publisher of Jim Marlboro Fan Club and I answer fan questions about Jim and his career.

THE MARVELETTES

See The Supremes

KATY MOFFATT

Katy Moffatt World Headquarters

Roger Devore
PO Box 334
O'Fallon IL 62269-0334 USA
Phone: 618-632-0278
Fax: 618-632-0278
Web address: http://members.aol.com/klmoffatt/index.html
E-mail address: Kmwhq@mclcodusa.net
Cost: $0
Frequency: As needed
Description: Provide information about Katy's career including album releases and tour information.

THE MONKEES

See also Davy Jones, Michael Nesmith, and Peter Tork

Head Of The Monkees

Teresa Jones
262 Baltimore Avenue
Baltimore MD 21222-4205 USA
Cost: $12 USA and Canada; $17 overseas
Frequency: Quarterly (Jan., Apr., July, Oct.)
Special features: News of the guys, ongoing tour dates, pen pals & photos
Description: I am the president/editor of HTM F.C. I run the club and make all newsletters ready for copy.

Monkeein' Around Fan Club

Janet Marie Davis
41297 CC Road
Ponchatoula LA 70454 USA
Phone: 504-845-3449
Best time to call: Daytime
Cost: $6
Frequency: Quarterly (Mar., June, Sept., Dec.)
Special features: At times, I have a Partridge Corner about one of the Partridge Family such as David Cassidy.
Description: I'm the President of the club. I started the club to show support to The Monkees, and it's like a pen pal sort of club. I do, at times, add extra features like Partridge Corner for Monkees fans who are Partridge Family fans, like myself.

THE MOODY BLUES

***Higher & Higher* — The Moody Blues Magazine**

Mark Murley, editor
PO Box 829-G
Geneva FL 32732 USA
Phone: 407-349-BLUE (2583)
Best time to call: Blue Line (info line) 24 hrs/day
Web address: http://Moodies-Magazine.com
E-mail address: hhemail@aol.com
Cost: $35
Frequency: Two to four times per year
Special features: Album retrospectives, news, interviews
Description: *Higher & Higher* is an independent magazine for Moody Blues enthusiasts. Since late 1983, *Higher & Higher* has chronicled the history and current achievements of the Moody Blues with articles & photos. Back issues available. Send SASE for brochure or $10 for a sample issue.

The Moody Blues Official Fan Club

Ivy Stewart
53-55 High Street
Cobham Surrey KT11 3DP England
Phone: +44-1932-868337
Fax: +44-1932-868997
Best time to call: 10 a.m. to 4 p.m. U.K. time
Web address: www.moodyblues.co.uk
E-mail address: info@moodyblues.co.uk
Frequency: Three magazines per year
Special features: Tour dates, merchandise, latest news, band photos
Description: The Moody Blues Fan Club secretary in charge of all matters concerning the fan club.

ALLISON MOORER

The Allison Moorer International Fan Club

Brandon Dorton
PO Box 150626
Nashville TN 37215 USA
Web address: www.allisonmoorer.com
E-mail address: amfanclub@aol.com

MOTT THE HOOPLE

***Two Miles From Heaven* — Mott The Hoople Appreciation Society**

CeeDee Mail Order
PO Box 14
Stowmarket Suffolk IP14 4UD England
Phone: +01449-770138
Fax: +01449-770133
E-mail: 113115.115@compuserve.com
Cost: £14 U.K.; £16 Europe; £22 elsewhere for four issues
Special features: Interviews, concert reports, reviews, discographies

N

NAZARETH

Razamanewz — The Official Nazareth Fanzine

Joe Geesin
Headrest Street End Lane
Broadoak Heathfield
East Sussex TN21 8TU United Kingdom
Phone: +01435-863994
Fax: +01435-867027
E-mail: razamanewz8192@hotmail.com

CHUCK NEGRON

Chuck Negron Fan Club

Kathy Reese
PO Box 30806
Portland OR 97294 USA
Web address: www.negron.com
E-mail address: negronfan@aol.com
Cost: $20 USA; $25 overseas
Frequency: Quarterly
Special features: Autographed photo, weekly America Online chats, backstage passes, special members-only events and discounts.
Description: Chuck Negron, former lead singer of Three Dog Night, now a solo artist. Also author with a new book, *Three Dog Nightmare*.

MICHAEL NESMITH

Dedicated Friends (The Official Michael Nesmith Fan Club)

Donna Bailey
1807 Millstream Drive
Frederick MD 21702 USA
Phone: 301-694-8064
Best time to call: Daytime
Web address: www.nezfriends.com
E-mail address: NezFanClub@aol.com
Cost: $12 USA; $20 overseas
Frequency: Quarterly
Special features: Newsletter with color photos of Michael, information direct from Michael and his staff.
Description: I'm Donna Bailey, Michael's official club president. I help promote his company, Videoranch, through the newsletter and web site. I answer fans' questions and assist them in whatever way I can. I have also put together a Michael Nesmith Tribute Band.

NEW KIDS ON THE BLOCK

Face The Music

Katrina Walker
PO Box 10193-GM
Fullerton, CA 92835 USA
Cost: One-time fee of $12 USA; $17 overseas. Dues of $5 two times per year USA; $10 overseas

O

ROY ORBISON

Roy Orbison International Fan Club

Phone: 615-242-4201
Fax: 615-242-4202

P

JOHN PATRICK

John Patrick Fan Club

Laurie Ewald, president
2140 W Cass City Road
Unionville MI 48767 USA
Web address: IFCO jttp:www/ifco.org
E-mail address: johnpat@centuryinter.net
Cost: $8
Frequency: Three times yearly
Special features: 8x10 picture, update schedule
Description: National recording artist, songwriter.

PETER AND GORDON

The International Peter And Gordon Fan Club

Kathy Holland
22742 Roscoe Boulevard
West Hills CA 91304 USA
E-mail address: GWPA1234@aol.com
Cost: $15
Description: The International Peter and Gordon Fan Club is now up and running. With Paul McCartney's recent induction into the Rock And Roll Hall Of Fame, it should be noted that Paul was a terrific songwriter even when he was writing songs for other folks besides The Beatles.

TOM PETTY

Web address: http://tompetty.com

PINK FLOYD

see Syd Barrett

GENE PITNEY

Gene Pitney International Fan Club

David P McGrath
6201 39th Avenue
Kenosha WI 53142 USA
Phone: 414-652-1964
Fax: 414-657-1049
Best time to call: After 6 p.m. (CDT)
Web address: www.genepitney.com
E-mail address: PitneyFan@aol.com
Cost: $10 USA; £10 U.K.; $20 Canada and Australia
Frequency: Three times per year
Special features: Letter from Gene each issue, interviews, archive photos
Description: I am the President of Gene Pitney Music & Merchandising, which runs the Gene Pitney International Fan Club (close to 1,000 members internationally). We also produce and sell Gene's tour merchandise for his U.S.A. shows. Approximately every two years we organize/produce a fan club convention.

POCO

A Good Feeling To Know — Poco Fanzine

Steven Casto
575 Lewisville Road
Woodsfield OH 43793 USA
Phone: 740-472-1863
Best time to call: Before 10 p.m. EDT
Cost: $14
Frequency: Three issues per year

Special features: Excl. interviews, endorsed by most members of band.
Description: Fanzine is to promote current and past members of Poco. We supply current and updated information, timeline articles, record reviews, various feature articles and concert reviews.

COZY POWELL

NaNaNa Newsletter — The Cozy Powell Information Service
Joe Geesin
Headrest Street End Lane
Broadoak Heathfield
East Sussex TN21 8TU United Kingdom
Phone: +01435-863994
Fax: 01435-867027
E-mail: razamanewz8192@hotmail.com

ELVIS PRESLEY

Elvis Arkansas Style Fan Club

Beverly Rook, president
PO Box 898
Mabelvale AR 72103 USA
Phone: 501-455-1273
Best time to call: Evenings
E-mail address: tcb@aristotle.net
Cost: $0
Description: The EASFC works on several charity projects during the year. #1 Elvis Presley Memorial Dinner benefits more than 10 charities.

Elvis Teddy Bears Fan Club

Mary Ann Parisi
744 Caliente Drive
Brandon FL 33511 USA
Phone: 813-684-6522
Best time to call: Evenings, weekends
Cost: $6
Frequency: Quarterly
Description: Elvis fan since the '50s. Saw him in concert five times, got a scarf, have had club since 1976.

The Presley-ites Fan Club

Kathy Ferguson, president
6010 18th Street
Zephyrhills, FL 33540
Phone: 1-813-788-9133
Cost: $5.40 plus 20 stamps, USA; $15 Canada; $20 overseas
Description: Founded in 1972; we support many charities, scholarship funds, endowment funds, and the Elvis Presley Memorial Trauma Center.

Sharing The Memory

Elvis Presley Fan Club Of Vermont
Pharilda Galloway, president
99 Hayes Avenue
South Burlington VT 05403 USA
E-mail: EPFCOFVT@compuserve.com
Web site: http://ourworld.compuserve.com/homepages/EPFCOFVT

We Remember Elvis Fan Club

Priscilla A. Parker, president
1215 Tennessee Avenue
Pittsburgh PA 15216-2511 USA
Phone: 412-561-7522
Best time to call: After 11 a.m.
Cost: $10 USA; $12 Canada; $25 overseas
Frequency: Bi-monthly

Special features: Memories of Elvis Presley, stories from the fans
Description: We are remembering Elvis Presley with pride and dignity through our works of charity. We keep the Elvis fans informed with our bi-monthly newsletters, of all the news about new Elvis items, books and recording releases.

(THE ARTIST FORMERLY KNOWN AS) PRINCE

Uptown Magazine
Harold E. Lewis
PO Box 43
Cuyahoga Falls OH 44222 USA
Web address: www.uptown.se
E-mail address: uptown@gwis.com
Cost: $50
Frequency: Five times a year
Description: The *Uptown Magazine* is produced by a team of dedicated fans and collectors. Many of the leading Princeologists all over the world contribute to the magazine, making it the definitive, authoritative guide. *Uptown* is not an authorized fan club. Since its inception in 1991, *Uptown* has established a name for itself as the leading authority on Prince.

R

EDDY RAVEN

Eddy Raven Fan Club

Sheila Futch
PO Box 2476
Hendersonville TN 37077 USA
Phone: 615-230-7414
Web address: www.eddyraven.com
Cost: $10 USA; $14 elsewhere
Frequency: Quarterly
Special features: Photos, road dates

HELEN REDDY

Helen Reddy Fan Club — East

Lorraine Breault
204 Thunder Circle
Bensalem PA 19020 USA
Phone: 215-702-1421
Best time to call: 9 a.m. to 9 p.m. EST
E-mail address: DL1990@aol.com
Cost: $10 USA; $18 overseas
Special features: Autographed picture of Helen when joining.
Description: This is an official fan club recognized by Helen. The club has been around for 13 years. Newsletters, postcards, e-mail updates and Christmas cards are sent out.

MARTHA REEVES AND THE VANDELLAS

See The Supremes

REO SPEEDWAGON

REO Fans News
Kathy Stover, president
PO Box 511316
Milwaukee WI 53203-0221
Web address: www.speedwagon.com/reofans.html
E-mail: reofans@aol.com
Cost: $15 USA; $20 Canada and overseas
Frequency: Quarterly
Special features: 8x10 photo, 30-page newsletter containing interviews,

concert and backstage photos, studio updates and tour information; annual REO Fans convention in Kansas City

Description: This is REO Speedwagon's largest approved fan club.

SMOKEY ROBINSON AND THE MIRACLES

Smokey Robinson & The Miracles Fan Club

8 Hillside Road
Narragansett RI 02882-2821 USA
Phone: 401-789-8992
Fax: 401-789-8992*96
Web address: www3.edgenet.net/smokey_miracles
E-mail address: srmfc@edgenet.net
Cost: $13 USA; $20 overseas
Frequency: Quarterly
Special features: Tour dates, Motown news, etc.
Description: Official authorized fan club for Smokey And The Miracles. Also covers other classic Motown artists.

ROOT BOY SLIM

Root Boy Slim Memorial Fan Club

Duane Straub, director
3834 Sheffield Circle
Danville CA 94506 USA
Phone: 925-736-1480
Fax: 925-736-7844
Best time to call: 6 p.m. to 10 p.m. PST M-F; 6 a.m. to 10 p.m. weekends
Web address: www.exanet.net/rbs
E-mail address: rootboy@exanet.net
Cost: $0
Frequency: Whenever something merits an announcement
Special features: Newsletters and information package, offers for "Root Loot," rare video and audio tapes, T-shirts, etc., proceeds of which go toward restoration of historic Slim recordings.
Description: This official club, whose namesake passed in 1993, is devoted to the continued rememberance of Root Boy Slim and his music. People loved this man — and a bizarre man he was. Many have a special story about Root Boy Slim — most have more than one! This club is devoted to tracking down episodes and tie-ins to a man with the strangest of messages — untangling the web, removing the cloak… day by day, documenting and saluting the life and times of Root Boy Slim. You can't quit this club! We're here because you're there.

RUSH

A Show Of Fans — Fanzine For And By Rush Fans

Mandy Riffle
PMB # 309, 5411 E State Street
Rockford IL 61108 USA
Phone: 815-398-1250
Best time to call: 10 a.m. to 10 p.m.
Web address: www.asof.com
E-mail address: syrinx67@aol.com
Frequency: Out of business — back issues still available; web site is still operating
Special features: Interviews with Geddy, Alex and Neil of Rush
Description: International fan magazine with lots of tour photos, artwork, information, interviews, feedback, Ask Big Al column, puzzles, surveys — a real collectible for the diehard Rush fan.

S

SANTANA

Santana International Fan Club

Stefani Charles
PO Box 881630
San Francisco CA 94188-1630 USA
Web address: www.santana.com
E-mail address: fanclub@santana.com
Cost: Lifetime membership — $25 USA; $35 international
Frequency: Quarterly (Winter, Spring, Summer, Fall)
Description: The Santana International Fan Club is the official fan club of Carlos Santana.

SAVOY BROWN

Shades Of Savoy Brown — The Official International Journal

128 Shelly Road
Glen Burnie MD 21061 USA
Alan Pearce, managing editor
PO Box 727
Cardiff Wales CF14 1YQ England
Phone: +44-1656-743406
Fax: +44-1656-743406
Best time to call: U.K. time up to 8 p.m.
E-mail address: shadesofsavoybrown@ntli.net
Cost: $22 USA and Canada; £12 U.K. and Europe; £15 overseas
Frequency: Three times a year
Special features: Conn-Ex-tions (ex-members of Savoy Brown, chat, interviews, etc)
Description: The only official Savoy Brown information outside Kim Simmonds' own web page. We talk to Kim regularly. Also do mail order for Savoy Brown & ex-members of Savoy Brown music.

SPARKS

Sparks International Official Fan Club
Mary Martin, secretary
Box 25038
Los Angeles CA 90025 USA
Cost: $10 USA and Canada; $15 Europe and Asia
Frequency: Six large glossy issues
Special features: Photos of Ron & Russ and articles from all over the world.
Description: Write newsletters, ship articles such as T-shirts, caps, magnets, etc. I have been a great fan of Sparks for 20 years.

BRUCE SPRINGSTEEN, OTHER JERSEY SHORE ARTISTS

***Backstreets* — The Boss Magazine**
PO Box 51225
Seattle WA 98115 USA
Phone: 206-728-7603
Fax: 206-728-8827
Best time to call: 9 a.m. to 5 p.m. PST M-F
Web address: www.backstreets.com
Cost: $18
Frequency: Quarterly
Special features: Subscriber-only telephone news hotline number.
Description: For nearly 20 years, *Backstreets Magazine* has covered the music of Bruce Springsteen and other Jersey Shore artists like no other publication.

STEPPENWOLF

***The Howl* — Newsletter of The Wolfpack, official fan club of John Kay and Steppenwolf**
PO Box 271495
Nashville TN 37227-1495 USA
Tour info hotline: 615-780-3579
Fax: 615-367-1320
Web address: www.steppenwolf.com
E-mail: wolfpack@steppenwolf.com
Cost: $10, renewal: $8 USA; $15, renewal: $12 overseas
Frequency: Quarterly

SUPREMES, MARVELETTES, MARTHA REEVES AND THE VANDELLAS

SMV Fan Club
Frances Baugh, president
PO Box 100671
Vanderveer Station
Brooklyn NY 11210 USA

T

THREE DOG NIGHT
see also Chuck Negron

Three Dog Night Fan Club
Madonna Nuckolls, president
PO Box 1975
Rowlett, TX 75030
Web address: www.threedognight.com
E-mail: mad4tdn@aol.com
Cost: $12 USA; $15 overseas

THUNDER ROAD

Thunder Road Fan Club
Barbara Gentry
215 Valley Court
Smyrna TN 37167 USA
Phone: 615-816-8277
Best time to call: Anytime
Web address: www.1-2-free.com/mypage/entertainment/thunderroad
E-mail address: thunderroadband@mindspring.com
Cost: $0
Frequency: Quarterly
Special features: Free 8x10 autographed picture of band, contests, etc.
Description: I am Barbara Gentry, head of the Thunder Road fan club. Our purpose is to make the fans a part of the band by offering free pics, newsletters, web site, and e-mail to contact the band.

PETER TORK

***Torkaholics Anonymous* — NJ's Foremost Peter Tork Fanzine**
Patti Shields, president
74 Main Street Suite 113
Woodbridge NJ 07095

T. REX
see Marc Bolan

TUBES

Official Tubes Fan Club
Marilyn Wood, director
PO Box 13111
Oakland CA 94661 USA
Phone: 510-339-1922
Fax: 510-339-9066
Best time to call: 7 p.m. or later PST
Web address: www.tubesrock.com
E-mail address: fanclub@tubesrock.com
Cost: $0
Frequency: Internet updates
Special features: Band updates, bios, tour dates

Description: Been working since 1982 with the Tubes, keeping the world informed of the whereabouts and performances of the greatest rock 'n' roll band of the century.

TINA TURNER

Simply The Best Tina Turner Fan Club
Mark Lairmore
4566 S Park Avenue
Springfield MO 65810 USA
Phone: 417-881-3746
Fax: 417-865-7304
Best time to call: 6 p.m. to 11 p.m.
Cost: $15 USA; $20 overseas
Frequency: Three publications a year
Description: Tina Turner fan club originally started 1989; members in U.S.A. and Europe; fan club features stories, articles, pictures. Issue dates Dec., April, Aug. 1999.

U2

U Stay 2
The Edge
PO Box 11913
Chicago IL 60611-0913 USA
E-mail address: u2sat@hotmail.com, ustay2@att.net, the-edge@att.net
Special features: Multimedia, videos, U2 look-alike tribute band and more
Description: U Stay 2 created eight years ago in Europe with a unique goal to gather all U2 fans of the world in a network to honor the rock group U2, pay tribute, share information using the latest technology and best programs.

V

GENE VINCENT AND THE BLUE CAPS

Web address: www.athenet.net/~genevinc/index.html

VOODOO MONKEY CHILD

V.M.C./1753
Laurie Stansbury or Amy E. Allan
PO Box 2546
Glenview IL 60025-6546 USA
Phone: 847-758-9868
Fax: 847-758-9868
Best time to call: Anytime
Web address: www.elknet.net/venom/vmc.htm
E-mail address: allencat@worldnet.att.net
Cost: $13 lifetime
Frequency: At least twice yearly
Special features: Limited-edition posters, clothing, vinyl, etc... available.
Description: We are the official fan club for the rock music group, Voodoo Monkey Child. V.M.C./1753 works closely with the band members, offering photos, interviews, artwork, clothing, stickers and other promotional items. We also have exclusive interviewswith the band members and the stage crew.

WALKER BROTHERS/ SCOTT WALKER

Walkerpeople
Lynne Goodall
71 Cheyne Ct Glengall Road
Woodford Green Essex 1G8 0DN England
Phone: +0181-505-4316
Best time to call: 8 p.m. to 10 p.m. U.K. time
Cost: £16 U.K.; £19 Europe; £22 USA, Australia, New Zealand, Japan
Frequency: Quarterly
Special features: Containing latest news relating to Scott's ongoing career. Walkerpeople is the official support organization for Scott Walker/Walker Bros.
Description: I edit *Walkerpeople* quarterly illustrated newsletter and run the appreciation society. *Walkerpeople* was established in 1981; since then I have also been involved in Scott/Walker Bros. record reissues and in TV/radio profiles of Scott.

ROGER WATERS

REG — The International Roger Waters Fan Club
Michael Simone, president
128 Onyx Drive
Watsonville CA 95076 USA
Phone: 831-768-9694
Best time to call: Evenings
Web address: www.rogerwaters.org
E-mail address: regpinky@jps.net
Cost: $20 USA; $25 overseas
Frequency: Three to four issues per year
Special features: Our club is totally nonprofit. It is our magazine that differentiates us from a fanzine, for though it contains rare articles, news, information, interviews and tidbits as well as exclusive interviews, it's through members' contributions and letters that our members around the world can communicate their thoughts and feelings with one another.
Description: The International Roger Waters Fan Club is in its eighth year of operation. REG is a club belonging to all of its members and formed so that we can share with one another our love for Roger Waters and his music.

JUDY WELDEN

Judy Welden Fan Club
Nancy Tetro, president
PO Box 7382
Port St. Lucie, FL 34985 USA
Web address: www.flinet.com/~jwelden
E-mail address: jwelden@flinet.com
Cost: $12 USA; $15 overseas
Frequency: Quarterly
Special features: Album first year, gift with renewals, autographed 8x10, discography, meet and greets, bio, fact sheet, preferred concert seating

DENNIS WILSON

Friends Of Dennis Wilson Club
Chris M. Duffy
1381 Maria Way
San Jose CA 95117 USA

Cost: $7 for four issues; $12 for eight issues
Frequency: Quarterly
Special features: Articles, reviews, poems, etc. for and about Dennis Wilson, The Beach Boys and Jan & Dean
Description: A lover of Beach Boys' music and enjoys writing to others who enjoy their music and present a positive, upbeat memorial magazine for Dennis and now Carl Wilson too, I am the editor and founder of FODW.

Y

NEIL YOUNG

Neil Young Appreciation Society
Alan Jenkins
2A Llynfi Street
Bridgend Wales CF31 1SY England
Fax: 01656-661825
Web address: http://ourworld.compuserve.com/homepages/nyas
E-mail address: nyas@compuserve.com
Cost: $25
Frequency: Quarterly

Z

NORMA ZIMMER

Norma Zimmer National Fan Club
Frances I. Young, president
1604 E Susquehanna Street
Allentown PA 18103-4362 USA
Phone: 610-797-9383
Best time to call: 6 to 8 p.m.
Cost: $6
Frequency: Quarterly
Special features: Membership card, pictures of Norma, lots more.
Description: Norma is the champagne lady with the Lawrence Welk Orchestra. She sings both religious and secular songs.

VARIOUS ARTISTS

***Ballbuster Magazine* & Ball Buster Hard Online Metal**
David LaDuke
PO Box 58368
Louisville KY 40268-0368 USA
Phone: 502-995-3396
Fax: 502-995-3396
Best time to call: After 12 noon
Web address: www.yft.com/ballbusterhard/
E-mail address: ballbusterhard@webtv.net or sbcomm@webtv.net
Cost: $4.25 USA; $5.25 Canada and Mexico; $6.50 overseas
Frequency: Two times per year
Special features: Power Rage, Disc Busters, Demo Busters, Eternal Wailings, Metal Messengers, etc.
Description: My name is David LaDuke. I'm publisher/editor of Ballbuster (the official int'l underground hard music report). I do promotion, publicity, write reviews and do interviews, etc.

Sh-Boom
Sue McIntosh
PO Box 746
Beattyville KY 41311 USA
Phone: 606-464-0513
Best time to call: After 5 p.m.
E-mail address: shboom46@hotmail.com
Cost: $19.95/13 issues
Frequency: Monthly
Special features: Covers all types of music.
Description: A 20-40 page tabloid covering all aspects of record collecting.

Foundations, Societies, Special Interest Clubs And Other Things Worth Knowing About

The following is a selected list of music organizations and museums. The information here comes more or less verbatim from the organizations, their literature or their web site and is not individually verified by *Goldmine*.

A

Academy Of Country Music
6255 Sunset Boulevard Suite 923
PO Box 508
Hollywood CA 90028
Phone: 213-462-2351
Web address: www.acmcountry.com
Description: Works to promote and enhance country music on behalf of its approximately 4,000 members. The academy hosts an annual awards show to recognize outstanding achievements in the industry. The academy was established in 1964.

The Alabama Music Hall Of Fame
David Johnson, executive director
P.O. Box 709
Highway 72 West
Tuscumbia, AL 35674
Phone: 800-239-AMHF
Web address: www.alamhof.org
E-mail info@alamhof.org

The Alabama Record Collectors Association (ARCA) Journal Newsletter
PO Box 11733
Birmingham AL 35202

American Classical Music Hall Of Fame
The Herschede Building
David A. Klingshirn, executive director
4 West Fourth Street
Cincinnati OH 45202-3602
Phone: 513-621-3263 (FAME)
Fax: 513-381-4130
Web address: www.classicalhall.com
E-mail: davidk@one.net

American Federation Of Jazz Societies, Inc.
Administrative Office: 2787 Del Monte St.
West Sacramento CA 95691
Phone: 916-372-5277
Fax: 916-372-3479
Web address: http://worldmall.com/wmcc/afjs/
E-mail: dhampton@worldmall.com
Description: An international resource and networking organization serving jazz societies, festivals, presenters and related jazz organizations since 1985. It includes a quarterly newsletter, a Washington legislative watch, a panel of experts available for consultation and an annual directory of society and festival officials.

American Federation Of Musicians
1501 Broadway Suite 600
New York NY 10036
Phone: 212-869-1330
Fax: 212-764-6134
Web address: www.afm.org
Description: Represents, negotiates, administers and protects the contractual rights of its 130,000 professional members in the United States and Canada.

American Jazz Museum
Dr. Rowena Stewart, executive director
1616 East 18th Street
Kansas City MO 64108
Phone: 816-474-8463
Fax: 816-474-0074

American Music Center
30 West 26th Street Suite 1001
New York NY 10019
Phone: 212-366-5260
Description: Fosters the creation, performance and appreciation of contemporary American music on behalf of its 2,500 members.

American Music Conference
5790 Armada Drive
Carlsbad CA 92008
Phone: 619-431-9124
Fax: 619-438-7327
Web address: www.amc-music.com
Description: A nonprofit organization founded in 1947, AMC is dedicated to promoting the value of music, music making and music education to the general public. AMC's media campaigns promote the benefits of music in education, recreation and cultural activities; encourage the support, continuation and improvement of music education standards in schools; and increase appreciation of the value of music in the home as an avocation and character-building activity for children.

The ARChive Of Contemporary Music
54 White Street
New York NY 10013
Phone: 212-226-6967
Fax: 212-226-6540
Web address: www.arcmusic.org
E-mail: arcmusic@inch.com
Description: The ARChive of Contemporary Music is a nonprofit music library, containing more than one million recordings and approximately two million photographs, press kits and other materials. Recordings are catalogued on a computer database and preserved. We are available to scholars and entertainment professionals for visits and to the general public by mail and over the telephone.

Association For Recorded Sound Collectors (ARSC)
PO Box 543
Annapolis, MD 21404-0543
Web address: www.arsc-audio.org
Description: A nonprofit organization founded in 1966 and dedicated to research, study, publication and information exchange surrounding all aspects of recordings and recorded sound.

Association Of Vogue Picture Record Collectors

PO Box 1356
Springfield MO 65801
Web address: www.voguepicturerecords.org
E-mail: info@voguepicturerecords.org
Special features: Newsletter, price guide
Description: An international organization of enthusiasts and collectors of Vogue picture records.

B

The Big Band And Jazz Hall Of Fame Foundation

Harold Van Roy, president
1560 North Santa Fe Avenue
Vista CA 92083
Phone: 619-457-8122
Fax: 619-457-2473

Blues Foundation

49 Union Avenue
Memphis TN 38103

Blues Music Association

PO Box 3122
Memphis TN 38173
Phone: 901-572-3843
Description: A professional organization devoted to expanding the marketplace for blues music.

Boston Rock And Roll Museum

Web address: www.dirtywater.com
Description: A web site dedicated to Boston rock.

Boswell Museum

Vet "Chica" Boswell Minnerly
Route 20
East Springield NY 13333
Phone: 607-264-3321
Fax: 607-264-3321
Web address: www.boswellmuseum.org/
E-mail: boswell@boswellmuseum.org
Description: The Boswell museum is a not-for-profit corporation to preserve and present popular music, jazz and social history of the 1920s and 1930s. It presents it in historical context with its present-day relevance and supports live performance by both students and professionals. Educational programs include workshops and classes in music, dance, theater and related arts for children and adults, radio show presentations, student performances and traveling exhibits for schools. Special events include guest artists, sing-alongs, film showings, dance-a-thons and vaudeville shows. The organization is a proud sponsor of the annual Not Still Art Festival, Cooperstown, N.Y.
Listed on the State And National Register Of Historic Places, as of fall 1999 we are currently closed to the public, pending renovation. Museum presentations continue at outreach locations.

C

The Corcoran Gallery Of Art

David Levy, president and director of Harlem Jazz Museum

17th Street and New York Avenue, NW
Washington DC 20006-4899

Country Music Association

One Music Circle South
Nashville TN 37203
Phone: 615-244-2840
Web address: www.country.com
Promotes and develops country music worldwide. The CMA has approximately 7,000 members, hosts the annual CMA Awards, SRO Entertainment Expo and co-sponsors Fan Fair. Among many other initiatives, the organization is also active in legislative affairs pertaining to the music industry.

Country Music Hall Of Fame And Museum

A Division Of The Country Music Foundation
4 Music Square East
Nashville TN 37203
Phone: 615-256-1639
Fax: 615-255-2245
Web address: www.countrymusichalloffame.org
Description: The Country Music Hall Of Fame, on Nashville's Music Row, operates two historic sites, Studio B and Hatch Show Print. The Hall Of Fame has a full-time staff of 25 divided among museum, library, education, research, marketing, special projects and administrative services. The museum serves more than 20,000 students each year with free education programs and assists hundreds of journalists, educators, music industry professionals and researchers by providing access to their library and archives.

D

Delta Blues Museum

114 Delta Avenue
Clarksdale MS 38614
Note: As of fall 1999, soon to be moving three blocks away to 1 Blues Alley
Phone: 601-627-6820
Web address: www.clarksdale.com/dbm
Best time to call: Mornings during the week
Description: The Delta Blues Museum is dedicated to the presevation and perpetuation of the Delta Blues in its birthplace, the Mississippi Delta. Established in 1979, the museum is located near the legendary crossroads of highways 49 and 61.

Doo-Wop Society Of Southern California

1158 26th Street, PMB 244
Santa Monica CA 90403
Phone: 310-493-9058
Phone: 562-493-9058 (24-hour hotline)
Web address: http://electricearl.com/dws/
E-mail address: Jimddddd@aol.com
Special features: Three concerts per year, quarterly newsletter *The Echo*.
Description: A nonprofit, tax exempt California organization formed in 1988 and dedicated to the preservation and exposure of the group harmony sounds of the 1950s and early 1960s.

E

Experience Music Project

Pete Blecha, senior curator
110 110th Avenue NE Suite 400
Bellevue WA 98004
Phone: 425-990-0575
Phone: 425-450-1997
Fax: 425-462-9242
Web address: www.experience.org
E-mail: experience@experience.org
Special features: Musicians' resources
Description: Experience Music Project celebrates and explores creativity and innovation as expressed through American popular music and exemplified by rock 'n' roll. The philosophical basis for EMP can be traced back to Jimi Hendrix's idea of Sky Church, a place where artists could exchange ideas, write and make music without the distractions and constraints of the music business. Museum to open in Seattle in mid-2000, at Seattle Center, next to the Space Needle and Monorail.

F

Fender Museum Of Arts Foundation and the Fender Museum Of Music And The Arts

PO Box 6555
Corona CA 91718
Description: A museum and performing arts education center under development as of fall 1999; Preview Center opened in June.

Free Expression Network

918 F Street, NW Suite 609
Washington DC 20004
Phone: 202-393-2787
Description: Supports free expression and free access to the artistic expression of others. The group is a national coalition of organizations that includes record producers, musicians, record and video retailers, artists, publishers, public interest groups and individuals.

Friends Against Musical Exploitation Of Artists, Inc. (FAME)

Pat Benti, executive director
2 Montmorenci Avenue
Boston MA 02128
Phone: 617-567-7722
Fax: 617-561-8900

G

Georgia Music Hall Of Fame

Rob Blount, executive director
200 Martin Luther King, Jr. Blvd
PO Box 870
Macon GA 31201
Phone: 912-750-8555
Fax: 912-750-0350
Web address: www.gamusichall.com
Special features: The Music Hall Of Fame contains a Georgia village, affectionately named "Tune Town" where there's a perpetual music festival. Visit the Jazz & Swing Club, the Rhythm & Blues Revue, the Skillet Licker Cafe (serving up piping hot country music), Vintage Vinyl (Rock 'n Roll Record Store), Gospel Chapel, Gretsch Theater, and the Coca-Cola Drug Store, each featuring your favorite Georgia artists. Listen to the music. See the concert videos. Discover memorabilia, instruments and photos of hundreds of Georgia's greats.

Gospel Music Association

1205 Division Street
Nashville TN 37203
Phone: 615-242-0303
Fax: 615-254-9755
Web address: www.gospelmusic.org
Special features: Gospel music week, Dove Awards, Academy of Gospel Music Arts educational seminars
Description: Founded in 1964, the organization promotes all forms of gospel music, including Christian music, on behalf of its 5,600 members in the United States and abroad.

Graceland

Jack Soder, CEO
PO Box 16508
Memphis TN 38186-0508
Phone: 901-332-3322
Web address: www.elvis-presley.com
Description: Walking through Graceland Mansion and touring its related attractions is an intriguing, moving, intimate, and entertaining look at the career and private life of one of the 20th century's most colorful and culturally influential people. But, the scope is larger than that. It is also a journey back through time, a look at who we were in America during the three decades of pop culture that Elvis Presley lived through.

Grateful Dead Museum

Dennis McNally
PO Box X
Novata CA 94948
Phone: 415-648-4832

I

The International Bluegrass Music Association

207 East Second Street
Owensboro KY 42303
Phone: 888-GET-IBMA
Web address: ww.ibma.org

The International Bluegrass Music Museum

Beck Schofield Glenn, administrator
207 E Second Street
Owensboro KY 42303
Phone: 502-926-7891
Fax: 502-686-7863

Iowa Rock 'N Roll Music Association And Their Hall Of Fame

PO Box 100
Spirit Lake IA 51360
Phone: 319-382-2256
Web address: www.iowarocknroll.com
E-mail: webmaster@iowarocknroll.com
Devoted to promoting the history of Rock and Roll Music in Iowa; no permanent site established as of fall 1999.

J

Jimmie Rodgers Museum

Jean Bishop, executive director
1725 Jimmie Rodgers Drive
PO Box 4555
Meridan MS 39304
Phone: 601-485-1808

K

Keystone Record Collectors, Inc.

PO Box 1516
Lancaster, PA 17608

M

Mammoth Music Mart For Lou Gehrig's Disease

3325 Main Street
Skokie IL 60076
Phone: 847-674-MART
Fax: 847-679-9109
Web address: www.lesturnerals.org/music.htm
E-mail: info@mammothmusicmart.org
Description: The Mammoth Music Mart, a giant tent sale, is the largest fund-raising event of its kind in the nation. More than 400,000 musical and electronic items are offered for sale, including compact discs, records, cassettes, videotapes, musical instruments, sheet and book music, and audio and video equipment. All of the products are donated. Proceeds benefit the Les Turner ALS Foundation in its fight against amyotrophic lateral sclerosis (ALS), better known as Lou Gehrig's disease.

The Motown Museum

2648 West Grand Boulevard
Detroit MI 48208-1285

N

National Academy Of Popular Music

330 West 58th Street Suite 411
New York NY 10019-1827
Phone: 212-957-9230
Description: Sponsors the annual Songwriters Hall of Fame Awards dinner. The organization is actively seeking a new site for the Songwriters Hall Of Fame Museum. It also organizes quarterly songwriter showcases and workshops.

National Academy Of Songwriters and the Songwriters Guild Of America

6430 Sunset Boulevard #705
Hollywood CA 90028
Phone: 323-462-1108
Fax: 323-462-5430

National Music Museum And Center

Jim Weaver
1155 15th Street NW
Washington DC 20005
Phone: 202-223-9721
Fax: 202-659-8621

The Nebraska Music Hall Of Fame

Web address: www.nebrocks.org
E-mail: pinky@teknetwork.com
Description: The Nebraska Music Hall of Fame was formed in 1995 to honor Nebraska-based musicians who have made a contribution and impact as a part of Midwestern, national and international music history.

New York Sheet Music Society

Sam Teicher
PO Box 354
Hewlett NY 11557
Phone: 516-295-0719
Description: The society attempts to preserve American popular music and recognize the personalities that have contributed to its success, i.e. songwriters, singers, authors, publishers and bandleaders. We publish a newsletter.

O

Old Town School Of Folk Music And Chicago Folk Center

4544 North Lincoln Avenue
Chicago IL 60625
Phone: 773-728-6000
Fax: 773-728-6999
Special features: Children's Center at 909 West Armitage Avenue
Description: The Old Town School Of Folk Music serves as a resource for the teaching, presentation and encouragement of folk music and folk culture of all countries.

R

Rhythm And Blues Foundation

1555 Conecticut Avenue NW Suite 401
Washington DC 20036-1111
Phone: 202-588-5566
Fax: 202-588-5549
Web address: www.rhythm-n-blues.org
E-mail address: RandBFdn@aol.com

Rhythm And Blues Rock 'N Roll Society, Inc.

PO Box 1949
New Haven CT 06510
Phone: 203-924-1079
Description: Founded in 1974 as a nonprofit tax-exempt organization.

Rockabilly Hall Of Fame

Bob Timmers, owner, site curator
E-mail: bob@rockabillyhall.com
Rod Pyke, U.K. and European agent
E-mail: rodney_pyke@msn.com
Box 70

Kimberly WI 54136 USA
Phone: 920-739-2503
Fax: 920-739-9443
Web address: www.rockabillyhall.com
Description: An Internet web site with more than 5,000 legends listed —
many with their own pages — and more than 500 individual pages in all.
Veteran performers, new talent, daily news, features, gig schedules,
reviews, reference sections, hundreds of rockabilly links, mp3 down-
loads and much more. The #1 rockabilly web site on the net, according
to the major search engines. The Rockabilly Hall Of Fame even has its
own label.

Rock And Roll Hall Of Fame

Terry Stewart, Executive director and CEO
1 Key Plaza
Cleveland OH 44114
Phone: 216-515-1204
Fax: 216-515-1284
Web address: www.rockhall.com
Description: A museum honoring the artists who have made unique con-
tributions to the energy and evolution of rock 'n' roll.

V

Vocal Group Hall Of Fame And Museum

Linda Stewart-Savach
98 E State Street
Sharon PA 16146
Phone: 724-983-2027
Web site: www.vocalhalloffame.com
Special features: Readers of *Goldmine* magazine have a voice in the
selection of inductees.
Description: A museum dedicated to honor the greatest vocal groups of
all time.

Rock The Vote

10950 Washington Boulevard Suite 240
Culver City, CA 90232
Phone: 310-237-2000
Fax: 301-237-2001
Web address: www.rockthevote.org
E-mail: field@rockthevote.org
Description: A organization that encourages 18- to- 24-year-olds to
become involved in the political process by exercising their right to vote.
Rock The Vote is a nonprofit, nonpartisan organization founded by
members of the recording industry.

WHAT ARE YOUR ALBUMS REALLY WORTH?

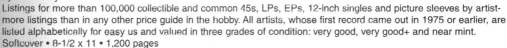

Standard Catalog of American Records
by Tim Neely
Listings for more than 100,000 collectible and common 45s, LPs, EPs, 12-inch singles and picture sleeves by artist-more listings than in any other price guide in the hobby. All artists, whose first record came out in 1975 or earlier, are listed alphabetically for easy us and valued in three grades of condition: very good, very good+ and near mint.
Softcover • 8-1/2 x 11 • 1,200 pages
200 b&w photos
REC1 • $29.95

Goldmine Record Album Price Guide
by Tim Neely
Find out which albums are worth collecting with this new price guide from Goldmine magazine. Now you can value record albums with confidence and celebrate 50 years of the LP ,the 1940s through the 1990s. More than 40,000 albums, valued at $20.00 or more, are listed and priced in up to three grades of condition, plus thousands of record albums not listed in other price guides. Easily find the album you want to value with the alphabetical listings by artist.
Softcover • 8-1/2 x 11 • 544 pages
100 b&w photos
REA1 • $24.95

Goldmine Price Guide to 45 RPM Records
2nd Edition
by Tim Neely
A new, larger format makes room for many new artists and 20,000 new listings - 50,000 records in all. All prices have been reviewed, providing the most accurate values in three grades of condition. Learn more about your favorite artists with the updated discographies from the '50s through the '90s. The handy checklist format helps you inventory your favorite records.
Softcover • 8-1/2 x 11 • 544 pages
100 b&w photos
R452 • $22.95

Goldmine's Promo Record & CD Price Guide
2nd Edition
by by Fred Heggeness, Edited by Tim Neely
More than 10,000 total individual promotional 45s, 78s, LPs, LLPs, EPs, 12-inch singles and sleeves and covers from 1950 to 1997 are listed. Easily identify your records with 1,100 photographic replications of labels, sleeves and covers.
Softcover • 8-1/2 x 11 • 464 pages
1,100 b&w photos
PRC02 • $24.95

Goldmine 45 RPM Picture Sleeve Price Guide
by Charles Szabla
Record collectors have discovered that it's not just their vinyl that has value - 45 RPM picture sleeves are also in high demand. Now you can quickly identify, date and value your collection-in two grades of condition with the first and only comprehensive price guide available. Alphabetical listings for more than 10,000 sleeves, covering more than 40 years of U.S. releases.
Softcover • 8-1/2 x 11 • 320 pages
1,200 b&w photos
RPS01 • $19.95

Goldmine Price Guide to Rock 'n' Roll Memorabilia
by Mark Allen Baker
Identify, authenticate and value non-recorded music collectibles with this comprehensive guide. Features 800 artists and includes descriptions and values for 10,000 items from guitar picks of music legends to magazines and instruments, plus bonus tips on collecting autographs, posters and other souvenirs.
Softcover • 8-1/2 x 11 • 768 pages
300 b&w photos • 8-page color section
RRM • $24.95